CHINESE THOUGHT

An Introduction

EDITED BY
DONALD H. BISHOP

CONTRIBUTIONS BY

Jeff Barlow   Shu-hsien Liu
Donald H. Bishop Fred Sturm
Chung-ying Cheng Yuk Wong
S. Y. Hsieh   Joseph Wu
Sung-peng Hsu   David C. Yu

KANSAS SCHOOL OF RELIGION
UNIVERSITY OF KANSAS
1300 OREAD AVENUE
LAWRENCE, KANSAS 66044

South Asia Books

SOUTH ASIA BOOKS
Box 502, Columbia, Missouri, 65205

© MOTILAL BANARSIDASS

First Edition : 1985

ISBN : 0–8364–1130–7

Printed in India by Shantilal Jain at Shri Jainendra Press,
A-45, Phase I, Naraina, New Delhi 110 028 and published by
Narendra Prakash Jain, for Motilal Banarsidass, Delhi 110 007.

181.11

Kansas School of Religion
At the University of Kansas
Smith Hall, Rm. 109, Library
Lawrence, Kansas 66045-2164

CHINESE THOUGHT
An Introduction

CONTENTS

PREFACE vii

I. ANCIENT PERIOD

1. CHINESE THOUGHT BEFORE CONFUCIUS
   Donald H. Bishop, Washington State University 3

2. CONFUCIUS
   Shu-hsien Liu, New Asia College 14

3. TAOISM
   Joseph Wu, California State University, Sacramento 32

4. MO TZU
   Donald H. Bishop, Washington State University 59

5. THE LEGALIST PHILOSOPHERS
   S. Y. Hsieh, University of Denver 81

6. MENCIUS
   Chung-ying Cheng, University of Hawaii 110

II. MEDIEVAL PERIOD

7. INTRODUCTION
   Donald H. Bishop, Washington State University 153

8. CHINESE BUDDHIST PHILOSOPHY
   Fred Sturm, University of New Mexico 184

9. NEO-CONFUCIANISM
   David C. Wu, Colorado Women's College 235

10. WANG YANG-MING
    Yuk Wong, New Asia College 276

III. MODERN PERIOD

11. INTRODUCTION
    Donald H. Bishop, Washington State University 305

12. WANG FU-CHIH
    Donald H. Bishop, Washington State University 311

13. KANG YU-WEI
    Donald H. Blshop, Washington State University   323
14. SUN YAT-SEN
    Jeff Barlow, Lewis and Clark College   340
15. HU SHIH
    Sung-peng Hsu   364
16. MAO TSE-TUNG AND THE CHINESE TRADITION
    Donald H. Bishop, Washington State University   392
17. CONTEMPORARY PHILOSOPHERS OUTSIDE THE MAINLAND
    Joseph Wu, California State University, Sacramento   422
18. THE CHINESE CONTRIBUTION TO WORLD THOUGHT
    Donald H. Bishop, Washington State University   441

INDEX   481

PREFACE

With the entrance of China into the world arena again, it is essential that people have a better understanding of the philosophies which have determined Chinese culture. The authors of the essays in this volume hope their work will be a contribution to this end. Each writes from his own perspective, of course; however, the editor has attempted to introduce uniformity in the work, although discrepancies remain.

Chinese philosophy has been divided into three periods and chapters have been included linking one with another so as to provide background and continuity to the text. In order to make the volume as timely as possible, chapters have been included on both Mao and thinkers outside the mainland.

This volume might well be used as a text in conjunction with original sources, many of which, are available now in English in paperback. It will be of value, also, to the general reader, who wishes a basic understanding of the Chinese tradition.

The story of Chinese thought, beginning with the early people in the upper Yellow River region is most interesting. Chinese civilization is one of the world's oldest, and a tradition which has lasted so long must have enduring values it can contribute to today's world, as the concluding chapter points out.

Washington State University   DONALD H. BISHOP
Pullman, Washington

I
Ancient Period

1
CHINESE THOUGHT BEFORE CONFUCIUS

DONALD BISHOP

One characterization of the Chinese tradition has been "The Three Ways", referring, of course, to Buddhism, Taoism, and Confucianism.[1] Buddhism in China has been widely and authoritatively documented. For Taoism we have the *Tao Te Ching* and the *Chuang Tzu*, books attributed to Lao Tzu and Chuang respectively, along with other early writings, while the four books, *The Analects, Doctrine of the Mean, The Great Learning* and *Mencius* provide a core of writings for Confucianism.

As to early or pre-Confucian China, our knowledge in general has come from a literary tradition consisting of the five classics, the *Shu Ching* (Book of History), the *Shih Ching* (Book of Odes or Poetry), the *I Ching* (Book of Changes), the *Li Chi* (Book of Rites or Rituals) and the *Ch'un Ch'ui* (Annals of Spring and Autumn), a history of Confucius' home state Lu, from 772 B.C. to 481 B.C. The Five Classics are traditionally believed to have been compiled by Confucius and his followers from earlier sources, written and oral, and were reconstructed by the Han historians in the period following the burning of the books by the first emperor of the Ch'in dynasty which lasted from 221 B.C. to 206 B.C.

The Five Classics had been long accepted as authoritative, but doubts as to their authenticity were raised by a group of historians in the second decade of the twentieth century. Perhaps overzealous and influenced by an empiricist trend, they turned for evidence from literature to archeology, the progress of which was expanding in China in the nineteen twenties and thirties. In time, paradoxically, the discoveries of archeologists more often tended to verify rather than refute the contents of the classics and other early writings, leading one author in the seventies to note that " ... old Chinese historical accounts in documents dating from about 1000 B.C. to the considerable surprise of skeptical historians, have been remarkably well confirmed by the past half century of archeological research."[2] At present, then, archeology and the classical literature are both profitable sources of a growing knowledge of the ancient Chinese world.

What those sources tell us is that China is indeed an ancient and continuous civilization. Its earliest settlements were in the river basins where there was fertile soil and plentiful moisture, a major settlement being, according to archeological evidence, in the middle-lower stretch of the Yellow River between Yang Shao and An Yang. Excavations of Yang Shao sites show people living in villages as early as the beginning of the second millennium B.C. Farming was the main occupation. Animals domesticated were pigs, dogs, goats, sheep and the horses which were used to pull chariots in battles. Food grains such as millet, rice and perhaps wheat were raised. Oracle bones show there was a fully developed language and a script as well. Metals were in use, bronze earlier and iron by the seventh century B.C. The former, being more highly prized, tended to be used for special purposes such as vessels for ceremonial occasions and rulers' tombs. Silk and jade were in use as luxuries. Knowledge of pottery-making was advanced, the unique black pottery of the Lung Shan culture being one example.

Chinese religion in this early period was characterized by belief in spirits and nature deities, and ancestor reverence or worship, divination and sacrifices. More will be said about this later. As to the Arts, the literary tradition provides us with examples of poetry both for enjoyment and social protest.[3] Ivory was carved with elaborate patterns. A variety of musical instruments were played. An early writer, noting that the "... music of the lute prospered under the Emperors Yao and Shun during the three dynasties," lamented its decline in the Warring States Period.[4]

Archeologists now suggest that the Chinese civilization in the Yellow River basin before the beginning of the Chou dynasty in 1122 B.C. went through three cultural periods or epochs, the Yang Shao, Lung Shan and Shang extending over a period of approximately one thousand years. As people were no longer wandering nomads, an increasing refinement of all those things which make up a culture was possible. That civilization, centered first in the

Chinese Thought Before Confucius

Yang Shao-Anyang region of the Yellow River gradually spread throughout most of the area comprising contemporary China.

This expansion of culture can be correlated with the political history of China, which is segmented or divided chronologically according to dynasties; a dynasty being a period of time in which a hereditary family ruled. The Classical literature asserts the existence of three ancient dynasties, the Hsia, Shang, and Chou, the last two having been documented archeologically. As to the Sage Kings Yao, Shun and Yu, the debate as to whether they were actual or fictitious persons goes on. If the former, they undoubtedly lived in the Hsia dynasty from c. 2200 B.C.–1766 B.C. Yu is purported to have been the founder of the Hsia dynasty in the region of the Yellow River noted above.[5] The corrupt emperor Chieh was the Hsia's last ruler. He was overthrown by K'ang Tang who set up the Shang dynasty c. 1766 B.C.

The Shang dynasty continued for several centuries, its last emperor being the degenerate Chou. It was succeeded by the Chou dynasty c. 1122 when the armies of Wu, head of the increasingly powerful Chou tribe and state, captured the Shang capital. At his death, the Duke of Chou, his younger brother, became the real power behind the throne occupied by Wu's thirteen-year-old son. On his coming to power, King Wu distributed the conquered territory among his relatives and clan members, between whose descendants concord at times turned to discord. Within a century after the conquest of the Shang, the power and influence of the royal family had waned while that of the heads of the numerous states waxed. One result of the decline was an invasion by outsiders from the West forcing the Chou family in 771 B.C. to move the capital eastward to contemporary Loyang in Honan province, the dynasty then becoming known as the East Chou.

The centuries from the mid-800's B.C. to 221 B.C., the end of the Chou dynasty, have been called the Age of Feudalism for at least two reasons. One is that China became divided into a number of princely states, each with its own court and nobility. The second is that society became separated into two groups variously characterized as the aristocracy and the commoner, the noble and serf, the landowner and the laborer; the few with political-military power and the many without.[6]

In the last three centuries of the Chou dynasty tension and open conflict between the feudal states increased, as each sought to dominate the other, leading the era to be called the Warring States period (480-227 B.C.) in contrast to the time before it known as the Spring and Autumn era (722-481 B.C.). The uncertainty, disorder and suffering during the Warring States period led people to search for causes and remedies to the chaos and the period of the Hundred Philosophers or Hundred Schools of Thought came into existence, among them being the Confucianists, Taoists, Mohists and Legalists, each with its diagnosis and proposed cure.

However, none could prevent the demise of the Chou dynasty in 221 B.C. and the ushering in of the Ch'in, the first of the so-called Imperial Dynasties. It was in the Ch'in from 221 B.C. to 206 B.C. that the process of amalgamation into an ever larger territorial unit was climaxed and China became unified at last as one entity under a single, all-powerful ruler.

This, then, is a brief outline of the history and formal aspects of China to the Ch'in dynasty. A knowledge of them alone is insufficient, and we turn now to early China's philosophical tradition or traditions. For no culture, no matter how early, is without a philosophy, or, more broadly, a guiding thought pattern.

In understanding it we might begin with the significant statement Confucius made about himself that he was only a transmitter, not a creator or founder of a new philosophical system.[7] If true, this means that we must go beyond Confucius (551 B.C.–479 B.C.) to an earlier tradition, an "ancient wisdom" which Confucius and the other philosophers dealt with in various ways—one accepting, rationalizing and passing it on; another stalwartly opposing it, another modifying it—as they searched for solutions to the pressing problems of the times.[8]

As to this "ancient wisdom" itself, as it existed in China, let us say c. 2000 B.C., information about its content can be gained in at least three ways. One is by examining the five classics and other works making up the Literary Tradition; another is by inferring from archeological finds. A third way of reconstructing the thought patterns of the early Chinese is through what I would call sympathetic, imaginative but disciplined insight based on a particular type of experience becoming increasingly rare, especially in the urbanized, industrialized, scientific, technological West.[9] For we must remember, as has been rightly pointed out, that the

Chinese have always been a people of the land. Even now eighty per cent of her population live in the countryside and are involved in agriculture; and, as one flies over the vast expanse of China today, one sees the landscape, much as it has been for centuries, dotted with small villages set in fields of rice or other crops.

Because environment is extremely influential in the formation of beliefs, we must, then, take into account the effect of a close association with the earth upon the thought patterns or the philosophical outlook of the people of ancient, pre-Confucian China. We need to ask ourselves how persons spending a lifetime tilling the land and living closely with nature would view nature and the world around them. This means that our first and foremost concern is with cosmology or, more broadly, metaphysics along with epistemology. What is the nature of reality and how is it known become the two central questions.

For the early Chinese immediate, direct experience is one answer to the epistemological question. Each day, as the farmer plants his fields and tills the land, he is directly aware of and apprehends the working of nature. But, and very important, intuitive insight is present also. Closely identifying himself with her, the farmer unconsciously knows or is aware of the nuances of nature. He is sensitive to her inner forces. Knowing what the day would bring weatherwise, when the right time to plant the seed is, whether the coming winter will be harsh or mild was a skill so highly developed, among some, that it seemed as if they had an almost miraculous insight into the ways of nature or mother earth.

As to the nature of reality, how do a people closely attuned to the earth view it? Reality is seen in terms of a certain set of attitudes on the one hand and a basic set of concepts on the other. Experiences with nature give rise to attitudes of awe, fear, wonder, respect, dependence, joy and gratitude. On a deeper level those relationships generate such fundamental metaphysical concepts as order, regularity, correlates, interrelatedness, cause and effect, parts and whole, harmony, vitalism, change and beneficence.

Take the concept of order. How would early man arrive at it? The answer is obvious. As one example, a person living close to the land has a lifetime of experience with the seasonal sequence of nature. Spring, summer, autumn and winter follow each other in a regular, orderly pattern. As a person works the land in conjunction with this natural cycle, he would readily arrive at the basic notion itself of order as a primary attribute of nature.

Order is related to a concept of time involving sequence, and a space concept of everything in its place. In north China the coolness of autumn and the cold of winter inevitably follows the heat of summer. Harvesting follows planting. The stars have their fixed places in the sky or heaven. Rivers and mountains, forests, flowers, animals, birds, all have their rightful place in the universe. All make up, and are important in the orderly scheme of things.

Other concepts associated with order are interrelatedness, correlation and mutual influence. To the early Chinese it was obvious that nature is related reciprocally. Her various aspects are intertwined and act upon each other. In the monsoon season rain falls and floods come. There is a direct relationship between flooding and the monsoon season, and there is an inevitable correlation between rain and growth. Without the first there is not the second. For the tree will not leaf and plants will not grow without rain and, in addition, sun. Thus for the early Chinese living close to the land the various aspects of nature are interrelated. The relationship between Heaven and Earth, and the forces of each, is the most basic one.

Interrelatedness involves interdependency or dependency. That nature was thus related was obvious to the early Chinese tillers of the soil. The sun shining on the earth in the springtime warms the earth making it suitable for planting. The seed is put in the ground. Its growth depends on a sufficiency of moisture, sunshine and other factors. There is, then, a direct cause-effect relationship between the various aspects of nature and between man and nature. If there is no monsoon, there is no plowing, sowing, growing and harvesting. The latter depends on the first.

The concept of harmony was an important one held by the early Chinese also. If the manifold aspects of nature are interrelated rather than isolated, interdependent rather than independent; if they exert a mutual influence on each other and work in conjunction to achieve ends, then the notion of harmony and a recognition of the harmonious relationship between nature's various parts would come naturally. Growth is a result of the harmonizing or working together of several elements. The movement of heavenly bodies is orderly, regular and harmonious. And the primary harmony found in nature was believed to be between heaven (or the sky) and the earth and the forces of each. Heaven and earth are harmoniously associated because the sky is the locus for the sun which acts upon the earth. It is from the earth that the mist rises; from the heaven rain falls.

The idea of harmony is associated with the distinction between one part and another; and between parts and the whole. The early Chinese distinguished between the one and the many, the particular and the universal, diversity and unity. The former requires the latter. For harmony to exist there must be parts to be harmonized. For there to be a whole there must be parts. There can be no universals without particulars. The Chinese farmer dealt first with particular things in a particular context. His experience did not stop there, however. He dealt not only with one particular rice plant but with a large number of them which made up a particular field. That field was one of several which made up a totality which he called his or his family's fields or land. To readily go from the particular to the universal, the many to the one, the notion of parts to the notion of the whole, would be quite in keeping with the early Chinese experience.

That there are distinctions, then, would be a primary observation of the early Chinese farmer. Nature is characterized by difference or differences. There is light and dark, short and tall, stones which are heavy and bamboo wood which is light. But what is the major feature of this difference between things, or what is the nature of the relationship between the different sets? It is dialectical or non-dialectical, antagonistic or non-hostile, competitive or cooperative, one of opposites or supplementaries?

The early Chinese answered in terms of the second. The various aspects of nature stand in a complementary relationship to each other. Rain, sun, and soil, supplement one another and work together to enable a seed to grow. The forces of heaven supplement the forces of earth to bring about production and change. Seeing the various aspects of nature supporting one another led the early Chinese to view reality non-dialectically in terms of continuity, extension and gradation rather than separation, opposites, irreconcilability and conflict. Change is the result of the forces of nature working, not antagonistically, but in harmony with one another. Nature is a rhythm, a melody of congruent notes, not an assortment of dissonant sounds.

It was the habit of seeing reality as a whole or synthetically which led the early Chinese to the concept of "nature's way", the "natural", or the "way of nature". It is "nature's way" that birds fly and fish swim and not the opposite. It is only natural that cold accompany winter and heat summer, darkness night, and light day. What we designate each may be relative; the phenomena themselves are not. The normal way of nature is that of growth through a continuum of successive stages from conception to death, from the coming into being to the going out of existence. Heaven has its ways and earth hers. "Nature" is itself an inclusive type concept and is a result of the farmer experiencing his environment, in all its diverse aspects, totalistically.

It is nature's oneness which, among other things, makes for its beneficence. That nature is good would be obvious to the Chinese farmer. For when he plants the seed in season and nurtures the plant properly as it grows, the harvest is abundant. True there are times when there is too much or too little rain, but this only stimulates the farmer to take precautionary measures. Thus what one might be tempted to call evil in the end leads to good. The fact still remains that there is the earth, sun, wind and rain. These primary ingredients, always present, are what makes nature beneficent.

To a people living close to the land, the view that the earth is alive, animated or filled with power or life force is a natural one. Noticing new life coming from the soil in the springtime, seeing water issuing from springs in the earth and other such phenomena would lead easily to such a belief. Nature is not passive or inert but is characterized by fecundity, creativeness or creativity. The farmer experiences this all around him. Early man's symbolizing the earth as mother illustrates this. His belief in fertility gods does also.

Vitalism was no doubt at the root of the belief that spirits dwell in the earth and in various forms of life. One was the dragon, associated with the storm and cloud and symbolizing kingly power; and early man attempted in a variety of ways to communicate with the indwelling spirits. The early Chinese sought to explain nature as much as possible in terms of what we would call natural laws, although forces or events might be more desirable or accurate terms. Change was a basic phenomenon, not yielding novelty but the expected. It was a matter of growth or development through a series of modifications to maturity. It is a result of the cause-effect relationship characterizing nature, a relationship directly experienced and intuitively apprehended by those living closely with her.

The cosmos, then, was not viewed by the early Chinese in narrow, mechanistic terms but as a vibrant organism, pulsing with life and activity. Nature is to be experienced directly, worked with, nurtured. It is not known analytically as an object to be exploited but synthetically as a reality to be cherished. Early man saw himself as a part of nature and it is this which enabled him to see within or gain insight into her. Communion with nature led him to view himself not as her conqueror but co-worker.

In summary, the "early wisdom" of China was that of an agrarian people. It was conceived in and drew its sustenance from the land. It was rooted in people's immediate experience with the earth. From the world of nature around them came such concepts (although we should recognize that the western term "concept" is really not the right descriptive term) as order, interdependence, harmony, cause and effect, change, wholeness and beneficence.[10] By means of those concepts the early Chinese were able to both understand and deal positively with their world. Experiences with nature evoked at least three responses. The sense of mystery and experiences with nature's harsher forces elicited awe and fear. The beauty, splendor, grandeur and plentitude of nature excited joy and gratitude. A third was a realization of man's littleness or finitude because of his dependency on the great forces of nature around him which he could not control.

The period of the Chou dynasty beginning in 1122 B.C. and especially the latter part of it, the Age of the Hundred Schools from 481 B.C. to 256 B.C., has been often called China's Classical Age comparable to the Golden Age of Greece. In both it was a time of unrest and uncertainty causing people to be concerned with ultimate questions. Among them were the following: What is the nature of man? What kind of society is natural to him? What is the best kind of society? How is it to be brought about? How is it to be ruled and by whom? On what basis? Is nature really what it was purported to be by the Ancient Tradition? How can the earlier views of reality be related to the life of an individual and his society? Is man unique in nature? Or is he a microcosm of the universe so that what is characteristic of or true of the universe is also true of him? If there is a "way of nature", is there not also a comparable "way of man"? Are there not some things which are natural to man and some which are not?

If reality is harmonious, would not a harmonious society be the ideal one, and how can it be created? If nature is non-dialectical or characterized by supplementaries, should not the society of man be likewise? If nature is characterized by change, man's life is as well; and how should the individual cope with those inevitable changes? If there is a "vital force" in nature, how can man relate to it and make it a part of himself? If nature is beneficent or good, what should man's response to it be? Is there not a "good" for man, which he can identify and bring into being? Does not a moral universe have as a correlate moral individuals and a moral society or society based on morality? What is the nature of that morality.

In China, as in ancient Greece, there was no unanimous answer given to each of these questions. Confucius did not agree with Lao Tzu. Mo Tzu differed with both, while the Legalists disagreed with all three. As noted earlier, none diagnosed the contemporary situation quite the same and each suggested his own cure. Each dealt with the earlier or ancient tradition in his own way, as we shall see, even as the tradition itself continued on.

NOTES

1. Arthur Waley's *Three Ways of Thought in Ancient China*, published first in 1939 is a good example of this characterization.
2. Frederick W. Mote, *Intellectual Foundations of China*. Alfred A. Knopf, New York, 1971, p. 7. An example of this is given in Paul Wheatley's *The Pivot of the Four Quarters*, Aldine Publishing Company, Chicago, 1971, p. 4, where he notes, "By revealing on oracle inscriptions the names of no less than twenty-three of the thirty Shang kings mentioned in literary sources, Tung Tsu-pin and others reaffirmed the potential worth, though not the factual accuracy of the literary tradition so far as the Shang was concerned."
3. Two examples of poems of social protest, "Big Rat" and "The North Wind" are given in Wm. Theodore De Bary, *Sources of the Chinese Tradition*, Volume 1, Columbia University Press, New York, 1960, pp. 13-14. An-

other from the *Book of Odes* is quoted in Ch'u Chai and Winberg Chai, *The Changing Society of China*. New American Library of World Literature, New York, 1962, p. 66.

    4. R.H. Van Gulik, *The Lore of The Chinese Lute*. Sophia University, Tokyo, in cooperation with the Charles E. Tuttle Company, Vermont, 1969, p. 56.

    5. Whether or not there was actually a Hsia dynasty continues to be debated. As pointed out by C.P. Fitzgerald in *China, A Short Cultural History*, archeology has confirmed the existence of the Shang dynasty but not the Hsia although the Classics accept the Hsia dynasty as historical.

    6. Chai and Chai use another set of terms to distinguish the two groups, "mind-laborers" and "body-laborers". Wheatley writes of Shang society, "On the stratified character of Shang society archeology, oracle bones, and later literary records are in agreement.", op. cit., p. 63.

    7. James R. Ware, translator, *The Sayings of Confucius*, New American Library, New York, 1955, p. 50.

    8. Used by Bede Griffiths in his book *Return to the Centre*. Collins, London, 1976, p. 100, the term "ancient wisdom" refers in the Indian tradition to the Sanatana Dharma, the Hindu term for the Eternal Religion preceeding any specific, formalized religion in India. Aldous Huxley referred to it as "The Perennial Philosophy" and related it to Taoism in the Chinese tradition. In a general sense it refers to the primal nature philosophy of early man everywhere living in close conjunction with the earth.

    9. The kind of experience early man had as he tilled the ground and worked the soil is not found even today among farming people in the west, simply because agriculture has become highly mechanized. The farmer today proudly proclaims himself a practitioner of scientific, mechanized agriculture. His outlook and attitudes vary from his ancestors of even a generation or two ago, to say nothing of a much earlier time.

    10. The reason "concept" is not a suitable term given by Conrad Schirokauer in his *A Brief History of Chinese and Japanese Civilizations*, Harcourt Brace Jovanovich, Inc., New York, 1978, p. 45, is that it "... implies inertia and passivity rather than the dynamism and self-movement in the Chinese conception." Donald Munro in his book, *Concept of Man in Early China*, suggests that, regarding such concepts, "it is best to consider them as forces." Stanford University Press, Stanford, 1969, p. 30.

2
CONFUCIUS

SHU-HSIEN LIU

Confucius (c. 551-479 B.C.) was born in the small state of Lu, which was located in what is now Shantung province. His family name was K'ung; his given name was Ch'iu, and Chung-ni was his literary name. "Confucius", the name widely used in English-speaking countries, is the Latinized form of K'ung Fu-tzu, which means the grand master K'ung. His great grandparents were immigrants from Sung, the descendant state of the ancient Yin dynasty. The lineage of the family can be traced back to the ducal house of Sung; but when Confucius was born, the family had become poor. According to his testimony, when he was young, he had to learn a number of skills needed for petty jobs.

Concerning the formal education of Confucius we know virtually nothing. He seemed in the main, a self-taught man who accumulated his vast knowledge through all possible sources that were open to him. He had started his teaching career early. As a young teacher not yet thirty years old, under the sponsorship of the Duke of Lu, he went to the king's capital, Chou, to study the ancient rites and ceremonies. After he came back, he became a renowned teacher; and more and more disciples came to study under him. Moral education was the backbone of his educational programme. He also taught his disciples how to serve as officials on all levels in government.

Between the years 502-496 B.C., during the reign of Duke Ting of Lu, Confucius gradually rose to power. He was appointed the Minister of Crime, and under his direction Lu soon became a model state. Unfortunately, this state of affairs aroused the fear and jealously of the other states. Ch'i, a powerful adjacent state, called a "good will" conference between the two states with the intention of plotting against Lu. But with Confucius as the acting Chief Minister at the occasion, Lu scored a decisive diplomatic victory. This dramatic event climaxed Confucius' short political career. Soon afterwards, the Duke of Lu indulged in the enjoyment of beautiful dancing girls and of handsome racing horses, presented to him as gifts, from the Duke of Ch'i and alienated himself from the good men in his government. Confucius sadly resigned from his post and began his thirteen years of wandering in various states. He kept hoping that some ruler might use him to realize his lofty political ideals but was disappointed. Finally, he returned to Lu in the year 484 B.C., but he never had another chance for practical politics.

He spent his last years teaching in Lu and died in the same state where he was born, which also happened to be the state of the descendants of the Duke of Chou. Confucius loved and esteemed the Duke of Chou as his spiritual father and as the great sage-minister who laid down the foundation of the glorious Chou system of rites and ceremonies.[1]

Most scholars today agree that *The Analects*, a collection of the master's sayings and conversations recorded by his disciples, is the best source which can be relied upon to study Confucius' philosophical ideas. However, *The Analects* is a most difficult book to read. Especially to a Western reader, the book may appear to be just a collection of disconnected aphorisms. Not only does Confucius rarely give a definition of any term, but also he often pronounces his judgements without producing any arguments. At times it seems that he contradicts himself.

It is here that a most significant difference between Western and Chinese philosophical approaches is found. In a typical Western philosophical treatise sophisticated logic is used to construct a metaphysical system. In *The Analects*, however, there is neither sophisticated logic nor a grand metaphysical system. And, strikingly enough, most traditional Chinese thinkers follow the example of Confucius Some Western scholars tend to think that no systematic philosophy has ever been developed in the Chinese tradition and that Chinese philosophy is no more than practical ethics. However, if we would not limit ourselves to a narrow Western view of philosophy, which overemphasizes theoretical sophistication and system-building, then we would realize that the Chinese have developed a distinguished philosophical tradition of their own. Their primary concern is an existential, not a theoretical one. What Confucius teaches is a situational ethics having to do with the ultimate commitment of our lives, an ethics which cannot be reduced to a system of abstract formulas. If there is any unity in Confucius' thought, it is a dynmaic unity of life rather than the static unity of a theoretical system.

As rightly pointed out by traditional scholars, the only way to read *The Analects* with any profit is to recite the text over and over again until one can almost relive the life of the master. If one can find out the particular context in which a certain statement is made, and, most important of all, can correlate his own moral experience with that of the master, then he may have a chance to be enlightened about the basic principles underlying the whole of *The Analects*. And it is only through a proper reading of the messages contained in *The Analects* that we can hope to reach an understanding of Confucius' ultimate commitment and religious philosophy.

Let us start with a paradoxical statement in *The Analects* which has puzzled the minds of scholars throughout the ages. Confucius said:

" 'Ts'an, there is one thread that runs through my doctrines.' Tseng Tzu said, 'Yes.' After Confucius had left, the disciples asked him, 'What did he mean?' Tseng Tzu replied, 'The Way of our Master is none other than conscientiousness (chung) and altruism (shu).' "[2]

Although Confucius asserts that there is a central thread that runs through all his doctrines, yet nowhere in *The Analects* does he mention what this thread is; and Tseng Tzu's answer seems to be wide off the mark, as chung and shu are apparently two threads rather than one. This apparent paradox cannot be resolved until we have studied carefully the whole text of *The Analects* and grasped the basic spirit of Confucius' philosophy.

Even a casual reader of *The Analects* cannot fail to notice the central position of the concept of jen in Confucius' philosophy. Jen has been rendered into English in varied ways such as: benevolence, man-to-manness, perfect virtue, human-heartedness, humanity. Not only has jen been mentioned more often than any other virtue in the book, but all evidence points to the fact that it has been regarded as The Virtue in Confucius' system of thought. Ceremonies and music are the two most important means of education for Confucius, and yet he declares:

"If a man is not humane (Jen), what has he to do with ceremonies (li)? If he is not humane, what has he to do with music?"[3]

Obviously Jen is being regarded as none other than the principle underlying the performances of ceremonies and music. Moreover, Confucius said:

"Wealth and honor are what every man desires. But if they have been obtained in violation of moral principles, they must not be kept. Poverty and humble position are what every man dislikes. But if they can be avoided only in violation of moral principles, they must not be avoided. If a *superior man* departs from humanity, how can he fulfil that name? A *superior man* never abandons humanity even for the lapse of a single meal. In moments of haste, he acts according to it. In times of difficulty or confusion, he acts according to it." (Italics mine)[4]

From this evidence it seems that the principle of jen is Confucius' ultimate commitment. But what is the exact meaning of jen. Here, again, the same difficulty that characterizes the reading of the whole text of *The Analects* occurs. In the book, Confucius does not give a formal definition of jen; instead he gives only various answers to questions about jen in different circumstances for students with different temperaments and with varying degrees of understanding. Since it is impractical to list here all the statements about jen in *The Analects*, only a few key statements from the book are selected and subjected to analysis, in order to uncover the layers of meaning contained in Confucius' teachings about jen. The five statements selected here are arbitrarily listed with numbers for the sake of convenience in discussion.

(1) Fan Ch'ih asked about humanity. Confucius said, 'It is to love men.'[5]

(2) Confucius said, 'Only the man of humanity knows how to love people and hate people.'[6]

(3) Fan Ch'ih asked about humanity. Confucius said, 'Be respectful in private life, be serious (ching) in handling affairs, and be loyal in dealing with others. Even if you are living amidst barbarians, these principles may never be forsaken.'[7]

(4) Yen Yüan asked about humanity. Confucius said, 'To mas-

ter oneself and return to propriety is humanity. If a man (the ruler) can for one day master himself and return to propriety, all under heaven will return to humanity. To practise humaniity depends on oneself. Does it depend on others?' Yen Yuan said, 'Although I am not intelligent, may I put your saying into practice.'[8]

(5) Tzu-kung said, 'If a ruler extensively confers benefit on the people and can bring salvation to all, what do you think of him? Would you call him a man of humanity?' Confucius said, 'Why only a man of humanity? He is without doubt a sage. Even (sage-emperors) Yao and Shun fell short of it. A man of humanity, wishing to establish his own character, also establishes the character of others, and wishing to be prominent himself, also helps others to be prominent. To be able to judge others by what is near to ourselves may be called the method of realizing humanity.'[9]

The simplest statement which Confucius makes about jen is that jen *is* to love men. In this sense jen seems to be an equivalent of benevolence. But to love without a principle means also to spoil. Therefore, on another occasion Confucius points out that only the man of jen knows how to love and how to hate people. Although no men are intrinsically hateable, yet, in order to really love men, we have to hate their evil-doings so that they may be forced to become educated as better men.

Thus jen is a much more profound kind of love than that of a devoted mother who lavishes all her fondness upon her children. True love in jen involves profound wisdom and sound judgement. In the third statement Confucius goes even further and gives concrete advice about realizing jen in life. It is a surprise to find that the first item Confucius lists, "be respectful in private life", does not even concern one's attitude towards others, but rather his attitude toward himself. Jen in this sense cannot be interpreted merely as benevolence or love. It is more like Schweitzer's reverence for life. Jen seems to imply a profound reverence for one's own life as well as a concern for other human lives, and for the transactions of human society. Its meaning is far wider than mere benevolence or altruism; rather it is the root of benevolence or altruism. Moreover, realizing jen is not merely empty talk. The principles involved in jen should be practised even when one lives amidst barbarians. They are universal principles not to be renounced simply because one happens to live in a different environment.

The foregoing discussion leads to an understanding of the true message conveyed in the fourth statement, which is perhaps one of the most profound statements Confucius makes about jen. "To master oneself" is the translation of the Chinese term *k'o-chi*, which may also be interpreted as "to overcome oneself". Although Confucius himself does not specify what is to be overcome in ourselves, it seems that the Sung philosophers are not far wrong in suggesting that we have to overcome the selfish desires within ourselves.[10] If we could discipline ourselves so that we would, in no circumstance, be swayed by unrestrained selfish desires, and hence become master of ourselves, then our outward behavior would also conform naturally with the rules of propriety. Therefore, the most important thing about jen is that we must cultivate the heart of jen or the mind of jen within ourselves, so that we can extend it to every aspect of our lives.

Thus, the term "propriety" in the text certainly does not mean merely external rules of propriety or social conventions which have been imposed on our behavior. It is rather that in our heart we have a natural love for propriety. Once our selfish desires are under control, the good will towards one's own life, as well as towards other lives, flows out without any obstruction. We are then able to recover our normal state of existence which is none other than a life of propriety.

Here we see clearly that there are parallels between Socrates' and Confucius' thought: the excellent moral nature of man is within himself rather than imposed upon him from any external source. Although in *The Analects* Confucius never mentions that human nature is good,[11] he is firmly convinced that there is tremendous potentiality in man. To develop such potentiality is to follow the natural course of things. Therefore it becomes the primary duty of a man not to follow his animal instincts or selfish desires. As for the detailed items which Confucius lists in his answer to Yen Yüan's further questioning, these are the means which help to recover our true selves. Since what Confucius refers to as propriety is the spirit of propriety rather than a rigid code of external rules of propriety, the chain of negative statements he makes should not be interpreted in such a priggish way as would please only the heart of a moral bigot.

Finally, in the fifth statement Confucius gives his view of the ideal commitment of a man. A man of jen wishes to establish his own character as well as that of other people. The spirit of this statement is similar to that of the Golden Rule, and the formulation of the statement is more detailed than its Western counterpart. Not only should you do unto others what you would like others to do unto you, but you should mold yourself into an ideal character and help others to do the same. Ideally, everyone in society should find his own way to become a healthy individual, with an ultimate commitment to jen and to develop a great concern for society at large and for the happiness of fellow human beings.

From the analysis above we should now have a fairly clear notion of jen. It certainly indicates a benevolent attitude towards people, but it is also much more than that. It implies the wisdom to distinguish what is good from what is evil. It is the realization of the intrinsic value of each individual life, and it shows an inalienable commitment to an ideal principle in life. The principle of jen allows for divergent manifestations. Once a man has grasped the spirit of jen, he should be able to find out what he must do in a given situation. Since each concrete situation is somewhat different from every other, the best one can do is to give a description of certain concrete situations as manifestations of jen. In this way people may learn from these examples and may realize the dynamic principle of jen in their own lives. This is exactly what Confucius does in *The Analects*. If he does not attempt to define jen, it is not because his mind is unsystematic, but because jen is itself beyond definition.

Moreover, the paradox involved in Tseng Tzu's answer to the question about the central thread in Confucius's philosophy can now be resolved. Since chung means none other than the full development of the heart of jen within the self, and shu the extension of this heart to others, they are beyond any doubt the two most important manifestations of jen. Therefore, Tseng Tzu's answer cannot be said to deviate from Confucius's own teaching. There is no paradox because jen cannot be defined neatly in any case and because the two threads of chung and shu are merely two aspects of jen.

Precisely because the moral discipline of the self and the search for the well-being of people cannot be artificially separated, Confucius refuses to draw a sharp line of distinction between ethics and political activities. In other words, politics would be an extension of ethics. To establish the character of the self is one's own moral aspiration, and to help to establish the character of others is the aim of political activity. But this aim cannot be achieved by imposing severe punishments upon other people. Therefore Confucius said:

> "Lead the people with governmental measures and regulate them by law and punishment, and they will avoid wrong doing but will have no sense of honor and shame. Lead them with virtue and regulate them by the rules of propriety (li), and they will have a sense of shame and, moreover, set themselves right."[12]

This statement certainly does not mean that law is altogether useless. It simply points out the fact that law alone is not an adequate means to lead people. How amazingly well Confucius' teaching fits in with the principles of modern educational psychology which emphasizes love and encouragement rather than hate and coercion. A ruler must set an example for his people, and a father must set an example for his son. From a Confucian point of view the highest ideal of a man is what later Chinese scholars phrase as "the way of inward sageliness and outward kingliness."

Although what Confucius teaches is a thoroughgoing practical type of philosophy, the realization of it in one's life is by no means easy. Confucius said:

> "I have never seen one who really loves humanity or one who really hates inhumanity. One who really loves humanity will not place anything above it. One who really hates inhumanity will practice humanity in such a way that inhumanity will have no chance to get at him. Is there anyone who has devoted his strength to humanity for as long as a single day? I have not seen anyone without sufficient strength to do so. Perhaps there is such a case, but I have not seen it."[13]

In other words, although everyone should be able to collect sufficient strength within himself to realize jen within his life, yet very few people are able to do so. Since realizing jen is an endless process, not even Confucius himself dares to claim that he is a sage or a man of jen. The Master said:

"The sage and the man of perfect virtue, how dare I *rank myself with them*? It may simply be said of me, that I strive to become such without satiety, and teach others without weariness.' Kung-hsî Hwâ said, 'This is just what we, the disciples, cannot immitate you in.' "[14]

It is instructive to note Confucius' own observation of the educational process he experienced in his life. Confucius said:

"At fifteen my mind was set on learning. At thirty my character had been formed. At forty I had no more perplexities. At fifty I knew the Mandate of Heaven (*T'ien-ming*). At sixty I was at ease with whatever I heard. At seventy I could follow my heart's desire without transgressing moral principles."[15]

It must have been at the later stages of his life that Confucius was able to declare: "Is humanity far away? As soon as I want it, there it is right by me."[16]

Although Confucius firmly commits himself to the principle of jen and has great faith in its application, this does not mean that jen will prevail in every case. In fact, one needs to sacrifice much in the process of realizing jen. Confucius said:

"A resolute scholar and a man of humanity will never seek to live at the expense of injuring humanity. He would rather sacrifice his life in order to realize humanity."[17]

His point of view is also clearly expressed in the statement that, if one seeks for humanity and gets it, then there is nothing for him to regret. His disciple, Tseng Tzu, develops further the master's teaching by saying:

"An officer must be great and strong. His burden is heavy and his course is long. He has taken humanity to be his own burden—is that not heavy? Only with death does his course stop—is that not long?"[18]

Confucius has always been pictured as an incurable optimist by temperament. The quotations above should serve as evidence for rejecting such an erroneous opinion. Confucius fully realizes what the actual conditions of life are, that what is contrary to jen has always been practised in real life. Indeed, at times he shows a great despair of life, but he is unshaken in his ultimate commitment to jen.

If a man has his ultimate commitment in jen, does he still need a religious faith? This question cannot be answered in a simple, straightforward way. In the following passages from *The Analects* Confucius comments on traditional religious beliefs and practices in his day.

Fan Ch'ih asked about wisdom. Confucius said, 'Devote yourself earnestly to the duties due to men, and respect spiritual beings but keep them at a distance. This may be called wisdom.'[19]

Wang-sun Chia asked, 'What is meant by the common saying, it is better to be on good terms with the God of the Kitchen [who cooks our food] than with the spirits of the shrine (ancestors) at the southwest corner of the house?' Confucius said, 'It is not true He who commits a sin against Heaven has no god to pray to.[20]'

Confucius was very ill. Tzu-lu asked that prayer be offered. Confucius said, 'Is there such a thing?' Tzu-lu replied, 'There is. A eulogy says, Pray to the spiritual beings above and below.' Confucius said, 'My prayer has been for a long time [that is, what counts is the life that one leads].'[21]

Confucius never discussed strange phenomena, physical exploits, disorder, or spiritual beings.[22]

Chi-lu (Tzu-lu) asked about serving the spiritual beings. Confucius said, 'If we are not yet able to serve man, how can we serve spiritual beings?' "I venture to ask about death.' Confucius said, 'If we do not know about life, how can we know about death?"[23] Moreover, Confucius further declared that " 'It is man that can make the Way great, and not the Way that can make man great."[24] Because of such passages many regard Confucius as an irreligious, agnostic, humanistic, moralistic thinker. On the other hand, we find in many instances that Confucius acts very much like a reactionary traditionalist. He insists upon keeping up the performance of traditional religious rites in a minutely detailed fashion. The following incident was reported:

"Tzu-kung wanted to do away with the sacrificing of a lamb at the ceremony in which the beginning of each month is reported to ancestors. Confucius said, 'Tz'u! You love the lamb but I love the ceremony."[25]

The most puzzling as well as the most important statement Confucius makes about sacrificial rites is perhaps the following:

> "When Confucius offered sacrifice to his ancestors, he felt *as if* his ancestral spirits were actually present. When he offered sacrifice to other spiritual beings, he felt *as if* they were actually present. He said, 'If I do not participate in the sacrifice, it is *as if* I did not sacrifice at all.'"[26] (Italics mine)

Is Confucius, after all, a pragmatic make-believer who would like to keep the traditional ritual ceremonies for the sake of invoking a sense of piety in people? And yet Confucius does seem to show a genuine belief in Heaven. On more than one occasion, when he was in great danger, he placed his faith in Heaven. Several times he said something like this: "Heaven produced the virtue that is in me; what can Huan T'ui do to me?"[27] Statements like this induce certain scholars to conclude that Confucius still believes in the traditional concept of Heaven as a supreme personal God who has dominant power over the cosmic order as well as over the moral order of man. There seems to be little doubt that Confucius did show a deep sense of mission in his life. Does this mean that, after all, Confucius was a religious man?

Apparently there are many contradictions involved in these varied interpretations of Confucius' religious philosophy. Is it the case that the old gentleman was such a muddle-headed thinker that he could hardly think anything through? Or is it the case that our interpretations are questionable? Upon closer examination, one must conclude that Confucius does have a coherent view which is consistent with his general commitment to jen. The difficulty is with the interpreters who have one-sided views of his religious philosophy and who lose sight of the central thread which runs through his doctrines. Hence, they fail to understand his philosophy as a whole.

Statements concerning religious matters cited above need further analysis. Let us first start with an examination of Confucius' attitude towards spiritual beings. It seems clear that Confucius does not care either to assert or to deny the existence of spiritual beings. He simply refuses to talk much about the subject, apparently because of an implicit belief that it has nothing to do with the more important aspects of life. Therefore, he is determined to practise an attitude of *epoche* against the topic. At a time when a host of spiritual beings were both believed in and worshipped on the local as well as on the national level, it required great insight and courage to point out that these do not have any concern with the core of our existence. Indeed, Confucius was introducing something revolutionary in his own day. As a man who lived some twenty-five hundred years prior to our time, and long before the development of modern science, he must be appreciated, because it was he who discovered a most intelligent attitude towards the subject-matter. This attitude, properly interpreted, could be adopted by modern man. Do spiritual beings exist? Paradoxically enough, Confucius's great contribution lies not in his giving an answer to the question, but in his refusal to answer the question. An avowed atheist today would be dissatisfied with Confuius' attitude, because Confucius was not radical enough to deny altogether the existence of spiritual beings. However, to deny the existence of such beings without inquiry is as irrational as to affirm the existence of such beings. Instead, we should hold an open mind towards the subject. It is no shame to confess our ignorance and to suspend our judgement on the topic until we find more decisive evidence which would enable us to say something definite about the matter. But to be ready to concede the existence of spiritual beings whenever decisive evidence could be produced certainly does not imply that we should do any bargaining with these beings in case they should exist. The ruling commitment of a man is to live as a man of jen. One cannot violate moral principles in order to seek gains gotten even from bargaining with spiritual beings. This is why Confucius declares that if one has sinned against Heaven, there is no god to pray to. Sacrifice for Confucius is definitely not a form of bribery, either to appease or to please the spiritual beings. Then what are we sacrificing for? This is a question we must answer in the following discussion.

By reflecting carefully upon the three *as if* statements Confucius makes about sacrifice, we have to conclude that for Confucius making sacrifice is an integral part of our lives which has a this-worldly rather than an other-worldly function. There were two main forms of sacrifices: sacrifices to ancestors and to Heaven. For Confucius it is out of our own inner demands that we make these sacrifices. We need to make sacrifice to our ancestors because they were the origin of our lives; and we need to make sacrifice to Heaven because Heaven is the origin of all things in the world. In fact it is for the same reason that we must be filial when our parents are still alive. Not only were they the origin of our lives, but they brought us up and took care of us when we were young. Thus naturally we have a feeling of filial piety towards them. Once we have realized the intrinsic value of life through our commitment to jen, it is only natural for us to appeal to forms of ritual ceremony to express our reverence for life and the world.

And the performance of these ceremonies, in turn, would enhance our feeling of piety towards this life. Moreover, the performance of these sacrifices would have great educational value for the common people. Thus the real foundation for ritual performances lies deep in the self rather than in the outside world. Confucius seems to imply that there is a profound depth dimension in man, and it is only through the realization of this depth dimension that he is able to develop into a full man.

All the ritual ceremonies thus have the function of helping man to develop this aspect of his life. They do not have much to do with the objective existence of the spiritual beings, and they do not have to presuppose Heaven as being a supreme overlord. The crux of the problem lies in whether we can extend our heart of jen to the whole universe or not. It is here that we have to make our existential decision. The apparent riddle of the *as if* statements made by Confucius is thus resolved.

It should be clear at this point that the concept of Heaven is not to be confused with the concept of god in his philosophy. As we have already noticed, although the existence of gods or spiritual beings is by no means certain in Confucius philosophical scheme, he does show a tremendous faith in Heaven. The only logical conclusion for us to draw is that Heaven is an important part of Confucius' philosophy, whereas god is not. However, many people were misled by a statement which they found in *The Analects* :

Tzu-kung said, 'We can hear our Master's [views] on culture and its manifestation, but we cannot hear his views on human nature and the Way of Heaven [because these subjects are beyond the comprehension of most people].'[28]

On the basis of this statement, they then declare that Confucius holds an agnostic attitude towards Heaven. But to accept such an interpretation would make Confucius' faith in Heaven completely incomprehensible. In fact the above-quoted statement says only that the disciples did not hear or understand the master's view of the Way of Heaven. It does not necessarily imply that he does not have a view of the Way of Heaven. Elsewhere in *The Analects* Confucius said:

> "I do not wish to say anything.' Tzu-kung said, 'If you do not say anything, what can we little disciples ever learn to pass on to others?' Confucius said, "Does Heaven (*T'ien*, Nature) say anything? The four seasons run their course and all things are produced. Does Heaven say anything?"[29]

The meanings contained in this passage are extremely rich. Confucius seems to imply that Heaven silently communicates with man. The universe as a whole is an orderly and creative universe, and human beings should imitate the example of Heaven. Hence they would be able to live in harmony with nature, not being alienated from nature. Therefore, Heaven, conceived as personal or impersonal, is intelligible to man. It stands for the symbol of the cosmic order as well as of the moral order in the universe, both of which we can experience in our daily lives without requiring recourse to any mystical vision of things. This explains why Confucius has so much faith in Heaven and has expressed a profound sense of mission in his life. The important thing is not to live a successful life according to external standards, but to live according to the Way. Hence, in spite of all the hardship one might suffer in actual life, Confucius cheerfully declares that "In the morning, hear the Way; in the evening, die content!"[30]

From the above discussion the threads of Confucius' thought are emerging. He does not rely primarily on metaphysical speculation. The most important thing for him is our experience of and commitment to jen. But once the central scheme of thought has been firmly established, it is not necessary for him to hold an hostile attitude toward metaphysical thinking. The universe is to be considered as an orderly and creative universe with intrinsic values in it. Man will be happy only if he lives according to the Way, and also according to his true nature. The speculations about gods, strange phenomena, and so forth, do not belong to the core of our existence. A man may lead a miserable life according to ordinary standards, but he may live a spiritually rich life according to the Way and die content!

If the above analysis of Confucius' philosophical thought is correct, we must caution against the temptation of applying any clichés to his thought. The Westerner likes to draw a sharp line of distinction between the supernatural and the natural, the sacred and the profane, the world of ideals and the world of facts, the pious and the atheistic. But in China there are no such sharp dichotomies. A humanist in the West is often an atheist. In spite of Confucius' mistrust of traditional deities, he did not lose his natural sense of piety. It is through the demand of the depth dimension of our souls that we have faith in the natural as well as the human world. Confucius has sown the seeds of a philosophy of union between Heaven and man which was further developed by his followers in the *Book of Changes*.[31]

Now we are ready to answer the question whether Confucius was a religious man or not. If religion is defined in the narrower sense as a belief in a personal God or spiritual beings, then Confucius was certainly not a religious man. If, on the other hand, religion is defined in the sense of ultimate commitment which gives satisfaction to the demands of our inner selves, then Confucius was a deeply religious man. Today when there is a growing tendency towards secularization in theology, Confucius' religious philosophy merits a reappraisal.[32] The sage of the past may prove to be a prophet for the future.

In a way Confucius' position in Chinese civilization may be compared with that of Jesus Christ in Western civilization. Confucius did not achieve anything great in the practical world, and he must have considered himself a man of failure. The paradoxical thing is that his thought has dominated Chinese civilization. Even today most Chinese intellectuals adopt Confucius attitude: that of a through-going this-worldliness which falls neither into unrestrained hedonism on the one hand nor rigorous moralism on the other.

Confucius has set up a personal ideal for later generations. On the one hand he has a tremendous respect for the past and a sense of continuity. On the other hand, he is definitely not a traditional reactionary. It is through him that the traditional system of rites received new spirit. And it is also through him that education for the first time was extended to all classes. Within the limits of this chapter, important aspects of Confucius' philosophy must be omitted. The emphasis has been on his discussion of his ultimate commitment and religious philosophy. To maintain the continuity with the past and to open up new possibilities for the future were Confucius' great contributions to Chinese civilization.

Notes

1. Ssu-ma Ch'ien, the great historian who lived about three hundred years after Confucius, wrote a complete biography of Confucius in his monumental *Historical Records*. Modern scholars, however, tend to challenge the authenticity of a number of facts as recorded in the biography. Creel, for example, doubted that Confucius had ever held any high governmental post in Lu at all. He believed that these were stories concocted by later Confucian scholars in order to give more prestige to their master. Cf. H.G. Creel, *Confucius and the Chinese Way* (New York: Harper & Brothers, 1960), pp. 37-71. For our present purpose, however, it is not necessary for us to pass any judgement upon these varied theories. We shall be contented with giving a brief account of Confucius' life as accepted by tradition.
2. Wing-tsit Chan, *A Source Book in Chinese Philosophy* (Princeton: Princeton University Press, 1963), p. 27. Chan has translated many key passages from *The Analects*. I shall use his translations unless otherwise indicated. Hereafter the book will be referred to as *Source Book*. Tseng Tzu was one of Confucius most important disciples. Ts'an was his private name.
3. Ibid., p. 24.
4. Ibid., p. 26. Humanity, is Wing-tsit Chan's translation for jen, and superior man for chun tzu, which literally means gentleman. Before Confucius, a gentleman was determined by his status of birth, but Confucius radically changed the meaning of the term by defining a gentleman in terms of his moral achievement.
5. Ibid., p. 40. Fan Ch'ih was Confucius' pupil.
6. Ibid., p. 25.
7. Ibid., p. 41.
8. Ibid., p. 38. Yen Yuan was Confucius' pupil. When he asked for detailed items to practice humanity, Confucius' answer was: "Do not look at what is contrary to propriety, do not listen to what is contrary to propriety, do not speak what is contrary to propriety, and do not make any movement which is contrary to propriety."
9. Ibid., p. 31. Tzu-kung was Confucius' pupil. Yao and Shun were

legendary emperors who flourished in the third millennium B.C., according to traditional accounts. Confucius traced his own moral and political ideals to these two-sage-emperors of ancient time.

10. Man has a natural tendency to seek for his own physical gratification and material gains, and hence is tempted to do much evil in his life. But Confucius said, "If you set your mind on humanity, you will be free from evil." See *Source Book*, p. 25. Also man tends to cling to his personal biases and prejudices. But Confucius was reported to have been free from four things: He had no arbitrariness of opinion, no dogmatism, no obstinacy, and no egotism. Cf. ibid., p. 35. The Sung dynasty was between 960-1279 A.D. and Neo-Confucian philosophy was the dominant trend during that period.

11. The only thing Confucius explicitly says about human nature is that by nature men are alike; through practice they have become far apart. Cf. *Source Book*, p. 45.

12. Ibid., p. 22.
13. Ibid., p. 26.
14. James Legge, tr., *The Four Books* (New York: Paragon Reprint Corp., 1966), p. 93. *The Analects* was selected by the great Sung philosopher Chu Hsi (1130-1200) as one of the Confucian *Four Books*. "Perfect Virtue" was Legge's translation for jen. Hereafter, the book will be referred to as *The Four Books*.
15. *Source Book*, p. 22.
16. Ibid., p. 33.
17. Ibid., p. 43.
18. Ibid., p. 33.
17. Ibid., p. 30.
20. Ibid., p. 25. Wang-sun Chia was a great officer and commander-in-chief in the state of Wei.
21. Ibid., Tau-lu was Confucius' pupil.
22. Ibid., p. 32.
23. Ibid., p. 36.
24. Ibid., p. 44.
25. Ibid., p. 25. Ta'u was Tau-kung's private name.
26. Ibid. Legge's translation of the paragraph is as follows: "He sacrificed *to the dead*, as if they were present. He sacrificed to the spirits, as if the spirits were present. The Master said, 'I consider myself not being present at the sacrifice, as if I did not sacrifice." See *The Four Books*, p. 30.
27. *Source Book*, p. 32. Human Tuui was a military officer in the state of Sung who attempted to kill Confucius by felling a tree. Confucius was then 59.
28. Ibid., p. 28.
29. Ibid., p. 47.
30. Ibid., p. 26.
31. *The Book of Changes* (*I Ching*) is one of the basic Confucian Classics. It is divided into the texts and commentaries. The texts consist of sixty-four hexagrams and judgements on them. These hexagrams are based on the Eight

Trigrams, each of which consists of three lines, divided or undivided, the divided representing the weak, or yin, and undivided representing the strong, or yang. Each of these eight corresponds to a direction, a natural element, a moral quality, etc. For example, *ch'ien* (☰) is heaven, *k'un* (☷) is earth. Each trigram is combined with another, one upon the other, thus making sixty-four hexagrams. These hexagrams symbolize various possible situations. There are seven commentaries, but three of them have two parts, thus constituting the "ten wings" of the book. Tradition has ascribed the Eight Trigrams to the legendary sage-emperor Fu-hsi, the sixty-four hexagrams to King Wen of Chou (r. 1171-1122 B.C., and the "ten wings" to Confucius. Most modern scholars have rejected this attribution, but they are not agreed on when and by whom the book was produced. Most probably it is a product of many hands over a long period of time, from the fifth or sixth century B.C. to the third or fourth century B.C. See *Source Book*, Ch. 13, pp. 262-270.

32. Cf. Shu-hsien Liu, "The Religious Import of Confucian Philosophy: Its Traditional Outlook and Contemporary Significance", *Philosophy East and West*, XXI (April, 1971), pp. 157-175.

3
TAOISM

JOSEPH WU

I

To begin with the author of this chapter would like to point out that there is no Chinese word which is exactly equivalent to the English word "Taoism". This term has been used ambiguously to refer to both *Tao Chia* and *Tao Chiao* in the Chinese cultural tradition. In fact, *Tao Chia* denotes a school of thought of which Lao Tzu[1] and Chuang Tzu[2] were the main representative philosophers. *Tao Chiao*, on the other hand, denotes a religion founded by Chang Tao-ling of the Han Dynasty.[3] This chapter will ignore *Tao Chiao*, as it will be taken up later, and will aim at an exposition of *Tao Chia*.

It will be based primarily on the *Tao Te Ching*[4] of Lao Tzu and the authentic works of Chuang Tzu,[5] with occasional references to later philosophers. In order to avoid unnecessary specific details and controversial issues, the author of this chapter will focus on the explication of three important Taoist Concepts: *Tao*, *Freedom*, and *Non-action* (wu-wei), which will constitute the three main sections of this chapter.

II. The Relative and the Absolute

The distinction between types of knowledge seems a favorite method in the writings of philosophers, both East and West. Plato made a distinction between opinion and knowledge which opened the way to further distinctions like appearance and reality, the empirical and conceptual, and rational and factual truth. A dramatic distinction between relative and absolute knowledge was given by a recent French philosopher, Henri Bergson, who wrote in the opening paragraph of his well-known little book *An Introduction to Metaphysics* :[6]

A comparison of the definitions of metaphysics and the various concepts of the absolute leads to the discovery that philosophers, in spite of their apparent divergencies, agree in distinguishing two profoundly different ways of knowing a thing. The first implies that we move round the object; the second, that we enter into it. The first depends on the point of view at which we are placed and on the symbols by which we express ourselves. The second neither depends on a point of view nor relies on any symbol. The first kind of knowledge may be said to stop at the relative; the second, in those cases where it is possible, to attain the absolute.

This is the very distinction the Taoists had attempted to make two thousand years ago. The distrust of linguistic symbols has been shared by both Bergson and the Taoists. The opening chapter of the *Tao Te Ching* launched an attack on language: "The Tao that can be spoken of is not the absolute Tao; names that can be given are not adequate names." Chuang Tzu joined this theme and maintained that "Speech by its very nature cannot express the absolute."[7] Thus the Taoists distrust argumentation as a means of attaining reliable knowledge or approaching truth. This has challenged a deep-rooted habit of Western philosophers who are inclined to think that argumentation is a necessary element of philosophy. Chuang Tzu says :[8]

> Suppose that you argue with me. If you beat me, instead of my beating you, are you necessarily right and am I necessarily wrong? Or, if I beat you and not you me, am I necessarily right and are you necessarily wrong? Is the one of us right and the other wrong? Or are both of us right and both of us wrong?

The criticism of argumentation is only a logical consequence of a very fundamental characteristic of Taoism, which is a distrust of language. A language is only a particular set of habits growing out of a cultural context, and the adequacy of the beliefs and knowledge as embodied in that language is only relative to that particular culture. If one is accustomed to thinking in terms of a subject-predicate sentence structure, he would certainly have a difficult time in grasping the meaning imbedded in a language which has no subject-predicate distinction. When one has grown up in a language where there are strict tense distinctions, he will fall to grasp the meaning as represented by a language which defies tenses. In a word, a language is a set of limitations imposed upon the individual by the social and cultural environment in which he grows up.

If a natural language is a set of limitations which represent a provincialism of cultural habits, would the construction of a universal language above all languages break such a limitation? The Taoist answer is that, even if such a language were possible, it would still be restricted by a finite viewpoint; for after all it is a human language. What is true of the human world may not be true of other worlds, the worlds of birds, monkeys, deer, fish and the like. Thus Chuang Tzu explained :[9]

> Now I would ask you some questions. If a man sleeps in a damp place, he will have a pain in his loins, and half his body will be as if dead. But is it so with an eel? If a man lives up in a tree, he will be frightened and all in a tremble. But is it so with a monkey? Of these three who knows the right way of habitation? Men eat flesh; deer feed on grass. Centipedes enjoy snakes; owls and crows delight in mice. Of these four, who knows the right taste? Monkey mates with monkey; the buck with the doe; male fish with female. Mao Ch'iang and Li Chi were considered by men as the most beautiful of women; but at the sight of them fish dived deep in the water, birds soared high in the air, and deer hurried away. Of these four, who knows the right standard of beauty?

Again, Chuang Tzu told an allegorical story of the death of a seabird. The Marquis of Lu, falling in love with the bird, gave it a top quality wine, entertained it with delightful music, and ordered a bullock slaughtered to feed it. But instead of enjoying good music and delicious food, the bird was dazed and frightened. In three days it died.[10] Wine may be delightful to a human individual but it is almost a poison to a bird. Likewise, "Water, which is life to fish, is death to man."[11] In short, for the Taoists, human knowledge is a limited knowledge and the human viewpoint is only a finite viewpoint. Human culture is but a crystallization of human bias, finitude, and partiality.

Then what is absolute knowledge? The Taoist answer is that absolute knowledge is the knowledge of Tao. What is Tao? If we asked a Taoist such a question, the answer would most likely be: "If I were to tell you, it would no longer be Tao." Nevertheless the Taoists did not intend to close their doors to communication. Instead, they have tried their best to explain the meaning of Tao to us.

The term "Tao" in the Chinese language, has a vast range of meanings. It is not only a key concept in Chinese philosophy but also has a very important usage in both literary and colloquial Chinese. The character for Tao is composed of two main parts. One of them, being an image of a human head which has been interpreted as a phonetic symbol, may also have contributed some meaning. The other part means "going" or "that which is for going". The combination of the two yields the meaning of "the way" or "the leading way." In Confucian classics it connotes dominantly the meaning of "social order" or "the most fundamental moral principle". For example, we can observe in the *Confucian Analects* the following:

"The superior man seeks Tao rather than a mere living.... He worries about Tao rather than about poverty." (15:31)

"If one can hear Tao in the morning, he can die in the evening without regret." (4:8)

"When Tao prevails in the society, then show yourself: when it does not prevail, then hide." (8:13)

"If Tao prevailed in the world, there would be no need for me to reform." (18:6)

In ordinary Chinese, tao has even greater varieties of meanings. It can mean "interest". "People of the same tao" means "people of the same interest". The phrase "tao yu", for some mysterious reason, means opium smokers. The phrase *"pu neng jen tao"* means "impotent" or "being unable to perform a man's function." "Tao li" means "reason". However Chinese Christians often call a preacher's sermon by this phrase, and *"t'ing tao li"* has thus become a synonymous term for "going to church". *"Kuei tao shan"*, or "going back to the mountain of tao", is a euphemistic expression for death. The last example reflects the influence of Taoism, which is our main topic here.

Tao as a metaphysical concept stands for the ultimate reality of the universe. Unlike such Pre-Socratic concepts as water, air or fire, Tao does not imply any notion of material substance. Unlike the Platonic forms, Tao is not entirely abstract. Because of its immaterial nature, it cannot be properly qualified or predicated by words which usually characterize material or corporeal objects. Ordinary language performs its function adequately in describing ordinary matters of life and our daily perceptual world. But it becomes very restricted and limited when it is applied to the characterization of Tao. This is why Lao Tzu says that "The Tao that can be spoken of is not the absolute Tao." Nevertheless Lao Tzu did not give up his effort to communicate with us. He has tried to use hints, suggestions, and metaphors to characterize Tao.

> Tao, being a hollow vessel,
>   Is never exhaustible in use.
> Fathomless,
>   Perhaps the fountainhead of all existences. (*Tao Te Ching*, 4)

What is meant by a hollow vessel? Does it suggest that Tao is emptiness, nothingness, or, using our familiar philosophical jargon, Non-being? According to the *Tao Te Ching*, Lao Tzu seems to have suggested that Tao is virtually Non-being.[12] But, what is Non-being? Does it mean the absence of all forms of existences? The clue to the answer to this question is found in the following passage:

> The thing that is called Tao
>   Is vague and elusive.
> Elusive and vague,
>   Latent in it are forms.
> Vague and elusive,
>   Latent in it is something.
> Shadowy and dim,
>   Latent in it is the vital force.
> The vital force being very pure,
>   Latent in it is something real. (*Tao Te Ching*, 21)

From this passage it is obvious that Tao is by no means the absence of any form of existence. The words "vague" and "elusive" simply mean that Tao is not a sharply demarcated corporeal substance or determinate being. The words "forms", "something" and "vital force", positively suggest that Tao is "something" rather than pure "nothingness". A later Taoist, realizing the difficulties in characterizing Tao, comments: "If we want to say it is Non-being, yet things from it gain completeness. If we want to say it is Being, yet we do not see its form."[13]

From the viewpoint of the present author, the nature of Tao cannot be settled in terms of Being and Non-being; for these two terms are among the most obscure concepts in human history. If we have to use this pair of traditional jargons, what we can say is that Tao is both Being and Non-being; or that it is neither, depending on how you define these two problematic terms.

Now what we are most certain of is that Tao is not the absence of any form of existences; and it cannot be Non-being if we mean by Non-being pure nothingness. Certainly Tao is something. The question then is: What are the characteristics of this something? Lao Tzu gives us a preliminary answer:

> There was an undifferentiated actuality.
>   Prior to Heaven and Earth it had existed.
> Lonely, inactive,
> Independent, and unchanging,
> Revolving unfailingly,
>   Can be considered the mother of the universe.
> I know not its name, and call it Tao. (*Tao Te Ching*, 25).

Again he says:

> Tao gave birth to the One.
>   The One produced the Two.
> Out of the Two came the Three.
>   And out of the Three came all existences. (*Tao Te Ching*, 42).

These two passages seem to suggest that Tao created the universe and gave birth to all that exists. This is probably why many scholars, both Western and Eastern, have tried to compare Tao with God in the Judaic-Christian tradition. Such a comparison, from the viewpoint of the present author, although not entirely mistaken, is very misleading. We should understand that Chinese culture is far less religious as compared to Western and Hindu cultures. If we interpret Tao in terms of God or a Divine Being, this is to force Chinese culture to be as religious as the Hebrew or Hindu tradition.

It follows that this comparison will undermine the humanistic spirit of Chinese culture and the naturalistic flavor of Taoism. Too much attention to the superficial resemblance between Tao and God can be a great hindrance to an adequate understanding of Chinese culture. Therefore, from the viewpoint of this author, the differences between the two, at the present stage of intercultural understanding, should receive more attention. These two concepts are different in many ways, but the following are the most important.

First of all, the most significant difference between the concept of Tao and the concept of God in the Judaic-Christian tradition is that the latter is a Deity of tremendous action, while the former is an embodiment of the principle of non-action. The *Tao Te Ching* explains very clearly that "the Tao never does anything." (37). Nevertheless, when we read the *Bible*, we easily notice that God has done many things. In addition to his labor in creating the world, he has exercised power to punish people, legislate commandments, give orders and make announcements.[14] But one can never find in the Taoist classics that Tao took any action of this kind. In the history of China, Tao has never become angry and destroyed two cities. Tao has never attempted to convert any 'pagan' into a Taoist like the dramatic conversion of St. Paul. Tao has never legislated any laws or commandments to restrict the behavior of mankind or other forms of creatures, but just lets them follow their own way. Chuang Tzu has pointed out that "Things are transformed of themselves"[15], and Lao Tzu emphatically declared that "the principle of Tao is spontaneity."[16]

A second difference follows the first. Or it might be better to say that it is the precondition of the first. God in the Judaic-Christian tradition is a personal Deity while Tao is impersonal and naturalistic. In the Christian context we often talk of or hear about "the will of God." But in the Taoist tradition, we never hear of "the will of Tao." Tao has never exercised authority (in fact it does not have one) to assert its power like the God in the *Old Testament*. Nor did Tao love mankind and send its beloved son to save the world. Tao has never performed miracles. Probably a Taoist would think that miracles represent a deviation from or violation of Tao.

A third difference is that God is an object of worship, while Tao has never been one. Tao would not listen to prayers, probably because it does not have ears. Even in the Taoist religion, the supernatural Taoists pray to some deities who were originally from the human world.[17] But they do not pray to Tao. In a strict sense, Tao is neither religiously available; nor is it even religiously relevant.

If scholars were to compare Tao with the concept of God as interpreted by some philosophers like Spinoza or Whitehead, I would have no objection. But when God is interpreted in terms of a metaphysical principle rather than a personal deity with authority and love, he is no longer the God of the Judaic-Christian tradition. Han Fei's interpretation of Tao reveals that Tao is a metaphysical principle rather than a deity. Here is a passage from his commentary :[18]

> Tao is that whereby all things are so, and with which all principles agree. Principles (*li*) are the markings (*wen*) of completed things. Tao is that whereby all things become complete. Therefore it is said that Tao is that which gives principles. When things have their principles, the one (thing) cannot be the other .... All things have each their own different principle, whereas Tao brings the principles of all things into single agreement. Therefore it can be both one thing and another, and is not one thing only.

Since Tao is a metaphysical principle, it requires philosophical talent to understand the meaning of Tao. Some people only have some vague feelings of it. Vulgar men would even laugh at it as too abstract, impractical, or irrelevant. Realizing this, Lao Tzu comments on the different levels of man's understanding of Tao:

> When men of superior understanding hear the Tao,
>   They try hard to live in accordance with it.
> When the common folks hear the Tao,
>   They seem to be appreciative but do not understand it.
> When the lowest type hear the Tao,
>   They simply break into loud laughter. (*Tao Te Ching*, 41).

Since men of superior understanding are very rare, the principle of Tao can hardly be popularized. The Taoists seem to be aware that common people are more receptive to Confucian values such as *jen* (human-heartedness), *yi* (righteousness), *li* (proprieties), *hsiao* (filial piety), etc.. From Lao Tzu's viewpoint, "On the decline of the Great Tao, the doctrines of human-heartedness and righteousness arose."[19] When the absolute is unattainable, we have to be content with the relative. The Absolute for the majority of mankind remains an unrealized goal.

III. BONDAGE AND FREEDOM

The topic of freedom has constituted a fundamental philosophical issue for both East and West. Western philosophers, legal scholars, political theorists, revolutionaries and religionists have explored this concept in many different directions. But the most general and dominant notion of freedom in the West is its implication of being free from external constraint, being able to satisfy one's own needs and desires. However, the concept of freedom in the East is very different. Professor E.A. Burtt has pointed out that:[20]

> According to the dominant orientation of the East, one who is merely free from external constraint is by no means really free; for this he must be liberated from the internal forces that drive him to make wrong choices or are revealed in unrealistic and ego-centered desires. When an inquirer asked Sri Ramakrishna, "When shall I be free?" the saint replied, "When the 'I' shall cease to be." He meant the ego that is in bondage to these forces; only when liberated from this bondage is a man truly free.

Professor Burtt's presentation, however, represents much more of the Hindu than the Chinese view of freedom. Although Chinese culture has been influenced by Buddhism and although there are striking similarities between Buddhism and Taoism, the Taoist concept of freedom is uniquely different from that of Buddhism or Hinduism.

What is the Taoist concept of freedom? A simple answer is that freedom can be acquired only by following Tao. Following Tao is not the same as "following the will of God" or "identifying oneself with Brahman." The Taoists do not favor the suppression of the individual. Freedom for them is not the denial of the ego or individuality. The Taoists recognize the importance of individuality or the unique qualities of individual existences, for the individuality of a particular existence is endowed by Tao. Therefore, to suppress individuality is a violation of Tao or the Natural Way. Chuang Tzu explains this to us in an interesting allegory.

There was once a regional emperor called Hun-tun who had two emperor friends, Shu and Hu. Hun-tun treated both of them kindly and generously. Shu and Hu always thought of repaying his kindness but had little idea of what should be done. Finally they came up with an idea. They thought all men had seven openings (sense organs) so that they could see, hear, eat, and breathe. But Hun-tun was born defective for he did not have even a single one. So they decided to bore him some. Every day they bored one hole. When they accomplished their enormous plan, Hun-tun returned to the mountain of Tao.[21]

This story suggests the importance of individuality or a particular existence. Hun-tun was endowed by Tao with no sense organs; yet he could live happily by following his own nature. Nevertheless, his friends, with a good intention and kind heart, tried to change what was born by nature, and this led to disaster.

What then is individuality? Individuality is the embodiment or particularization of Tao. The Taoists call it by the Chinese term *te* which has been translated into English as "virtue", "character" or "power". Te is the principle underlying each individual existence. Chuang Tzu explains: "When things obtained that by which they came into existence, it was called their *te*."[22] Another ancient Chinese philosopher, Kuan-tzu, calls it "the dwelling place of Tao."[23] This metaphor suggests that Tao and Te are intimately related. The basic distinction between the two is the one of universality and particularity. Spontaneity is no doubt a universal principle, the principle of Tao. The te of a fish is its ability and inclination to swim, and the te of a bird is its ability and inclination to fly. In other words, it is spontaneous for a bird to fly, and for a fish to swim. If we force a bird to swim and a fish to fly, this is violation of the principle of spontaneity. The term "authentic existence" in modern existentialism seems a very interesting counterpart of te in Taoism. For the existentialists, freedom lies in the assertion of one's authentic existence; and, for the Taoists, freedom is the full realization of one's *te*. In our discussion here, for the sake of communicational convenience, these two terms will be used interchangeably.

In order to understand what freedom is, we should first understand the nature of bondage; for freedom can be defined negatively as the conquest of, or liberation from bondage. For Spinozoa bondage is formed by our passions. For the spiritualists, whether Buddhists or Christians, the material world constitutes a bondage on us. The Taoists have synthesized both viewpoints. First, let us listen to Lao Tzu :

> The five colors blind man's eyes;
> The five sounds deafen man's ears;
> The five flavors spoil man's taste;
> Horse-racing and hunting madden man's mind;
> Goods hard to get impede man's actions. (*Tao Te Ching*, 12)

Chuang Tzu explains in less poetic but more clear language saying:[24]

> There are five ways in which we lose our original nature. First, the five colors confuse the eye and obstruct our vision. Second, the five notes confuse the ear and obstruct our hearing. Third, the five smells assail our nostrils and block up our forehead. Fourth, the five tastes foul the mouth and hurt our taste. Fifth, desires and occupations confuse our mind and cause agitation of our spirit.

The fifth item in Chuang Tzu's statement suggests that not only the material world can constitute a bondage upon us, but our desires and occupations can equally cause the loss of our authentic existence. In a certain sense, our sharp sensitivity or awareness of the difference between ourselves and others can also form a bondage. For example, I am now a poor college professor, and I am aware that many of my high school friends already have become top executives, attorneys and medical doctors earning over fifty thousand dollars a year. I might regret that I did not go to medical school, law school or into the business world. If I had, with my talents, I could have been as successful as they. Now, my monthly paycheck cannot even satisfy my basic needs, house payments, groceries, utility bills, my wife's necessary dresses, and my children's educational expenses.

Such an awareness may become severely binding on me and thus cause the loss of my freedom—the freedom to realize myself. Why? The reason is simply this. I am a philosopher, and being a philosopher has been my own choice based on my ability and inclination. But, if I were tempted by the business world and gave up my philosophical and scholarly commitment in order to become a high-paid executive, I would be losing my authentic existence.

Chuang Tzu, realizing such a crisis confronting man, teaches us with an interesting story of a mythical bird. In the first chapter of his work he tells us of a huge bird and two small creatures. The huge bird, which is called *peng*, can fly up to ninety thousand miles and can endure a continuous trip of six months. However the small cicada and dove, with a maximum of effort, can go only up to the top of some trees. Sometimes they even cannot go that far, and they fall to the ground midway. But there is no point in the two small creatures envying the peng. Kuo Hsiang wrote an excellent comment on this allegorical story saying :[25]

> Although the great is different from the small, yet if they all indulge themselves in the sphere of self-enjoyment, then all things are following their own nature and doing according to their own capacity; all are what they ought to be and equally happy. There is no room for the distinction of superior and inferior.

Therefore there is no point in a poor school teacher envying the Ford and Rockefeller families; and there is no point in a poor housewife envying Mrs. Jackie Onasis. I learned of one couple who tried to press their son, who was a talented artist, to go to medical school; for they did not want him to suffer financial hardship. This is quite typical of many parents in this modern society. But, from a Taoist's viewpoint, this is to force a fish to fly and a bird to swim. It is a deprivation of one's *te* or authentic existence.

I hope my readers are not given the impression that Taoism is a philosophy of self-interest or individualism in the vulgar sense. The Taoists are concerned with self-interest, but their kind of interest does not mean material gain or reputation. They are concerned with individuality, but their way to assert individuality is not to do whatever the individual pleases. Paradoxically enough, the Taoist way to assert one's individuality is self-forgetting, to affirm one's own interest in disinterested action. The topic of disinterested action will receive more attention in the next section. Here my topic is self-forgetting, or simply forgetting.

A popularized version of the Taoist thesis of forgetting is found in the English translation of the famous Chinese novel *Dream of the Red Chamber*. A depressed, aging man called Chen Shih-yin, after a series of family misfortunes, heard a Taoist sing the following song:[26]

> We all envy the immortals because they are free,
> But fame and fortune we cannot forget.
> Where are the ministers and generals of the past and the present?
> Under neglected graves overgrown with weeds.
>
> We all envy the immortals because they are free,
> But gold and silver we cannot forget.
> All our lives we save and hoard and wish for more,
> When suddenly our eyes are forever closed.
>
> We all envy the immortals because they are free,
> But our precious wives we cannot forget.
> They speak of love and constancy while we live,
> But marry again soon enough after we are dead.
>
> We all envy the immortals because they are free,
> But our sons and grandsons we cannot forget.
> Many there are, of devoting parents, from ancient times—
> But how few of the sons are filial and obedient!

Without fully understanding all the subtle meanings in this song, Shih-yin greeted the Taoist saying: "What did you try to say? What I can get is 'free' and 'forget'." "That's what you need to get," answered the Taoist. "For if you are free, you'll forget, and if you forget, you'll be free. In other words, to forget is to be free and to be free is to forget."[27]

What is the implication of this song? This song suggests a way from bondage to freedom. Fame, fortune, gold, silver, spouses, and offspring all can constitute worldly ties upon us. How do we liberate ourselves from all these ties? By forgetting. What does "forgetting" mean here? How is such a control of memory possible? A student may try to memorize something for the test. But how can we forget something as we wish?

According to modern psychology, to forget an event is to suppress it into one's subconsciousness. But this is by no means the intent of the Taoists. Deliberate and artificial forgetfulness leads to bondage rather than freedom, for it is a violation of the principle of spontaneity. Then how can we forget something spontaneously, when its impression has already been deposited into our memory?

For the Taoists, forgetting has a special meaning. To forget something is to transcend the customary view or conventional interpretation of its value. The customary view of money is that it contributes to one's well-being, living comfortably in a mansion with a heated swimming pool, owning the latest Continental or Rolls Royce, and enjoying a luxuriously planned vacation spent in the Bahamas or Miami Beach. The customary view of children is that they ought to perform their filial duty and repay your favor of supporting and educating them when they are young. Perhaps someone may say that examples like money and children are more or less socially or culturally determined and thus are not universal to mankind; and this is the basic reason that the Taoists would like to transcend the common views of them. Americans value money the most, and Chinese people are greatly concerned with offspring; and the elevated value of money and the excessive concern for filial piety can be considered the product of some particular tradition. But, if we find something which is universally held by mankind, should we still consider it merely a conventional or customary view?

Perhaps the notion of death meets such a universal standard. What is death? No matter how it is defined by different people, it creates anxiety and fear in all mankind. The immanent purpose common to all religions is the spiritual conquest of death, and medical professionals aim at deferring its arrival. Is death something really dreadful? Chuang Tzu's answer is found in the implication of a story:[28]

> Lady Li was the daughter of the border warden of Ai. When the lord of Ch'in first got her she wept until the collar of her robe was thoroughly drenched with tears. But when later she

went to live in the palace of the lord, shared with him his elegant couch, and shared the delicacies of his dining-table, she regretted that she had wept. How do I know that the dead will not regret that they formerly craved for life?

From the Taoist viewpoint "death and life are never ceasing transformation." Since death is the natural result of life, to feel bitterness against it is to violate the principle of Tao.[29] If we can grasp this basic principle we can understand that life and death are basically the same. It is only customary views which have separated death from life and have valued one and feared the other.

In short, all the conventional views of things and their relation to us impose upon us standards of valuation which constitute a subtle and sophisticated bondage binding us both physically and psychologically. This is why, from the viewpoint of the Taoists, Confucian values like jen, yi and li, are only relative and ought to be transcended. This has been fully illustrated in the fictional conversation between Confucius and his best student Yen Hui.[30]

> Yen Hui said to the Master, "I made some progress."
> "What do you mean?" asked Confucius.
> "I have already forgotten human-heartedness (jen) and righteousness (yi)."
> "Very well," replied Confucius, "but you still haven't got it."
> They met again another day and Yen Hui said, "I have made further progress now."
> "What do you mean?"
> "I can now sit into forgetfulness," replied Yen Hui.
> Confucius was a little startled, then asked: "What do you mean by sitting into forgetfulness?"
> "I have abandoned my body," replied Yen Hui, "and gave up my knowledge, and so have become one with the Great Path (ta tung). This is what I mean by sitting into forgetfulness."

When a person achieves the state of sitting into forgetfulness, he experiences only pure phenomena or uninterpreted reality. He does not see things as he saw them before. He does not see things as other people do. Delicious food will no longer stimulate his appetite. Beautiful music will no longer please his ears. A nude female body will no longer arouse his sexual desire. Death to him is no longer a threat or an object of fear. Danger to him is not something to be worried about.

Chuang Tzu calls such a personality chih jen (ultimate person or person of the highest level). This is the ideal personality of Taoism. Chuang Tzu characterizes this kind of personality as the following :[31]

> The chih jen is spirit-like. Even when the great lakes burned up, he would not feel hot. Even when the great rivers were frozen, he would not feel cold. Even when the mountains were riven by thunder and the seas thrown into waves by storm, he would not be frightened. A person like this could mount upon the clouds, could ride upon the sun and the moon, and thus wander beyond the four seas. Neither life nor death can affect him, much less gain and loss.

I hope my readers will not take Chuang Tzu's characterization as literally descriptive. "Riding on clouds", "the moon", and "the sun" and "wandering beyond the four seas" should be understood as metaphorical expressions. In a certain sense the chin jen is an ideal person depicted imaginatively rather than an existing person literally described. *Chih jen* is an absolutely free man, but he is not aware of his own freedom. When one is aware of his freedom or his need for freedom, then he is not absolutely free. The Taoists believe that such a state of absolute freedom can be attained. The question is, by what way can we attain such a spiritual level? The answer is that it is a twofold path: the understanding of Tao and the practice of *wu-wei*. The former has been already expounded in Section I, and the latter will receive full attention in the next section.

IV. Action and Non-action

No one would deny the fact that American life is full of unceasing action. Speeding cars fill the interstate highways continuously day and night. Out of the chimneys of large factories smoke comes twenty-four hours a day, signifying the unfailing action of their engineers and their capitalist operators. In metropolitan areas there are restaurants and service stations open round the clock to accommodate the needs of this society of unceasing action. People in industry value productive action. Medical doctors are busy acting upon the body of their patients. Lawyers are always ready for some legal action in the courts.

An average American, no matter what he is, cannot avoid three important kinds of action—filing income tax returns, "celebrating" Christmas, and presidential elections. As a spectator of Western culture from the Orient, the present author observes that action is an immanent value permeating most, if not all, aspects of Western culture. It is probably a logical consequence of the fact that Western men from the very beginning have had a Judaic-Christian concept of God as a Deity of tremendous action.

The Taoist thesis of wu-wei seems diametrically opposed to the American way of life. Wu-wei literally means "non-action"; but it implies a great deal more than what it appears to mean. My preliminary interpretation of this concept is that it is a Chinese version of Ockham's Razor. It is a principle of simplicity or economy. For Ockham, entities or principles should not be unnecessarily multiplied (*Entia non multiplicanda praeter necessitatem*).[32] While Ockham's razor is directed primarily toward purely metaphysical and epistemological issues, the Taoists are concerned with an economy of action and a simplicity of life. Confucius shared this fundamental thesis when he said: "In hearing cases, I do not differ from others (i.e., other people who assuming the role of a judge). But I maintain, however, the important thing is to have no cases to hear." (*Lun Yu*, XII, 13)

There is, in Chinese legal history, a famous story which illustrates this point very well. Two brothers were disputing the distribution of some properties they inherited from their father. Both of them went to court for a decision. If this kind of case had taken place in contemporary American society, no doubt it would have taken months to settle. In addition to the complicated procedures of filing documents by the attorneys of both the plaintiff and the defendant, the court would probably employ accountants and real property appraisers and summon witnesses for testimonies and evidence.

Moreover, the judgment issued by a local court may not be final; for the defeated party can file an appeal to a higher court. Nevertheless, the Chinese judge, as the story tells us, handled the case in a very different way. He was reported as saying to the brothers: "The most valuable thing in the world is harmony in the family, while the most valueless thing is material possession. Why do you two brothers sacrifice the most valuable for the most valueless? Go home and have no more fight. Be good brothers again." It was said that a case settled in this manner is settled forever. To American readers especially, this may sound incredible, probably for two reasons. First, our modern society is one of action and complication; and we have already gotten used to complicated ways of life. It is highly implausible that we could go back to this kind of judicial simplicity. Secondly, Western society is governed more by law than by morality; and, in court a judge usually refrains from giving moral lessons. Nevertheless, Chinese philosophers would hold that morality and law are not to be separated and that law-enforcement is only the last resort.

When this principle is applied to politics, as some scholars have already observed, government should adopt a laissez-faire policy. It is a principle of non-interference. This interpretation can easily gain textual support from Lao Tzu who said: "I do nothing and the people will follow the course of self-transformation." (*TTC*, 57) Again he made a gradation of governments:

> The best government is one of which people know nothing more than its mere existence. The second best is one loved and praised by people. The next is one that they fear. And the last is one which people despised. (*Tao Te Ching*, 17)

This passage suggests that the best government is one which acts least, legislates the least number of statutes, entertains the least number of court cases, and, probably the most important of all, taxes the people the least.

Now the paradoxical situation is that, if a government should have no action or reduce its action to the minimum, what is the justification for its existence? Does Lao Tzu mean to suggest that the ideal society is one without a government? Throughout the *Tao Te Ching* he did not make this point clear. What we are certain of here is that, assuming that it is impossible to do away with government, the best form of government is a government of wu-wei or non-action. Then, what would such a government be? The answer to this question depends on our interpretation of the term "wu-wei" or non-action. Negatively speaking, a government of non-action is one which spares unnecessary procedures, reduces unnecessary labor, and cuts unnecessary expenditures. Positively it is a government of maximum efficiency through minimum administrative work. If we use some common usages of the American business world, it is managing with the best result through minimum supervision.

I am afraid that the foregoing interpretation may have twisted Taoism into a form of common-sense pragmatism or utilitarianism. The Taoists are not philosophers like Bentham who was concerned about the maximum good of the maximum number of people. A Taoist, nevertheless, does not unconditionally reject the goal of efficiency. But, for them, efficiency is only a by-product or something incidental. It is not the main concern of their philosophy. No doubt, the essence of Taoist philosophy is non-action, but it is not aiming at the promotion of administrative or managerial efficiency.

Then what is the essence of the philosophy of non-action in Taoism? As the present author observes, the basic spirit of this philosophy lies in the notion of hsu and ching as found in Chapter 16 of the *Tao Te Ching*: "Attain the utmost in hsu and hold firm to the basis of ching." The term ching does not cause serious difficulty in translation and has usually been translated into words such as "silence", "calmness", "quietude", and "tranquility". But the term hsu defies accurate English translation. It has been translated into terms such as "void", "vacuity", and "nothingness", which do not reveal its positive significance at all. Some examples of its use in ordinary Chinese may probably lead to a better understanding of this term. "Modesty" in Chinese is called hsu hsin (vacuous heart/mind). Syncategramatic words are called hsu tzu (insubstantial or dynamic words). These two examples clearly show us that this term has a positive meaning. The first example suggests receptivity and the second flexibility.

The concept of calmness or tranquility is symbolized by water. "The nature of water is that it becomes clear when left alone and becomes still when undisturbed."[33] Lao Tzu speaks of water as possessing the virtues of non-competition and non-aggression,[34] which are of course derived from its fundamental spirit of calmness or quietude.

Receptivity is symbolized by the female metaphor. A female exhibits the characteristics of gentleness and capacity for reproduction. Because she is receptive, she is therefore reproductive; and, because she is receptive, she is never aggressive. Although she is never aggressive, she overcomes the male by tranquility.[35] In spite of her being gentle and weak, her receptivity is a strong seductive power which overcomes her male partner. Because of her receptive nature, she performs no action; nevertheless an act is performed.

Flexibility is symbolized by the infant metaphor. Together with flexibility, there come potentialities, opportunities, hopes, and potencies. Thus Lao Tzu says:[36]

> He who possesses virtue in abundance
> May be compared to an infant.
> Poisonous insects will not sting him.
> Fierce beasts will not seize him.
> Birds of prey will not strike him.
> His bones are weak, his sinews tender, but his grasp is firm.
> He does not yet know the union of male and female,
> But his organ is aroused,
> This means that his essence is at its height.
> He may cry all day without becoming hoarse,
> This means that his (natural) harmony is perfect.

In addition, an infant signifies the utmost innocence, the virtue of being uncorrupted by culture or social conventions. Perhaps among these three metaphors, the infant is the best one signifying non-action: for it does not know how to complicate life but acts spontaneously. This is probably why the great Confucian philosopher Mencius shared this view and said: "The great man is one who retains an infant's heart."[37]

Thus far I have presented the Taoist theory of non-action under first, the principle of economy, and second, the concepts of hsu and ching. The first interpretation is, of course, very preliminary. The second one, nevertheless, is not yet thorough or final. The essence of wu-wei lies in the depth of Taoist philosophy. Concepts such as simplicity, hsu and ching are but derived from this underlying essence. What is the underlying essence of non-action? As the present author observes, the underlying principle of non-action is disinterested action. Lao Tzu speaks of the Taoist sage (man of non-action) as one who:

> Manages affairs without action.
> Preaches doctrines without words,...
> Produces but takes no possession.
> Performs but takes no pride.
> Accomplishes but claims no credit. (*Tao Te Ching*, 2)

This is the attitude of a great artist who creates simply for the sake of creativity. This kind of philosophy is very different from utilitarianism or common-sense pragmatism. It is an esthetic attitude rather than a religious resignation, intellectual deliberation or practical calculation. It was Kant who first used the term "disinterested" to characterize the activity and attitude of an artist.[38] Many recent philosophers follow Kant and have developed this thesis more thoroughly and systematically. For example, Richards and Wood explains :[39]

> Our interest is not canalized in one direction rather than another. It becomes ready instead to take any direction we choose. This is the explanation of that detachment so often mentioned in artistic experience. We become impersonal or disinterested.

Our impersonal or disinterested attitude is created through distancing ourselves from the objects involved or given.[40] The Spanish philosopher Jose Ortega Y Gasset has given us a very meaningful illustration explaining degrees of distances as related to the same given event or reality.[41]

Suppose an illustrious man is dying and several people are around him. This group of people include his wife by his bedside, the doctor counting his pulse, a reporter waiting for news and a painter who happens to be there. These four people are witnessing the same fact but their impressions of this fact are different because of different levels of involvement or different degrees of distance. To the wife of the dying man, the distance is almost reduced to zero; for she is facing the permanent departure of her life partner. The physician is a little more distant. He may not have the feeling of agony and despair the woman has. It is nevertheless to him either success or failure in his professional performance. He may feel that his reputation or prestige is at stake. The newspaper reporter is far more distant from that agonizing situation. For him, the dying man is only a scene which is to be reported later in the newspaper. He is, nonetheless, still not completely free from the emotionality of the situation; for he has to describe the scene to his readers for the purpose of interesting or moving them. Lastly there comes the painter. He is miles away from the painful reality. He considers only perceptual phenomena—lights and shadows, colors and shapes. His attitude is purely contemplative, and the agonizing elements are left outside of his field of perception. "With the painter," says Ortega Y Gasset, "we have reached a point of maximum distance and of minimum sentimental intervention."[42]

It is quite understandable that the painter, being a spectator of the scene, can be entirely unattached or disinterested in the situation. But can the dying man's wife become as non-attached as the artist? Can a person detach himself from the situation in which he is in fact a participant rather than a spectator? It is hard for an ordinary person to do so. But this is exactly the very life attitude of our Taoist philosopher, Chuang Tzu. It was recorded about his attitude toward the death of his wife :[43]

> When Chuang Tzu's wife died, Hui Tzu went to condole with him and, finding him squatted on the ground drumming on the basin and singing, said to him:
> "When a wife has lived with her husband and brought up children and then dies in her old age, not to wail for her is enough. When you go on to drum on this basin and sing is it not an excessive and strange demonstration?"
> Chuang Tzu replied, "It is not so. When she first died, was it possible for me to be not affected by the event? But I reflected on the commencement of her being: not yet born to life, she had no bodily form; not only had she no bodily form, she had no breath. During the intermingling of the waste and dark chaos there ensued a change, and there was breath; another change, and there was bodily form; another change, and there came birth and life. There is now a change again, and she is dead. The relation between these things is like the procession of the four seasons from spring to autumn, from winter to summer. Now she lies with her face up, sleeping in the great chamber between heaven and earth. If I were to fall sobbing

and go on to wail for her, I should think that I did not understand what was appointed for all. I therefore restrained myself.

Chuang Tzu was not simply restraining his emotions by means of reason, as some scholar suggested.[44] It is a state of mind attained through long-term metaphysical cultivation and a development of an esthetic attitude toward life.

The concept of Tao to Chuang Tzu is not only an object of understanding but has become a conviction and a guidance for life. Because of this, Chuang Tzu is beyond life and death. In Christianity, the conquest of death is possible through believing in Christ's resurrection and an after life in the kingdom of God. In Hinduism, particularly in the Bhagavad-gītā tradition, the conquest of death lies in the belief that the physical body does not affect our real self. Both Christianity and Hinduism are forms of religion and the conquest of death in both relies very much on some supernatural beliefs or religious dogmas. But the Taoist philosophers' conquest of death rests entirely on a naturalistic basis, a metaphysical foundation and an esthetic attitude. This reflects a unique characteristic of Chinese culture.

Someone may ask if such a disinterested attitude is the same as indifference. The answer is clearly negative, if by indifference we mean having no concern at all. Being disinterested in something is different from being unconcerned about it. Chuang Tzu did not feel any agony or despair when his wife died. It does not mean that he never loved her or that he had no concern for her well-being when she was living. His love for her and his detachment from her death are not contradictory at all. The principle of disinterestedness as a way of life can best be interpreted as "with full concern but without attachment". My readers may have a vague feeling that this phrase sounds self-contradictory. This is simply because we usually think of "concern" and "attachment" as implying each other. This is a matter of psychological association rather than logical necessity. Likewise, disinterested action is not without action at all. It can be action at its peak, but it is a purposeless action with hsu and ching. It is purposeless in the sense of having no anticipation of practical results.

Lao Tzu has explained this very well when he said that a sage performs without taking pride in it. The action is performed simply for its own sake, in accordance with the ultimate principle of Tao. When an individual attains such a level, he is free from both external and internal restraints. He can sit into forgetfulness and is not affected by life or death. He then becomes absolutely free. Thus, the understanding of Tao, the cultivation of wu-wei, and the attainment of freedom are interrelated themes in Taoist philosophy. Theoretically speaking, the attainment of freedom is the goal, while the understanding of Tao and the cultivation of wu-wei are means. But, we have to remember, the Taoist philosophers do not even have the concept of freedom in their mind; so they are even free from freedom. This is absolute freedom.

V

In this chapter the author has presented the philosophy of Taoism by describing the three cardinal concepts of Tao, Freedom and Wu-wei. In concluding he would like to comment on the label "mysticism" as applied to Taoism by many scholars. The term "mysticism" is a typical product of the religious tradition of the Western world; and, when it is used to label Taoism, it is highly misleading. The Chinese cultural tradition by its very nature is humanistic and naturalistic. To associate Taoism with "mysticism" is to force Chinese culture into the religious mould of Hebrew or Hindu culture.

The term "mysticism", however, has acquired more liberal meanings in contemporary philosophy. William James has characterized mystical experience as having the following four characteristics: (1) ineffability, (2) noetic quality, (3) transiency, (4) passivity.[45] This general characterization can certainly apply to the kind of experience which was called "sitting into forgetfulness" by Chuang Tzu. But James made no distinction between the experience of a Christian mystic who had achieved a union with God and the experience of a naturalist poet who was self-forgettingly intoxicated with the radiance of the sunset. Therefore, in order to use this term more properly, a distinction needs to be made. My proposed distinction is one between religious mysticism and esthetic mysticism. The former applies more to Christianity, Hinduism, Islam, and Buddhism, while the latter applies to Taoism.

Nobody would deny the obvious fact that Taoism is a product of Chinese culture. Thus it follows that a correct understanding of Taoism requires an adequate understanding of Chinese culture. About a quarter century ago George Rowley made a very interesting comment on the Chinese view of life: "The Chinese way of looking at life was not primarily through religion, or philosophy, or science, but through art."[46] To me this is the most penetrating single statement of Chinese culture ever made by a Western scholar.

In Chinese culture, art is a permeating quality in all aspects of life. In the contemporary West, there is a tendency for art to become a science. In China, however, even a science is an art. There is no question that medical science is, by definition, a science. But in China it is sophistically artistic. I do not need to mention the art of acupuncture and other healing techniques as examples. A striking example is that many of the texts of prescriptions were written in verses or poetic form. In short, it is not religion but art which has played the most important role in Chinese culture. Therefore, my conclusion is: only through this concept of Chinese culture can one truly understand Taoism.

Notes

1. Lao Tzu literally means "the old man" or "the old master". According to a celebrated historian, Ssu-ma Ch'ien, Lao Tzu's real name was Li Erh. He was a senior contemporary of Confucius who once paid him a visit to learn about the principles of propriety. Being a curator in the capital library of Chou, Lao Tzu wrote the five-thousand word text *Tao Te Ching* upon retiring from his post. However some recent scholars have challenged the reliability of this account. Up to the present, there has not yet been agreement on the identity of Lao Tzu.

2. Chuang Tzu, whose personal name was Chuang Chou, was according to Ssu-ma Ch'ien, a contemporary of Mencius. His doctrines were based on the sayings of Lao Tzu. It is said that he declined an invitation to become the prime minister of the state of Ch'u in order to follow his own interests and inclinations. Some recent scholars suspected that Chuang Tzu was later than Lao Tzu, but no substantial evidence supports this suspicion. His writings include a group of essays anthologized under the title after his name, Chuang Tzu.

3. Chang Ling or Chang Tao-ling (d. A.D. 157-178) started a cult for

healing the sick. Soon this was developed into a religious movement known as Tao Chiao. Tao Chia and Tao Chiao are separate entities in the history of China; yet some of the doctrines are shared by both.

4. *Tao Te Ching* has numerous English translations and quite a few of them are highly readable. However, in this chapter, with only a few exceptions, quotations from this book are translated by the author.

5. According to recent scholars, only the seven essays grouped as Nei P'ien (Inner Part) are authentic. As the present author observes, these seven essays are sufficient to represent Chuang Tzu's thought. Quotations from Chuang Tzu are primarily from these Nei P'ien essays.

6. Henri Bergson, *An Introduction to Metaphysics*, tr. by T.E. Hulme, New York: The Library of Liberal Arts, 1949; originally published in 1908, p. 21.

7. Lin Yutang, *The Wisdom of Laotse*, New York: The Modern Library, 1948, p. 53.

8. This is from the second chapter of *Chuang Tzu*. The translation is Derk Bodde's. Quoted in Fung Yu-lan, *A History of Chinese Philosophy*, tr. Derk Bodde, Princeton: Princeton University Press, 1952, Vol. I, p. 231.

9. Quoted in Fung, Vol. I, p. 230.

10. Ibid., p. 228.

11. Ibid.

12. *Tao Te Ching*, Chapter 40.

13. This is Wang Pi's comment, quoted in Fung, I, p. 179.

14. All these are clearly and commonly known to those who read the *Bible*; therefore no specific documentation is provided here.

15. Quoted in Fung, I, p. 226.

16. *Tao Te Ching*, Chapter 25. Using "spontaneity" to translate *tzu jen* is originally Alan W. Watts'. Cf. Alan W. Watts, *The Way of Zen*, New York: Vintage Books, 1957, p. 17.

17. Joseph Wu, "Some Humanistic Characteristics of Chinese Religious Thought," *Religious Studies*, Vol. 5, No. 1 (August, 1969), 101.

18. Quoted in Fung, I, p. 177.

19. *Tao Te Ching*, Chapters 18 and 38.

20. E.A. Burtt, *In Search of Philosophic Understanding*, New York: The New American Library, Inc., 1965; mentor book paperback, 1967, pp. 287-88.

21. This story is in the last section of Chapter 7 of *Chuang Tzu*.

22. Quoted in Fung, I, p. 225.

23. Ibid., p. 180.

24. Lin, *The Wisdom of Laotse*, p. 90.

25. *Chuang Tzu*, tr. Yu-lan Fung, New York: Paragon Book Reprint Corp., 1964; originally published in Shanghai, 1933, p. 27.

26. Tsao Hsueh-chin, *Dream of the Red Chamber*, translated and adapted from the Chinese by Chi-chen Wang, Garden City; Doubleday & Company, Inc., 1958, p. 13.

27. Ibid., pp. 13-14.

28. *Chuang Tzu*, Chapter 2.
29. Quoted in Fung, I, p. 237.
30. *Chuang Tzu*: *Basic Writings*, tr. Burton Watson, New York & London: Columbia University Press, 1964, pp. 86-87.
31. *Chuang Tzu*, Chapter 2.
32. Frank Thilly and Ledger Wood, *A History of Philosophy*, 3rd edn. New York: Holt, Rinehart and Winston, 1963, p. 248.
33. Lin, *The Wisdom of Laotse*, p. 77.
34. *Tao Te Ching*, Chapter 8.
35. Ibid., Chapter 61.
36. *Tao Te Ching*, Chapter 55. This is Wing-tsit Chan's translation, from his *A Source Book In Chinese Philosophy*, Princeton: Princeton University Press, 1963, p. 197.
37. *Mencius*, Book 4B, Chapter 12.
38. Immanual Kant, *Critique of Judgment*, tr. by J.H. Bernard, (New York: Hafner Publishing Company, 1951), p. 38.
39. Melvin Rader, ed., *A Modern Book of Esthetics* 3rd ed., New York: Holt, Rinehart and Winston, 1960, p. 445.
40. Regarding this thesis, the best discussion in the author's knowledge has been Edward Bullough's article " *'Psychical Distance' as a Factor in Art and an Esthetic Principle*", in British Journal of Psychology, Vol. V, 1913, reprinted in Rader, pp. 394-411.
41. Rader, pp. 413-15.
42. Ibid., p. 415.
43. *Chuang Tzu*: *Genius of the Absurd*, arranged from the work of James Legge by Clae Waltham, New York: Charter Communications Inc., 1971, p. 207.
44. Fung, Vol. I, p. 237.
45. Williams James, *Varieties of Religious Experience*, New York: The New American Library, 1958, paperback, pp. 292-93.
46. George Rowley, *Principles of Chinese Painting*. Princeton: Princeton University Press, 1947, p. 3.

4
MO TZU

DONALD BISHOP

Mo Tzu is believed to have been a native of Confucius' state of Lu. It is generally accepted that he was born when Confucius was in his later years and that he died in the early part of the fourth century B.C.[1] He was brought up in Confucian principles but rejected a number of them in adult life.[2] Like Confucius he went from one state to another offering his services to rulers. Only once was he appointed to office which he held for but a short time. Afterwards, he started a school, one of its aims being to train leaders for government service.[3]

Mo Tzu's pronounced views attracted a group of loyal and dedicated followers who banded together to spread his doctrines throughout the land. For two centuries after his death, Mohism became widespread in China, its pre-eminence stimulating a strong attack from Mencius; it then gradually faded as a distinct movement. However, its influence on Chinese culture continued in many ways, as we shall see, with a renewal of interest in his thought in the nineteenth and twentieth centuries.

The characterization of Mo Tzu as a proponent of universal love, in contrast to Confucius as an advocate of "graded love" is a common one.[4] Mo Tzu said we should love all men equally. Confucius, on the other hand, claimed that it is natural to love those nearest one or related to oneself more than those distant, or unrelated to oneself.

We are also familiar with the claim that Mo Tzu grounded his concept of universal love on a pragmatic or utilitarian principle. The reason that one should love all men is because of the practical benefits that follow from such. Was this the only or the major reason that Mo Tzu advocated universal love? Before answering the question let us examine the principle of utility itself, for it is an important one in ethical thought.

There are at least three types of ethical utilitarianism. One is the egoistic. The good is that which is good for me, whatever is for my benefit or gain. A second uses the criterion of majority good. Bentham and Mill, the English philosophers, propounded this view that the good is whatever will promote or insure the well-being of the majority in a given society. This is considered more laudable because it takes into consideration a larger number. One is concerned about not only his own but the good of others also. A third type is what may be called universalistic utilitarianism. The main concern or criterion it uses is the good not of some no matter how many, but all. Nothing less than the good of everyone must be the aim of an action, if it is to be a truly virtuous one.

Let us now go on to examine the notion of usefulness or utilitarianism itself. It is a sufficient criterion of virtue? Those who say no do so on at least three grounds. Utilitarianism associates virtue with well-being but does not, in itself, give us any criteria to determine what well-being is; it does not give us any qualitative criteria or grounds for judging what the good is. It only gives us a quantitative measurement, the number of people whose well-being is to be taken into account.

In the second place, utilitarianism does not give us any criteria for determining what means should be used for achieving the end sought. There may be some means one could use which would negate the end or make reaching it impossible. Some means may be better than others for enhancing well-being. How are we to determine this? Utilitarianism offers us no critique.

The third criticism is the most devastating, for it declares that utilitarianism is not a doctrine of virtue but of expediency. Utilitarianism uses the test of consequences. An act is good or bad depending on the consequences which follow from it. However, if my motivation for acting is consequences, am I acting ethically? One answer is, no; I am acting simply in terms of expediency. Whether or not I do the good or right is determined by the consequences to me which follow from it. If good consequences are expected to follow, I shall do it. If other, I shall not. But this is not only acting expediently but selfishly. If everyone acted in such terms, the amount of good done in the world would be limited, because we would not do the good, as Kant pointed out, at those times, which are many when there is no reward in sight for doing so.

There are at least four questions the ethicist deals with: "What is the good? What is the good grounded in? Why do the good? What are the means to the good?. How would Mo Tzu or a Mohist answer these questions?"

The first actually consists of two parts. That is, when we ask what is the good, what we really want to know is, what is the nature of the good and whose good is to be considered. We are seeking a qualitative and quantitative answer. Mo Tzu's answer to the second part is obviously, all. Mo Tzu was concerned for the good, not of himself alone, not a few or even many, but of everyone. He would claim that, if one acts out of a concern for less than all, he is not acting truly virtuously. In this sense, Mo Tzu was a universalistic utilitarian. As to the first part of the question, Mo Tzu pointed to a number of things which all men find good when they are true to themselves or which all men want—a state of peace and harmony in society, a society in which individuals have a sufficiency of material things, a life filled with joy and happiness. These are what every normal person wants or considers good. One may note that in terms of Mo Tzu's answer the good has the character of the universal, not the particular. The good of one person does not differ radically from that of another.

The second question the ethicist is concerned about is the basis of the good. What is the good grounded in? Three immediate answers are, that which is less than man; man; and that which is more than man. They may be referred to as sub-humanistic, humanistic, and trans-humanistic foundations. Mo Tzu forthrightly rejected the first, and ultimately the second as well. From the first point of view the good is grounded in nature seen from a Darwinian "law of the jungle" perspective. From a humanistic standpoint, the good is grounded in man himself. Man is the source, the determinant, the creator of the good. The good is what he wills it to be. In this case, the good takes on the nature of particularity. Each person determines for himself what the good is and sets about on his own to bring it into being. The individual tends to be concerned primarily about his own good. He tends to view it as being dialectical in relation to others, that is, his good differs from and is in conflict with that of others.

From a trans-humanistic standpoint, however, the good already exists and man simply discovers it. Having discovered it, he then goes ahead to create a society in which the good may find expression or be made manifest. He is interested in bringing about conditions which lead to the growth of individuals whose attitudes are such that the well-being of all will be realized.

For Mo Tzu the good is grounded in a trans-human reality; namely, Heaven or God. One knows what the good is when one knows what God is, for God is goodness. Goodness originates in God, is created by him. Man does not create the good; he discovers it, in Heaven or God. In Mo Tzu's words, "Heaven is honourable; Heaven is wise. So then, righteousness must originate with Heaven."[5]

This answers the question of motive also. Why should I do the good? From the trans-humanistic standpoint, because God wills me too. I do the good because God wishes that I should, and not only because of results which follow from my actions. Since God or Heaven is the model for man, we turn to Him to answer the question of means also. What means does one use to achieve the good or make goodness realizable? The answer is love, universal love. Heaven or God is love. God's love is universal. It goes out to all. It is impartial and non-discriminating and it goes out equally to all. It is unbounded, unlimited. God is beneficient. Heaven "loves the world universally and seeks to bring mutual benefit to all creatures" and its will is "to love all people in the world universally."[6] Since such is the nature of God, and since God or Heaven is the pattern man follows, love, as indicated in the quote above, is the means one uses in doing the good or the right.

For Mo Tzu, then, one acts virtuously only when he acts self-transcendently, when he gives himself to that which is greater than himself, is motivated ultimately by that which is beyond himself, and accepts a norm or standard which is other than or outside himself. That is, one is virtuous when he acts on the level of or in terms of the universal, not simply the particular.

Does this mean that the self-transcendentalist fails to take into account the results or consequences of an act? Obviously not. At this point we need to introduce another aspect of Mo Tzu's philosophy, namely, his metaphysics or views of reality. Mo Tzu believed reality to be orderly, dependable, harmonious, beautiful and good. We see this in his statements: "Thus Heaven sent forth its heat and cold in season, the four seasons proceeded in order, the yin and yang, rain and dew were timely, the five grains ripened, the six types of domestic animals grew to maturity, and disease, pestilence, and famine did not occur.... Heaven sets forth one after another the sun and moon, the stars and constellations to lighten and lead them; it orders the four seasons.... it sends down snow and frost, rain and dew to nourish the five grains.... it lays out the mountains and rivers.... it establishes kings and lords ....from ancient times to the present this has always been so."[7]

One aspect of nature's orderliness is that it acts in terms of what is called the principle of cause and effect or what the Buddhist calls the principle of dependent origination. Every cause gives rise to a similar and equivalent effect. An effect is as great as, and is like the cause. Given this, that follows. The that is determined by the nature of the this. This is an irreversible characteristic, principle or law of nature.

Mo Tzu believed reality is this way because Heaven created it thus. Nature is a mirror or reflection of God, a being whose essence is wisdom, righteousness and justice.[8] God's justice and righteousness is realized in the cause-effect principle. When man acts in terms of it, good results; when he acts in disregard of it, evil accrues. Justice is inherent in reality. When man acts in conformity with nature, the intrinsic becomes extrinsic, the potential becomes actualized. Universal love is the means by which the potential becomes the actual, the channel through which the justice inherent in reality as a whole is realized on the level of human affairs.

While not the only, the basic stimulus or determinant of action for the self-transcendentalist, then, is not consequences or results. Instead nature, and ultimately Heaven, is. The virtuous man is one who knows what the nature of reality is and, once knowing it, consciously or freely chooses to act in accord with it. When he acts thus, certain consequences inevitably follow.

Several items which may be inferred from this may be noted at this point. One is that the supernatural does not act as a sanction but rather as an inspiration or stimulus. Heaven is or sets forth a paradigm which is so attractive that, once man knows what it is, he will naturally or voluntarily follow it. But Heaven does not compel man to follow it. Man is given the choice of accepting or rejecting the nature and will of Heaven.

In this context, man's basic choice on the human level is between universal love and graded love. What happens when man chooses the latter, that is, loving those nearest him most and those farthest away least? Mo Tzu's reply is disorder, enmity, violence, and war. All these, Mo Tzu believed, are the effect of a single overall cause, partiality or graded love. Mo Tzu states this very clearly when he says: "When we inquire into the cause of these various harms, what do we find has produced them? Do they come about from loving others and trying to benefit them? Surely not. They come rather from hating others and trying to injure them. And when we set out to classify and describe those men who hate and injure others, shall we say that their actions are motivated by universality or partiality? Surely we must answer, by partiality, and it is this partiality in their dealings with one another that gives rise to all the great harms in the world. Therefore, we know that partiality is wrong."[9]

Mo Tzu asserted that the ultimate, logical, and actual end of graded love is self-love. In *The Works*, Wu Matse is pictured as the unabashed proponent of such a view: "Wu Matse told Motse: I differ from you. I cannot love universally—I love the people of Tsou better than the people of Ch'u, the people of Lu better than the people of Tsou, the people of my district better than the people of Lu, the members of my family better than the people of my district, my parents better than the other members of my family, and myself better than my parents. This because of their nearness to me. When I am beaten I feel pain. When they are beaten the pain does not extend to me. Why should I resist what does not give me pain but not resist what gives me pain? Therefore I would rather have them killed to benefit me than to have me killed to benefit them."[10]

Wu Matse's view may be brought out by means of a diagram. Start by putting a point in the middle of a piece of paper. Draw a number of concentric circles around it. The farther from the center of the circle one gets, the more diffused one's love becomes, the less there is for anyone within the outer rings. If one turns the whole thing around, so to speak, or starts with the outside circle and works in, we see that love gets stronger as one draws nearer the center of the diagram. That is to say, inversely, the greatest love one has is for one's self. Thus the cumulation of graded love is self-love.

The idea is indicated differently in a statement quoted by Liang Chi-Chao, "Love exists only when it has reached everybody. Love has disappeared the moment it fails to include all. When love is not pervasive, it cannot be called love."[11] Anything less than universal love leads to self-love. When love is not universal, it is not love; in fact, it is simply selfishness. Even if it is on the level of the group and not just a single individual, it is still selfishness. One does not act virtuously, when he acts for himself or his group only. Virtue requires acting on the level of the universal or mankind.

It might be suggested that universal love has as a corollary, unlimited love while graded love has limited love as its counterpart. The adherent of graded love says that I have only so much love to give or offer. When it is gone, there is no more. Therefore, I shall portion it out, giving the least to those I hardly know, more to those I know well, even more to my distant relatives, still more to my closest ones, and of course saving the most love for myself.

Suppose, on the other hand, one took the view that the more one loves, the more love he has to love with. That is to say, love is self-renewing. Or it is unbounded. There is an unlimited reservoir of love in existence. It exists as a potential; it is in a potential form in all persons. It exists in actuality, in actual form in God or Heaven. One taps this reservoir of love only by loving; and the more one loves in breadth and depth, the greater one's love becomes because the supply is inexhaustible in so much as its origin is Heaven.

One might carry the point further by suggesting that this is the reason Mo Tzu or the Mohist could accept the principle of returning good for evil or love to non-love. Only by love can the potential love in the other person be brought out. Only by doing so is the cause-effect character of reality maintained also. For, if we show love to another, even though he has not to us, then ultimately a similar reaction will follow. Love will give rise to love, hate to hate. This is why Mo Tzu rejected the principle of reciprocity or returning like with like, i.e., hate with hate. He was quite aware of the traditional teaching that good evokes good for he quoted from the *Book of Odes*: "There are no words that are not answered, no kindness that is not requited. Throw me a peach, I'll requite you a plum."[12]

The second, self-renewing, kind of love indicated above may offer another reason than the pragmatic one often suggested for Mo Tzu's well known assertion that one should treat or love another person's parents as much as one's own.[13] First, if one's love is infinite in amount, one can easily do so. Secondly, to love other parents as much as one's own does not mean that one loves his own parents less. This would be true if one held the first view of love as limited. But it is not true in terms of the second type. And the suggestion here is that Mo Tzu conceived of love in the second sense. What Mo Tzu wanted to see was a leveling up, not down, of society. If loving other parents as much as one's own would reduce one's love for one's own parents, Mo Tzu would have rejected it. He did not believe it would, however, because of his concept of love. He pointed out to his contemporaries the many beneficial results which would naturally follow if all loved other parents as much as their own. This was not the major reason for loving them so, however. The reason was because that is the nature of real love, or that is what genuine love calls us to do.

One of the central questions of ethical philosophy is the relationship of means and ends. Again in regard to the characterization of Mo Tzu as a utilitarian, another note might be added. Mo Tzu's argument is not that self-interest, being concerned about one's own well-being as an end, is immoral. There is nothing wrong with it. It is quite natural. The questions he raised were, are you concerned about other's too, and how or what means will you use to achieve their well-being? The ethical question, then, concerns both means and ends. Mo Tzu would argue that a person is unethical if he is concerned only about his own well-being and if he reaches it at the expense of others. Both his ends and means are immoral. Mo Tzu asserts that to be ethical, a person must be concerned about others' good as well as his own; as much or equally concerned about their good as his own, and must use the right means of achieving their good.

The means must be inclusive in nature. They must be such that the good of all is enhanced at the same time the good of any one individual is.[14] That is to say, the ends must be of a universal type and the means must be of the nature of the universal also. Particular type means will not lead to universal ends, nor will negative type means lead to positive type ends.[15] This is why Mo Tzu rejected war as the means to peace. This is why he held up love as the means. Only love has the character of a universal; love is the only universal. Only it has unity power or the capacity to unite rather than divide. One sees this in such statements as Mo Tzu's reply to the question, "But what is the way of universal love and mutual aid? Motse said: "It is to regard the state of others as one's own, the houses of others as one's own, the persons of others as one's self. When feudal lords love one another there will be no more war; when heads of houses love one another there will be no more mutual usurpation; when individuals love one another there will be no more mutual injury. When ruler and ruled love each other they will be gracious and loyal.... When all the people in the world love one another, then the strong will not overpower the weak, the many will not oppress the few...."[16]

Mo Tzu wanted to see a society in which individuals were constantly "enlarging not restricting one's consciousness of others."[17] He wanted to see, as a contemporary sociologist has said, the fundamental duties and attitudes one has toward one's own group "gradually extended to larger groups" until they include all mankind.[18] Within the context of the Chinese tradition it might be said that both the Confucianist and the Mohist believed in Jen in its broadest sense. One difference was that for Mo Tzu it was derived from God or Heaven while for Confucius its source was man; and the Confucianist tended to limit its expression to his own kin while the Mohist would extend it to all mankind.

Confucius and Mo Tzu differed also in their concept of man. From Mo Tzu's viewpoint universal love is natural to man. It is as natural, let us say, for an individual to love other's parents as much as his own. One reason is that universal, impartial love has been implanted in man by Heaven.[19] Another is that the individual is a microcosm of Heaven and, since Heaven is characterized by universal love, so is the individual. The fact that individuals did not love thus did not deter Mo Tzu. In the first place, he declared that if their leaders would set an example, people would follow.

He pointed out several instances of such in the past. King Ling of Ching loved slender waists, and to please and emulate him, the people ate only one meal a day. King Kou-chien of Yueh admired bravery and his soldiers and people were so brave "the soldiers trampled each other down in their haste to go forward." Duke Wen of Chin liked coarse clothing so the men of the state of Chin "wore robes of coarse cloth, wraps of skeepskin, hats of plain silk, and big rough shoes." Thus if the rulers would practice "universal love and mutual benefit," the people "would turn to universal love as naturally as fire turns upward."[20]

In the second place, Mo Tzu believed that partiality was so characteristic of society at his time that few children could escape its influence. Family, clan and village were the three foci of each person's life. To be oriented to any broader or more universal perspective was the exception rather than the rule. This does not mean that persons could not be true to their nature. It only means that they were not. One is reminded at this point of a statement associated with Mencius:

> The trees on the Bull Mountain were once beautiful. But being too near the capital of a great state, they were hewn down.... Even so, nourished by the rain and dew and with the force of growth operating day and night, the stumps sent forth fresh sprouts. But soon cattle and sheep came to browse on them, and in the end the mountain became bare again. Seeing it thus, people now imagine that it was never wooded. But is this the nature of the mountain?

> So it is with human nature. How can it be said that man is devoid of human-heartedness and righteousness? He has only lost his good feelings in the same way that the trees have been felled. Assailed day after day, can the heart retain its goodness? Even so, nourished by the calm air of dawn and with the force of life operating day and night, man develops in his heart desires and aversions that are proper to humanity. But soon these good feelings are fettered and destroyed by the inroads of the day's activity. Thus, fettered again and again, they wither until the nourishing influence of night is no longer able to keep them alive. So in the end man reverts to a state not much different from that of birds and beasts, and seeing him thus, people imagine that man never had good feelings. But is such the nature of man?[21]

The question being raised is in regard to the nature of man. One point of the Bull Mountain story is that a person's nature cannot necessarily be deduced from what he is or is actually doing at a particular time, since under other conditions he might be or act quite differently.

What else may be inferred from Mo Tzu's writings regarding his concept of man? Mo Tzu believed in the essential goodness of man. He would have rejected a Darwinian view of man as an organism intent only on fulfilling biological needs. Man is of the category of the ontological not the empirical. He is a being not a thing. Also he is a divine not just human being as noted before. Man is a being seeking to realize his essence. In essence, he is o the category of the universal, in accident the particular. That is, while externally or physically individuals are different, internally or psychologically they are alike in that they have the same needs, hopes and desires.

The essence of man is his universal nature, what he has in common with others, what unites rather than separates him from his followers. Only through universal love is this communality realized. Man fulfils or realizes his true self, his a priori self, only as he transcends himself. He transcends himself when he lives in terms of universal love. On that level individuality is not annihilated. Indeed only then is it fully realized. Mo Tzu took a monistic view of man. This view does not deny individualism or the self as an individual existent. Such discrimination is natural. What monism emphasizes is the self "and" others, not the self "against", others. Mo Tzu believed the individual's natural relationship to his fellows to be a non-dialectical one. Harmony not its opposite is natural to man. Conflict arises when man does not know his true self, seeks more than he needs, is motivated by exorbitant pride and rampant greed.

Mo Tzu's faith in the common man and his willingness to follow a good example has been noted already. Other aspects of Mo Tzu's social philosophy may be mentioned at this point. Mo Tzu viewed society as analogous to an organism made up of many parts, each dependent on the other, each contributing to the whole n its own way and thereby ensuring both its own and the wellbeing of the whole. Mo Tzu's analogy to building a wall illustrates his organicism. He wrote: "What is the greatest righteousness in conduct? Let those who can lay the bricks, lay the bricks, let those who can fill in the mortar fill in the mortar, and let those who can carry up the material, carry up the material. Then the wall can be completed. To do righteousness is just like this. Let those who can argue, argue, let those who can expound the doctrines expound the doctrines, and let those who can administer, administer. Then righteousness is achieved."[22] As with Plato, justice (righteousness) and harmony in society is secured when each contributes to society in the way he is naturally fitted to. From such a viewpoint, the good of one individual and the good of another and the good of the individual and the good of the group or whole are not exclusive or in opposition. It is not necessary to deny the one or the individual in order to affirm the many or the whole. In both cases the relationship between the two is a complementary not conflicting one.

Mo Tzu had no desire to deny the individual or individualism. From his viewpoint genuine individualism is reached through the group not apart from it; the latter is the way of selfishness. He believed that an individual has no right to do what may be pleasing to himself if it is harmful to the group or a larger whole. Mo Tzu opposed individualism achieved at the expense of the group. It was not genuine individualism in the first place, and the wrong means were being used to reach it.[23]

Mo Tzu also favored an a-legalistic society, that is not one in which there were no laws or rituals, but one in which human relations were not excessively formalized and stereotyped.[24] In a formalistic society, the natural goodness of man and its spontaneous expression is often stifled. In such a society a particular type of reciprocity is the basis of human relationships and this is a limiting factor, too. One interacts with only those he expects will reciprocate. And reciprocation is always in kind. As indicated earlier, in such a society individuals will do no more than return like with like. There will be no going of the second mile and one will go only one mile even with one's kin. This was Mo Tzu's criticism of graded love. It restricts the expression of one's love both in depth and breadth.

The matter might be stated differently by saying that Mo Tzu wanted to see a society based on not a legalistic but an attitudinal ethics. He believed a good society to be one in which individuals have certain attitudes such as good will, compassion, love (i.e., righteousness) so much a part of them that they act naturally or spontaneously in terms of them, in all their relations with the fellow men. The important point is, of course, that society be grounded in virtue not expediency. What, for Mo Tzu, is the nature of or the way to practice such virtue? Mo Tzu's answer is: "Let him who has strength be alert to help others, let him who has wealth endeavour to share it with others, let him who possesses the Tao (the way of nature and life) teach others persuasively. With this, the hungry will be fed, the cold will be clothed, the distributed will have order."[25]

An organic society such as Mo Tzu advocated is a non-stratified one. It is a society in which classes or groups and group loyalty is not developed to the detriment of the whole. A society may be stratified horizontally or perpendicularly; that is, it may be divided in terms of classes or groups. In both cases the loyalty of the individual is given to something less than the whole. Mo Tzu wanted to have a society in which there were no barriers to a person giving his greatest allegiance to that which is of the nature of the universal. Thus for him an all-encompassing brotherhood or society is the final universal which demands man's fullest allegiance. Anything less than mankind—nations, states, districts, clans, are artificial or man-made constructs and cannot validly command man's final loyalty. Mo Tzu would claim that loyalty to the universal is natural to man, for man is by nature of the category of the universal, while loyalty to the particular is taught or conditioned. He would point out that societies like individuals must transcend themselves in order to fulfil themselves.

Mo Tzu believed that human societies should be a microcosm of nature and Heaven. They both provide man with a suitable pattern to follow, Heaven in its love and righteousness and nature in its beneficence, orderliness and harmony. On the socio-ethical level, this means that a society to endure must be rooted in religious values. Self-interest is not sufficient to bind people together, nor even enlightened self-interest. Stable, enduring human relations must have self-giving and universal love as their basis.[26]

We can see now why Mo Tzu opposed so many aspects of his society. It was stratified perpendicularly and horizontally. The aristocracy cared little about the common man. Family and clan loyalties had precedence over larger loyalties. Partiality and self-interest was the norm set by the rulers.[27] There were many inequalities. A double standard existed. As Mo Tzu pointed out, actions considered wrong for an individual were accepted as right when performed under the guise of the state.[28] Excess rather than moderation was often the rule.[29] Thus Mo Tzu opposed not music per se but the inordinate part it often played among the aristocracy who idled their lives away in amusement, rather than being concerned with the good of those they held power over.[30]

It should be emphasized that Mo Tzu's sympathies were for the common man who bore the brunt of excessive taxation, indulgent egoism and unbridled militarism. Like K'ang Yu-wei in the nineteenth century, Tzu was deeply concerned over the suffering of the masses, especially that caused by wars of aggression;[31] and he gave his life to the search for its causes and remedy.

One finds parallels to Confucius in Mo Tzu's political philosophy, for both upheld the traditional views of the Mandate of Heaven, the necessity of the ruler being moral, and setting a good example, and the "elevating of the worthy" or the "superior man" to social and political leadership.[32] Mo Tzu wrote of the "Superior Man": "So if the superior man wishes to be a generous ruler, a loyal subject, a kind father, a filial son, a comradely older brother, and a respectful younger brother, he must put into practice this principle of universality. It is the way of the sage-kings and a great benefit to the people."[33] This statement reminds us of the three tests Mo Tzu insisted on: "....the test of its basis, the test of its verifiability, and the test of its applicability."[34]

This has been a resume of Mo Tzu's thought from a philosophical point of view. It has questioned the usual picture of Mo Tzu as a utilitarian and suggested that his concept of universal love had much deeper roots. One cannot but wonder why his philosophy declined from the eminent position it apparently held for two or three centuries after his death. We are familiar with Mencius' opposition. He criticized Mo Tzu on specific points such as his insistence that a person loves other's parents as much as one's own.[35] He opposed Mo Tzu's philosophy also as being in general too extreme and declared that "The adhering to the mean is nearer to the truth."[36]

No doubt one reason for the decline of Mohism was that there were too many vested interests who would lose were it taken seriously. Professor Chan writes: "The centuries of war in which Mohism thrived was no time for intellectual hair-splitting and sophistry, and their condemnation of war did not endear them to the rulers."[37] In a similar vein Professor Mei states:

> "Another reason is internal, to be found in the specific tendency in Mohism. It was an age of greed and covetousness. Under one pretence or another every lord maintained a large army and started a war when he had a chance to win. While these lords could not help but admire the idealism of a warless order on their lips—it is quite possible they anticipated our modern slogan of 'war to end war'—in their hearts they hated the men who disturbed their conscienceless equanimity."[38]

Suzuki refers to Mo Tzu's "economic views which brought about the vehement accusations of the Confucians resulting in the downfall of his whole system." By this he meant Mo Tzu's opposition to the financial extravagances of the rulers, their "luxurious habits as to dwelling, clothing, eating, and travelling." It is true that Mo Tzu advocated and practiced a life oriented toward asceticism, frugality, and simplicity; and there are many in every age and clime who do not find such appealing.

Thus a number of reasons may be given for the decline of Mohism. They may not be a sufficient explanation, however. For one wonders if Mo Tzu's ideal of universal love may not have been too demanding of human nature. Professor Mei reflects this when he writes:

> Every integrated personality and every organized society has its centre of reference, focus of orientation, or singleness of purpose. This heart of life and activity exhibits a religious quality. For this, Motse has discovered a great moral principle and is wholly convinced that in that alone the individual and the community in the period of storm and stress are to find their salvation. But it is quite foreign to the habit of thought and conduct of the time, and of any time, shall we not say?[39]

Others might point out that Mo Tzu was simply ahead of his time, as have been others who proclaimed his doctrine of universality. They stand out as candles in the dark, but men fail to see their glow because their eyes are dimmed by selfishness. However, since their eyes are not completely closed, some of the flame comes through and has an effect. Thus Liang Chi-Chao notes that Mohism contributed to the unification of China:

> What then accounts for the unification in China? The physical environment has had its share, but the most potent factor has been the psychological influence which the teachings of these ancient philosophers has exerted. It has been observed before that one's consciousness of others should be enlarged rather than restricted. If our ancestors had encouraged the people of Tsin to love their country only, and the people of Yu to love their country only, then the attitude of the people today would not be better than that of the Germans and French. But the Chinese made it a point to nourish this consciousness, so differences have been merged into a united whole. As Europeans encouraged a discriminatory attitude towards other nations, the differences between them have become accentuated. The psychological effect is unnoticeable, but how real and powerful a factor it can become![40]

And in speaking of the effects of Mo Tzu and his philosophy, Professor Mei wrote:

> But this is quite different from saying that it left no lasting influence in any other way. In fact, it did this in a most profound manner. The virtues of industry and frugality were at least strengthened by the Moist emphasis. And the altruistic conduct which characterizes the old type of family life as well as the specific temperament which marks off the national attitude of the Chinese are to no small degree a legacy from Motse. As a conscious system of philosophy, Moism flourished only for a short time, but as a habitual way of life it has taken deep roots in the soil of the nation and the fibre of the people. Even today the peasants who till the land and their consorts who nurse their aged parents as well as their babies, are unknowingly practicing much of the Moist ideal. It is only through a comparative study of civilizations that we begin to appreciate the rare excellence in such crude folks. They do not know what beautiful verses they are composing with their lives; perhaps they will never

know. But each masterpiece of culture is after all a pattern of these unsophisticated lines. And, we submit, the Chinese pattern cannot be deciphered without some clear insight into the teachings and personality of Motse, who has been our poets' constant, if unconscious, source of inspiration.[41]

Finally, one might note Professor Lung's comments on Mo Tzu "that Motse's system of thought is probably the most 'logical, rational, and extremely useful' in the history of Chinese philosophy. Though most of his teachings are now impracticable and are to be discredited, yet his doctrine of Universal Love and his Condemnation of Offensive war will ever remain as inspiring elements in the mind of man."[42]

One may take issue with the latter part of his statement, for, is something inspiring necessarily impractical and is not the practice of universal love and the condemnation of offensive war needed as much if not more today as in Mo Tzu's time? We shall not disagree, however, when Professor Lung states, "Motse was one who dared say and act what he believed to be right, one who dared go on with his divine message for humanity even though humanity was against him."[43]

Notes

1. Mei proposes 470-391 B.C. as dates for Mo Tzu, Chan 479-438 B.C. and Watson "sometime between the death of Confucius in 479 B.C. and the birth of Mencius in 372 B.C." Watson also points out that some say Mo Tzu was a native of the state of Sung.

2. D. Howard Smith writes: "In his early years, Mo-tzu studied under the Confucian scholar, Shih-chio, a man well versed in the rites and ceremonies which were carried out at the ancestral temples and at the border sacrifices. But Mo-tzu became extremely critical of the Confucians of his own day." *Chinese Religions*, New York, Holt, Rinehart and Winston, 1968, p. 61.

3. See Yi-Pao Mei, *Motse The Neglected Rival of Confucius*, London, Arthur Probsthain, 1934, p. 45, for details. Hereafter will be referred to as *Rival*.

4. Typical is Hu Shih, *Development of the Logical Method in Ancient China*, Shanghai and London, 1922, p. 57. Mo Tzu characterizes the Confucian view thus: "The Confucianist says, Love among relations should depend upon the degree of relationship, and honour to the virtuous should be

graded. This is to advocate a discrimination among the near and the distant relations and among the respectable and the humble." *Works*, p. 200.

5. Yi-Pao Mei, *The Ethical and Political Works of Motse*, London, Arthur Probsthain, 1929, p. 141. Hereafter will be referred to as *Works*.

6. Burton Watson, *Mo Tzu Basic Writings*, New York, Columbia University Press, 1963, p. 89. In the three chapters on the Will of Heaven Mo Tzu gives several reasons for his belief that "Heaven loves the people generously." He describes what he believes Heaven's will is in a general sense in his statements "Now what does Heaven desire and what does it abominate? Heaven desires righteousness and abominates unrighteousness" and "To obey the will of Heaven is to be universal and to oppose the will of Heaven is to be partial in love." (*Works*, pp. 136, 155). He becomes more specific in other statements when he says "Now that we must obey the will of Heaven, what does the will of Heaven desire and what does it abominate? Motse said: The will of Heaven abominates the large state which attacks small states, the large house which molests small houses, the strong who plunder the weak, the clever who deceive the stupid, and the honoured who disdain the humble —these are what the will of Heaven abominates." (*Works*, p. 142). Its counterpart is found in Watson, p. 85.

7. Watson, op. cit., pp. 87-8.

8. Smith states that Mo Tzu "....objected to a tendency, already manifest in Confucianism, to depersonalize heaven by substituting for it a doctrine of an inexorable fate." (op. cit., p. 65) and Mei writes "Now this conversion of heaven from a personal will to a cosmic law in Confucianism was just what Motse felt compelled to combat." (*Rival*, p. 160).

9. Watson, op. cit., p. 39. The corresponding statement in Mei is on p. 87, *Works*.

10. Mei, op. cit., p. 219.

11. Liang Chi-Chao, *A History of Chinese Political Thought*, London, Kegan Paul, Trench, Trubner and Co. Ltd., 1930, p. 94.

12. Watson, *op. cit.*, p. 47. Its equivalent in Mei is on p. 95, *Works*.

13. In the three chapters on universal love, Mo Tzu offers a number of arguments for it and on one occasion takes up objections to his views by discussing with a critic whom the critic would trust his parents with if he had to go off to war: an advocate of partial or universal love. In amusing fashion, Mo Tzu says: "It seems to me, on occasions like these, there are no fools in the world. Even if he is a person who objects to universal love, he will lay the trust upon the universal friend all the same." Mei, *Works*, p. 90.

14. Liang Chi-Chao writes of Mo Tzu, "According to him nothing is profitable unless it profits the whole of mankind.", op. cit., p. 102.

15. In this respect, Mo Tzu very cleverly brings out the distinction between a passive and active good will in a conversation with Wu Matse, Wu Matse said to Motse: "Though you love universally the world cannot be said to be benefited; though I do not love universally the world cannot be said to be injured. Since neither of us has accomplished anything, what makes you then praise yourself and blame me?" Motse answered: "Suppose a conflag-

ration is on. One person is fetching water to extinguish it, and another is holding some fuel to reinforce it. Neither of them has yet accomplished anything, but which one do you value?" Wu Matse answered that he approved of the intention of the person who fetches water and disapproved of the intention of the person who holds fuel. Motse said: "In the same manner do I approve of my intention and disapprove of yours." Mei, *Works*, pp. 213-14.

16. Mei, *Works*, p. 82.

17. Liang Chi-Chao, op. cit., p. 171.

18. W. T. Jones et al, *Approaches to Ethics*, New York, McGraw Hill Book Company, Inc., 1962, p. 486.

19. Mo Tzu wrote, "Every creature living between Heaven and earth and within the four seas partakes of the nature of Heaven and earth and the harmony of the Yin and the Yang." and "Even the tip of a hair is the work of Heaven." Mei, *Works*, pp. 26, 145. The latter statement is found in Watson, p. 88.

20. Watson, op. cit., p. 49.

21. Ch'u Chai, *The Story of Chinese Philosophy*, New York, Washington Square Press, 1961, pp. 56-7.

22. Mei, op. cit., p. 213.

23. One wonders if Mo Tzu is not often misrepresented on this point. Liang Chi-Chao for example wrote, "Motze's theory does not consider the individual at all. According to him nothing is profitable unless it profits the whole of mankind. To secure this mutual profit it is necessary that all individuals should sacrifice their personal profits...." op. cit., p. 102. One might argue that Mo Tzu's strong stand against fatalism illustrates his individualism or his belief that the individual can control his own destiny. See his three chapters on Anti-Fatalism in Mei's *Works*.

24. Mo Tzu opposed excessive court formalities for example, because they were often carried on hypocritically or insincerely. He objected to the formulized rituals associated with death such as expensive burial practices and the three year mourning period not because he was disrespectful, but because he felt they were not beneficial to society. Moreover it was contrary to the law of the ancient sage-king that "There shall be no extended mourning after burial, but speedy return to work and pursuit in what one can do to procure mutual benefit." Mei, *Works*, p. 130.

25. Mei, op. cit., p. 52. Watson's translation is, "It desires that, among men, those who have strength will work for others, those who understand the Way will teach others, and those who possess wealth will share it with others." p. 85.

26. One finds an interesting parallel between Mo Tzu and Hobbes in their view that in a state of nature or "pre-society" man lived in a condition of constant fear, strife and war. Human societies were formed to enable man to get out of such a state. The difference between them is that for Hobbes man is the creator of society while for Mo Tzu, "Knowing the cause of the confusion to be in the absence of a ruler who could unify standards in the world, Heaven chose the virtuous, sagacious and wise in the world and

crowned him emperor, charging him with the duty of unifying the wills in the empire." Mei, *Works*, p. 59. See Watson, pp. 34-5 for an equivalent statement.

27. Mo Tzu characterized the rulers of his time thus, "Those whom the rulers now are enriching and honouring are all their relatives, the rich without merit, and the good-looking." Mei, *Works*, p. 52.

28. Mo Tzu's description of the double standard is found in his statement condemning offensive war: "Suppose a man enters the orchard of another and steals the other's peaches and plums. Hearing of it the public will condemn it; laying hold of him the authorities will punish him. Why? Because he injures others to profit himself. As to seizing dogs, pigs, chickens, and young pigs from another, it is even more unrighteous than to steal peaches and plums from his orchard. Why? Because it causes others to suffer more, and it is more inhumane and criminal. When it comes to entering another's stable and appropriating the other's horses and oxen, it is more inhumane than to seize the dogs, pigs, chickens, and young pigs of another. Why? Because others are caused to suffer more; when others are caused to suffer more, then the act is more inhumane and criminal. Finally, as to murdering the innocent, stripping him of his clothing, dispossessing him of his spear and sword, it is even more unrighteous than to enter another stable and appropriate his horses and oxen. Why? Because it causes others to suffer more; when others are caused to suffer more, then the act is more inhumane and criminal. All the gentlemen of the world know that they should condemn these things, calling them unrighteous. But when it comes to the great attack of states, they do not know that they should condemn it. On the contrary, they applaud it, calling it righteous. Can this be said to be knowing the difference between righteousness and unrighteousness? The murder of one person is called unrighteous and incurs one death penalty. Following this argument, the murder of ten persons will be ten times as unrighteous and there should be ten death penalties; the murder of a hundred persons will be a hundred times as unrighteous and there should be a hundred death penalties. All the gentlemen of the world know that they should condemn these things, calling them unrighteous. But when it comes to the great unrighteousness of attacking states, they do not know that they should condemn it. On the contrary, they applaud it, calling it righteous. And they are really ignorant of its being unrighteous. Hence they have recorded their judgment to bequeath to their posterity . If they did know that it is unrighteous, then why would they record their false judgment to bequeath to posterity?" Mei, *Works*, pp. 98-9.

29. Excess in clothing on the part of the rulers is one example as the quote below indicates. He criticized them also "in constructing boats and carts excessively" and their indulging "in retaining too many women" in their households. "The present rulers are quite different from this when they make their clothes. Having what is warm and light in winter and what is light and cool in summer, they would yet heavily tax the people, robbing them of their means of livelihood, in order to have elaborately embroidered and gorgeous garments. Hooks are made of gold and ornaments on the girdle consist of pearls and jades. Women are employed to make the embroidery and men to

do the carving. All these are for the adornment of the body. They really add little to its warmth. Wealth is squandered and energy wasted all for naught. So, then, when clothing is made not for the body but for brilliant appearance, the people will be wicked and unruly and the ruler extravagant and deaf to good counsel. It will be impossible to keep the country out of disorder. If the rulers sincerely desire the empire to have order and hate to see it in disorder, they must not indulge in making clothing excessively." Mei, *Works*, p. 24.

30. Mo Tzu's attitude toward music is found in three chapters titled "Condemnation of Music" in Mei's *Works*. (also pp. 110-116 of Watson) While it is usually said Mo Tzu was completely opposed to music, one should be reminded of Mo Tzu's statement, "If musical instruments also contribute to the benefit of the people, even I shall not dare condemn them." Mei, *Works*, p. 176.

31. Mencius said of Mo Tzu, "Motse loved all men; he would gladly wear out his whole being from head to heel for the benefit of mankind." (*Works of Mencius*, Book VII, Part I, ch. 26) Mo Tzu often made extensive journeys to rulers to disuade them from embarking on proposed wars and several times persuaded rulers to stop wars in progress.

32. Mo Tzu's emphasis on "elevating the worthy" is found in chapters VIII, IX, and X of the *Works* and pp. 18-33 of Watson.

33. Mo Tzu enlogized the "sage-kings" of antiquity (Yu, T'ang, Wen, Wu) in declaring, for example, that they "....gave all their thought to finding worthy men and employing them...." (Watson, p. 25); they "....loved the people of the world universally...." (Mei, *Works*, p. 15); They were "....very judicious and faithful in their punishments and rewards" (*Works*, p. 61); and "They engaged themselves in universality and not partiality in love. Loving universally, they did not attack the small states with their large states, they did not molest the small houses with their large houses." (*Works*, p. 147).

34. Describing the three tests Mo Tzu wrote, "How is it to be based? It is to be based on the deeds of the early sage-kings. How is it to be verified? It is to be verified by the testimony of the ears and eyes of the multitude. How is it to be applied? It is to be applied by being adopted in government and its effects on the people being shown. These are called the three tests." (Mei, *Works*, p. 194) Mo Tzu's primary concern for the good of the people is reflected in these three tests, as is his pragmatism or utilitarianism and his insistence on government being concerned for the ctitizens' welfare.

35. Mencius' criticism of Yang Chu and Mo Ti is, "Yang's principle of 'each one for himself' amounts to making one's sovereign of no account. Mo's principle of 'all-embracing love' amounts to making one's father of no account. To have no father and no sovereign is to be like the birds and beasts." Fung Yu-Lan, *A Short History of Chinese Philosophy*, New York, Macmillan Company, 1962, p. 71.

36. See D.T. Suzuki, *A Brief History of Chinese Philosophy*. The Monist, April, 1908, No. 2, p. 271. Lin Yutang makes the same criticism in his book *The Wisdom of India and China*, New York, Random House, 1942, p. 787.

37. Wing-Tsit Chan, *A Source Book in Chinese Philosophy*, Princeton, Princeton University Press, 1963, p. 212.

38. Mei, *Rival*, p. 180.

39. *Ibid*, p. 191.

40. Liang Chi-Chao, op. cit., p. 177.

41. Mei, *Rival*, p. 182.

42. Kwan-hai Lung, The Social Philosophy of Motse, *China Today*, Vol. IX, No. 1. Jan., 1966, p. 24.

43. Ibid. This chapter has focused mainly on Mo Tzu's views. The Mohist Logicians of a later time will be taken up elsewhere in this volume. Three discussions of Mo Tzu not referred to above are Creel H.G. *Chinese Thought From Confucius to Mao Tse-Tung*. (Mentor Books, New York, 1953, ch. 4); Day Clarence B., *The Philosophers of China*, (Citadel Press, N.Y., 1962, ch. 4); Fung Yu-Lan, *The Spirit of Chinese Philosophy*, (Beacon Press (paperback), Boston, 1962, ch. 2.).

5
THE LEGALIST PHILOSOPHERS

S.Y. HSIEH

Legalism refers to a way of thinking which gained acceptance toward the end of the Chou dynasty. "Legalist Philosophers" is a term used to denote a group of thinkers in China who belonged to the "Fa-chia." If, by merely looking at the translation of "Legalist Philosophers", one conjectures that all these philosophers are fond of attaching "undue importance to the strict letter of the law or to legal forms", then he is wrong.

The word "chia" ordinarily means a family. When referring to a group of philosophers, it means a school. Thus "Fa-chia" means a group of thinkers who emphasized the importance of "fa." But what does "fa" mean? According to Professor H.G. Creel, the word "fa" has a series of meanings ranging from model, method, technique, rule and regulation to law.[1] Moreover the word was often used to imply not only one meaning but two or more at the same time, thus making it difficult for a reader to understand its exact meaning in a specific context.

However, insofar as the bulk of the "Fa-chia" writings are concerned, the word "fa" mainly means two things: penal law and administrative techniques. The former was used mainly to rule or control the people, while the latter were the instruments by which a ruler controlled the officials.[2] It is because the "Fa-chia" included exponents of both law and administrative techniques who did not necessarily endorse each other's view that Professor Creel considers it advisable to label those who emphasize administrative techniques either administrators, methodists, or technocrats.[3]

However, the latter two names already have meanings which have long been in use and connotations which make Professor Creel hesitate to adopt them. But his point is clear: "Legalist Philosophers" is not a proper translation for the thinkers of "Fa-chia". In this chapter we shall call these thinkers Legalist/Administrative Theorists.

During the Warring States period, especially in the third and fourth centuries B.C., when the most outstanding Legalist/Administrative Theorists appeared one after the other, the intellectual community in China was basically a kind of free market each school competing with others for the patronage of those who were in power. Although the actual number of schools that existed during that period was numerous, one Han Dynasty historian who lived in the second century B.C. subsumed them under six schools, and the Legalist/Administrative School was one of them.[4]

This means that that School had unique teachings which distinguished itself from all others. It also differed in that it did not have a recognized founder. Moreover it became, through the person of and reforms initiated by one of its leaders, Shang Yang, the official ideology of a peripheral state, the Ch'in, and Ch'in finally unified all of China in 221 B.C. This identification of Shang's teachings and policies of a unifying state certainly meant a victory for the Legalist/Administrative School, but such a glorification lasted only for a short while. From 207 B.C. onward, because of its harshness and severity, it never again won official patronage in Chinese history.[5]

Traditionally, the standard dynastic histories' section on literature conveniently serves as a guide for the identification of thinkers of the various schools. Opinions expressed in the *Historical Records of Ssu-ma Ch'ien* and the *Former Han History* of Pan Ku are particularly authoritative because they are the first two voluminous histories of China. According to the latter, there were seven Legalist/Administrative works which were written or compiled during the Warring States Period.[6] However, among the authors of these seven works, four are especially noteworthy. They have each contributed to the Legalist/Administrative School as a whole. They are Shang Yang, Shen Pu-hai, Shen Tao, and Han Fei.

Shang (d. 338 B.C.) is believed to be an illegitimate descendant of the ruler of a small state called Wei. His original surname was therefore Wei. According to the then prevailing custom, such descendants also frequently adopted the surname of Kung-sun, meaning the descendants of dukes. Therefore Wei Yang was also known as Kung-sun Yang. The surname of Shang has been associated with him because of his enfeoffment by the ruler of Ch'in as the Lord of Shang. Shang was a place name.[7]

Shang is known in Chinese history as a great reformer. Although he was by no means the first reformer in China,[8] his name has been brighter than others because the state which he served and strengthened, the Ch'in, later unified all of China in 221 B.C. The laying of the foundation of the Ch'in power has been attributed to none other than Shang.

There are two reforms in Ch'in which were initiated by Shang. Both were aimed at consolidating the power of the central government and enriching the state. The first was promulgated in 359 B.C. and had several components. It took away the privileges enjoyed by hereditary nobles and selectively bestowed them on the people. Anyone who expected to have political and social privileges had to earn them by fighting on the battleground. To kill an armed enemy soldier, for instance, would entitle a person to one grade of rank, one hundred units of land, nine units of residence, and one slave. Or, alternatively, one might choose to become an official with fifty catties of rice each year as one's salary. Of course, the more enemy heads taken, the higher the rank and the salary. As a corollary to this idea of rewarding those who contributed to the public, especially on the battleground, Shang prohibited the people from fighting for private causes. Nor would he tolerate anyone who either defected or surrendered to the enemy. A second component of the reform had an economic purpose, but the means used was, strictly speaking, a manipulation of the people's desire for social status. The government promised to free slaves if they would devote themselves to either farming or weaving. On the other hand, those who gave up farming and turned themselves into merchants would be enslaved. Thirdly, Shang forced everyone in the state to be an informant for the government by requiring all households to be mutually responsible for each other's behavior. Crimes committed by the members of one family would have to be reported to the government by its neighbors if known to them; otherwise they would be punished as severely as the criminals. This system of mutual responsibility would certainly have to be preceded by a series of preparatory measures. Every household in the state was registered and every five families were organized into a unit. Law and order was achieved through tight social regimentation. Finally, Shang eliminated the ideological basis of the learned scholars' resistance to his reform by burning the Confucian books of poetry and history. Moreover, he restricted scholars and officials from moving about in the country.

The second large reform was announced in 350 B.C. It was basically a continuation of the policies Shang had put into effect nine years previously, and was similarly aimed at reducing the power of the noble class. First, it destroyed the economic base of these nobles by breaking down the boundaries of the then prevailing land enclosures and by encouraging the people to till any uncultivated land they could find. Institutionally, this measure meant that the well-field land system, which allotted land to the nobles whose slaves would then cultivate it, was abolished.[9] Land possession would become public, and the state, by disclaiming ownership of land, would be contented with collecting revenues from the farmers in the form of taxes. The assumption underlying this policy was that human beings are basically selfish and that they will work extremely hard for themselves but not for others, or for the public weal. Thus, by breaking up the well-field system and by permitting free sale of tillable land, Shang expected to see economic productivity multiplied. Actual development, of course, proved the accuracy of Shang's predictions, although with lamentable long-range side-effects, one being the concentration of land in a few hands.

A second component of reform was the universal bureaucratization of the administrative apparatus of Ch'in. By providing an intermediate organizational unit, the *hsien*, Shang consolidated the administrative control of all villages and towns in Ch'in. Heads of the *hsien* were directly appointed by, and solely responsible to the ruler. Hereditary leadership in localities was therefore destroyed. However, the idea of establishing such an administrative unit at the intermediate level was probably initiated by the southern state of Ch'u.[10] A third component of the reform was to relocate the capital eastward from Yung to Hsien-yang. If Ch'in had been weak, such a move would certainly have exposed it to threats and even attacks from its neighbor Wei.[11]

But Ch'in was actually expanding. Therefore the movement of

the capital could serve only as a clear signal of its ambition to expand eastward, though not necessarily indicating a desire for the total conquest of all the states in the middle and lower Yellow and Yangtze river basins. Internally, changing the capital further consolidated the power of the central government. Former hereditary nobles and their descendants either moved with the government to the new capital and thereby left their own power bases, or stayed behind in a town destined to diminish in wealth and importance.

The reforms were effective and successful. According to Ssu-ma Ch'ien, the people in Ch'in appreciated Shang's policies ten years after they had been put into practice. The whole state was so law-abiding that if anyone happened to drop something somewhere, he could hope to recover it on the very spot where he lost it. Thieves disappeared and robbers went out of existence. Everyone had enough to eat and every household was self-sufficient. Moreover, the people were eager to fight for the state and were always timid in starting a feud for private causes. Whether in towns or in villages, everything was orderly.

Shang's contribution to the Legalist/Administrative theories lies mainly in his emphasis on law. When the information in the *Book of Lord Shang*, a book which was probably compiled by the followers of the Legalist/Administrative School after Shang's death,[12] and which contained many authentic sayings of Shang, is pieced together, a full picture of the Legalist side of the Legalist/Administrative theories emerges. Shang's preference for law as a tool of government was based on his conviction that a government had to be concerned, not with the few individuals in society who could discipline themselves without any outside influence, but with the greatest majority. His preference was also influenced by his dissatisfaction with moral virtues which had been much emphasized by the Confucian philosophers.

To begin with, he thought that the Confucians were not realistic enough. They had failed to see that the greatest majority of the people shared certain physiological needs and psychological characteristics which an intelligent ruler should use as the starting point of his policies—when they are hungry, they strive for food; when they are tired, they long for rest; when they suffer hardship, they seek enjoyment; and when they are in a state of humiliation, they strive for honor. In ordinary situations, they always try to take advantage of others—when measuring, they take the longer part; when weighing, they take the heavier; and when making selections, they choose whatever is profitable. This being the case, a ruler can easily manipulate the people if he can control what they love or hate. "If the people are brave, they should be rewarded with what they desire; if they are timorous, they should be put to death in a manner they hate. In this way, timorous people, being incited by punishments, will become brave; and the brave, being encouraged by rewards, will fight to the death."[13] And the most effective way of enabling the people to have a clear idea of the conditions leading to either rewards or punishments was to stipulate everything clearly and unambiguously in black and white, i.e., in the form of law. Thus, if laws are concise, the punishments will be multitudinous; if the laws are multitudinous, punishments will be scarce.

The second reason that Shang preferred law was that, compared with moral virtue, it could be more effective as a tool of government. Shang was aware that morally superior people could behave themselves, but that the scope of influence of these people would be limited. Thus, to rely upon moral virtue as a means of government would mean that, insofar as the masses are concerned, everything would be precarious. Chance rather than certainty would be the predominant factor.

Shang was a person who liked to see everything develop according to his original design; he wanted to rule out the element of uncertainty. This strong desire to be a manipulator stretching his vision into and thereby controlling the unknowable and unpredictable future was Shang's leading characteristic. To attain his goal, he found he had to do a great deal of calculation, in order to discern the necessary development of every knowable factor. This was the price which Shang was always willing and always had to pay. Projected into the person of a sage, Shang expressed his ideal: a state in which all citizens are in total compliance with the law. "A sage knows the right principles which must be followed, and the right time and circumstances for action. Therefore the rule, which he exercises, always leads to order, the people, whom he employs in war, are always brave and the commands, which he issues, are always obeyed."[14] Shang maximized the power of human reason vis-a-vis the vicissitudes of human life.

On the other hand, Shang justified his hatred of moral virtues as an effective tool of government by his philosophy of history. Things in this world change with time, including the ways of governing the people. To adopt certain views and adhere to them as if they were good for all situations as the Confucian scholars had done, without realizing that time has already changed, is anachronistic. Shang believed, instead, that in remote antiquity, when the structure of society was matriarchal, it was the affection between the mother and her children that served as the basic bond in society. Primary relations were given high regard; and private considerations surpassed all others. However, as time went on, it was discovered that the practice of putting primary relations above all others led to disorder among social groups. Whenever a conflict between two parties arose, there being no other criterion for settling a dispute, brute force was often the final arbiter. Some virtuous men therefore suggested that impartiality and uprightness should be used as the distinctive characteristics of referees to be chosen for the resolution of disputes, and that unselfishness should serve as an overriding principle for all individuals. These suggestions turned out to be very useful and the people came to appreciate the contributions made by virtuous men.

This stage of honoring the virtuous men was certainly a big step forward in the history of human civilization. It meant, among other things, the mobilization of human reason to discover ways to deal with difficulties in human life. Natural feelings, especially the affection generated among relatives, were now replaced by rational thought. It also meant the restraint of private considerations and the emergence of a sense of the public.[15]

However, such a stage had its usefulness as well as its limitations. When history evolved still further, it was discovered that what the virtuous men did was not always the best. In the first place, the virtuous men were often different from average people, and the way in which they differed from others was not always predictable. Secondly, they tended to compete with one another by affirming and reaffirming only their unique virtues. The former bewildered the people, while the latter meant practically a reversion to the first stage in which there was no publicly acknowledged standard. Both eventually led to disorder. This, of course, contradicted the original purpose of setting up virtuous men as referees.

A new stage was ushered in when a few sages appeared. They found a way out of the dilemma faced by the virtuous men. Many quarrels were eliminated when the concept of ownership was established. Thus, land and properties, when declared to belong to a particular person, would in most cases not attract those who might otherwise be tempted to claim them. Similarly, when a man was acknowledged as the husband of a certain woman, or when a woman was admitted by others to be the wife of a certain man, sexual disputes could be avoided. However, the mere concept of ownership was not sufficient.

It was also necessary to accompany it with a series of prohibitions and restraints—if you violate so-and-so's ownership, then such and such evil consequences will follow; therefore, it would be better if you would refrain from violating other people's ownership. However, mere threats themselves would not frighten away any mortal soul. It would also be necessary to have someone to reinforce such prohibitions. Hence officials were produced to serve as executioners of such prohibitions. Yet the officials themselves were human beings. How could one be sure that they would always faithfully carry out their duties? It was necessary to establish a supreme ruler whose orders would be obeyed by the officials. Once such a fountain of justice was set up, the third stage of human history began. This was the stage in which subjective feelings were surpassed as well as protected by objective rules. Virtuous men were replaced by officials who were supposed to be recruited, not because of their blood relations with the royal house, nor because of their virtuous behavior, but because of their qualifications—competence, ability and devotion to the public weal, which could be objectively measured, i.e., measured by law :

> "(An intelligent ruler) does not hearken to words, which are not in accordance with the law; he does not exalt actions, which are not in accordance with the law; he does not perform deeds, which are not in accordance with the law."[16]

Objectivity was therefore one of the primary goals of Shang's preference for law, as expressed in his philosophy of history. He wanted to be rid as much as possible of the subjective element in the process of public affairs. Thus, in ruling a country, a ruler should make clear the laws governing the officials. He should not rely either on his own personal knowledge or deliberation or on those of his officials when discharging his duties.[17]

Ideally, a country should rely upon the self-functioning of the laws to such an extent that even the appearance of sages should not make it necessary to make any new law.[18] Nor should there by any need for a mediocre ruler to delete anything from the code of law. Everything should simply be done by following the law, and therein would lie justice. Thus, to execute a person because he has violated the law is not considered cruel, and to reward another person because he has rendered services to the state should not be viewed as showing him any particular affection.

Although Shang justified his preference for law in general terms, his special interest lay in the penal law. Here, he repudiated the theory that the penalty should increase in accordance with the severity of the crime, a rationale accepted by most of the people of his time. He argued that severe crimes had often been committed, not by innocent people, but by the habitual criminal who had regularly committed light crimes but also had not been deterred by the penalties which followed. If a government really wanted to see penalties acquire a deterring effect, it should severely punish those who had done misdemeanors. Such a disproportion between crime and punishment would scare the people to such an extent that all the links in the escalating scale of crimes would be broken. No criminal habit could ever be formed by anyone; therefore, few serious crimes would ever occur, and a state could hope to remain in good order. This is called "to abolish penalties by means of penalties."

It means at least two things. First, it enabled Shang to claim that his philosophy was basically based upon a passion for the people's welfare. If this claim can be sustained, then the Legalist philosophy is as noble as the Confucian one which upholds a constant adherence to moral virtue. Second, it reveals that Shang subscribed to the view that ends justify means. Although it is possible and also legitimate to ask the theoretical question: "Is there any end which is not also a means in another context?" Shang did not seem to have been bothered by it.[19]

While Shang believed that laws were binding, not only upon the people in general, but also upon the officials and even the ruler, the primary object for the application of laws remained the people. The thinker who specifically discussed the techniques by which a ruler can manipulate his ministers and officials and thereby protect himself was not Shang, but Shen Pu-hai.

Information concerning Shen's life is very scanty. However, by piecing together bits of scattered information, it can be safely said that he was probably born in 400 B.C.,[20] became the Chancellor of the State of Han in 354 B.C., and served in that position up to his death, which was between 340 and 337 B.C.

The concept which has most frequently been associated with Shen's name is the concept of hsing-ming[21]—correspondence between one's performance and his title. Underlying such a concept is a set of assumptions: that when a large group of human beings are living together, it is necessary to have some form of government; that the government has to be responsible for a wide range of things so as to enable the group to live together peacefully; that the government is not composed of one individual only, it has to be a group of people; that in this group, one of them is a leader who issues orders to other members of the group, i.e., officials, and also assigns responsibilities to them; that in assigning responsibilities to officials, the leader has to know the exact nature of such responsibilities as well as the capabilities of the officials involved; that ideally, there should be a close correspondence between responsibilities, symbolized by a title, and the assignee's capabilities, concretely demonstrated by his performance; that such a correspondence is not only a measure of how successfully the problems encountered by the people are solved, but also a method of controlling the officials—when there is a match between performance and title, the leader should give rewards to officials; that, since it is virtually impossible for a leader to find from among his relatives the many and varied talents needed to carry out all the jobs pertaining to government, it is necessary for him to recruit such talents from among the whole population; that once such a system of recruitment is put into practice, it marks the passing away of feudal government and heralds the appearance of bureaucratic government.

Shen is therefore a theoretician who made great contributions to the bureaucratic government in historical China by calling a ruler's attention to an indispensable aspect of government affairs, i.e., the usefulness and necessity of administrative techniques. The gist of Shen's teachings has been succinctly summarized under the

The Legalist Philosophers

heading of "Instructions to the Ruler" by Professor H.G. Creel who has spent a long time collecting and analyzing what he himself has labelled as the fragments of Shen's teachings:

> Be independent, impersonal, and impartial.
> Depend upon technique, not sagacity.
> Firmly hold the controls, but leave action to your ministers.
> Appear inactive and complaisant—but when you do act, act decisively.
> Be completely informed, but do not bother with details.
> Hide your motives and your actions.
> Do not vaunt your power or intelligence.
> Inspire sympathy and affection.
> Give office only on the basis of ability, achievement, and seniority.
> Let no one minister gain predominant power.
> Do not give orders that will not be obeyed.[22]

It is apparent from a reading of such Instructions that Shen did not include law in his administrative theory. Indeed, the word "law" seldom appears in the Shen fragments. Therefore, it is correct to view Shen as a member of the "Fa-chia", if "fa" is interpreted as meaning both law and method. But, it is incorrect to call him a Legalist Theorist because law was not his favorite topic.

One question that has interested as well as puzzled historians of Chinese thought is the exact relationship between the Legalist/Administrative Theorists and the Taoists. Briefly, there are two theories. On the one hand, Ssu-ma Ch'ien suggests that Legalist/Administrative Theorists were greatly influenced by the teachings of "Huang Lao." By "Huang," he probably meant the legendary ruler Huang-ti, who lived in remote antiquity; and by Lao, he meant Lao Tzu. For two thousand years, Ssu-ma's statement has been accepted by scholars as authentic.[23]

This discovery in 1974 of the four classical treatises attributed to Huang-ti together with the two sections of the *Lao Tzu* leads scholars in China to believe that these six treatises as a whole constitute the essential teachings of Huang Lao and that Ssu-ma's aforementioned conclusion has acquired another support. Their reasoning is that the four treatises were probably composed in the early half of the fourth century B.C.,[24] while the *Lao Tzu* had been composed even earlier; that both "tao" and "fa," the key terms in Taoism and Legalist/Administrative theories, frequently appear in the first four treatises; that the concept of hsing-ming, which has so far been identified with Shen Pu-hai, is actually the most important concept of the four treatises; and that both Shen and Han Fei came from the same area where there is a tradition to emphasize the "fa."[25] In short, they think that the *Lao Tzu* appeared first, then came the four treatises attributed to Huang-ti; that the latter represent the transition or at least the beginning of transition from Taoism to Legalist/Administrative theories, and that these six treatises together influenced the Legalist/Administrative Theorists, especially Shen and Han.

On the other hand, Professor Creel casts doubt on the validity of Ssu-ma's argument. His reasons are that the correct dating of the book *Lao Tzu* should be the third century B.C., and that a close examination of the ways in which two key terms were used by the Legalist/Administrative Theorists and the Taoist philosophers has revealed a different story. In the first place, if the *Lao Tzu* is really a product of the third century B.C., then it could not have influenced people who had lived in the fourth century B.C., such as Shen Pu-ahi. Secondly, the meaning of the "way," which has been frequently used by the Taoist philosophers and which has made them unique, is cosmic in nature, i.e., the Way as the totality of all things. Although there are nine occurrences of the word "way" in the Shen fragments, none of them had such a cosmic meaning.[26]

Moreover, regardless of the identity of the words used, the concept of "non-action" (Wu-wei) meant different things for Legalist/Administrative Theorists and the Taoist philosophers. When Shen used the word, he meant that a ruler, while vigilant, should not interfere with the duties of his ministers, especially the details of such duties. However, non-action as used by Chuang Tzu meant letting nature take care of everything in this world. It stood for complete abstinence from the activities of the world. It is only in the *Lao Tzu*, a book which was composed in the third century B.C., that non-action in the sense Shen used it, i.e., as a technique of government control, appeared frequently. It is reasonable, therefore, to assume that it was Shen who influenced the author(s) of *Lao Tzu*, rather than the other way around.

Professor Creel's view regarding the relationship between the Legalist/Administrative Theorists and the Taoists, especially the purposive Taoists, is both interesting and significant.[27] If it is sustained by further research, it will reverse or at least modify a conclusion which has been accepted by countless scholars for the last two thousand years.[28]

If Shen is counted as an administrative theorist who contributed significantly to the personnel side of the art of ruling for a ruler, then Shen Tao, or at least the book carrying his name, can be viewed as having pointed out an impersonal yet indispensable element of leadership for the Legalist/Administrative theories.

There is little information concerning the life of Shen Tao. Professor Creel speculates that he was probably a younger contemporary of Shen Pu-hai, but the book attributed to him may be a forgery.[29] Moreover, unlike both Shang Yang and Shen Pu-hai, he lacks a recognizable group of followers in later Chinese history and therefore is not important. Vitali Rubin suggests that the concept of power and position (shih), which has traditionally been attributed to Shen Tao, may have been borrowed by Han Fei, the greatest Legalist/Administrative theoretical synthesizer, from the *Book of Lord Shang*.[30] Rubin's reasoning is that in the book of *Hsun Tzu*, Shen's name is mentioned three times; yet although Hsun Tzu is known for his ability to characterize other thinkers, never is the concept of power and position referred to in connection with Shen.

Upon close examination, one finds weaknesses in both arguments. Forgery or not, the book *Shen Tzu*, being a less refined work than the *Han Fei Tzu*, clearly existed before the *Han Fei Tzu*. That is why it was possible for the author(s) of *Han Fei Tzu* to write a critical comment on the concept of power and position.[31] Moreover, the very fact that, after criticism, the concept was incorporated into Han Fei's political theory indicates that, the actual number of its subscribers notwithstanding, the concept was important. Rubin's reasoning can also be questioned. Since Han is an author who unhesitatingly acknowledges every intellectual debt he owes his predecessors, there is no need for him to fabricate a certain Shen Tao in order to attribute to him something he has borrowed from the *Book of Lord Shang*. Indeed, what purpose does it serve Han to act as Rubin has suspected? And one certainly cannot assume that Hsun Tzu's failure to quote something necessarily means the non-existence of such a thing. In fact, there is no claim in the book of *Hsun Tzu* that it includes every significant theory.

Insofar as the book itself is concerned, a careful reading of extant remnants of the *Shen Tzu* reveals that it actually embodies, in addition to the familiar theory of power and position, virtually all the elements of Legalist/Administrative theories. After it defends the necessity of law,[32] the *Shen Tzu* goes on to discuss the origin of law as well as its functions. It states that, whenever one talks about matters related to law, it is the positive law made by human beings that should be the object of discussion. The contention is that people accept laws because they find laws agreeable to them. By implication, it rules out the possibility of a divine or natural origin of law. Ideally, it says, a government should carry out its daily functions by referring all decisions to the law. By doing so, officials will not be partisan toward their own relatives and no one in the state will be denied his due attention. Thus everything will presumably be orderly as if nothing deserves any special attention of the occupants of the whole hierarchy of government.

However, regardless of the fact that everyone in the country has to live under the law, one's political status determines his basic attitude toward the law. The people have to fulfil their obligations as stipulated by the law by providing physical strength to the state. The officials have the responsibility of defending the law and also carrying out its regulations even to the extent of sacrificing their own lives. It is the ruler who has to see to it that laws are changed in accordance with the Way. Thus the important elements of Legalist theory are all present.

When it comes to the actual performance of duties in the government, the *Shen Tzu* is also revealing. It says that an intelligent ruler should seek loyal officials to serve the state. Yet loyalty is not defined in terms of officials' subjective state of mind expressed in their devotion to the ruler's person. It means dedication to their duties, and the duties are attached to their titles. If every official can understand this definition of loyalty and can try to fulfil it, then all the duties will be automatically carried out by the official while the ruler himself has no specific function. In other words, the ideal official's way of service is to look after his duties and actually perform them while the ruler's way is to have no specific responsibility in the handling of any concrete affair. Thus the skeleton of Shen Pu-hai's theories of *hsing-ming* and non-action are already present in the *Shen Tzu*. Viewed in this way, Han historian Pan Ku's comment on Shen Tao, that Shen preceded both Shen Pu-hai and Han Fei and has been praised by both of them may have some factual basis and may be extremely significant.[33]

The concept which has been most frequently identified with Shen Tao is the concept of power and position, i.e., shih. Now shih has at least half a dozen meanings. It means power, force in action, opportunity, position, gesture, and genitals. The way it is used in the *Shen Tzu* is political in nature, meaning power and position, as such, is interchangeable with two other characters, ch'uan (power) and wei (hierarchical position). The essence of the concept is that an individual's moral refinement is not sufficient to influence evil men, while power and position should enable one, regardless of his moral character, to subdue all others, including the morally perfect.

The life story of Yao, a sage ruler in antiquity, can serve as a telling example. Before he ascended the throne, he could not, regardless of his fine moral character, influence even his neighbor's behavior. However, as soon as he became a ruler, his orders were obeyed by everyone in the country. It is concluded in the *Shen Tzu*, therefore, that, in ruling a country, it is neither an individual's subjective efforts directed toward moral refinement nor his actual moral achievement that counts. Rather, it is the position he occupies and the power he holds that really matters.

This theory is significant because it repudiates the Confucian theory of government which puts so much emphasis upon an individual's subjective efforts toward moral refinement. Recognizing the existence of numerous factors that lie beyond one's control, yet which are influential in shaping one's life, the Confucian philosophers decided to urge everyone to look into himself and concentrate on what lay within his own power. A man, they advised, should try to cultivate his own person so that once opportunities avail themselves, he can make the fullest use of them and establish a career of his own which would leave a mark on posterity.

But the Confucian philosophers had no way of telling whether opportunities would come at all or, if they did, when they would arrive. So they coined the concept of the Decree of Heaven to subsume all the unknown forces. Moreover, once a person is recruited by the government on the basis of his moral character and ability, the Confucian philosophers would continue emphasizing the invisible force of moral character as a guarantee of one's devotion and dedication to his work. Implied in such a view is the belief that if one has done his best, it is likely that he will do a good job. If he fails, it means that there is a gap between the requirement of the work on the one hand and the actual ability of the particular person on the other, and a ruler should not severely punish such a person who has failed. Compared with this approach, the one suggested in the *Shen Tzu* immediately looks much colder and stricter. Moreover, even though the Legalist/Administrative Theorists' approach may be a bit more efficient in the short run, it is doubtful how long it can actually last.

Viewed from another perspective, the concept of power and position fits nicely into, although it is not explicitly based upon, the philosophy of history as suggested in the *Book of Lord Shang*. Subjective moral efforts as well as the end product of such efforts are abandoned because they are useless and out-of-date. They are useless in the sense that to possess a moral character does not lead one anywhere in terms of the power relationship; and they are out-of-date because history has already advanced from the stage in which moral virtues are elevated and has moved into another in which force and hierarchy are honored.

Thus, if the *Shen Tzu* really represents Shen Tao's ideas, then Shen should be considered as a predecessor for both Shen Pu-hai and Han Fei. Before Shen Pu-hai, he had already caught sight of the importance of administrative techniques. Before Han Fei, he had already tried to put all leading elements of Legalist/Administrative theories together into a book. However, his treatment of such ideas was still rudimentary. For a more sophisticated synthesis of all leading Legalist/Administrative theories, one has to read the book attributed to Han Fei.

Han Fei (d. 233 B.C.) was, according to Ssu-ma Ch'ien, one of the princes of the state of Han. As an adult, he was very much concerned with the affairs of his own state. However, the many memorials he submitted to the throne, which contained remedies for policy defects as he saw them, were neglected; and he never had an opportunity to gain political power in Han. Ironically, it was the ruler of the expanding Ch'in, a rival of Han, who appreciated his mental capacity. Thus, when the Han ruler dispatched him to Ch'in as a special envoy, the ruler of Ch'in wanted very much to give him an office. But his former fellow student, Li Ssu, who together with him had studied under Hsun Tzu, was envious of his analytical talent and persuaded the ruler of Ch'in to fabricate a case against him. He was poisoned in prison in 233 B.C., much to the regret of the ruler of Ch'in who later lamented his own approval of the fabrication.[34]

If it is true, as Pan Ku claimed, that Shen Tao preceded both Shen Pu-hai and Han Fei and that his works were praised by both of them, and, if the ideas in the *Shen Tzu* are genuinely those of Shen Tao, then the *Han Fei Tzu*, a book that has been attributed to Han Fei, can be taken as an elaboration upon, though a much more sophisticated version of *Shen Tzu*. In the *Han Fei Tzu*, the good points of all the three foregoing Legalist/Administrative Theorists are included and critically synthesized.[35] The importance of law, much emphasized by both the *Book of Lord Shang* and the *Shen Tzu*, is sustained. Heavy punishment for minor crimes, forceful leadership, and single-minded devotion to agriculture and war, points which characterize Shang Yang, are approved. However, Shang's idea of bestowing political positions to persons with military merits was scorned. Shen Pu-hai's advocating that a ruler needs administrative techniques to protect himself against the intrigues of his own ministers is taken for granted. In fact, the theory of *hsing-ming*, which is an integral part of Shen's theory of administrative control, is better preserved in the *Han Fei Tzu* than in the fragments of Shen's writings ever since such writings as a whole were lost. But Shen is charged with the fault of not having paid close enough attention to the importance of law. Consequently, the state of Han which Shen served never achieved military supremacy among the contending states in the seventeen years when Shen was the Chancellor of Han. Finally, Shen Tao's theory of the necessity of power, position, and circumsances for rulers and officials is incorporated into the *Han Fei Tzu* as an indispensable ingredient. Indeed, for the governing of a state, power, position, and circumstances are as important as the law.

However, Han questions the validity of Shen Tao's view which, in order to show the indispensability of power, position, and circumstances, has completely eliminated the role of moral character. Han thinks that both virtue and position are necessary. Only when virtuous and capable people occupy high political positions will a state be orderly.[36] The reasons are simple. Power, position, and circumstances are impersonal. They cannot function by themselves. Nor can they possibly choose their own masters. All depends upon who controls them. Thus when sages like Yao and Shun ascended the throne, the whole country was in good order; when despotic rulers like Chieh and Chou took over the throne, the country was in great trouble. Han's criticism is reasonable and convincing. But it creates a theoretical difficulty. The moral element, which had been consistently excluded from the *Book of Lord Shang* and the writings of the two Shens, now found a way back into the Legalist/Administrative theories of Han Fei by becoming an indispensable element of the concept of power, position, and circumstances.

In addition to synthesizing the theories of the *Book of Lord Shang* and the writings of the two Shens, the *Han Fei Tzu* also exhibits a tendency to systematize the advice to a ruler. It cautions a ruler against the eight possible means by which ministers try to gain influence over their lord (chapter 9), and the ten possible mistakes he himself may commit (chapter 10). There are seven techniques which can enable a ruler to attain peace in the country (chapter 25), six things he should avoid by all means (chapter 25), and seven ways by which he can hope to control his subordinates firmly (chapter 30). Thus the ideas in the *Han Fei Tzu* are unusually systematic, yet the effort of systematization seems to have been confined to the chapter level. There does not seem to be an overall plan for the book. Earlier chapters do not gradually lead to the later ones and there is no development *per se* for the work as a whole.

In two respects, the *Han Fei Tzu* superseded the works attributed to his predecessors, especially the *Book of Lord Shang*. He refined the philosophy of history inherited from the *Book of Lord Shang* and clearly coined the concept of sage-king.

The Legalist Philosophers

There are at least two versions of the theory of evolution for human civilization in the *Han Fei Tzu*.[37] The first one is very general in nature, and it can be viewed as a summary of the version in the *Book of Lord Shang*. It attributes the difference in thought and institutions between antiquity and contemporary time mainly to the increase of population. The second version divides the evolution of human civilization into two stages. Belonging to the first stage are the remote and middle antiquities, when human beings had to fight for their survival against forces of nature—birds, beasts, insects, reptiles, and deluge. The second stage is characterized by the struggle among men themselves. Despots like Chieh and Chou, who wantonly killed innocent people, were removed from their thrones by folk heroes like T'ang and Wu, who each founded a new dynasty.

It is in the second version that the concept of sage-king, which already appears in the *Mencius* and the *Hsun Tzu*, is clearly defined.[38] In remote antiquity, when human beings were few, they had to fight for their existence against attacks from beasts and reptiles. They also had to ward off harassments from birds and insects. But, being inexperienced, they did not know how. It was with the help of a sage, who was kind enough to be concerned with the sufferings of these people, and also intelligent enough to be able to devise remedies which would ward off the attacks and harassments, that the people were enabled to lead a better life.

The sage fashioned nests of wood in the trees and the people, by following his lead, survived and were free from harassments. They called him the Nest Builder. In order to express their gratitude toward him, and also believing that he could improve their lives in other respects, the people made him their ruler. As time went by, and probably after the death of this first sage, the people felt that they could no longer tolerate another serious problem. While they could enjoy eating fresh fruits, berries, mussels, and clams, these food turned rank and evil-smelling if not immediately consumed. If they ate them in their decayed condition, the people became sick. But they did not know how to overcome such difficulties.

Then another sage appeared. Concerned and intelligent, he drilled with sticks and produced fire by which the people could cook their food. Some of the food became delicious when cooked, and many other kinds could be kept longer after cooking. The people were greatly delighted, and, as they did before, called this sage a Drill Man and gave him power to rule over them.

Historically, this theory probably cannot be substantiated.[39] What is interesting about it is that it has significant implications. A theory of popular sovereignty can indeed develop out of it. Although the people were rather ignorant compared with the sage who was intelligent enough to make a cultural breakthrough, they nevertheless had the power to rule themselves. It was only when the sage had made a significant contribution to them as a whole that they, being pleased, voluntarily gave the sage the power to rule them. Basically, such a power was given away as a trust. In theory, they could recall it if they thought necessary. But nothing of this sort is mentioned in the *Han Fei Tzu*. What is implied is that after the Nest Builder passed away, the power that had been given to him seemed to have been returned to the people so that when the Drill Man appeared and made a significant contribution to their life, they gave such a power to him, again at their pleasure. If these are indeed the true implications of this passage in chapter 19 of the *Han Fei Tzu*, then the book at least contains the germs of a potentially democratic theory. As is, it is merely a handbook for the prince. It may be favored by the ruling class, but definitely not by the people.

Regarding the significance of the Legalist/Administrative theories, they have been criticized as being much too harsh for the people to accept. The fact that the Ch'in applied such theories to politics and thereby became so strong that it unified all of China does not seem to have impressed many people in China.[40] What they remember most is the historical eventuality that after all of China was unified in 221 B.C., the Ch'in lasted for only fifteen years. Among the literati, few have openly praised either the Ch'in or the Legalist/Administrative theories since the Han dynasty. It is only since the early 1970's that the Chinese Communists have led a movement which honours the Legalist/Administrative Theorists and practitioners and denounces the Confucians. The movement has had a short history however.

From the perspective of Chinese thinkers, the Legalist/Administrative theories are significant for many reasons. First of all, it was a new, distinctive school of political thought. Its amoral approach, its emphasis on law, administrative techniques, and hierarchical position, and its conscientious use of the philosophy of history as a justification for political views was unique and unprecedented. It is true that the Taoists also despised morals, but they did so for different considerations. While the Legalist/Administrative Theorists discarded morals because the morals were out of date and would probably not be an effective means of government, the Taoists looked down upon the morals of the time as symptoms of a decaying age.

On the other hand, Hsun Tzu also gave law a very high place in his philosophy.[41] To him, the appearance of law means the beginning of order. At one point, he considered the setting up of laws and regulations as important, insofar as their social functions were concerned, as the exaltation of rituals.[42] Both were indispensable means for the attainment of a constant order. However, to him, superior men, as initiators of laws and new regulations, were even more essential to a state than the laws. Thus it was only the Legalist Theorists who gave first priority to laws instead of to men. According to the *Han Fei Tzu*, any state which follows the Legalist theory can afford to be led by a mediocre ruler without the danger of perishing. Finally, there is a kind of philosophy of history in the *Mencius*. While it could have served as a basis for his overall philosophy, the cyclical view merely provided an explanation for Mencius' constant engagement in debates and arguments.

Secondly, like the founder of the Moist school, Mo Tzu, the Legalist/Administrative Theorists identify human selfishness as the single most important source of all social evils, and they try to eliminate it as much as possible. Indeed, in their view, human beings are so self-centered that not only the ruler and his ministers have different interests, even fathers, and sons and husbands and wives are not of one mind. Thus Mo Tzu suggested replacing selfishness with universal love, while the Legalist/Administrative Theorists thought of objectifying everything. They resorted to the power of reason and wanted to have as many things made public as possible. And the most convenient means by which their wishes could be fulfilled was the making and promulgation of laws and regulations. Laws and regulations touched almost every aspect of human existence—the do's and don't's in every man's life, the recruitment of officials, and the bestowing of rewards and the meting out of punishments.

They can be seen, read, and known, and they do not change in accordance with each individual's subjective wishes or mood. Like Mo Tzu's remedy, which is purely intellectual in nature, the remedy suggested by the Legalist/Administrative Theorists is also intellectual in nature. Although the teachings of both schools were in vogue for a while, they have been rejected by the majority of the Chinese people throughout most of Chinese history. One probable reason for such a negative reception is that by eliminating the emotional, sentimental, and private dimensions of human life, human existence simply becomes too pure, cold, and inhuman.[43] And to expect human beings to be inhuman is just asking for too much, at least insofar as the majority of the Chinese people are concerned.

Thirdly, the vision of the Legalist/Administrative Theorists is not broad enough. They are concerned solely with things that are political in nature. It is true that because they are so, they have succeeded in seeing points which have escaped the attention of Confucians—the ineffectiveness of the moral approach, the need for a government being concerned with the majority of the people, and the necessity of giving heed to what is probable. However, their single-mindedness has made them blind to such a degree that they fail to see the desirability of leading a diversified and rich life. In order to attain national prosperity and strength, they urged the people to become either farmers or soldiers, and discouraged them from reading either odes or history, or learning either rites or music. They frowned upon sophistry and cleverness, and despised kindness and benevolence.

A legitimate concern is what should follow after becoming prosperous and strong. The *Book of Lord Shang* states that territorial expansion under the supervision of an awesome sovereign should be the ultimate goal. The fragments of Shen Pu-hai's writings and the *Shen Tzu* have little discussion on this.[44] It is only in the *Han Fei Tzu* that one detects an ideal beyond prosperity and strength, a society in which the honorable and the mean each keeps his own place without the one infringing upon the other, and in which all the people, regardless of their unequal intellectual endowments, can peacefully compete by doing their best.

However, this ideal is completely overshadowed by the talk of devotion to agriculture and war, statecraft, and techniques of administrative control, and one wonders how important such an ideal actually is. If Han Fei had really been serious about the ideal, he would, at the very least, have allocated one chapter to explain all the questions related to the ideal. But he did not. The casual and insignificant way in which such an ideal is portrayed leads one to doubt its real status in Han Fei's mind.

Fourthly, the relationship between Taoism and Legalist/Administrative theories is more complex than is ordinarily assumed or understood. Based upon the statement made by Ssu-ma Ch'ien,[45] it is generally agreed that Legalist/Administrative Theorists were influenced by Taoists and that the former borrowed many key terms from the latter. The new dating of the time of composition of Taoist classics, the study of the development of Taoist thought, the collection and analysis of the fragments of Shen Pu-hai's writings, and the scrutiny of the key terms used by both Taoist and Legalist/Administrative Theorists have modified Ssu-ma's statement. It is now accepted by many scholars that the *Lao Tzu* is a work of the third century B.C. As such, it was composed later than the earliest part of the *Chuang Tzu*. Moreover, many of the tenets of the *Lao Tzu* are distinctly different from those of the earliest part of the *Chuang Tzu*. While the latter are mostly contemplative in nature and show a tendency to rebel against all kinds of human devices, including institutions and values, the former reflect a deep interest in getting involved in human affairs under the guise of an overtly contemplative but inwardly scheming **sage.**

Professor Creel has named this branch of Taoism purposive Taoism, and on the basis of his examination of the Shen Pu-hai fragments, claims that it can be concluded that, contrary to the common assumption, it was Shen who influenced the author(s) of the *Lao Tzu* and not the other way around. This is so because Shen never used the term Tao in the sense typical of contemplative Taoism, although the term appeared at least nine times in the Shen fragments. On the other hand, Shen used the term non-action in a way different from that of both Confucius and early contemplative Taoists. By non-action, Shen meant that a ruler should keep away from intervening in the details of the conduct of government, yet should constantly be alert. To Confucius, it meant that a ruler should delegate his power to his virtuous and capable ministers. To the contemplative Taoists, it meant that a person should not obstruct the flow of things natural. It is only in the later part of the *Chuang Tzu*, which is believed to be a later addition, and throughout the whole *Lao Tzu*, that the term is used in the sense Shen used it, i.e., as a technique of control.

Since Shen existed in the fourth century B.C. and the *Lao Tzu* was composed in the third century B.C., it is logical to think that the former probably influenced the latter rather than the other way around. Thus, the relationship between Legalistic/Administrative Theorists and the Taoist philosophers is twisted. Ideas in the oldest part of the *Book of Lord Shang* as well as in the Shen fragments probably developed independently from those in the earliest part of the *Chuang Tzu*, but the author(s) of *Lao Tzu* borrowed from both sources. The themes of the *Lao Tzu* then served as one of the starting points of the *Han Fei Tzu*, crystallizing in the twentieth and twenty-first chapters which are devoted to an explanation of the important terms in the *Lao Tzu*. Since Han was the great synthesizer of Legalist/Administrative theories and he borrowed several themes from the *Lao Tzu*, Ssu-ma Ch'ien probably gained the impression that Legalist/Administrative Theorists were indebted to the Taoists, without realizing that the teachings of the *Lao Tzu* were already deviating from the original contemplative branch of Taoism.

However, Ssu-ma's conclusion has been accepted by Chinese scholars for two thousand years without serious challenge. It has been given further support by the 1974 discovery of the four classic treatises attributed to Huang-ti. If it can be firmly proven that these four treatises had actually existed before Shen Pu-hai's maturity, Professor Creel would probably have to reconsider his own theory. As it is, Professor Creel's argument sounds quite convincing.

By applying Marxist economic determinism to Chinese history, scholars on the China mainland in the 1970's advanced the theory that the Legalist/Administrative Theorists, especially Shang Yang and Han Fei, should be viewed as champions for the then emerging landlord class whose interests were opposed to those of the nobles, who had been the slave owners. By breaking the boundaries which had formerly defined and protected the nobles' lands, by allowing slaves to till the waste lands and pay taxes to the central government, and by permitting free sale of lands among the people, Shang had, so these scholars claim, actually deprived the nobles of their economic power base and had advanced the interests of the landlords. This theory is plausible, although it has its weak points; and mainland scholars may have overstretched themselves by applying economic determinism to Legalist/Administrative theories.

That mainland scholars became interested in Legalism illustrates how that school of thought has always been a factor to take into account, especially in the political realm. Professor Creel states that "Legalism seems to have steadily infiltrated Confucianism over a long period" and Fung Yu-lan writes that "both Confucianism and Legalism have had their proper sphere of application." That each has its sphere can be seen in such attitudes in the Chinese mind as one needs to be realistic as well as idealistic.

While one may believe man to be essentially good, it is wise to keep in mind that it is man's nature to "seek profit and avoid harm"; thus men will look to rewards and fear punishment. The function of government, then, is as much to direct and manage people as it is to enlighten and enoble them. While harmful, perhaps, if extreme, social control is necessary. The subordination of the individual to society is unavoidable. Power is a reality, and its concentration in the hands of a ruler is necessary. Otherwise laws will be on the books only and not effectively administered. While a society made up of individuals who voluntarily act morally would be ideal, we do not have such a society yet and, until then, laws and their equitable enforcement is necessary.

Although an exemplary, moral ruler and moral people in office is desirable, it is also necessary to have a ruler who has "shu", who can exert power and who has subordinates who execute laws fairly and equitably. We need to judge by deed and results, not by word. And one needs to be realistic in recognizing that there is change as well as non-change. New conditions arise and must be taken into account and new ways devised to meet them, as old ways will not always do.

Notes

1. H.G. Creel, *Shen Pu-hai, a Chinese Political Philosopher of the Fourth Century B.C.*, Chicago: The University of Chicago Press, 1974, p. 148.
2. K.C. Hsiao has made a penetrating analysis into the distinction between law and administrative techniques. See K.C. Hsiao, *Chung kuo cheng chih ssu hsiang shih* (History of Chinese Political Thought), Taipei: Chung hua wen hua ch'u pan shih yeh wei yuan hui, 1965, p. 242.
3. H.G. Creel, "The Fa-chia: 'Legalists' or 'Administrators'?" in H.G. Creel, *What is Taoism?*, Chicago: The University of Chicago Press, 1970, pp. 92-120. For the term "technocrats" see Shen Pu-hai, p. 162, n. 121.
4. Ssu-ma T'an, who is the father of the great historian Ssu-ma Ch'ien. The six schools were (1) Yin-yang; (2) Confucian; (3) Moist; (4) Names; (5) the Fa-chia; and (6) Taoist. See Creel, *Shen Pu-hai*, p. 156, n. 97.
5. F. Mote has labelled the Ch'in ideology "un-Chinese" to reflect the unvarying Chinese assessment of the Ch'in experiment. See Federick W. Mote, *Intellectual Foundations of China*, New York: Alfred A. Knopf, 1971, p. 114.
6. Pan Ku, *Han shu* (The Former Han History), Po na edition, ch. 30. See also J.J.L. Duyvendak, *The Book of Lord Shang*, Chicago: The University of Chicago Press, 1963, pp. 68-69.
7. He was enfeoffed fifteen towns, headed by Shang and Wu. They are situated in the border area between Ho-nan and Shensi provinces.
8. There had been at least two leading reformers who preceded Shang. They were Li Kuei (455-395 B.C.) and Wu Ch'i (d. 381 B.C.). See Yang, *Shang Yang*, pp. 14-15; Shih, *Shang Yang*, pp. 3-6.
9. The well-field system (Ching-t'ien chih) is said to have worked in the following way. A large piece of land would be equally divided into nine units in the form of two crosses overlapping each other, 井, which happened to be the shape of the top of a Chinese well. The nobles had their slaves till the land, and the crops from the center unit would be submitted to the central government as revenues.
10. H.G. Creel, "The Beginning of Bureaucracy in China: The Origin of the Hsien," in Creel, *What is Taoism?*, pp. 121-59.
11. This state was previously a part of the state of Chin. Although romanized the same, it is different from the Wei where Shang Yang was born.
12. Kao, *Shang chun shu*, p. 11. See also Duyvendak, *Lord Shang*, p. 159.
13. *Shang chun shu*, ch. 5. Here, I have used Duyvendak's translation. See Duyvendak, *Lord Shang*, pp. 209-10.
14. *Shang chun shu*, ch. 18; Kao, *Shang chun shu*, pp. 144-45. Here I have used Duyvendak's translation. See Duyvendak, *Lord Shang*, p. 292.
15. K.C. Hsiao reached a similar conclusion when he commented on Han Fei's rejection of moral virtue. See Hsiao, *Cheng chih ssu hsiang shih*, p. 233.

16. *Shang chun shu*, ch. 23; Kao, *Shang chun shu*, p. 172. Here, I am using Duyvendak's translation. See Duyvendak, *Lord Shang*, p. 317.

17. *Shang chun shu*, ch. 3; Kao, *Shang chun shu*, p. 35; Suyvendak, *Lord Shang*, p. 188. My interpretation here is slightly different from that of Duyvendak. I have included both the ruler and the officials in discussing knowledge and deliberation.

18. *Shang chun shu*, ch. 17; Kao, *Shang chun shu*, pp. 134-35. Cf. Duyvendak, *Lord Shang*, p. 283. My translation here is different from that of Duyvendak. Here, there seems to be a self-contradiction in the *Book of Lord Shang*. Earlier, Shang criticized the Confucians' attitude of sticking to a set of conclusions as if they were eternal truth. Here, the author of the book seems to be making the same mistake.

19. Mote noted that Legalists in general had no speculative interest in anything inapplicable. See Mote, *Intellectual Foundations*, p. 122.

20. Creel, *Shen Pu-hai*, p. 21.

21. For an explanation of the term, see H.G. Creel, "The Meaning of Hsingming," in H.G. Creel, *What is Taoism?*, pp. 79-81. See also Fung Yu-lan, *A History of Chinese Philosophy*, Princeton: Princeton University Press, 1952, Vol. 1, p. 324.

22. Creel, *Shen Pu-hai*, p. 63.

23. Fung Yu-lan has apparently accepted this view. See Fung, *Chinese Philosophy*, Vol. 1, p. 334.

24. T'ang Lan "Huang-ti ssu ching ch'u t'an," (A Preliminary Explanation of the Four Treatises of Huang-ti), in the *Wen wu*, No. 221 (Issue No. 10, 1974), p. 50. On the same page, T'ang states that, in general, teachings attributed to early legendary heroes such as Shennung and Huang-ti were probably forged in the middle and late stages of the Warring States Period. If he takes 403 and 256 B.C. as the beginning and ending dates of that period, then the five decades between 354 and 305 B.C. will be the middle stage. This will weaken his earlier statement that the four treatises were probably composed in the early half of the fourth century B.C.

25. Shen was originally born in the state of Cheng, which produced two famous Legalist thinkers, Tzu Ch'an and Teng Hsi. In 376 B.C., Han conquered Cheng and absorbed its culture. This is the Han which Shen served. It is also the same Han where Han Fei came from.

26. Creel, *Shen Pu-hai*, p. 176.

27. In an article written in 1954, Professor Creel suggested that early Taoism could be divided into at least two aspects, contemplative and purposive. The first was interested in the search of peace of mind, while the second was interested in seeking power. In Professor Creel's judgment these two aspects were logically incompatible. See H.G. Creel, "On Two Aspects in Early Taoism," in Creel, *What is Taoism?*, pp. 37-47.

28. K.C. Hsiao, however, pointed out that the differences between the Taoists and the Legalists were fundamental while the similarities shared by them were superficial. See Hsiao, *Cheng chih ssu hsiang shih*, p. 246.

29. Creel, *Shen Pu-hai*, p. 137, n. 11.

30. Vitali Rubin, "Shen Tao and Fa-chia," in the *Journal of the American Oriental Society*, 94.3 (1974), pp. 337-46.

31. I am referring to ch. 40 of the *Han Fei Tzu*. See Wang Hsien-shen, *Han Fei Tzu chi chieh* (The Han Fei Tzu, with Collected Annotations), Taipei: I wen yin shu kuan, reprint, n.d., chuan 17, pp. 1-5. Ch'en, *Han Fei Tzu*, pp. 886-98.

32. Shen Tao, *Shen Tzu* (Taipei: Shih chieh shu chu, 1958), p. 2.

33. Pan Ku, *Han shu*, ch. 30, p. 17; Ch'en, *Han Fei Tzu*, p. 889, n. 1.

34. Ssu-ma Ch'ien, *Shih chi*, ch. 63, pp. 1-8b; W.K. Liao, tr. *The Complete Works of Han Fei Tzu*, London: Arthur Probsthain, 1939, Vol. 1, pp. xxvii-xxix.

35. That Han Fei is the greatest synthesizer of the Legalist/Administrative School is universally admitted by Chinese and English writers. See Fung, *Chinese Philosophy*, p. 320; Hsiao, *Cheng chih ssu hsiang shih*, pp. 227, 229-30; Mote, *Intellectual Foundations*, p. 121.

36. Ch'en Ch'i-yu insists that this is Han's true view. He charges that most scholars have neglected this point. See Ch'en, *Han Fei Tzu*, p. 891, n. 8.

37. The one-sentence summary in the fourth paragraph of ch. 49 of the *Han Fei Tzu* may be counted as a third version. See Wang, *Han Fei Tzu*, chuan 19, p. 3b; Ch'en, *Han Fei Tzu*, p. 1042.

38. *Mencius*, IIIB:9. Wang Hsing-ch'ien, *Hsun Tzu chi chieh* (The Hsun Tzu, with Collected Annotations), Taipei: I wen yin shu kuan, reprint, n.d., chuan 12, p. 3b.

39. Fung Yu-lan did not think that such a division into three stages was sustenable. However, he believed that it was historically relevant. He viewed the Warring States Period as well as the Spring and Autumn Period immediately preceding it as reflected such a procession of evolution. See Fung, *Chinese Philosophy*, Vol. 1, p. 316.

40. Mote noted the imbalance between the traditional criticism against the Ch'in ruler, the "First August Supreme Ruler", and the great deeds the ruler did to China. He attributed such an imbalance to the particular cultural values of the Chinese. See Mote, *Intellectual Foundations*, p. 127.

41. Hsun Tzu thinks that if scholars, in ruling a state, can abide by the laws which have been tested time after time, they can achieve lasting order. See Wang, *Hsun Tzu*, chuan 7, p. 5b.

42. The ritual (*li*) plays a very important role in Hsun Tzu's political philosophy. It may even be said that Hsun Tzu's ideal government is one based upon the ritual. The *li*, in its expression, means formality, convention, manners, etiquette, customs, folk ways and mores; ceremonial, ritual, and rite. As a quality, it means decorum, gentiality, refinement, and culture. See Y.P. Mei, "Hsun Tzu's Theory of Government," in the *Tsing Hua Journal of Chinese Studies* (Taipei: Tsing Hua hsueh pao she), Vol. VIII, Nos. 1 and 2 (Aug. 1970), p. 70.

43. Mote attributed the failure of Legalism to its being too rational and too self-enclosed to comprehend all the mysteries of the human heart. See Mote, *Intellectual Foundations*, p. 122.

44. The last paragraph of the "missing texts" attached to the *Shen Tzu* does talk about the state of affairs when a sage-king is ruling. The ideas in it are very interesting. But they are so incompatible with the themes in the rest of the book that it is dubious whether they should belong there. See Shen, *Shen Tzu*, p. 14.

45. Ssu-ma Ch'ien, *Shih chi*, ch. 63, p. 1.

6
MENCIUS

CHUNG-YING CHENG

I

In the years following his death, Confucius' philosophy became widely established and attracted many able disciples. Mencius was one of them. The *Shih Chi* states that he received instruction from Tzu Ssu, who is believed to be the grandson of Confucius. If this is so, Mencius lived in the middle of the Warring States period. Its beginning is said to be 403 B.C., and Mencius is believed generally to have been born in 371 B.C.

Before turning to Mencius' philosophy, it might be pointed out that Warring States Confucianism differed in several ways from the Confucianism of the Spring and Autumn period. One is its adoption of the debate form to express ideas. The writings of Warring States Confucianists are mainly in propositional form rather than collections of thoughts expressed in phrases and sentences as in the *Analects*. The clarifying and unifying of basic concepts is a second. Positive debates on question concerning the Way of Heaven (T'ien-tao), nature (hsing) and fate (ming), principle (li) and essence (chi) is a third. Confucius was hesitant to discuss such metaphysical questions. Confucianists in the Warring States period had no such reluctance however. This led to a fourth characteristic, the establishing of a metaphysical basis for political and social philosophy. The Confucianists of the Warring States period recognized both the lack and the need of such and thus spent much effort in meeting that need. A fifth characteristic is the proposing of new social patterns that were in fact plans for reform. Mencius' philosophy reflects these developments in Confucianism.

II

As to the dates of Mencius, the *Shih Chi* does not record the dates of Mencius' birth and death. However, according to the biographies of Mencius by Ming scholars and the biography by Ch'eng Fu-hsin of the Yuan dynasty, Mencius was born in the fourth year of King Lieh (375-369 B.C.) of the Chou dynasty and died in the twentysixth year of King Nan (314-256 B.C.). These dates correspond to the years 371 and 289 in the Western calendar.[1] If we consider that Mencius was fifty years old when he travelled to Ch'i, our calculations of the dates of his birth and death agree with the above. By these calculations, Mencius was born exactly one hundred years after the death of Confucius; and if we take thirty years to be one generation, Mencius lived three generations later than Confucius. The *Shih Chi* states that "Meng K'o was a native of Chou and received instruction from Tzu Ssu." The state of Chou was close to that of Lu, and for Mencius in his youth to have studied with Tzu Ssu, making him a fourth or fifth generation disciple of Confucius, is a definite possibility.

Mencius considered himself a self-trained disciple of Confucius. He said, "I could not be a disciple of Confucius, I privately studied all men."[2] He said too, "What I desire most is to study Confucius." He devoted his whole life to Confucian orthodoxy. He discussed it everywhere and with everyone which illustrates that he "tried to correct men's hearts, rejected heterodox theories, opposed one-sided actions, eliminated extravagant speech, and thus succeeded to the teachings of the Three Sage Kings." He himself said that he had no alternative but to argue them. "Is it just that I like to argue then? I have no alternative."

Just as Confucius had done earlier, Mencius travelled to the various states to visit the feudal lords. He did so in the hope of being employed and given the opportunity to put his theory of humane government into practice. Mencius considered the world his responsibility. He said: "If one were to establish peace in the world, in this generation if I am rejected, who else is there?" When Yin Shih criticized him for making known his intention to leave Ch'i in three days, Mencius replied:

"How can Yin Shih not know me? Travelling a thousand li to see the king was something that I desired. Is leaving because I did not have the opportunity to do so also something that I desire? I have no alternative. I am leaving after three days because I consider it urgent. The king almost reformed. If the king had reformed, he certainly would have summoned me. When I left and the king did not come after me, I knew at once that there had been a change of will. In those circumstances, how could I have lodged in the king's realm? By using of means appropriately, a king practises virtue. If the king used me, then how could the people of Ch'i fail to be at peace and the people of the world fail to accept peace? The king almost reformed. I hope for it every day. Could I be of so little spirit?"[3]

This illustrates that Mencius was devoted to and suffered for virtue. In fact, throughout his life, Mencius was a failure. Although King Hui of Liang invited him to be a minister and treated him with great courtesy, he did not accept his recommendation to practice the "kingly Way" and "humane government." Mencius then served as a minister in Ch'i, but he could not realize his ambition there either, and left. From there he returned to Chou by way of Hsieh. Subsequently, he was invited to Hsi, but Hsi was a small state between Ch'i and Ch'u and there was no way that Mencius could put what he advocated into practice, so he left. Finally, he retired and, together with students such as Kung-sun Ch'ou and Wan Chang, gathered his own thoughts and his discussions with others into the seven chapters of the *Mencius*.[4] The "Biographies of Mencius and Hsun Ch'ing" in *Shih Chi* records the following:

"Meng K'o was a native of Chou. He received instruction from Tzu Ssu. When he was well versed in the Way he went to serve King Hsuan of Ch'i, but King Hsuan was unable to use him. He then went to Liang, but King Hui of Liang was not satisfied with what he had to say and considered it both impractical and inapplicable in the current circumstances. At that time Ch'in employed Lord Shang, enriching the state and strengthening the armies. Ch'u and Wei employed Wu Ch'i and fought both superior and weak adversaries. Kings Wei and Hsuan of Ch'i employed the disciples of Sun Tzu and T'ien Chi, and all the feudal lords went eastward to the court of Ch'i. The world was engaged in making vertical and horizontal alliances, and aggression was considered a virtue. Meng K'o, however, transmitted the virtues of T'ang, Yu, and the Three Dynasties. Because the common virtues did not accord with those of the past, he retired and with the disciples of Wan Chang wrote prefaces to the *Odes* and the *Documents*, recorded the thoughts of Confucius, and compiled the *Mencius* in seven chapters."[5]

III

Mencius' discourses can be divided into three categories according to their content: the kingly way and humane (*jen*) government, the notions that nature is good and wisdom can be cultivated, the historical facts concerning Yao, Shun Yu, T'ang, Wen, Wu, I Yin, Po I, the Duke of Chou and Confucius and criticism of the disciples of Yang, Chu, Mo Ti and Hsu Hsing.

Discourses on the kingly Way and humane government. The feudal lords of the Warring States period seized territory and sought power. States practiced tyrannical government internally, and the relationship between states was motivated by profit and loss, and toward that end vertical and horizontal alliances were formed. Governments plotted to appropriate the wealth of individual households, concerned themselves only with the privileges of the minority and dismissed the welfare of the people without a thought. In seizing cities and territory, they fearlessly sacrificed the lives and property of the people. To save the people from these calamities, and to enable them to live peacefully and work happily, Mencius argued strongly the relative merits of righteousness and profit. He made a distinction between the Way of kings and the Way of dictators (*pa*) and advocated humane government that obeyed Heaven and cherished the people. Mencius' discourses were aimed directly at the current rulers' emphasis on profit and disregard of righteousness, the way of dictators, and the evil governments that were being established.

Discourses on the notions that nature is good and that wisdom can be cultivated. Mencius maintained that basically man's nature has the beginnings of all the virtues and that these beginnings of the virtues are good. Human nature has within it the beginnings of humaneness, righteousness, propriety, wisdom, and so on; there is no need to seek for these externally. In seeking goodness all men must follow their natures, "extend and complete them." The merits of the notion that "wisdom is cultivated" is that it is a constant bringing out of the goodness in human nature and that it guides all actions; it enlarges upon the beginnings of all virtues and enables them to be fully realized in practice. Ultimately, it leads to the point of being unwavering, the state where one is not influenced by external things. Mencius' discourses were directed at the theories of Kao Tzu that "human nature is neither good nor not good" and that "humaneness is internal, righteousness is external."

Discourses on historical facts. Mencius assumed the responsibility for passing on the truths that he had inherited. He took Yao, Shun, Yu, T'ang, Wen, and Wu as examples of humane rulers and I Yin, Po I, the Duke of Chou, and Confucius as representatives of the sages. Consequently, whenever anyone expressed doubt about their actions, or about regarding them as being representative of their ages in their entirety, Mencius never wearied of carefully explaining and defending them. We can observe this in Mencius' explanations that "Yao did not give the world to Shun," and that "Yu did not transmit the world to a worthy man but to his son," and in his defense of the facts that "Shun took a wife without announcing it," and that "Shun did away with the hsiang [music]."

Also, in Mencius' view T'ang overthrew the Hsia dynasty and King Wu overthrew the Shang to save people from cruelty. He said: "I have heard of punishing a man called Chou; I have not heard of killing a ruler." He explained, too, that "I Yin did not employ his skills in slicing and boiling in making an agreement with T'ang," and that "Confucius did not lodge with Yung Tan or with the servant, Chi Huan, in Ch'i." What is important in these clarifications and elucidations of historical facts by Mencius is that he did not want the words and deeds of Yao, Shun, Confucius, and others to be misrepresented or distorted by later generations; he wanted later generations to know whom to follow in practicing humane government and the Way of kings.

Discourse criticizing the disciples of Yang "Chu," "Mo Ti" and Hsu Hsing. There were many scholars in the time of Mencius, but the followers of Yang Chu and Mo Ti were the most numerous. Mencius assumed the responsibility for orthodox Confucianism and maintained that the Hundred Schools of Learning were "heterodox theories" and "extravagant speech." He wanted to establish as the model to be followed the spirit of the Spring and Autumn period expressed by Confucius in the dicta, "correct men's hearts, reject orthodox theories, oppose one-sided actions, eliminate extravagant speech" and therefore he criticized all strange principles and heterodox theories. He said that both Yang Chu and Mo Ti were "without father and ruler like the beasts", and that one had to "become an earthworm to grasp the theories of Ch'en Chung-tzu." He criticized Kao Tzu's immorality. He maintained that Hsu Hsing devoted his energy to plowing only; he did not apply his mind or enjoy discussions; he caused men "to lead each other into falsehoods" and, therefore, he was not qualified to govern the state.

IV

We shall now discuss Mencius' method of discourse; we shall examine how he discussed things and people, how he established and proved his theories, and how he faulted others. These points have been ignored in previous discussions of Mencius, but in fact they are quite important.

Some people have pointed out Mencius' skill in observation.[6] This is the starting point in Mencius' discussions of problems: he always makes direct observations with the proper attitude. In his faith in men, Mencius believes that man is originally guided by his inborn nature toward goodness. As time went on, habits and desires often obscure these basic dispositions toward good and become the source of his own faults. Nevertheless, under certain circumstances these basic predispositions can reassert themselves. Mencius was skilled in the investigation of these inherent elements and in enlarging on them. He thereby could prove that man's nature originally has the beginnings of all virtues; that there is no need to seek for them outside. He could also explain thereby that the means of expanding and completing the beginnings of all virtues is government and acting as men. Mencius employed the intuitive method to enlarge upon his theory of government and acting as men. This is illustrated in the following two examples:

"I have heard Hu Ho say: "Your majesty was seated in the hall when an ox was led by the hall. Your majesty saw it and asked: "What is going to be done with the ox?" The reply was: "It will be used to consecrate a bell." Your majesty said: "Release it. I cannot bear its shuddering. It looks like an innocent man being led to the execution ground".... This is the art of humanness.... Now your kindness is sufficient to extend to the birds and beasts, but your merit does not reach to the people. How can you make this exception?"

"Mencius said: "All men have hearts that cannot bear [the suffering of] others. The former kings had hearts that could not bear [the suffering of] the people, and they had governments that could not bear [the suffering of] the people. When one who has a heart that cannot bear [the suffering of] the people and who practises humane government that cannot bear [the suffering of] the people, governs the world, he can turn it around in the palm of his hand. To illustrate that all men have hearts that cannot bear [the suffering of] others, let us suppose that at this moment a man sees a child about to fall into a well; he will feel frightened and distressed, and this will not be because of his intimacy with the child's parents nor because he hopes thereby to gain friends in the district and village."

These two passages, one about King Hsuan of Ch'i being unable to bear the shuddering of the ox and the other about a man being unable to bear the sight of a child falling into a well, contain important examples of the expansion of the beginnings of all virtues. Mencius said: "Extend kindness and you will have the means of guarding the four seas; do not extend kindness and you will not have the means of guarding your wife and sons." He said further: "If you can complete them you can thereby guard the four seas; if you do not complete them you will not have the means whereby to serve your parents."

In addition, he used stories such as that of the man of Sung, who pulled up the sprouts to assist them in their growth, and of the man of Ch'i, who had a wife and a concubine, as concrete examples that could be compared directly with abstract principles. They are deeply penetrating and easily understood; and, therefore, they correctly portray the extreme cases in real life. The chapter in which Mencius discusses funerals with Mo Che-i reflects a similar method:

"In earlier times there were people who did not bury their relatives. When their relatives died, they threw their corpses into a ditch. Later, as they passed the ditch they saw foxes eating the corpses and gnats gnawing them. Perspiration formed on their brows and they could not look at them. That perspiration was not ordinary perspiration; it was the heart reflected in their faces. They returned, turned over the corpses with herbs, and buried them. Burying them was proper and right; therefore, there must be principles whereby a filial son or a human man buries his relatives."

This chapter describes and traces the origins of the burial ceremony. What it describes is an involuntary response of the heart that is reflected in the face and motivates all actions. It proves that "ritual" is not an empty form or rule. The most primitive, the most direct experiences in a person's life, are always directly linked to the beginnings of the virtues. This is an important premise in Mencius' discourses.

There is a relationship between this "intuitive" method and another that Mencius employed in discussing his theories. This latter we call "fulfilling feelings and knowing classification." Mencius maintained that man's nature contains the beginnings of all virtues, and naturally it contains also the possibility of their completion and realization. According to this principle, to prove the existence of the beginnings of certain principles, there need only be the possibility of their fulfilment and completion within them. Whether or not they are realized is not a question of possibility or impossibility; it is one of whether or not they are evident in the individual's actions. Mencius maintained that by being unable to bear the shuddering of the ox, King Hsuan of Ch'i demonstrated that he had within him the beginnings of humaneness which cannot bear [the suffering of] others; and, therefore, he had the wisdom "to be able to" practice humane government. His not practicing humane goverment was due to later influences. He let selfish desires conceal the beginnings of humaneness, or he had the wisdom but did not practise it. He did not give the beginnings of humaneness the opportunity to be fulfilled.

What we have called the principle of "fulfilling feelings and knowing" is only the principle of the unity of knowledge and action. Thus in discussing the four beginnings, Mencius said: "Each of us has the four beginnings within us. Wisdom is the expansion and completion of them. They are the same as the start of a fire or the source of a spring. If you can complete them you can thereby guard the four seas; if you do not complete them you will not have the means whereby to serve your parents."

The concept of "classification" occupies an important position in Mencius' thought and discourses. It is used no less than thirty times in the book of *Mencius*. Furthermore, the concepts of "classification" and analogy are applied directly or indirectly in the discourses on humane government, the notion that nature is good, and the origins of all virtues. "Classification" means classification of all things in the world according to their similarities and differences or the definition of the common qualities of each category of things. When Mencius discussed a problem, he employed analogy to illustrate the abstract; and difficult to comprehend conditions for the same class of things as inferred from obvious examples, and he applied the logic of classification. Mencius was very skilful in the application of the logic of classification. First, he accepted the premise: "All things of the same class are similar." Then he stated the specific conditions, and from the conditions he isolated the common qualities of one class of things and constructed a concept which he used in drawing "analogies" with similar conditions elsewhere. Mencius employed two particular sets of circumstances to distinguish between the concepts of "can not" (*pu-neng*) and "do not" (*pu-wei*), and he concluded that King Hsuan's not protecting the people of Ch'i belonged to the category of "do not." Mencius' argument is as follows:

"Question: 'What is the difference between "do not" and "can not?"' Answer: 'If it is grasping Mount T'ai and leaping over the northern sea with it that you say to others "I can not," it really is a case of "can not." If it is breaking twigs for elders that you say to others "I can not", it is a case of "do not", not of "can not." The king's not being a king is not in the category of grasping Mount T'ai and leaping over the northern sea with it; the king's not being a king is in the category of breaking twigs.'"

In this chapter of *Mencius*, the category of "do not" includes the following four sets of circumstances: "Strength enough to lift a hundred catties but not strong enough to lift a feather";

vision sufficient to examine the tips of autumn down but cannot see a cartful of firewood"; "kindness extends to the birds and beasts but its merit does not reach to the people"; and "breaking twigs for elders." "Humane government" that protects the people is not something that can not be done; humane government's not being realized is the result of those who govern "not doing" it.

On the premise that "all things of the same class are similar," Mencius said: "The sages and I are in the same category." This led to the conclusion: "What kind of man Shun was, I am. It is the same with those who act." This conclusion was logically necessary. It also led to the statement in the *Mencius*: "What the unicorn has in common with the walking beasts, the phoenix with the flying birds, Mount T'ai with the hills and mountains, the rivers and seas with the navigation streams, is the category. What the sages have in common with people is also the category. To be more excellent than his category, to be more talented than his group, since the beginning of man there has been no one more outstanding than Confucius." Within the same category there are common characteristics. Only one who can fulfil them can "be more excellent than his category, more talented than his group."

Mencius provided the following examples of not knowing the categories:

"Here is the third finger; it does not bend freely and we blame it on disease or injury. If it can bend freely, it does not consider the distance from Ch'in to Ch'u long because the finger is not the person. To say that the finger which is not the person knows evil, while the mind which is not the person does not know evil, is called not knowing categories."

Both the finger not being the person and the mind not being the person belong to the same category of things—not being the person. Mencius tried to show that men have knowledge of and make the same responses to the same class of things. Only when one can distinguish that one is not three can he be considered to have knowledge of categories.

The "intuition" and "experience" described above are the sensations that one is made aware of in particular circumstances.

For these experiences to be extended and made comprehensible it is necessary to generalize the particular circumstances. At such times, we are applying the principle of "knowing"; we extend the knowledge gained in limited experience and apply it generally to things of the same class. "Knowing," therefore, is an extension and application of knowledge; it is the richest logical meaning reached inductively or deductively. "Fulfilment" of feelings is realized in each person's actions; it is the realization of the extension and completion of all the good elements in knowledge in the individual's personality. Consequently, if there is to be "fulfilment of feelings," there must be "knowing of knowledge." "Fulfilment of feelings" and "knowing of knowledge" support and complete each other. Knowledge is the basic action and action is the manifestation and the completion of knowledge. Neither of the two can lack the other. This is an important point in Confucian thought.

The third method Mencius used in discussions of his theories we shall call "rectification of names" or "correct definition of terms." This method derives from the disintegration of Confucius' notion of "correct names."[7] "Rectification of names" and "correct definition of terms" applies to dissimilar things and conditions. It covers dissimilar terms and definitions. Ultimately it is the basis for assigning different moral values to dissimilar terms and definitions. There are many examples of Mencius' use of this method. A few are as follows:

> "Desertion, alliances, vulgarity, decadence, all are things that grieve the feudal lords. If it is 'desertion from' which leads to indifference and rebellion, it is called 'desertion.' If it is 'desertion to' which leads to indifference and rebellion, it is called 'alliance.' Lack of disgust with animal-like behavior is called 'vulgarity.' Lack of disgust with drunkenness is called 'decadence.' In the time of the former kings there was no pleasure in desertion or alliance, and no vulgar or decadent actions."

> "One who robs humaneness is called a thief. One who robs righteousness is called a murderer. A thief and murderer is only a ruffian. I have heard of the ruffian, Chou, being killed; I have not heard of a ruler being killed."

"Correctness through obedience is the Way of women. To live in the extended place of the world, to establish a correct position in the world, to practise the Great Way of the world—if one attains his aim he abides by it with the people; if he does not attain his aim he practises the Way alone. One whom wealth and honor cannot make immoral, poverty and contempt cannot send away, military power cannot intimidate, is called the great man of spirit."

Now we shall explain in detail one example of Mencius' application of "rectification of names" or "correct definition of terms." On the premise that when a humane man occupies the throne, he definitely can with "a heart that cannot bear [the suffering of] others practise government that cannot bear [the suffering of] others", Mencius asked: "How can a humane man be on the throne and deceive the people?" Mencius explained that "to deceive the people" means "to entrap them and then punish them." How does he entrap them in crime? Mencius said: "The people's attitude toward the Way is this: If they have a constant livelihood, they have a constant heart. If they do not have a constant livelihood, they do not have a constant heart. If they do not have a constant heart, they disregard the laws and are dishonest and wasteful. They cannot be any other way."

It follows that if the ruler does not provide a constant livelihood for the people, he can entrap the people in crimes; he can create the conditions in which "to deceive the people." On the premise that a humane ruler does not deceive the people, and the above explanation of "deceiving the people", it is of course possible to deduce the principle that "the enlightened ruler regulates the people's livelihood." This illustrates the application of the device of "rectification of names" or "correct definition of terms." The key to the discourse is bound up with the definition of "deceiving the people." The relationship between "to practise humane government" and "to regulate the people's livelihood" involves the concept of "deceiving the people" and its implications in the context in which it is expressed.

Besides being applicable in this discourse, the device of "rectification of names" or "correct definition of terms" provides the basis for defining many concepts in Confucian thought. For instance, the following definitions indirectly aided Mencius in formulating his theories of the goodness of nature and fate,

> "One who is desirable is called good; one who has possession of himself is called sincere; one who is complete is called beautiful; one who is complete and outstanding is called a sage; a sage who cannot be known is called a deity."

By establishing definitions and clarifying concepts the whole system of thought acquires a firm base.

V

Mencius' theories of fate and of the goodness of nature. We have said above that when political, social, or moral philosophy reaches a certain stage it, of necessity, is faced with the question of its metaphysical basis. Confucius could remain silent about the Way of heaven and fate; the Confucians or the Warring States period could not. Mencius discussed not once, but twice, and even three times, the problems of "nature," "fate," "heaven", "the Way," "mind," 'vital force," "righteousness," "principle," etc. On the one hand, his understanding of man's existence and his basic nature certainly derived from his own intuition and experience. On the other hand, they arose out of the need which had developed in Confucianism to explain these basic questions. Consequently, Mencius' discussions of nature, fate, heaven, the Way, mind, righteousness, principle, etc., were significant at that time. He advanced Confucius' thought to new heights; he ascribed an inherent fundamental principle and a metaphysical system to the teaching of Confucius.

Although both "nature" and "fate" derive from heaven, there is a very important difference between them. "Nature" is a creative force animated by the individual himself. "Fate" is an external restriction upon the individual; it is an objective condition which the individual cannot control. We may say that "nature" and "fate" represent two different tendencies. The former animates the development of the individual; the latter restricts the development of the individual. In the development of personality, both "nature" and "fate" are necessarily blended and assimilated. If the power of the individual is not developed, it cannot be said to have been restricted by objective conditions. However, if he does not know how to avoid objective, external causes which obstruct, even constant effort on the part of the individual is in vain. Consequently, man should assimilate external causes to the utmost extent and, within the limits placed on him by objective conditions, strive to attain the highest degree of activity and creativity. It is in this sense that we shall discuss Mencius' theory that nature is good.

"Nature" is man's original mind (*hsin*), the "child-like mind" that Mencius spoke about. This child-like mind is derived from heaven and is received in its entirety at birth; it is not something to be found externally. It includes a sympathetic mind, a mind that knows shame, a respectful and yielding mind, and a mind that knows right and wrong. Mencius said:

"All men have minds that are sympathetic; all men have minds that know shame; all men have minds that are respectful and yielding; all men have minds that know right and wrong. A sympathetic mind is humane; a mind that knows shame is righteous; a respectful and yielding mind [reflects] propriety; a mind that knows right and wrong [reflects] wisdom. Humaneness, righteousness, propriety, and wisdom are not imposed on us from outside; we really do possess them, we just do not think about them. Therefore, it is said: 'Seek and you shall attain it; neglect and you shall lose it.' We can multiply them endlessly but we cannot exhaust their qualities. The *Odes* state: 'Heaven produced all people. There are affairs and regulations [for them]. The people maintain their natural dispositions and love what is right, excellent, and virtuous.' Confucius said: 'The author of this ode really knows the Way! Because there are affairs, there must be regulations [for them]. The people maintain their natural dispositions: therefore, they love what is right, excellent, and virtuous.'"

"Nature is the general source of morality or the beginning of 'nature'"; it is the law that where "there are affairs there must be regulations" for them; it can be found in one's self. All people have natures; therefore, "nature" has a finite existence. When it is developed, it gradually approaches "goodness," "sincerity," "beauty," "greatness," "sageliness," and "spirituality." It fulfills itself. If it does not fulfil itself, this original mind may degenerate into selfishness. Nevertheless, "nature" can be destroyed even by later influences. "We really do possess them [virtues], we just do not think about them." "Seek and you shall attain them; neglect them and you shall lose them." "Attain" and "lose" refer to the attainment and loss of what the mind knows, not to its existence or non-existence in reality. Accordingly, Mencius said:

> "The nature of the gentleman cannot be increased even by prosperity, nor ruined even by poverty; it is predetermined. The nature of the gentleman is the roots of humaneness, righteousness, propriety, and wisdom in the mind; it is characterized by a mild harmony in the countenance and a rich fullness in the back; it is moved by the four limbs. The four limbs do not speak but they know."

"Nature" is also what Mencius called natural ability and innate knowledge. He said:

> "That which man is capable of doing without having to learn it is natural ability. That which man knows without being anxious about is innate knowledge. The measure of the child is that he loves his parents and, when he grows up, he respects his elder brothers. Treating parents as parents is humaneness; respecting elder brothers is righteousness."

What Mencius called "nature" was man's original mind; consequently, in *Mencius* the two terms, "mind" and "nature" are often used interchangeably. Mencius maintained that to develop his active and creative nature, the individual must "employ his mind to its utmost." To "employ his mind to its utmost" he must first "know his nature." How can he "know his nature"? Mencius exhorted people to seek earnestly within themselves for that knowledge. He said: "The function of the mind is thought. Think and you will attain it; do not think and you will not attain it. This is what heaven has given to us".

Here Mencius exhibits a particularly extreme tendency toward idealism. He maintains that "all things are within us." Consequently, one need only "retreat to the mind to find the truth", energetically strive to "know his mind" and to "employ his mind to its utmost." To extend the beginnings of goodness in the mind is, "to treat parents as parents and be humane to the people; to be humane to the people and be careful about affairs." Seek humaneness and you certainly will attain humaneness; seek knowledge and you certainly will attain knowledge. Because "nature" is what "Heaven" had given to him, one can "employ his mind to its utmost" and know nature, and of course, he will "know heaven" as well. Mencius said: "One who employs his mind to its utmost knows nature; when he knows nature he knows heaven. He preserves his mind and nourishes nature; therefore, he serves heaven."

"Heaven" combines the two mutually exclusive forces, "nature" and "fate". "Nature" is what heaven confers and "fate" is what heaven decrees, but both are received from heaven. "Heaven" gives to the individual active and creative abilities. At the same time, heaven also places external limits upon him. Thus "nature" and "fate" attain a unity and a harmony in "heaven." In *Mencius* the two terms, "heaven" and "fate", are often used interchangeably. Although "nature" is also a part of "heaven", it is always used in the sense of an external force or the natural element that represents "heaven" in the realm of human power. The "decree of heaven" (*t'ien-ming*) is not something that can be led or regulated by human power; it is a limitation on the active and creative nature of man. Although they appear together in the phrase, "know nature and you know heaven," the two terms, "heaven" and "nature", seldom are found together in *Mencius*. Mencius provided a further definition of "heaven and fate." He said: ".... all are heaven, they are not what man is able to do. That which is done without anyone doing it is heaven; that which arrives without being sent is fate."

The way in which man can relate heaven and fate is only to "obey heaven and know fate." What does it mean to "know fate"? Many laws of nature can be known inductively from experience. Knowing these laws, whenever one encounters similar conditions he can consider them in terms of those laws and arrive at the same conclusions. People can depend on these possibilities and select appropriate actions and thus avoid encountering objective conditions which lead to disaster. Although "fate" is beyond the scope of our control, it is within the scope of our knowledge; although we cannot "oppose fate", we can "know fate". Therefore, Mencius said:

"There is nothing that does not have a fate; everything conforms to what is proper for it. Therefore, one who knows fate does not stand beneath a high and dangerous wall. One who reaches the end of the road and dies, accords with fate. One who dies in fetters and handcuffs does not accord with fate."

To obey heaven and "know fate" is nothing more than the following principle: If fate can be avoided, avoid it; if it cannot be avoided, obey it. The conclusion to be drawn from the dictum, "know fate", is that "fate" can be divided into the known and the unknown. The known can be further divided into that which is already known and that which is not yet known. On the one hand, within known, objective limits, man fully develops his active and creative powers to employ his mind to its utmost in order to know nature; on the other hand, in unknown or not yet known, objective conditions, he can only wait and then make the appropriate changes according to the occasion. Thus we do not blindly obey and follow objective conditions; in all circumstances we must strive and engage in the greatest activity. Therefore Mencius said: "A gentleman administers the laws as to avoid fate."

Mencius often used historical events and crises in the life of an individual to explain examples of unknowable and unavoidable decrees of heaven which one can only submit to. The following statements explain why Yao and Shu yielded the throne and why Yu transmitted it to his son; and why I, I Yin, the Duke of Chou, and Confucius, although virtuous, did not possess the world.

"One who is unlike Tan Chu is also unlike Shun. Shun resembled Yao and Yu resembled Shun in that they ruled for many years and extended benefits to the people for a long time. Ch'i Hsien was able to respectfully inherit the Way of Yu. I resembled Yu in that each ruled for only a few years and did not extend benefits to the people for a long time. Shun, Yu, and I were separated from each other by a long time. That the virtue of their sons was not like their own was all decreed by heaven; it was not something that men could bring [about]."

"For an ordinary person to possess the world, he must have the virtue of Shun and Yu and be recommended by the Son of Heaven; consequently, Confucius did not possess the world.

When after successive generations have possessed the world, the means whereby heaven destroys the line must be one like Chieh or Chou; consequently, I, I Yin, and the Duke of Chou did not possess the world."

Mencius explained the fact that these men's talents and virtues were the same, but the circumstances were different, by "heaven and fate." "When heaven chooses to confer the world to a worthy person, it confers it to a worthy person; when heaven chooses to confer the world to a son, it confers it to a son. All is decreed by heaven; it is not something that man can bring [about]." Mencius said that Confucius' statement that "The righteousness of T'ang, Yu, Shan, Hsia Hou, Yin and Chou Chi were all the same" had the same meaning.

We have said above that "nature" represents the active force which animates the individual's self-development, and that "fate" represents the force which restricts the individual's self-development. Mencius maintained that although humaneness, righteousness, propriety, and wisdom originate in heaven, they do not belong to the category of "fate" but to the category of "nature." Conversely, although desires and likings are granted at birth, they do not belong to the category of "nature" but to that of "fate." This is because humaneness, righteousness, propriety and wisdom are the real sources and the direction of the individual's activity; desires and likings, on the other hand, are regulated by things and restrict individual development. Mencius said:

"The reactions of the mouth to flavour, of the eye to beauty, of the ear to sound, of the nose to scent, and of the four limbs to comfort and ease, are their nature and there is a fate in them; the gentleman does not call them nature. Humaneness between father and son, righteousness between ruler and subject, propriety between guest and host, wisdom to the worthy person, and a sage to the Way of heaven are matters of fate and there is nature in them; the gentleman does not call them matters of fate."

The meaning of fate in regard to the desires and likings by the organs of sense is different from that of "fate" in general. With the exception of the knowable and known natural laws, fate in general cannot be actively controlled or avoided by man. Desires and likings, on the other hand, can and ought to be. Mencius advocated "cultivating the mind and reducing desires" in coordinating "nature" with "fate". This should increase the development of humaneness, righteousness, propriety, wisdom and other virtues while desires and likings would become regulated and fewer. Accordingly, Mencius said: "In cultivating the mind, nothing is better than reducing desires. There are few men with few desires who are not preserved by them; there are few men with many desires who are preserved by them."

There is another point worth mentioning in Mencius' explanation of fate. For the individual, "fate" includes the desires and likings, partialities and enjoyment of the senses. But overall "fate" also includes a mandate of heaven which reflects the will of the people. There is a relationship between this characterization of it and the emphasis on the notion of "obey heaven and you obey the people" in Mencius' political thought. We shall discuss this subsequently.

The desires and likings which belong to the category of "fate" should be moderated and the virtues in the category of "nature" should be expanded. How should the virtues be expanded? I maintain that when in the chapter, "Kung-sun Ch'iu," Part II, Mencius said, "do not waver in mind," "know the force of words (yen)," "cultivate the natural disposition (ch'i)," and "restrain the will," he had in mind the methods of expanding and maintaining the virtues. What does "do not waver in mind" mean? We said earlier that Mencius considered nature to be man's original mind; consequently, "do not waver in mind" means "do not waver in natural disposition." By "do not waver in mind," Mencius meant grasp firmly the principle of goodness; do not be influenced or excited by external things; do not rely on external difficulties and fears. How can one attain the condition of unwavering in mind? We can find the answer in Mencius' criticism of Kao Tzu's understanding of not wavering in mind: "If you do not acquire it by the force of words, do not seek for it in the mind; if you do not acquire it by the mind, do not seek for it in the natural disposition." Mencius said:

"If you do not acquire it by the mind, do not seek for it in the natural disposition, is permissible; if you do not acquire it by the force of words do not seek for it in the mind, is not permissible. The will is the leader of the natural disposition; the natural disposition is the fulfillment of the body. The will is primary and the natural disposition is secondary; therefore, it is said: 'One who restrains his will does not expose his natural disposition.'"

It is clear that here Mencius is dividing the mind into two parts, "will" (chih) and natural disposition.[8] "Will" is the active part of the mind. "Natural disposition" is the life-giving force of the human body, and it is secondary to the mind. The "will" can influence the "natural disposition," and conversely, the "natural disposition" can influence the "will." "Do not waver in mind", therefore, means preserving the active part of the mind and, at the same time, guarding a fulfilled life-giving force. Mencius said: "When the will is united it moves the natural disposition; when the natural disposition is united it moves the will. That which is excitable and hasty is the natural disposition, which in turn moves the mind."

This will cannot unthinkingly pass on proposals which it cannot accept, or principles which it cannot affirm, to the natural disposition thereby simply wasting the life-giving force and, at the same time, letting slip away the activity of the will. Accordingly, Mencius agreed with one part of Kao Tzu's statement, "if you do not acquire it by the mind do not seek for it in the natural disposition." The other part of Kao Tzu's statement, "if you do not acquire it by force of words do not seek for it in the mind," Mencius found difficult to accept. Kao Tzu maintained that judging a thing right or wrong, righteous or unrighteous, depends on the external thing.[9] There thus is no direct, cause-and-effect relationship between "words" and "mind."

For Mencius, on the other hand, the mind contains universal morality and truth, of which humaneness, righteousness, propriety and wisdom are primary. To "know the force of words" is to acknowledge that basic morality and truth include the right and wrong, the righteousness and unrighteousness of things. If one "knows the force of words", he will of course seek for it in the mind. If a person "does not acquire it by the force of words", this reflects the obscurity that still remains in his mind; he still, has not revealed the truth which certainly is contained in his mind, and he must "turn inward and seek within himself" or "turn to himself and be sincere." Thus there is an exceptionally close relationship between "mind" and "words." It shows that Mencius not only opposed Kao Tzu's statement "if you do not acquire it by the force of words do not seek for it in the mind", but he, in fact, insisted that "if you do not acquire it by the force of words you [must] seek for it in the mind."

In the following two statements, Mencius defines "know the force of words" as the ability to distinguish between right and wrong, true and false. He said:

"What is meant by 'know the force of words'? Answer: When words flatter, we know what they conceal; when words are extravagant, we know what they betray; when words are evil, we know what they are straying from; when words are evasive, we know they reflect poverty of thought."

"It is born in his mind and destroyed by his government; it is manifest in his government and destroyed by his affairs. When a sage arises again he must follow these sets of words."

The ability to make known positively the truth, to distinguish between truth and falsehood and between right and wrong, depends on nourishing the "great natural disposition." What is the "great natural disposition"? Mencius' reply was:

"It is difficult to describe. To be great and constant, the natural disposition is maintained by honesty and is not harmed; it serves as a stopper in the world. The natural disposition corresponds to righteousness and truth, and it cannot be without them. It is born in the aggregate of righteousness; it is not something that is appropriated by righteousness. When action is hateful to the mind, it is not satisfied with it."

A natural disposition that is maintained by goodness and is magnanimous probably describes the mind that promotes and extends the beginnings of all virtues. Thus "a natural disposition that is magnanimous" is one that "corresponds to righteousness and truth," one that is "born in the aggregate of righteousness."

It is man's extension of virtue, the expansion of results arrived at subjectively. When "the natural disposition is magnanimous", actions are not only satisfying; even when they follow desire they do not exceed what is right. This then is the state of being "unwavering in mind."

'We have been discussing Mencius' concepts of nature and fate. The concepts of "nature" and "fate" lead to Mencius' view of "heaven" and "mind." Heaven is the source of fate; mind is what depends on nature. Mencius' theory of man's life is to "obey heaven", "know fate" and "fulfil nature." Obedience to heaven and knowing fate require that in cultivating himself, the individual have few desires and that informing a new government in the state the ruler follow the will of the people. Fulfilling nature means extending the beginnings of the virtues within man's nature and reaching the state of being "unwavering in mind." To be unwavering in mind ultimately depends on "knowing the force of words," "restraining the will," and "maintaining the natural disposition." Thus we can see the line of Mencius' thinking—the correspondence between the "Way of heaven" and the "Way of man." There is also a correspondence between "nature" and "fate." Looking at it this way, we realize that Mencius' discussion of the goodness of nature and his theory of humane government are also constructed on his concepts of "nature" and "fate."

A central idea in Mencius' discussions of the goodness of nature is the idea that there is in "nature" an active faculty which develops virtue. This active, creative faculty of the individual is expressed in a natural flow of virtue. Mencius maintained that man has within himself latent virtues and he must develop them. Hsun Tzu said that goodness is an "acquired" characteristic, but he did not deny that man has the potential for goodness or the latent faculty for accepting change. Thus both Mencius and Hsun Tzu acknowledged the existence of man's latent faculty for goodness; but, in fact, there was a great difference between Mencius and Hsun Tzu.[10] Because Mencius thought that the tendency toward goodness in man's nature is active, he maintained that the way to attain goodness is to return to the original mind. Hsun Tzu, on the other hand, thought that the tendency to goodness in man's nature is passive, and he maintained that the way to attain goodness is to set an external mould. Thus the theories of Mencius and Hsun

Tzu are such that one seeks within while the other seeks without; one is active and the other is passive. Consequently, in their discussions of the goodness and evil of nature, each maintains his own principles.

Mencius' argument for the goodness of nature is entirely a statement of the person's intuitive experience. He says, "Nature can be good and so it is said to be good." The goodness of nature belongs to the basic substance of nature; "it is not imposed on us from outside." Mencius said, "because there are affairs there must be regulations for them"; that is, the goodness of nature is the norm for nature. The goodness of nature embraces the four beginnings: sympathy and aloofness, good and evil, respect and yieldings, right and wrong. Mencius maintained that these four beginnings, in the right circumstances, can be experienced intuitively, which proves that man's nature is good.

In the chapter entitled, "Kao Tzu," Mencius criticized Kao Tzu's theory that "nature is neither good nor not good," and he replied to Kao Tzu's criticism of the theory that nature is good. In these criticisms and arguments, it is obvious that Mencius understood the "goodness of nature" to be a latent faculty inclined to goodness and to attaining goodness. He said, "Man's nature is good, it is like water flowing downward; there is no man who is not good, just as there is no water that does not flow downward." Mencius maintained that in normal circumstances this faculty to attain goodness will emerge naturally and is the beginning of all virtues; man's nature will develop the faculty for goodness in accordance with humaneness and righteousness.

But what are normal circumstances? What are the natural circumstances in which something can develop without external influences? These are rather difficult questions. Mencius' statements were based on intuitions; he did not analyze them or consider whether or not such intuitions contained within them elements of later habits. Nor did he examine further the so-called natural circumstances to see whether or not they contained "acquired" element. This is a shortcoming in his discussions of the goodness of nature.

If we regard Mencius' theory of the goodness of nature as an exaggeration necessarily erected by the individual's active and self-motivating nature, we disregard several questions for which there are no satisfactory answers. Mencius' theory of the goodness of nature does not lack hypotheses which can lead to good conclusions. Like William James' "will to believe," the "nature is good theory" has both practical and metaphysical value.

To sum up, because Mencius emphasized the goodness of nature, the beginnings of all virtues have their source within. When nature has an active, self-motivating faculty, morality becomes a subjective, practical prescription for the individual. "Goodness" is wholly attainable in the mind; it is not constructed out of the knowledge of external things. This is Mencius' basic argument in refuting Kao Tzu's theory that "humaneness is internal, righteousness is external."

VI

Mencius' theory of humane government. People of the Warring States period lived in the midst of great dangers. The rulers of the age loved warfare; they loved material things; they loved music, women, good horses. They exacted levies and sent out expeditions; the people were exhausted and fled for their lives. Because rulers wanted to extend their powers, they encroached upon this country and that; the people became the sacrificial victims in wars for control of cities and seized territory.

> "Disputes over land take the form of war,
> Corpses fill the fields;
> Disputes over cities take the form of war,
> Corpses fill the cities."

Mencius made the following observations about the livelihood of the people at that time:

> "In your kitchen there is fat meat and in your stables there are fat horses; yet the people look hungry and there are starving bodies in the fields. This is leading animals to eat people."

> "Now you regulate what the people produce. On the one hand, they do not have enough to serve their parents; on the other hand, they do not have enough to nourish their wives and sons. At the end of a good year, their bodies suffer; in a year of misfortune, they cannot avoid death."

"Your majesty snatches the people's time, preventing them from ploughing and hoeing in order to support their parents. Parents are cold and hungry; elder and younger brothers, wives and sons, are scattered."

"Years of misfortune are years of starvation. Of Your Majesty's people, those who are old and weak turn over and die in the gutters and ditches; those who are strong scatter to the four directions by the thousand. Your Majesty's storehouses are stocked with treasures, and his kitchens and stables are full; but the civil officials do not report that those above are remiss and oppress those below."

"In order to gain territory, King Hui of Liang wastes his people in wars."

There was no protection for the people's lives and property. The rulers were concerned only with satisfying their own rapacious ambitions and desires and cared not if the people lived or died, enjoyed fortune or suffered misfortune. This was the course followed by all rulers of the Warring States period; it also was what Mencius called "cruel government" and the "way of dictators." Mencius maintained that those who practice cruel government and the way of dictators could in the end be rushing along the road to destruction. There are not two ways to "rule the world"; the ruler should practise humane government and protect the people as sons.

Mencius observed in history the destruction of cruel rulers, and he observed in the contemporary and political and social conditions the dangers of establishing states for profit and of forcing the submission of the people. In the following quotation, Mencius states forcefully the principle reasons why cruel government cannot be practised and states cannot be established for profit:

"Why must Your Majesty talk about profit? There are humaneness and righteousness too. If Your Majesty asks, 'How can I profit my state'; the nobility ask, 'How can we profit our families'; and the officials and common people ask, 'How can we profit ourselves'; those above and those below attack each other for profit, and the state is endangered. The one who kills the ruler of a ten thousand chariot state must be one who has a hundred chariots. Taking ten thousand with one thousand, and taking one thousand with one hundred, cannot be said to be little. When righteousness is secondary and profit is primary, then [people] are not satisfied if they are not snatching."

"Confucius said: 'There are only two Ways, humaneness and the absence of humaneness.' When one oppresses his people, in extreme cases, he himself will be killed and the state will perish; in less extreme cases, he himself will be in danger and the state will be cut up. They are given dark and oppressing names which filial sons and compassionate grandsons cannot change in a hundred generations. The Ode states: 'The warring of the Yin is not far away. It is found in the age of the Hsia.' This is an illustration of it."

"The means whereby the three dynasties obtained the world was humaneness. The means whereby the world was lost was absence of humaneness. The means whereby the state prospers and is preserved or is lost and perishes are both possible. If the Son of Heaven is not humane he does not protect the four seas. If the feudal lords are not humane they do not protect the altars of soil and grain. If the ministers and officials are not humane they do not protect the ancestral temples. If the scholars and common people are not humane they do not protect the four limbs. To hate death and destruction but to enjoy lack of humaneness is the same as hating drunkenness but insisting on wine."

"There has never been an instance where a subject thinks only of profit in serving his ruler, a son thinks only of profit in serving his father, a younger brother thinks only of profit in serving his elder brother, which has ultimately led to humaneness and righteousness between ruler and subject, father and son, older brother and younger brother, when thinking only of profit they were united and did not perish."

In pointing out the current fondness for profit, Mencius held up the fundamental principles of humaneness and righteousness. In pointing out the selfishness and private profits of the current rulers of state, he held up the ideal of humane government which showed love for and protected the people.

Confucius did not explain clearly the origins of the ruler's power; but he does not appear to have denied that the ruler's power is determined by "heaven" and "fate". Although Mencius did not deny that power is something given or denied by heaven and fate, in the following quotations he explains that the ruler's power is derived from the people. The people are the source of political power and the foundation of the state. Mencius said, "The people are the most important, the altars of soil and grain are second, and the ruler is the least important. For this reason one who comes into being by the altars and the people is the Son of Heaven, those who come into being through the Son of Heaven are the feudal lords, and those who come into being through the feudal lords are the officials."

The "mandate of heaven" (*t'ien-ming*) is seen in the "will of the people." Therefore, what belongs to the will of the people also belongs to the mandate of heaven. As Mencius said, "Formerly, Yao recommended Shun to heaven and heaven accepted him; he introduced him to the people and the people accepted him. Therefore, it is said: 'Heaven does not speak; it is revealed by actions and affairs.... When he manages the sacrifices and the hundred spirits are pleased, then heaven accepts him. When he manages affairs and the people are peaceful, then the people accept him. Heaven approves and the people approve.'"

"Heaven does not speak" because the "mandate of heaven" is expressed in the "will of the people"; "heaven sees as my people see, heaven hears as my people hear." The mandate of heaven is not impossible to attain; it is made manifest in actual conduct and affairs.

Since the Son of Heaven inherits both the mandate of heaven and the will of the people in succeeding to his position, in conducting the government he accords with both the mandate of heaven and the will of the people. To accord with the mandate of heaven means to practise humane government; that is, "Treating the kindred as the kindred should be treated, he treats the people humanely; treating the people humanely, he loves things." Stated briefly, it means extending the beginnings of humaneness and righteousness. Mencius said: "There are things which no man can endure; substituting these with what all men can endure is humaneness. There are things which no man can do; substituting these with what all men can do is righteousness." What does it mean to accord with the will of the people? It means to act in compliance with the people's feelings in employing the virtuous and able and in punishing those who are wicked. Mencius said:

"When those on the left and right say that a man is virtuous there is some doubt in it; when all the officials say that a man is virtuous, there is some doubt in it; when the people say that a man is virtuous, examine him and if you observe his virtue, employ him. When those on the left and those on the right say that a man cannot be employed, do not listen to them; when all the officials say that a man cannot be employed, do not listen to them; when the people say that a man cannot be employed, examine him and if you observe that he cannot be employed, dismiss him. When those on the left and the right say that a man may be killed, do not listen to them; when all the officials say that a man may be killed, do not listen to them; when the people say a man may be killed, examine him and if you observe that he should be killed, kill him. Therefore, it is said, 'the people killed him'. Only when it is thus can you be called the parents of the people."

If a ruler can accord with the will of the people, he "honors virtue and respects scholars; when a virtuous person is on the throne, the capable are in office." He considers this to be the first step in establishing humane government. This leads us to our discussion of the principles and the form of a humane government.

The fundamental principles of humane government are those of obeying heaven and loving the people, honoring humaneness and emphasizing righteousness. In addition to employing the virtuous and capable, Mencius mentioned two other principles: (1) "Take no pleasure in killing people," and (2) "Share your pleasures with the people." "Take no pleasure in killing people" means do not use the people as tools in wars to gain control of cities or to appropriate territory. When King Hsiang of Kiang asked Mencius, "How can the world be settled?" Mencius said: "Settle it by uniting it." "But who could unite the world?" Mencius replied: "One who does not take pleasure in killing people can unite it." His argument was very simple:

"Does Your Majesty know about the sprouts? During the seventh and eighth months, if it is dry, the sprouts wither. If the heavens produce moisture-laden clouds, and the rain falls copiously, the sprouts open out and flourish. It is so and who can stop it? Now of those who are shepherds of the people, there is not one who does not take pleasure in killing people. If there was one who did not take pleasure in killing people, the people of the world would stretch out their necks and look to him. It really is thus. Just as water flows downward, the people turn to him in great numbers; and who can stop them?"

"Sharing pleasures with the people" means "grieve over the people's sorrows" and "rejoice over the people's joys." Mencius explained the difference between "enjoying pleasure alone" and "enjoying pleasure with the multitude" to King Chieh of Ch'i as follows:

"Now Your Majesty is presenting music here. The people hear the sounds of Your Majesty's bells and drums and the notes of your reed pipes and flutes, and they raise their aching heads with knitted brows saying to one another, 'The music which our king enjoys, why has it brought us to this extreme? Father and son do not see each other; older brother and younger brother, wife and son, are scattered.' Now Your Majesty is hunting here. The people hear the sound of Your Majesty's chariots and horses, they see the beauty of your feather pennons; they raise their aching heads with knitted brows and say to one another, 'The hunting which our king enjoys, why has it brought us to this extreme? Father and son do not see each other; older brother and younger brother, wife and son, are scattered.' Again, Your Majesty present music here, and the people hear the sounds of bells and drums and the notes of reed pipes and flutes. They raise their happy and delighted faces and say to one another, 'Our king is almost free of serious ailments, or how could he present music?' Again, Your Majesty is hunting here, and the people hear the sound of chariots and horses and see the beauty of the feather pennons. They raise their happy and delighted faces to say to one another, 'Our king is almost free of serious ailments, or how could he be hunting?' This is nothing more than sharing pleasures with the people. When Your

Majesty shares his pleasures with the people, then he is their king."

The park of King Wen (of the Chou dynasty) was seventy *li* square, but the people considered it small; the park of King Hsuan of Ch'i was forty *li* square, and the people considered it too large. This was because although "King Wen's park was seventy *li* square, the grass and reed cutters and the fowl and rabbit hunters could enter it; he shared it with the people, and the people considered it small. Is this too not proper?" It was not so with the park of the King of Ch'i. King Wen used the people's strength to build the Spirit Tower and the Terrace Lake; but the people not only did not begrudge it, they were happy and rejoiced over it. Because he "enjoyed them with the people, he really did enjoy them."

If the ruler does not share his pleasures with the people, when the people see the ruler travelling for pleasure, they naturally resent it; "when the people do not attain something, they blame the ruler." Mencius felt that it certainly was not right for the people to blame the ruler if they did not attain something; nevertheless, he said:

"One who is the people's ruler but does not share his pleasures with the people is also blamed by the people. If one rejoices over the people's joys, the people also rejoice over his pleasures; if one grieves over the people's sorrows, the people also grieve over his sorrows. There has never been one who rejoiced with the world and grieved with the world who was not a king."

In fact, the two principles, "take no pleasure in killing people" and "share pleasures with the people," reflect "a heart that cannot bear the suffering of others" and they are extensions of the goodness of nature. The basis of humane government is no more than the ruler's developing the goodness in his own nature in order to practise the Kingly Way. Mencius maintained: "Extend kindness and it will be sufficient to protect the four seas; do not extend kindness and it will not be sufficient to protect your wife and son." To extend kindness means to enlarge the area of application of "a heart that cannot bear the suffering of others" from "serving one's relatives" and "obeying one's elder brother" to "benefiting the people and loving things." Ultimately it means, "extend that which you love to that which you do not love."[11]

Since Mencius considered political power as deriving from the people, it followed that if the ruler does not practice humane government, the people can get rid of him. Thus he said:

"One who robs humaneness is called a robber; one who robs righteousness is called a thief. One who is a thief and a robber is called a ruffian. I have heard of a ruffian called Chou being killed; I have not heard of a ruler being killed."

"When the feudal lords endanger the altars of soil and grain, they change their order. The sacrificial victims are ready and the millet vessels have been cleansed; but when it is time for the sacrifice the grass is dry and the water overflowing: then they change the order of the altars of soil and grain."

Because the ruler plunders and robs humaneness and righteousness, the people cannot depend on him for their lives; they may then change the order he established and dispose of him. This is a revolutionary idea of government on the part of Mencius.

The means that Mencius proposed for putting humane government into practice was based entirely on Confucius' principles of "ordinary people", "enrich the people", and "kill the people." He maintained that the ruler must first of all attend to the fortunes and prosperity of the people. He should make their livelihood peaceful and prosperous, free from hunger and cold; then he can teach them filial piety and brotherly love and thereby, in addition to making their livelihood rich in material ways, maintain their livelihood in a harmonious social and ethical order. Mencius proposed the following:

"If the agricultural seasons are not opposed, there will be more than enough grain to eat. If the close-meshed nets do not enter the pools and ponds, there will be more than enough fish and turtles to eat. If hatchets and axes do not enter the mountain forests at all times, there will be more than enough wood for use. When there is more than enough grain and more than enough fish and turtles to eat, and when there is more than enough wood for use, the people live and die without regret. To live and die without regret is the beginning of the kingly

Way. If a five-*mou* plot is planted with mulberry trees, those over fifty can wear silk. If the young of fowl, pigs, dogs, swine are not lost before their time, those over seventy can eat meat. On a hundred-*mou* plot, if you do not appropriate its time, a large family can be without hunger. Pay attention to the teaching of the schools of aged scholars, extend it by the righteousness of filial piety and brotherly love; then those who are white-headed will not be carrying burdens on their backs on the roads. There has never been an instance when those who were seventy wore silk and ate meat, when the common people were not hungry and cold, and there was no king."

How is this social ideal to be realized? Mencius' prescription was: "Regulate what the people produce." Mencius maintained that if the people do not have a fixed livelihood, they cannot settle down and pursue productive occupations without anxiety. If the people do not have the energy to plan their lives, they may do anything to disturb the social peace. Therefore, if the government does not provide livelihood for the people, it puts them in a position where they cannot plan their lives and waits for them to do wrong so it can punish them according to the criminal law. This is extremely unfair. Mencius said:

"Only an official can be without a fixed livelihood but maintain a fixed heart. The people, if they do not have constant livelihoods, do not have constant hearts. When they are without constant hearts they are perverse, depraved, and licentious. There is no other alternative. To lead them into crimes and then punish them is to ensnare the people. How can there be a humane man on the throne and the ensnaring of people be possible. This is why the enlightened rulers of the past regulated the people's livelihood. They required them to produce enough to serve their parents, and produce enough to store for nourishing their wives and sons, so that at the end of good years their bodies were satiated and in years of misfortune they were able to avoid death. Then they urged them to goodness, and it was easy for the people to follow them".

How does one "regulate the people's livelihood?" Mencius maintained that the three dynasties of the past, the Hsia, the

Shang, and the Chou, had already established a fairly good system which could be used as a model:

"The Hsia levied taxes on groups of fifty families; the Yin levied services from groups of seventy people; in the Chou people cultivated one hundred *mou* plots on the tithing system. In fact, all of them are the same. Those who cultivated land on the tithing system gave tithes; those who gave services made their contribution. Lung Tzu said: 'In governing land there is nothing better than levying services; there is nothing better than levying taxes....' The Ode says, 'When it rains on our public fields, it extends to us personally.' Even those who provide services do so for the public fields. When you look at it this way, even in the Chou dynasty services were provided."

We shall not go into whether or not the Yin and the Chou had already established the well-field system to replace the Hsia taxes. The fact is that as a result of buying and selling land in the Warring States period, the earlier land systems were destroyed and the boundaries defining territories were no longer clearly drawn. Returning to the earlier land systems would have required a redistribution of the land. This is what Mencius called "the division of land into fields." He said: "Humane government must begin with a division of land into fields. If the land is not divided into fields correctly, the well-fields will be unequal and the grain will be unevenly distributed. Because the rulers are cruel and the officials corrupt, it is necessary to proceed slowly in dividing their land into fields. After the land has been correctly divided into fields, and the fields are regulated, you can remain seated while deciding matters." Mencius' ideal well-field system was as follows:

"Require that one of the nine uncultivated fields be used for levied service; one tenth of the country would be a levy for yourself. Ministers and below must have a plot of land to supply the means for sacrifices. This plot of land should be fifty *mou*. All others should have twenty-five *mou*. When one dies his plot does not leave the village. This village plot becomes the common plot. Those that come and go are friends; they look to each other for protection and assist each other; they support each other in sickness; all the people are related and friendly. One square *li* forms a plot; the center of each 900 *mou* is a public field. Eight families each have a 100 *mou* plot; they work the public field together and do not dare to attend to their private affairs until the public work is done. Thus they can distinguish the rustic person. This is the general outline."

It is obvious that in Mencius' time, if one had wanted to put such a system into operation, he would have had to regain control of land that had been sold and redivide it. But would the landowners of that time have been willing to return their land to the public? Futhermore, by then the population had increased considerably from that of the early dynasties, and could the land still have been divided as it had been? Mencius does not appear to have considered these questions, and his plan for a humane government contains impracticalities. Perhaps Mencius did see these difficulties, and he did not recommend the well-field system for large states such as Ch'i and Wei but only for a small state such as Ten.

In summary, although Mencius' ideal of humane government has a new theoretical foundation, the overall plan that Mencius proposed is ultra-conservative. In discussing Mencius' ideal of humane government, we should evaluate the ideal principle and the practical separately.

VII

Mencius' Criticism of Contemporary Scholars. Mencius did his best to promote the Confucian teaching at a time when there was a great variety of teaching by the hundred schools of philosophy. Mencius adopted a very severe attitude toward the teachings of the hundred schools. He maintained that all of the teachings of the hundred schools were "heterodox theories" and "licentious speech"; furthermore, all of them reflected "one-sided actions" and therefore were not the correct teaching. What Mencius had in mind as the correct teaching was the teaching of the former kings—Yao, Shun, Yu, T'ang, Wen and Wu—the teaching of humaneness and righteousness. To publicize the correct teaching and to correct men's hearts, he showed a willingness to follow the spirit of the Spring and Autumn period expressed in Confucianism: "Put a halt to heterodox theories, oppose one-sided actions, and abolish licentious speech." Consequently, in his criticisms of the hundred schools of philosophy, he spared no effort and left no alternatives.

Of the hundred schools, the teachings of Yang Chu and Mo Ti were the most popular; and, therefore, Mencius directed his strongest attacks at them. He said:

> "The sage kings did not practise them; the feudal lords introduced them and scholars everywhere discuss them. The words of Yang Chu and Mo Ti fill the world. In the world, if a statement does not derive from Yang Chu it derives from Mo Ti. Master Yang teaches hedonism; he is without a ruler. Master Mo teaches universal love; he is without a father. Without father and ruler, one is an animal .... If the teachings of Yang [Chu] and Mo [Ti] are not stopped, if the teaching of Confucius is not set forth, heterodox theories will deceive the people and completely block humaneness and righteousness."

Mo Tzu's teachings were formulated before the time of Mencius. Mo Tzu maintained that "when there is mutual love in the world there is order; when there is mutual hate there is rebellion."[12] His aim in governing the world was to make "states not attack one another, families not rebel against one another, thieves and robbers disappear, ruler and subject, father and son, could then be filial and kind." His goal was quite close to Mencius' ideals of the kingly Way and humane government. He wanted people in the world to practice mutual love, and to work for each other's benefit. His theory did not contain a statement of the notion of being "without father," but there are problems with his methodology. It provided the basis for Mencius' criticism that Mo Tzu's discussions of mutual love amounted to discussions of being "without father." Mo Tzu explained mutual love as "regarding another's home as one's own home," "regarding another's person as one's own person," "regarding another's family as one's own family," "regarding another's state as one's own state". If we consider this concept of mutual love further, does it not lead to "regarding another's father as one's own father,"? "regarding another's ruler as one's own ruler"? If we delete the adjective from the two phrases, "another's father" and "one's own father," the case of mourning the loss of "one's own father" becomes just mourning the loss of a "father," and there is nothing on which to build the moral relationship between father and son. This is the reason why Mencius criticized Mo Tzu's mutual love as being "without father." We can see that in all of his criticisms of Mo Tzu, Mencius did not refer to Mo Tzu's goal of "governing the world" or "condemning attacks"; he referred to his methods and prescriptions.[13] Mencius' criticism of Mo Tzu's disciple, Sung Ch'ing, also concerned method. He said, "Your purpose is great but your justification of it is not permissible."

Mencius was not opposed to Sung Ch'ing's going to urge Ch'in and Ch'u to stop their hostilities. On the contrary, Mo Tzu advocated condemning attacks and Mencius, too, condemned war. He said, "One who considers war good should be punished in the highest degree." What he was displeased with was Sung Ch'ing's "justification", his method. Mencius maintained that Sung Ch'ing should not have discussed profit with the kings of Ch'in and Ch'u; he should have discussed humaneness and righteousness.[14] In this chapter, Mencius explained that the difference in method can lead to different results.

Very few people, other than Mencius, discussed Yang Chu's "hedonism."[15] According to Mencius' record of it, Yang Chu's hedonism is contained in the statement, "If pulling out one hair would benefit the world, I would not do it." This is the exact opposite of Mo Tzu's theory of mutual love which said, "If wearing the whole body smooth from head to foot will benefit the world, do it." The earliest statement of Yang Chu's "hedonism" is probably that which is recorded in *Huai Nan Tzu*, "Devote your whole life to guarding truth, do not trouble the body with material things."[16] Yang Chu's disciples, however, interpreted the phrase, "Devote your whole life to guarding the truth," as extreme "selfishness"; and by Mencius' time it was explained as, "If pulling out one hair would benefit the world, I would not do it." According to this interpretation, if a person is unwilling even to pull out one hair to benefit the world, he certainly could not offer himself for service to the state or society. This is why Mencius criticized him saying, "Yang [Chu] is a hedonist, he is without a ruler." Because the relationship between "ruler and subject" is fundamental to Mencius' ideal society, he could not but attack Yang Chu's implication that one should be "without ruler." It seems, however, that Mencius considered Yang Chu's theory easier to correct than that of Mo Tzu; that is, he considered it to be closer to Confucian thinking, because he said: "Those who abandon Mo [Tzu] of necessity turn to Yang [Chu]; those who abandon Yang [Chu] of necessity turn to the Confucians."

Besides Yang Chu and Mo Ti, Mencius criticized the contemporary agriculturists, Hsu Hsing and Ch'en Hsiang.[17] The age of Hsu Hsing and his teaching have not been recorded in any ancient text other than that of Mencius. His theory emphasized that the ruler and the people should cultivate the fields together; it considered agricultural matters important. Mencius pointed out that this was impractical; "the work of a hundred artisans certainly cannot be done by ploughing." Hsu Hsing was a farmer, not a potter or a weaver; he had to depend on the potter for his utensils and on the weaver for his clothes.

It can be seen that in the whole social structure, a division of labor and of work is definitely necessary. This was the basis for Mencius' opposition to the notion that the ruler and the people should cultivate the fields together. Mencius made a distinction between "mental" labor and "physical" labor. He maintained that "the one who labors mentally governs others, one who labors physically is governed by others." The one who labors mentally has his own duties; he definitely need not join the people in the physical ploughing to be considered as having benefited the people. In antiquity, the sages—Yao, Shun, Yu, Chi—belonged to the category of people who labored mentally; they drove away the savage beasts, regulated the great rivers, taught the people sowing and reaping, established moral standards, and sought out the worthy and talented in the world. Even though they did not join the people in cultivating the fields, their work was important and cannot be underrated. If the ruler joins the people in cultivating the fields, who will have the time to govern the state?

Mencius maintained that things in the world are not all alike. Among men there are those who are intelligent and those who are dull, those who are worthy and those who are degenerate. However, when there is a division of labor and a worthy man is on the throne, the strong labor in the fields, the talented apply their talents for the benefit of the people, and the state is well managed. Consequently, he said: "Here is an uncut jade; although it weighs ten thousand *taels* it requires a jeweller to polish it. When it comes to the government of the state it is said: 'Drop what you study and follow me.' Is this any different from teaching a jeweller to polish jems?"

Mencius also criticized his contemporary, Ch'en Chung-tzu. According to what Mencius said about him, Ch'en Chung-tzu came from an old and honorable family in Ch'i. He probably belonged to the then popular "holy and pure" group. His "pureness" is illustrated in this account : "Because he considered his elder brother's emolument to be unrighteous emolument, he would not accept food from him; because he considered his elder brother's house to be an unrighteous house, he would not live with him; he withdrew from his elder brother and abandoned his mother and went to live in Yu-ling." What Mencius emphasized in his criticism of Ch'en was that his "pureness" could not "fulfil the category."

He pointed out that Ch'en Chung-tzu's conduct was not entirely consistent, and that his actions were contrary to human nature; only an earthworm could do such a thing. Ch'en Chung-tzu would not eat his elder brother's food or live in his elder brother's house, but the house that he lived in in Yu-ling certainly was not built by someone who was pure and the millet that he ate certainly was not cultivated by someone who was pure. His pureness led him to pay attention to minor matters of deportment, but if he wanted to practice it strictly—"to carry out his principle"—people said that he definitely could not live in a house or eat millet. Would one not have to become an earthworm to practice it?

Finally, we shall mention Mencius' criticism of Kao Tzu. Kao Tzu insisted that life (*sheng*) is nature (*hsing*); that nature is neither good nor not good. His ideas approached those of Lao Tzu and Chuang Tzu. Mencius' position on the goodness of nature, which has been discussed above, is a criticism of Kao Tzu's theory. Kao Tzu also insisted that "humaneness is internal, righteousness is external," which was the opposite of Mencius' theory in which the basic mind alone is the source of humaneness and righteousness. Kao Tzu maintained that righteousness is recognized in external things and affairs; something "is long and we consider it long, the length is not within us; something is white and we see it as white by observing it from the outside; therefore, I say it is external."

Mencius maintained that "righteousness" issues from the inner mind; it is an evaluation and a feeling perceived in response to external things, and he therefore said it is internal. Kao Tzu, on the other hand, said: "What warms the men of Ch'in is no different from that which warms us. The same is true with things; the things that cause warmth are also external." There seems to have been a difference between what each of the two men, Mencius and Kao Tzu, meant by "righteousness."[18] But not only was there a difference between what each of them meant by "righteousness," what they meant by "humaneness" was not exactly the same either. Mencius maintained that "humaneness" issues from the goodness of nature. Since Kao Tzu maintained that nature is neither good nor not good, he probably understood humaneness to be the natural emotions.

NOTES

1. In *Hsien Ch'in chu tzu hsi nien*, Ch'ien Mu has established definite dates for all the scholars, and he maintains that Mencius lived from 390 to 305 B.C. and that he lived to be eighty-six.

2. There are a number of English translations of *Mencius* available in which the quotes used here can be easily found. The Mentor series one by James Ware is a familiar one.

3. *Mencius*, "Kung-sun Ch'ou," B. 12; *Shih-chi* (Shang-wu yin-shu kuan yu wen k'u hui-yao), 74.14. This is recorded in the biographies of Mencius and Hsun Tzu in the *Shih-chi*.

4. The theory that Mencius and his disciples, Wen Chang and Kung-sun Ch'ou, wrote seven books of the *Mencius* is based on the *Shih chi*. See *Shih chi*, ch. 74, "Biographies of Mencius and Hsun Tzu," No. 14 (Shang-wu yin-shu kuan wan yu wen k'u hui-yao), 14.60.

5. Ibid., 4.60.

6. See Ch'ing Shan, "Meng tzu ching ch'a shih" (Chung-hua ts'ung-shu p'ien wei-yuan hui Meng tzu yen-chiu chi, Taiwan, March, 1963), pp. 217-218. The original article was published in *Ta-lu tsa-chih*, 8.4 (February, 1954).

7. For the development and application of Confucius' theory of the correction of names, see my, "Kung tzu cheng-ming ssu-hsiang". (Chia Po Monthly, March, 1967).

8. Hu Tsan-yun, "Chih yen,' 'ch'ih chih,' yu 'yang ch'i.'"

9. This is Kao Tzu's theory that "righteousness is external." For details see Ch'en Ta-ch'i, "Kao Tzu chi ch'i hsueh shuo," (*Meng tzu yen-chiu chi*, pp. 145-180). For a discussion of Kao's Tzu's theory that righteousness is external, see ibid., pp. 139-144.

10. In his comparative study of Mencius' theory that nature is good and Hsun Tzu's theory that nature is evil, Ch'en Ta-ch'i pointed out that "Mencius' theory that nature is good and Hsun Tzu's theory that nature is evil are the opposite of each other, but the degree of opposition between them is not as great as the terminology of their theories indicates" (*Chung-yang wen-wu kung ying she Chung-kuo wen-hua ts'ung-shu*, Taiwan, 1953, pp. 37-38).

11. Mencius maintained that "One who is humane extends that which he loves to those whom he does not love; one who is not humane extends that which he does not love to those whom he loves." Mencius, "Chin hsin," B.1.

12. Sun I-hsiang, *Mo tzu hsien-ku*, ch. 4, "Chien ai," No. 4.

13. The book of *Mencius* contains criticisms of all of Mo Tzu's basic principles. For instance, Mencius criticized Mo Tzu's stinginess in mourning and Mo Tzu's indiscriminating love. See *Mencius*. "hsi Wen-kung," A.5.

14. It is possible that Mo Tzu's "profit" and Mencius' "profit" did not mean the same thing. The concept of "profit" is used also in *Lun Yu*, "Tzu Han," No 9, where it does not have the same meaning.

15. In the book entitled "Yang Chu" in *Lieh Tzu*, Yang Chu's theory appears to be emphasizing the enjoyment of a material livelihood, which is not what Yang Chu meant; it is a forgery of the Wei-Chin period.

16. In general *Huai nan tzu* is in agreement. (Chung-hua shu-chu chu tzu chi ch'eng, Vol. 7, *Huai nan tzu*, ch. 13).

17. According to Lu shih ch'un ch'iu, "Ai t'ui", the teaching of Shen Nung was: "If there are boys who come of age but are not ploughing, there may be hunger in the world; if there are girls who have come of age but are not weaving, there may be suffering of cold in the world." The ruler, therefore, "personally ploughs and his consort personally weaves; thus they extend benefit to the people." This agrees with Hsu Hsing's theory. Thus Mencius said: "The one who promotes the teaching of Shen Nung is Hsu Hsing" (Chung-hua shu-chu chu tzu chi ch'eng, Vol. 6, Lu shih ch'un ch'iu, *ch.* 21).

18. Ch'en Ta-ch'i, "Kao tzu chi ch'i hsueh-shou" (Meng tzu yen-chiu chi, pp. 145-80).

II
Medieval Period

7
INTRODUCTION

Donald Bishop

We shall take the fourth through the sixteenth centuries as the Medieval Period. It began with the time Buddhism was winning an increasing number of converts, and ends with Wang Yang-ming (1472-1529), the last outstanding Neo-Confucianist.

What was the nature of Chinese civilization at the beginning of this period? Geographically, by the fourth century A.D. China had become a territorial entity, in extent almost what it is now. The feudal states united under the Ch'in (221-206 B.C.) were more firmly consolidated under the Han dynasty from 206 B.C. to A.D. 220. Thus China's political history up to this time was a transition from tribal government to a feudal system made up of numerous petty states nominally under one, the Chou, their reduction by conquest and assimilation to seven at the beginning of the Ch'in when they were made into one headed by the emperor as the Son of Heaven. The Han further consolidated the empire and a monarchical hereditary form of government marked by centralized power, a large and influential bureaucracy and a single ruler continued in general as the accepted, expected type until 1912.

Cultural progress in the pre-Medieval Period was constant and increasingly homogeneous as well, a result of natural growth and the desire of Ch'in and Han rulers for political unity based on a common culture.[1] Kuang Wu Ti, the first emperor of the Eastern Han illustrates the later. His generals reconquered Chinese possessions in the South in the Red River Delta later known as Annam and Sinocized the area. The Yangtze river culture was gradually overlaid by the earlier Shang culture of the Yellow River in the north. In addition to the local traditions and cultures of the earlier feudal states a national culture arose pervading the whole empire.

Advances in literature included, as noted already, the work of the Han historians in collecting and editing the Classics which survived the burning of the books. In doing so commentaries were added, making more difficult the labors of later historians in sorting accretion from the original. Conflict between the "New Script School" and the "Old Script School" compounded matters also. The first's version of the Classics was written in the form of the then current script. The "Old Script School" claimed it possessed the original texts which existed before the burning. The two groups differed in their interpretation of Confucius also, the first exulting him as a saviour and king without a throne; the second viewing him only as the traditional Sage, teacher and transmitter of the past.[2] Writing itself was facilitated by the invention of the brush pen and the making of paper (c. A.D. 100).

A major literary, historical work of the first century B.C. was the Shih Chi or Historical Memoirs, by Ssû-ma T'an and his son Ssû-ma Ch'ien. An important dictionary was the Shou Wên compiled in the Eastern Han. The writing of poetry flourished, two well known poets being Ssû-ma Hsiang-ju and Yang Hsuing. Carving on stone became a new art medium in the Han with the appearance of bas-relief. A proto-porcelain ware was developed in the late Han and archaeological excavations at Lak Lang in north Korea have unearthed lacquered vessels, a new development of the Han dynasty. Painting of everyday scenes on tiles was common, painting often serving a moral purpose as illustrated by the portraits of eminent and virtuous persons painted on the walls of the Cloud Terrace and Unicorn Pavilion in the Han capital. Landscape painting, emphasizing the unity of man and nature, was beginning to come into its own at this time also.

The consolidation of wealth and power in the Han enabled an imperial architecture to develop consisting of extensive palaces, ancestral halls, pavilions and other buildings following symbolic patterns. In science a noted mathematician was Chang Heng who calculated the value of pi. Water clocks, sundials and seismographs were made. A new type of plow and new methods of sowing helped increase agricultural production. Extensive canals and irrigation works allowed new land to be brought under cultivation and stimulated trade. The Great Wall, incorporating parts of existing walls, was vastly extended in the reign of the Ch'in emperor Shih Huang Ti. He also introduced a uniform system of weights and measurements. Generally cultural and technical advances reinforced the growing attitude of China as the "Middle Kingdom", the belief that Chinese civilization, as it developed first in the middle-lower Yellow river and spread outward, was the highest.

As to Chinese society at the beginning of the Medieval Period it may be pointed out again that it was still primarily an agricultural and village one. The "root and branch" distinction made by Chinese philosophers is an example of this, the root being symbolic of agriculture which is of supreme importance because it involves production and the branch referring to the merchant who lives off the profit made from the goods produced.[3] It is interesting to note that the first Han ruler followed the "root and branch" philosophy for he enforced an old law prohibiting merchants from occupying any official office.

The tendency to make distinctions seems a universal phenomenon and Chinese society at this time was no exception. According to a number of scholars the distance between classes or the upper and lower strata of society noted earlier became more pronounced in the Ch'in and Han dynasties. Urbanization may have been a causal factor, as there seems to be a correlation between urbanization and classes.[4] In China at this time cities accompanied the growth of empire, becoming centers of wealth and power. We find repeated proposals and efforts to alleviate the oppressed conditions of the poor. Mencius' well field system, the Han emperor Wu's efforts in 7 B.C., under Tung Chung-shu's goading, toward land reforms favoring the peasants and Wang Mang's similar attempts two decades later, are but three examples.[5]

Family and clan were the basic social units to which primary loyalty was given. The social and political order was a macrocosm of the family which was paternalistic and authoritarian. Just as there could be only one sun in the sky, there could be only one head of the family, the father, and one political head, the emperor. Formalistically, society was based on Li, broadly defined as the accepted customs, mores or rules of conduct covering all aspects of life for the purpose of achieving social order and harmony. For example, according to Confucianism relations between people were categorized into five with a definite set of reciprocal attitudes characterizing each; love in the father and filial piety in the son, gentleness in the elder brother and respect in the younger, kindness in the husband and obedience in the wife; humane consideration in elders and deference in juniors, benevolence in the ruler and loyalty in the subject. Five ch'ang or ethical norms incumbent on all were upheld by Confucianists as conducive to a good society, they being jen (human heartedness), yi (righteousness), li (propriety), chih (wisdom) and hsin (sincerity).

As to intellectual activity or Chinese thought preceding the Medieval Period, the Warring States Period was one of intense activity while the Ch'in dynasty was a time of stagnation due to the repressive measures of the Legalist oriented rulers. With the relaxation of restrictions at the beginning of the Han a reawakening occurred for the rest of the dynasty. While Taoism was important, Confucianism became the dominant school, being proclaimed the state or official philosophy in 136 B.C. by the emperor Wu Ti. For example, a start was made to make the Classics the basis of examination for those entering the bureaucracy and in A.D. 175 the Classics were engraved in stone at the state university in the capital.

Ch'in and Han Confucianism was a continuation of the old with new elements added due in part to the transition from feudalism to empire. As noted in the chapter on Confucius, ethics and politics were his major concerns. They continued to be among his followers, as we have seen in the chapter on Mencius. Tsou Yen (305-240 B.C.), shortly after Mencius, stressed the Confucian emphasis on self-rectification and cultivation, applying the principle to rulers especially; thus the famous phrase, "the ruler must be moral", i.e. he must exhibit jen, chung and shu. Tsou Yen was interested in metaphysics also and was an exponent of the Yin-Yang view.[6]

According to one scholar that view of reality originated with the occultists of pre-Chou days. Earlier occultists had offered a supernaturalistic interpretation of the universe in terms of spirits. A different type of occultism developed in the Chou dynasty named the Yin-Yang School which tended to interpret the universe rationally in terms of natural forces. Its early writings viewed the universe cosmologically as an ordered structure of five interrelated elements, water, fire, wood, metal and soil. The Appendices of the Book of Changes developed a cosmogony incorporating the Yin-Yang theory of the origin of the world, namely that all things are produced by the intermingling of the two forces. Thus in the one case reality is a group of five elements and in the other pairs of opposites. As noted above Tsou Yen was an important third century B.C. representative of the Yin-Yang School. At the same time he helped in amalgamating the two views, a fuller union of which is evident in the important Confucianist Tung Chung-shu (179-104 B.C.).

Tung was a renowned teacher at the National University and was known for giving his lectures from behind a screen. It is largely due to his influence that Confucianism became held in official esteem. He suggested the examination system and, as counsellor to the Han emperor Wu, advocated, as noted earlier, land reform measures.

Tung's ready synthesis of the five elements and Yin-Yang views was possible because he conceived of reality as an organic whole. This means that reality is a totality of interdependent, harmoniously interacting parts and man is a part of that whole. Thus the five agents or forces act upon each other. Wood produces fire; fire produces earth, earth produces metal, metal produces water, water produces wood. They have spatial-temporal, ethical, social, political and other correlates. Wood is associated with east, spring and benevolence; fire with south, summer and propriety; metal with west, autumn and righteousness; water with north, winter and wisdom; the earth with the center, sincerity and is all inclusive. Each agent had a color correlate and became of political significance when the emperor Wu adopted the agent earth and its color yellow for his rule.

Tung viewed man as a microcosm of the universe and went to extreme lengths to demonstrate it. He has four limbs corresponding to the four seasons, and the alternate opening and closing of the eyes corresponds to night and day. In comparing man with Heaven and Earth he declared that man's head is round and resembles the shape of the Earth. What is above the neck is noble and manifests Heaven; what is below is humble and manifests Earth. Since man is representative of both Heaven and Earth, he is therefore both Yang and Yin.

Tung's high view of man is seen in his statement that "Of the creatures born from the refined essence of Heaven and Earth, none is more noble than man." Moreover, "Man receives the mandate from Heaven and is therefore superior to other creatures. Other creatures suffer troubles and defects and cannot practice humanity and righteousness; man alone can practice them."[7] Tung promulgated the Confucian emphasis on self-rectification and development. Man is to perfect himself with the aid of Li or rituals and music. He is to realize his essential humanity which he defines in Mencian terms as loving people "with a sense of commiseration."

Tung continued the Confucian doctrine of the Mandate of Heaven which asserts that the ruler receives the right to rule from Heaven and keeps it only as long as he rules on behalf of the people and their welfare. Such a theory exults the king, which the Han rulers no doubt found pleasing. It requires they be virtuous however, a task some rulers found difficult. According to Tung the function of the king and government is to help man perfect his goodness. The four ways of ruling are through beneficence, rewards, punishments and executions. The concept of correlates comes in again as wood is associated with the minister of agriculture, fire the minister of war, soil the minister of work, metal the minister of the interior, water the minister of justice. While Confucianism in this period tended to strengthen the hand of the ruler as Heaven's representative, there was a natural check on him also. Since man, Heaven and Earth are interrelated, if there are unnatural or undesirable natural occurrences it may be due to man's upsetting the natural harmony or balance. Thus the floods, droughts, and earthquakes causing distress among people are visitations of Heaven angered by the misdeeds of the ruler and can be avoided only if the ruler is moral.

Tung's philosophy also included a metaphysical basis for the social order. As noted above, it was commonly accepted that there are five major relationships among people. Tung emphasized three of these relationships or bonds and correlated them with Yin and Yang. Yang was associated with the ruler and Yin with subject, Yang the husband and Yin the wife, Yang the father and Yin the son. Yang is the superior, active, dominant principle and Yin the passive, subordinate. Thus in all social relationships there is a definite locus of authority giving order and stability to society which is itself grounded in the Tao or the way of Heaven and Earth.

The type of naturalistic, rationalistic Confucianism advocated by Tung continued but by the first century A.D. a new element had become strong. It was based on the spurious literature of the New Script School mentioned earlier containing distorted interpretations of the Classics which deified Confucius and infiltrated Confucianism with mystery and superstition. One of its opponents was the Confucianist Wang Ch'ung (c. A.D. 27-100). His was the attitude of the sceptic who insists on concrete evidence as proof. He opposed superstition and appeal to mystery and said that natural calamities are not an act of Heaven but simply a result of natural forces. He disclaimed the existences of ghosts and rejected the claim of a person becoming a spirit at death. His outlook no doubt was influential in preparing the way for a revived rationalism and naturalism in Confucianism in the post-Han era.

Regarding man's nature Wang declared that "some people are born good and some born evil" just as "some people's capacity is high and some people's is low."[8] Earlier Yang Hsuing (53 B.C.-A.D. 18) had declared that man is a mixture of good and evil and he who cultivates the good in himself will become a good man just as he who cultivates the evil will become an evil person. Both compare with Mencius who, we may say, declared all persons are essentially good while Hsun Tzu asserted the opposite.

Hsun Tzu (298-238 B.C.) is usually characterized as a representative of the naturalistic or realistic wing of Confucianism. He was the mentor of Han Fei Tzu and Li Ssu, the chief minister of the Ch'in emperor Ching or Shih Huang Ti. The appellation of naturalism to Hsun Tzu is quite appropriate if one uses it as a denial of belief in supernatural influences and a minimizing of Heaven. Hsun Tzu said, for example, that "the superior man is anxious about what is within his power, and does not seek for what is from Heaven", and he observed that it rains both when people do and do not pray for it, and it cannot be validly asserted, therefore, that it rains because one prays. Realism is appropriate if used, as contemporary political theorists do, who say let us be realistic and recognize that nations like individuals act primarily in terms of self interest.

Hsun Tzu was Confucianist in a number of ways. He opposed superstition and belief in ghosts and spirits. When you see a star falling, do not think of it as the work of unseen forces or an abnormality and fear it but simply understand and marvel at it as one of the rare occurrences of nature. He valued education on Confucian lines. He emphasized self cultivation and music as a means of it. He advocated the typical Confucian virtues of humanity and righteousness saying that "Among men's virtues there are none higher than propriety and righteousness." He encouraged filial piety and looked on the traditional mourning rites and sacrifices to ancestors as manifestations of it.

Hsun Tzu's naturalistic interpretation of Heaven was perhaps more Taoist than Confucianist. Heaven was the natural order of things in which all aspects of nature operate in a systematic, Yin-Yang fashion. Work in harmony with Heaven or the Tao and good effects will come; fail to do so and the opposite follows. There is no capriciousness in this but rather the working of the principle of cause and effect. Good comes from acting morally, evil from immoral action. In a similar vein he minimized fate, declaring that what happens to persons is a result of their own efforts or lack thereof rather than fate. We see this in his statement "To neglect human effort and admire Heaven is to miss the nature of things."[9]

Hsun Tzu differed with traditional Confucianism in several ways. He placed greater stress on wisdom than humanity. He held to the overcoming or controlling of nature much more than to the harmonizing of man and nature. He stressed Li more strongly and thought of them more in terms of social control mechanisms.

The major departure from the Confucian tradition was Hsun Tzu's pessimistic view of man seen in his statement, "The nature of man is evil; his goodness is a result of his activity." What Hsun Tzu asserted is that man can become good through self effort. The sage, for example, is one who has done just that. If in his practices and studies day after day for a long time he concentrates his mind, has unity of purpose, thinks thoroughly and discriminately, and accumulates goodness without stop, he can then be as wise as the gods and form a trinity with Heaven and Earth. Thus the sage is a man who has reached this state through accumulated effort. When asked why everyone else does not do the same, Hsun Tzu replied, "They do not do so because they do not want to." In Kantian terminology it is a matter of the will and Hsun Tzu refers to this in his statements "When a person's character is formed according to rule and his will is firm. . . . he can be called a strong scholar" and, "When a man's mind knows the right, then only can he will to do the right. When he can will to do the right, then only can he do the right and abstain from doing wrong."

Hsun Tzu, like Confucius, believed that the minority of "Superior Men" knew the good, had the will to do it and, in fact, through self-effort had achieved sagehood. The masses need unbiased, unprejudiced sages as their example and teachers who will show them the correctness of law and the desirability of being law abiding. Thus Hsun Tzu was willing to give greater power to government which rules through efficiency of force and law rather than moral example. In his view law is the medium through which the principle of moral cause and effect is carried out in society. For laws make people do what is good with the result that society is orderly and people prosper. Such a condition would not exist without firmly enforced laws for "man's inborn nature is to seek for gain.... it is the original nature and feelings of man to love profit and seek gain." This means that the stronger will take advantage of the weak, some will use others for their own profit unless preventive laws exist.

Hsun Tzu did not disassociate morality from government however. In Confucian fashion, he held that a "real king" is earnest about his state, nourishes the people and is moral himself. His goal is to bring about a society or kingdom characterized by "Great Equableness", that is, one in which everyone does well whatever his particular task is. The ethical question as associated with the nature of man is, of course, a universal and age-old one. Will man willingly do the good once he knows what it is; or must he be coerced into doing so? Hsun Tzu answered in terms of the latter.

Hsun Tzu's epistemological views are of significance and interest. He begins his essay on Prejudices by saying that "everything that men suffer is from being prejudiced". How can one avoid being prejudiced or biased and become like Confucius and the sages? It is through knowledge of the right or the Tao. That knowledge comes through the empty or unperturbed mind. Everyone has a mind which on the one hand collects data and stores away sense impressions or data. On the other hand the mind is characterized by emptiness defined by Hsun Tzu as that which does not allow what is already stored away to be injured by that which is about to be received.

The mind has the capacity to make distinctions and perceive a plurality of things. Yet it also has a unity defined as that which keeps the knowledge of the plurality of things from blinding us to the unity of things. The mind is always in motion, even dreaming when asleep. Yet it is characterized by unperturbedness defined as that which does not permit dreams to disturb one's knowledge. In seeking knowledge of the Tao, one's mind must be characterized by emptiness, unity and unperturbedness. When one's mind is such, he will "follow right principle and be illustrious in virtue." This is the kind of mind or knowledge the ruler should have. Laws are an expression of the type of mind or knowledge. When carried out they insure fairness, equality and justice in the kingdom rather than favoritism, nepotism and opportunism. The core of Hsun Tzu's political philosophy was his belief in rule by law to insure equality, a view transmitted through his students Han Fei Tzu and Li Ssu who attempted to put it in practice in the Ch'in dynasty. As has been noted sufficiently already, the Legalists provided a philosophical basis for the Ch'in and Han dynasties. However Legalism came into disrepute due to the harshness of the Ch'in rulers and by the middle Han had lost much of its overt influence, although its positive contributions such as the minimizing of social distinctions, a uniform law and the equality of all before the law, the acceptance of change and looking to the present and future rather than the past continued on.

Mohism experienced a decline also but for different reasons noted in the chapter on Mo Tzu. What might be said about Mohism after Mo Tzu is that it was fairly influential even in Mencius' time, as he felt compelled to deal with it, that elements in Mohism such as its universalistic emphasis continued on as a part of the Chinese tradition even up to the present and that Mohists developed a keen interest in Logic not only to validate Mohism but for the sake of logic itself.

The last six chapters of Mo Tzu's works as we have them now are called the Mohists Cannons. They are presumed to be additions and deal with types of knowledge, definitions, causation and dialectics. In addition they seek to justify Mo Tzu's hedonistic, utilitarian ethic which asserts that the good is what is useful in enhancing man's happiness. The Cannons also counter statements in the Tao-te Ching about banishing learning and in the Chuang Tzu on winning and losing.

A group in this period called the Logicians or School of Names had in common with the Mohists an interest in the doctrine of universal love and knowledge for its own sake. Two of its leaders were Hui Shih (c. 380-305) and Kung-sun Lung (c. 380). As a rationalist Hui Shih attempted to validate his metaphysical monism through reason or rational knowledge. Hui and Kung-sun differed on two important points, the former viewing immediate reality as changing and relative, the latter seeing it as permanent and absolute.

The Logicians did not become an important and permanent school in Chinese thought. Several reasons may be given. They lived in times of unrest and distress which their activities and views were not concerned with or relevant to.[10] The lack of general interest in logic and epistemology *per se* is a second. To the vast majority of Chinese, paradoxes such as "the South has no limit, yet has a limit"; assertions like "the egg has hair" and whether it is valid that a "white horse is not a horse" were topics too vague, nonsensical, unrelated to common sense, of no practical value and therefore not worth wasting time on.

Taoism, of course, is an integral part of the Chinese tradition in the pre-Medieval Period, its fortunes varying with the times, the early Han being an especially favourable one. It was pointed out in the chapter on Taoism that freedom is the goal and understanding the Tao and practicing wu-wei are the means of realizing it. As was noted earlier, wu-wei is associated with economy of action and was interpreted as non-action or disinterested action. When the concept of wu-wei is applied to the social and political, it has at least two major implications. The ethical is that society must be grounded in virtue not utility. People are to act unselfishly rather than doing what is only for their benefit. The political is a minimum of government and a society characterized by simplicity of life, few Li and direct face to face relations. It is not to be wondered that Taoism was opposed in the highly politicized, legalistic Ch'in dynasty, although Legalists found attractive some elements of Taoism.

One aspect of freedom is the freedom to realize one's unique selfhood. The Tao is present in all things and persons. Each person is a unique assemblage or manifestation of the Tao. The essential Tao in the self often becomes covered over. By freeing oneself from the artificialities and superfluities of civilization one regains one's original pure state, which is one of union with Tao. One returns to the root. It was the contention of later Taoists like Kuo Hsiang and Wang Pi that a society based on extensive Li promotes both artificiality or insincerity and classes. People act in terms of convention rather than from an inner motive. Li inevitably intensifies the superior/inferior distinction which is at the root of a class system and creates envy and jealousy among people. It is not to be wondered that the Taoist is often compared to those who believed that society corrupts and man should withdraw from it. Not that the Taoists accepted the extreme to which Yang Chu (440-360 B.C.) went in that direction. The validity of the "Yang Chu Chapter" has been questioned; but in it we find the idea of withdrawing from the cares of the world, being concerned only about one's own sensual pleasures, not "plucking out a single hair" even if doing so would benefit the whole empire. In Yang Chu the Taoist doctrine of inaction or taking no artificial action was debased to the level of no effort except that of a selfish nature, and it is not to be wondered that his views were attacked by Mencius, as noted in that chapter.

The concept of wu-wei defined as disinterested action is central to Taoist ethics as the author of the chapter on Taoism has pointed out. Wu wei deals with the important question of motives or why one does the good or the right. The Taoist's disdain of Li was due in part to the belief that motivation should come from within. If one does out of propriety what is commonly accepted as right, one does it because it is the proper or socially acceptable thing to do and, in addition, one may profit from doing so. Both such motives are external, utilitarian and impure. They do not characterize genuine moral action whose motive is doing good for its own sake rather than some ulterior motive.

Good deeds done for reward are a sign of a person who has not yet attained inner purity and union with the Tao. Lao Tzu, like Mencius, advocated discarding profit or the profit motive. In poem 19 he advocated other, often called "passive" virtues, although it should be pointed out that the appellation is questionable, especially from the Taoist point of view. For instance he advocates embracing simplicity and having few desires. He emphasized contentment, tranquility, not putting oneself forward, sitting quietly, not pursuing fame, honor and other such goals commonly upheld in today's world. He might even be called an apostle of non-violence, for in poem 67 he declares that he has three treasures, the first being love, and says that "deep love helps one to win in the case of attack...."

It may not be too far amiss to call Taoism a transcendentalist philosophy if by transcendental we mean, first, going beyond the usual or ordinary and, second, excelling or being excellent in oneself. For Lao Tzu wanted to see each person realize his potentialities to the fullest and he recognized that to do so would mean often going beyond what is ordinarily required or expected.

One can point to a number of ways Lao Tzu and the Taoist is a transcendentalist. As indicated already, one ought to transcend Li or social convention. The result will not be that one acts always in unconventional ways, although there may be times when one does. But one will act conventionally because one believes one should, because it will bring about social harmony and not because it will benefit one. One should transcend or go beyond conventional morality, too, as noted above, both in regard to content and motive. One should transcend the self in the sense of transcending selfishness, self-centered motives and action. One should transcend the world or worldliness in that one should not be so closely tied to the things of this world that one thinks it impossible to get along without them. Without denying it, one should transcend the part and be one with the whole; for instance, one should be concerned for the good of all, not just one's own. One should transcend distinctions, in the sense that one should not look on persons from the superior-inferior distinction or the good-bad one. The first leads to classes, the second to categorizing a person as either all good or all bad.

Taoism emphasizes metaphysical and epistemological transcendentalism also. Transcend appearances to get at the heart of things. Transcend or go on from the particular to the universal. Transcend disharmonies and recognize the harmonies in reality. Transcend opposites as they are momentary and not permanent. Transcend dualities in order to recognize the oneness of all things. By these and other transcendings a person becomes one with the Tao.

Epistemological transcendentalism is reflected in the view that the senses or sense knowledge is to be transcended or gone beyond. The senses are limited, even as words are in describing the Absolute. As we know, Lao Tzu disdained learned knowledge. It is superficial and should be gone beyond. Egoistic motives, when it comes to knowing, should be transcended also. Do not know in order to exploit or manipulate, Chuang Tzu cautioned. Restrain the "scheming mind". Transcend prejudices, be impartial; in Chuang Tzu's words, "Exercise fully what you have received from nature without any subjective viewpoint." Analytical or discursive reasoning is to be transcended also, as it is reductive. It breaks reality into parts and any reconstruction is never true to the original whole. We are reminded of Chuang Tzu's statement that "Great knowledge embraces the whole; small knowledge, a part only. Great speech is universal; small speech is particular."[11] Genuine knowledge is all inclusive; false knowledge is exclusive. Finally, an epistemological subject-object dualism is to be transcended, for knowing is viewed ontologically as being, being or becoming one with that which is being known. Knowing is also associated with realizing. To know the Tao is to realize it within.

In the centuries after Chuang Tzu and prior to the Medieval Period Taoism continued as an essential and influential element in Chinese civilization. It was a source of inspiration for poets and artists and solace for weary court officials.[12] One of its prominent, second century B.C. leaders was Huai-nan Tzu who continued the Taoist themes of tranquility, the all-pervasiveness of the Tao, the harmony of reality and man's need to harmonize with reality. His statement that "....he who comprehends evidences will not be fooled by strange phenomena," illustrates his opposition to corrupted forms of Taoism creeping in at the time.

A renewal of interest in Taoism occurred in the second and third centuries A.D. leading to a movement called Neo-Taoism.[13] Three of its leaders were Wang Pi (A.D. 226-249), Ho Yen (d. A.D. 249) and Kuo Hsiang (d. A.D. 312). Wang emphasized transcending distinctions—"The ten thousand things have ten thousand different forms but in the final analysis they are one. How do they become one? Because of non-being...." Viewing ultimate reality as nameless, Ho Yen cautioned that we not be beguiled by words;

thus words and forms are to be transcended. In his treatise on the Tao he wrote "Being, in coming into being, is produced by non-being. Affairs, as affairs, are brought into completion by non-being. When one talks about it and it has no predicates, when one names it and it has no name, when one looks at it and it has no form, and when one listens to it and it has no sound that is Tao in its completeness." Kuo emphasized transcending opposites and extolled the sage as one who, by doing so, lives in the world and is quite able to handle it. He wrote "This and that oppose each other but the sage is in accord with both of them. Therefore he who has no deliberate mind of his own is silently harmonizing with things and is never opposed to the world. This is the way to occupy the central position and to be in union with the profoundly mysterious ultimate in order to respond with things from any direction they may come."[14]

In the chapter on Taoism the author distinguishes between philosophical and religious Taoism and centers his discussion on the former. Such a distinction encounters the problem of definition. How do we define religion? What is religion? One answer is that an emphasis on transcending and the Transcendental is an element of religion universally. Does this mean, then, that Taoism, even so-called philosophical Taoism, is really a religion, since that element is found in it? Moreover ethics is commonly associated with religion and the statement is often made that a person is not truly religious if he is not virtuous. We have already seen that both a personal and social ethics is an inseparable part of Taoism. Perhaps, then, we should be cautious about making too rigid a distinction between philosophical and religious Taoism. We shall follow tradition, however, and do so and thus discuss the rise and character of what is called religious Taoism in the centuries following Lao Tzu and preceding the Medieval Period.[15]

Religious Taoism is said to have arisen soon after the passing of Lao Tzu and Chuang Tzu whose writings provided the first scriptures of religious Taoism. It should be kept in mind, however, as Professor Chan points out, that "the practice of divination, astrology, faith healing, witchcraft, and the like had existed from very early days." Thus religious Taoism may be said to have had its roots in antiquity, although it was undoubtedly given an impetus by the fang-shih of the third and second centuries B.C. who picked out passages in the Lao Tzu and Chuang Tzu, nebulous, vague or ambiguous in character, and associated them with belief in immortals, the prolongation of life, alchemy and other such practices then becoming popular.

While this makes it possible to view religious Taoism as popularized degeneration or corruption of a "pure" philosophical Taoism, there are other ways of looking at the matter. Religious Taoism may be viewed as a schema containing elements, lacking in philosophical Taoism, which man has always found essential in life. For example, while philosophical Taoism appeals to the mind or reason, religious Taoism appeals to man's feelings, emotions or sentiments. While philosophical Taoism does not, religious Taoism plays on the sense of awe, mystery and wonder found in man everywhere. Granted this makes it more susceptible to misuse; at the same time it is a dimension of man's being which cannot be disregarded or suppressed. Thirdly, religious Taoism is concerned with the spiritual aspect of man's nature.

The two streams of Taoism may be compared in regard to their view of the Tao also. The philosophical Taoist conceives of the Tao as the impersonal Absolute, as a rational principle, while the religious Taoist attributes personality to the Tao or sees it as personal in some sense. This is a significant difference, for to the religious Taoist the Tao is a supreme being or reality which one can interact with, pray to, call upon in times of distress, rest on in moments of weakness, appeal to in terms of one's hopes and longings, offer sacrifices to, revere and praise in chant and litany. Such a Tao is much more meaningful to the majority of people. The Tao as the Impersonal Absolute is of meaning to only a few.

Religious Taoism became associated with a belief in a large number of deities. In the language of metaphysics we may say that for the philosophical Taoist the Tao as the Ultimate, the Absolute, the One, the Indescribable and Ineffable is the single Universal of which all particulars are manifestations. The religious Taoist, however, does not go beyond the level of particulars. He associates the Tao as Deity with particulars thus making possible and giving rise to the popular belief in innumerable deities.

While religious Taoism became widespread among the masses with a particular interpretation of certain passages of the two Taoist classics, its growth was due to other factors as well. One was the disintegration or decline in power of the Han dynasty in the second century A.D. The economic accompanying the political chaos brought widespread suffering among the masses who turned to Taoist religious communities and Taoist magical cults for help and comfort. Moreover the ethical impulse of religious Taoism brought many converts. It taught the ideal of universal brotherhood and insisted on the performing of acts of virtue such as caring for orphans, the sick and aged. A third factor strengthening religious Taoism was its leadership of popular revolt movements aimed at improving the conditions of the masses. One occurred in A.D. 184 in the Shantung-Hopei region and became known as the Yellow Turbans revolt. Another followed in A.D. 189 in Szechwan under the leadership of Chang Ling, founder of the Five-Peck-Rice sect of Taoism. Both movements became powerful and widespread, requiring a great deal of effort on the part of the rulers to put down, and it was to a large extent due to them that Taoism became popular as a religion among the masses.

Religious Taoism should not, therefore, be looked upon or be looked down on as a degenerate form of philosophical Taoism, vulgarized for the masses. Rather it should be seen as a tradition which offered the Chinese that which was lacking in both Confucianism and philosophical Taoism. While it may be lamented that it became associated with magic, superstition, the cult of immortality and other such features in the pre-Medieval Period and after, its positive value and contributions should not be overlooked. It made the present more bearable by providing people solace in periods of distress and hope in times of despair. It provided a religious impetus and sanction for social protest movements. It upheld a high ethical standard insisting on inner purity and virtuous deeds. It advocated meditation as a means of attaining a right view of one's self and the world. It emphasized bodily and spiritual health and continued the theme of living simply and naturally or in conformity with nature.

In the first chapter very little was said about religion in ancient China. Since religion has been an important aspect of Chinese culture for centuries, a summary of its basic features up to the Medieval Period is in order. Religion in pre-Medieval China was characterized by sacrificing, divination, ancestor reverence or worship and belief in spirits, fate and many gods as well as a single, supreme one.

Spirits were believed to be numerous and powerful, interfering in man's activities and determining his destiny as the Classics and inscriptions on oracle bones indicate. We read in the *Book of History*, for example, that the Shang king T'ang was "fearful and trembling" because he was not sure but what he might have offended "the powers above and below." The spirits approved or disapproved and to gain the former and avoid the latter sacrifices were offered and rituals performed. Before undertaking an important venture the blessings of the spirits were sought and they were praised at its successful culmination. The *Book of Rites* states that, when the "Son of Heaven" is "about to go forth on a punitive expedition," he should sacrifice "specifically, but with the usual forms to God" and records that king Wu, after a victorious battle, reared "a burning pile to God; prayed at the altar of earth, and set forth his offerings in the house of Mu."

Because spirits could intercede for good or ill in human affairs it was incumbent on the emperor especially that he perform the sacrifices correctly. He offered seasonal ritual sacrifices such as the spring plowing ceremony and the "great summer sacrifice for rain to God when all the instruments of music are employed." While heads of states in the Chou dynasty offered lesser sacrifices, only the emperor could offer the "united sacrifice to all ancestors" at the capital and the grand sacrifice to Heaven and Earth. According to the royal regulations in the *Book of Rites* a tenth of the year's expenditure was to be spent on sacrifices and "in sacrifices there should be no extravagance in good years and no niggardliness in bad."

Failure to sacrifice to the spirits and leave unattended the spirits of the hills and rivers was considered an act of irreverence and might cost a head of state his territory. The building of altars and special places of worship became important in sacrificing to and propitiating the spirits and deities. The emperor Shun, we are told, divided the empire into twelve provinces and "raised altars on twelve hills in them." A main altar was built at the capital where the emperor sacrificed. Sacrificial worship characterized the religion of the aristocracy and common people alike. The *Book of Rites* notes that in the second month of spring a special day of sacrificing was designated by the emperor when people are to "sacrifice at their altars to the spirits of the ground."

Early Chinese religion was polytheistic and naturalistic. The gods believed in were numerous and were nature deities, as might be expected among people living close to the land. Each family had a deity presiding over its land. There was a god of each district and state, as well as the national earth god the emperor sacrificed to. River junctions and high places were believed especially sacred. The emperor was required to sacrifice to "all the famous hills and great streams under the sky, the five mountains receiving sacrificial honours like the honours at the court to the three ducal ministers, and the four rivers honors like those paid to the princes of states." Since spirits were influenced by virtuous behaviour also, it was incumbent on rulers especially that they be virtuous so that there would be no calamities from Heaven.

A hierarchical relationship was believed to exist among the deities providing a model for human society. Moreover, each god had a specific function such as the door god and the hearth god. In the pantheon of deities Heaven (T'ien) eventually became the supreme one. Many scholars point out that in earlier Chinese history God was conceived of as personal and later as impersonal.[16] As "anthropomorphic," God looks and acts like man. He distinguishes between the virtuous and evil, rewarding one and punishing the other. He approves and disapproves and sees and hears as people do. He becomes angry, grants and withdraws his blessing and is to be praised and supplicated. He has a will which man is supposed to carry out.

As impersonal being God is associated with the powerful forces people sensed in natural occurrences which evoked such reactions as "reverence for the majesty of Heaven." God was identified with the creative and other principles believed to be indwelling in nature. According to the cosmogony of the *Book of Rites* the origin of all things is in Heaven and earth and through the united action of the two all things are created. The "directing power of heaven and earth" is referred to and Heaven is believed to manifest the principle of harmony as earth does distinctions.

A belief in the power of God and his arbitrary nature and influence over man and the cosmos along with the notion of the mysteriousness of the universe may have been two sources of the early belief in fate. Man's experience with the great power of natural phenomenon such as the rain and wind, which led him to realize his insignificance and powerlessness in the grip of such forces, strengthened this belief, as did his populating this world with all manner of spirits and mysterious forces.

One function of divination was dealing with fate. By being able to foretell the future one hoped to avoid unpropitious events. Archaeological evidence as well as the literary tradition indicates what was used to divine with. The *Book of Rites* states that "The ancient kings made use of the stalks and the tortoise shell; arranged their sacrifices; buried their silk offerings, recited their words of supplication and benediction and made their statues and measures." Only when divination was favourable would they take action. According to the *Book of History*, Yu consented to the throne only after such had occurred; and the *Book of Poetry* records that, when T'an-foo wished to move his people to the plain of Chou, he went there first and received a favourable response divining with a tortoise shell.

A major aspect of early Chinese religion was ancestor reverence or worship which took the form of elaborate mortuary rites and sacrificial offerings. Ancestor worship was predicated on the belief in a soul which was released from the body on death and continued in a subterranean existence. Because of its continuity the dead were involved in the affairs of the living, sharing their joys and misfortunes, and influencing their destiny. As the dead had needs like the living, food and drink offerings were made to them regularly. Moreover, if the dead could interfere for good or ill in the affairs of the living, as much as possible should be done to insure their contentment, thus evoking their favour. The ancestral hall or temple was the locus of ancestor worship, for the aristocracy at least, while an altar in the home served the same purpose for others. Mortuary rites were held in the hall as well as at the grave site. Ancestral tablets were kept in the temple and it was a place for monthly and seasonal sacrifices.

Both archaeological and literary evidence indicate that ancestor worship was widespread in early times.[17] Tombs of Shang aristocracy with numerous artifacts have been unearthed. Buried with the royalty were food utensils, weapons and sacrificial vessels, all deemed necessary for the soul's continuance and bliss. Ancestral halls were used for non-religious purposes also. Yu received his appointment in "the temple of the Spiritual ancestor" as Shun had before him. In them officials transacted business and carried on affairs of state. They served for festive occasions as well.

Ancestor worship was thought of as a means by which a link between the living and the dead was maintained. It was a vehicle for expressing filial piety. It offered a way of perpetuating the memory of the dead and demonstrating one's feeling of respect and gratitude to them. Ancestral worship contributed to the continuity and unity of society and the integration and perpetuation of the family as the primary social unit. It is not to be wondered we read in the *Book of Rites* "that no other business should interfere with the rites of mourning was a thing extending from the son of Heaven to the common people," that "the mourning rites of three years for parents extend from the son of Heaven to all" and that "where there had been neglect of the proper order in the observances of the ancestral temple, it was held to show a want of filial piety, and the rank of the unfilial ruler was reduced."

Religion played an important, perhaps even a dominant role in ancient Chinese culture and thought. Seasonal gatherings of family, clan and village had religious overtones. As in other societies, religion became inseparable from politics in that the chief authority, the emperor, became a religious as well as a political potentate.[18] Political unity in the Chou was reinforced by religion. T'ien was the supreme ruler in Heaven just as the emperor was on earth.

Religion and ethics were inseparable also. T'ien, a paradigm of virtue, required the same from his followers. Ancestor worship as a religious act was the highest expression of the virtue of filial piety. Early art forms had religious themes. It is significant that religion took a pluralistic rather than a monolithic form in early China.[19] There was no single religion demanding the loyalty of all. The function of religion was not only to insure virtue but to maintain a harmonious relationship between heaven, earth and man. The centrality of religion is seen in man's attitude toward the earth; it was a religious not a solely utilitarian one. The land was considered sacred, to be respected and reverently cared for. Thus the relationship between God, man and nature was a reciprocal one. Each influenced the other for good or ill.

Religion was predicated on a view of reality as monistic and moral and a belief in the continuity of life and organic natural processes. There was no sharp division between a person and his ancestors. Life flowed on from one generation to another. Similarly, there was no absolute break between past, present and future. Moments merged into each other. The cosmos was viewed as in constant process. Further, since no sharp separation was made between heaven and earth, T'ien was not conceived of as an utterly holy, transcendent Deity who must manifest himself in special ways, as in western religious thought. Finally, non-scientific explanations of the cosmos were not objectionable but were, instead, quite acceptable, reasonable and satisfying to the early Chinese.[20]

The preceding discussion illustrates several problems which arise in any attempt to describe early Chinese religion—the evidence to be used, differences as well as similarities between the several time periods, distinctions between the religion of the masses and that of the few, the relationship of the state to religion. The analysis above used both the classical literature and archaeological findings as evidence. In regard to the time element and differences and similarities, one might point to continuities characterizing religion in China from the pre-Shang to the end of the Han. They would include belief in spirits in general and in the spirit or soul of the individual in particular, and the view that spirits of both types had an influence on the living. Ancestor reverence or worship with its attendant rites would be a second. One might make a valid claim for time variations in both cases, but it would be one of degree only. In the Chou dynasty sacrificial ritual was carried out by the kings, for example, and thus became more elaborate and pompous than in the Shang, just as ancestral halls became more numerous and elaborate in the feudal era.

Divination may be noted as a third constant. It was carried on by people of all ranks, as an interest in future happenings in order to better deal with them is common to all. Black pottery inscriptions indicate its practice in pre-Shang times, oracle bones and tortoise shells its continuation in the Shang, Chou and succeeding periods. Belief in nature deities, the associating of gods with streams, rivers, valleys, mountains, along with belief in gods associated with agricultural processes is a fourth constant, although again some variations may be noted. No doubt the number of such deities believed in increased through time, and new ones were added with sociological changes. A god of the hearth, for example, would be found in a settled but not a nomadic society.

One change which is quite evident is the rise of the belief in the Mandate of Heaven. It became prominent in the Chou period as rulers used it to justify dynasty. The official theme was that Heaven, the dispenser of rewards and punishments, had become disgruntled with the unworthy Shang rulers and had given over authority to rule to the Chou kings. From then on it became customary to view the ruler as the Son of Heaven and as Heaven's earthly authority. Out of this grew a state cult of religion in which certain rituals, the Feng and Shan sacrifices for example, were to be performed only by the emperor while heads on other levels of authority were to perform the other rituals.[21] The state religion often differed and even came into conflict with the people's religion.

Two other changes may be noted. One is a transition in the concept of deity from Shang-ti as a tribal god in the Shang to T'ien as a universal God or to God of everyone in the Chou. It would seem that the change in the view of God paralleled political changes. A second development, or perhaps simply change, is in the concept of God as anthropomorphic or manlike to the more philosophical view in the late Chou of God as impersonal (T'ien). In this case, we are reminded of the need to distinguish between the religion of the many and the few, as it was the more philosophically minded minority who accepted the more abstract view.

A similar distinction is to be kept in mind when noting the increasing association of the ethical with the Deity occurring in the Chou dynasty. Writers refer to the ancient religion being rationalized in this period, the Mandate of Heaven being one rationalization, the substitution of the ethical for ritual another. In earlier times sacrificial rites were believed to be the means of appealing to the Deity, while later it was believed that what the Deity wishes is virtuous behaviour. This was the Confucian view, as has already been pointed out; and it paralleled the growth of a different view of fate which placed an increasing emphasis on man, not spirits, controlling his destiny. Similarly there was a growing belief that the universe operates on the basis of natural laws or forces rather than being under the control of spirits. Again we need to be reminded that this humanistic approach to religion arising in the Chou period was that of the educated elite and not the majority.

Philosophers concerned with society and history present us with at least three explanatory theories; that societies change very little, at least up to the Modern Period, that change is only in appearance or on the surface but underneath is continuity or non-change; that change is constant and pervasive. We need not debate here which one, if any, of those three best explains pre-Medieval China. That there were changes cannot be doubted.

Two inter-related changes are the growth of cities and the appearance of class consciousness and classes.[22] Classes or class distinctions were a result of increasing specialization of labor, growth of trade, private ownership of land, conquest and the institutionalization, expansion and centralization of political power as well as other factors; distinctions being ones such as those between the "barbarian" and the true Han Chinese, the aristocracy and the commoner, the landed owner gentry and the peasant laborer, the ruling court hierarchy and the ruled masses, the educated minority and the uneducated, illiterate majority. Thus class was determined by position, birth, wealth and occupation, and the superior/inferior dichotomy was a basic one.

Reasons for the growth of classes were hinted at above. One, the philosophical, was omitted; by turning to it new answers to the questions raised at the end of chapter one may be suggested. In looking at the various schools of thought let us begin with Confucianism. One problem facing us is whether there are significant differences at least between the tenets of the later Confucianists such as the Han and the teachings of Confucius himself. We find numerous examples in history of a founder's views being changed, even distorted by later followers. Did this happen in the case of Confucius? The answer suggested here, tenuously and with the recognition that the problem warrants much more investigation by scholars, is that it did not. If the answer is valid, we are then forced to conclude that Confucius' own teachings provided

Introduction

a rationalization of the class society we find on Chinese soil in subsequent centuries.

Several such teachings can be pointed to. One is Jen defined as human-heartedness or love, love of one's own kin coming first and it then being extended outward to others. The difficulty with this kind of love is that in actual situations we tend to restrict or give most of our love to our kinsfolk and thus end up leaving little, if any, for those farther away. Such love in practice then becomes graded or discriminating love and, reinforced by an emphasis on filial piety, results in a society characterized by partiality, prejudice, favoritism and nepotism or inequality and injustice.

A second teaching of Confucius centers on his acceptance and promulgation of Li conceived on the one hand as correct performance of religious and other rituals and on the other as proper social conduct. These Li or formalized rules of behavior covered a wide range of activities and not only took into account but augmented differences of social status or station. Li tended, then, to strengthen rather than minimize classes. Furthermore, at least one aspect of Confucius' view of man reinforced Li and a class system. Confucius tended to distinguish between the superior and inferior man. We find many statements in the *Analects* describing the superior man as one with greater intellectual, physical, moral and other capacities who, by virtue of them, rightfully leads the majority endowed with lesser capacities. Thus there are natural gradations among men and to characterize some as superior and others as inferior is quite natural.

Most basic, however, is Confucius' metaphysical view of reality as stratified or hierarchical and pluralistic. A person who accepts metaphysical pluralism conceives of reality as made up of a multitude of particulars or particular entities. When the two notions of hierarchy and superior-inferior are added in, this means that those particulars can be grouped into levels or a hierarchy going from bottom to top, the upper being thought of as superior to the lower. Moreover, it is not illogical, in conjunction with this pluralism and hierarchism, to view reality as composed of such sets of dualisms as Heaven and Earth and Yang and Yin and to attribute superiority and higher status to one half of the dualism and inferiority and lower to the other.

An epistemological empiricism and particularism as a correlate of metaphysical pluralism holds that knowledge is of particulars or individual things. This means that knowledge is based on or is knowledge of distinctions. It is empirical in that it is knowledge derived from the senses and takes as its object the physical, tangible world of distinct, separate, particular material objects or entities surrounding one. Confucius' metaphysics and epistemology is the empiricism, pluralism and dualism described above, classes being its sociological correlate or implication and authoritarianism the political. To the Confucianist, then, a society characterized by a differentiation of groups or classes is quite a natural or valid one. Through the correct performance of Li, group distinctions are maintained and social order should result.

When we turn to Lao Tzu, differences are quite apparent. For Lao Tzu, and Chuang Tzu as well, real knowledge is trans-sensual and trans-rational or intuitive. They held that sense knowledge and rational knowledge, which may be called ordinary knowledge, involve the categorization, compartmentalization, classification or bifurcation of reality and thus the making of distinctions. One of the best statements illustrating this, noted already, is Chuang Tzu's—"Great knowledge is all-embracing and extensive; small knowledge is partial and discriminative." Lao Tzu and Chuang Tzu emphasize and laud the non-discriminating mind, the mind that does not make hard and fast distinctions, the mind that recognizes there are differences but does not take them to be ultimate, the mind that rejects the superior-inferior distinction. They would define knowing as insight or seeing immediately and directly into the essence of reality which is characterized by similarity not difference. To them true knowledge is knowledge of the whole or universals which incorporate but always transcend the particular or particulars. For Lao Tzu, man errs in creating a society which is a correlate of empiricism and rationalism. It should be based instead on an epistemology of intuition whose ethical correlate is sympathetic identification. Such an intuitive epistemological process does not involve the fracturing of reality and inducing from particulars but is one in which conclusions are arrived at directly, immediately and totalistically.

Lao Tzu's epistemology of intuition has as one of its logically implied metaphysical correlates the view that ultimate reality, the Tao, is beyond form and name. The Tao, known intuitively, is

Introduction

beyond distinction, division, multiplicity or categorization; and it is this Tao which one should seek to identify with. It cannot be fully named or denoted because language itself or words themselves are human constructs and are therefore limited as a means to reach the end sought for. Lao Tzu's metaphysics may be further described as a monistic pluralism, i.e., a combination of pluralism and monism or a combining of particularism and universalism. Reality consists, to begin with, of observed, experienced particulars and particular entities. They are not separate, isolated or independent but are integrated, synthesized or parts of a larger whole. Put differently, particulars make up universals, which universals in turn become one in a single Universal which is the primordial Tao.

For the Taoist it is important to start with the universal rather than the particular; for then all particulars in the end are manifestations or extensions of the same, the one Tao. Any distinctions are of a second order. They are superficial and inconsequential and pertain to the "mundane world". They should be transcended or not entertained in the first place. Society should be based on or should be a manifestation of universals and, ultimately, the one universal Tao. The Taoist believes the Confucianist mistakes the part for the whole; he does not transcend or go beyond the limiting, distinction creating type categories which reason or the rational mind creates in order to understand and deal with reality. The result is that a Confucian type society is based on a metaphysics of a second order.

At this point Lao Tzu's view of man may be brought into the picture. A central point is his assertion that the Tao is found in all, no matter one's origin, livelihood or birth. As to individual differences, Lao Tzu would certainly admit them. On the level of the empirical, the observable, we recognize that some are more intelligent or capable than others. But this does not allow us to conclude that they are superior. To do so would be to draw a qualitative type conclusion from quantitative type evidence. This is invalid; the most it allows us to do is to conclude that people are different. This, of course, is a vacuous tautology and may as well not be drawn at all. The important thing is that people are ontologically alike; in their essential nature they are all Tao. Any conclusion drawn should be in terms of the ontological not empirical; for example, whether or not a person is fully realizing his essential self or tao. Also involved in Lao Tzu's view of man is the idea that the individual never lives, indeed cannot live, isolated and self dependent. The human like the natural world is an interdependent, inter-related one. Lao Tzu too drew a picture of the ideal man or sage. The Taoist and Confucian sages differ in that sense knowledge of the empirical world and its socio-political correlate characterized the latter in contrast to the transcendental knowledge of the former. For Confucius the sage is one who is wise in the ways of the world; for Lao Tzu the sage is one who is wise in the ways of the spirit. The contrast is one, of course, which should not be pushed too far; and, in the case of both, the sage is a model of virtue.

In describing further the social implications of Lao Tzu's metaphysics, epistemology and view of man, organicism becomes an appropriate term. Society is made up of a number of functional or occupational groups not classes, each necessary for the well being of the whole. As with Plato, harmony is a result of each person doing the work he is best suited for and using his capacities to the fullest. In such a society wu-wei, defined as non-attachment, and not self interest would be the basic motive, for it would be a society of primary or face to face relations characterized by mutual sympathy and understanding. This means that the "we and our" would replace to a large extent the "I and mine" orientation of individuals. There would be no classes, for there is a minimum of Li which gives rise to distinctions. Li would not be necessary as the individual is inner rather than outer directed. It is the Tao within the person, not external rules, which prompt behaviour.

We are familiar with Lao Tzu's characterization of the ideal society as made up of a large number of semi-independent, self-contained villages. In that society there are not rural-urban distinctions, as there are not large urban centers. While Lao Tzu's proposed society may be explained as a reaction against the growing classes, urbanization and institutionalizing of Chinese society in his time, a full explanation would require that one take into account its philosophical or cosmological basis also.

Mo Tzu too was concerned with the questions raised at the end of chapter one. To see what answers he gave to them it is best to go directly to his metaphysical position. It will be recalled that

Introduction

Heaven is Mo Tzu's starting point. Is Mo Tzu's Heaven identical with Lao Tzu's Tao or Confucius' T'ein? The answer is no, for Mo Tzu conceived of Heaven as a more personalized or anthropomorphic entity. Heaven is an omniscient, impartial, all-loving, willing Being, and his will is that man be and do what He is and does. Thus since Heaven loves all people equally, man should also. Since Heaven is impartial and treats all alike, individuals should likewise. Since Heaven is compassionate toward everyone, we should be too. Since Heaven does not make distinctions, man should not either.

In sum, Mo Tzu's metaphysics is not the naturalism of Lao Tzu or the empirical, rational humanism of Confucius but is, rather, what we can call a theistic or religious metaphysics because it is centered on a personalized Deity. Its ethical and social implications are much like those of Lao Tzu however. For the society Mo Tzu advocated which was based on universal love would be one in which there are no inequalities of rank or position to provoke envy, no flouting of wealth to stimulate jealousy, no selfish striving to get ahead of others, no seeking for glory and fame, no competing for courtly honors, appointments or titles which magnify the superior-inferior distinction. Lacking partialities and inequalities, there would be genuine justice leading to real and lasting peace. Society would be characterized by unlimited love, mutual sympathy, empathetic understanding, non-aggressiveness, cooperation and harmony. It would be a society in which what is valued and sought after are those things which unite rather than divide, which are for the common rather than the solely self-good, which stimulate the best, the divine like and atrophy the worst in human nature. The harmony prevailing would not be a tenuous and artificial one based on Li, but a genuine one grounded in love and respect for one another.

We are now in a position to make a final statement regarding the "ancient tradition" or the "early wisdom" of pre-Confucian days and what happened to it. The thesis here is that Lao Tzu and Mo Tzu, the latter perhaps more than the former, were the ones who came closest to continuing that tradition in circumstances which increasingly made its practical realization difficult. This conclusion is drawn on the basis that both took the organicist view of reality as an interrelated whole; both accepted the presence of a vital force at work in reality, one viewing it naturalistically and the other theistically; both related man to a reality other than, greater than, deeper than, beyond man himself which he could have meaningful relations with and which served as a model for living. Both accepted a non-dialectical metaphysical pluralism-cum-monism, i.e., all particulars are in the end bound up in the one Universal and thus with each other. Both took an organic type society, one made up of a number of interdependent entities, as its implication. Both refused to see reality, whether natural, human or social, in terms of the superior-inferior dichotomy. Thus both advocated an egalitarian type society.

Circumstances in Lao Tzu's and Mo Tzu's time did not favour the continuation of the "ancient tradition" or the practical realization of the "early wisdom", although there is evidence that some communal type societies existed. There was increasing urbanization. There were wars between states. There were those who cheated and deceived others. Rulers were envious of each other. There were too many motivated by self-interest rather than the common good. But Lao Tzu and Mo Tzu would not be dissuaded by those circumstances, for they believed that one's philosophy should be derived from the ideal, not the real, from the possible not the actual; and the real should not deter one from proclaiming the ideal.

Notes

1. For a discussion of Ch'in and Han culture see Schirokauer, Conrad, *A Brief History of Chinese and Japanese Civilizations*, New York, Harcourt Brace Jovanovich, Inc., 1978, pp. 62-71.

2. Ch'u Chai and Winberg Chai, *Confucianism*, New York, Barron's Educational Series, Inc., 1973, pp. 5,100.

3. For a discussion of this see Fung Yu-lan, *A Short History of Chinese Philosophy*, New York, The Free Press, 1948, p. 18.

4. For the growth of cities in the Ch'in and Han see G. William Skinner, ed., *The City in Late Imperial China*, Stanford, Stanford University Press, 1977.

5. As an example see Tung Chung g-shu's memorial as quoted in Li, Dun J., *The Civilization of China*, New York, Charles Scribner's Sons, 1975, pp. 90-91.

6. For a summary of Tsou Yen's views and the Yin-Yang School see

Introduction

Chan, Wing-Tsit, *A Source Book of Chinese Philosophy*, Princeton, Princeton University Press, 1963, pp. 244-246.
    7. Chan, op. cit., p. 280.
    8. Chan, op. cit., p. 295.
    9. Chan, op. cit., p. 122.
    10. Chan, op. cit., p. 233.
    11. Chan, op. cit., p. 180.
    12. For a discussion of Taoism and its concept of the Tao as related to Chinese art se Sze, Mai-Mai, *The Way of Chinese Painting*, (Bollingen Series XLIX, 1956), chapters 1 and 2. The book *Creativity and Taoism, A Study of Chinese Philosophy, Art and Poetry* by Chang Chung-yuan is also very good on this topic. New York, Harper and Row, 1970.
    13. For a discussion of Neo-Taoism see Fung, op. cit., chapters 19 and 20 and Chan, op. cit., ch. 19.
    14. Chan, op. cit., p. 329.
    15. Frederick W. Mote writes, for example, "China's intellectual life was not as highly compartmentalized into separate and sometimes competing categories like philosophy, religion, and science as were most others." *Intellectual Foundations of China*, New York, Alfred A. Knopf, 1971, p. V.
    16. Chai and Chai give the rise of humanism as the reason for the change: "The religious beliefs of the Shang people were gradually transformed during the Chou period.... in simplifying and modifying them, the Chou give them all humanistic interpretations.", op. cit., p. 123.
    17. For the archaeological evidence see Wheatley, *Pivot of the Four Quarters*, pp. 40, 55, etc.
    18. This has led some scholars such as Eberhard, Goodrich and Watson to use the term Theocracy to describe the Shang era.
    19. Joseph Wu points this out in *Clarification and Enlightenment, Essays in Comparative Philosophy*, Taichung, Tunghai University Press, 1979, p. 15.
    20. There are, of course, many good discussions of religion in China. A single book devoted completely to it is D. Howard Smith's *Chinese Religions*, New York, Holt, Rinehart and Winston, 1968. A sociological approach is found in C.K. Yang's *Religion in Chinese Society*, Berkeley, University of California Press, 1961. An interesting survey is found in K.S. Latourette, *The Chinese, Their History and Culutre*, 4th edition, New York, The Macmillan Company, pp. 520-564.
    21. See Fitzgerald, C.P., *China, A Short Cultural History*, Catham, W. and J. Mackay Limited, 4th edition, p. 222.
    22. It should be noted that there are differences in views held regarding the question of classes in Chinese culture and whether or not Confucianism tended to support a class system.

8
CHINESE BUDDHIST PHILOSOPHY

FRED STURM

It is impossible to exaggerate Buddhism's impact on Chinese thought and culture. The influence has been so profound and far-reaching, it is surprising to discover that at first Buddhism was a virtually unintelligible import from the totally foreign culture of India. It took almost five centuries from its introduction on Chinese soil before the Chinese people were prepared to accept Buddhism as a viable intellectual alternative. Much of that viability resulted from the gradual transformation of Buddhist doctrine and practice into an authentically Chinese tradition.

Siddhārtha Gautama, the Buddha, was a contemporary of the founders of Confucianism and Taoism, the two most important and durable Chinese intellectual traditions. The problems which confronted Indian and Chinese thought during the sixth century B.C. were quite literally worlds apart. Both groups were seeking a "way"—mārga in Sanskrit, and tao in Chinese—but the "ways" which they were looking for were very different. The Chinese were after a way out of the growing social and political chaos accompanying the disintegration of the Chou empire, which led to attempts at articulating the Way (Tao) of socio-political order and stability. The Indians, on the other hand, were seeking a way of coping with a human existence characterized by suffering and frustration and apparently doomed to an interminable series of re-births, which led many of them to articulate Ways (mārga) of liberation (mokṣa) from such existence and the cycle of transmigration.

Buddhism first came to China mid-way through the long-lived Han dynasty which seemed to have resolved the quest for socio-political order and which recognized Confucian philosophy as the official state ideology. There were no facilities for translating Buddhism's message into Chinese; both adequate vocabulary and conceptual apparatus were lacking. Even had adequate translation been available to make Buddhism intelligible to Chinese scholars, the message conveyed would have been irrelevant for the problems of the day. Buddhism was offering answers to questions the Chinese were not raising! It was only with the collapse of the Han empire almost two centuries later that the Chinese situation began to change sufficiently for Buddhism to be relevant. It took a re-articulation of the Taoist position in the wake of that change to prepare the ground linguistically and conceptually for an intelligible translation and interpretation of the Buddhist Way.

1. Origins: Indian Buddhism

Buddhism was part of a widespread movement, including Jainism and Materialism (Lokāyata) as well, protesting the orthodox Vedic and Upaniṣadic tradition. These three major protest movements differed as much from each other as they did from the orthodoxies against which they ranged themselves. Each of the positions, "orthodox" as well as "unorthodox", was motivated by the search for a way of coping with the predicament of human existence. The traditional story of Siddhārtha Gautama's quest before Enlightenment suggests that he was familiar with the major alternatives, and that he rejected each in turn: the hedonism of the materialists, the intellectualism and yogic practices of the Brāhmaṇas, and the asceticism of the Jains.[1] His unique experience of enlightenment, as communicated in his famous sermon at the Deer Park near Banaras,[2] consisted of four basic insights called "Noble Truths": (a) all existence is suffering, (b) the direct cause of suffering is desire, (c) suffering can be overcome through the elimination of desire, (d) the way of liberation from desire, and hence from suffering, is a "middle way", i.e., a way of moderation which avoids extremes applied to each of the eight major categories into which the total range of human existence and activity can be divided.

In the realm of intellect this involves holding "right" or "correct" views, i.e., an understanding of what is as it is without assumptions or speculation. Phenomena are as they appear to be, continually changing so that each state of being is momentary. The view that there is permanence, that objects and events persist in some self-identifiable fashion stems from ignorance. In a process of dependent origination, where each stage is dependent upon a prior stage for its origin, ignorance gives rise to a disposition toward action which results in consciousness. Consciousness intends "name-and-form", i.e., the objective realm of awareness, which is turn produces the six sensory fields (5 perceptual and 1 conceptual). Given these fields, sensory contact with them is produced, followed by inner feeling of such contact. The stage is now set for the key element in what proves to be a twelve-level process. Thirsting or desiring, as inner feeling attaches itself to the objective range of awareness, produces the phenomenon of grasping for, or clinging to. This tendency gives rise to the karmic process of becoming, which leads to birth and re-birth, resulting in decay, suffering, and death.[3]

The chain, which is self-perpetuating, can be broken most effectively at the point of desiring. To be without desire is to be "nirvāṇa", literally "without the flame of passion."[4] When the flame is blown out, passions are cooled and there is no more desire; then the "self", which is dependent upon that desiring, withers away, and there is no more pain and frustration, no more "losing". Through the intellectual formulation of right views which dispel ignorance, and through right practice in the other seven dimensions of the eight-fold Middle Way, nirvāṇa is realized.

Of all the "ways" proposed to resolve the basic problem of liberation, the Buddhist proved to be the most satisfactory, or at least the most popular. Indeed, by the third century, when Aśoka created an empire which encompassed most of the sub-continent,[5] Buddhism had taken on the aspect of state ideology, although without any suppression of Jainism and Hinduism, and Indian culture bore its unmistakable imprint. This was true of intellectual activity, with the appearance of monastic schools of university stature within which the great philosophical traditions of Indian Buddhism took their rise. The pursuit of the Middle Way, as it applied to intellectual life, led to the articulation of a new problematic. The way of liberation was no longer the burning issue. It had been resolved, although it was to re-surface later in Chinese Buddhism under the guise of "spiritual cultivation: its nature and efficacy."

The new question for second generation Indian Buddhists who concerned themselves with "right understanding" was directed to the realm of phenomenal experience which was grounded in ignorance. To ascribe desire and suffering to ignorance was understandable, but this did not seem to be an adequate explanation of the undeniable realm of phenomenal experience. Such experiencing, the essence of all waking and dreaming moments, appears to be bi-polar, having both a subjective and an objective dimension. The naive assumption is that there is a subject—the "self" or "soul"—which accounts for subjective experiencing, and an object—"things" and "events"—which constitutes the objective pole of experiencing.

Sophisticated philosophical reasoning proceeds to the affirmation of a ground of subjectivity, viz. the realm of mind in-itself or pure consciousness, and to the affirmation of a ground of objectivity, viz. the realm of pure matter or physicality. To accept both grounds as real yields an ontology of dualism; denying one of them leads either to an ontology of idealism (declaring that mentality or ideation accounts for all phenomena), or to an ontology of materialism (insisting that materiality underlies all phenomena). Theological reasoning goes further in proposing a divine base for all realms of existence and essence.

The initial Enlightenment revealed neither divinity nor a self independent of phenomenal experiencing. Since everything is momentary and impermanent, no underlying substance—mental or ideal, material or physical—can be posited in which appearances can be said to inhere, or from which they can be said to arise. Mental phenomena do not imply a mind; physical phenomena do not imply a material substratum; actions do not imply an actor; perceptions do not imply a perceiver. How, then, is experiencing to be explained.

The first satisfactory effort to respond to this new problematic was attempted by a group of intellectuals whose several positions taken together have been termed Abhi-dharma, literally "concerning the elements."[6] The fullest statement of the position was given four centuries later in the Vibhāṣā Śāstra ("analytical commentary"), leading to a new designation: Vaibhāṣika ("those who analyze"). Analyze they did! Experiencing was seen to consist in five categories of objective combinations, five heaps (skandhas) of subjective combinations. Combining was interpreted in terms of ten causes. All the combinations do indeed exist, but only as momentary combinations, relative to causal process and hence impermanent, real in any given moment of experiencing, but without continuity. There is no inherence in some fundamental and abiding mental or material substance, and hence only existence without essence. The elements or dharmas which are related causally within the subjective and objective states of experience are real insofar as past, present, and future moments of existence are concerned. This interpretation of phenomenal experiencing is best known by a descriptive name: Sarvāstivāda ("everything exists school").[7]

A reaction to this position was soon forthcoming, although its fullest articulation was not written until the latter half of the third century A.D. The *Satyasiddhi* was a "completion of the truth": the doctrine of a two-fold void. Not only is the self void, but the dharmas themselves were analyzed as being void of any self nature. The earlier analysis held good only for a lower, naive view of experience. It was the "truth of ignorance" to perceive the dharmas as real. At this level the analysis was pushed even further to distinguish 84 dharmas, but it was emphasized that the elements of phenomenal experience were "real" only in the present moment. "Past" moments are real only in memory (a present mental state); "future" moments are real only in anticipation (also a present mental state). The "truth of ignorance" refers to only the present momentary phenomenal existence of the elements. The "truth of enlightenment" reveals the total emptiness of these experientially momentary "elements." Opposed to the declaration "sarvam asti" ("everything exists") was affirmed "sarvam śūnyam" ("everything is empty").[8]

The third outstanding effort to resolve the problem of phenomenal existence arose within the Mahāyāna branch of Buddhism through the sharp mind of Nāgārjuna (A.D. 150-250), the first in a great line of Buddhist logicians. Agreeing with the notion that there are two levels of truth, the truth of ignorance and the truth of enlightenment, he argued that the articulation of either, separated from the other, necessarily results in error. "Without relying on everyday ordinary activities," he insisted, "the truth of enlightenment cannot be expressed.... A wrongly conceived 'emptiness' can ruin a dim-witted person.... like a poorly-grasped snake." Strict adherence to the intellectual Middle Way is demanded. For this reason, the school to which he gave birth is called "Mādhyamika". To affirm the reality of experiential data is one-sided; to deny the reality of experiential data is likewise one-sided. Neither statement is true. One does not avoid one-sidedness by affirming the truth of both statements when uttered as a conjunction, nor is one-sidedness avoided by denying the truth of both statements when uttered as conjunctive. Whatever results from the process of dependent origination is empty, having no nature of its own because of total derivation from external causes. It is emptiness, then, which appears under the guise of the phenomenal realm of dependent origination. In other words, there is no difference between phenomenal existence and emptiness. "Since all dharmas are by nature empty, why declare them to be 'finite' or 'infinite', 'both finite and infinite', 'neither finite nor infinite'? Why declare them to be 'permanent' or 'impermanent', 'both permanent and impermanent', 'neither permanent nor impermanent'?" Phenomenal experiencing is illusory; but the illusion cannot be denied; it exists; it is relationally real, although basically empty. What is real, is empty; and concerning emptiness, words fail and only silence suffices. This has been designated, therefore, Śūnyavāda ("the emptiness school").[9]

Finally, in the fifth century A.D., two brothers, Asaṅga and Vasubandhu, provided the classic articulation of a philosophical position which seemed to offer the most satisfactory resolution of this long-standing problematic.[10] If the phenomenal world is to be accepted, yet affirmed to have no substantial base, then emptiness is the ground of experiencing. Were "emptiness" to be equated with pure-consciousness, consciousness taken in and of itself without reference to the intentionality of awareness, then an adequate explanation for phenomenal appearing can be given. Sensations, perceptions, conceptions, and feelings constitute the objective range of conscious experiencing. The power of imagination shows that consciousness itself is sufficient to account for all the objects of conscious experience.

There is a consciousness of the visual, of the auditory, of each of the five types of sensation, as well as consciousness of intersensory phenomena, and consciousness of thought-processes. In each of these seven instances of conscious experiencing the focus is on the phenomenal objects of awareness which have their roots in the conscious act of projection and intentionality. To focus on consciousness-itself, pure-consciousness without its intentional objects, is to encounter that which is Śūnya, empty, void. Viewed as the ground of the phenomenal, pure consciousness is said to be ālaya-vijñāna ("the granary of discriminate consciousness", i.e., the storehouse of seeds of conscious objectification), the grounding of and potentiality for all phenomenal occurring. Viewed apart, it came to be known as tathāgata-garbha ("womb of the gone-this-way", i.e., the ground of "thus-ness" or "such-ness"), the state of complete detachment from anything projected beyond itself."[11]

At the same time this philosophical activity was taking place in India, other Buddhists concerned themselves with the non-discursive dimension of the Middle Way. The fourth Noble Truths in the articulation of the Buddha's Enlightenment included much more than correct understanding of the human predicament. It describes an eightfold path, indicating that liberation through moderation involves not only the intellect—correct understanding—but the entire range of psycho-physiological existence within the phenomenal realm. Strong emphasis is placed on correct ethical and social behaviour. This is made very explicit in the recitation of the *Triratna* ("Three Jewels"), the traditional Buddhist affirmation of faith: "I take refuge in the Buddha; I take refuge in the Dharma; I take refuge in the Sangha."

The establishment of the Sangha, a community of those who had committed themselves to the thorough search for liberation and to a strict adherence to the principles of the Middle Path, resulted from the recognition that human existence is caught up in a web of social relationships which cannot be easily eliminated. The way of the muni, the solitary hermits who lived in seclusion and were pledged to silence, was not the way which pointed to liberation, any more than the way of the Jaina ascetic. In this transitional state of being in, yet not of, the phenomenal world, a society within society had to be created, a society which dispensed with caste distinctions, but which respected sexual differences, a society which had its own rules and regulations, providing the necessary supportive structures for those who consciously were seeking the freedom of nirvāṇa. The Dharma came to refer to standards for moral actions, standards designed to guide Buddhists both within and outside the Sangha. Dharma became articulated in terms of proximate norms, and even highly specific practical rules applicable to the widest possible range of daily mundane activities and situations. The *Dhammapada* is best known, and one of the earliest, documents in which such articulation took place, serving as a useful guidebook for those embarked upon the Noble 8-fold Middle Path which leads to full liberation.[12]

The underlying precept of moderation implied an avoidance of extremes and any sort of one-sidedness, not only in matters of understanding but also in modes of activity and behaviour. To state fully a given moral norm, therefore, it is necessary to give it positive expression, as a virtue, and negative expression, as a vice to be avoided. The norm for correct speech, then, is stated in two complementary ways: (a) to speak the truth at all times; (b) to refrain from all falsehood and deception. Because the human predicament is characterized essentially in terms of pain, the basic norm in Buddhist ethics, functioning almost as an expression of the Kantian categorical imperative, has to do with attitudes and actions relating to suffering, its infliction and its alleviations. The two complementary sides of this fundamental moral norm are (a) to act compassionately toward any suffering on the part of a sentient being; (b) to inflict no injury upon any sentient being. The other virtues and norms of Buddhist ethics can be shown to derive from this. Thus the norm for determining correct livelihood counsels occupations which lessen the level of pain in the world and prohibits occupations which result directly or indirectly in the infliction of injury. Regarding individual involvement in activities which promise sensual pleasure, the proximate norm counsels prudence and temperance and prohibits the over-indulgence which strengthens desire.

There was much room for disagreement in how proximate norms were to apply to specific situations. Matters of diet provide a clear example. Given the fundamental prohibition of injury to sentient beings, was meat-eating eliminated automatically, or might there be a way of justifying its inclusion in the Buddhist cuisine?

There were those who argued that if the animal had not been killed by the Buddhist who was to eat it, nor even killed for the explicit purpose of feeding the Buddhist, then there was no harm in eating the meat because the Buddhist eater was responsible neither directly nor indirectly as causal agent in the pain and death of the slaughtered beast. Others argued that any participation in animal-slaughtering and meat-eating, however oblique, constituted involvement in a pattern of activity which raised the level pain in the world.

Control over mental and other psychic activity was enjoined as well in the eight-fold Middle Path, and resulted in the appearance of a variety of disciplinary approaches designed to provide the ability for becoming increasingly free from the distracting processes of sensation, perception and intellection in which psychic and mental suffering is rooted, and for achieving perfect detachment from the "objects" of such processes. Such dhyāna or samādhi disciplines involved practitioners in levels of meditation and concentration leading to the enjoyment of peace unmarred by outward sensations and inner thoughts. Often techniques of meditation were correlated with Buddhist schools of philosophy and accompanied them on Buddhism's journey through Central Asia and into China.

2. Preparation: Neo-Taoism

When Buddhists from India and Central Asia first arrived in China, the Chinese were totally unprepared to appreciate their faith-stance, or to understand the philosophical expression of that stance as presented by any one of the many divergent philosophical schools. The problems for which these purported to be resolutions were not Chinese problems. As indicated earlier, Buddhism provided answers to questions the Chinese had not raised. Furthermore, both questions and answers were given in the grammatical framework of a highly inflected Indo-European language structure, fundamentally different from the linguistic structure of Chinese.[13] Technical terminology had evolved over the course of centuries to express distinctions which had been made in the course of continuing Buddhist conversation and argumentation. There were few, if any, equivalent concepts or distinctions in Chinese intellectual history up to that point, and the Chinese language, therefore, did not contain the vocabulary necessary for intelligible translation of Buddhist texts and discourse.

At the time of Buddhism's advent, during the first century c.e., the Han dynasty was flourishing. Confucianism, as re-articulated for the purpose by Tung Chung-shu (197-104 b.c.), served as the official state ideology.[14] The Chinese were concerned with good government, sound social institutions and the development of culture. For centuries of intellectual development they had created a technical vocabulary to meet the needs of an on-going conversation which addressed itself to the elaboration of these concerns. It was not until the downfall of the long-lived Han dynasty and an ensuing period of three hundred and sixty nine years of political and social instability that the ground could be prepared intellectually and existentially for intelligible interpretations of Buddhism and meaningful translations of Buddhist documents.

Legalism had served as the ideological base for the short-lived Ch'in dynasty which had unified China, and Confucianism provided the intellectual underpinning for the Han. Now, in the wake of the latter's collapse, and what came to be judged as the bankruptcy of Confucianism, the Taoist tradition reappeared as the most popular intellectual position, serving both as a reaction against Han dynasty Confucianism and as a promising perspective from which to deal adequately with highly unsettled times.

Taoism had arisen initially as an effort to provide a resolution for the same problematic of how to determine the correct way of establishing and maintaining socio-political order which concerned Confucianism, Legalism and the other classic schools of Chinese philosophy.

The *Tao-Ten-Ching* argued that human beings, human society and government are natural, and that the way of structuring and directing human behaviour ought not to deviate from the way of natural structure and processes. Although one can distinguish "ways" for each of the myriad kinds of natural phenomena, each of these is rooted in the Way itself. The fundamental characteristic of natural processes, stated negatively, is to act without intentionality.[15]

"Reversal is the way",[16] and when this is applied to individual behaviour, social institutions, or political governance, this means to be rid of artificial, contrived structures, norms, and processes—all results of intentional activity which marks deviation from, and hence disruption of, the natural.

Two centuries later the *Chuang-tzu*, noting that "reversal" leads to "spontaneity", proceeded to an analysis of the underlying natural process—the Tao—that continual flow of transformation within which all things find themselves. To be at one with the Tao, the spontaneous process of the natural, is to reject artificial standards imposed for purposes of uniformity by external agencies, whether princely decree, legislative act or customary tradition. A fundamental problem faced is how to harmonize, existentially as well as intellectually, the experiential uniqueness of individuals with the basic insight that each is integrally related to the unified process of transformation which is the Tao.[17]

In the decades following the collapse of the Han dynasty there was a decided resurgence of interest in the thought of Lao and Chuang. Wang Pi (A.D. 226-249) and Ho Yen (d. A.D. 249) concerned themselves with an explication of the *Tao-Te-Ching*, supplemented with the earlier *I Ching*. At the same time Hsiang Hsiu (d. A.D. 250) and Kuo Hsiang (d. A.D. 312) were attempting to interpret the text of the *Chuang Tzu*. The work in which they were engaged, which was more than an academic exercise of scholasticism, was known as "Dark Learning" (hsuan[2] hsueh[2]), not because they were dealing with matters of the "occult", but because they were attempting to shed light on the mysteries of fundamental reality through the understanding of the nature of the Tao. Lao and Chuang had been concerned with social, political, and ethical philosophy; the Neo-Taoists of the post-Han period were grappling with ontological issues.[18]

This does not mean that the Neo-Taoists had turned their attention completely away from political matters. The revival of interest in Taoist thought during the post-Han period was occasioned by both a disillusionment with Confucianism which had been the official ideology of the Han dynasty, and a concern for explaining the disintegration of what had appeared to be a highly successful and firmly grounded political structure. The initial concern of the Neo-Taoists can be interpreted as sociopolitical, but the tradition which Lao and Chuang had developed during an earlier period led them to a consideration of more fundamental issues relating to existence and essence.

Throughout his commentary on the *Tao-Te-Ching*, Wang Pi emphasizes that all that exists[19] is rooted, or has its origin, in emptiness.[20] The many shapes and objects in the world are reducible to a fundamental unity. A truly unique "one", or a "one" over against which there is no other, cannot be described, because description is of necessity limiting and relational, necessarily entailing delimitation and contrast. Therefore unity is rooted in wu,[2] lacking all determinative characteristics.[21]

When Wang Pi concludes that fundamental reality is empty (Tao[4] is wu[2]), he means that the ground of being is devoid of distinguishing characteristics. Otherwise it would be a thing among other things. Hsiang Hsiu and Kuo Hsiang, working on the *Chuangtzu* text, take a radically different position. "The Tao is everywhere, but everywhere it is Wu." Because "Wu is Wu"—"Emptiness is Emptiness"—the Tao cannot be said to create all the things that there are (yu). If there is anything, it is responsible for its own being. All Yu comes to be through its own spontaneous act (tzu[4] jan[2]). Spontaneity refers to the naturalness of all things. They are what they are according to their own inner nature without any external causation. "The creating of things has no sovereign. Everything creates itself, and does not derive from anything else." In like manner Hsiang and Kuo understand Chuang-Tzu to be suggesting that the unending process of transformation which characterizes phenomenal existence is not dependent upon a prime mover, a final goal or an external director of any kind. This is the principle of tu[2] hua[4] ("self-transformation"), viz. that each individual is responsible for its own process of change.

Despite this radical independence of all existents, there is a nonintentional matrix of relationships such that everything is related to every other thing, just as lips are related to teeth. Lips are lips, and do not exist for the sake of teeth. Yet without lips the teeth would be sensitive to the cold. "Though mutually opposed, they are mutually indispensable at the same time." So is the mutual relationship of reciprocity between existent and ultimate! The ultimate is empty, non-purposive, nothingness. There is no Tao! Yet each individual is related to that Tao and dependent upon that Tao. The perfect human being, chih[4] jen[2] "has no ego ....forgetting all distinctions: life and death, right and wrong.... he proceeds on to that which has no limits....He is a person who depends on nothing else."[22] The Tao is absolute Wu. What does it mean to suggest that it is prior to yu, all that there is? "So what can be prior to things"? Still things are being generated continuously. This indicates they are what they are spontaneously. Nothing (sic) causes them to be such as they are."

This development of Taoist ontological concepts, together with the redefinition of traditional terms, especially the attribution of wu to Tao, provided a matrix of concepts and terms which finally permitted translation of Buddhist ideas into a language and world of thought with which the Chinese had become accustomed.

3. ADVENT: BUDDHISM-IN-CHINA

The circumstances surrounding the early introduction of Buddhism into China are shrouded in the mystery of legend. The earliest development must have been slow and difficult, occurring as it did during the latter half of the Han dynasty. There were few, if any, points of contact, and we can only surmise that its early foothold was as an esoteric religious movement with a stress on practice. It was not until after the collapse of the Han dynasty and the articulation of Neo-Taoist positions, that there was the possibility of so foreign an intellectual import being understood in any satisfactory manner. The unsettled post-Han times, along with the new problems, concepts, vocabulary of the Neo-Taoists, finally provided an ambiance within which Buddhism had the opportunity to become intelligible to the Chinese mind and gain a real foothold in the context of Chinese culture.

An early Chinese Buddhist apologetic treatise, *Disposition of Error*[23] attempted to answer charges which were being brought against the movement and in so doing reveals some of the problems of understanding at that early period:

(i) Buddhism is not mentioned in the classics. The Chinese were accustomed to an appeal to tradition for the resolution of problems. From its inception Confucianism relied on classic literature which purported to convey wisdom from past ages, a wisdom which transcended temporal change and was believed to be relevant in any human situation. The Neo-Taoists were returning to the *Tao-Te-Ching* and the *Book of Chuang-Tzu* for answers to the questions which were puzzling them several centuries later. If there was any value in Buddhist thought, historic Chinese sages would have known it. Failure to locate mention of Buddhism in the classic literature of the past made this imported tradition highly suspect.

(ii) Buddhist monks renounce worldly joys. The idea of asceticism was foreign to the Chinese mind. Indeed, notions which frequently underlie ascetic practice, such as that of a dualism in which the body is viewed as the prison of the psyche, or an interpretation of experiencing in which the mind is viewed as introducing a category of casual nexus for the purposes of intelligibility, had not appeared in Chinese intellectual history. Although the Confucianists looked with disfavour upon officials who indulged in amusements at the expense of fulfilling responsibility, it was the neglect of duty which was frowned upon, not the enjoyment of pleasures.

(iii) Monks injure their bodies, thereby dishonouring their parents who gave them their bodies.

(iv) Monks do not marry. In both instances disregard of familial responsibilities would be shocking and cause for censure on the part of Confucianists. The "Great Renunciation," in which Siddhārtha Gautama abandoned his wife and new-born son, as well as turning his back upon his princely responsibilities, would horrify anyone educated in the Confucian tradition which placed high value on social structures, and made the assumption of social roles morally obligatory.

(v) Buddhism teaches that human souls do not die, but return to bodily existence. It is interesting that it was the doctrine of saṃsāra, the cycle of re-births, which caught the attention of the Chinese critics, rather than the concepts of anattā. The assertion that there is no real self, but only an aggregate of aggregates of feelings, mental states, etc., would seem to fly in the fact of the Confucian notion of social responsibility and the mutuality of relationships. However, the very idea of any form of transmigration or reincarnation would appear absurd to a Chinese whose view of human nature was non-dualistic.[24]

(vi) The ideas and practices of Buddhism come from barbaric lands of the west. This was an objection which continued to be raised throughout Chinese history. Buddhism is not only foreign, but its origin lies in the regions of darkness, far removed from the light of civilization. It was this deeply embedded concept of cultural superiority, supportable in terms of much empirical evidence, which probably gave rise to the legend that when Lao-Tan fled his native city in disgust at the corruption of his day, and rode off on the back of a black ox, he proceeded to a place far to the west where he found a perplexed man sitting beneath a banyan tree longing for enlightenment. According to that legend, whatever light may be shed by Buddhism came originally from China and the Taoist tradition! The fact is that had it not been for the language and conceptual schemata of Neo-Taoist thought, Buddhism might well have remained foreign to the Chinese mind and culture.

The most satisfactory method of transmitting Buddhist thought proved to be that of ko² i⁴ (literally, "reaching meaning") which rested on the establishment of analogies between Buddhist ideas and Taoist concepts, drawing upon terms which appear in the *Tao-Te-Ching*, the *Chuang-tzu*, and the *I Ching*, as these were interpreted by the Neo-Taoists.[25] Given the variations in viewpoint within both Indian Buddhism and Neo-Taoism, it is not surprising that there was wide divergence of views among the early Chinese Buddhists. At times it proved impossible to locate an apt Neo-Taoist word to use in translating a basic Buddhist concept, and the Sanskrit word was retained. Reduction of such words to writing proved to be exceedingly difficult. Spoken Sanskrit is highly inflectional and polysyllabic; spoken Chinese is non-inflectional, isolating, and basically monosyllabic. Written Sanskrit is an attempt toward phonetic transcription through use of the alphabet whereas written Chinese is non-phonetic and non-alphabetic. The problem was to select from a wide variety of Chinese written characters, each pronounced in the same way within a given region. The original meaning—and association of meanings, especially with regard to the visual gestalt which stems from the pictographic-ideographic origins—of the written character, had to be considered carefully.[26]

Difficulties with translation were eased when bi-and multilingual Buddhist scholars arrived on the scene, but not until a confusing variety of Chinese Buddhist philosophical positions had emerged, referred to in the literature of the time as the "seven schools and six houses", none of which remained as an identifiable movement for any length of time.[27]

The first of the truly great translators whose work combined to create a tradition of Chinese Buddhist textual and linguistic study and to produce the great Chinese *Tripiṭaka*, the most complete collection of Buddhist scriptural texts and commentaries that exists, was Kumārajīva (344-413 A.D.) of Kucha, located in what is now Chinese Turkestan.[28] Highly qualified by family background, linguistic abilities, and a profound knowledge of Buddhist texts and doctrines, he arrived in China as a military captive. The translations executed under his direction remain great literature to this day because of his insistence that the demands of Chinese intelligibility took precedence over literalness of textural rendition. Seventy two volumes were translated under his direction, none more influential than Nāgārjuna's *Middle Teaching Treatise*, which was thoroughly studied and promulgated by Kumārajīva's Chinese colleagues and disciples, the "Ten Philosophers". Two other works of the Mādhyamika or Śūnyavāda school supplemented that major work: Nāgārjuna's *Twelve-Gates Treatise* and Āryadeva's *Hundred Verses Treatise*. These three texts constituted the basic works in the articulation of the Chinese version of the Mādhyamika position. For that reason the movement has come to be known as San-Lun ("Three-Treatise") Buddhism.

It was the writings of Seng-chao (A.D. 374-414), one of Kumārajīva's "ten", which established San-Lun as the first major school of philosophical Buddhism in China.[29] Among his thesis is that of the "immutability of things".[30] Events occur and are real within their own time period. Past events are "at rest" in the past, and do not "move" into the present. Present events are "at rest" in the present, and cannot be said to "move" into the past. There is, then, no thread of continuity between moments, no temporal flow, no phenomenal movement. "Everything according to its own nature remains for only one time period. What thing is there, then, to come and go?" In an essay entitled "Non-real's emptiness", or "emptiness of the Un-Real",[31] he defends the thesis that: "All things are really in one way non-existent, and in another way not non-existent. Because of the first fact, although existent, they are non-existent; because of the second fact, although non-existent, they are not non-existent." He proceeds with the implication: "If 'to be' does not mean they are real, and 'not to be' does not mean they are wiped out totally, then 'to be' and 'not to be', although different terms, express the same meaning." To declare either that there is being or that there is non-being is to fall into one-sidedness. To follow the Middle Path demands we take the position that there is neither being nor non-being.

In another essay[32] Seng-chao demonstrates that the higher knowledge of an enlightened person is no knowledge. To know implies that there is something known. Knowledge is articulated in terms of the attributes of that which is known. Higher knowledge has as its object that which is without qualities. Knowledge illumines "that which is" (yu); higher knowledge (prajñā, or "sage" knowledge) illumines "that which is empty (wu)", but this wu is the profound mystery (hsuan). "Therefore the sage is like an empty hole. He desires no knowledge. He lives in a world of change and purpose, but he holds himself to the world of wu-wei (without purposive action). He is silent and alone, empty and open ....Nothing more can be said about him."

One of Seng-chao's contemporaries, Tao-sheng (A.D. 360-434) gained a reputation for original, if not radical, views, some of which were to be developed more fully by later Buddhist scholars.[33] This included his insistence that "Buddha-hood is achieved through sudden enlightenment (tun[4] wu[4]: literally, instant awakening or instant apprehension)." This was defended on grounds that lower knowledge entails a grasping of that which is differentiated and limited, a process which necessitates a chain of reasoning or inference, whereas higher knowledge is the grasping of that which is undifferentiated and without limits. The object of higher knowledge is grasped immediately or not at all. There is no connection between the two levels of knowing, no passing from one to the other; the gradual procedure needful of the lower level is totally inapplicable to the higher.

In discussing a second thesis, that "a good deed entails no punishment", he countered the Taoist ideal of wu-wei with the concept wu[2] hsin[1] ("without heart-and-mind"). Acts which are accomplished through a motivation which is void of all clinging, whether the desire of the heart or the goal-directed purpose of the mind, do not involve the self and are free from the wheel of dependent origination. He stirred up considerable controversy with the explication of his declaration that the Nature of the Buddha is inherent in all creatures. On the one hand, this implied that even persons who are diametrically opposed to all for which Buddhism stands are candidates for enlightenment or nirvāṇa. On the other hand, this meant that many cherished symbols were not to be taken seriously as absolutes. "Arrival at the other shore" was a goal, and therefore to be denied. "Seeing the Buddha" was an experience on the lower level of knowledge, and therefore to be avoided. There can be no "Pure Land", because that is a contradiction in terms. These symbols express certain concepts which may be useful as means, but like fish-nets, they are only good for catching the fish. Once the fish is caught, the nets had better be discarded lest we catch ourselves within them!

The great Chinese theoretician of the San Lun school was Chi-tsang (549-623) who lived to see the reunification of China under the short-lived Sui dynasty (590-617), and the opening of the glorious T'ang dynasty (618-906). His commentaries on the three treatises were cogent and served as the definitive statement of the school's position in China. He is best known for his elaboration of Nāgārjuna's dialectic in his *Essay on Double Truth*.[34] In it he posits three levels of dialogue concerning reality. On each level an affirmation is made from the vantage-point of "lower knowledge", and a negation of that thesis follows from the perspective of "higher knowledge". "These three levels of double truth," he wrote, "all consist in gradual renunciation, like a scaffolding which is built up from the ground. Why? Ordinary people say that the true report of things is that they exist; they do not understand that there is no cause behind their existence. Therefore Buddhas formulate the thesis that in the final analysis things are empty, and have no cause to exist.... Thus according to the knowledge of sages things are by nature empty.... to assist people to progress from the worldly into the real and renounce the ordinary state in favor of the sagely, this first level of double truth is proposed."

On the second level it is judged that both thesis and antithesis of the first level are one-sided statements. A middle-way is taken in affirming that everything is both existent and empty. This itself does not resolve the problem of one-sidedness, however, since it is only a dualistic affirmation. The anti-thesis which higher knowledge affirms is non-dualistic, viz. that everything is neither existent nor empty. At the third level of knowledge it can be seen that the distinctions made in the thesis and antithesis of the second level are one-sided. This leads to a middle-way affirmation that either there are the two extremes of existence and emptiness or there are not. Higher knowledge again judges that this is a dualistic statement, and affirms the antithesis that everything is neither both existent and empty, nor neither existent nor empty.

Note that what seems to be a middle-way statement at one level becomes one-sided at the next. Chi-tsang himself clearly states his purpose: "One-sidedness and centrality are two extremes.... They are, therefore, called 'worldly truth'. Only neither one-sidedness nor centrality can be regarded as the Middle Way or Highest Truth."

The other major Mahāyāna philosophical movement, Yogācāra, also made a slight inroad into China; but it was not until a younger contemporary of Chi-tsang began to espouse it that its roots became firmly embedded in Chinese soil. Gradually it eclipsed the San-Lun school in popularity and influence. Hsuan-tsang (596-664) was the great Chinese Buddhist genius who accomplished this. Many Chinese Buddhist monks could be described as peripatetic, literally (moving from monastery to monastery, city to city, and even country to country) and figuratively (accepting the doctrine of one movement within Buddhist thought for a while only to reject it in preference for another); but Hsuan-tsang was perhaps the most peripatetic of all. His journey of sixteen years, from 623 to 645, which took him across Central Asia, into Himalayan kingdoms and throughout the Indian subcontinent, has become a staple adventure tale in China. Not only do we have his own account, *Records of the Western Regions*,[35] but a later 16th century novel based on his journey, as fanciful as it was popular, incorporating folk art embellishments which had been added over the centuries.[36]

Hsuan-tsang was initially attracted to interpretations of Yogācāra texts by leaders of the She-lun school. The available translation of the texts was clumsy to the point of ambiguity. He was convinced that Asaṅga and Vasubandhu had uncovered the core of Buddhist teaching, and grew increasingly frustrated at ambiguities in textual rendering. Herein lay the motivation for his journey to India: to locate authentic texts, to secure adequate linguistic ability to read them and to receive tutelage from the leading exponents of the Indian school. To say that he was successful is an understatement. In India he engaged in the rigid program of studies in linguistics, logic, textual analysis and philosophical discourse at the great Buddhist university centre of Nālandā. His reputation as an authority on the school's position and as a skilful polemicist was widespread throughout the greater India region, and preceded him on his return to China. He returned with six hundred and fifty seven documents, including works in the various schools of Indian logic, as well as the canonical literature of six Theravādin sects and two hundred and twenty four Mahāyāna sūtras. He was greeted with an imperial commission to establish a centre for the fresh translation of Indian Buddhist texts. In the ensuing nineteen years Hsuan-tsang completed highly accurate and intelligible translations of seventy-five texts. What is perhaps the more important is his writing of a treatise, *Ch'eng-wei-shih lun*, a systematization of the Yogācāra position based on selections from the major writings of ten masters of the school along with his own perceptive commentary.[37]

It was Hsuan-tsang who designated the school wei[2] shih[4], a translation of one of the Sanskrit phrases used to refer to the position: "merely ideation". Hsuan-tsang writes, "The word 'wei' ('merely', 'only') is used to deny that there are any things apart from consciousness.... There are no 'fa' ('dharmas', 'material elements') outside of consciousness."[38] This is the basic thesis: that all phenomena, both the objective (materially, spatiality, temporality, from which the notion of '*fa*' is evolved) and the subjective (sensations, ideas, mental states, from which the idea of 'wo': the ego or self, emerges) exist only within the scope of consciousness.

But if the process of ideation alone exists without any external source of stimulus or causation, how can we explain the various distinctions which arise in conscious experience? The answer: "The evolution results from consciousness itself which contains the seeds within." Pure consciousness, i.e., consciousness considered apart from the objects of experience, is devoid of content, and yet the potentiality for a field of awareness is present. "Why are the seeds called such?", asks Husan-tsang. The answer: "The functions and differentiations in root-consciousness produce their own generation spontaneously."[39] It is this spontaneous germination of potentialities which gives rise to the other levels of consciousness, and the process of cross-fertilization, which Hsuan-tsang calls "perfuming", occurs. "In this way the other consciousnesses which perfume it, and the consciousness which is perfumed, arise and perish together, and the concept of perfuming is thus established.... As soon as seeds are produced, the consciousness which can perfume become in their turn causes which perfume and produce seeds."[40] Thus it can be said that "a seed produces a manifestation; a manifestation perfumes a seed. The seeds, the manifestations, perfuming, turn on and on, functioning at one and the same time as cause and effect."[41]

The analysis is complex and subtle. Hsuan-tsang's leading disciple, Kuei-chi (632-682) found it necessary to write a commentary on his master's systematic exposition! The school became known widely as Fa-hsiang, concerned as it was with the analysis of the elements of experience in terms of mutuality and differentiation.

4. Transformation: "Chinese" Buddhism

The corpus of Buddhist writings and teachings which came to China reported the efforts to provide answers to genuine questions arising in the course of Indian cultural and intellectual history. The problem of rendering them intelligible to the Chinese went far beyond the level of linguistic translation. A correct rendition into the Chinese language merely provided Chinese readers with a variety of answers to a set of questions they had not raised, and which, at the time, they were incapable of raising because of the fundamental differences in cultural and historical development of the two peoples. Buddhism provided ready-made answers; in order to render them relevant, the Chinese had to formulate right questions!

The situation was eased when current Neo-Taoist terms and concepts were introduced into the translations. Buddhism then seemed to be addressing itself to questions which Chinese were raising at the time. "Three-Treatise" and "Mere Ideation" Buddhist schools were the products of this first stage of Buddhist relevancy in China. The shadow of the Indian tradition still hovered over the thought and activities of these movements, however. A successful transmutation of Buddhism into a Chinese phenomenon occurred with the emergence of five new movements indigenous to China. An old Chinese expression classifies four of them: "T'ien-t'ai and Hua-Yen schools for teachings; Ch'an and Ching-t'u schools for practice!" It is my contention that T'ien-t'ai and Hua-yen (True Words Sect of Esoteric Buddhism), represents the Chinese appropriation of Buddhism on a popular level of religious practice. Ch'an itself represents a further stage in the total Sinicization of Buddhism.

The main thrust of T'ien-t'ai Buddhism, the "School of the Lotus Scripture", is a typically Chinese reaction.[42] Because the fundamental problematic of Chinese thought had been concerned with the re-establishment of order, which called for the harmonization of conflicting parties and interests, it is not strange that, when confronted with a welter of conflicting interpretations of Buddhist teaching, Chinese intellectuals would address themselves to the task of ordering the diverse strands into a unified whole. This was the self-proclaimed message of T'ien't'ai; and the emphasis upon harmonization permeates all aspects of its work, theoretical as well as practical.

Chih'i (A.D. 531-597), the "Great Master of T'ien-t'ai", is best remembered for his popular and authoritative commentaries on the *Lotus of the Wonderful Law* scripture.[43] T'ien-tai ("Heavenly Terrace") refers to the mountain where Chih'i built the great headquarters monastery of the school. A more accurate designation of the position is "Fa-hua" ("Flowery-Law") because of the central role the *Lotus-sūtra* plays in its thought and practice. That sūtra presents a view of liberation which represents most clearly the Mahāyāna perspective.

Yāna is Sanskrit for "ferry boat" which transports people to the opposite shore. The earlier interpretations of Buddhism by self-styled "elders" (thera), are classified Hīna ("small")-yāna by the Mahāyānists because they emphasize liberation of an elite through individual effort. The insight into Buddhism which the Mahāyānists claim to propagate provides a Mahā ("great")-yāna capable of carrying all beings to the other shore, which is Nirvāṇa. The *Lotus sūtra* declares: "The Enlightened Ones could never save all beings by using the Hīna-yāna. The Buddha himself is in the Mahā-yāna.... He saves all beings." Does this mean that the teaching of the "elders" is false? And since there are many Mahāyāna schools, each distinguished by a different version of Buddhist teaching, which one is genuine?

These were questions which Chinese had been raising as more and more sects of Indian Buddhism struggled to gain a hearing and allegiance from Chinese Buddhist converts. The Chinese mind insisted upon order and sought for order through harmonization.

In typical Chinese fashion Chih'i, in his commentaries, insisted that none of the contending teachings was false, that each could claim to be grounded legitimately in the discourses of Śākyamuni himself. The Four Noble Truths were intended for all creatures, but there is a wide range of intellectual and spiritual ability to comprehend and appropriate the revelation of truth represented by humanity as a whole at any given time. For this reason the Buddha intentionally adapted the articulation of Truth to the diverse capacities of his hearers.

Chih-i distinguished five historical periods, beginning with the Buddha's Enlightenment, and terminating in the full explication of the *Lotus-sūtra* through T'ien-t'ai teaching. On each level from the second through the fifth a fuller explication of Truth is given, and Chih-i identifies the methods used and the contents of the teaching at each of these levels. This effort at harmonization was called the analysis of the "five periods and eight doctrines." T'ien-t'ai teaching represents the final stage in the full disclosure of the Truth which was revealed to the Buddha. It is the Eka-yāna, the "One-and-Only", or "All-Inclusive" boat-to-Nirvāṇa, not because of a claim to exclusiveness, but rather because of its call to ecumenical synthesis.

The philosophical position of T'ien-t'ai Buddhism was formulated by Hui-wen (550-577) who was struck by a passage in the *Mādhyamika-śāstra*: "That which is produced by causes I say is identical with emptiness. It is also identical with mere naming. It is the significance of the Middle Way as well." From this Hui-wen derived the fundamental doctrine of the perfectly harmonious three-fold objective truth: the truth of emptiness, temporality, and the mean. It is the Truth of Emptiness that no fa (element of phenomenal existence) has any nature of its own since all fa result from external causation and are totally dependent for their being on something other than themselves. Therefore all fa, or the total range of phenomena, are empty and in themselves constitute a void. It is the Truth of Temporality that the fa exist momentarily just as they appear to be. Their ultimate reality, then, consists in chen-ju. This phrase, usually translated as "thus-ness" or "such-like-ness", means literally "as-if-genuine". In other words, the elements of phenomena themselves are empty; the realm of phenomenal existence itself is an illusion which appears to be real at the moment of appearance.

An analysis of phenomenal appearance reveals ten basic categories of Chen-ju. Since each category is related to the others, reference can be made to a hundred realms. Again, since each basic category is related to these hundred realms, reference can be made to one thousand of them. By adding three major divisions of spatiality, aggregate materiality, and vitality, which are related to each of the thousand realms, the total number of existential realms comes to three thousand! It is the Truth of the Mean that the worlds of phenomenal existence and their constituent elements are simultaneously empty and temporal. These three levels of truth are perfectly harmonious: "the three are one; the one is three", i.e., the three affirmations constitute a single truth; the single truth is triadic.

Hui-wen also encountered a passage in another of the Mahāyāna scriptures, the *Mahāprajñāpāramitā*, concerning three levels of knowledge: (i) "of the species of the way", (ii) "of all existence", (iii) "of the species of all existence". He saw in this the corresponding subjective dimension of his theory of the truth. Knowledge of "species of the way" clarifies distinctions and the names that are given to them. Knowledge of "existence" is the epistemological middle view that "what is" is neither "emptiness" nor "non-emptiness", neither distinction nor non-distinction. The fa have no self-nature, and are therefore void, yet they constitute momentary phenomenality. Appearance is characterized by distinctive multiplicity, and yet it is relationally unified. It can be said, therefore, that "the three thousand worlds are immanent in a single moment of thought".

This does not imply that phenomenal existence is produced by thought, but that all possible phenomenal worlds are involved in a single instance of thinking. "These three thousand realms are contained in a fleeting moment of thought. Where there is no mind, that is the end of the matter. If mind comes into being to the slightest degree, it immediately contains the three thousand. One may say neither that the mind is prior and the fa posterior, nor that the fa are prior and the mind posterior...If the fa were derived from mentality that would constitute a vertical relationship. If mentality contained all fa simultaneously, that would constitute a horizontal relationship...Neither position will do! All one can say is that mentality is all fa, and all fa are mind. Therefore, the relationship is neither vertical nor horizontal. Fa and mind are neither the same, nor are they different." The conclusion: phenomenality and mentality are mutually inclusive. In this way the apparently conflicting doctrines of the Buddhist schools are harmonized.

A third member of the first generation of T'ien-t'ai leadership, Hui-ssu (514-577) addressed himself to the problem of practice, the means of attaining to the state of enlightenment and nirvāṇa. He counseled the dual method of chih[3] and Kuan[1]. The usual translation: "concentration and insight" may be misleading. Chih means literally "stop" or "cease". "By chih," Hui-ssu wrote, "I mean to learn that all fa.... have no nature of their own. They neither come into nor go out of existence. Because they are caused by illusion and imagination they exist without really existing... Those who hold this view can stop the flow of erroneous thinking. This is called chih." Kuan means to examine thoroughly, to look deeply into the matter, thereby gaining an insight into its very nature. Through such examination we find that fa are like illusions and dreams which seem to exist but really do not... kuan means to ground one's attention on the one mind...the Mind-of-Pure-Self-Nature."[44]

Classic Chinese Buddhism reached its intellectual apex in the philosophical system articulated by Fa-tsang (643-712).[45] As a young monk he was a member of Hsuan-tsang's translation centre. He began to take issue with the Wei-Shih philosophy, however, especially after reading the *Avataṃsaka-sūtra*. His interpretation of that sūtra, known in Chinese translation as *Hua-yen*, provided the basis for the school of the same name. Despite its subtle intricacies, *Hua-yen* (Flowery-splendour) became an influential position not only in China but in Japan as well. Less than fifty years after Fa-tsang's death the emperor Shomu accepted Ke-gon (Japanese for Hua-yen or "wreath of flowers") as official Japanese ideology. The cosmic harmony about which it spoke seemed to him a perfect concept for supporting a universal Japanese state; the state itself supported the Buddhist school which promulgated the doctrine. The great Todaiji monastery with its temple housing the large bronze Sun Buddha remains a reminder of the acknowledged relevance of Fa-tsang's thought.

It was the interest of the Chinese empress, Wu-hou, that led to

Fa-tsang's most famous explication of his system. In 704 she commanded him to lecture on Hua-yen philosophy.[46] He pointed to one of the pair of golden lions "guarding" the door to the throne room of the palace in order to illustrate the ten fundamental principles of his system. (1) The gold itself symbolizes the realm of li[3], a word which signifies "principle," "rationality," "governance." The lion-figure symbolizes the realm of shih[4], a word which refers to "affair," "event," "thing," "that which is manager." The gold in itself has no manifested qualities; the lion-figure represents discriminate marks or characteristics. Yet the lion is dependent upon the gold for its existence; the gold is its primary cause, although the goldsmith is the secondary agent cause. The goldsmith could not form the lion without the gold, but the lion would not be formed out of the gold without the agency of the smith. This is the first principle: "Understanding the arousing of shih[4], the realm of phenomenal experience, through causation." (2) The second principle is called "Discriminating the emptiness of atomic reality." It consists in noting that there is nothing to the lion apart from its shape. The "lion," then, is empty of any nature apart from the gold. (3) The lion nonetheless does appear, and the third principle concerns its three characteristics: (i) from the vantagepoint of sensation it exists, this is its "imaginative-nature;" (ii) from the perspective of criticism it only appears to exist, this is its "dependency-nature;" (iii) from the viewpoint of grounding it is gold, this is its "basic reality." (4) Because the basic reality of the lion is its golden nature, there are no qualities which belong to the lion itself. Therefore the leonine characteristics are non-existent and merely products of the perceiving mind. (5) When the lion is created, there is no real birth of a lion. The gold of which the lion is crafted was before the crafting, and will remain after the destruction of the lion. There is, then, no real coming-into-existence nor passing-out-of-existence. (6) The sixth principle, "Discussing the five doctrines," follows the T'ien-t'ai attempt to harmonize all conflicting Buddhist positions according to an historical view of five periods of gradual unfolding of the full truth. (7) This principle introduces the idea of "Ten Gates to the Mysterious" through which perfect understanding can be gained.[47] (8) The lion embraces six qualities: (i) as a whole, generalness; (ii) as parts, speciality; (iii) as parts and whole stemming from a single cause, similarity;

(iv) as distinct in parts, diversity; (v) as a totality, integration; (vi) as a plurality of parts, disintegration. (i) Viewing the gold lion reveals that enlightenment and illusion are mutually related, pure mind and ignorance act simultaneously: "Once we have become enlightened, the illusory itself becomes the real, so that no other reality remains for us to enter. This is the harmonization of shih and li." (10) "Viewing the lion and the gold, the characteristics of both are extinguished completely, and the passions cease to be produced. .... The mind is as calm as the sea. Deluding thoughts are extinguished. .... We cast off our bondage, become free from hindrances, and abandon forever suffering's source. This is called 'entry into Nirvāṇa'."

It took a high degree of developed intelligence, along with dogged persistence, for Chinese to understand the subtleties of these four great philosophical schools of Buddhism—two of which came from India, and two which were products of Chinese Buddhist intellectual labour—which we have examined in all-too brief-fashion. It is not surprising that a movement emerged within popular Chinese Buddhism which, if not anti-intellectual, concentrated on practice to the neglect of philosophical theory.[48] The origins of Ching[4] t'u[3] ("Pure Land") are difficult to trace if the central practice of calling upon the name of Amitā-Buddha for assistance, or encouraging people to invoke the name, is taken as indicative of a movement's existence.

Evidence of nien[4]-fo[2] ("reciting the Buddha-name") can be found as early as the time of the Han dynasty's collapse. It was T'an-luan (476-542), however, who initiated the articulation of the position. T'an-luan was 24 when 80-year-old Vasubandhu died in India. This made a great impression on T'an-luan, the disturbing recognition that the end of an era had occurred. Nāgārjuna and Vasubandhu were the last of the great bodhisattvas in his estimation.[49] We were now living in an age far removed from the days of Śākyamuni. Conditions were such that there were no living bodhisattvas, but only ordinary human beings of mediocre, intellectual, moral and pious abilities. T'an-luan noted that Nāgārjuna had written: "When the bodhisattva seeks the stage of non-retrogression, there are two ways. One is difficult and one is easy." If any way is open in an age of decadence, it would have to be the easy way.

The clue to what the easy way entailed came from a desire uttered by Vasubandhu before his death that he be re-born in a land of happiness "with all beings, universally." The *Sukhāvatī-vyūha* ("Sūtra of the Land of Happiness") described the forty-eight vows taken by Dharmakāya when he determined to be a bodhisattva and began the arduous path toward enlightenment and nirvāṇa. Upon succeeding, he became known as Amitā-Buddha, i.e., "infinitely-enlightened one," and was viewed under two aspects: Amitābha ("infinite light") and Amitāyus ("infinite life"). The eighteenth vow was crucial for T'an-luan, who related it to the Vasubandhu desire. Dharmakāya vowed not to obtain perfect knowledge and enlightenment as long as there remained a single sentient being who, relying fully upon his grace, believing completely in his power and repeating his name, failed to be re-born in the Pure Land which he had ordained, the "Happy Land of the West." The twentieth vow promised to receive anyone who repeated his name with the intent to be re-born in the Pure Land of Amitā-Buddha. Here, then, was the easy way!

The other way, that of understanding the subtleties of the doctrine, was a difficult way. It relied solely upon self-power and the intellect. For this very reason it was treacherous, because self-reliance makes one subject to arrogance and pride, and may terminate in the cultivation of "ego-clinging," thereby proving to be a self-defeating method through "self" assertion. To appropriate the grace of Amitā-Buddha is to rely wholly upon Other-power. Whatever efforts are made in the name of O-Mi-T'o-Fo (Chinese pronunciation of Amitā-Buddha) are void of ego. It is true that a desire to be re-born is involved, but that does not matter. Vasubandhu had expressed the desire to be re-born with all creatures universally. Dharmakāya's vow included every single sentient being, including even those who in this lifetime are guilty of the "five deadly sins and ten evil acts!"

It is important to remember that the Pure Land is not to be confused with Nirvāṇa. The Pure Land is a world free of all temptations and defilements where a desireless existence is possible, thereby guaranteeing, through negative conditioning, the attainment of Nirvāṇa. T'an-luan reveals an affinity with his younger contemporary, Hui-ssū of the T'ien-t'ai school, in identifying a dual aspect of practice: chih and kuan. Chih is interpreted by T'an-luan as the concentration of thought on O-Mi-T'o-Fo and his Pure Land, trusting him to stop any tendency toward regression, and knowing that once re-born in Pure Land there will be an end to the influx of evil into body, mind, and mouth. Kuan is interpreted as the attainment of profound insight into the nature of Pure Land, and receiving after re-birth an immediate vision of O-Mi-T'o-Fo.

It was a memorial tablet to T'an-luan which led Tao-ch'o (562-645) to assume leadership in the *Ching-t'u* movement. He wrote after that experience: "T'an-luan is a great leading light of Buddhism, far surpassing me in understanding and insight, and yet he committed himself to the Easy Way." His *Compendium on the Happy Land* was an attempt to demonstrate the relevancy of Ching-t'u practice for the present age through citations from a wide variety of texts, but its primary importance lies in his reply to the critics of Pure Land Buddhism.[50]

The work of Shan-tao (613-681) established Ching-t'u as the recognized leading movement of popular Buddhism, a position which it continues to enjoy among Chinese, Korean, and Japanese Buddhists today. A disciple of Tao-ch'o, he lived in Ch'ang-an, the imperial capital, during the reigns of the first three T'ang dynasty emperors when Buddhism became the operative state ideology. He placed great emphasis as the motive for nien-fo upon personal consciousness of having committed acts of evil throughout an eternity of previous existences and the spirit of repentence which follows such awareness.

In his commentary, *Kuan'ching shu*, Shan-tao included a parable which became the hallmark of Ching-t'u expositions. Travelling westward, a pilgrim comes upon the confluence of two rivers, unfathomable, one of fire from the south, the other of water from the north. A single white path led between the converging rivers toward the west, only five inches wide, and threatened by waves of fire and water from each side. Highwaymen and wild beasts saw him hesitate and began to attack. In that moment of hesitation, convinced that to proceed in any direction would result in certain death, a voice came from the east encouraging him to take the white path toward the west, and a voice came from the west promising assistance if he would continue with singleness of purpose. The east is this world, "a house of flames;" the west is the Pure

Land. The beasts and highwaymen represent the five skandhas, the psycho-psysiological aggregates which constitute the self. The river of fire is anger and hatred; the river of water, greed and desire. The narrow white path is the singleminded aspiration to be reborn in Pure Land. Śākyamuni's is the voice from the east; O-Mi-T'o-Fo's the voice from the west. Trusting in the promise, the pilgrim persisted and completed the precarious journey through the grace of Amitā-Buddha.

Ryōsetsu Fujiwara, in his 1957 article "Nembutsu shisō no kenkyū," has pointed to the important influence of the practices of popular religious Taoism upon T'an luan's formulation of Ching-t'u. These practices included the chanting of formulae, derived from an esoteric interpretation of the *Tao-Te-Ching*, with an emphasis on the conviction that an intimate relationship holds between the speaking of secret names and the unleashing of hidden powers. It is equally possible, I believe, that T'an-luan and his colleagues were taking advantage of this popular Taoist practice in an effort to make Ching-t'u intelligible to the common people. The same relationship with popular Taoism could be maintained in the case of Chen-yen, the second great popular movement of Buddhism to develop in China.[51] Usually translated "True Word" Buddhism, a more accurate rendering would be "Words of Truth" or "Words of Genuine Reality." Reference is made in the name of the school to those meaningful sounds which, when voiced, not only reveal the hidden truth, but integrally relate the speaker to fundamental reality, evoking the power of Buddhahood through the very manifestation of that power.

The origins of Chen-yen can be traced to India's movement of Tantric Buddhism, the result of Buddhist appropriation of the *śākta* concept from the thought and practice of the extremely popular Śaivite and Vaiṣṇavite sects of Hindu mysticism. Śakti is the divine energy which was symbolized by the feminine consorts ascribed to the Hindu deities Brahmā, Viṣṇu, and Śiva. This is the cosmic energy which manifests itself in all acts of creativity and destruction, and which lies hidden within all human beings, waiting to be aroused through proper yoga disciplines.[52]

Two Indian Buddhists introduced the Tantra-yāna positions to China early in the eighth century. Śubhākarasiṃha (637-735), known as Shan Wu-wei, arrived in 716, and nine years later published his Chinese version of the germinal *Mahāvairocana-sūtra*. Usually translated as the "Great Sun Buddha," a better rendering for understanding would be "The Great Brilliance." D.T. Suzuki, in his essay "Passivity in the Buddhist Life,"[53] suggested that Buddhism's Mahāyāna movement represents a new phase of Buddhist thought in which the idea of anattā (non-ego) was replaced by the concept Buddhatā (Buddha-nature), implying a transition from emphasis on individuality and personal liberation to an outlook which is cosmological in scope.

If he is correct, then the ideas expressed in the *Mahāvairocana-sūtra* should represent the extreme limit of Mahāyāna thought because the "Great Brilliance" *is* the cosmos. It is a limitless reality, viewed under two aspects: (a) the Matrix Realm, or Cosmic Womb, the dynamic cosmic energy which unfolds as the world of myriad things, thereby enfolding all entities; (b) the Diamond Element, the self-contained potential energy, perfected individuation. The relationship between the historic Buddha and the cosmic Buddha, is expressed in terms of this "two-yet-not-two" dialectical view of cosmic Buddhahood. Śākyamuni appeared in history within spatiotemporal limits, and revealed the truth publicly in a relative and instrumental way. Mahāvairocana, on the other hand, does not appear, and remains hidden without limits, privately enjoying absolute truth as intrinsically valuable. Other scriptures and schools are esoteric, because they found their doctrines on the public discourse of the historic Buddha, an effort to communicate truth in intelligible terms. The *Mahāvairocana-sūtra* is esoteric scripture, however, because it purports to refer to the truth-in-itself as grasped in its entirety by the cosmic Buddha.

Vajrabodhi (663-741), known in Chinese as Chin Kang-chih, arrived in 720. It was he who began to interpret the doctrine and initiate disciples into the practice. Initiation required the building of sanctuaries for proper ceremonial ritual which necessitated the painting of maṇḍala, diagrams of the cosmic Buddha in both Womb and Diamond aspects. In the Womb maṇḍala fourteen hundred and sixty-one "beings," manifestations of creative energy, are pictured in spatial relationship to each other. Mahāvairocana Buddha is in the centre, surrounded by the Buddhas of the Four Cardinal Directions, each accompanied by a Bodhisattva, and also accompanied by the feminine counterparts of each, as well as varying personifications of the diverse functions performed by each of the major manifestations of cosmic energy.

From its beginning, Buddhism has described the self as nothing more than an association of five aggregates. Cosmic brilliance manifests itself in its aspect of unfolding energy in a five-fold association of "Enlightened Ones," each one of which is itself an association of Bodhisattvas. The Womb-maṇḍala pictures this in vivid detail. In the Diamond-maṇḍala the arrangement differs, but it still reveals a Buddha-body, the nine points arranged in diamond-shape in the centre to symbolize the personal or inner as over against the revealed and public symbolized in the Womb-maṇḍala. When cosmic energies are symbolized anthropologically, the maṇḍala reveals the Mystery of Body; when symbolized by Sanskrit letters, the Mystery of Speech is revealed; when symbolized by instruments appropriate to each, the maṇḍala reveals the Mystery of Mind. Both Womb-maṇḍala and Diamond-maṇḍala may be symbolized in these three ways.[54]

A third Indian, Amoghavajra (705-774), came to China as a disciple of Vajrabodhi's, and succeeded him to leadership of the school. It was his activity, especially at the imperial court, and his effort to interpret the position in terms intelligible to the Chinese, that made it the leading Buddhist sect in China for over a century and earned for him the ascription: "the great master of broad wisdom." Three emperors were initiated into the mysteries by him: Hsuan-tsung (713-755), Su-tsung (756-762) and Tai-tsung (763-779). He translated a hundred and ten texts of esoteric Buddhism into Chinese and wrote his own interpretation of the truths revealed through the school, *Memorials and Answers*. In this latter work he was able to explain the maṇḍalas in the light of the old classic schools of Yin-and-Yang, and of the Five Elements. The five central Buddhas in the maṇḍalas were interpreted as being symbolic of cosmic unfolding at the stage of the derivation of the basic elements—earth, water, fire, air and space. The inner side, the diamond elements, is identified with pure consciousness. Thus the material and the mental are viewed as inseparable, representing the objective and subjective dimensions of unitary experiencing: once again, "Two but not two."

Following in the wake of T'ien-t'ai and Hua-Yen practice, Amoghavajra attempted to relate Chen-yen to the other Buddhist schools which were known at that time in China. The unique, and consciously Chinese, feature of his account is that the second and third stages in historical unfolding of the truth are pre-Buddhist Chinese schools of philosophy. There are ten stages in all, grounded on the level of animal passions.

Confucianism, with its secular virtues put forth for the civilizing of humanity, and popular Taoism, with its hope for immortality and attainment of a heavenly existence, constitute the second and third stages. There follow two basic Hīnayāna schools which identify Nirvāṇa with personal extinction; the Wei-shih, the San-lun, the T'ien-t'ai, and the Hua Yen expositions of enlightenment. All these teach the exoteric, public gospel of the historic Buddha, with the purpose of providing an instrumental truth which will lead to Nirvāṇa. The tenth stage is that of Chen-yen, where the esoteric gospel is revealed, the inner, intrinsic truth of Nirvāṇa which characterizes Buddha-nature in its essence of self-enjoyment.

Because the exoteric truth is instrumental, and the esoteric is intrinsic, there is only one vehicle of liberation and it is only through Chen-yen that it is fully revealed. "Now there are nine kinds of medicine for the diseases of the mind, but the most they can do is sweep away the surface dust and dispel the mind's confusion. Only in the 'Diamond Palace' (a two-pronged reference to the *Diamond Head Sūtra* and to the Diamond Maṇḍala initiation) do we find the secret treasury opened wide to dispense its precious truths. To enjoy them or reject them—this is for everyone to decide in his own mind. No one else can do it for you; you must realize it for yourself."

After Amoghavajra's death one of his Chinese disciples assumed leadership as Abbot of East Pagoda Hall. Hui-kuo (746-805) was responsible for the initiation of Kūkai, the Japanese pilgrim who accepted the apostolate to carry Chen-yen to Japan. He was overwhelmingly successful in his mission, and "Shingon" Buddhism became very popular in Japan.[55] It has made an indelible mark on traditional Japanese culture, ranging from arts inspired in the maṇḍala symbolisms to the first syllabary of written Japanese.

The initiation Kūkai underwent under the direction of Hui-kuo involved two stages: the revelation of the mysteries of the Womb-maṇḍala, and the revelation of the mysteries of the Diamond-maṇḍala. It was during the ritual of the first stage that Kūkai learned the essential "Three Mysteries." These consist in the knowledge that Vairocana's cosmic manifestation is triple in nature: (i) bodily action, (ii) speech, (iii) mental thought. Now body, speech, and mind are characteristics of every man, which signifies that the secrets of Buddha-nature are hidden within every man. The great affirmation which is made in the revelation of the "Three Mysteries" is that Buddha-nature is present within human personality, that it is therefore "attainable" in this corporeal existence, and that this is accomplished through the manifestation of cosmic energy in body, speech, and thought, thereby expressing the esoteric truth: "Buddha-in-me; I-in-Buddha." The penetration of the mysteries of the body requires knowledge of the mūdrās, the proper hand symbols for invoking each of the Buddha and Bodhisattva energies, as well as the postures of meditation, and the proper method of handling ritual instruments. These are the "secrets of touch." To penetrate the mysteries of speech it is necessary to learn how to articulate correctly the "true words", the "secrets of sound" which, when uttered, place one's body in touch with the vibrations of the creative Word. The mysteries of mind require for their penetration an understanding of the five approaches for grasping the truth. After all this, however, Kūkai reported that Hui-kuo "informed me that the esoteric scriptures are so abstruse that their meaning cannot be conveyed except through art," an art which results from a mastery of the three mysteries. The process of artistic creativity evokes the Buddha-nature or cosmic energy which lies hidden within the artist. Truth works of art manifest that "Great Brilliance" in its purity.

5. TRIUMPH: C'HAN-NA—THE TOTAL SINICIZATION OF BUDDHISM[56]

The history of this Buddhist school is a stormy one. There remains serious controversy about the correct interpretaion of its development and the import of its teaching and practice. There is agreement that Ch'an has represented a truly revolutionary movement within Buddhism beginning with the re-interpretation of the position by Hui-neng (605-706), as recorded in the *Platform Scripture*.[57] Hu Shih and Daisetz Taitaro Suzuki engaged for years in bitter controversy over the nature of that revolution, a dialogue which reached a climax in their exchange of views in the third volume of the journal *Philosophy East and West* (1953).[58]

Hu Shih insisted that within the movement itself Hui-neng and his successors led an iconoclastic struggle for eventual control by radicals and heretics, signifying a Taoist revolt against Buddhism from within, successful enough to transform Buddhism into a thoroughly Chinese position. The revolt surfaced as a struggle for official leadership on the part of 8th century Ch'anists. In the previous generation Hui-neng had lost his bid to succeed to the patriarchate of Ch'an. His rival's disciple, P'u-chi, later assumed the mantle of leadership. Hu Shih described the challenge as beginning with "denunciation of the most highly honored school of the empire" and continuing with "a revolutionary pronouncement of a new Ch'an which renounces Ch'an itself and is therefore no Ch'an at all."[59] Shen-hui was exiled by the emperor, but returned in the wake of a rebellion, making fund-raising appearances to assist in the financing of the uprising. The revolt was successful, and the new emperor stripped P'u-chi of his office and named Shen-hui the legitimate seventh patriarch of Ch'an-na.

It was during his exile in 734 that Shen-hui abandoned the practice of "sitting in meditation" which had been normative practice for Ch'an-na, in favour of the cultivation of "no-mind" and "seeing one's original nature." To illustrate the extreme nature of the iconoclasm, Hu Shih cites the words of Hsuan-chien, a leading Ch'an master of the ninth century: "Here, there is neither Buddha, nor patriarchs. ....Bodhisattvas are only dung-heap coolies Nirvāṇa and Bodhi are dead stumps to tie your donkeys to. The twelve divisions of sacred scriptures are only lists of ghosts, sheets of paper fit only for wiping the pus from your boils. .... Have these anything to do with your salvation? The wise do not seek the Buddha. The Buddha is the great murderer who has seduced so many people into the pitfalls of the prostituting devil."[60]

Suzuki, in reply, agreed that "the meaning of Ch'an as meditation or quiet thinking or contemplation no longer holds good after Hui-neng. ....It was Hui-neng's revolutionary movement that achieved this severance."[61] The Chinese words Ch'an-na have been used to reproduce the sound of the Sanskrit word dhyāna which referred to "meditation," an eight-staged spiritual exercise which began in single-minded concentration and ended in total mental calmness, the elimination of even the consciousness of making-no-distinctions. Both Hu Shih and Suzuki agree that Chinese Ch'an rejects the very core of the Indian meditation tradition which gave it birth and for which it is named. For Suzuki, however, this does not represent an iconoclastic movement which in final analysis is a rejection of Buddhism, but rather a stripping away of all the accretions of philosophy and practice which constitute the total history of Buddhism in India and China, to return directly to the very heart of Śākyamuni's enlightenment experience. "In Zen," writes Suzuki, "there must be a general mental upheaval which destroys the old accumulations of intellectuality and lays down a foundation for a new faith; there must be the awakening of a new sense which will review the old things from an angle of perception entirely and most refreshingly new. In dhyāna there are none of these things, for it is merely a quiet exercise of the mind."[62]

This interpretation of Ch'an agrees that the first satisfactory articulation of the true enlightenment experience occurs only in China, whether the articulation is attributed to the semi-legendary Bodhidharma, to whom tradition ascribes the founding of Ch'an-a late in the fifth century, or to Hui-neng late in the seventh. Bodhidharma is identified as twenty-eighth in the line of individuals who secretly and orally transmitted the full truth which the Buddha himself could convey at the time only privately to a single disciple, and even then not through speech but merely through the subtle gesture of smiling while holding a lotus-flower. According to this tradition, or legend, the first public exposition of full Buddhist truth occurs on Chinese soil! In other words, there is no evidence of the position in Indian records—there could not be. On the other hand, Hui-neng is pictured as a lay neophyte in Hung-jen's monastery, who wins out over Shen-hsui, acknowledged by all members of the community as the monk who had the most profound insight into the secret teaching. The implication of this is that from Bodhidharma, the first truth patriarch, to Hung-jen, the fifth legitimate patriarch, the doctrine was misunderstood!

In this regard, it is interesting to note that the Ch'an-na tradition espoused in turn three scriptures as the basic source of true understanding. Each substitution marked not only an advance in understanding, but an apparent rejection of the interpretation which had gone before. That the third "scripture" was not part of the Indian Buddhist corpus, but a document written out of the Chinese controversy over correct understanding, indicates the purely Chinese nature of the Ch'an-na school from the late 7th century on.

Bodhidharma introduced the *Laṅkāvatāra-sūtra* to China in 470 and based his teaching on it.[63] The *sūtra* represents as critique of the two major techniques advocated by traditional Mahāyāna schools, intellectual analysis and multi-staged meditation yoga. The Buddha had avoided these one-sided extremes in favour of the middle way of intuitive grasping of inner truth. Bodhidharma considered the verse: "Avoid the erroneous reasonings of the philosophers and seek this self-realization of noble wisdom" to be the major thesis of the sūtra, and is reported to have expanded on the statement with the following commentary: "There is no Buddha but your own thoughts. Buddha is Tao. Tao is Ch'an-na. Ch'an-na cannot be understood by the definitions of the intellectuals. Ch'an-na is a person's successful seeing into his own fundamental nature. ... I have come from India only to teach you that Buddha is thought. ... I have no interest in monastic rules nor ascetic practices, nor miraculous powers, nor merely sitting in meditation."[64] Bodhidharma did recommend a dhyāna exercise however: Pi[4] Kuan[1] ("wall-concentration") which literally involves sitting before a blank wall to so concentrate the mind that it purges itself of all sensations, memories, imaginings, and ideas, and becomes pure, without "external defilement."

It was Hung-jen, self-proclaimed 5th patriarch following a rift within the movement in mid seventh century, who substituted the *Vajracchedikā-sūtra* with the remark that it was "easier" to comprehend.[65] Its main thrust was the description of how to engage properly in the six ideal activities from the stance of emptiness or egolessness. Phenomena were interpreted as projections of the mind which in turn defile the mind. From this concern Hung-jen formulated his major theme: "Keep watch over your original mind!" This entailed continual wiping off the "dust" which settled on the mind in the form of perceptions and ideations, obscuring the clarity of originally pure mind, so that original mind could continue to shine forth. The technique was called k'an[4] chin ("look at, or, watch purity"). There was the necessity to wipe the mirror of the mind clear of accumulated "dust" before the "loo ing at" or "guarding" could occur. Implicit was a position of "gradual enlightenment."

Another rift occurred immediately after Hung-jen's death. It was the new Chinese document which surfaced out of the polemic that became authoritative for the splinter movement which triumphed finally in the next century, *The Platform Scripture of the Sixth Patriarch*, ascribed to Hui-neng. Contained in this new document is the account of the competition for succession to the patriarchate. It took the form of rival efforts to state the true Ch'an-na position in poetic quatrains. Shen-hsiu, who represented the normative interpretation according to the way in which Hung-jen's disciples understood his message, wrote:

"The body is the tree of enlightenment;
The mind is the stand for a clear mirror.
Keep it polished at all times;
And do not permit dust to settle on it."[66]

Hui-neng's reinterpretation of the position was stated in direct opposition:

"There is no tree of enlighenment;
The clear mirror has no stand
From the beginning there is nothing,
What can any dust settle on?"[67]

To "look at" original purity implies a distinction which reveals being at a distance from full enlightenment, and furthermore involves an activity which prevents enlightenment, so that it cannot be considered even a partial stage on the road to enlightenment. Hui-neng proposed that K'an-ching be replaced by chien[4] hsing[4] ("seeing original nature"). This is immediate insight, implying sudden enlightenment." In place of Hung-jen's "Keep watch over our original mind," Hui-neng, denying that it is possible to watch" one's "original mind" (what is there to watch? and what is it that watches?), demanded: "Show me your original face before birth!"

The proliferation of Ch'an-na sects was rapid and confusing. Kuih Tsung-mi (780-841), a Ch'anist by persuasion, has provided us with his comparative analysis of the "various schools of Ch'an mutually conflicting with each other." He identified 100 "houses." "The doctrines preached by these established sects are contradictory and obstructive to each other. Some of them regard 'emptiness' as the foundation; some regard 'wisdom' as the source. Some say that only silence is true; some that walking and sitting are right. Some claim that from morning to evening all actions arising from the view of discrimination are false; some say all discriminate doings are real. Some preserve all the myriad practices; some suppress even Buddhas. Some give free course to their will; some restrain the mind. Some respect the sūtras and vinayas (i.e., the original documents of Buddhist teaching) as authorities to rely on; others regard both of them as obstacles to the Tao." (the translation is by Jan Yum-hua.)[68]

In true Chinese fashion, Tsung-mi attempts to interpret these ten houses of Ch'an-na as being limited perspectives on the truth, but capable of harmonization. Again, in a different passage, he suggests that the differences might be interpreted in quite another way (the underlining is mind): "I compared each of these sects and found out their doctrines as described. Should one take my words and ask the scholars who belong to those sects, all of them would refute my view. If one asks about existence, the reply would be emptiness; or to a question about emptiness, they would answer existence. Some of them may say that both alternatives are wrong, or both are unobtainable, or cultivation and non-cultivation are the same, or some similar answers. The reason is that these scholars are always afraid to be trapped by words, or to be hindered by what they have obtained. They therefore, reject the questions, whatever is asked."[69]

This refusal to be "trapped by words" is emphasized in the "four theses of Ch'an" ascribed to Bodhidharma:

"A special transmission outside the scriptures;
No dependence upon words and letters;
Direct pointing to the soul of man;
Seeing into one's nature and the attainment of Buddhahood."

Suzuki finds in these four statements the complete doctrine of Ch'an: "In a word they mean that Zen (Japanese transcription of Ch'an) has its own way of pointing to the nature of one's own being and that when this is done, one attains to Buddhahood i which all the contradictions and disturbances caused by the intellect are entirely harmonized in a unity of higher order."[70]

Fung Yu-lan, dean of modern historians of Chinese philosophy, suggests that "all Ch'anists.... irrespective of which interpretation they accept, emphasize five main points: (1) 'The highest truth is inexpressible;' (2) 'Spiritual cultivation cannot be cultivated;' (3) 'In the last resort nothing is gained;' (4) 'There is nothing much in Buddhist teaching;' (5) 'In carrying water and chopping wood: therein lies the wonderful Tao.'"[71] The four "theses" of Bodhidharma and the five propositions cited by Professor Fung express very clearly the way in which the Ch'an-na movement can be viewed as standing at the end of a centuries-long effort to comprehend Buddhist enlightenment on the part of concerned Chinese. At the outset there was a perplexing array of sūtras and sects, each one purporting to present and interpret the words of the Enlightenment One through a language and a logic radically at variance with Chinese modes of literary expression and philosophical argument. It was necessary for the earliest Chinese Buddhists to become intellectually Indianized. The work of the Neo-Taoists provided a linguistic and problematic framework into which the Buddhist sūtras and commentaries could be translated and made intelligible to the Chinese mind. Such translation resulted in a reinterpretation of the positions and the earliest division between an Indian Buddhist tradition and a Chinese Buddhist tradition occurred. Still the Chinese Buddhists remained perplexed at the great diversity of interpretation to be encountered in the seemingly endless stream of documents which was to constitute the multi-volumed Chinese Tripiṭaka.

The first efforts to deal creatively with such a wide range of apparently inconsistent interpretations involved the typically Chinese concern with history, the chronological ordering of the sūtras and commentaries, with the suggestion that the Buddha not only tempered his teaching in accordance with the relative ability of specific audiences to understand, but also provided a graded sequence of expositions, beginning with the simpler Theravāda positions and gradually progressing to more complex Mahāyāna teachings. T'ien-t'ai and Hua-yen schools adopted this technique for the harmonization as a base for their new systematic presentations of Buddhism. In Ch'an these problems of translation from Sanskrit to Pāli, of interpretation of positions rooted in an Indian intellectual milieu, and of diverse historical traditions, are set aside as not only irrelevant but potentially harmful to a truly existential concern with being enlightened. Given this somewhat anti-intellectual and strongly experimental stance, a Ch'an-na Buddhist is liberated from the historical tradition, and Chinese Buddhism finally reaches the stage of standing apart from Indian Buddhism. A comparison of the four "theses" and the five propositions cited above with certain ideas which had been expressed by Chuang-tzū indicates that, whether conscious or not, Ch'anists came close to doing what Hu-shih has suggested did occur, viz. instigating a Taoist revolt from within the Buddhist movement and, in a sense, transforming Buddhism into a new New-Taoist philosophic position.

6. Conclusion

At the outset of this chapter I suggested that the successful transplantation of Buddhism to the soil of Chinese culture was made possible by a re-articulation of Taoism at the time of the Han dynasty collapse. This renewal of Taoist thought prepared the ground linguistically and conceptually for an intelligible translation and interpretation of Buddhism to the Chinese mind and spirit. The high point of Chinese Buddhist development is reached with the articulation of a full Taoist-Buddhist synthesis in Ch'an-na thought during the 8th and 9th centuries. In the process of developing that synthesis, Taoism itself was transformed through association with Buddhist thought and practice, just as Buddhism had been thoroughly transmuted into a Chinese movement through interpretations which relied heavily upon Taoist words and concepts. From henceforth Chinese "gentle persons" would be good Confucianists and Legalists when engaged in official public business or family responsibilities, yet become Buddhists and Taoists at times when it was propitious to withdraw from the world of politics and economics and social institutions and enter upon a period of private retirement.

The impact which Taoism and Buddhism had on the development of Chinese civilization has been profound and manifold. The Buddhist influence in Chinese cultural history ranges all the way from techniques and subject-matter of traditional brush-stroke painting to the analysis of Chinese phonology; from the composition and performance of works for traditional woodwind and stringed musical instruments to the study of logic. This strong Buddhist presence in subsequent Chinese civilization can be seen most clearly in the history of the arts. Noting that "Buddhist works make up the vast majority of existing Chinese sculpture, if we exclude pottery tomb figures," Fong Chow, Associate Curator of Far Eastern Art at the Metropolitan Museum of Art, suggests that "the effect of Buddhism on China accounts for some of the greatest religious sculpture in the world."[72]

Chinese Buddhist sculpture begins with the monumental stone carvings in the famed cave temples constructed in North China under the auspices of the Turkish Wei dynasties. Central Asian pieces, created after the style of the Indian Buddhist Mathurā and Gāndhāra traditions, served as the models. Later, during the post-Wei period, the Gupta tradition was introduced to further modify Chinese Buddhist sculptural style. Indeed, Hsuan-tsang included nine Gupta pieces along with the sūtras and commentaries in the items which he brought back to China in the early years of the T'ang dynasty. Throughout the T'ang, and continuing with the elegant Kuan-yin statuary of the early Sung, adaptations of these Indian styles created a Buddhist sculptural tradition which became distinctively Chinese. The same kind of artistic adaptation led in the construction of temples and pagodas to a uniquely Chinese Buddhist architectural tradition.

In the graphic arts Buddhist influence can be seen especially in the development of landscape painting and calligraphy. It has been customary to divide T'ang landscapists into two schools named after the break which occurred in the Ch'an-na tradition because of the controversy concerning who was the authentic Sixth Patriarch, Shen-hsiu or Hui-neng. The "Northern School" of landscape painting took on a "realistic" or "naturalistic" appearance in its depictions of "mountains-and-water;"[73] the "Southern School" was "impressionistic," concerned only with a "seeing-into-one's-own-nature" by means of the quickly executed depiction of the painter's initial instinctive reaction to "mountains-and-water." Wang Wei, the early 8th century landscape artist and poet, summed up the "Southern approach" in his well-known rule: "When you paint, use your instincts more than your brush".[74]

Much Chinese painting of this period is characterized by subject-matter which is explicitly Buddhist, but the profound influence of Buddhist mentality upon the graphic arts is found rather in the technique. The principle of economy in stroke, utilization of a few suggestive, yet decisive lines applied quickly, almost spontaneously, became popular during the latter part of the T'ang dynasty and arose out of the southern Ch'an emphasis on sudden enlightenment. Although the Imperial Academy of Art, organized during the Sung dynasty, was consciously neo-Confucian in its orientation, emphasizing a much more rational and intellectual appraoch to painting, the Buddhist influence was still at work as can be seen especially in the important Ma-Hsia school of landscape painting which took as its key principle: "Everything in one corner" or "Paint only one of the four corners." The idea of creating such an asymmetrical focal point, and merely suggesting—if not omitting altogether—incidental details, grew out of the insistence on the part of Ch'an masters that the mind be attentive and practice total concentration.

Outside the Sung Academy the great Ch'an graphic artists of the early thirteenth century, Mu Ch'i, Liang K'ai, Ying Yu-chien, and others, were at work in Buddhist monasteries. For them there was no concern with the subject matter per se, whether they were engaged in painting or calligraphy, but only with the use of the brush in transferring ink to paper, a use arising out of the flash of sudden insight and characterized by disciplined spontaneity.

A parallel development occurred in poetry. Many poets suffered a similar influence from Ch'an insight and concerned themselves more with the technique of working with words in "spontaneous" and lyrical fashion, having little concern with subject-matter, while other poets focused attention consciously on Buddhist themes. The best known of the latter to English readers is Po Chu-i (772-846).[75] Po was a government official by profession, a poet by vocation, and a Buddhist by persuasion. During most of his mature life he was an ardent Ch'anist, but in his later years became a devotee of the Pure Land School. His poetry includes works in which the essence of Buddhist doctrine is set forth, works in which experience is explicitly interpreted through Buddhist eyes, and works which do not deal directly with matters Buddhist but in which there is continual employment of Buddhist terms, phrases, images.

Chinese Buddhism reached an apogee during the T'ang dynasty, but its mark was made so profoundly upon the Chinese mind and spirit that subsequent developments in philosophy, religion and the arts must be viewed as efforts to weave Buddhist insights and images into a rich synthesis which took as its major strands the Confucian, Taoist, and Buddhist traditions.

The Confucian tradition was affected deeply by the permeation of Buddhist ideas and concepts. A resurgent neo-Confucianism was to become the dominating intellectual force during the long-lived Sung dynasty (960-1279). Its beginnings can be traced to some isolated Confucian voices raised in protest against Buddhist dominance during the T'ang dynasty.[76] The very protests reveal the appropriation of Buddhist language and presuppositions. This unconscious utilization of Buddhist thought continues in the work of the Sung "cosmologists"[77] so that, when Chu Hsi works out the great Neo-Confucian "Summa", the imprint of Buddhism cannot be hidden or denied!

Notes

1. For brief accounts of the life of Siddhārtha Gautama v. Wm. Theodore de Bary (ed.), *Sources of Indian Tradition*, New York: Columbia University Press, 1958, chapter 2; Henry Clarke Warren (tr.), *Buddhism in Translations*, New York: Athenaeum, 1963, chapter 1.

2. The text of the Deer Park sermon in English translation appears in Wm. Theodore de Bary, op. cit., pp. 15 ff.; S. Radhakrishnan and C.A. Moore (eds.), *A Source Book in Indian Philosophy*, Princeton: Princeton University Press, 1957, pp. 274 ff.

3. For texts in which "dependent origination", "momentariness", and "impermanence" are discussed v. Wm. Theodore de Bary, op. cit., pp. 17 ff.; S. Radhakrishnan and C.A. Moore, op. cit., pp. 278 ff.; Henry Clarke Warren, op. cit., chapter 2.

4. *Van* means "to hold dear", "to desire", "to love", "to seek", "to obtain". The Greek goddess *Venus* derives her name from this same root: "the loved one", "the desired one". The English word "win" is related to the root as well, signifying the satisfactory termination of a grasping process begun in desire. *Nir* is the form of *nis* which appears before a sonent, meaning "out", "forth"; in compounds: "without", "not", "lacking".

5. For information about Aśoka's conversion to Buddhism and his application of Buddhist principles to law and politics. *v.* Wm. Theodore de Bary, op. cit., pp. 142 ff.; A.L. Basham, *The Wonder That Was India: A Survey of the Culture of the Indian Sub-Continent Before the Coming of the Muslims*, New York: Grove Press, 1954, pp. 53 ff.; E. Hultzsch (ed.), *Inscriptions of Aśoka*, London, 1925; V.A. Smith, *Aśoka* (3rd ed.), Oxford, 1920.

6. The word *dharma* (a variant of *dharman*) has several associated meanings as it is used in Buddhist writing. *dhṛ* is the root, meaning "to hold or support", "to carry", "to make firm", "to hold fast", "to withstand", "to decree", "to remain or continue". *Dharman* then, is (a) that which holds fast, persists, endures, or (b) that which is established or decreed. It comes to be used to refer to (a) permanent reality, those basic elements which resist change and transformation, and also to (b) regularity in behaviour, whether fixed custom, legal ordinance, or ethical norm. Arthur Waley, however, argues, in a note to his *The Real Tripiṭaka* (London: George Allen & Unwin, 1952, p. 267) that 'category' is the best translation: "The categories of Buddhist philosophy are mainly concerned with the abstract and mental.... The common European translation of *dharma* by words such as 'element', 'component', etc., is therefore misleading."

7. For a fuller discussion of this position *v.* H.V. Guenther, op. cit., *Philosophy in Theory and Practice*, Baltimore: Penguin, 1972, chapter II; David J. Kalupahana, *Buddhist Philosophy: A Historical Analysis*, Honolulu: The University Press of Hawaii, 1976; Junjiro Takakusu, *The Essenitals of Buddhist Philosophy*, Honolulu: The University Press of Hawaii, 1956, chapter IV.

8. For a fuller discussion of this position *v.* H.V. Guenther, op. cit., chapter III; D.J. Kalupahana, loc. cit.; J. Takakusu, op. cit., chapter V.

9. For analyses of Mādhyamika *v.* H.V. Guenther, op. cit., chapter V; D.J. Kalupahana, op. cit., chapter 11; T.R.V. Murti, *The Central Philosophy of Buddhism: A Study of the Mādhyamika System* London: George Allen & Unwin, 1955; Richard H. Robinson, *Early Mādhyamika in India and China*, Madison: University of Wisconsin Press, 1967. Selections in English translation from the *Mādhyamika-śāstra* appear in Radhakrishnan and Moore, op. cit., pp. 340 ff.

10. For analyses of their system *v.* Surendranath Dasgupta, *Indian Idealism*, Cambridge: Cambridge University Press, 1962, chapters, 4, 5; H.V. Guenther, op. cit., chapter IV; D.J. Kalupahana, op. cit., chapter 12; P.S. Sastri, *Indian Idealism* (2 volumes), Delhi/Varansai: Bharatiya Vidya Prakashan, 1976 in which Vijñānavāda Buddhism is compared with Mādhyamika and Advaita Vedānta. A translation of Vasubandhu's basic writing was done by Clarence H. Hamilton from the Chinese version prepared by Hsuantsang: *Wei Shih Er Shih Lun or The Treatise in Twenty Stanzas on Representation-only*, New Haven: American Oriental Society, 1938.

11. The term *tathāgata-garbha* was used sparingly in the literature of this tradition. It was not fully developed until the Chinese school of *Huayen* Buddhism adopted the short treatise on the Awakening of Faith (said to have

been translated into Chinese in 551 c.e., but probably written by a Chinese Buddhist at that time). V. the "Introduction" to *The Awakening of Faith Attributed to Asvaghosha*, translated with commentary by Yoshito S. Hakeda, New York: Columbia University Press, 1967, p. 10.

12. *Dhamma-pada* is the Pāli equivalent for *Dharma-pada*, perhaps best rendered into English as "correct pathway" or "Guide to Right Behavior". Sarvepalli Radhakrishnan's translation into English is available with the Pali text: *The Dhammapada*, New York: Oxford University Press, 1954, or without the original: Radhakrishnan and Moore, op. cit., pp. 292 ff. Narada Thera's translation into English accompanied by the Shih Liao-Chan Chinese text appears in *Bilingual Buddhist Series: Sutras & Scriptures*, volume one, Taipei: Buddhist Culture Service, 1962, pp. 29 ff.

13. This radical contrast in grammatical structure is evident whether we use the older nineteenth century language structure classification of flectional, isolating, agglutinative, or adopt a more modern method which positions postitive languages along an analytic-synthetic scale ranging from free forms (Chinese appears at this extreme) to bound forms (classic Indo-European toward this end).

14. For analyses of the work of Tung Chung-shu v. Fung Yu-lan, *History of Chinese Philosophy*, New York: Macmillan, 1960, pp. 191-203; Yao Shen-yu, "The Cosmological and Anthropological Philosophy of Tung Chung-shu" in *Journal of the North China Branch of the Royal Asiatic Society*, volume 73 (1948), pp. 40-68. Selections in English translation from his writings appear in Wing-tsit Chan, *A Source Book in Chinese Philosophy*, Princeton: Princeton University Press, 1963, chapter 14; Wm. Theodore de Bary, *Sources of Chinese Tradition* New York: Columbia University Press, 1960, pp. 162-8, 201-03, 216-8; E.R. Hughes, *Chinese Philosophy in Classical Times*, London: Dent, 1954, pp. 293 ff.

15. Wri[2]-wei[2]-; wri signifying "being empty of" and wei meaning "purposive or causative action". v. chapter 2, 3, 10, 37 *et possim*.

16. v. especially chapter 40.

17. v. chapter 8 and the reference to the Marquis of Lu and the Seabird in chapter 18.

18. Selections in English translation from the writings of these Neo-Taoists can be found in Wing-tsit Chan, op. cit., chapter 19. For analyses of the Neo-Taoist position v. Kenneth Chen, "Neo-Taoism and the *Prajñā* School during the Wei and Chin Dynasties" in *Chinese Culture*, volume 1 (1957), pp. 33-46; Fung Yu-lan, *History*, volume 2, chapters V and VI; V.T. T'ang, "Wang Pi's New Interpretation of the *I Ching* and Lun-Yu" in *Harvard Journal of Asiatic Studies*, volume 10 (1947), pp. 124-61.

19. Yu[3]: the word means "there is", "there are", "to have", "to be present".

20. Wu[2]: the word means "without" or "lacking".

21. His commentary on the *I-Ching* helps to clarify his position. Appendix One refers to the twenty-fourth hexagram *FU*[2], "Going back", "returning". "Don't we see the core of Heaven and Earth in *FU*[2]?" writes Wang. "*FU*[2]

stands for the reversal to the original body. That origin is the mind-and-heart of Heaven and Earth." There are a multitude of things, an endless process of changes and transformations, associated with Heaven and Earth, and yet the root-origin, the heart-and-core of Heaven and Earth, is absolutely quiet, perfectly empty. It must be made clear that the tranquility which marks the end of activity is not opposed to activity, nor is the silence which marks the end of speech opposed to speech. Activity is grounded and completed in tranquility; speech is grounded and completed in silence; multiplicity is grounded and completed in unity; fullness of being is grounded and completed in emptiness. Appendix Three refers to fifty "units", only forty-nine of which are used. Wang Pi suggests that this represents the relationship between the ground of being and the beings that there are. "One" is both the origin of numerical series, and the ultimate number. Yu^3—all that there is—is multiple, and like a series finite. The unity which orders multiplicity, and upon which multiplicity depends, is non-finite, and hence empty of all relationships.

22. $Chih^4 jen^2$ is perhaps most literally rendered into English as a "person who has arrived at the ultimate limit of person-hood."

23. Selections in English translation can be found in Wm. Theodore de Bary, *Sources of Chinese Tradition*, pp. 274-280.

24. For a brief analysis of the discussion which arose concerning the doctrine of saṃsāra v. Fung Yu-lan, *History*, volume two, pp. 284-292. Fuller treatments can be found in Derk Bodde, "The Chinese View of Immortality" in *Review of Religion*, volume 6 (1942), pp. 369-374; Hu Shih, "The Concept of Immortality in Chinese Thought" in *Harvard Divinity School Bulletin* (1946), pp. 26-43; Walter Liebenthal, "The Immortality of the Soul in Chinese Thought" in *Monumenta Nipponica*, volume 8 (1952), pp. 327-397.

25. *v.* T'ang Yung-t'ung, "On 'Ko-yi': The Earliest Method by which Indian Buddhism and Chinese Thought were Synthesized" in W.R. Inge (ed.), *Radhakrishnan: Comparative Studies in Philosophy*, London: George Allen & Unwin, 1951, pp. 276-286.

26. Two examples will suffice to illustrate the problem. Nirvāṇa was rendered $nieh^1 p'an^2$ in some documents, *nieh* signifying "knead", "make", "fabricate", and *p'an* meaning "stop", "happiness", "retirement cottage". This made possible a wide range of interpretation of the significance of the state of *Nirvāṇa* from the minimal "cessation of desire" to the maximal "paradise". *Dhyāna*, the word for "meditation" which was derived from "thinking about" or "setting the mind upon," was "transliterated" by $ch'an^2 na^4$. *Ch'an* referred to the levelling of land for construction of an altar, to the sacrifices associated with fertility rites pertaining to mountains and springs, and also to abdication or resignation from political responsibilities. *Na* meant "there", "that", "where", "what", "which", "tranquil", "quiet". On the one hand there is implicit reference to withdrawal and quiet resignation, on the other an intended reference to worship. As many observers have pointed out, *dhyāna* changed its basic nature in Chinese *ch'an-na* tradition. Other factors were involved, of course, including disciplinary techniques in popular religious Taoism, but the very nature of "transliteration" into Chinese played an im-

portant role. These early difficulties of interpretation through correlating concepts and symbols portended the failure of efforts to introduce Indian Buddhism successfully into Chinese thought and culture. In the long run a greater success was registered, however, because these problems of language and concept transmission forced the Sinicization of Buddhism, thereby making it an integral part of Chinese intellectual and cultural history from that time forward. What has been said thus far might give the false impression that the Sinicization of Buddhism was effected exclusively through the Taoist intellectual tradition. Confucianism played a role as well. For a study of this dimension of Sinicization v. Hajime, Nakamura "The Influence of Confucian Ethics on the Chinese Translations of Buddhist Sutras" in *Sino-Indian Studies*, volume 5, part 3/4 (1957), pp. 156-170.

27. For a discussion of the "7 schools and 6 houses" v. Fung Yu-lan, *History*, volume II, pp. 243-257. Selections in English translation from these traditions appear in Chan Wing-tsit, op. cit., chapter 20.

28. v. Richard H. Robinson, *Early Mādhyamika in India and China*, Madison: University of Wisconsin Press, 1967, chpater III.

29. v. Fung Yu-lan, *History*, volume II, pp. 258-270; Walter Liebenthal, *Chao Lun: The Treatises of Seng-Chao* Hong Kong, 1968,; Richard H. Robinson, op. cit., chapter VI.

30. v. Chan Wing-tsit, op. cit., pp. 344-349; R.H. Robinson, op. cit., pp. 228-232.

31. Chan, Wing-tsit, op. cit., pp. 350-356; R.H. Robinson, op. cit., pp. 222-227.

32. v. R.H. Robinson, op. cit., pp. 212-221.

33. v. Fung Yu-lan, *History*, volume II, pp. 270-283.

34. v. Chan Wing-tsit, op. cit., chapter 22; Fung Yu-lan, *History*, volume II, pp. 293-298.

35. Translated by Samuel Beal, New York: Paragon Reprints, 1968. For reconstructions of the life and travel of Hsuan-tsang v. Rene Grousset, *In The Footsteps of the Buddha*, London: G. Routledge & Sons, Ltd., 1932; Hui-li, *The Life of Hsuan-tsang*, Peking, Foreign Languages Press, 1959, (an older translation re-printed in India: *Hwui-Li, The Life of Hiuen-Tsang*, Delhi: Academica Asiatica, 1973); Arthur Waley, *The Real Tripiṭaka*, London: George Allen & Unwin, 1952.

36. Hsi-yu chi, *Monkey* (tr. by Arthur Waley), London: George Allen & Unwin, 1942.

37. A full translation along with resume and critical introduction has been done by Wei Tat under the title *Ch'eng Wei-Shih Lun: Doctrine of Mere Consciousness*, by Tripitaka-Master Hsuan Tsang, Hong Kong: The Ch'eng Wei-Shih Lun Publications Committee, 1973,. Selections in English translation appear in Chan Wing-tsit, op. cit., chapter 23.

38. Wei Tat (tr.), *Ch'eng Wei-shih Lun*, p. 505 (Book V, para. I, no. 1).

39. Ibid., pp. 105 ff. (Book II, paras. I, II).

40. Ibid., pp. 129 ff. (Book II, para. II, no. 4).

41. A traditional summation of the *Wei-shih* doctrine. For an analysis

v. Fung Yu-lan, *History*, volume II, pp. 299-338.

42. For analyses of *T'ien-t'ai v.* Kenneth Ch'en, *Buddhism in China*: A *Historical Survey*, Princeton: Princeton University Press, 1964, pp. 303-313; Fung Yu-lan, *History*, volume II, pp. 360-385; J. Takakusu, op. cit., chapter IX. Selections in English translation from *The Method of Concentration and Insight*, a work by Hui-ssu, one of the "patriarchs" of the school, appear in Chan Wing-tsit, op. cit., chapter 24.

43. For selections in English translation of *The Profound Meaning of the Scripture of the Lotus of the Wonderful Law v.* Wm. Theodore de Bary, *Chinese Tradition*, pp. 317-321.

44. For selections in English translation from *The Method of Concentration and Insight in the Mahāyāna v.* ibid., pp. 314-317.

45. For analyses of the system *v.* Fung Yu-lan, *History*, volume II, pp. 339-359; Takakusu, op. cit., chapter VIII.

46. A complete translation into English of Fa-tsang's lecture appears in Chan Wing-tsit, op. cit., pp. 409-414.

47. The ten gates are (a) the gold and the lion are completed simultaneously; (b) the eyes of the lion could represent the entire lion, as could any other part of the lion, every part thereby becoming the perfect whole: "One is All and All is One". In itself the part is "pure", but seen as involving the others it is "mixed"; (c) although the gold is singular, and the lion multiple, when viewed in terms of characteristics, the two are mutually compatible; (d) each part of the lion is only part of the unity of the gold so that each part is identical to every other part. The parts are mutually identified, then, and yet exist as they are freely and easily without hindering each other; (e) attending to the lion, the lion is clear, the gold obscure; attending to the gold, the gold is clear, the lion obscure; attending to both simultaneously, each is both clear and obscure. This is the "gate" of obscure-and-manifest correlation; (f) both gold and lion may be evident or obscure, one or many, pure or mixed, active or powerless: therefore the one is the other, and neither one disturbs the other. This is the "gate" of peaceful compatibility of the subtle and the minute; (g) in each part the whole lion is present, in each hair the whole lion which is present in every other hair is present, therefore there is an endless series of infinitizing lions: "Thus these many hairs contain an infinitude of lions, and this infinitude of lions of these many hairs is further contained within each single hair." This is a restatement of the old Indian image of Indra's fish-net, where a jewel placed at each knot reflects every other jewel as well as the reflections in every other jewel, *ad infinitum*; (h) discourse about lions illustrates ignorance, talk about gold illustrates true nature. This is the "gate" of dependence on phenomena for revealing truth; (i) the lion appears momentarily, each moment involving past, present, and future, but each of these momentary divisions itself involves past, present, and future, so that there are nine "ages" involved in each momentary appearance: a single instant is equivalent to the ages of history, and all the ages of history constitute only a single instant; (j) the lion arises and the gold is concealed when the mind attends to lion, the gold arises and the lion disappears as the mind attends to gold. Neither has

a nature of its own, each is dependent upon transforming of the mind alone.

48. For analyses of this popular movement *v.* Kenneth Ch'en, op. cit., pp. 338-350; D.T. Suzuki, *Shin Buddhism*, New York: Harper & Row, 1970; Takakusu, *op. cit.*, chapter XII.

49. Selections in English translation from T'an-luan's *Commentary to Vasubandhu's Essay on Rebirth* appear in Wm. Theodore de Bary, Chinese Tradition, pp. 336-340.

50. For selections in English translation v. ibid., pp. 341-346.

51. For a discussion of this movement *v.* Takakusu, op. cit., chapter X.

52. Discussions of Tantrism in China appear in Kenneth Ch'en, op. cit., pp. 325-337, and in Chou I-liang, "Tantrism in China" in *Harvard Journal of Asiatic Studies*, volume VIII (1945), pp. 241-332. For additional information concerning Tantric Buddhism *v.* B. Bhattacharya, *An Introduction to Buddhist Esotericism*, London: Oxford Univeristy Press, 1932; Agehananda Bharati, *The Tantric Tradition*, London: Rider, 1965; S.B. Das Gupta, *An Introduction to Tantric Buddhism*, Calcutta: University of Calcutta Press, 1950.

53. Essay IV in *Essays in Zen Buddhism, Second Series*, New York: Grove Press, 1961.

54. *v.* Giuseppe Tucci, *The Theory and Practice of the Mandala*, London, Rider, 1961.

55. *v.* Yoshito S. Hakeda, *Kūkai: Major Works, Translated, with an account of his life and a study of his thought*, New York: Columbia University Press, 1972. Selections from the works in English translation can be found in William Theodore de Bary (ed.), *Sources of Japanese Tradition*, New York: Columbia University Press, 1958, chapter VII.

56. The literature in English concerning this position is extensive. The following discussions are recommended: Kenneth Ch'en, op. cit., pp. 350-364; Heinrich Dumoulin, *The Development of Chinese Zen*, New York : The First Zen Institute of America, 1953; H. Dumoulin, *A History of Zen Buddhism*, New York: Pantheon Books, 1963; Fung Yu-lan, *History*, volume II, pp. 386-406; D.J. Kalupahana, "Reflections on the Relations between Early Buddhism and Zen: in *Buddhist Philosophy*, Honolulu: The University Press of Hawaii, 1976, pp. 163-178; K'uan Yu Lu (Charles Luk), *Ch'an and Zen Teaching*, London: Rider, 1960; D.T. Suzuki. *Essays in Zen Buddhism*, 3 volumes, New York: Grove Press, 1964; Suzuki, *Introduction to Zen Buddhism*, New York: Grove Press, 1949; Suzuki, *Manual of Zen Buddhism*, London: Rider, 1960; Suzuki, *Studies in Zen*, New York: Dell Publications, 1955; Suzuki, *Zen Buddhism*, New York: Doubleday, 1956; Takakusu, op. cit,, chapter XI.

57. The most recent translations into English are by Chan Wing-tsit, *The Platform Scripture: the basic classic of Zen Buddhism*, New York: St. John's University Press, 1963 and Phil B. Yampolsky, *The Platform Scripture of the Sixth Patriarch*, New York: Columbia University Press, 1967.

58. Hu Shih, "*Ch'an (Zen) Buddhism in China: Its History and Method*"; Diasetz Teitarō Suzuki, "Zen: A Reply to Hu Shih", in *Philosophy East and West*, volume 3 (1953), pp. 3-24, 25-46.

59. Ibid., p. 7.
60. Ibid., p. 19.
61. Ibid., p. 45.
62. *Essays in Zen Buddhism*, First Series, p. 262.
63. D.T. Suzuki has published a translation in English of this *sūtra*: *The Laṅkāvatāra Sūtra; a Mahāyāna text*, London: Routledge and Kegan Paul, 1956.
64. Cited on pp. 234 f. in D. T. Suzuki, *Essays in Zen Buddhism*, First Series.
65. Among the translations into English are Edward Conze, *Buddhist Wisdom Books*, London: George Allen and Unwin, 1958, pp. 21-71; Lu K'uan-lu (Charles Luk), "The Diamond Sūtra" in *Bilingual Buddhist Series: Sutras and Scriptures*, volume 1, Taipei : Buddhist Culture Service, 1962, pp. 109-132; Shao Chang Lee, *Popular Buddhism in China*, Shanghai: Commercial Press, 1939, pp. 27-52.
66. *Platform Scripture*, chapter 6.
67. Ibid., chapter 8.
68. "Tsung-mi, His Analysis of Ch'an Buddhism" in *T'oung Pao*, volume LVIII, p. 36.
69. Ibid., p. 35.
70. *Essays, First Series*, p. 176.
71. *History of Chinese Philosophy*, volume II, p. 390.
72. "Chinese Buddhist Sculpture" in *The Metropolitan Museum of Art Bulletin*, volume 23 (1965), pp. 303, 301.
73. The Chinese name for landscape painting is "mountain/water".
74. Cited by Jean A. Keim in *Chinese Art*, volume I, London: Methuen, 1961, p. 8. For an English translation of Wang Wei's brief essay, "Introduction to Painting" v. William Theodore de Bary, *Sources of Chinese Tradition*, p. 225.
75. For accounts of the life of Po Chu-i and selections in English translation from his poetry v. Kenneth K. S. Ch'en, *The Chinese Transformation of Buddhism*, Princeton: Princeton University Press, 1973, pp. 184-239; Arthur Waley, *The Life and Times of Po Chu-i*, London: George Allen and Unwin, 1949.
76. Notably Han Yu and Li Ao. For an analysis of their thought v. ibid., pp. 408-412; for selections from their writings in English translation v. Chan, op. cit., chapter 27.
77. Chou Tun-i, Shao Yung, Chang Tsai, Ch'eng Hao, Ch'eng I. For an analysis of their thought v. Fung Yu-lan, *History*, volume II, chapters 11, 12; for selections from their writings in English translation v. Chan, op. cit. chapters 28, 29, 30, 31 and 32.

9
NEO-CONFUCIANISM

DAVID C. WU

I. THE RISE OF NEO-CONFUCIANISM

Genetically speaking, Neo-Confucianism refers to the Confucian renascence in the Sung period (960-1279). But in a broad sense it means the development of Confucian thought since the Sung dynasty; it covers a tradition of a thousand years. The term, Neo-Confucianism, was actually coined by Western sinologists in the nineteenth century, who used it to designate a new Confucianism as distinct from the Confucianism of Han and pre-Han China. The prefix implies at least two notations: the synthesis of classical Confucianism with Buddhism and Taoism and, consequently, a philosophical movement that is more metaphysical and more comprehensive than classical Confucianism. Historically, Neo-Confucian philosophy was named by its followers as the Philosophy of Tao (*Tao-hsueh*) or the Philosophy of Principle and Nature (*Hsing-li hsueh*).

In order to have a sense of history vis-a-vis the rise of Neo-Confucianism, we shall dwell briefly on the political and ideological situation of Sung China. Throughout this period China was besieged with the threat of foreign conquests. During the Northern Sung period (960-1126) it faced the rivalry of the Liao (Khitan) empire which occupied present Mongolia and Manchuria as well as part of North China. And during the Southern Sung era (1127-1279), the Liao empire was overthrown by the Chin (Jurchen) kingdom which also controlled North China above the Huai River, while the Chinese were only able to hold onto China along the Yangtze River and south of it. In addition to these two foreign powers, China also had to face the ominous eastward threat of the kingdom of Hsi-hsia in present Tibet. The Sung dynasty was not only unable to regain North China but finally lost the whole country to the Mongols who established the Yuan dynasty (1260-1368).

This cursory review of the political situation of Sung China shows that the Chinese were then living under the constant strain of national annihilation. This experience forced their leaders to confront the problem of how to strengthen the nation in the face of foreign adversaries. Out of this concern came the deep conviction that the recovery of the nation must depend on the revival of Confucianism—the moral and spiritual fiber of Chinese civilization. External threats and national humiliation drove the Chinese towards self-reflection. And Neo-Confucianism in the Sung period was its intellectual expression.

In order to appreciate the ideological picture of Sung China, a recapitulation of the Chinese philosophical and religious scene prior to the 11th century is necessary. The ascendancy of Confucianism came to an end with the collapse of the Han dynasty (202 B.C.-A.D. 220). In the next few hundred years Buddhism increasingly captured the philosophical and religious attention of the Chinese. Meanwhile, Taoism also became influential among different strata of society. During the Northern and Southern dynasties (265-587), when China was politically divided and socially in chaos, Taoism had a great appeal to the troubled Chinese; its concept of non-being (*wu*) as the ultimate reality in nature and life gave the elites a philosophical basis for a life of non-attachment and escape. The Taoist doctrine of becoming a physical immortal (*hsien*) through taking drugs and cultivating breath control was also in vogue among the literati who desired some sort of personal survival. Also, as Buddhism became more rooted in the Chinese soil, its rituals and priesthood and its doctrines of bodhisattvas and celestial realms contributed towards the establishment of the Taoist religion, which eventually began to rival Buddhism in the T'ang dynasty (618-907). But it was Buddhism that attracted the learned Chinese the most. Many gifted literati entered the monastic order in order to study and meditate. They wrote numerous commentaries on the Buddhist scriptures and produced many works of Buddhist philosophy and history. It is interesting to note that, although the T'ang dynasty was noted for its share of the best poets and artists in China, it did not produce a single Confucian philosopher comparable in stature to such scholar-monks as Tu-shun, Fa-tsang, Tao-hsuan, Hsuan-Tsang, or K'uei-chi. These learned monks were also versed in the Confucian classics, although they tended to interpret them from the Buddhist perspective.

Not only was Buddhism the dominant intellectual-religious

movement in T'ang China, it also constituted a great economic power. Many of the large monasteries became huge land-owners through donations and commercial activites (e.g., loans, hostels). On top of that there were privileged monasteries which through official recognition were exempted from taxation.[1] Because of the tax-exempted privilege, these monasteries were also the "recipients" of estates purported to be donated by prominent families who used this device for a tax-shelter purpose. Thus there was an unhealthy alliance between privileged monasteries and prominent families in many parts of the country. The increase in the number of monks in T'ang China also meant a decrease in the number of able-bodied men who could otherwise work in the fields or be conscripted. In late T'ang, monasticism had become an economic and social threat to the state. And it was mainly from the economic and social point of view that Buddhism was under assault at that time. Han Yu (768-824), the great Confucian essayist, attacked Buddhism in his famous essay "Inquiry into the Nature of Tao" on the ground that monks and nuns failed to fulfill the Confucian ethics of obligation to the family and to the state. The great persecution of Buddhism in 842-845 by the state was caused by the fear that Buddhism was threatening the economic and social wellbeing of the state.

By the eleventh century, the creative phase of Buddhism had reached a plateau and Neo-Confucianism was about to emerge. But the rise of Neo-Confucianism was due to long years of preparation through mutual influences between the Confucianists, Taoists, and Buddhists. Confucianism, despite its built-in relationship with the bureaucracy through the civil examination system, was certainly in retreat in the period we are studying. But generations of Confucian scholars were actually assimilating many metaphysical ideas of Buddhism and Taoism, of which classical Confucianism was deficient, as they pondered the fate of their tradition. By the eleventh century the Confucianists were ready for their task of reconstruction and the foreign invasions of the time provided the right momentum for the outpouring of their long-brewed thought.

II. GENERAL FEATURES OF NEO-CONFUCIANISM

Before discussing the views of individual Sung thinkers, we shall present the features of Neo-Confucianism common to them all.

1. SELF-CULTIVATION

The Neo-Confucianists regard the cultivation of the self as (hsiu-shen) the basis of philosophy.[2] This is an affirmation of the view of Mencius that man's nature is good; it embodies jen (benevolence, humanity, goodness) which can be intuited by the mind (hsin). If man cannot intuit his nature, it is because his mind has been obstructed by selfish desires or evil thoughts. The cultivation of the self involves the mind's return to its original purity so that it can intuit its real nature. This method requires a person to be under constant self-examination (fan-sheng); he must "rectify" his mind so that it can function spontaneously and he must make his will sincere so that he can bring out the best from within. This state of self-introspection enables him to become conscious of his innate nature. When this innate nature is in command, his thoughts and actions will be in accord with the principles of righteousness (yi), propriety (li, ritually correct), and wisdom (chih, thought and action following the dictum of intuitive knowledge). As the *Great Learning* says, cultivation of the self is the root of learning.[3] The Neo-Confucianists have faith in the perfectibility of man. The will to be good and to intuit the good in Neo-Confucianism is comparable to the epistemological inquiry into the nature of the objective world in Western philosophy.

So far, all that has been said about self-cultivation can be found in classical Confucianism. But the Neo-Confucianists also emphasize the idea of seriousness (ching, concentration on what one is doing) as a mode of self-cultivation. Here we detect some influence of Buddhism. Becoming serious or being inwardly concentrated reminds us of Buddhist meditation. It is known that the leading Neo-Confucianists such as Ching Tsai and Ch'eng Yi practiced daily sitting although they distinguished their "seriousness" from the Buddhist or Taoist concept of tranquility (also pronounced ching). Ch'eng Yi told his students that seriousness implies tranquility but tranquility does not imply seriousness.[4]

2. SPIRITUALITY OF THE MIND

The Confucian perception of mind (literally, "heart") goes back to the tradition of Mencius who conceived the mind as the agent of spirituality and morality. He spoke of "preserving the mind," "nourishing the mind," and of the "innate knowledge" of man.[5]

He believes that if one keeps his mind pure, then it can inform the subject about what is the right thing to do in a given situation. Mencius says, "He who exerts his mind to the utmost knows his nature. He who knows his nature knows Heaven."[6] Mind is the spiritual agent; human nature (hsing) is goodness, and Heaven is the transcendent reference of goodness. If one exercises the mind, he knows both his own nature and Heaven.

It can be seen that the Confucian view of the mind is quite different from the Western view, beginning with Plato, which emphasizes its cognitive and intellectual functions. Neo-Confucianism follows the classical tradition by asserting the spiritual and moral functions of the mind.

Insofar as the cognitive function of the mind is concerned, classical Confucianism did not say much, except for the notion that the mind can directly intuit. When Buddhism came to China, it brought with it the emphasis on the cognition of the mind. Its doctrine of the non-substantiality of the phenomenal world is based on a rigorous analysis of the mental process (the formation of perceptions and thoughts). The Buddhist view that believing in the substantiality of things is due to man's delusion is predicated on a sophisticated theory of the mind. The Fa-hsiang school (Mere ideation), the Chinese version of the Yogācāra Buddhism of India, exerted a great philosophical influence at one time through its doctrine of the mind. Its speculation definitely influenced the Hua-yen school of Buddhism (Flower splendor) which conceives absolute reality as Mind. Under the influence of Buddhism, the Neo-Confucian conception of the mind was much broadened. But at times the Buddhist analysis of the mind seemed to overwhelm the Sung Confucianists' intellectual appetite. As Chu Hsi decried, "The Buddhists only grind and rub this mind away to its finest essence, as if it were a lump of something. Having scraped off one layer of skin, they then scrape off another until they have scraped to a place (Emptiness) where they can no longer scrape."[7]

The Neo-Confucian understanding of the mind combine the Confucian interest in spirituality and morality with the Buddhist interest in cognition. But in the last analysis the former seems to be more basic in it than the latter.

3. PRINCIPLE OF CREATIVITY

Neo-Confucianism not only continued to reiterate the classical concept of jen, but also raised it to a metaphysical status. Jen was not viewed as a generic attribute shared by all sentient beings, although this trend had already started with the Confucian metaphysician Tung Chung-shu (179-104 B.C.). In Neo-Confucianism, jen is equated with life (sheng) or vitality. It can also mean the pit of the peach or apricot, implying the idea of growth. Jen is like water which flows naturally downstream; it functions in terms of spontaneity (tzu-jan) and effortlessness (wu-wei). Thus jen has moved beyond its earlier ethical conception to a new metaphysical meaning. Here we see the influence of Taoism upon Neo-Confucianism, for water is the metaphor of Tao, and that Tao as creative and destructive forces operates spontaneously in nature; it endures and overcomes its adversaries by just being what it is.

Jen in Neo-Confucianism thus conveys the meaning of creativity—spontaneous living or doing what a thing is naturally fitted to do. This is the generic meaning of jen. There is also a derivative meaning which refers to the goodness of human nature. Moral or human nature is now understood as having a cosmic source. The morality of humanity must be continuously nourished in the cosmic life of constant changes. This is why the Neo-Confucianists emphasize the importance of being open-minded (kung), which means putting the self in a mode of cosmic relatedness. They also say that, when one is open-minded, he is in jen; namely, the state of spontaneity and vitality.

It appears that the Neo-Confucian drive to make jen a metaphysical concept was also stimulated by Buddhism. Mahāyāna Buddhism through the doctrine of bodhisattvas made compassion (karuṇā) a cosmic concept. These bodhisattvas (saviour-beings), who postpone their own entrance to Nirvāṇa in order to assist many more sentient beings to enlightenment in this world and others, in fact symbolize dramatically what cosmic compassion is all about. The universe is infused with compassion by virtue of the goodwill and sacrificial deeds of these bodhisattvas.

Because of the doctrine of non-substantiality (niḥ-svabhāvatā) or impermanence in Buddhism, even compassion is ultimately nonsubsisting; it is empty (śūnya) and has no self-nature. It is here that Neo-Confucianism parted company with Buddhism. From the Confucian perspective, jen, as life, is the general character of Ultimate Reality, called the Great Ultimate. To say that jen is ultimately empty and non-substantial would be unthinkable to the Neo-Confucianists.

4. COSMOLOGY OF ORGANISM

Classical Confucianists emphasized society and government but did not develop a cosmology (theories of the universe) because of their fascination with nature and their interest in Tao as the source of creation. Other ancient Taoist cosmological treatises are included in the *Huai-nan-Tzu* (Collection of writings by Prince of Huai-nan), compiled in the second century B.C. In addition to Taoism, the *Book of Changes* and the school of yin-yang also were concerned with cosmological theories. The *Book of Changes* (compiled in the fourth century B.C.) expounds the complementary modes of yin (passive) and yang (active) forces as the primordial modality for the production of things and explains the sixty-four hexagrams as the hypothetical natural-human situations in which the complementary modes of yin and yang interact. The school of yin-yang, attributed to Chou Yen (305-240 B.C.), combines the two modes of yin and yang with the five phases of nature (Wood, Fire, Soil, Metal, Water).[8] These five phases do not denote the five elements as such but refer to their respective functions (e.g. Wood grows, Fire ascends). The school of yin-yang explains how myriad things come into being through the mutual producing functions of these five phases in cycles of succession. The cyclical movements of the five phases follow this pattern: Wood produces Fire and is overcome by Fire; Fire produces Soil and is overcome by Soil; Soil produces Metal and is overcome by Metal; Metal produces Water and is overcome by Water; Water produces Wood and is overcome by Wood. The mutual productivity of these five phases is actually a further explanation of the complementary modes of yin and yang.

Both the *Book of Changes* and the school of yin-yang belong to the syncretistic tradition of Taoism and Confucianism—the synthesis of Taoist cosmology (nature) with the Confucian concern for man and society (morality). The classical representative of this syncretistic tradition is the Han metaphysician Tung Chung-shu who developed an elaborate cosmology which attempts to relate the basic cosmological categories with their human counterparts. He worked out a pattern of correlation among seasons, directions, colors, sounds, virtues, physical organs, political powers, historical periods, and human conduct and relations. This is a kind of organistic thinking in which everything is related to everything else, and the whole becomes the part and the part becomes the whole. The total picture forms a harmonious whole. Tung Chung-shu's organistic cosmology represents an extreme type of correlational thinking. Although it never became as dominant in later times as it was in the Han dynasty, its basic mode of correlation remains the typical way of philosophical reflection, namely, thinking in terms of complementariness, of whole and part, and of reciprocal relations.[9]

As the Neo-Confucianists in the eleventh century were attempting to revive Confucianism in face of the dominance of Buddhism and Taoism, they were wrestling with the prospect of reconstructing a philosophy that could stand the competition of its rivals. This means that the new philosophy must somehow embrace the best of its rival system while rejecting those elements that are unacceptable to a Confucian perspective and values. The first generation of Neo-Confucianists agreed that in order to repudiate the Buddhist metaphysics built around the notion of nonsubstantiality, Confucian metaphysics must begin with a cosmology that explains the substantial and orderly pattern of creation. This Neo-Confucian cosmology they appropriated from The Taoist cosmology of yin and yang.

The Neo-Confucianists conceived of the creative source as fundamentally one and unitary but as functioning in the binary mode of opposite movements. This creative source is called ch'i (material force, ether, matter-energy), the physical basis of all things. And the yin and yang modes are the conceptual reference to the operation of Ch'i in things and events, which can be more concretely described in other binary expressions such as motion and rest, arising and combining, dispersion and consolidation, being stimulated and being responsive, being vacuous and being filled. These bi-polar concepts are different expressions of the reciprocal relation between the two modes of activity. For example, "dispersion" refers to the receptive mode in which the subject appropriates the world (object) into its own experiencing and "consolidation" refers to the productive mode in which the subject completes its act by including the world as part of its own being. "Reciprocal" means that these two modes affect each other rather than a one-way kind of affecting. Thus the "dispersion" mode affects the "consolidation" mode, but the "consolidation" mode also affects the "dispersion" mode by qualifying what has been received.

As Westerners, we have no difficulty in understanding how the "dispersion" mode affects the "consolidation" because this is our way of understanding causality: A, being prior to B, causes B. But we might have some difficulty in understanding how the "consolidation" mode affects the "dispersion" because this implies that B as the later occurrence causes A as the antecedent.

Causality in this reverse order is not a common habit of thinking in the West. Here we confront a basic difference in causality, between Western philosophy and Neo-Confucianism. Western philosophy, based on both scientific and theological traditions, assumes that cause A is external and prior to effect B. From this viewpoint, the proposition, B causes A, is certainly logically absurd. But on the basis of the yin and yang modes of thinking, all relations and entities are internally related. This is the basic meaning of organism; the subject is part of the whole (universe) but, at the same time, the whole also becomes a part of the subject. The world and the subject are internally related and their distinctions are relative only. From this point of view, causality means mutual correctedness or immanence among things or activities. It is not like the billiard ball view of causality "in which the prior impact of one thing is the sole cause of the motion of another."[10] Also, according to the yin and yang modes of cosmology, time is cyclical instead of linear. A, as the cause, is not viewed as prior to B; A and B are viewed as a cylical or reciprocal relation. It is as correct to say that A causes B as to say that B causes A. In essence, causality is conceived primarily as a reference to the phenomenon of mutual attraction among things rather than the phenomenon of some external force (past) that impinges upon a passive object (future).[11]

The foregoing discussion on cosmology shows that the Neo-Confucian picture of the world is dynamic and harmoniously patterned. It is a naturalistic cosmology in that the world is self-creating through the alternating process of yin and yang, and the concept of a creator external to nature is conspicuously absent. The Neo-Confucian interest in cosmology appears in part to be an answer to Buddhism which does not have an explicit cosmology.

5. Metaphysics of the Great Ultimate

Cosmology is not the sole aspect of Neo-Confucianism; it also has a metaphysics. By metaphysics we mean a general theory of reality or existence which conditions the different areas of investigation within the same philosophical system. In this sense, the previous discussion on cosmology must be subsumed in metaphysics. The most general metaphysical principle in Neo-Confucianism is the Great Ultimate which qualifies all other concepts of existence.[12] From the viewpoint of the school of Principle, the Great Ultimate refers to the totality of moral and natural principles that are eternal and are to be embodied in the world of flux. From the viewpoint of the school of Mind, the Great Ultimate is the mind which ontologically is the source of morality and spirituality and epistemologically the agent of cognition which unites the self with the world. Because of the dominant moral and spiritual meaning associated with the concept of Great Ultimate, the naturalistic cosmology of Neo-Confucianism must be qualified. Neo-Confucianism goes beyond naturalism if by "naturalism" is meant a worldview devoid of the transcedent and of spirituality in man and nature.

6. Criticism of Buddhism

On the whole, the Neo-Confucian criticisms of Buddhism are superficial and can easily be repudiated by a Buddhist scholar. The defect of their criticisms is that they argued from the Confucian viewpoint rather than from a genuine attempt to understand Buddhism.[13] Although Confucian spokesmen such as Chou Tun-yi and Lu Hsiang-shan had personal contacts with scholar-monks of the day, their criticisms reflect their deficiency in Buddhist knowledge. By and large, their attacks on Buddhism can be summarized as follows: (1) Philosophical. The doctrine of Emptiness has deprived the Buddhists of their ability to see that the universe is inherently intelligible and moral. This in turn has led Buddhists to disavow the view that man is a moral and rational agent co-equal with Heaven and Earth.

By contrast, the Confucianists believe that the world is rational and intelligible because there are inherent principles and laws in it. As Chu-Hsi said, "We Confucianists say that all principles are real while the Buddhists say that all principles are empty."[14] (2) Attitudinal. The Buddhists think that the life-death process (saṃsāra) is a chain of sorrow and misery that man must break through; thus their attitude towards the world is basically negative. As Chang Tsai said, "The Buddhists consider the existence of mountains-rivers and the great space as the outcome of one's subjective delusions; the six senses (five senses plus the mind) as the particles of dust; and the world as a dream!"[15] By contrast, the Confucians view the world as the arena where eternal principles are actualized through the activities of man and nature. (3) Sociological. The Buddhists attempt to avoid the basic five human relationships (father and son, king and ministers, husband and wife, elder brother and younger brother, elder friend and younger friend) as well as the moral obligations demanded by these relationships. Consequently a normal society would be impossible in Buddhism. The Buddhists are selfish because they desire their personal salvation by neglecting their obligations to society. As Lu Hsiang-shan said, "The distinction between the Confucians and the Buddhists is that the Confucians practice public-spiritedness and righteousness whereas the Buddhists work for selfishness and profit!"[16]

III. BIOGRAPHIES OF NEO-CONFUCIAN PHILOSOPHERS

We shall briefly introduce the lives of seven prominent Neo-Confucianists whose views will be discussed below.

1. CHOU TUN-YI

The Neo-Confucian movement is generally traced to Chou Tun-yi (1017-1073) as its founder. He was born in Honan province and served in various government posts as a mid-ranking administrator. His love for nature was so great that he would not allow the grass grown in front of his study to be cut. While serving as an officer in Nan-an in North China, he also tutored the two Ch'eng brothers for a year, who in posterity became even better known than Chou. The major contributions of Chou were his two works: *An Explanation of the Diagram of the Great Ultimate (T'ai-chi't'u shuo*) and *Penetrating to the Book of Changes* (*T'ung-shu*). The first is a short essay on cosmology and the second is a treatise on metaphysics based on insights derived from the *Doctrine of the Mean* (*Chung-yung*) and the *Book of Changes*.

2. Chang Tsai

Chang Tsai (1020-1077), a contemporary of Chou Tun-yi and a native of Shensi province, was a man of independent mind and uncompromising spirit. As a youth, he met Fan Chung-yen (982-1052), a famous political reformer, who advised him to study the *Doctrine of the Mean*. Although Chang Tsai was also a mid-ranking official and once even had an audience with an emperor, he did not have an uninterrupted public career because he was at odds with Wang An-shih (1021-1086), then the prime minister and a radical reformer. (Chang and his contemporary Neo-Confucians favored the moral rectification of the scholar-officials as the first step towards any national reform, whereas Wang advocated the institution of new economic and agricultural programs.) Chang was a relative of the two Ch'eng brothers who visited him occasionally and attended his public lectures on the *Book of Changes* at the city of Lo-yang. Chang's major contribution was his book, *Correcting Youthful Ignorance* (*Chang-meng*) and his essay, *The Western Inscription* (*Hsi-meng*). The first deals with cosmology, metaphysics, and ethics, whereas the second is about the cosmic status of man and filial piety. Both are extremely influential in Neo-Confucian thought.

3. Ch'eng Hao

Ch'eng Hao (1032-1085) and Ch'eng Yi (1033-1107) were brothers of a distinguished official's family in Lo-yang. While youths they received instruction from Chou Tun-yi, associated with Chang Tsai, and befriended Shao Yung (1011-1077), a cosmologist who built his system on the basis of numbers (numerology) which reflects strong Taoist influence. The elder brother was a very conscientious official, serving in different posts as a magistrate, censor, and military judge. He even acquired a reputation as a competent irrigation engineer who built dikes to stop the floods of the Yellow River. Due to a disagreement with Wang An'shih's radical reforms, he resigned his office and returned to Lo-yang where, with his brother, he taught for the last decade of his life. Together with Ch'eng Yi, he gathered a large number of disciples. It was in Lo-yang that Neo-Confucianism actually started, and the Ch'eng brothers were its indisputable leaders.

The elder brother left the world without having written a book himself. However, his recorded sayings and other literary ramains are included in *The Complete Works of the Two Ch'eng* (*Erh-ch'eng ch'uan'shu*).

4. CH'ENG YI

Ch'eng Yi was reputed to be a serious student, had a high calling, and read voluminously. He declined several government's offers and remained a teacher (Wang An-shih was then in power). Only after the death of his brother did he join the conservative forces of government. In 1086, at the age of fifty-three, he was made lecturer to the young emperor. One of his memorials to the emperor reads: "If, everyday, more time is devoted to receiving men of good character, and less time to wives and eunuchs, there should ensue a good transformation of character and habit."[17] However, he was at this job for only twenty months. His own uncompromising moral attitude, as well as his critical opinions, antagonized another group of officials headed by Su Shih, the noted poet and writer, which caused him to be dismissed. In 1092, he was called back to head the directorate of education in Lo-yang. But again, factionalism gave him trouble, only this time it was worse. The group which was once loyal to Wang An-shih had regained power under a new prime minister and attempted to remove the officials who were once against Wang. Ch'eng Yi was accused of teaching heterodoxy. In 1097 his teaching was banned and he was banished to Szechuan for three years. Although he was pardoned in 1106, his teaching continued to be banned until 1155. By then Chu Hsi, at twenty-five, was quietly preparing himself for a revival of the teaching of Ch'eng Yi. The last decade of Ch'eng Yi's life was exceedingly harsh; his disciples left him at his own request and he had no close friends around. At his burial only five persons (disciples) were present.

Most of Ch'eng Yi's teaching is contained in *The Complete Works of the Two Ch'eng* which includes his major philosophical work, *Studies of the Book of Changes* (*Yi-ch'uan i-chuan*). Many of Chu Hsi's works also include the sayings of Ch'eng Yi.

5. Chu Hsi

Chu Hsi (1130-1200), the most influential Neo-Confucian philosopher, was born in the province of Fukien, although his family came from An-hwei province. His life parallels the first half of the Southern Sung dynasty when there was much political instability. He received the degree for the highest level of civil service examinations at the age of eighteen, a rare accomplishment in the Chinese academia. His teacher was Li T'ung, a follower of Ch'eng Yi. He was far more interested in studies than success in public career. He completed his first book at the age of twenty-nine, and when he was forty-three he had written a total of thirteen books. This made him a highly regarded scholar while still in middle age. Because of his national reputation and broad scholarship, he was supported for most of his life by government subsidies (sinecures) through appointments as "temple guardian."

On the other hand, he was constantly confronted with offers for public offices, which he declined in most cases on account of sickness or family reasons. The real reason seems to be his unwillingness to hold offices under higher officials whom he considered morally unworthy; for to accept such appointments would be interpreted as collaborating with them. Although he did hold several offices during his writing career, they total about nine years only. When he did accept a position, he was conscientious and exacting in carrying out his duties. For example, for two years he was prefect of Nan-K'ang in Kiangsi, where he performed relief work during the famine. It is in this tenure of office that he restored the White Deer Grotto Academy as a public school where many visiting lecturers were invited, among whom was Lu Hsiang-shan, his philosophical opponent.

Although Chu Hsi tried hard not to become involved in politics, it was impossible to remain aloof due to his prestige and reputation. In 1194 he was appointed lecturer to the newly enthroned emperor. He accepted it reluctantly. After arriving in the capital, he warned the emperor against favoritism in the court, which became interpreted as an attack against General Han T'o-chou who was in charge of palace security and the most powerful man then in office. This left him with no choice but to resign after being an imperial lecturer for only forty-six days. Immediately after Chu's departure, Han and his supporters launched a campaign against Chu Hsi and his philosophy, which was stigmatized as "false learning." For two years Chu's teaching was banned and a number of officials known as his associates lost their positions. When Chu died in 1200, his teaching suffered because of official denunciation. But nine years after his death, he was posthumously honored by the state. After that his philosophy became increasingly influential and eventually was identified as the Neo-Confucianism of the Sung period.

Chu Hsi selected the *Analects of Confucius*, the *Works of Mencius*, *Great Learning* (*Ta-hsueh*) and the *Doctrine of the Mean* as the "Four Books" of Confucianism. He wrote a commentary on each of them. He also wrote many other commentaries on the Confucian classics.[18] In 1313 (Yuan dynasty) the emperor ordered that Chu Hsi's commentaries on the Four Books and the Five Classics be the authoritative interpretation and the basis of the civil service examinations. They remained the authoritative books until the abolition of the examination system. For nearly six hundred years Chu Hsi's interpretation of the Confucian texts was the orthodox thought of Confucianism.

Although Chu is chiefly known as a philosopher, he also wrote more than 1,000 fine poems, numerous essays on literary criticism, and books on history. In all, he wrote about one hundred books, although many of them are no longer extant. The following selected works may indicate the wealth and diversity of his teaching: (i) *Classified Conversations of Master Chu* (*Chu-tzu-yu-lei*), (ii) *Surviving Works of the Ch'eng Brothers of Ho-nan* (*Ho-nan ch'eng-shih i-shu*), (iii) *Original Meaning of the Book of Changes* (*Chou-i pen-i*), (iv) *Commentary on the Songs of Ch'u* (*Ch'u-tz'u chi-chu*), (v) *Outlines and Details of Chinese History* (*Tzu-chih t'ung-chien*).

6. Lu Hsing-shan

Lu Hsing-shan (1139-1193), a native of Kiangsi province and a friend of Chu Hsi practiced archery and horsemanship in his teens because he wanted to prepare himself for combat against the Jurchen invaders. He was primarily a teacher and was periodically supported through government subsidies. For five years he was a professor at the government academy and for some time he was a commissioner of military affairs in Ching-mennear, the border of Hupei province, where he established a military system against local bandits and restored peace and prosperity. Lu Hsiang-shan is known in history as a philosophical opponent of Chu Hsi. It appears that the fundamental difference between them is one of philosophical method. Chu Hsi emphasized the investigation of things externally and the study of books in order to acquire knowledge, whereas Lu Hsiang-shan emphasized intuition of the mind (self) and the practice of virtues in order to attain knowledge. Their mutual friend Lu Tsu-chien (1137-1181) arranged a meeting between Chu and Lu at the Goose Lake Temple in Kiangsi in 1175 in order to enable them to understand the philosophy of each other better. At the four-day meeting several poems were exchanged between them. These poems seem to show that Chu criticized Lu's method as being too easy and simple whereas Lu criticized Chu's method as being too laborious and giving too much attention to details. Later, Chu and Lu exchanged letters twice to express their differences on the nature of the Great Ultimate. When Lu died in 1193, Chu attended his funeral. In the last years of Chu's life, in letters to his friends he accused Lu of being a Ch'an (Zen) Buddhist!

Lu did not write a book. His letters, short essays, poems and recorded conversations were compiled in *The Complete Works of Lu Hsiang-shan* (*Hsiang-shan ch'uan-shu*). Lu's philosophy was more carefully worked out by his best known disciple, Yang Chien (1141-1226). However, Lu's philosophy of mind did not become influential until the appearance of Wang Yang-ming, his most outstanding interpreter.

7. WANG YANG-MING

Our rationale for including Wang Yang-ming (1473-1529) in the biographies of Sung Neo-Confucianism is that (i) he was, next to Chu Hsi, the most influential Neo-Confucian thinker and that (ii) he was the proponent of the school of Mind of Lu Hsing-shan. Wang, the foremost philosopher of the Ming dynasty, was probably the most colorful and most interesting thinker among the leading Neo-Confucianists. Also, among the historical figures we have considered, Wang was the most active and prominent public official. His life seems to fit well with the Confucian scholar-official model. His father was at one time minister of personnel. Wang was married at the age of sixteen. On the night of his wedding day, he went to visit a Taoist priest. Their conversations on the topic of longevity (how to nourish life through Taoist breath control) so enwrapped him that he spent the entire night at the temple. This anecdote indicates something of his unconventionality. In the early decades of his life, he was interested in both Buddhism and Taoism (internal alchemy or breath control); however, he was never converted to any.

In 1506, while a government official, Wang recieved forty strokes of beating at the imperial court and was banished for three years to Kweichow, a province then populated mostly by the aborigines because of his protest against the imprisonment of a courageous censor who censored the evil conduct of an influential eunuch. It was in exile (1508) at the age of thirty-six that Wang was awakened to the conviction that principle (li) and mind are identical. The next year he propounded the identity between knowledge and action. In 1516 he was made Governor of Southern Kiangsi and its adjacent districts, where bandits and rebels abounded. He was able to pacify them and encouraged them to be "new citizens." Then in 1519, he confronted the rebellion of Prince Ning in Kiangsi, who was threatening to replace the reigning emperor. Although Wang subdued the rebellious force and also captured the Prince, his great victory turned out to be a pain.

The men in power at the capital were jealous of his military success and reputation and were determined not to let him reap the harvest of victory. The group, consisting of eunuchs and courtiers, accused Wang of conspiracy with Prince Ning on the grounds that there had been prior exchanges of personnel between them. Thus for several years his life was in danger. It was in this period (1521) that Wang discovered the doctrine of the innate good knowledge (liang-chih) which informs man what is right. He confessed that it was "achieved after a hundred deaths and a thousand sufferings."[19]

After a period of retirement, Wang was recalled to service in 1527 as chief of military affairs in the four provinces of South—central China. His main task was to subdue the bandits and rebels who infested that vast area. But he died in 1529 en route home in East China after submitting his resignation due to illness. Instead of rewarding him posthumously, his superiors accused him of leaving office without permission and of teaching false doctrines. His thought was proscribed until 1567.

Wang had many disciples during his active career, some of whom attained important government positions. After his death, his school was divided into many branches, two of which were influential in the Ming dynasty. Wang left us with his *Instructions for Practical Living* (*Ch'uan-hsi lu*) which represents the most developed ideas of the school of Mind in Neo-Confucianism.[20]

IV. NEO-CONFUCIAN SCHOOLS

We shall now delineate the three groups of Neo-Confucianism: the original Neo-Confucianism (Chou Tun-yi, Chang Tsai, Ch'eng Hao); the school of Principle (Ch'eng Yi, Chu Hsi); the school of Mind (Lu Hsiang-shan, Wang Yang-ming). While the ideas of each thinker will be emphasized, the common features of each group shall also be noted. Since Wang Yang-ming will be discussed in the next chapter, the treatment of the third group will be very brief.

1. THE ORIGINAL NEO-CONFUCIANISM
(1) Chou Tun-yi

According to Chu Hsi, Chou Tun-yi is the pioneer of Neo-Confucianism. This does not mean that there were no other Neo-Confucianists prior to him, for instance in the thought of Li Ao (died 844) we see evidence of ideas that anticipate Neo-Confucianism. For Chu Hsi, the task of Neo-Confucians was to rediscover classical Confucian thought, particularly the school of Mencius. It was Chou Tun-yi who succeeded in the line of Confucius which was broken after the death of Mencius, so claimed Chu Hsi. What Chu Hsi really meant was probably that Chou Tun-yi was the first Sung thinker to reinterpret the Confucianism of the Mencian tradition by making use of intellectual resources outside of Confucianism. This qualifies him as the pioneer of Neo-Confucianism because its task was precisely this.

A. *Mutuality Between the Non-Ultimate and the Great Ultimate in Cosmology*

In Chou's *Explanation on the Diagram of the Great Ultimate*, he conceives the creative source in terms of the polar concepts of the Non-Ultimate (Wu-chi, literally, "without pole") and the Great Ultimate (T'ai-chi, literally, "great pole"). The "Non-Ultimate" refers to the vacuous and tranquil nature of material force (ch'i), the physical source out of which individual things are formed. Ch'i as vacuous and tranquil does not mean that it is non-existent; it is real potentiality or energy prior to any conception of intelligibility or orders; thus the Non-Ultimate in Chou's mind is something like the chaos (h'un-t'un) out of which the cosmos emerges. In contrast, the "Great Ultimate" refers to ch'i that alternates between the yin and yang. Through their complementary movements the five phases of nature (Wood, Fire, Soil, Metal, Water) are produced and through the cyclical movements of these five phases myriad things are created. In Chou's system, the Great Ultimate is ch'i as the order of yin and yang and the Non-Ultimate is ch'i as potentiality or energy. But these two sides are cosmologically co-equal and inseparable. The Non-Ultimate is the depths (ungrund) of the Great Ultimate. The correlation between the two poles depicts both the rhythm-like process of nature and its inexhaustibility and mystery (miao). This is why Chou's *Explanation* begins by saying: "[There is] the Non-Ultimate [in itself]; and [this is] then the Great Ultimate [for everything else] (*wu-chi erh t'ai-chi*)."[21] It also says, "The Great Ultimate is fundamentally the Non-Ultimate."[22]

Since the Non-Ultimate is a Taoist concept (*Tao-te ching*, Chapt. 28) and since the cosmology of yin and yang was historically more akin to Taoism than to Confucianism, the Taoist influence in Chou's cosmology is beyond question. However, the Confucian element is also clearly visible; it lies in the cosmological origin of man's morality. Man is produced by the yin-yang force just like any other living thing, but he is endowed with the pure and spiritual force which has the potentiality for actualizing the five principles of his nature (humanity, righteousness, propriety, wisdom, faithfulness). When these five principles of man react to the external world, they can distinguish good from evil for him. Therefore the material force in man for Chou is not merely physical; it is also moral. Man stands at the head of the cosmic process in terms of the progressive grades of the material force endowed by the myriad creatures. He is also at the center of the cosmos because his moral nature is basically the same as that of Heaven and Earth. Thus, "his brilliance is identical with that of the sun and moon, his orderly existence is identical with that of the cycles of the four seasons, and his good and evil fortunes are identical with the benign and bad spirits."[23] The synthesis of Taoist and Confucian elements distinguishes Chou's cosmology from that of Taoism, where morality is only a human design and where man, as another natural species, is not the center of the cosmos.

B. Sincerity as the Ontological Principle

Chou Tun-yi in his *Penetrating the Book of Changes* attempted to relate the cosmic order with the concept of sincerity (ch'eng). This term, developed in the *Doctrine of the Mean*, conveys ideas far beyond the English word "sincerity." It also means reality, truthfulness, ever-creating and ever-accomplishing, and right intuition. It refers to a pervasive quality underlying all sentient beings. The *Doctrine* says, "Sincerity is the end and beginning of things; without sincerity there would be nothing."[24] Also, "Sincerity is the way of Heaven. The attainment of sincerity is the way of man."[25] Chou developed this concept further by relating it to the origin of the cosmos (ch'ten-k'un) which is none other than the Great Ultimate. Because the Great Ultimate is the order of yin-yang, everything which contains this order also embodies sincerity. Thus it is an ontological principle. "Sincerity is the foundation of the five constant virtues and the source of all activities."[26]

However, Chou also added a Taoist flavor to it by stating that sincerity is a state of non-being (wu) and pertains to "non-activity (wu-shih)." "Sincerity in its original substance engages in in-action (wu-wei)."[27] It is the inherent nature of a thing. In the case of man, it is his original nature. When man is aware of this state, then whatever action he does would be good. The notion of sincerity, as Chou used it, anticipated the doctrine of the original good knowledge of man later developed by Wang Yang-ming.

C. Tranquility as the Method of Realizing Sincerity in Actions

Since sincerity is the source of man's moral activities, we must constantly guard it in order to function morally. In this context, Chou introduced the notion of tranquility (ching), the mental discipline of calmness. When man masters tranquility, then he is in the state of sincerity. In describing the sincerity of the sage, Chou quoted a passage from the *Book of Changes*: "[The sage] is silent and undisturbed (concentrative). [Being in this state, his mind], stimulated [by Heaven], penetrates to all things in the world."[28] Chou used this quote to amplify the psychological and ontological implications of sincerity: when the sage is in perfect tranquility, he is in complete harmony with all things under Heaven.[29] Therefore, the corollary follows: what he does is always morally right.

Chou's concept of tranquility was no doubt influenced by Buddhism, particularly the Ch'an school, whose meditation as a mental discipline was essential for enlightenment. But his interest in tranquility must be viewed in the context of his total philosophy. The sage—every man is a potential sage—practices tranquility in order to return to sincerity so that he may engage in actions beneficial to others and society. This is a correction to the monastic life of Buddhism which rejects active social involvement.

(2) Chang Tsai
A. *Doctrine of Ch'i*

Chang Tsai was the first Neo-Confucian to build his philosophy primarily on the doctrine of material force (ch'i). The world ch'i literally means breath, vapor, gas, or air. These meanings suggest that it has the character of amorphousness and of filling spaces. It is the primordial substance in the universe. (The concept of mind in Chang's thought must be viewed in the context of ch'i; hence the traditional dualism between body and mind in Western thought is not present in him.) He conceived the activities of ch'i chiefly in terms of the polar movements of dispersion (san) and consolidation (chu). When the ch'i disperses, it is incorporeal and invisible. When it is consolidated, it is mixed with solid matter (chih, literally, sediments), being corporeal and visible. The invisibility of ch'i is also called the Great Vacuity (t'ai-hsu) which is formless, being the original essence of the material force. The visibility of ch'i is also called the Great Harmony (t'ai-ho), referring to the presence of ch'i in a concrete object. All physical phenomena can be generically explained in terms of the polar movements of ch'i. Its fluctuations among the innumerable living things depict the cosmos in constant changes and transformation. Ch'i in Chang's philosophy is the Great Ultimate and its fluctuating movements are the yin and yang of the Great Ultimate.

B. Heaven and Earth as the Father and Mother of Mankind

In Chang's famous essay, *Western Inscription*, he views Heaven (ch'ien) and Earth (k'un) as the universal parents, all people as brothers and sisters, and all creatures as one's companions.[30] This notion of universal love, including brotherly love for the handicapped, the sick and the rejected, was probably influenced by the doctrine of compassion in Mahāyāna Buddhism. However, the idea that Heaven and Earth are father and mother of mankind was already expressed in the *Canon of the Great Peace* (*T'ai-p'-ing ching*), an important Taoist work of the second century A.D.[31] We may also recall that the doctrine of universal love (chien-ai) was a basic teaching of Mo Tzu (479-381 B.C.) who opposed the Confucian idea of graded or preferential love. In affirming universal love did Cheng Tsai reject graded love?

In the *Western Inscription*, the key idea is filial love (hsiao), the son's unswerving love for his parents, which is the root of human love in Confucianism. Chang has combined the universal love of Mo Tzu and Buddhism with the graded love of Confucianism. Love (jen) in theory, is universal. Therefore, one should extend his love to include all sentient beings. But in practice love is to be realized in accordance with different human relations, the chief of which is that of the son to his parents. It also should be noted that Chang's claim that Heaven and Earth are universal father and mother is essentially anthropocentric.

C. Two Levels of Human Nature

Man, like other sentient beings, is also the product of the reciprocal movements of the ch'i. But man is co-terminous with Heaven and Earth. Thus Chang said, "that which fills the universe (ch'i) I regard as my body and that which commands the universe (principle) I consider as my nature."[32] This original nature of man is called the Heavenly Nature (*T'ien-ti chih hsing*) which refers to the pure aspect of the material force in dispersion.[33] But because the pure aspect of ch'i in condensation is always mixed with matter, man's original nature is contaminated with evil. This mixture of the incorporeal aspect of ch'i with the corporeal matter in man is called Physical Nature (ch'i-chih hsing) which is the source of evil. Chang identifies Heavenly Nature with the dispersion of the material force. This refers to the mental state when man is devoid of material desires (wu-yu); hence his mind does not discriminate his self from others. In this state, one "forms one body with the universe."[34] Physical Nature is identified with the condensation of the ch'i because in the act of production the producer is attached to what he has produced. This attachment is called the material desires which create separation between the self and others and prevent the self from actualizing its Heavenly Nature.

These two levels of human nature are Chang's attempt to reaffirm the original goodness of human nature according to the Mencian tradition, while recognizing that the source of evil is also in man. In his explanation of these two levels of human nature, however, he seems to have identified goodness with primordial matter, pure and formless, and evil with a mixture of primordial and corporeal matter. Therefore there is a "Neo-Platonic" tendency in his understanding of the human body. Although Chang did say that Physical Nature can be transformed into Heavenly Nature, he did not tell us just how this is to be done. Later we shall see that Chu Hsi made some improvement on Chang's theory of evil by equating the goodness of human nature with principle (li) instead of the pure aspect of the material force. In this way, evil becomes the result of not fully actualizing the principle in man rather than of the corporeal nature of the human body.

D. *Spiritual Function of Mind*

Like other physical things, mind is also made of ch'i, hence it is basically a material substance. But mind is physical in a very special sense because it directs human nature and feelings (hsin-t'ung ch'ing-hsing) and it embodies the Heavenly Nature and possesses consciousness (chih-chueh). Mind directs human nature because its Heavenly Nature has direct insight into things. The primary function of the mind for Chang Tsai is not the production of sense knowledge (wen-chien chih chih) but the intuition of moral knowledge or virtuous nature (te-hsing). This moral knowledge for Chang refers to the principle of jen; more specifically it consists of the five Confucian virtues. The mind also directs feelings because it possesses the Physical Nature which enables it to produce sense knowledge; namely, perceptions of the world as known. They make up the empirical knowledge derived from the cognitive function of the mind—the domain of epistemology in Western philosophy. Although Chang Tsai recognizes the cognitive activity of the mind, he nevertheless feels that sense knowledge obstructs the development of moral knowledge. "The sage, however, fully develops his nature and does not allow what is seen or heard to fetter his mind."[35] This is because sense knowledge which depends on external things and activities would cause the mind to be ensnared by them. The mind therefore becomes egoistic and thus produces material desires. Due to these material desires, the mind is unable to exercise direct moral intuition in response to human relations.

Chang believes that "by enlarging one's mind, one can enter into all things in the world."[36] This certainly does not mean in the cognitive sense; it can only mean in the moral and spiritual sense. That is to say, when the mind is completely free, it can respond to each and every thing adequately because it is endowed with Heavenly Nature or is co-terminous with the universe. "Therefore, the mind that leaves something outside is not capable of uniting itself with the mind of Heaven (Heavenly Nature). Knowledge coming from seeing and hearing is knowledge obtained through contact with things. It is not knowledge obtained through one's moral nature. Knowledge obtained through one's moral nature does not originate from seeing or hearing."[37]

We can see that Chang Tsai's main interest in the mind is spiritual, not epistemological. However, he has sown the seed for the later developments of the school of Mind in Neo-Confucianism. We might also mention that although the philosophy of Chang is generally viewed as materialism by Chinese Marxists today, it should not be understood as "materialism" in the Newtonian sense as being mechanistic and passive. The conception of ch'i for him is dynamic and spiritual.

(3) Ch'eng Hao
A. *Jen as the Principle of Life*

In Chang Tsai's philosophy, we already see the operation of universal love (jen) among myriad things through the alternations of the yin and yang forces. In Ch'eng Hao's thought, jen becomes the principle which underlies and unites all things; it is life or the tendency to grow. The Confucian virtues are now viewed as specifications of this principle. Ch'eng Hao's concepts of Tao or Heaven-Earth also refer to jen. But jen as the principle is not independent of nature and man (such as the eternal ideas of Plato); it is immanent in nature and provides both differentiation and unity for things. Because this principle is also the nature of man, "all things are already complete in oneself (man's nature),"[38] a saying of Mencius quoted by Ch'eng. This quote, for him, seems to mean that, because this principle which unites all things is also in man, man can intuit it directly. And this intuition gives him a sense of affinity with the world. It does not require a great deal of intellectualism to understand jen. All one needs is to practice sincerity (to be absolutely real to himself) and seriousness (to be attentive to what he is doing).

Ch'eng Hao uses a medical illustration to explain what the opposite of jen is: Not-jen is analogous to man's paralysis which involves an obstruction in the circulation of blood in his body. By the same token, the inability to have the feeling to unity with the world is due to man's disease of the spirit caused by egotism and intellectualism. These two attitudes create the sense of distinction between the self and not-self; hence the feeling of oneness is lost.

It can be seen that li (principle) for Ch'eng is fundamentally an ontological concept, explaining the relatedness of things. Whereas the experience of li at a higher level involves intellect or reason, at the generic level of experience jen is the oneness of the world.

B. *Nature as Process of Growth*

The concept of nature (hsing), the embodiment of principle in material force, is viewed by Ch'eng Hao as the creative process. "All things have the impulses of spring (spirit of growth)"[39] due to the operation of jen in them. Nature, as viewed by Ch'eng, is dominated by changes, not necessarily in the sense of producing novelty but according to the fluctuation between the yin and yang forces. The inter-penetration of these two poles in reciprocity is the means by which things and individuals are created. Thus "production and reproduction is what is meant by changes," a phrase derived from the *Book of Changes* often quoted by him. Human beings are part of this creative process, although they can fully actualize the principle by cultivating a sense of the unity of things.

For Ch'eng Hao, reality is one; material force and principle are inseparable. But when principle is embodied in material force, it becomes the nature of a particular thing; hence nature is the endowment of material force. He says that "what is inborn is called the nature,"[40] meaning that it is material force that gives birth to nature. We can see that "nature" for him is a psycho-physical concept; therefore, he does not identify nature with the good in a metaphysical or moral sense. Indeed, he says that nature is both good and evil.[41] By good he is referring to the mean or the state of equilibrium in material force and moral actions. Conversely, evil is understood as dis-equilibrium. He says, "What is called evil is not fundamentally evil; it is as it is only by going too far or not far enough."[42] This statement implies that imbalance, at least at the human level, can be transformed into balance through spiritual cultivation. According to him, only the alternation of yin and yang as the principle or Tao is beyond good and evil. But the function of this principle in the concrete world nevertheless entails evil because the alternation of yin and yang invariably produces both harmony and disharmony in things.

Nature for Ch'eng Hao is basically one; both good and evil belong to it. Because of this conviction, he rejects the two-level theory of nature as propounded by Chang Tsai which distinguishes between Heavenly Nature and Physical Nature. He believes that Physical Nature alone can explain the source of both good and evil. His view of nature also differs from that of his brother, Ch'eng Yi, who follows Chang Tsai's view. Because Ch'eng Yi has a dualistic conception of reality (li and ch'i), he identifies Heavenly Nature with li and Physical Nature with ch'i. Li is entirely good; therefore, the Heavenly Nature of man is good. Ch'i is a mixture of good and evil, therefore, the Physical Nature of man entails evil. It can be seen that, according to this dualistic view, good and evil come from two distinct sources. This would be unacceptable to Ch'eng Hao who believes that both good and evil come from Physical Nature, which for him is identical with material force.

C. Problems of Emotion

In the foregoing discussion, we emphasized two essential aspects of Ch'eng Hao's philosophy: the principle of life as the unity of all things and nature as the process of growth. The first shows the ontology of the li, and the second shows that this ontology is characterized by process. Man as part of this process is to "regard Heaven and Earth and all things as one body. To him there is nothing that is not himself." The mind of man must enter into things and form spontaneous relations with them. By this is meant that man should respond to things and events positively as they come along but, at the same time, he should not let the effects of these responses remain in his mind. Otherwise, the mind would constantly be upset by emotions such as joy, anger, sorrow, and gladness. Emotions should be tied with things and events but not with the mind. When one is angry, he is angry at a thing or event; he should not transfer that anger to the mind. This is the way to keep the mind pure and tranquil (like the mirror when it is not reflecting things). Hence the sage can relate to all the things although his mind is emotionally free from them. "The normality of Heaven and Earth is that their mind is in all things, yet of themselves they have no mind. The normality of the sage is that his emotion follows the nature of things, yet of himself he has no emotion."[43] It should be noted that Ch'eng does not say that emotion is bad; what he means is that the storing of emotions is bad.

This interesting method of eliminating emotions also implies Ch'eng Hao's answer to what our attitude towards external things should be. According to him, Chang Tsai, by teaching that man should not become ensnared by external things so that he may be free from material desires, still has a fear of external matters (hence implying a distinction between external things and the internal mind). But man need not fear external things because the principle which underlies his mind also underlies external things. Therefore, one should respond to them naturally. It seems that the basic factor which made Ch'eng Hao criticize Chang Tsai is the latter's identification of the source of evil with the physical nature of things. For Ch'eng Hao, this would prevent people from having spontaneous relations with external things, for fear that there is something intrinsically evil in them (he believes this is a Buddhist attitude). In all fairness, we must say that the difference between these two men regarding external things is not great. Both believe that one should form one body with all things and there is no real separation between the external and the internal at the level of direct intuition.

In our discussion of the original Neo-Confucianism as represented by Chou Tun-yi, Chang Tsai and Ch'eng Hao, we have introduced the germinal concepts of Neo-Confucianism and its locus of philosophical concerns. Although there are differences in their interpretations of the same concepts, by and large their philosophical emphases are the same: a monistic world view centered around the notions of the Great Ultimate, material force and principle; a process understanding of the world in terms of the alternation of yin and yang; an ontology of creativity under the notion of jen; the dominance of intuition as the function of the mind; the emphasis on moral and spiritual cultivation as the primary task of philosophy and mysticism, in sofar as they believe that the source of existence is indefinable, ineffable, and inexhaustible. What remains to be done is a characterizing of the school of Principle and the school of Mind, which represent modifications of the original Neo-Confucianism by emphasizing some concepts already present in it through refinement and reconstruction.

2. The School of Principle

Ch'eng Yi, a contemporary of the three Neo-Confucians we have reviewed, is best known as the pioneer of the school of Principle. Chu Hsi studied the thought of all these four men as well as other thinkers and constructed a coherent Sung Neo-Confucianism. But Ch'eng Yi undoubtedly influenced him the most. His own philosopny can be said to be an articulation of these four Confucians from the perspective of Ch'eng Yi. Because there is a close affinity between him and his mentor, we shall here review the thought of Chu Hsi only with the assumption that it represents both the ideas of himself and Ch'eng Yi. Where differences exist between them, they shall be pointed out.

(1) Li and Ch'i as the Metaphysical and Existential Entities

Li is the metaphysical entity because it by itself is invisible, devoid of physicality, and without consciousness; it "exists before the physical form" in that, considering li as thought per se, it exists before ch'i, is unchanging and supremely good. The term "supremely good" (chih-shan) here should be understood in the ontological rather than the moral sense. Li is supremely good because without it there would be no order and meaning in the physical world. Although both Ch'eng Yi and Chu Hsi view li and ch'i as depending on each other and inseparable in the physical thing,

Chu Hsi appears to have some difficulty in determining the ontological priority of li. But whenever he was pushed by his disciples on this issue, he did not hesitate to state the priority of li. He said on one occasion, "Fundamentally principle and material force cannot be spoken of as prior or posterior. But if we must trace their origin, we are obliged to say that principle is prior. However, principle is not a separate entity. It exists right in material force."[44] In this passage the logical priority of li is asserted. But he also appears to admit the priority of li in terms of time. Once, a student asked him whether there was principle before the existence of the physical world. He answered, "Heaven and Earth come into existence because of li; and without it they could not have come into existence, nor men, nor other things—everything would have lacked support and foundation."[45] (We shall refer to individual principles as li uncapitalized and to Principle in the unitary sense as li capitalized hereafter.)

Ch'i is the existential entity which "exists after the physical form [and is therefore with it]."[46] It is both incorporeal and corporeal; the former refers to its pure and clear aspects which are capable of penetrating into other material things and the latter to its impure and turbid aspects which consolidate into separate things. Ch'i is perceptual and can have consciousness; but it cannot be an individual thing without the embodiment of li. These two entities are inseparable for the composition of a physical thing. The depiction of their mutuality constitutes the polar nature of the phenomenal world.

The relation of li and ch'i reminds us of Aristotle's form and matter, the former being conceptual and the latter perceptual, the combination of which constitutes a sense-object. But because Aristotelian form and matter are understood in terms of the relation between the universal and the particular, they are not the same as li and ch'i. The form is the universal through which matter or the particulars are subsumed as a sense-object. Also because the universal as form is viewed as the actual (active) in contrast to matter as the potential (passive), the universal is therefore metaphysically higher than matter on the scale of natural process. Moreover, in Aristotelian logic, the universal is the substance or the theoretic substratum of the sense-object.

But, although the sense-object displays the various qualities or "accidents" of the substance, they can in no way qualify the substance, because that which is changeable cannot influence that which is permanent (substance). In comparison, Chu Hsu's conception of li and ch'i does not presuppose the relation of the universal and particulars or the logic of subject-predicates, as implied in the duality of form and matter. Li is static and passive and ch'i is dynamic and active. Their relation is viewed primarily in terms of that of "substance" (t'i, not in the Aristotelian sense) and "function" (yung); the former refers to the static or the non-perceptual principle embodied in the thing and the latter to the manifestations of the principle in the sense-object. The conceptions of "substance" and "function" seem to imply an equal relation between li and ch'i in the phenomenal world.

Chu Hsi was certainly aware of the distinction between principle in the moral and the natural sense; the former he called "that which should be so" (so-tang-jan) and the latter "that which is naturally so" (so-i-jan). In the moral sense, for instance, the principle of father is benevolence to his children; the principle of son is filial piety to his parents and the principle of the government official is loyalty to his emperor. In the natural sense, for example, the principle of fire is being hot and that of water being cold.[47] "The armchair is an object (literally, instrument), that it can be sat in is its principle; the human body is an object, that it speaks and moves is its principle."[48] Even dried and withered things (inorganic) still have their principles for their specific existence. For example, each kind of rotten wood, when burned, produces its own fragrance. "It is [its] li which originally constitutes it so."[49]

Li in Chu Hsi's thought generally refers to the functional aspects of a thing; in the moral sense it denotes how the person should act in a social relation and in the natural sense it denotes how a thing functions according to its usefulness. Li by and large does not connote scientific knowledge that is deductively formulated and through which a sense-object is defined. However, both scientific knowledge and li have one thing in common: they refer to knowledge not directly perceived by senses. In scientific knowledge, it is the concepts that must be formulated in order to define sense objects, and those concepts are not directly perceived, although their validity must be tested through perceptual devices such as laboratory experiments. Likewise, the li of a thing is derived through intuition or direct thought (nien) and not perceived externally, but it corresponds to the meaning of the sensed object. Because this kind of mental intuition (chih-chueh) is fundamental for both moral and natural knowledge, the cultivation of mind becomes the paramount task. Here Chu Hsi follows in the steps of his predecessors. Man's mind is innately pure and spiritual; it, through its pure aspect of ch'i, can enter into things. But because egotism and desires for things dominate the mind, it becomes cluttered (as the pure water is obstructed by the mud). Its intuitive power is therefore undermined. In order to understand the li of things, man must first of all practice the method of seriousness (chu-ching) which makes the mind vacuous and tranquil, leading to a restoration of the original mind. This original mind, being none other than goodness or benevolence, is also the metaphysical Li or the oneness of the universe. When man discovers this goodness within himself, he is in the state of cosmic sincerity—a perfect condition for responding to things or events.

Although Chu Hsi recognizes the distinction between moral and natural knowledge, he views the principles of things as primarily moral in nature. This is because the cultivation of the mind is a prerequisite for both kinds of knowledge and because the principles of things are fundamentally unitary and one.

Sense-knowledge is viewed in Neo-Confucianism as somewhat trivial because it is not derived from intuition. As Ch'eng Yi says, "Knowledge derived from the sense is not the knowledge derived from the moral nature. When the body makes contact with things, knowledge of them is not from within. This is all that is meant nowadays by 'wide information and much ability.' The knowledge which comes from the moral nature does not depend on seeing and hearing."[50]

However, on occasion Chu Hsi seems to indicate that there are ways of obtaining principles other than intuition. Once he said, "If one reads [books] in order to understand virtues, then the principles lie in books. If one discusses about ancient and modern personalities to distinguish the right from the wrong, or the true teaching from the false, then the principles lie in the deeds of ancient and modern personalities. If one handles affairs and wishes to know whether he has executed them properly, then the principles lie in the handling of affairs."[51] Here Chu Hsi suggests three ways principles may be deduced: (1) reading books, (2) learning the deeds of historical personalities, (3) handling daily affairs. Of these three, the second also refers to learning from books because historical writings are a main source from which Chinese scholars learn about the virtues of the historical personalities in which the principles are embodied.

On one occasion, Chu Hsi's great love for books drove him to say, "Things under Heaven cannot exist without principles. But their essence is already contained in the books of the sages. Hence one must begin pursuing them from here (books)."[52] Principles deduced from books are from things external to the mind. Although they are embodied in the thought of these books, they are nevertheless learned through "seeing and hearing," namely, through perceptions of sights and sounds. Thus sense-knowledge seems to be one of the cognitive processes for the obtaining of principles in Neo-Confucianism. Whereas the creative thinkers of the Sung period, such as Chu Hsi emphasized intuition as the chief method for the discovering of principles, followers of Neo-Confucianism in later times, tended to identify li with the moral precepts of the Confucian classics viewed as veritable truth. Thus Chu Hsi's famous dictum "Investigation of things in order to extend one's knowledge" (chih-chih-ko-wu) was equated with mere book learning in later periods. This is certainly not Chu's original intent.

(2) The Oneness of Li in Things

In our discussion of Ch'eng Hao, we mentioned jen (life, growth) as the Li which unites the myriad things in oneness. On the basis of this idea, Ch'eng Yi developed the well-known dictum: Principle is one, but its manifestations are different and divided (li-i fen-chu). Li is jen—the Principle of growth—but is manifested diversely in each and every thing. In other words, while things are different in their actualities, they are in fact the multiple manifestations of the same jen. Chu Hsi followed in the steps of Ch'eng Yi by elaborating this notion further. Hence jen is identified with the totality of the Confucian virtues. In the moral sense, all the li are viewed as the specific principles to be actualized in men and, to a far lesser degree, animals. In the natural sense, all the li are viewed as the specific principles of life or growth. And both moral and natural phenomena are related because essentially all actualities manifest the reciprocal movements of yin and yang—the universal pattern of Li. The word li etymologically means the markings in jade or the texture of muscles; it is like the strands in a thread or the grain in a bamboo block.[53] Thus li suggests the notion of pattern in things.

For Chu Hsi this unitary Li is potentially in the mind because mind is the original goodness of man. "The principle of the mind is the Great Ultimate," as he tells us.[54] The "Great Ultimate" here refers to the Li in the unitary sense. Thus man potentially can understand all the li in the world. However, Chu Hsi insists that man must investigate external things and events in order to extend his knowledge, for the accumulation of principles is a way to regulate the intuitive power of the mind.

Chu Hsi's emphasis on the "investigation of things" distinguishes his school from the school of Mind under the influence of Lu Hsiang-shan and Wang Yang-ming. For the latter, the mind is li which is none other than original good knowledge (liang-chih). When the mind is in its original nature, it can directly inform the knower about the external world. Chu Hsi feels that the school of Mind overemphasizes the internal reality of Li as mind; he thinks that the external reality of li is mind; he thinks that the external reality of li in individual things also should be investigated. Thus both the cultivation of mind and the investigation of things are equally important for the understanding of Li. Insofar as the intuitional power of the mind is concerned, there is basic agreement between the school of Principle and the school of Mind.

Chu Hsi's conceptions of li and ch'i are definitely influenced by Hua-yen (Flower-splendor) Buddhism which propounds the interpenetration between Li and shih. Li refers to the Tathatā (Suchness), the Emptiness or Buddha-nature which underlies the world and shih to the multiple events and things that are manifestations of Li. Events and things are interrelated because they all manifest Emptiness which refers to the Buddhist doctrine of dependent co-origination which asserts that the rise of a thing depends upon the existence of many other things; hence all things are interdependent for their existence.[55] Thus the Hua-yen school is a philosophy of totalism; the world is pictured as an organism in which things are interrelated by virtue of the interfusion between Emptiness and phenomenal things. The organistic structure of li and ch'i in Chu

Hsi's thought certainly reminds us of the totalistic philosophy of Hua-yen. But, either because he did not know the metaphysical meaning of Emptiness or did not wish to dwell on it, for Chu Hsi Li is not empty but substantial, meaning that it as a unitary Principle contains many norms and standards in the moral and natural sense. In spite of the Buddhist influence on him, Chu Hsi's organistic worldview of li and ch'i is predominantly Taoistic and Confucianistic.

(3) *The Great Ultimate and the Non-Ultimate as the Polar Concepts of Being and Non-Being*

In our discussion of Li and ch'i as metaphysical and existential entities, we already mentioned the fact that on several occasions Chu Hsi conceives of Li as prior to ch'i. If we take these passages in question seriously, then both in the logical and ontological sense Li is higher in status than ch'i. Therefore, the polarity tends to give more weight to Li. It is when Li is understood in this metaphysical sense that Chu identifies it with T'ai-chi, the Great Ultimate.[56] T'ai-chi is Li as the totality of principles. It may be recalled that Chou Tun-yi is the first to view T'ai-chi as ch'i; namely, the force of yin-yang and the five phases of nature. Chang Tsai also identifies ch'i with T'ai-chi. Thus both men, and to some extent Ch'eng Hao, belong to the tradition of the monism of ch'i as the ultimate source of cosmology. Chu Hsi differs from this by conceiving T'ai-chi as the Principle that exists prior to the material world. This is because he takes pains to distinguish the physical ch'i from the conceptual Li and commits himself to the position that the source of cosmology is dualistic and that the physical order depends on the conceptual order for its meaning and existence. There must be the principle of yin and yang before we can understand how these forces work. Likewise there must be the principle which governs the relation between the father and son before we know how they should act to each other. Thus the concept of T'ai-chi in his system does convey an a-priority.

However, Chu Hsi does say explicitly in the following passage that T'ai-chi is also ch'i:

The myriad things, the four seasons, and the five phases all originate from the T'ai-chi. T'ai-chi is none other than ch'i.

When it spreads, it is divided into two forces. Between the two, that which moves is called yang and that which rests is called yin. They are further divided into five phases which are further expanded to produce the myriad things.[57]

We must admit that the passage above, which at its face value appears to follow the monistic tradition of ch'i, is certainly contrary to the spirit of Chu Hsi's philosophy. But if we interpret it as representing his conscious attempt to re-interpret Chou Tun-yi's *An Explanation of the Diagram of the Great Ultimate*, then what it actually means is that because T'ao-chi is the Principle of yin and yang and the five phases, the existence of ch'i must be explained in terms of this Principle. The phrase "T'ai-chi is none other than ch'i" should mean that T'ai-chi is the Principle of ch'i. Likewise, the notion that myriad things are originated from T'ai-chi, means that because T'ai-chi is the foundation of cosmology, multiple things must depend on the prior state of T'ai-Chi for their existence.

Although T'ai-chi refers to the ultimate, it is not meant to be the absolute in the sense that its limit can be rationally conceived. For this Great Ultimate is also called the Non-Ultimate. This is because the principle of yin and yang is the most general character of T'ai-chi. The yang becomes yin by being absorbed and the yin becomes yang by being overtaken; one reverts to the other. The principle of reciprocal movement cannot imply an ultimate limit. The quote below clearly shows that the Great Ultimate is the Principle of alternation of yin and yang:

> Question: Does the Great Ultimate begin with the yang (principle of motion)?
>
> Answer: It seems as though the yin (principle of rest) is the foundation of the Great Ultimate; but in reality the yin also is derived from the yang. These principles of motion and rest are like the opening and closing of doors [in spiral succession]. You can always trace this [series] of opening and closing further back because there is no end to it, no matter how large [a cycle of] opening and closing you begin. Therefore, you cannot say that there is actually a "beginning" for the cycle.[58]

It may be said that the Great Ultimate is the principle of yang and the Non-Ultimate is the principle of yin; each entails the other in alternation. Thus in one sense the Great Ultimate has a limit by virtue of the principle of yin and yang; but in another sense it does not have an ultimate limit because the reciprocity between yin and yang implies a denial of any sense of ultimacy.

Because of the polarity between the Great Ultimate and the Non-Ultimate in the conceptions of Li, Chu Hsi's metaphysics involves both being and non-being. Being refers to his emphasis on the moral and rational principles that are viewed as eternal and good. Non-being refers to his emphasis on the reciprocity of the yin and yang which implies that changes and perishing are the marks of existence. Because the reciprocity of the yin and yang is the most general principle, other principles must be qualified by it. That principles are permanent should be understood to mean that they are used to explain the phenomenon of change in the world. The value of permanence is not the fact that principles are permanent, but the fact that permanence is required in order to explain the phenomenon of change. In Chu's system, "permanence" reflects Confucianism and "change" reflects Taoism.

(4) *Nature and Mind and the Problem of Evil*

We have said in our discussion of Chang Tsai that he views nature (human) in terms of two levels: Heavenly Nature and Physical Nature. And evil arises in Physical Nature because of the mixture between these two natures. Then in our discussion on Ch'eng Hao it was said that nature for him is basically one, which is the embodiment of principles in the material force. Thus nature is the process of growth which is both good and evil. Hence for Ch'eng Hao nature corresponds to the Physical Nature of Chang Tsai. For both men, evil is associated with Physical Nature.

Chu Hsi continues to use the dichotomy of Heavenly Nature and Physical Nature but manages to modify their respective meanings. "Heavenly Nature" now becomes the Principle or T'ai-chi itself. Being supremely good or transcending both good and evil, this original nature of man is the same for all human beings. But this nature is obstructed, because of its mixture with the physical nature of man at birth, though its potentiality for restoration is always there. "Physical Nature" now refers to the combination of

Principle with material force in man.[59] This is the nature which comes with the birth of the individual, not identical with Principle itself. Chu Hsi attributes the goodness of human nature to Principle and the relation between good and evil to physical nature. Although human beings receive the same Principle, they differ in their endowments of the material force which varies in accordance with its degree of clearness and turbidity, refinement and coarseness. "The nature of all men is good and yet there are those who are good from their birth and those who are evil from their birth. This is because of the difference in material force with which they are endowed."

It should be noted that Chu Hsi does not mean that material force per se, is evil. Evil is due to the inability to actualize principle by individuals. Those who are born with turbid and impure material force would have a great deal of difficulty in actualizing them. Between these two extremes there lies the largest number of individuals whose physical endowments differ in degree of clearness and refinement. They are strong in actualizing certain principles but weak in actualizing others; hence they are both good and evil.[60]

Although Chu Hsi's view of material force appears to be deterministic regarding man's potentiality for good, this determinism is removed in his conception of the mind. He says, "The mind is the germinal and the clear aspect of the material force."[61] It is this mind which contains the Principle or the potentiality to actualize it. Thus, although individuals are endowed with material force of different degree of clearness and purity, it can be transformed and refined through the process of spiritual cultivation which is the practice of sincerity and seriousness. Such cultivation would enable a person to restore his mind. Man's original nature or mind is like the pure water that has become impure due to its contamination with mud (a reference to physical endowment). Just like the impure water which can be made pure by the removal of the mud, so the original mind can be restored through the transformation of the material force of man. When this is accomplished, man can naturally intuit the principles of the external world. Thus through both will and intellect man can be made good.

3. THE SCHOOL OF MIND

The school of Mind was initiated by Lu Hsiang-shan and was

fully developed by Wang Yang-ming. A fundamental difference which sets it and the school of Principle apart is a difference in philosophical assumption regarding the ultimate character of the universe. One asserts that the universe is monistic whereas the other views it as di-polar. Thus for the school of Mind the ultimate is mind and Li is identical with it. For the school of Principle, reality is the polar relation of li and ch'i. By identifying Li with mind, the highest quality of ch'i, the school of Mind says that the original mind has innate knowledge of principles. On the other hand, the school of Principle appears to envisage Li as an a-priori reality of thought, though it is never separated from the physical world. Thus Chu Hsi's di-polar world view assumes that there is a transcendent order that gives meaning and value to existence. It is precisely this transcendent order that Lu Hsiang-shan is questioning and this is the reason why he insists that Li is the mind. Based on the same argument, Lu criticizes the use of the concept of Non-Ultimate. As he understands it, the Non-Ultimate could mean "non-physicality" or "thought," thus suggesting a separable metaphysical realm in contrast to the ch'i.

Because the human mind is Li, the school of Mind says that it is wrong to emphasize the "investigation of things" externally. Instead, the proper way is the "rectification of mind," that is, the continuing correction of our conduct in order to restore the original mind which embodies the principles. We may recall that Chu Hsi also says that the mind contains principles, but the process of knowing for him is dual: spiritual cultivation and investigation of things. Chu is afraid that the school of Mind would over-emphasize the cultivation of the mind at the expense of study and thinking.

In retrospect, it is probably correct to say that whereas the school of Principle has developed a philosophy that is well-reasoned and carefully worked out, it is the school of Mind, both in method and intent, that appears to be closer in spirit to the original thought of Mencius. It also has a greater affinity with the original Neo-Confucianism as represented by Chou Tun-yi, Chang Tsai, and Ch'eng Hao, in its monism and in its epistemological concern for intuition.

NOTES

1. For a good study of the economic influences of the Buddhist monasticism in the T'ang dynasty, see: Kenneth K.S. Ch'en, *The Chinese Transformation of Buddhism* (Princeton: Princeton University Press, 1973), pp. 125-178.
2. The Confucian tradition of self-cultivation (*hsiu-shen* or *hsiu-yang*) appears to begin with Mencius. James Legge (tr.), *The Works of Mencius* in *The Chinese Classics*, vol. 2 (Hong Kong: Hong Kong University Press, 1960 rep.), pp. 448-449; 452-453: hereafter referred to as *The Works of Mencius*.
3. Wing-tsit Chan, *A Source Book in Chinese Philosophy* (Princeton: Princeton University Press, 1963), p. 86: hereafter referred to as the *Source*.
4. Wing-tsit Chan (tr.), *Reflections on Things at Hand: The Neo-Confucian Anthology*, compiled by Chu Hsi and Lu Tsu-ch'ien (New York: Columbia University Press, 1967), p. 143.
5. For "preserving the mind" and "innate knowledge," see: *Source*, pp. 78, 80. For "Nourishing the mind," see *The Works of Mencius*, p. 479.
6. *Source*, p. 78.
7. Fung Yu-lan, *A History of Chinese Philosophy*, vol. 2, tr. by D. Bodde (Princeton: Princeton University Press, 1953), pp. 569-570; hereafter referred to as *Philosophy*, vol. 2.
8. *Source*, p. 250. This particular reference to the correlation between yin and yang and the five phases is derived from the *Lü-shih ch'un-ch'iu* (Commentary on the *Spring-Autumn Annals* by M . Lü).
9. Chung-ying Cheng, "Model of Causality in Chinese Philosophy: A Comparative Study," *Philosophy East and West*, 26, 1 (January 1976), p. 14.
10. Joseph Needham, *Science and Civilisation in China*, vol. 2, *History of Scientific Thought* (Cambridge, England: Cambridge University Press, 1956), p. 289; hereafter referred to as *Needham*.
11. For a lucid discussion on causality in Chinese thought, see: Chung-ying Cheng, "Model of Causality in Chinese Philosophy," *op. cit.*, pp. 1-20.
12. The term Great Ultimate first appears in the *Book of Changes* (*I-ching*) where it does not have a moral connotation; it suggests the sense of being the pivot of the world through which the yin and yang movements alternate.
13. For an illuminating discussion on the Neo-Confucian criticisms of Buddhism, see: Charles W.H. Fu, "Morality or beyond: The Neo-Confucian Confrontation with Mahayana Buddhism," *Philosophy East and West*, 23, 2 (July 1973), pp. 375-396.
14. *Ibid.* p. 384.
15. Chang Tsai's particular references to Buddhism herewith mentioned are derived from the *Śūraṅgama Sūtra* (*Leng-yen ching* or sūtra of heroic deed), translated into Chinese in the 8th century. It has been one of the most influential Mahāyāna sūtras in Chinese Buddhism. For a synopsis of this work, see: D.T. Suzuki, *Manual of Zen Buddhism* (New York: Groave Press, 1960), pp. 64-72.

16. *Source*, p. 576.

17. Carsun Chang, *The Development of Neo-Confucian Thought*, vol. 1 (New York: Bookman Associates, 1957), p. 210.

18. The Five Classics are: *Book of Songs* (*Shih-ching*), *Book of History* (*Shu-ching*), *Book of Rites* (*Li-chi*), *Spring and Autumn Annals* (*Ch'un-ch'iu*), and the *Book of Changes*.

19. Wing-tsit Chan, "Wang-Yang-ming: A Biography," *Philosophy East and West*, 22, 1 (January 1972), pp. 63-74.

20. The *Ch'uan-hsi lu* has been translated into English. See: Wang Yang-ming, *Instructions for Practical Living and Other Neo-Confucian Writings*, tr. by Whing-tsit Chan (New York: Columbia University Press, 1963).

21. This translation is by Chung-ying Cheng. See his review of the *Reflections on Things at Hand: The Neo-Confucian Anthology*, tr. by Wing-tsit Chan, *Philosophy East and West*, 20, 4 (Oct., 1970), pp. 423-426.

22. *Source*, p. 463.

23. *Ibid.* pp. 463-464 with modifications.

24. *The Works of Mencius*, p. 418.

25. *Ibid.*, p. 413.

26. *Source*, p. 466. The five constant virtues are the five principles of human nature: humanity, righteousness, propriety, wisdom, faithfulness. The fifth virtue was added to the original four in early Han dynasty.

27. *Source*, p. 466 with slight change.

28. *Ibid.* p. 467 with some modifications.

29. Chou Tun-yin was not the first Neo-Confucian to use this passage from the *Book of Changes* (see note 28). It was first quoted by Li Ao, a forerunner of Neo-Confucianism in the ninth century, who interpreted this passage with a conscious adoption of Buddhist ideas. He seemed to equate "silent and undisturbed" with the Buddhist notion of "concentration" (chih or śamatha) and "is stimulated, [the mind] penetrates to all the things in the world" with the Buddhist notion of "insight" (kuan or vipaśyanā).

30. *The Western Inscription* is translated in entirety in the *Source*, pp. 497-498.

31. "So Heaven is known as father, the life producer, and Earth is known as mother, the life fosterer," a quote from the *Canon of the Great Peace*. See: Ying-shih Yu, "Life and Immortality in Han China," *Harvard Journal of Asiatic Studies*, vol. 25 (1965), p. 85.

32. *Source*, p. 497.

33. Siu-chi Huang, "The Moral Point of Vew of Chang Tsai," *Philosophy East and West*, 21, 2 (April 1971), p. 147.

34. *Source*, p. 499.

35. *Ibid.* p. 515.

36. *Ibid.*

37. *Ibid.*

38. *Ibid.*, p. 79.

39. *Ibid.*, p. 532.

40. *Ibid.*, p. 529.

Yang-ming's faith in Confucianism. One of Wang Yang-ming's other names is *Shou-jen*, meaning to preserve one's humanity, especially to hold to integrity under stress. Confucius had once stated that people are usually intelligent enough to understand a moral principle but not sufficiently humane to act on it. Wang Yang-ming's life was given to the developing and practicing of that which is implied by the term Shou-jen; and the results are reflected in his other name *Yang-ming* meaning "brilliance of the sun" or "as splendid as the sun."

In revolting against Chu Tzu, Wang Yang-ming adopted Chuang Tzu's attitude toward the deliberate pursuit of empirical knowledge. Chuang Tzu wrote at the beginning of the chapter "Nourishing the Essence of Life": "There is a limit to our life, but to knowledge there is no limit. Using the limited to pursue the unlimited is perilous." Chuang's view was that it is impossible, and impracticable to inquire into the principles of innumerable things. The insatiable desire to know, endangers and shortens life. Hence the tragedy of Dr. Faustus under Goethe's mighty and passionate pen. Outward and forward research is irrelevant to inward and backward reflection. Western philosophy since Thales and Aristotle has more often stressed the former. Eastern thought since Confucius and Śākyamuni has treasured the latter. Wang Yang-ming exemplifies the tendency towards the inner in his reinterpretation of ko-wu as rectifying the function of the moral will or the transcendental affection of the original mind.

While dissatisfaction with Chu Tzu was the ultimate cause of Wang Yang-ming's new theory, the immediate one was insult and persecution from the vicious eunuch Liu Chin. Quite often, Chinese rulers placed castrated youths in charge of thousands of official mistresses. Thus humiliated, eunuchs often focused their remaining vitality on accumulating wealth and power. Most of them played the role of political clowns and scoundrels, from whom people suffered bitterly and unworthily. Employing Hegel's dialectical wisdom in "cunning of reason"[2] however, we may conjecture that, but for the eunuch's usurpatory command to beat him forty strokes in the emperor's presence and to banish him to Lung-ch'ang, which was inhabited by aboriginals and haunted by epidemics, Wang Yang-ming might not have been so thoroughly and promptly enlightened. Thus the king and the eunuch indirectly promoted the Wang School, just as the emperor Herod and the governor Pilate aided the spread of Christianity in a negative way.

At the age of thirty-seven, while in banishment, Wang Yang-ming instantaneously realized what chih-chih and ko-wo should mean, an experience corresponding perhaps to Descartes' ecstasy in suddenly perceiving the rigour of mathematics. At thirty-nine Wang Yang-ming's fortunes took a new turn. He was raised from the magistrate of a prefecture to an executive assistant in the Department of Justice at Nanking. Meanwhile, Liu Chin, the eunuch, was executed as a national criminal. After crushing the rebellion of Prince Ning, Wang Yang-ming was appointed governor of Kiangsi. In 1521, the new emperor made him minister of military affairs, but only in the capacity of planner and consultant. Except for subduing several mutinies in 1527, Wang Yang-ming spent his final years in quasi-retirement in Yueh where he was born and brought up. During this period, his fame spread and many scholars became his followers. He was not without adversaries, however. His radicalism and his refusal to accept the text of *The Great Learning* as rearranged by Chu Hsi created much opposition. His major work, *Inquiry on the Great Learning* was written about a year before Wang Yang-ming's death and contains his essential beliefs.

The New Meaning of Ko-wu

Wang Yang-ming's monistic idealism has always been misunderstood as the Chinese version of Berkeleyan subjective idealism. It should be kept in mind that these two systems are vastly different in problem, approach, method and consequence. The former adopted the moral-ontological approach of Mencius and Lu Hsiang-shan (1139-1193); the latter took the onto-cosmological approach of scholastic theology and the epistemological approach of John Locke. For Berkeley, to be is to be perceived occasionally by finite minds but continuously by the infinite divine Mind of God, who and only who can guarantee the existence of an object even when no finite mind perceives it. God enables man to cognize the object thru bestowing upon him the order of ideas. Karl Popper considered Berkeley to be the forerunner of Ernst Mach. In fact, both Berkeley's empirical cognitive mind and Mach's mechanical materialistic mind are devoid of moral content. Their ultimate concern is cognition and epistemology instead of morality and moral metaphysics, as in the case of Wang Yang-ming.

In Chinese philosophy, only orthodox Confucianism possesses a moral metaphysics. Hsun Tzu, the eminent heterodox Confucian, transformed the Taoistic aesthetic mind into cognitive mind. Among Confucians, it is Hsun Tzu whose concept of mind is most akin to the British empiricists. Like Mencius, Yang-ming is a transcendentalist, apriorist, and rationalist who need not appeal to a superhuman power, since Liang-chih is already intellectual intuition with the inherent capacity to apprehend both phenomenon and noumenon. Interpreters are often fascinated by the two following passages:

The Master roamed the South Town. A friend of him, pointing at the blooming trees amid crevices, said, "There is nothing outside the mind (according to you). Such blossoms of the trees bloom and fall by themselves in deep mountains. Have they anything to do with my mind?" The Master replied, "Before you saw these flowers, they receded to tranquility with your own mind. When you are looking at them, their colours become immediately apparent. It is known that these blossoms are not outside your mind."[3]

(Someone) asked, "Human mind and objects have the same body (according to you). If blood and vital force (ch'i) fluently flow thru my body, then they share the same body; but other people and I have different bodies, not to mention animals, plants, and me. Why are they regarded as having the same body?" The Master said, "you may simply observe from the viewpoint of the activating subtle incipience of transcendental affection. Not only animals and plants, but also heaven and earth, ghosts and gods have the same body (substance) as mine." When asked again, the Master said, "What is the mind of heaven and earth as you see amid heaven and earth?" He answered, "I have heard that human mind is the mind of heaven and earth." The Master asked, "What is mind as called by man?" He replied, "it is merely an illuminating spirit (ling-ming)." The Master said, "Thus we know what fills heaven and earth is solely this spirit. Man alienates himself from the universe by his own body. My spirit is the master of heaven and earth, ghosts and gods. Without my spirit, who deems heaven high? Without my spirit, who deems earth deep? Without my spirit, who discerns between blessings and disasters to be brought by ghosts and gods? Apart from my spirit, there are no heaven and earth, ghosts and gods, and myriad things; apart from heaven and earth, ghosts and gods, and myriad things, there is no my spirit. Thus, one vital force flows thru everything, how can one be alienated from it"? The student asked again, "Heaven and earth, ghosts and gods, and myriad things exist from time immemorial. Why do they become nothing without my spirit?" The Master said, "Now look at dead men. As soon as their essential spirits (ching-ling) dissipate, where are their heaven and earth, and myriad things?"[4]

For Yang-ming, the whole universe has the same substance—moral mind or liang-shih. But in Chinese, the word t'i means both pen-t'i and shen-t'i, substance and body. No wonder that in the dialogue quoted above the student misunderstood that the whole universe had a human body. It is his human body, not substance, that alienates man from the universe. Although my body and external flowers share the same substance, yet before and after my sense organs perceive flowers, there is only an internal rather than an external relation between the flowers and my sense organs which perceive flowers thru my mind.

In this sense Yang-ming vividly explained that my mind and flowers recede to serenity. When I look at those blossoms, they and my mind enter into an external relation to render their colours apparent at once. What is inside my mind must be the image and principle of flowers rather than objective flowers themselves. For Wang Yang-ming recession to tranquility is to maintain an internal relation without an external one; in other words, to eliminate the subject-object dichotomy. Wang Yang-ming never denied the existence of external objects independent of human consciousness. Even in the state of tranquility, i.e., non-duality, both flowers and human minds exist by themselves. Hou Wai-lu ridiculously labeled Wang Yang-ming a solipsist.[5] However, this is not Hou's unique mistake. Irrational attacks on both ancient and modern idealists prevail in China.

Wang Yang-ming observed that it is uniquely human mind that can evaluate everything, especially heaven and earth and ghosts and gods. Chinese philosophy has not generally postulated a supreme God with a Divine Mind because it holds that the human mind occupies the loftiest status in the value hierarchy. Like Buddhism, in which gods and goddesses are under Buddha's instructions, Confucianism and Taoism mentioned ghosts and gods as a concession to folk religion or convictions. The human mind can be diviner than that of ghosts or gods. Being absolutely autonomous, moral mind is free from the control, intervention, and interference of external deities. It is solely in this negative sense that Wang Yang-ming elevated human spirit to be the master of ghosts and gods. He did not positively assert the master-slave relationship between man and god. The man-god relationship in Confucianism is far from that of the Brāhman-Śūdra one. On the contrary, men, gods, and ghosts are in interdependence on a moral-ontological ground, sharing one and the same substance.

Further, Confucianism does not postulate the immortality of the human soul to be rewarded or punished after corporeal death. Like Aristotle, in contrast to the Pythagoreans and Plato, man's spiritual side vanishes with his physical life. Confucian immortality merely refers to a person's lasting influence upon later generations. In China only Taoism as a folk religion believes in both physical and spiritual immorality. According to Confucianism, the after-death human mind loses its function and identity. No longer can it make moral and value judgments, not to mention perceiving external objects like blossoms, heaven and earth. Images, ideas, and impressions, percepts and concepts cannot be retained by a dead man's brain or mind. It fact, a dead man has no mind.

For this reason, Wang Yang-ming denied the existence of a concept of heaven and earth and myriad things in dead people's minds or spirits. Unfortunately, readers are apt to mistake Wang Yang-ming's phrase "their heaven and earth", which means their individual subjective worlds, for "heaven and earth themselves" which means the external objective world common to all people. That there is nothing outside the mind is definitely not an epistemological statement, but a record of moral experiences stressing the mastership of the human mind in the universe.

A problem arises here as to what Wang Yang-ming meant by

"thing" or "objects". Wang Yang-mings's "thing" as a philosophical term did not mean physical object. It meant what volition aims at, or what liang-chih transcendentally affects, which was explicitly identified with human events, especially ethical and political affairs. He gave four instances: (a) serving parents: the Chinese word "shih" as a noun means event and as a verb means to serve or to treat properly. Thus to treat parents with filial piety is one of the cardinal ethical events, (b) governing people: a statesman is at the same time ethically inferior to his parents but politically superior to his subjects. To rule over the whole or a part of a nation is a political event to be aimed at or transcendentally affected by liang-chih. (c) reading books: despite Lao-Chuang's belittlement and contempt, to read books is in Confucianism an essential means to realizing ethico-political ideals. (d) listening to lawsuits: a judge should discern between right and wrong and good and evil thru his liang-chih in order to ensure justice.

Wang Yang-ming's identification of object and event as ethical-political was new in Chinese thought. We may shed light on its significance by a comparison with Western philosophy. In general, an object is an ob-ject or opposite-ject in opposition to a subject, not an "e-ject" as an e-ject that emerges by itself with no need of any subject. Strictly speaking object presupposes subject, while eject does not. Necessarily situated in either a cognitive or ethical context, every object is nothing but an event itself. Western thinkers concentrate on the cognitive aspect, whereas Chinese people are absorbed in the ethical aspect.

Four hundred years after Wang Yang-ming, Einstein advocated the concept of physical "events" instead of the traditional concept of "matter". Under his influence Whitehead and Russell promulgated neutral monism, the view that the most fundamental element of the universe is event, from which mind, matter, space and time may be defined or derived. Natural monists managed to evade the difficulties and absurdities involved in idealism and materialism. But Chinese metaphysicians seldom probed into such difficulties. Not being an exception, Wang Yang-ming created a coherent system without an awareness of the difficulties in idealism. What he anxiously avoided is Chu Hsi's separation of mind and object. Appealing to moral volition, Yang-ming joined mind as ethical agent and object as ethical event at the cost of narrowing the content of object to a level above pure physical objects or physical events.

Still following the Western cognitive tradition, Husserl suggested that any object is inevitably within a structure of intentionality. Developing his teacher Brentano's original emphasis on intentionality, Husserl succeeded in thoroughly refuting naive realism. Thru transcendental ego and inter-subjectivity he propagated a transcendental idealism free from solipsism. His transcendental ego is conscious, while Freud's super-ego is unconscious. Yang-ming's liang-chih is morally conscious or conscientious, functioning more vividly than Freud's unconscious superego. And concerning moral content, liang-chih is stronger than Husserl's transcendental ego.

We may call liang-chih the Confucian transcendental ego, equivalent to the "mind of the Tao" (Tao-hsin) in Taoism and "Buddha-nature" in Buddhism. Husserl, however, did not regard object as event. Yang-ming stressed that parents, sovereigns, people, books, and lawsuits are not authentic objects, whereas serving parents and superiors, governing people, reading books, and listening to lawsuits are. If your volition lies in seeing, hearing, speaking, and moving, then seeing, etc., is an object. His object is never purely external since it is always in an ethical relationship. *The Doctrine of Mean* already said, "Without sincerity there is no object." From this Wang Yang-ming acquired the inspiration to define object as ethical event. Being individual and universal, liang-chih implies intersubjectivity.

Adopting Husserl's phenomenological method, Heidegger established the concept of Being-in-the-world. The relation between the world and man born as being-thrown-there, is both opposition and interdependence or mutual appropriation. My personal world is not only private but is also in interaction with others' private worlds. The individual's world as various structures of meaning will dissipate with the individual's life. This may also illumine Wang Yang-ming's saying that nothing exists outside or beyond the mind. The thing refers to principles pretended (in Whitehead's terminology) by individuals and events performed by individuals.

Nevertheless, Heidegger's authentic self of unconcealment and Sartre's authentic self free from bad faith or self-deception[6] are still weaker than liang-chih as unconditional goodwill and categorical imperative. Sartre's analysis of bad faith excels the Confucian advocacy of sincerity in its psychological aspects and practical utility. Western philosophers never enhance sincerity to the level of metaphysical substance. Confucians are unique in identifying sincerity-substance (ch'eng-t'i) with humanity-substance (jen-t'i) and mean-substance (chung-t'i). Owing to Kant's influence, Heidegger's "call of conscience"[7] has a moral implication like the awakening of liang-chih. But Heidegger's concept of sincerity consists in positively facing reality rather than the negative elimination of self-deception. Compared to Sartre, he is more heroic in thought and theory but less heroic in action or practice. Confucian sincerity may include heroism, which ranks lower than morality in the Confucian value hierarchy. To the Confucian, the hero is the manifestation of vitality and passion, while the sage exemplifies moral reason. Wang Yang-ming as a heroic sage and sagely hero excelled all other Chinese sages, in part because of his military feats in suppressing bandits and rebellions. His moral volition lay in seeking to restore national peace and order. What he called thing or object is virtually moral objective, or rather, ethico-political objective. Some scholars considered Yang-ming's term "volition" ambiguous or equivocal, moral and amoral (non-moral). Judging from all his writings and deeds, I firmly believe that the term is politico-ethical and that volition and object (objective) must be homogeneous.

Innate Goodness (liang-chih) as Intellectual Intuition

Berkeleyan subjective idealism and other types of empiricism assert sensory experience to be the only source of knowledge. Radical empiricism incurred the difficulty of what the neo-realist Perry called the "ego-centric predicament". Chinese philosophy has never overstressed the sense organs as the unique means of obtaining knowledge. On the contrary, Eastern thinkers, like medieval Western theologians, always scorned sensory experience and sensualism. Chinese philosophy fully accentuates the role of intellectual intuition in moral and aesthetic cultivation. Lao Tzu, for example, asserted that one can acquire the truth of the universe without going outdoors, reading books or asking teachers.

Chuang Tzu, who followed Lao Tzu, coined a new term, "knowing without knowledge" (wo-chih chih-chih). In this paradox "knowledge" is on a lower plane of the relative, empirical, mundane world but "knowing" is on a higher realm of the absolute, transcendental, supramundane world. From this viewpoint one may dispense with sense-experience and grasp the supreme truth that both the universe and myriad things are natural "ejects" rather than "objects".[8] In Taoism, the aesthetic mind as authentic self acquires this absolute knowledge. Authentic man illumines transcendental knowledge without the aid of empirical knowledge. Thru intellectual intuition, man masters the supreme truth that everything is contingent aggregate without permanent selfhood, thinghood, is-ness, identity, substantiality. This absolute transcendental, supramundane truth ranks higher than empirical knowledge.

It is extremely interesting to compare views of the supreme truth in Taoism and Buddhism. Chuang Tzu's aesthetic mind illumines myriad things as e-jects free from causal chains, while Buddhist wisdom observes everything as ob-jects chained by causality, from which only Buddhas in Nirvāṇa have emancipated themselves. Confucians, like Taoist philosophers, treasure this actual life, this world, this shore and put otherworldliness into a Husserlian epoche and refrain from judgments on and aspirations for an afterlife on other shores. No wonder they mystified human intellectual intuition. Mencius said, "Expanding the mind to the full, one understands human nature and heaven." This understanding or knowing dispenses with sensory experience. The Confucian *Commentary on the Book Changes* remarked, "Ch'ien (first hexagram) understands the great beginning." In Confucianism one understands not thru sensory but thru intellectual intuition or moral reason. Chang Tsai, the Northern-Sung Neo-Confucian, rigorously distinguished between two levels of knowledge: in the higher realm, knowledge pertains to morality; in the lower realm, knowledge is confined to what one sees and hears, as in Russell's "knowledge by acquaintance."[9]

From Mencius' liang-chih and liang-neng (intrinsic original good knowledge and capability) and Chang Tsai's "knowledge of virtuous nature (moral reason)" Wang Yang-ming expounded his own doctrine of innate goodness or intrinsic knowing in which he too asserted that knowledge of the good is the highest form of knowledge and that such knowledge is gained intuitively and not through the senses. Look within oneself and discover one's original character which is of the nature of good, not evil. A comparison may be made with Kant's system wherein only God possesses that intellectual intuition which grasps all noumenal truth consisting of thing-in-itself, the soul, freedom, and God himself. Man was so underestimated that, miserably equipped with only sensible intuition in addition to general understanding and reason, he can never acquire the truth or full understanding of noumena.

For Mencius and Wang Yang-ming, liang-chih is a metaphysical entity which needs no logical proof or empirical verification. It exists in and of itself. Even today one finds two types of Chinese thinkers, as the following anecdote illustrates. Fung Yu-lan, the Western oriented realist, once claimed that liang-chuh is a postulate. Hsiung Shih-li, the Eastern oriented idealist, immediately retorted that liang-chih is an actual presentation.

The Cosmological and Ontological Significance of chih-liang-chih

Wang Yang-ming said, "Liang-chih is the essential spirits of the universe. These essential spirits created heaven and earth, produced ghosts and heavenly sovereigns (gods)...It is really non-dual with objects. Regaining it, man will be perfect without the slightest defect. Spontaneously and unconsciously he will wave his hands and dance, not knowing within heaven and earth what pleasure can displace such exaltation."[10] Earlier the Taoist Chuang Tzu had asserted that Tao (Chinese logos, dharma, and rita) "created heaven and earth, mystified ghosts and heavenly sovereigns (gods)." Yang-ming changed the subject Tao into liang-chih and the verb "mystified" into "produced" and then claimed that liang-chih is the one eternal existent from which all things come.

In philosophical Taoism the supreme principle Tao is viewed as impersonal, unconscious cosmic reason instead of omniscient personal God. Being omnipotent and omnipresent or ubiquitous. Tao naturally produced the universe from undifferentiated chaos. Ghosts and gods are considered as simply unnecessary by-products which adorn and enrich the world. While the Tao of the Taoist is both transcendent and immanent, Wang Yang-ming's liang-chih is equally transcedent but more immanent. Wang Yang-ming believed it is the creator of the universe and that it is definitely not in a state of duality or opposition to myriad things. In a sense, this non-duality is stressed by Lao-Chuang, for he said one may deliberately oppose, resist, or estrange oneself from the Tao; but, in order to survive, one had better retrieve the abandoned Tao. Likewise for Mencius, whoever lost his moral mind ought to regain the missing mind (ch'u fang-hsin), and joy will result—"when myriad things (principles) are already complete in me (my mind), I reflect upon them to become sincere, and this exaltation (delight) could not have been greater." Wang Yang-ming also agreed that by reflection upon liang-chih one can regain it with unsurpassable pleasure or ecstasy.

In passing, it might be pointed out that many critics condemned Mencius and Wang Yang-ming for oversimplifying the difficulties involved in the recovering of innate goodness. Actually, Confucians are not naively over-optimistic. Doing full justice to the bright side of human nature, they are reluctant to elaborate upon its dark side. Orthodox Confucians do not regard animal instincts, physiological desires, and psychological emotions, as human nature. On the other hand, Lao Tzu and heterodox Confucians like Hsun Tzu denied intrinsic goodness to human nature, accepting only instincts and desires as its content. Hence they held to the doctrine that human nature is evil.

According to Chinese cosmological thought ghosts and gods, despite their spiritual aspects, mainly belong to material force (ch'i) rather than reason or principle (li). Being physical, they pertain to noumena, are subject to eventual dissipation and are subordinate to liang-chih. In the early classics, especially the *Book of Odes* and the *Book of History*, the Chinese concept and God resembles the Judaic-Christian belief in God as personal. Confucius believed in both a metaphysical God (Heaven-Tien) and physical ghosts and gods. Mo Tzu, who propagated the quasi-religion of God as Heavenly Will (T'ien chih), revered ghosts and gods more than Confucius did. Undoubtedly Mencius and Chuang Tzu disbelieved in God. So did Lao Tzu, Hsun Tzu and Han Fei Tzu.

The Confucian principle of creativity or humanity (jen), was thoroughly internalized by Mencius to become the chief content of innate goodness or the top item of the "four beginnings" (ssu tuan). For Mencius and the Neo-Confucians, including Wang Yang-ming, gods and ghosts have no cosmological or metaphysical status, and God as the supreme being does not exist at all. It may be noted that in Buddhism, Śākyamuni negated the Hindu concept of Brahman as personal God but adopted the Hindu gods as instruments for preaching compassion (karuṇā). Chinese philosophy and Buddhism are similarly atheistic as a whole. It is man-God figures like Confucius and Buddha instead of God-man beings like Jesus that the Chinese aspire after. We can easily understand, therefore, why China assimilated and revolutionized Indian Buddhism but rejected all other foreign religions, especially those whose cosmology stressed a dominant, frightening, inaccessible God who threatens human dignity.

Analogous to Lao-Chuang's (Lao Tzu and Chuang Tzu taken together) Tao and Te, Wang Yang-ming's liang-chih is also ontological essence. A student asked, "It is mankind with vacuous spirit (empty mind, hsu ling) who possesses liang-chih. Do grass, tree, tile, stone, etc., have liang-chih?" The Master replied, "Human liang-chih is the very liang-chih of grass, tree, tile, stone, etc. Without the former, grass, tree, tile and stone cannot be grass, tree, tile and stone. Not only grass, etc., but also heaven and earth cannot do without liang-chih. For heaven and earth are originally the same substance as man's. The most essential part of its beginning is a little illumining spirit (spiritual light, liang-ming) of human mind. Wind, rain, dew, thunder, and sun, moon, star, and animal, plant, and mountain, river, soil, rock are one and the same substance as man's. Therefore, the five cereals, animals and the like can maintain human life; medicine and minerals can cure disease. It is due to having the same material force that they permeate and penetrate one another."[11]

Obviously liang-chih, the unique ontological entity which makes reality one, is all-pervasive and all-binding. In this sense it is like the Taoistic Tao, the mystery of all mysteries. The Taoist Chuang Tzu, for example, said, "Heaven and earth live together with me, while myriad things and I are one." Even his rival Hu Shih, the logician, asserted, "universally love myriad things, since heaven and earth are one body (substance)." However, both Chuang's aesthetic mind, metaphorically the spiritual storehouse or spiritual terrace, and Hui's cognitive mind, lack the moral implication Wang Yang-ming give liang-chih. They see in reality only the perpetual transformation of myriad things in material cycles of life and death, formation and destruction.

In comparison with Hui and Lao-Chuang, Mencius' philosophy

is weaker in pure metaphysics but stronger in moral metaphysics. Mencius said, "Upwards and downwards I flow together with heaven and earth; however, this be deemed small complement." For Mencius everyone is endowed with the transcendental ground of sageliness and is a potential sage; that is, a person of great moral and intellectual character. Wang Yang-ming followed Mencius in his view of man, as we see in Wang Ken's (a disciple of Wang's) observation that streets were crowded with potential sages.

In the early Sung, the Neo-Confucianist Chang Tsai taught people to fully expand the moral mind so that it may coincide with the heavenly (cosmic) mind. Chang Tsai outshone the Neo-Confucianist Chou Tun-i because he absorbed Mencius' thought. Inheriting Mencius' spirit, Ch'eng Ming-tao, Chang's second nephew, quoted his epigram "myriad things (principles) are complete in me (my mind)" and added, "Not only men, but also things (other animals, plants, minerals, etc.) are so. All of them go out from here (the mind). Man differs from things in his ability to expand his mind. Having expanded the mind to the utmost, humane (human-hearted, benevolent) man regards heaven and earth, and myriad things as whole (one body or substance), nothing but himself." It may be pointed out that, unfortunately, most people adhere to their "small bodies" (Mencius' term, meaning physical frames) but neglect the expanding of their "great bodies" (Mencius' term, meaning moral minds). Cheng Ming-tao claimed, "Humanity and heaven and earth are one thing. Why do people belittle humanity?", and in his article "*To Understand Humanity*" he taught, "Learners should understand humanity at first Humane (humanistic) man undifferentiatedly has the same body (substance) as that of things. Righteousness, propriety, wisdom, and trustworthiness are all humanity...This Tao is not in duality with objects...All functions of heaven and earth are my function...If my reflection upon myself (my inherent goodness) has not yet attained sincerity, then myriad things and myself are still two objects in opposition."[12] Ch'eng Ming-tao urged his disciples to merge themselves into the creative flux of the universe by expanding individual mind to universal mind. This is possible because, as Ch'eng Ming-tao wrote in his "*Letter on Stabilizing Nature*", "The constant principle of heaven and earth is that cosmic mind pervades myriad things mindlessly (without its own mind)."[13]

Since the *Commentary on the Book of Changes* remarked, "The great virtue of heaven and earth is to produce", creativity and humanity have long been identified by Chinese philosophers. The sage models himself after creativity, the supreme principle of the Ch'ien hexagram. It is considered a moral obligation to create a new self or to renew oneself everyday.

The Neo-Confucianist Chu Hsi fashioned a monistic system of no distinct hierarchy but of dynamic creative principle (li) or Supreme Ultimate (T'ai Chi) in which everything shares. In his view even insentient or inanimate things have their nature, principle or reason. We must bear in mind that cosmic reason or natural (Heavenly) principle is transcendently insentient being's substance but is never immanently its nature. Besides, principle and material force, being noumenon and phenomenon respectively on two levels, cannot be fundamental elements of any dualism. Li precedes Ch'i cosmologically, ontologically, epistemologically and axiologically. Like Aristotle's "form", li does not contain matter; unlike Aristotle's "matter", which must be formless, ch'i may have form or no form. The vast scope of ch'i includes formless matter, either undifferentiated chaos, differentiated material, instrument (another ch'i), air, gas, temperament, disposition, morale and spirit. Chu Hsi's emphasis on the difference between li and chi was not incited by the seventh century Buddhist Hua-yen School's principle (li) and event (shih). Fourteen centuries before Chu Tzu, Chuang Tzu distinguished between the metaphysical Way (Tao) and physical object (wu) and gave the name Hun T'un to undifferentiated chaos or material with indeterminant forms. It is in this sense that Chuang is Chu's forerunner.

Lu Hsiang-shan, a forerunner of Wang Yang-ming and Chu Hsi's chief opponent said, "The principle pervades the universe. It is said that there is no event beyond Tao, no Tao beyond event." The Neo-Confucian Tao is more dynamically creative than Taoistic Tao. Confucian li is extremely substantial, whereas Buddhistic li refers to radical non-substantiality. Confucian event (shih) has a moral implication affirmed in both principle and function, while Taoistic and Buddhistic event without moral implication is affirmed only in function as expediency or contingent illusory occurrence of dependent origination. The Tao and its manifested event are two aspects of the same substance. They cannot be separated from each other. "The universe has never confined and divided people, it is people who confine and divide themselves!"[14] exclaimed Lu Hsiang-shan. To cultivate oneself is to eradicate all prejudice of the sick mind and recover the original mind (Tao Hsin). When meaning "without concealment and recession" Tao reminds us of the original Greek concept of truth—aletheia (a-lethe-ia) or unhiddenness, unconcealment, or self-blossoming emergence, being or eject, a theme on which the late existentialist Heidegger elaborated. Taoistic Tao as Chinese logos is metaphysical reality and truth. Confucian Tao is moral-metaphysical reality and truth as seen in the statement, "To investigate object (ke wu) is to inquire into this (moral principle)." Lu Hsiang-shan preceded Wang Yang-ming in specifying the meaning of object. Yang Chien, Lu's chief disciple, commented, for example, that the mind consists of myriad particulars of righteousness and propriety.

Refining the thought of Mencius and later thinkers such as Ch'eng Ming-tao, Lu Chiu-yuan, Ch'en Pai sha and Chan Jo-shui, Wang Yang-ming wrote in the *"Inquiry on the Great Learning"*:

> The great man regards heaven and earth and myriad things as one body. He deems the world one family and the country one person. Whoever cleaves to objects to distinguish between others and himself is a small man...He himself makes it (his mind) small...even the mind of the small man necessarily has the humanity that forms one body with all. Such a mind is rooted in his nature endowed by Heaven, and is naturally intelligent, lucid, and not blurred...The highest good (*summum-bonum*) is the ultimate principle of manifesting character and loving people...As the highest good emanates and reveals itself, we will consider right as right and wrong as wrong.[15]

This is Wang Yang-ming's mature doctrine of inherent goodness which is vastly different from Plato's idea of Highest Good (Hikenon), the leading Idea of Ideas, all of which are non-creative and non-inherent in the human mind.

Wang Yang-ming then went on to condemn three schools of thought. In reference to the Ch'eng Chu School of Neo-Confucianism he wrote: "Later generations do not understand that the highest good is intrinsic in their own minds, but exercise their selfish opinions and cunning to grope for it outside their minds, believing that every event or every object has its particular definite principle. For this reason the law of right and wrong is obscured; the mind becomes concerned with fragmentary, trivial details and broken pieces; the selfish desires of man become rampant, while Heavenly (natural) principle ceases to operate."

Of the Buddhists and Taoists Wang Yang-ming said, "In the past there have, of course, been people who wished to reveal their clear character. However, merely because of not knowing how to abide in the highest good, they drove their own minds toward excessive nobility, and thereby lost them in illusions, delusions, void, and quiescence, performing no work of the family, the state, and the world." Regarding the Moist and Legalist Strategists-Militarists, he wrote, "There have, of course, been those who wanted to love their people. But simply because they did not know how to abide in the highest good, and instead immersed their own minds in base and petty things and thus lost them in scheming strategy and cunning techniques devoid of the sincerity of humanity and commiseration. Such are the followers of the Five Despots (in the Spring and Autumn period)."[16]

Except for Legalism, all Chinese philosophies denounced cunning. Lao-Chuang used the word chih on three planes: transcendental wisdom or intellectual intuition on the upper plane, empirical knowledge on the middle plane, and Machiavellian trickery or chicanery on the lower plane. Liang-chih as conceived by Wang Yang-ming is also transcendental intuition and lies in direct opposition to cunning. Emphasizing the cognitive, empirical mind rather than the moral, transcendental mind, the Neo-Confucianists Ch'eng I (I-ch'uan) and Chu Hsi unconsciously sided with the Pre-Ch'in Hsun Tzu instead of Mencius and also disagreed with Wang Yang-ming. Hsun Tzu's moderate Hobbesian pragmatism and utilitarianism was influenced by Mo Tzu, but his naturalism went one step further than Lao-Chuang's spiritual naturalism.[17] The Taoistic and Buddhistic highest good, namely, Tao-mind and the Buddha-nature are morally much weaker than liang-chih, Wang Yang-ming's categorical imperative.[18]

In Wang Yang-ming's eyes, Moistic and Legalistic imperatives must be solely technical and pragmatic, and hence hypothetical and heteronomous, resorting to external authorities like sovereigns and God. The Taoist's and Yang Chu's imperative overstresses advisory prudence or self-love. From Wang Yang-ming's view even Hsun Tzu and the Ch'eng-Chu School posit imperatives not sufficiently categorical and autonomous. The Lu-Wang School, as represented by Wang Yang-ming, asserts that "The Mind is principle (reason)." This is an analytical proposition, since the universe is the manifestation or embodiment of liang-chih, and it resembles Hegel's doctrine that the universe with human history is the manifestation of Absolute Mind, Absolute Spirit, Absolute Reason, despite the latter's non-morality. For the Lu-Wang School, the mind and objective reason are necessarily identical. But the mind is neither Fichte's Ego (God) who posits the Non-ego (Nature) to be dialectically reconciled with Ego, nor Yogācāra's ālayavijñāna (the eighth consciousness or seed-ideation) that transforms and manifests itself into illusory phenomenon. In contrast to the Lu-Wang School, Chu Tzu defined the mind as the "spirit of vital force" (ch'i chih ling), and degraded the mind from the moral, transcendental realm into the cognitive, empirical realm. Thru moral cultivation, this mind may asymptotically approach objective principle but can never coincide with it. Strictly speaking, Chu Hsi's proposition "nature (hsing) is principle" is analytic, whereas his proposition, even if permitted to assume that "the mind is principle", is synthetic aposteriori. The Chinese verb to be (chi) has tight and loose meanings. The former is to be one and the same (identical) with, as in Lu-Wang's hsin chi li and Chu's hsing chi li; the latter is to be close, near, akin and even equal to, as in Chu Shi's possible saying hsin chi li and Buddhistic aphorisms like "everyday-mind is Tao."

GOOD AND EVIL IN THE FOUR-EPIAGRAM TEACHING

Having accused Chu Tzu of separating mind and principle, Wang Yang-ming condensed his essential teachings into four lines with "good and evil" in common:

In the mind as substance, there are no good and evil,
When the volition (will) is motivated, there are good and evil;
Liang-chih is to know (discriminate between) good and evil,
The rectification of things is to perform good and remove evil.

The original substance of the moral mind, being highest Good, transcends the bifurcation between good and evil. This substance is tranquil, while its function is active, bringing about the distinction between good and evil to be coped with by innate goodness, the supreme Good. For Chu Hsi, ko wu may be cognitive or moral investigation of things. Wang Yang-ming swept away the cognitive aspect, restricting ko wu to a moral rectification of the object to which the will is oriented.[19] Moral law amounts to liang-chih or principle of reason, which guides us to do good and ch'u evil. Ch'u means to remove or to shun, to avoid or prevent.

What is the origin of evil? Like Spinoza and Leibniz who defined evil as a deficiency in the good and doing evil as the abusing of the free will endowed by God, Wang Yang-ming considered evil to be a deviation from the liang-chih endowed by nature: "The highest good is the original substance of the mind. As soon as one deviates slightly from this original substance, there is evil. It is not that there is good and there is also an evil to oppose it. Hence good and evil are one thing."[20] Wang Yang-ming admitted this idea had been expressed in Ch'eng Ming-tao's saying: "Good and evil in the world are both the Principle of Nature. The so-called evil is not originally evil. It becomes evil merely on account of deviation from the Mean." The supreme good is beyond good and evil. When the vital force is perturbed, the dichotomy between good and evil arises. This perturbation causes the deviation from the Mean, liang-chih or original substance. The duality between good and evil is not absolute, but relative. Wang Yang-ming observed, "The spirit of life of heaven and earth is the same in flowers and weeds. Where have they the differences between good and evil? When you want to enjoy flowers, you will deem flowers good and weeds evil. But when you want to use weeds, you will then consider them good. Such good and evil are products of the mind's likes and dislikes..." Outsiders accuse Wang Yang-ming of stealing the Buddhist ideal of transcending good and evil. Actually, before the Indian ingression of Buddihsm, Pre-Ch'in Taoists and Confucians already yearned for the supramundane realm beyond good and evil.

The relativity between good and evil does not consist in subjective selfish desires, and habits but in the unselfish moral judgment of liang-chih. Let us quote Spinoza: "...if anything in nature seems to us ridiculous, absurd, or bad, this is because we know things only in part, being almost entirely ignorant of how they are linked together in the universal system of nature, and because we want everything to be directed in accordance with the precept of our own reason. Yet what reason declares to be bad is not bad in relation to the order and laws of nature as a whole, but only in relation to the laws of our nature in particular."[21] For Spinoza, reason is inferior to intuition; for Wang Yang-ming, moral reason is intellectual intuition. Long before Spinoza, the Chapter "Heaven and Earth" of *Chuang Tzu* depicted the Virtuous Man (te jen, quasi-authentic man inferior to the Man of Tao or Tao-Man) as "thoughtless when staying at home, deliberationless when going outdoors, without storing right and wrong, good and evil (in his mind)." Authentic and quasi-authentic men abstain from the partial and relative knowledge which both Chuang Tzu and Spinoza condemned.

Following Chou Tun-i's catchword "to concentrate on tranquility and establish the human ultimate" Chu Hsi's teacher Li Yen-ping urged the young Chu Tzu to sit down silently and purify his mind until attaining the state of "ice dissolved and coldness relieved" as suggested by Lao Tzu in the Chapter "*Keng Sang-Ch'u*" of the *Chuang Tzu*. Inspired by both philosophical and religious Taoists in addition to Ch'anists and Neo-Confucians, Wang Yang-ming instructed his students to sit in quiescence and to purify and stabilize their minds disturbed or confused by mundane trivial affairs. Unfortunately, many of his disciples became attached to tranquility, and averse to creative activity. In view of this development, Wang Yang-ming substituted "refining and training oneself in concrete affairs" for sitting in total quiescence.[22]

Summary and Evaluation

In summarizing Wang Yang-ming's views, we may begin by pointing out what he had in common with the Confucian tradition. He shared its belief in the essential goodness of man and the need for man to exert himself, its concern for the rectification of affairs and of oneself and its stress on the significance and value of life here and now. He accepted the Confucian assumption of the knowability of the world and its inter-relatedness, its placing of man in a position of centrality and its insistence on the importance of virtue. He agreed with the Confucian emphasis on the harmony of man and nature, Heaven as an over-arching principle, the need for order and the primacy of wisdom or sageliness. These, and other elements, which make up the Confucian tradition Wang Yang-ming found quite congenial.

The Neo-Confucianists too accepted those aspects of Confucianism, and to that extent their and Wang Yang-ming's view are compatible. Basic differences are evident, however, to which we now turn. Among the Neo-Confucianists, as among philosophers generally, there were those who advocated beginning with the external world or looking without and others who stressed beginning with oneself or looking within. There were those who conceived of knowledge as facts, data or information about the world around them; others believed knowledge to consist of principles found in the mind. Some Neo-Confucianists declared that principles are in the external world and one finds them by analyzing that world; others held that principles are already in the mind and are distilled out, known or intuited directly by the "innate knowing faculty."

Furthermore, there were dualists who separated mind and nature, knower and known, perceiver and the perceived and non-dualists who insisted on a close unity or affinity of the sets. Chu Hsi may be taken as an exponent of the first and Wang Yang-ming of the second in each of the above cases. Chu Hsi was a dualist in his separation of man and nature, mind and principle, substance and function. Wang Yang-ming viewed reality as a totality, as one. It has a single ontological essence, Liang-chih; and its existential implication is the unity of all things.

A further, important distinction is to be noted. Not only is there a divergence as to what knowledge is or consists of but there is disagreement also as to the purpose of knowledge. There are those who, as noted above, define knowledge as information regarding objects or things, and there are those who see knowledge as knowing what direction to take in human affairs. That is, for some the purpose of knowledge is an understanding of the material world; for others it is normative, not informative. We seek knowledge in order that we may be more virtuous or have a better world.

For Wang Yang-ming ko-wu is the second type and purpose. To him investigation is rectification—"the investigation of things is the work of abiding in the highest good." Or, as he puts it in the fourth axiom, "The rectification of things is to perform good and remove evil." Wang Yang-ming conceived of knowing as not a scientific, rational investigation of things but as the elimination of "what is incorrect in the mind so as to preserve the correctness of its original substance."

This was the reason for Wang Yang-ming insisting, contrary to Chu Hsi, that sincerity of will precede or be held superior to the investigation of things and the extension of knowledge. In order to extend one's knowledge, one must begin by purifying oneself rather than by investigating things. The will must be made sincere or pure, first of all. It must be purged of selfish desires for, when one is no longer motivated by such desires and wishes to do only what is the good or right for all, he will investigate things in an unbiased and impartial fashion and his knowledge inevitably will be greater. Approaching a problem or situation selfishly or with only one's own interest in mind leads to a partial or limited rather than full understanding of the problem. If one's will is pure, however, if one is sincere or unselfish, one's knowledge will be extended and the investigation of things will be complete. One's mind will transcend good and evil because one will be motivated by impartiality rather than by either, as implied in the first of the four-epigram teaching. One's mind will be in a state of equanimity or unperturbability. The faculty of innate knowledge will fulfil its true role of knowing good and evil, and one will be stimulated to act with the intention of promoting good and eradicating evil.

It is evident from the above that for Wang Yang-ming knowledge and action are one and not separate, as Chu Hsi maintained. In asserting that "knowledge is the beginning of action and action the completion of knowledge, Wang Yang-ming makes several points. When one knows the good, one will be so attracted by it that he cannot help but do it. Knowing is itself an activity. One learns through acting or doing. Knowing does not take place in a vacuum but in a specific context. Action should not be based upon impulse but on deliberation and self-examination. The attitude that one should know first and then put knowledge in practice is erroneous. Wang Yang-ming likened it to an incapacitating disease and he claimed his "advocacy of the unity of knowledge and action is precisely the medicine for that disease."

Wang Yang-ming pointed out that, when we talk about knowledge and action we talk about them as separate, but in fact they are not. It is not to be wondered that he declared they "should proceed simultaneously." Such a view is inevitable, given Wang Yang-ming's definition of thing as event and his belief that the purpose of knowledge is normative or his conceiving of knowledge as "the direction for action."

The Lu-Wang school (School of Mind) which was initiated by the Neo-Confucianist Ch'eng Hao (1032-1085), and continued by Lu Hsiang-shen (1139-1193) reached its culmination in the early Ming with Wang Yang-ming. Mencius was its earliest ancestor, and Wang-Yang-ming's contribution was his ordering and systematizing of the views of the two earlier Neo-Confucianists. He was to Chinese philosophy in the early Ming, what Kant was to European philosophy in the nineteenth century.

Wang Yang-ming was influenced by Buddhism, as seen in his emphasis on meditation, forming one body with not only human but other forms of being and reality being in constant flux. But like many Neo-Confucianists he criticized Buddhists for being overly pessimistic and escapist, "having nothing to do with the work of the family, the state and the world." And while in many ways a universalist himself, he criticized Mo Tzu's universal love as lacking in distinction and having no starting point. Love must begin somewhere, and the proper place is one's own parents and family as distinguished from others.

Two outstanding disciples of Wang Yang-ming were Wang Chi and Ch'ien Te-hung. The latter was the more faithful of the two. Wang Chi was influenced by Hui-neng's emphasis on abrupt enlightenment. He maintained that not only mind-in-itself but will, knowledge and things are all beyond good and evil and that sagehood is attained through a sudden awakening. Ch'ien Te-hung stressed Wang Yang-ming's last instead of the first of the four teachings and claimed attaining sagehood through doing good and undoing evil must be a gradual, stage-by-stage process. Wang Yang-ming resolved the difference between the two by maintaining that the first way was suitable for those of gifted intelligence and the second for those of lesser or average intellect. The way which is appropriate is determined by the nature of each individual.

Important among Wang Yang-ming's critics were Chan Jo-shui who, rejecting the stratification of absolute and relative good, repudiated the first of the four teachings claiming that mind-in-itself can only be good and cannot be beyond good and evil. Another was Lo Ch'in-shun who revived Chu Hsi's objective rationalism and attacked Wang Yang-ming's interpretation of liang-chih as knowing merely subjective mind-in-itself at the expense of excluding the objective nature of the mind.

Lesser critics were Lü Nan who adhered to the traditional distinction made in the *Book of History* between knowledge and action.[23] Huang Wan also criticized Wang Yang-ming and presented a pragmatic and utilitarian revision of his philosophy. A third, Lin Chih-ya, opposed Wang Yang-ming's views on the grounds that they discouraged an investigation of the external world and thus impeded what we call the growth of science and scientific outlook, a criticism gaining increasing favor today.[24]

Despite his critics, many of whom were followers of Chu Hsi, Wang Yang-ming's influence was extensive. His emphasis on the close relation of knowledge and action, and his conceiving of knowledge moralistically had immediate repercussions politically. They aroused opposition to corrupt officials and stimulated much needed reform activity on the part of many of his followers. Wang Yang-ming's philosophy of action was carried to Japan where it became influential in the seventeenth century and again in the period of the Meiji restoration.[25] And in the twentieth century Sun Yat Sen found his activist philosophy relevant and appealing, as did Chiang K'ai-shek.

Unfortunately differences arose among Wang Yang-ming's followers over his doctrine of innate knowledge especially. Using it as a guise, some of his disciples engaged in a number of extreme views and practices which led critics to blame the collapse of the Ming in part on Wang Yang-ming's philosophy.

Nevertheless, despite his critics and the capriciousness of some of his followers, Wang Yang-ming and his philosophy stirred great admiration among followers of the Chinese tradition. His philosophy of forming one body with all things was appealing both to those of a sensitive nature and to people who recognized the need for national unity. Believing that virtue comes from within and is not necessarily dependent on promptings from without, Wang Yang-ming helped people to recognize that self-rectification, while difficult, is always a necessary task.

Wang Yang-ming was applauded for his concern for his fellowmen, as he wished all men a full, happy life. His portraying of the highest good as "manifesting character and loving people" was recognized as highly commendable and much needed in practice. His belief that man can know good and evil, if he wills to, many found valid. His unquenchable faith in man's essential goodness, even though it may be clouded over at times, inspired large numbers. Wang Yang-ming envisioned a society in which individuals were concerned not solely with their own ambitions and ends. He believed many people, government leaders for example, had become mired in selfish desires and petty details with resultant social chaos, and he offered his philosophy of idealism and magnanimity as its cure.

Notes

1. Chang Hsi-chih, *Yang-ming hsueh-chuan* (Academic Biography of Yang-ming) (Taipei: Chung Hua, 1961), pp. 19-20.

2. Hegel, *Lectures on the Philosophy of History*, tr. Wang Tso-shih (Peking: Triad, 1958), p. 72. Hegel is not completely right in saying: "Both these (China and India) lack...the essential consciousness of the conception of freedom." and "The Orientals do not know that the spirit is free in itself, or that man is free in himself." At least Mencius and Yang-ming knew that conscience is absolutely free to choose between options. See Hegel, "Introduction to the *Philosophy of History*," tr. C.J. & P.W. Friedrich, in *The Philosophy of Hegel*, ed. C.J. Friedrich (New York: The Modern Library, 1954), pp. 11, 34. Although Hegel created the term "cunning of reason," Wang Fu-chih (1619-1692) first conceived the idea that Heavenly (natural) Tao made impartial accomplishments thru the selfish desires of Ch'in-shih-huang (First emperor of the Ch'in dynasty) and Empress Wu-tse-t'ien. See Wang Ch'uanshan, *Tu T'ung-chien lun* (Reading the *Mirror of Universal History*) (Taipei: Chung Hua, 1970), vol. 1, 1:2a; vol. 3, 21:12b. Ch'uan-shan, the most dynamic thinker after Yang-ming, is also the best philosopher of history in China.

3. *Wang Yang-ming ch'uan-shu* (Complete Works of Wang Yang-ming) (Taipei: Cheng Chung, 1970), vol. 1, p. 90. Hereafter cited as *WYCSI*.

4. *WYCSI*, pp. 103-4.

5. Hou Wai-lu and others, *Chung-kuo ssu-hsiang t'ung-shih* (General History of Chinese Thought) (Peking: People: 1960) vol. 4, lower section, pp. 884-7.

6. Sartre, *Being and Nothingness*, tr. Hazel E. Barnes (New York: Philosophical Library, 1956), pp. 47-50; Hazel E. Barnes, *An Existentialist Ethics* (New York: Alfred A. Knopf, 1968) part one.

7. Heidegger, *Being and Time*, tr. J. Macquarri & E. Robinson (New

York: Harper and Row, 1962), p. 307; *Sein and Zeit* (Tubingen: Max Niemeyer Verlag, 1953), pp. 295-301.

8. Heidegger, *Kant and the Problem of Metaphysics*, tr. James S. Churchill (Bloomington and London: Indiana University Press, 1968), pp. 30-9. Concerning "uncovering and truth," see pp. 260-71, 300-1. Truth is uncoveredness of entities, Being-disclosive, or the way in which Dasein behaves. As to aletheia, see Heidegger, *An Introduction to Metaphysics*, tr. Ralph Manheim (New York: Doubleday, 1961), pp. 86, 102, 154-5, 159, 161. About "standing-in-itself," see pp. 52, 86. Later Heidegger (Heidegger II) coined the term "event of appropriation" which has a touch of Eastern philosophy. See his *Identity and Difference*, tr. Joan Stambaugh (New York: Harper & Row, 1969), pp. 36-7. This book shows how metaphysics cannot but be derived from theology and logic. Chinese moral metaphysics, however, dispense with theology.

9. Wang Fu-chih, *Chang-tzu cheng-ment chu* (Commentary on Chang Tzu's *Rectifying Youthful Ignorance*) (Peking: Chung Hua, 1975), pp. 121-3.

10. *WYCSI*, p. 87.

11. *WYCSI*, pp. 89-90. Also see my essay "The Transcendence and Actuality of Chang Tzu's Tao," in the *Journal of the Institute of Chinese Studies of The Chinese University of Hong Kong*, vol. VI, no. 1 (1973): 109-42.

12. *Erh-Ch'eng Ch'uan-shu* (Complete Works of the Two Ch'engs) (*Ssu-pu pei-yao* or Essentials of the Four Libraries edition), vol. 1, I-shu, 2a:3.

13. *Ibid.*, vol. 5, *Ming-tao wen-chi*, 3:1.

14. *Hsiang-shan ch'uan-chi* (Complete Works of Hsiang-shan) (*Ssu-pu pie-yao* or Essentials of the Four Libraries edition), vol. 4, 34:5b.

15. *WYCSI*, pp. 119-20.

16. *WYCSI*, p. 120.

17. See my essay "Han Fei Tzu's Development and Revision of His Forerunners' Works and Distortion of *Lao Tzu*," in *New Asia College Academic Journal*, vol. XVII (Hong Kong, 1975): 189-220.

18. For Kant, "the maxim of self-love (prudence) only *advises*, the law of morality *commands*." Having classified the principle of volitions into three planes: rules of skill, counsels of prudence, and commands (laws) of morality, Kant said, "We might also call the first kind of imperatives *technical* (belonging to art), the second *pragmatic* (to welfare), the third *moral* (belonging to free conduct generally; that is, to morals). *Kant's Critique of Practical Reason and Other Works on the Theory of Ethics*, tr. T.K. Abbott (London: Longmans, 1967), pp. 126-34.

19. Kant, the Western Mencius or Prussian Wang Yang-ming, also declared, "The only objects of practical reason are...those of *good* and evil. For by the former is meant an object necessarily desired according to a principle of reason; by the latter one necessarily shunned, also according to a principle of reason...But *good* and *evil* always implies a reference to the *will*, as determined by the *law of reason* to make something its object; for it is never determined directly by the object and the idea of it, but is a faculty of taking a rule of reason for the motive of an action (by which an object may be realized).

Good and evil, are properly referred to actions, not to the sensations of the person, and if anything is to be good or evil absolutely (i.e., in every respect and without further condition), or is to be esteemed, it can only be the manner of acting, the maxim of the will, and consequently the acting person himself as a good or evil man that can be so called, and not a thing...it is the moral law that first determines the concept of good..." *Ibid.*, p. 17.

20. *WYCSI*, p. 84.

21. *Spinoza: The Political Works*, ed. and tr. A.G. Wernham (Oxford: at the University Press, 1965). *Tractatus Politicus* (Treatise on Politics), p. 273.

22. *WYCSI*, p. 87.

23. Huang Tsung-hsi, ed. *Ming-ju-hsueh-an* (Selected Works of Ming Scholars) (Taipei: The World Press, 1965), p. 56.

24. For Wang Yang-ming, liang-chih is the first principle or highest truth covering moral metaphysics and natural scinence. Moral truth may be found only thru inward and backward reflection, while scientific truth should be discovered by painstaking observation and experiment. Orthodox Confucians, philosophical Taoists and Buddhists condemn all outward and forward pursuit of physical truth as trifling with matter at the cost of losing the moral will or authentic self. Nevertheless, superb scientists like Einstein and Sakarov maintain their life long goodwill. For Kant, "nothing can possibly be conceived in the world, or even out of it, which can be called good, without qualification, except a Good Will." Unconditional good will is compatible with investigation of external objects. Yang-ming did not exclude natural science on purpose, but this exclusion unavoidably followed from his basic theories.

25. As to Yang-ming's influence on Japan, see: Carson Chang Chun-mai, *Pi-chiao Chung-Jih Yang-ming-hsuen* (A Comparative Study of Wang Yang-ming's Philosophy in China and Japan) (Taipei: Publishing Committee of Chinese Cultural Enterprise, 1955); Chu Ch'ien-chih, *Jih-pen ti ku-hsueh tsi Yang-ming-hsueh* (The Ancient Learning of Japan and the Philosophy of Wang Yang-ming) (Shanghai: Shanghai People, 1962).

Note: Those citations which are not annotated in this essay can easily be found in popular books like Fung Yu-lan's *History of Chinese Philosophy* and Wing-tsit Chan's prolific translations.

III
The Modern Period

11
INTRODUCTION : THE MODERN PERIOD

D. BISHOP

The two main dynasties of the Modern Period are the Ming (1368-1644) and the Ch'ing (1644-1912). The Medieval Period likewise witnessed two major ones, the T'ang (618-917) and the Sung (960-1279). The T'ang, immediately preceded by the short lived Sui (581-618), which was important because its initiation marked the end of three hundred and sixty years of internal division, was one of the greatest of Chinese dynasties. It was a period of general prosperity during which the empire reached a new level of power and wealth. Land reforms were initiated which aimed at equalizing holdings. An extensive canal system facilitated trade and the movement of goods. The increasing revenues of the state made possible a flourishing capital at Ch'ang-an which became a center of culture and the arts, as did Loyang also in the north and major cities in the south as well.

Sculpture reached its peak in the first century of the T'ang. Its poetry and calligraphy is esteemed by many as China's finest. Few Chinese poets can equal Li Po (699?-762) and Tu Fu (712-770).[1] Printing was taken up and porcelain appeared. T'ang culture influenced China's neighbors, not only Japan but Korea and Indo-China as well. The T'ang was open to outside influences and forces also. Zoroastrianism, Nestorian Christianity, Manichaeism and Islam came into China at this time.[2] T'ang society had as its pillar the extended family system, Confucian in orientation. The government was staffed by an extensive bureaucracy enlisted through the examination system centered on the traditional Confucian writings.

It was in the T'ang that Buddhism, attracting the best minds, reached its peak. This is one reason for the flourishing of the arts and culture[3]. Monasteries became centers where thinkers and artists alike could carry on their creative work. The very success of Buddhism, however, its extensive land holding for example, made it subject to attack and led in the end to its demise. In his edict of 845 the emperor Wu-tsung accused Buddhism of poisoning "the customs of our nation", "destroying law and injuring mankind" causing "men to abandon their lords and parents", beguiling and confounding "men's minds so that the multitude have been led astray" and building temples and chapels of "elegant ornamentation sufficient to outshine the imperial palace itself."[4]

Five dynasties ruled China from 907 to 960 when the Sung was instituted. The Sung dynasty was also one of many achievements. Landscape painting has often been proclaimed as its greatest, one writer claiming that it "touched perfection and has never been surpassed or even equalled in later times." The printing and porcelain which appeared in the T'ang continued to be improved. In literature the writing of histories became popular and advanced, Ssu-ma Kuang (1019-1086) being the most noted historiographer. There was a steady expansion of commerce and trade which, along with sound agriculture, provided an economic basis for cultural growth, the increasing number and size of cities being the loci for it.[5] The rise of Neo-Confucianism is emblematic of a changing viewpoint, Chinese culture becoming less cosmopolitan and tending to look inward. Although Buddhism was still influential—many Neo-Confucianists practised meditation for example it and Taoism both tended to decline. The Neo-Confucian revival was a result, in part, of their demise. It was due to practical circumstances also. Some areas of China were at times under foreign control and there was a constant threat from without which led Chinese intellectuals to search for a philosophical foundation for national strength and unity. Furthermore, improvements in printing enabled education to become more widespread and academies and other centers of learning, each usually headed by an outstanding scholar, sprang up all over the country, replacing Buddhist monasteries as centers of learning.[6]

Hu Yuan (993-1059) is one of the best known of these independent scholars. While Buddhist in his use of Buddhist terminology, he was a thorough Confucianist in his exposition of traditional Confucianism. He stressed a close relationship between teacher and pupil, saw as one of his duties the ethical indoctrination of his students and had as a primary concern the application of Confucian ethics to politics and everyday life. The study of the Classics had this as its goal, for the truths in them, he claimed, were relevant to all times, places and people. To him the Way was an all-inclusive concept and reality with a threefold manifestation. The first, substance, consisted of the age-old bonds and rituals of society; the second, literary expression, is the Classics which describe and perpetuate them; the third, function, is the practical application of the Way so as to bring about prosperity and order in the empire.

Hu Yuan was critical of the formalism he believed characterized the literary examination system and asserted it yielded only mediocrity. Although he continued throughout his lifetime in the role of teacher, not administrator or government official, he offered practical measure for enhancing social welfare, improving agriculture and strengthening the country's defences. Wang An-shih (1021-1086) was also one of this class of scholars, and he had close ties with the leaders of the Confucian revival. But he was more of an administrator and he became the leader of a movement of political renewal which was both thorough and not without opposition.

Of the Sung Neo-Confucianists it was Chu Hsi's interpretation which became the official state ideology and the basis of the examination system in much of the Sung and a large part of the Ming (1368-1644) dynasty. While giving continuity to Chinese philosophy, the domination of Chu Hsi's views resulted in little creativity or innovation as well. The Ming dynasty itself was more an era of cultural consolidation than innovation. Few heights were scaled in literature and the arts in the Ming, although there were advances in carpet making, bronze casting and especially in ceramics. There was much building also, so that architecture flourished. The military power of the empire increased. It was also a time of the coming of the Europeans, the Portugese to Macao, the Spanish to Formosa and then the Dutch and the British to Canton. In Christian circles the Jesuits were the most ambitious and successful. Francis Xavier arrived in China in 1552 and Matthew Ricci in 1582.[7]

As the Ming period progressed the examination system under the influence of narrow minded and dogmatic scholars became increasingly rigid and stereotyped, the famous eight legged essay being an epitome of it.[8] A reaction against both this trend and Chu Hsi's philosophy resulted in the formation of the Lu-Wang School initiated by Ch'ing Hao, carried on by Lu Chiui-yuan (1139-1193) and culminating with Wang Yang-ming, also known as Wang Shou-jen (1472-1528).

While one may begin by labelling one a rationalist or an advocate of intellectual speculation and the other an idealist or proponent of introspection, the differences between Chu Hsi and Wang-Yang-ming may be summed up briefly as follows. Chu Hsi asserted we should begin with all the many particular existing things to determine the principles inherent in them. Such a view entails a separation between things, the mind and principles. Wang Yang-ming on the other hand asserted that things are not external but internal or in the mind and that mind and principle are likewise one rather than separate. A mind which separates things from itself and becomes concerned with externals becomes a "little mind" dealing only with triflings and the inconsequential and this is what had happened to the Neo-Confucianists in the end, Wang believed.

Furthermore, Chu Hsi interpreted or viewed the mind from an intellectual standpoint, while to Wang Yang-ming mind was or involved will. Will is primary, for one must will or choose to investigate things first, if one is to acquire knowledge. Moreover, while Chu Hsi was more intellectual in approach, Wang was more moral. We learn or investigate things not for the sake of knowing only or in itself but in order to bring about improvement by supporting the good and opposing evil. Wang Yang-ming is noted especially for, first, his doctrine of the extension of the innate knowledge of the good and, secondly, for his doctrine of the unity of knowledge of action. We can know intuitively, directly or immediately what the good is and, once knowing what it is we can also know how to apply it or put it into practice.

The transition in philosophical thought from Chu Hsi's rationalism to Wang Yang-ming's idealism was continued in the seventeenth and eighteenth centuries with a new emphasis among many scholars on practicality or practical learning and truth as objective, not subjective. Basic in this emphasis was the assertions that there is no principle apart from material force, that knowing should have practical ends and that the investigation of things involves learning through practical experience and the solving of practical problems.

In the text Wang Fu-chih (1619-1692) illustrates this trend. Others like him who may be briefly acknowledged at this point are Ku Yen Wu (1613-1682), Yen jo-ch'u (1636-1704) and Yen Yuan (1635-1704) especially.[9] Yen Yuan believed the sitting in meditation adopted from Buddhism by many Confucian scholars was useless and unproductive. He claimed principles are not self-existent or do not exist apart from material forces or things. The implication of this is that truth in the form of abstract principles or concepts is learned only through actual experience or interaction with the physical world of concrete objects. And truth or knowledge must be actively sought out; it does not just come to one.

Yen Yuan also, in believing man "the purest of all things", rejected the view that man's physical nature is the source of evil, and admitted it is only a means thereof. Like Plato and Mencius, he saw evil as being a result of external influences. Yen Yuan's practicalism was reflected in the academy he set up which had four halls, one each for history and the Classics, literature, military arts and practical affairs. This made it possible for him to teach not only literature, history and the Classics but such practical subjects as agriculture, which he himself engaged in. Interestingly, he was an advocate of the early well-field system favored by Mencius.

The questions agitating thinkers in the Sung and Ming continued to perplex Ch'ing thinkers as well. What is the nature of reality-material, immaterial or both? Which is primary and which is secondary? What is knowledge and its sources? What does it originate in, the internal, the external or a source transcending both? Is truth or concepts a product of culture or do concepts determine culture? Is truth of the nature of the particular or the universal? Is there universal truth or truths or only particular truths? What is the role of the philosopher? To seek knowledge for its own sake or satisfaction, or to know in order to reform? Is the morality the philosopher is to be concerned with only a personal or private one, or is there what we might call a social ethics or ethics for society philosophers ought to be concerned with? What is man himself? Is he but a particular among a multitude of particulars? Or does he have a universal nature or share in a universal one too? If the latter, what is the nature of that universal nature? What about past, present and future? Should we press for continuity or discontinuity? Is the past a suitable model for the present and future or do changing conditions require a new one or ones? How are new and alien views to be dealt with? Accepted critically, uncritically or not at all? These are some of the issues Chinese thinkers dealt with as we shall see in the following chapters.

NOTES

1. Li, Dun J., *The Civilization of China*, New York, Charles Scribner's Sons, 1975, p. 148.
2. Latourette, Kenneth Scott, *The Chinese, Their History and Culture*, New York, The Macmillian Company, 4th edition, 1962, pp. 155-6, 218-219.
3. A good study of Buddhism in China is Kenneth Chen's *Buddhism in China: A Historical Survey*.
4. De Bary, Wm. Theodore, *Sources of The Chinese Tradition*, Vol. I, New York, Columbia University Press, 1960, pp. 380-381.
5. Marco Polo in his travels in China at this time was impressed by its cities. De Bary, *op. cit.*, p. 383.
6. De Bary, *op. cit.*, p. 384.
7. Latourette, *op. cit.*, pp. 235-237.
8. See Levenson, Joseph R., *Confucian China and Its Modern Fate*, Berkeley, University of California Press, for a discussion of the eight legged essay.
9. See Chan, *Source Book in Chinese Philosophy*, pp. 703-704.

12
WANG FU-CHIH

D. BISHOP

The Neo-Confucianism which arose in the Sung and Ming dynasties took two major forms, the earlier rationalism of Chu Hsi and the later subjective idealism of Wang Yang-ming. Rationalists such as Chu Hsi asserted that universals are prior to particulars, principles precede material force or that there is a realm of the unchanging behind over-changing phenomena. Thus an objective reality exists independent of the mind cognizing it. Wang Yang-ming held that truth lies in the mind and we attain it through intuition independent of the phenomenal world.

Wang Fu-chih's opposition to both, and to Buddhism and Taoism as well, was precipitated by the downfall of the Ming at the hands of the invading Manchus, a demise which Wang blamed on the Neo-Confucianists whose starting point was the mind rather than the real world.[1] They had become involved in contemplation and abstract speculation to such an extent that what they thought, said and did offered little guidance to man and his existential concerns. Their rationalism and idealism had not been "realistic enough to provide decisive thinking and patriotic, victorious action."[2] Moreover immorality had set in due in part to one wing of the Wang school which "...went so far as to proclaim that wine, women and song were no obstacle to attaining Enlightenment."[3] The ultimate result was a weakening of the state, its decadence within making it an easier prey of enemies from without.

The philosophical reaction which set in took the form of a materialistic outlook or an empirically oriented school of thinkers, prominent among whom was Wang Fu-chih (1619-1692). They were solicitous for the here and now, for this world and this life and how it can be improved; and no metaphysical or epistemological positions were acceptable which were unrelated to that concern. They insisted that philosophy and philosophers must ever keep in mind the needs of this world and its betterment. Scholars should concern themselves with only what is useful to that end.

Wang Fu-chih was born in Human province, was the son of a scholar, and received the chu-jen degree at the age of twenty four. When the Manchu army invaded the province, he became involved in military operations against them, but to no avail. Rather than being a part of the ruling hierarchy he retired to the neighboring mountains, living anonymously and writing profusely. His writings were first published for public perusal in 1842 but it was not until the latter part of the century that his views attracted wider attention and interest.

As an empiricist Wang declared that the first step we must take is to admit as primary the existence of the external world. Knowledge does not consist of innate ideas. Nor is it gained through sitting in meditation or through abstract contemplation. It is, instead, a result of the contact of the mind with objects in the world. Whatever knowledge we acquire comes from an investigation of things or a critical, detailed, objective study of the visible, tangible world around us. We should begin, then, by looking without and not within. Our starting place should be the real world and not the contents of the mind.

As we experience and investigate the external world, we notice, Wang says, that it consists "only of concrete things."[4] Those things have attributes or properties, and it is those characteristics which determine a thing's nature. A fish has fins enabling it to swim, a bird feathers allowing it to fly. Seeing each we say it is natural or it is a fish's nature to swim and a bird's to fly. The nature of a concrete, particular thing, then, is not determined by some a priori, metaphysical principle discoverable through contemplation or intuition but is determined by the specific attributes each thing possesses which enables it to act in its own unique way.

This position might be restated by saying that, according to Wang Fu-chih, the physical cannot be separated from the metaphysical, or principle (li) from material force (ch'i). Wang wrote, "the so-called metaphysical does not mean 'non-physical' or shapeless.". Where the physical is, there also is the metaphysical, which goes beyond it. To imagine something metaphysical without a physical basis is impossible. Such a monstrosity has never been met with, either in human history, or in the history of natural objects...If one puts aside these concrete objects and searches for a non-physical entity, one can go through history, past and present and one will find nothing to which one can attach a designation, to say nothing of attributing reality."[5]

According to Wang the metaphysical arises from or is inherent in the physical. Physical objects are not manifestations of principles, or particular things expressions of universals. Principles do not take the form of universals, transcending and existing apart from and prior to things, and manifesting themselves in things. There is no "Way" apart from concrete things. The "Way" is in the thing, is determined by the nature of the things. And we know a thing and its nature by observing, investigating and experiencing it. Thus Wang urges us to "hold on to concrete things and its Way will be preserved. Cast aside the concrete things and its Way will be destroyed."[6]

From Wang's standpoint the order of things is not from the universal to the particular, or even from the particular to the universal, since the two are one or the universal and the particular cannot be separated. Principles are or lie within things. They have no separate existence. They arise from things. We conclude that there is a principle of growth, for example, from seeing things grow. Similarly the concept of impartiality comes from acts of rewarding and punishing and virtue from relations such as between father and son. And the notion of usefulness arises from man's interaction with "water, fire, metal and wood", of well being from the presence of "grains, fruits, silk and hemp."[7] In terms of such an empirical standpoint we recognize the existence of an entity through noting its usefulness (in Wang's words—"From their functions I know they possess substance"), and we understand its nature through seeing its characteristics. Seeing how a thing functions tells us about its nature or "Way" (Tao). Essence, then, is determined by its usefulness. Meaning is to be found in activity. Wang wrote that "What is operable is based on Being. From operation we infer reality. Because of being we have operation or function. Because of being we have reality, which produces the constitution of things. Reality and operation together build up truth by means of which the laws of nature and morality act."[8]

While Wang took a Positivist's view that reality consists of particular things, he argued at the same time as an organicist for the inter-relatedness and interdependence of things. In his commentary on the *Book of Changes* he asks, "Is there a thing in this world which is distinctly by itself and has no relation to anything whatsoever?" His answer was, "no such thing can be found in the universe. Neither can it be found in the mind...a thing or concept which is completely isolated, and related to nothing whatsoever outside itself, is impossible to find, either among the various kinds of physical things, or in mind."[9] In fact it is this inter-relatedness which enables us to talk about the "Way" in a broad sense or to even have a concept or understanding of the Way. There could be no "Way of Nature" without the unity of nature.

It is interrelatedness or correlations, moreover, which is the basis of or which makes possible both the orderliness or order we find in nature and the process of daily or constant renewal. Wang accepted the traditional view that yin and yang are constantly interacting and bringing about continuous change. He says that "nature repeatedly changes and is perpetually different." Through the interaction of the yin and the yang in the five elements, the myriad forms of life are constantly coming into being, being or existing and going out of existence. In this ever on-going process there is continuity of form but discontinuity of content. For example, "the water in a river stays water", but the water which is present at a given point in a river at one moment is not the same water that was there a moment before. Thus the elements change, although their shape, form or nature does not. There is outward change or change in ch'i but not inwardly or in li. The same is true of human beings. They too are being daily renewed. They continue to be made up of "skin and flesh" but "the skin and flesh of today are not the same as the skin and flesh of former days."[10]

Wang, then conceived of reality as being both organic and dynamic. It is a totality made up of many interrelated, interdependent parts or particular things working together for the good of the whole, and it is not static but is ever changing and constantly renewing itself. That process of change is not haphazard but is orderly, having no ultimate end or purpose external to itself but having only immediate, internal and pragmatic ends or purposes.

Wang also believed there is a direct relationship between nature and virtue. First of all the concept of good itself, as noted earlier, comes from the existence of things in the world such as wood and water which we use for our physical well-being. They make life possible and thus are good or through them we arrive at the notion of good. Goodness or virtue is also associated with the mean and we arrive at the notion of the mean through our experiences with nature. A good day is one which is neither too cold nor too hot. Wang's statement, "When the Way is fulfilled, we call it virtue", illustrates that he associated goodness with completion also.[11] When a plant grows and lives out its natural cycle of maturing and producing seeds, we call it a complete cycle and view it as good. Individuals should, in the same sense, achieve completion.

Goodness becomes associated with desires and desiring because, when we see things in nature that are useful for our well-being, it is only natural to desire them. Man, then, has desires. He is a desiring creature or being. If we look upon desires as ch'i, then we must admit that there have to be principles or Li correlated with them in such a way as to result in virtue. One such principle is found in Wang's statement, "Thus in sound, color, flavor and fragrance we can broadly see the open desire of all creatures, and at the same time they also constitute the impartial principle for all of them. Let us be broad and greatly impartial, respond to things as they come, look at them, and listen to them, and follow this way in work and action without seeking anything outside."[12] Impartiality is but one of a number of ethical principles, which are a part of the existing order of things. The chief or central one is sincerity. Both its physical and metaphysical connotations are evidenced in Wang's statements. "Sincerity naturally becomes solidified" and sincerity is the beginning and end of things. Without sincerity there will be nothing."[13] Sincerity in the form of the middle way or the mean is the guiding principle in regard to desires. As applied to them it means that, while man experiences within himself the whole range of emotions, feelings or desires, not all of them should be permitted expression and those that are should not be expressed beyond moderation.

Wang's moralistic approach to art is an interesting one. One function or value of poetry, for example, is as a medium to express man's feelings or emotions. However, it is not desirable that all feelings whatsoever be allowed expression in poetry. Only those which tend toward purifying and elevating man should be. For poetry is capable of leaving a permanent impression on the reader and it may, therefore, serve either as a good or evil force in society. Wang upheld the traditional view that the function of poetry is to refine character and reinforce morality in society by appealing to man's higher sentiments. Poetry which does not express man's loftier emotions becomes "rash" and "uncouth" and socially degenerating and should not be allowed.

Wang's metaphysical belief that man and the universe are one or inseparable is seen in his views on poetry and art also. There are two elements in painting or in the writing of poetry. One is the feelings of the artist or poet; the other is the scenery or scene being portrayed (the emotional and the visual). In the process of writing a poem or painting a landscape the two cannot be separated. If you divorce the artist's feelings from that which he is trying to portray (the emotional from the visual), what you end up with, if it is poetry, is crude and vulgar. If it is painting, it is artificial and superficial. The arist has to become one with the universe he is describing or painting.[14] If he is to be a great poet or painter, he must immerse himself in it until he has become fully integrated into it. The work of the artist, then, has a moral purpose and significance and is grounded in a metaphysics which emphasizes the organic nature of reality.

Wang applied his insrumentalism to human institutions also. Just as in the world of nature everything has a function or is useful for a good end, the eye for seeing for example, so man's organizations must be of some value. Thus the state exists to serve the people. Governments subsist to promote human welfare and the best government is one which is of the greatest service to its people.[15] When a government or ruling group does not promote the general well-being, it has no legitimate claim on the loyalty of its subjects. Wang said that rulers should be neither too harsh nor too lax. They should make use of "worthy men" and rule on the basis of jen. In dealing with people a government should "bestow humanity and love to the highest degree."[16]

Wang was noted for his extreme nationalism. He loathed a foreign ruler setting foot on Chinese soil. He refused to hold office under the Manchus, preferring a solitary life in the wilderness insstead. He was very much concerned about the preservation of the Chinese nation and culture. He believed that the Chinese had sufficient moral strength and integrity to carry them through any crisis. He never feared that "the Chinese nation would perish from the face of the earth."[17] He upheld the traditional distinction between the Chinese and the "barbarian" and believed Chinese civilization to be the highest in the world.

Wang's process metaphysics with its emphasis on continual change, led him to an evolutionary view of history. History constantly changes and does not repeat itself. Man's institutions are in constant transition. The old are being replaced by new ones. Each kind of institution is a result of the conditions of the age in which it came into being. Thus they are both inevitable and appropriate for their particular age or time. Wang wrote that "During the Han and T'ang dynasties there were no Ways as we have today, and there will be many in future years which we do not have now. Before bows and arrows existed, there was no Way of archery. Before chariots and horses existed, there was no Way to drive them."[18] Similarly the ancient feudalism and well-field system "which were designed to govern the ancient world...cannot be applied universally to the present day."[19] Because of the constancy of change what was suitable for the past is not for today, and "...what is suitable for today can govern the world of today but will not necessarily be suitable for the future."[20]

Moreover Wang believed that change was progressive. Societies advance in an evolutionary sequence from lower to higher stages of civilization. Chinese culture, for example, progressed from a "primitive bestial existence, through a barbarian stage, to a more or less civilized state, and finally to the existing state of high civilization."[21] This view, of course, was contrary to traditional Taoist and Confucian ones. The Taoist extolled the prehistoric state of nature and the Confucianist the golden age of the three sage kings.[22] Wang declared we have insufficient evidence to prove the glories of a prehistoric age, and his experiences with the mountain tribes he lived among may have made him dubious. As to the golden age, he said that people who extoll the past often see only the good and overlook the bad in it. He believed the founders of the Han, T'ang and Ming dynasties were as wise and virtuous as the sage kings.

In summary, Wang Fu-chih lived at a time when, because of the conditions existing in Chinese society, philosophical idealism was being disavowed and "practical Confucianism" revived. Scholars increasingly came to believe that learning should be practical, both in origin and purpose. The emphasis was more on practice than theory, on doing more than contemplating or meditating. The starting point was to be the real world and not the mind. Thinking should begin with and be more closely related to real life. Scholars should "study, teach and practice only what is useful."[23]

It was claimed that knowledge originates in experience, not introspection. Truth is objective, not subjective. The test to be used should be that of usefulness, results or consequences. It is not to be wondered that the schools or movements which arose in the seventeenth and eighteenth centuries in China which Wang was a part of have been termed variously "Investigations Based on Evidence", the "Empirical School", "Historical Criticism" and "New Learning."[24] "Han Learning" is another, for it was asserted that truth is to be sought "directly from the old classics" and the classics should be studied as "guides for practical ends."[25] Moreover those classics predated Buddhism and religious Taoism and thus were the authoritative literature of the Confucian tradition. That tradition had become overburdened with the doctrines of Buddhism and Taoism, and Wang and others sought to extricate Confucianism from the weight of that growth.

Wang and others like him emphasized the need for strong personal character and living a life of jen (human-heartedness).[26] The result would be no dishonesty in the household or corruption in government. China should be a strong nation, for she is still the center of the world.[27] National strength would be the result of personal virtue, integrity and character. Laxity and folly are not permissible. The common good, not self-interest, should be the motivating force. Society should be such that people can have their desires and wants fulfilled, as it is only natural for them to do so.

Wang was both a traditionalist and a non-traditionalist. He was the former in that he both inherited and transmitted the nationalist sentiment which had long been a part of the Chinese tradition.[28] He accepted traditional Confucian morality centered around the five great relationships and the accompanying virtues.[29] Like Motzu he accepted wars of defence and condemned wars of aggression.[30] He taught the central premise of political thought that the ruler must not be despotic; he must be moral and have the good of the people at heart. He was not a traditionalist, however, in that his materialism was more extreme than those before him. One author writes, for example, that though "Wang has been correctly described as Chang's (Chang Heng-ch'u, 1020-1077) successor...he actually went beyond Chang "for what Wang wanted "was not only materiality, but concreteness of materiality."[31] His empirical interpretation of history was a stringent one also. We are to learn practical lessons from history and any non-natural interpretations of history are to be immediately rejected.[32] Further, Wang presented an evolutionary as opposed to dynastical interpretation of Chinese history. Instead of accepting the usual division based on dynasties, he divided Chinese history into three periods based on the phenomenon of progressive change.[33] Moreover his view as to the relationship between principle and desires was one which had not been considered for several hundred years.[34] And his scepticism regarding the "Golden Age" of sage-kings was most untraditional.[35]

As noted earlier Wang's written works remained anonymous during his lifetime and did not receive public attention until the nineteenth century. His influence during his lifetime was not as extensive, as a result, as it was in the late eighteen hundreds. T'an Ssut'ung, a reformer who died in 1898, took many of his ideas on reform from Wang.[36] In the twentieth century Wang has influenced Chinese nationalist and revolutionary thought and activity.[37] He is believed to have had an influence on Mao Tse-tung and certainly many of Wang's views paralleled those of Chinese communists today.

Notes

1. Wang disliked Taoism for its emphasis on non-being (wu), inactivity (wu-wei) and vacuity (hsu). He was an authority on Buddhism, opposing it, however, for its views of the illusoriness of the world, its an-ātman or noself doctrine, its negation of life as filled with suffering and its goal it sets up for man of release and withdrawal from the world. For Buddhism in China see Kenneth Chen's *Buddhism in China: A Historical Survey*.

2. Clarence B. Day, *The Philosophers of China, Classical and Contemporary*, The Citadel Press, New York, 1962, p. 231.

3. Liang Ch'i-ch'ao, *Intellectual Trends in Ch'eng Period*, Harvard University Press, Cambridge, 1959, p. 5.

4. Wing-Tsit Chan, *A Source Book in Chinese Philosophy*, Princeton University Press, Princeton, 1963, p. 694.

5. Carsun Chang, *The Development of Neo-Confucian Thought*, Bookman Associates, New York, 1962, p. 270. Joseph Levenson in his book Modern China and *Neo-Confucian Past* has a rather technical philosophical discussion of empiricist thinkers of Wang's time which is interesting and informative.

6. Chan, *op. cit.*, p. 696.
7. Chan, *op. cit.*, p. 695.
8. Chang, *op. cit.*, p. 273.
9. Chang, *op. cit.*, p. 275.
10. Chang, *op. cit.*, p. 276.
11. Chan, *op. cit.*, p. 695.
12. Chan, *op. cit.*, p. 700.
13. Chan, *op. cit.*, p. 696.

14. One interesting analysis of Wang's views of Art is found in a University of Hong Kong Master's thesis by Song-Nian Yeo titled *A Reconstruction of Wang Fu-chih's Theory of Poetry* (1970). The classical contention that the artist's feelings must be purified and that he must become one with the universe is discussed in chapter two of Mai-mai Sze's *The Way of Chinese Painting*.

15. "He supported the theory that the state is organized for the sake of the people, and not for the rulers—the best form of government being, in his opinion, the one which can be of the greatest service to the people." Arthur W. Hummel, Editor, *Eminent Chinese of the Ch'ing Period*, U.S. Government Printing Office, Washington, 1944, vol. II, p. 818.

16. S.Y. Teng in an essay on Wang Fu-chih writes that Wang "...was extremely critical of the Ch'in and Sung dynasties for their despotism. The empire should belong to the public. The superior ruler is one who adopts policies ahead of time; the mediocre ruler merely keeps in step with the times, and the worst ruler is one who goes against his times." *Journal of Asian Studies*, Vol. XXVIII No. 1, Nov. 1968, p. 116.

17. Lin Mousheng, *Men and Ideas*, John Day Company, New York, 1942, p. 212.

18. Chan, *op. cit.*, p. 695.
19. Teng, *op. cit.*, p. 115.
20. Chan, *op. cit.*, p. 701.
21. Mousheng, *op. cit.*, p. 208.

22. Teng writes that Wang "...criticized Lao Tzu's exhortation to simplicity and a return to nature" because he thought "this would drive people back to the primitive stage." *op. cit.*, p. 116.

23. Day, *op. cit.*, p. 234.

24. Day's book has a chapter titled "The Return to Empirical Realism" which discusses the various schools or movements which arose in this period. *op. cit.*, pp. 229-260.

25. Liang Ch'i-chao, *op. cit.*, p. 23.

26. Others in this period of an empirical orientation are Ku Yen-wu (1613-1682), Huang Tsung-hsi (1610-1695), Yen Yuan (1635-1704) and Tai Chen (1724-1777).

27. Teng quotes Wang as writing of China, "her wealth is sufficient to be multiplied by the millions, her military power is adequate to make herself strong, and the wisdom of her people can win renown for them." *op. cit.*, p. 117.

28. Mousheng writes of Chinese nationalism, "It has often been said that Chinese nationalism is a new theory and a new movement, a resultant of China's contact and conflict with the West. This is an incorrect view. While Chinese national consciousness has certainly increased in recent decades, it began no less than twenty-five centuries ago...In no age has nationalism ever ceased to be a strong sentiment and a dynamic force." *op. cit.*, p. 213.

29. As an example of this one might point out that, while Wang accepted many points of the philosophy of Li Chih (1527-1602), he, in one author's words "...nevertheless reacted in horror to Li's total abandonment of moral standards." Wm. Theodore de Bary, *Self and Society in Ming Thought*, Columbia University Press, New York, 1970, p. 216.

30. Wang, for example, condemned Emperor Sui Wen-ti (581-604), for exhausting the nation by his attack on Korea. See Teng, *op. cit.*, p. 123.

31. Chan, *op. cit.*, p. 692.

32. Teng points out that Wang "...vehemently denied all divine or magical interpretations of history...Wang went on to repudiate fate, luck, and all other mysterious or supernatural forces as influences on the course of history. We may say that Wang aimed at no less than liberating history from China's ancient mysticism." Teng, *op. cit.*, p. 116.

33. Chang writes that "Wang Fu-Chih was one of the very few Chinese thinkers who recognized the importance of progressive change of renewal." *op. cit.* p. 291.

34. Liang Ch'i Ch'ao writes that Wang's idea that "the Rational Principle of nature resides in human desires and that without human desires there can be no discovery of the Rational Principle of nature may be considered an insight into what had not been thought of since the Sung (960-1277 A.D.)..." *op. cit.*, p. 39.

35. "Though Wang Fu-chih does not deny the greatness of the early sage-kings, he breaks sharply with tradition by asserting that the times in which they lived, despite their efforts, were crude and dark and that there has been a steady subsequent growth in civilization," Arthur F. Wright, editor, *Studies In Chinese Thought*, University of Chicago Press, Chicago, 1953, p. 34.

36. Liang Ch'i Ch'ao writes that "Later on, Wang substantially affected the thinking of a scholar from his native town, T'an Ssu-t'ung, who once said: Among the scholars of the past five hundred years, Wang alone was truly capable of comprehending natural and human causes." *op. cit.*, p. 39.

37. Teng in his article writes: "Since the late nineteenth century, Wang's work has been an inspiration to the nationalist and revolutionary Chinese. For

some time beginning in 1907, Wang Fu-chih was honored in Confucian temples. His *Tu T'ung chien lun* and *Sung lun* was said to have been in the hands of almost every student in school during the Republican period. Possibly as a result of Mao Tse-tung's early interest in Wang and his connection with the institute called Ch'uan' shan hsueh'she in Changsha, a large discussion meeting was held on November 18-26, 1962 at the Hunan capital, in which more than ninety scholars participated, commemorating the two hundred seventieth anniversary of Wang Fu-chih. *op. cit.*, p. 122. See also Chan, *op. cit.* p. 776.

13
KANG YU-WEI

D. BISHOP

K'ang Yu-wei lived from 1858 to 1927. He described himself as from a family "with a tradition of literary studies for thirteen generations."[1] Certainly he was widely read, as his written works, filled with reference to people and philosophies East and West, past and present, testify.[2]

K'ang was an activist as well, however. He was concerned about contemporary conditions in China and became a leader of reforms.[3] In 1883 he formed an Anti-Footbinding Society and sent a memorial regarding the custom to the Throne in 1898. This was but one of a number of petitions directed to the emperor, not all of which reached him.[4] In 1898 K'ang was finally able to meet the emperor and a number of edicts directed towards needed reforms followed. Becoming alarmed, the Empress Dowager put an end to the budding reform movement.[5] K'ang fled to Hong Kong and from there to Japan, America, and Europe, finally returning permanently to China in 1912.

The suffering of man was the primary impetus of K'ang's thought and activity.[6] He tells how, on returning to his native village in 1885, "...amid the pledging of wine among the villagers, the mutual helpfulness of the neighborhood women, the fondling of the children, and the manifestations of affection among family members, my ears heard all the sounds of quarreling, my eyes saw all the aspects of distress." He concluded that, while "All this grief and misery is termed peace, in reality in every household in the world, the overflowing of jealousies and the clashing of wills at cross-purposes is more poisonous than yellow fog and pervades the whole world."[7]

What was he to do in the face of this suffering, K'ang asked himself. Flee from the world, as the Brahmin resorts to his cave? K'ang found that impossible. Then go discover the causes of suffering and do something about its cure. What are they? In the end K'ang summed up the causes in one generalization. The nine boundaries are the cause of suffering; their abolition is the cure.

National, class, racial, sex, family, livelihood, and administrative along with the boundaries of kind and suffering are the nine. They predominated in early times in the Age of Disorder. They have been abolished to some extent and in some places, but still largely characterize the world in the present Age of Increasing Peace and Equality. In no place, however, has the third stage of man's evolution, the Age of Complete Peace and Equality, been reached.[8] This is the goal we should all seek to realize, for in it there will be no misery and suffering. All people will then be happy, prosperous and content.

K'ang conceived of the "boundaries" as limitations or barriers which kept man from becoming what he might be. What people are and what they might become, was an important distinction to K'ang. For he would not accept man or the world as it is. He believed it could be different, and he took as his two-fold task pointing out to his fellow men that world which might be, and practical activity aimed at bringing it into being.

What we have here, of course, is the problem of the nature of man. What is man's nature? Where does it come from? Can it be corrupted? Can it be improved? How? To what extent? Central to K'ang's concept of man is his belief that all people "proceed from Heaven," that the "...all-embracing Primal Ch'i created Heaven and Earth," that "Although individual forms may differ in size, still they are all but parts of the all-embracing ch'i of the ultimate beginnings of the universe."

K'ang proceeded to draw several implications from this initial premise. First, all men are brothers. This is because they have a common origin and a common birth. K'ang writes, for example, "Being that I was born on earth, then mankind in the ten thousand countries of the earth are all my brothers..." Second, all are equal. K'ang's insistence on the equality of women illustrates this very well. He wrote, "When we consider that all people are given birth by Heaven, and are all alike in body and intelligence, then it is extremely unjust and extremely unequal to honour men and repress women." Women are equal to men because they have a similar beginning in Heaven and are made of the same stuff.

A third implication drawn by K'ang was the interdependence of mankind. K'ang believed this was especially true in the contemporary world. What happens in one part may well have effects in other places. We share each others' happiness and sorrow. Thus we find K'ang saying regarding his fellowmen, "Do they progress—then I progress with them; do they retrogress—then I retrogress with them; are they happy—then I am happy with them; do they suffer—then I suffer with them." The fourth implication is K'ang's belief that man is in essence good. He could not be otherwise, for both the principle (Heaven) and the substance of which he is made (ch'i) is good. Since the creator is good, the created must be also.[9]

Two other components of K'ang's view of man may be mentioned. One is that man is both body and spirit. "Heaven," K'ang wrote, "is composed of a single soul substance; man is likewise composed of a single soul-substance...The earth began from spiritual ch'i; the spiritual ch'i was wind and thunder; the wind thunder flowed into form, and all things came forth to birth." The second is that pleasure and pain are the major determinants of man's actions. K'ang noted that, "under the firmament, all who have life only seek pleasure and shun suffering" and "man, already having experienced pleasure in his bodily soul, still more seeks eternal pleasure in his spiritual soul." It should be noted that K'ang's was not a crude or crass Hedonism.[10] He points out that in the Age of Complete Peace and Equality the pleasures sought will be the more refined ones involving the mind and spirit as well as body.

What, in summary, is K'ang's answer to the question of human nature? It seems that it is in essence the view, quite widely held today, of the malleability or plasticity of man. There is in each individual a basic "human nature" which is neutral at birth and which can be fashioned or led to become good, bad, or various mixtures of both. Man can be conditioned to be partial or impartial, compassionate or uncompassionate, loving or hating. In his book K'ang quite often asserted man is a product of time and circumstances. At the same time, he is not completely devoid of free will. He can choose; and it is this capacity which will enable him to reach the third level of human existence, the Age of Complete Peace and Equality.

K'ang also cautions us, again, to distinguish between what man is and what he might be. Man's true nature is the latter, not the former. K'ang was realistic in his observations of man as he is. He noted, for example, "In man's nature there is nothing but proceeds from selfishness," that "Man is the most selfish and uncompassionate of all creatures," that "...sages are not very different from tigers" because "each loves its own kind and not others." But in such statements K'ang is simply describing man as he is now. When he says, however, that "...in the Age of One World men will regard others as they regard themselves and there will be no barriers between them" and "In the Age of Complete Peace and Equality people will naturally love others, will naturally be without sin", he is pointing to man as he can and will be, since the factors or conditions which have made him the first will no longer be present.

When K'ang affirms man is good, what does he mean by "good?" What criteria does he use to determine the good? One is "that which more suits and better accords with man's spiritual soul and bodily soul." Whatever elevates the soul of man can be taken to be good. Secondly, that which "...heightens and expands man's enjoyment and pleasure" and minimizes suffering is to be considered good. K'ang defined suffering as "the spirit knotted-up, the body wounded, the soul melancholy and downcast" and declared that all "material inventions and social techniques" are to be judged by "the one criterion of the extent to which they have increased human happiness and decreased human suffering."[11]

From the above we see that K'ang's basic criterion is a pragmatic, theological one. The good is that which is useful for achieving desired ends. We do not find K'ang using the criterion of a personal God and the carrying out of God's will as the good. Nor does he associate the good with nature, or accept the Darwinian model of nature as a suitable pattern for the good. K'ang was thoroughly acquainted with Darwinian thought and the Darwinian view that nature is characterized by the law of "tooth and fang." That he was no devotee of such a philosophy is seen in his statement, "Should we follow the example of natural evolution, then among all mankind throughout the world the strong will oppress the weak, mutually gobbling each other up, and wars will occur daily, like fighting among quail." Obviously this is far from the ultimate state of Complete Peace and Equality.

In essence the good is that which is useful in helping the individual become what he may be and in a universal sense the world what it might be. This is what led K'ang to advocate abolishing boundaries or race and kind, for example. Kind boundaries are barriers which result from distinctions of "appearance and physique." K'ang pointed out that such distinctions are most unfortunate because of man's tendency to love his own kind but not others. He wrote that the common attitude among men is, "Those who are the same as I in appearance and physique, I am then intimate with and love; those who are different than I in appearance and physique, I then hate and kill." The result is two-fold, the oppression and subjugation of one race by another, wars which follow racial distinctions, and the wanton slaying of birds and beasts by men. When people throughout the world cease to make such distinctions among themselves and between themselves and animals, much suffering will be eliminated and a one world of peace and equality will be nearer realization.

It is significant to note K'ang's emphasis upon equality and how highly he extolled it as a practical virtue. He recognized that "the inequality of creatures is a fact" but the ideal is "that mankind should be equal, that mankind should be completely unified in the One World Era of Complete Peace and Equality." It is obvious from such a statement that K'ang believed equality is a prerequisite for unity. There will not be a brotherhood of man until all are equal. For a unity to be genuine, those who compose it must be equals.

This was a major reason for K'ang's advocacy of the abolition of sex, class, and family boundaries. Regarding the first, he was distressed by the suffering of women and wrote that "...within the world, from past to present, the way in which women have been treated is alarming, appalling, lamentable such as to make one weep. How can I describe this inequity? I cannot absolve men of their responsibility for the innumerable sufferings of women in the past." As to class boundaries, he wrote that, "Of the sufferings of mankind due to inequality, none compare to those which stem from a baseless distinction by classes," there being three types of inferior classes—races, slaves, and women. And in regard to family boundaries he wrote, "To have the family and yet to wish to reach Complete Peace and Equality is to be afloat on a blocked-up stream, in a sealed-off harbour, and yet to wish to reach the open waterway. To wish to attain Complete Peace and Equality and yet to have the family is like carrying earth to dredge a stream, or adding wood to put out a fire."

K'ang asserted several arguments against sex, class, and family boundaries. Classes are a denial of the universal right of self-determination and independence. Slaves as a class, for example, cannot exercise such a right and are not, therefore, treated as equals. Such boundaries are a denial of human dignity also. K'ang claimed that women often are only regarded by men "from the point of view of their beauty and sexual desirability" and "their dignity as human beings is ignored." The three types of distinctions are contrary to nature also. K'ang asserted that, despite the fact that men and women are equal by natural right, "women have long been subjected to men." K'ang's view seems to be that family, class, and sex distinctions are not natural but man created divisions. And if man has created them, he can also absolve them.

K'ang elicited two further arguments against the three boundaaries. They are based on and stimulate an undesirable and false dualism. He puts the matter succinctly in his statements, "...if there is that which is especially dear to us, then there is that which is not dear. If there is that which we love, then there is that which we do not love." Applying this to the Chinese tradition, K'ang declared that the presence of clans has led the Chinese "to hold dear those of the same surname and feel estranged from those of different surnames." Further, "those of the same surname care for each other...those of different surnames are enemies." Bifurcations of this type carry through all levels of Chinese society.

The unfortunate result of the three boundaries was a further and major argument K'ang used against them. Regarding sex discrimination, K'ang lamented that "the talents of women have been wasted through history" because women have not been allowed to become scholars or government officials. He declared that class divisions were responsible for "the thousand-year period of darkness and cultural stagnation" in Medieval Europe and that caste had led to the same results in India. Where the family system prevails, attitudes of selfishness and partiality are present since parents favour their own children more. The transmission of wealth through the family intensifies economic inequities. Disadvantages in education are a result also, since wealthy parents are able to afford their children a better education. Judged pragmatically in terms of results, then, sex, class, and family boundaries must be abolished if equality as a practical, social virtue is to be realized.

The view of society as an organism held by K'ang is a concomitant of the concept of equality. From such a standpoint society is made up of a variety of persons and groups, dependent on each other, and each doing the kind of work he or she is best fitted for. Thus, each in his own contributes to society as a whole. In such a society there are no gradations of "high and low" or distinctions of inferior and superior. All are treated equally or on the same level.

In the present Age of Disorder the opposite definition of society prevails, negative distinctions exist, and the result is disunity. Thus we have a further reason for abolishing caste, class, family and clan. In applying the organism concept to Chinese society, K'ang said that the failure to achieve national unity was due to the "corrupt practice of dividing the single nation into numberless nations, and from the whole we have made tiny pieces." Similarly on the international level, the assertion of absolute national sovereignty and independence has made world unity or a single world society impossible. Mankind, individually and collectively, must recognize its interdependence. Each person must see himself as part of a larger group.[12]

K'ang's view of society as an organism is one reason for his rejection of the principle of competition. For cooperation, not competition, is the basis of an organic society. He repudiated competition on other grounds as well. It is contrary to the nature of man. It may be true of nature, from a Darwinian standpoint. Therefore, while "those who advocate the theory of competition understand nature," they "do not understand man." For man is neither animal nor a product of nature. Man competes, as he does in the present Age of Disorder, not because it is his nature to but because he has been taught to or because of necessity due to the conditions of the present age. When the third age is realized, he will not compete because he will not have to.

K'ang described competition as "the greatest evil to the public existing in the world, past or present." He said "...eminent men pay their respects to it without shame" with the result that "the earth becomes a jungle, and all is blood and iron." Measured by the pragmatic test, then competition fails. It has brought, not peace and prosperity to all, but instead the opposite.

K'ang declared, furthermore, that competition has created a false illustion in the minds of many. It has led them to believe in a progress which does not really exist. K'ang's statement is insight of..."Those who discuss these matters nowadays hate the calm of unity, and exalt the hubbub of competition. They think that with competition there is progress; without strife there is retrogression." One notes the Darwinian influence here. Without competition there is no progress. How unfortunate to be caught in the web of such an illusion, K'ang says!

This brings us, of course, to K'ang's view of progress. In defining progress he wrote, "Daily to bend our thoughts more earnestly to means of seeking happiness and avoiding suffering: this is to progress."[13] Elsewhere he said that "The establishment of laws and the creation of teachings which cause men to have happiness and to be without suffering: this is the best form of the Good." Progress, then, is identified with maximizing happiness and minimizing pain. Moreover, progress must be universalized in the sense that all share in it. If a minority or even a majority reach a maximization of pleasure, this is not enough; for some are still left out.

As to how progress is best achieved, again, cooperation not competition is the best means. Where competition has prevailed, only the strongest have benefited. The majority have not. Further true progress is achieved through planning, organization and the passing of rules and laws whose aim is the general good.

Central to K'ang's social and ethical philosophy is his concept of compassionate love. He defined it as "attraction in action." When absent, man becomes an animal; its presence is what makes him truly human.[14] K'ang wrote, "...if men sever what constitutes their compassionate love, their human-ness will be annihilated. Those whose human-ness has been annihilated cease to be civilized and return to barbarianism." Compassionate love must be extended to all people equally. One sees a parellel to Motzu here. It is the key to the concept of equality. For a person will not treat others as equals if he detests or dislikes them. It is most necessary for a harmonious, enduring society. Permanent human relationships are possible only if grounded in love, not mutual self-interest. There is no real progress without it, for non-love is partial and exclusivist.

If compassionate love and equality are the keys, then a Darwinian view of society is obviously rejected. K'ang was quite aware of the "Social Darwinism" of the West in the nineteenth century and he staunchly opposed it. Darwinism does not extoll compassionate love but rather, opposite attitudes and insists on them as necessary for progress. In a Darwinian type society the strong prey on and use rather than succour the weak. It is a society of unequals in which each is out for himself. There is no concern for others or for the common good. In it society is defined as a sum of competing self-interests, not a totality of mutual or shared interests. No wonder K'ang rejected such Darwinism. It might be characteristic of the Age of Disorder; but no traces of it would be found in the Age of Complete Peace and Equality.

K'ang's anti-Darwinism is reflected in his political philosophy as well. He was quite aware of the current world consisting of independent, sovereign states quarreling and warring with each other like birds of prey. He wrote that under the "theory of natural selection" states "marshal their troops and look at each other, considering the swallowing up of another state as a matter of course." "Each state plans for its personal benefit" and "Everyone looks to the advantage of his own state and aggresses against other states." The Darwinian philosophy of self-interest is so dominant that "Even the good and upright cannot help but be partial each to his own state."[15] Armaments and slaying are accepted and justified—"They consider fighting for territory and killing other people to be an important duty; they consider destroying other states and butchering their people to be a great accomplishment." Such are the results of Darwinism combined with the sentiment of patriotism and nationalism.

K'ang would not accept such a situation as final, however. A "One World is the ultimate law of this world," he wrote. "It is certain that One World eventually will be reached." he added. It is a reality of the future and not "empty imaginings." One finds a strain of historical determinism here. It is based on the thesis "That to which the general state of affairs tends will in the future be attained." K'ang claimed the present general trend is toward unity, although the world has a long way to go to achieve it. But, because that is the prevailing direction, it will be reached some time.

What is required to reach that state? K'ang's general answer is the abolishing of national boundaries and states. Even more the "idea of state" must be discarded. As states are abolished, the national egoism and blind patriotism, which are an inevitable concomitant of "states having been established", will disappear. The selfishness due to "the fact of there existing sovereign states" will decline also, since its source is no longer present. "The laws of empires...piled on one another endlessly," the "oppression," the "quarreling over land and cities," the "grinding down of the people," such conditions will no longer exist.

K'ang asserted that there are three steps to world unity and a single world government. The first is disarmament. Nations must stop manufacturing further arms and destroy existing ones. The second is alliances, small states joining together to form constantly larger ones until there is finally only one. The third is a universal legislature representative of all the people.

Much emphasis was placed by K'ang on the method of federating as being a natural one. He stated, for example, that "the progress of state boundaries from division to union is a natural thing." K'ang believed that the amalgamation process, the going from disunity to unity, is the law of nature. "The parts becoming joined" is due to "natural selection." He would not accept the Darwinian method of amalgamation, however, in which increase is a result of conquest. Peaceful, voluntary federation is the method to be used, even though it may be a lengthy one, to bring about the third stage of world unity.

K'ang presented a pragmatic as well as naturalistic argument for his political philosophy. A single world government is the only way to "save the people" from widespread suffering, the folly of war, the unlimited waste and loss of production from "people being driven into being soldiers," the selfishness and self-centeredness nations and national sovereignty engenders and the "calamaties" of wars in human history which are so great "they cannot be calculated even."

The test of any government is results, K'ang asserted. "Goodness in the doctrine of government lies in causing the people to enjoy their happiness and benefit from their profits, in nourishing their desires and giving them what they seek," he wrote. He stated emphatically that "...the sole criterion for distinguishing the advancement or decadence of civilizations and the enlightenment or barbarism of governments is the degree of suffering or happiness of their people." He declared it to be a universal principle, saying that "Those which cause their people happiness, their civilization must be advanced and their government must be enlightened; those which cause their people suffering and resentment, their civilization must be decadent and their government must be barbarous."

Armed with the sword of pragmatism, K'ang asserted the true end of government to be the well-being of the people. It would be best achieved through the abolishing of all national boundaries, nation-states and nationalistic sentiment so that a genuinely universal spirit, outlook, and government could emerge to ensure universal happiness and welfare.

The doing away with economic as well as political barriers K'ang considered essential also. He believed "livelihood barriers" posed a serious obstacle to the Era of Complete Peace and Equality. By such boundaries he meant the prevailing economic institutions, systems and concepts on which they were based.[16]

K'ang singled out private property, capitalism, the profit motive and the attitudes they stimulated as the chief economic obstacles to progress. He criticized the first as leading to inequalities of wealth, selfishness and partiality. When property is owned privately and transmitted to successive generations, wealth inevitably becomes concentrated in the hands of the stronger, more talented, more ambitious. Having stimulates the urge to have more. Thus private property appeals to the latent selfishness in each of us and involves us in a vicious circle. Regarding this, K'ang wrote that "The practice of amassing being accepted as morally right, its violent evils become central in human nature: the original seed propagates itself and the desire to amass more is turned over endlessly in the mind."

K'ang's criticism of capitalism was as trenchant. The capitalist system was a concomitant of modern science and technology in which factory replaced home and shop production. It resulted in economic inequities and a new kind of struggle. A battle for raw materials and factories replaced the territorial struggles of an earlier period. Factory production requires a large initial investment, which only a few can afford, thus giving rise to a greater gap between rich and poor. Capitalism has led to a new struggle between haves and have nots, which has replaced the former struggles between weak and strong states.

K'ang criticized capitalism, not only because of the results accruing from it noted above, but for other reasons too. It is based on the profit motive. The capitalist produces goods for profit. This means that the capitalist is exploiting man's basic need for food, clothing, and shelter for his own gain. He is using people and their primary needs for his own end, a practice which is obviously immoral. Illustrative of K'ang's view of the profit motive is his statements, "...cleverness in deceit is also born, because of the contention for profits. Hence spurious goods are manufactured which injure the innocent public. In the case of medicines, foods, boats, and vehicles, the harm done is still greater. Even if the goods are not actually spurious, yet the merchant demands excessively high prices for goods of poor quality. They are satisified to cheat people; trustworthiness is non-existent; all shame is lost." K'ang's statement reflects more than the traditional Chinese distrust of the merchant. It was a commentary on contemporary economics as well.

Capitalism moreover, K'ang said, as it allows for the concentration of wealth, gives rise to positions of mastery and subordination and attitudes of pride and abasement. "Among the rich there is pride; among the poor there is obsequiousness," K'ang wrote, adding, "At the extreme of pride, the proud one gives orders with contemptuous gestures of chin and fingers; at the extreme of obsequiousness, the obsequious one becomes depraved, licking the sores of the rich man, for there are no limits to which pride and obsequiousness will extend." Such attitudes, K'ang declared are not ones to "cultivate human nature and perfect human character."

K'ang rejected capitalism also because it was based on the principle of competition. The capitalist believes that competition leads to improved methods of production and distribution, that it stimulates people to work harder and use their talents more fully. K'ang believed that the same ends could be achieved with even better results through cooperation. It, not competition, is the key to progress, economically as well as socially. It might be noted that K'ang also disagreed with the capitalist's contention regarding the greater efficiency of capitalism. He pointed to the wastefulness often found due to the lack of comprehensive planning, over-production at one time and under-production at another.

K'angs proposal for solving the problem was straightforward. In the One World Peace and Equality "...all agriculture, industry, and commerce will revert to the public." They will be publicly owned and controlled. His solution was based on the pragmatic criterion that other systems had not worked. Capitalism had provided some, but not all, with the physical things necessary for health and happiness.

K'ang's basic concern was that all have a just share in the abundance of nature. He wished to see disparities of wealth abolished or that economic equity be achieved, and he searched for a system he believed would bring it about. He believed the economic, political, and social to be inter-related. Equality must be the ruling principle for all three. For, everywhere, wealth and power go together. K'ang noted, for example, that "In the West, moreover, the importance of money, as regards power, position, and friendship, is even greater than in China." Where wealth is concentrated in the hands of a minority, power is also. A class and status society results. K'ang could accept none of the three and he would have none present in the Era of Complete Peace and Equality.

K'ang's economic are related to his metaphysical views in several ways. As one example, he believed in the sufficiency or even the plentitude of nature. Nature is such that there is enough for everyone. Since all are equal, every person should have a fair or equal share in the good things of nature. Actually, in his major writing, *Ta T'ung Shu*, K'ang does not deal extensively with metaphysical concepts. He accepts traditional metaphysical views and is more interested in their practical implications. He assumes, for example, that there is the Tao, loosely described as the way of Nature or Nature's or the natural way which man should seek to understand and put into practice. Act in accordance with, not contrary to, Nature's way.

For instance, nature is characterized by universality or universal principles. It does not vary from area to area. Yang and yin are universal or found everywhere. That women are everywhere equal to men is an implication of this universality. That slavery is contrary to the "universal principles of nature," since it denies self, will and determination, is a second example. Since there are universal natural principles, there are also universal moral principles. That "man should not use force to oppress others" is a typical one. Such a moral rule admits of no exception. K'ang would not, then, support ethical relativity. It would be contrary to nature as well as unfruitful.

As noted before, K'ang rejected Darwinism. Thus for him reality is characterized by supplementaries, not opposites. The social and economic implication of this is cooperation, not competition. Further, reality is characterized by harmony; and man's goal, because he is a part of nature, is harmony within and without. Body, mind, and soul are to be in harmony. Man should, further, work in harmony with his fellowmen.

K'ang assumed the oneness of reality also. The concept of society as an organism, the oneness of mankind and a One World are logical implications or correlates of the unity of nature. As characterized by unity in plurality, man and the creations he devises should be also. If oneness is natural to nature, so is it to man. Oneness implies or has harmony as its correlate. Just as harmony is natural in nature, so it is between men. Disharmony, conflict, and war is not natural but unnatural to man. Thus peace needs no justification; rather conflict and war do. Further, a divided or splintered world that is broken into competing political units is not natural. The opposite is. States are artificial or arbitrary divisions created by man. They are not natural distinctions.

K'ang was impressed by the impartiality of nature also. Its implication is the equality of man. All are equal before nature or God, as the theist would say. K'ang applied the notion of impartiality to relations between the sexes, stating, "All this restriction of women, and discrimination against them, is contrary both to nature and to the best interests of mankind." Since nature does not discriminate, man should not either. K'ang appealed to the concept of "natural rights" or rights endowed by nature also. He lamented, for example, the subjugation of women to men "despite the fact that men and women are equal by natural right."

That there is an "all embracing Primal Ch'i" from which all are created was accepted by K'ang. The implications which follow from it are those noted above, the natural harmony, unity or oneness of man, common goals or ends, and non-dialectical means of achieving them. K'ang also accepted the traditional belief in Heaven and emphasized the implications thereof. Since "all human beings have bodies given by Heaven," so "all human beings have the right of freedom given by Heaven." Individual freedom is a universal, natural inheritance just as one's physical being is.

This essay on K'ang Yu-wei may be concluded with a reminder that K'ang was a product of two traditions. Within the Chinese one he accepted and continued the Lu-Wang school of Lu Hsiang-shan and Wang Yang-ming. They represented an idealistic Neo-Confucianism which Professor Chan characterizes as "imbued with the spirit of purposeful action instead of Ch'eng-Chu's cold and abstract speculation."

But K'ang was part of a broader movement as well; namely, the universalist sentiment which was sweeping the world in the late 19th and early 20th centuries. Its emphasis was upon internationalism and world unity and its basic assumption was the oneness, brotherhood, and perfectibility of mankind. Advances in science and technology had made a realization of a "world brotherhood" possible at last. Organizations such as the League of Nations were being created to bring it about. Events had taken place aimed at leading mankind in that direction—the Hague Peace Conferences, World Parliaments of Religions.

All of these had influenced K'ang and he took as one of his tasks the popularizing of a world view among his countrymen. He urged his fellow Chinese to extend the traditional view that "all within the Four Seas are brothers", to "all within the world are brothers," and one of his contributions was that he broadened the scope of Chinese thought, forcing it to be more inclusive.

In this sense K'ang's was a philosophy of transcendence. He wanted individuals, nations, and cultures to go beyond present limitations or barriers. They are not insurmountable; they are eradicable. Once broken down, a new world of much greater joy and abundance lies before man.

In many ways, K'ang's era was one of hope. In numerous places people were caught up in a faith in a better future, a more peaceful world, the inevitability of progress of advance. Life and the universe was being affirmed. The injunction of Liang Chi-

Chao, K'ang's pupil, that "One's consciousness of others should be enlarged rather than restricted" was being taken seriously. K'ang joined in this affirmation. He urged men to act naturally; that is, to be one with nature, themselves, and others.

NOTES

1. K'ang's grandfather was superintendent of education in the District of Lienchow and devoted himself to the study of Neo-Confucianism. See Ch'u Chai and Winberg Chai, *Confucianism*, Woodbury, Barron's Educational Series, 1973, p. 159.

2. K'ang also dwelt on many world events from which he drew lessons in his constructing of his Utopia.

3. One tactic used by K'ang to get the support for his reforms of the orthodox Confucians who opposed them was his 1897 publication called *Confucius as a Reformer* in which he argued that Confucius was not an opponent of change but was a reformer who had brought about drastic changes in Chinese society, changes which were a revival of ancient ways and truths. See Creel H.G., *Confucius and the Chinese Way*, New York, Harper Torchbook, 1949, p. 101; also Wing-Tsit Chan, *Sources of the Chinese Tradition*, Princeton, Princeton University Press, 1963, p. 724; also Levenson Joseph R., *Confucian China and its Modern Fate*, Barkeley, University of California Press, 1968, pp. 80-85.

4. As an example see the memorial submitted January 29, 1898 in which K'ang urged the emperor to undertake reforms. Interestingly, he pointed to the Meiji reforms in Japan as the "model of reform." De Bary Wm. Theodore, *Sources of the Chinese Tradition*, Vol. II, New York, Columbia University Press, 1964, p. 73.

5. See Mousheng Lin, *Men and Ideas*, New York, John Day Company, 1942, pp. 216-217.

6. That K'ang started with the universal suffering of mankind demonstrates the influence of Buddhism on his thinking. In 1913 he started a monthly magazine called *Compassion*. Compassion (metta) is, of course, a virtue highly extolled by the Buddha.

7. The quotations in this chapter are taken from Thompson Laurence G., *Ta T'ung Shu, The One-World Philosophy of K'ang Yu-wei*, London, George Allen and Unwin Ltd., 1958.

8. K'ang differed from the Confucian tradition which assumed a cyclical view. Under Western influence he accepted the evolutionary view.

9. K'ang's view of the essential goodness of man is typically Confucian and contrasts with the orthodox Christian view. There is disagreement as to the degree to which K'ang was influenced by Christianity. Chai and Chai assert that the influence of Christian missionaries on K'ang "was Great." (*op. cit.*, p. 162.) Kang saw similiarities between Christianity and Confucianism, the

Christian doctrine of love and the Confucian concept of Jen being more or less identical, for example. K'ang, however, did not want to see Christianity adopted by the Chinese and he therefore undertook to make Confucianism the "state religion", a move which evoked opposition from Christians, Buddhists, Moslems and Taoists.

    10. K'ang's hedonism was much like that of John Stuart Mill's. Mill has often been misunderstood and misinterpreted on that score, for he exulted the "higher" over the "lower" pleasures.

    11. In this statement, we see the utilitarianism advocated by Mill, that men's machines are to be used for the enhancement of social well-being.

    12. K'ang stoutly advocated such organizations as the League of Nations and, on the request of President Wilson, submitted a statement to him on Confucius' views or a world state. See Creel, *op. cit.*, p. 128.

    13. Belief in inevitable progress was dominant in the West in the later 19th and early 20th centuries and must have been an influence on K'ang, although, of course, K'ang found the idea in earlier Confucian writings also. See Day Clarence B. *The Philosophers of China*, Secaucus, Citadel Press, 1962, p. 254; also Thompson, *op. cit.*, p. 47.

    14. Chan, *op. cit.*, p. 735, points out that K'ang, under the influence of Western science "identified jen with ether and electricity." An interesting essay titled K'ang Yu-wei's Excursion into Science is found in Jung-Pang Lo's *K'ang Yu-Wei, A Biography and Symposium*, Tucson, University of Arizona Press, 1967.

    15. Self-interest as the motivation of states is termed "political realism" today and K'ang would have repudiated it now even as he did then.

    16. An interesting account of K'ang's economic views is found on pp. 340-353 of Lo, *op. cit.*, in which a comparison is made with Marx's views. Lo's book contains an exhaustive listing of works by and about K'ang Yu-Wei, pp. 410-480.

14
SUN YAT-SEN

JEFF BARLOW

Despite major differences between individual thinkers such as Wang Yang-ming or Chu Hsi, the long tradition of Confucian philosophy exhibits remarkable continuity. The Confucian sages generally agreed on a core of seminal works, examined similar problems and utilized a largely common vocabulary. This continuous tradition was occasionally fractured, as by the thinkers of the "Wild Ch'an" school of the late Ming,[1] but always regained an equilibrium which would, in outline at least, have been recognizable to Chinese thinkers of much earlier periods. This continuity ended in the mid-nineteenth century when the traditional institutions and ideas of Chinese society proved unable to subsume the disruptive impact of the West.

Despite this mid-nineteenth century break in its historical development, Chinese thinkers for some time looked to the past for solutions to pressing problems, both social and philosophical. Although K'ang Yu-wei clearly belongs as much to the late nineteenth century as to the Confucian tradition, he still proceeded from a Confucian foundation in his search for a syncretic philosophy with which to re-establish social and philosophical stability.[2] From that point in time, the problems of the Confucian tradition become inextricably entwined with Chinese nationalism. Chinese thinkers with a nationalist awareness, men like Liang Ch'i-ch'ao, were less concerned with revivifying the Confucian past than with creating a universal world of ideas in which Chinese could be comfortable. To such men it was often satisfactory to point out commonalities in Western and Chinese thought rather than to attempt to assert the primacy of the Chinese tradition.

If we accept the assessment of both Chinese Nationalists and Communists, the primary Chinese political philosopher of the early twentieth century was Sun Yat-sen. Sun was, however, much more than a political philosopher; he was also the major Chinese political actor from the late-nineteenth century to the rise of Mao Tse-tung. Sun is often known as the *Kuo-fu*, the "Father of the Nation," and Nationalist and Communist alike trace their revolutions back in large part to him.

Sun's status as the *Kuo-fu* is a consequence of both his thoughts and his actions. This double involvement ranks him with such thinkers as K'ang Yu-wei and Mao Tse-tung, and makes him equally difficult to assess. The political thought of those men can only, with great hazard, be divorced from the context in which their thoughts were formulated. The Mao who wrote "On Contradiction" cannot be treated separately from the Mao who supervised the often violent process of land-reform after the creation of the People's Republic. Neither can the Sun Yat-sen who authored the series of essays known today as the "Three People's Principles" be discussed aside from the Sun who labored industriously to overthrow the Ch'ing Dynasty, often in league with strange allies ranging from apolitical opium smugglers to French imperialists.

Sun was born in Kwangtung province, South China, in November of 1866. China was then in the midst of the T'ung-chih Restoration, a last traditionalistic attempt to cure the many ills of Confucian society. China's problems were so many and so varied that they were to be insoluble for decades, and in some respects have not been completely resolved to the present. These difficulties can be roughly divided into internal and external ones. Internally, population growth had simply exceeded the capacity of the Chinese eco-system to support human life. An excess population of millions pushed and strained all aspects of the socio-economic system. There were more educated elite than there was prestigious employment and more peasants than arable land. Past solutions to such problems had always been dictated not by policy but by the Malthusian correctives of famine, plague and war. Whether traditional China might have regained a sort of equilibrium after suffering, death and dynastic change is a question rendered moot by the advent of the West.

Western nations, led by Great Britain and France, were pressing into every land and sea in search of colonies to provide sources of raw materials, cheap labor and markets for surplus industrial production. The prolonged contest between Britain and France had been decided with the defeat of Napoleon, and Great Britain was relatively free to arrange the world's economic order to her liking. To the British this meant first that China had to be forced to participate in trade. The problem was particularly acute because British imports of Chinese goods, especially tea, had caused a great imbalance of trade. China had to be opened to British exports to redress that imbalance and this meant that persistent Chinese refusal to engage in more than sporadic luxury trade had to be overcome. The result was the series of conflicts of the 1840's known collectively as the Opium Wars.

The major issue of the wars was the Chinese attempt to exclude opium produced by Britain in her Indian colonies. Opium was not only a terrible scourge to the Chinese peasant, to the point where missionary and travellers' accounts tell us whole villages were in a perpetual stupor in which they could neither farm nor trade effectively, but also a major drain on the Chinese currency. Millions of ounces of silver flowed out to pay for opium, disrupting virtually every aspect of the socio-economic system.

The Chinese lost the Opium Wars and the series of wars and battles which followed them. Exposed to international trade, but stripped by treaty of control over her tariff structure, China was more a victim of trade than a participant in it. Native industry was destroyed or stunted, the currency debased, control over many police powers lost and vast sections of territory alienated to foreigners. On the heels of opium came missionaries. As individuals, most missionaries were hard-working and sensitive, but as a group they were very disruptive to the Chinese social fabric. Many nations, notably France, also seized upon support for mission efforts as a tool with which to expand national economic and political interests at the expense of the Chinese central government.

In addition to suffering the many internal effects of the foreigner's presence, the Chinese also began to lose their traditional overseas dependencies. Okinawa, Taiwan and Korea were lost to the Japanese, Great Britain came to dominate Tibet, and France gained control over Viet-nam. Sun Yat-sen was to say that the origin of his drive to reform China was this loss of China's former grandeur and the alienation of her dependencies. A very strong element of antiforeignism was to remain a major aspect of the Chinese revolutionary movement. Sun himself, although the mos Westernized of the Chinese leaders, was not immune to this element and frequently sought support from various Asian anticolonial groups from the Philippine Islands to Japan.

Kwangtung Province, particularly the area around Canton where Sun was born, was a very vital and turbulent place, crisscrossed by foreign traders and missionaries, as well as by more familiar types such as opium smugglers and secret society organizers. The Cantonese had been engaged in coastal trade in Asian waters for some time, and it was relatively easy for them to go from that to emigration as a partial answer to overpopulation and lack of local opportunity. Tens of thousands of Cantonese young men, and some women, went out to foreign lands from Alaska to Peru along the Pacific Coast of the American continent, as well as to more distant lands where there was opportunity for hardworking and frugal people. Sun Yat-sen also followed this path and went to Hawaii in 1879. There he lived with an older brother, an earlier, well-established migrant.

In Hawaii, Sun received schooling in the English language and was so apt a pupil of Western ways that his brother sent him home to Kwangtung in disgrace because of his rapid alienation from the Chinese tradition. The following year, 1884, Sun continued his education in English in Hong Kong. For the next several years he shuttled back and forth between Hong Kong, Canton and Hawaii, before entering medical school in 1886 at a missionary college in Canton. In 1887 he transferred to a similar institution in Hong Kong where he stayed for five years.[3]

Sun, like most Chinese, anxiously watched the decline of Chinese sovereignty at foreign hands, and had been interested in political solutions to the problem for some time. In 1894, while living once again in Hawaii with his brother, he founded a radical group of Overseas Chinese, the *Hsing Chung Hui*, usually translated as the "Revive China Society."

Sun led the Hsing Chung Hui in two attempted revolutionary coups, one in 1895 at Canton, another in the adjoining Waichow district in 1900. Both risings failed due to insufficient preparation and lack of organizational cohesion. The attempts did publicize Sun's name as a revolutionary, and provided the cachet he needed to move freely among radical Chinese groups overseas for the next twelve years. In 1905 in Tokyo he joined in creating another political group, the *T'ung Meng Hui*, a united front of Chinese radical organizations, many of whose members were students in Japan.

For the next six years, Sun engaged in a series of armed risings, usually by providing funds and leadership from abroad. He was on Chinese soil but once before 1911, very briefly, at a rising along the Sino-Vietnamese border in December of 1907. It has sometimes been argued that Sun and the T'ung Meng Hui were a continuous and highly effective group which, by the series of armed risings, eventually created a revolutionary situation and overthrew the Manchu government in 1911. In fact this is much too simplistic an analysis. The T'ung Meng Hui was frequently split by factional disputes, and at some points existed in name only. Sun often chose not to rely upon the organization or the student-intellectuals who were its primary membership, but rather, worked with opium-smuggling secret society bandits and French imperialists who saw him as a means to increase their influence in Southern China.

During the period from 1900 to 1912 Sun's political goals also shifted back and forth. He sometimes planned for a united republic of China; at other times he worked for a separatist regime to be created in the border provinces along the Sino-Vietnamese frontier.[4]

Whatever Sun's relative contribution to the revolution, and it was certainly substantial, the Manchu regime finally fell in 1911. The dynasty collapsed as much from devolution, a progressive loss of power to provincial interest groups, as from revolution. Sun was the most widely known of living revolutionaries and also had foreign contacts who might facilitate the crucial tasks of gaining diplomatic recognition and securing loans. Thus, Sun Yat-sen was elected Provisional President of the Republic of China in December of 1911. Sun held the post for but a few months before yielding in favor of Yuan Shih-k'ai who could command wider foreign support, as well as the support of the Chinese traditional elites and the military.

The T'ung Meng Hui evolved and became the Kuomintang, the Chinese Nationalist Party. Led primarily by the young modernist Sung Chiao-jen it became the major source of opposition to Yuan

Shih-k'ai's increasingly dictatorial rule. In 1913 Yuan had Sung Chiao-jen assassinated and drove the Kuomintang into exile. Sun Yat-sen continued as head of the Kuomintang to work for a unified and modern Chinese Republic until his death in March of 1925.

The period of Sun's life from 1913 when he fled to Japan to work against Yuan to his death in 1925 is very episodic and discontinuous. He was often virtually without support; at other times he worked in close concert with local militarists, who were opposed to the rule of Yuan Shih-k'ai or his equally oppressive successors, the warlords.

Sun's basic strategy was for a "Northern Expedition," a military expedition to be staged from the south of China, where he sometimes had a secure base in the area around Canton, to march north, take Peking and unify the nation. Nothing could be done in China of the 1920's without foreign assistance. Even the central government was completely dependent upon foreign sources of loans and munitions, and rebel regimes naturally had even less stable a foundation. After seeking help from Western sources, including the United States, and meeting with indifference, if not active hostility, Sun turned to the world's newest revolutionary power, the Soviet Union. In January of 1923 Sun and a Comintern representative signed the Sun-Joffe agreement. Sun then began to receive substantial Soviet material aid and advice. Sun needed not only financing and munitions but also methods to better organize his efforts. The Russians encouraged Sun to adopt more strict Leninist organizational methods, to emphasize social reform, to create a modern party-army, and to cooperate with other revolutionary nationalist groups.

The Soviets then forced another ally in China, the young Chinese Communist Party, into alliance with the Kuomintang. The Kuomintang thus became a very broad "united front" incorporating nationalists of all stripes, from rather traditional military men to the fiery young labor organizers and rural agitators of the Chinese Communist Party and the left wing Kuomintang. After Sun's death this coalition was finally to unite China before falling apart in the bitter struggle which lasts to today, carried on by the People's Republic and the Republic of China, Taiwan.

This life of very active political involvement gave Sun Yat-sen little time for deep reflection or abstract thought. While he is undeniably a central figure of the time, from at least 1906 to his death in 1925, he remains curiously aloof from some of the most important aspects of that period. Sun made a lasting contribution to political life, but almost none to thought or philosophy. This is particularly noteworthy because many of the political struggles of the time were presaged by long and complex discussions and debates among intellectuals.

For example, 1919 was the height of the May Fourth period, a time marked by intensive discussions and active involvement of activist students and their professors. The year was also the beginning of an extended debate between the two major liberal philosophical camps of the time. This was the great debate over "Isms" joined by Hu Shih and Ch'en Tu-hsiu, major figures in the May Fourth period. Ch'en Tu-hsiu would, in 1921, be a co-founder of the Chinese Communist Party. In 1919 he was interested in Marxism as an ideology with which to organize and animate the masses of China for social and political reform. Ch'en thus upheld the utility of "Isms" or abstract bodies of thought. Hu Shih was the foremost Westernized intellectual of the time and had a Ph.D. from Columbia University where he had been a student of John Dewey. Hu Shih argued against narrow deterministic philosophies like Marxism.[5] This debate was to foreshadow the later break between Chinese radicals and liberals, and was extremely important in defining the issues of the time.

Sun Yat-sen made no contribution to the debate, both out of the nature of his own convictions, and because of the press of his own activities. We will discuss his philosophical attitudes and their determinants below. At this point we can best consider his immediate activities. In 1919 Sun was working on a book which he had begun in 1918 and was not to finish until 1921 due to the frequent interruptions caused by his political life. The book is one of his major works, *The International Development of China*.[6]

Unlike the very abstract debate raging in the liberal and radical Chinese press, Sun's work is overwhelmingly practical, a detailed and meticulous plan for developing China. It must also be said that it was simultaneously impractical as the funding necessary for the projects far exceeded that which China could possibly amass. Even Sun could see no real plan of action, beyond proposing that the world should unite to make of China a collective development project in order to prevent a major war over control of her economy.

In 1923 another titanic intellectual struggle was waged, this time initiated by what we might term Chinese Neo-traditionalists. Western horror at The Great War, and an assiduous search for its philosophical roots, temporarily revived traditionalist Chinese thought. Conservatives, led by Carsun Chang (Chang Chün-mai) seized this opportunity to counsel China against a continued process of modernization, arguing that even Westerners now admitted their intellectual tradition had proven bankrupt.[7] As this debate touched upon fundamental aspects of every spectrum of Chinese thought, from Confucian to Marxist, virtually every important Chinese thinker participated in it.

Perhaps the most conspicuous non-participant was again Sun Yat-sen, who was, as so frequently the case, struggling with more immediate problems relating to his political survival. Sun's writing at this time shows an exclusive pre-occupation with raising armies and the funds to pay for them, with forming alliances and devising tactics with which to oppose warlord enemies in the Canton area.[8] Sun was also involved in his alliance with the Soviet Union and in working out strategies with his Comintern advisor, Michael Borodin.

To place Sun Yat-sen in context with the other great Chinese thinkers of his time is consequently very difficult. He rarely engaged in the great discussions which animated them, being preoccupied with his attempt to create a modern Chinese Republic through political action. The one area where Sun can be said to have made a major theoretical contribution to Chinese thought is political philosophy. There his status rests almost entirely upon his creation of the "Three People's Principles." Sun developed or perhaps better, evolved, the Principles over time and set them forth as the solution to many of the problems which the Western impact had precipitated for China. In his words, the Principles would "...elevate China to an equal position among the nations, in international affairs, in government, and in economic life, so that she can permanently exist in the world."[9]

The Three People's Principles are conventionally defined as "Nationalism," "Democracy," and "Livelihood." The third Principle, "Livelihood," has been the source of much disagreement, but can perhaps be best understood as a form of Socialism. The origins in time of the Three People's Principles are also controversial. Sun himself traced them to his efforts in the Reading Room of the British Museum during 1897, and this is the date accepted by the Chinese Nationalist custodians of the Sun heritage.[10]

Feng Tzu-yu, who is widely accepted as the primary Chinese historian of the period, does not emphasize the importance of the Principles before the creation of Sun's major political organization, the T'ung Meng Hui, in 1905. Feng states only that Sun moved among the radical students and Overseas Chinese communities advocating *Min-tzu chu-i*, a term which can be translated as either "nationalism" or "racialism," and in context seems most often to imply the latter.[11] In the judgment of Harold Schiffrin, the major Western historian of Sun in this period of his life, the Principles did not take systematic form until 1905 and did not acquire a formal title until the following year.[12]

Specific references to the Three People's Principles before 1906 are very rare. The third issue of the T'ung Meng Hui's newspaper, the *Min Pao*, stated that organ's "isms" were six in number:

(1) To overthrow the Manchu regime.
(2) To establish a Republican government.
(3) Nationalization of land.
(4) Support true world peace.
(5) Cooperation between the Japanese and Chinese peoples.
(6) To demand—or request—that the World Powers agree to and aid the tasks of the Chinese revolution.[13]

Not until well after the revolution in 1911 did Sun begin to elaborate upon the Principles, and it was not until a series of lectures which he presented in 1924 that they acquired systematic form.

The intellectual origins of the Three People's Principles are as cloudy as is the chronology of their development. It is possible to find in them ideas which seem to be drawn from a number of Western and Chinese sources, particularly Henry George, Liang Ch'i-ch'ao and Yen Fu.[14] These ideas seemingly were incorporated with very little change or elaboration on Sun's part. Sun's conception of the Three People's Principles was more eclectic than creative.

The origins or the somewhat vague nature of the Three People's

Principles in no way disqualify Sun Yat-sen as a modern revolutionary thinker, nor does it suggest that he was too traditional, or too uncritical to devise a more systematic set of political ideals. Rather, it is because Sun's career was basically that of a political actor; and he had little leisure or opportunity to reflect upon abstracts, concerned as he usually was to find solutions to immediate problems facing both him and his country.

Perhaps an adequate symbol of that preoccupation can be seen in the context in which he finally succeeded in publishing the 1924 series of lectures on the Principles. Sun had been prepared to publish the Principles in systematic form in 1922 when his manuscript and library was destroyed in a battle with an opposing warlord. When the Principles were finally published in 1924, he was unable to present a completed discussion of the Principle of Livelihood because of the chaotic context of the times.

Sun Yat-sen's contribution to Chinese political thought, then, cannot be viewed as the creation of a highly-defined body of abstract political thought, for the Three People's Principles are not such. Rather, Sun, through his status and political power popularized the ideas and charged his successors with carrying them out. It is this legacy which has kept the Three People's Principles a viable political force in the Chinese world today, both as a guideline for policy and as a symbolic appeal for support.

Sun himself never really intended the Three People's Principles to be the animating force in the Chinese revolution of 1911 which overthrew the Ch'ing. Sun's political arguments at this time were in fact fairly traditional, and had little to do with the much more Demoractic and egalitarian Three People's Principles he emphasized later.

The question of the revolution was an overwhelmingly concrete one, how to overthrow a political system which had periodically reconstituted itself after the most extreme disorder for more than a thousand years. A major source of opposition to the Ch'ing dynasty was Chinese anti-Manchuism. The Chinese people in general identified themselves not as members of a modern state "China," but as members of the Han race, the ethnic majority of China. The Han believed themselves to be oppressed by an alien dynasty, the Manchu. To most Han Chinese, then, the problem was not so much one of the political form of the government, or which Western doctrines were most suitable to the Chinese environment, but of how to proceed with overthrowing the Ch'ing dynasty.

The south of China in particular had a long history of anti-Manchuism. It had been the last area to fall to the invading Ch'ing armies and the resistance had been long and sanguinary. In the mid-nineteenth century the central and southern provinces had burst into open rebellion, led by the T'ai P'ing movement which had adopted a visionary form of Christianity, so transformed as to be almost unrecognizable. The rebels were subdued only after years of victories against the central government. The Manchus tried vainly to reestablish themselves, upon a firm footing with the temporary palliatives of the T'ung-chih Restoration. The collapse of the dynasty accelerated once again with the defeat at the hands of the Japanese in 1895.

Anti-governmental violence rose to a crescendo, as a result of an extended series of droughts and famines in the south of China. It was in this context that Sun began his activist career in the fall of 1895 with the unsuccessful attack upon Canton.

Branded by the government as a dangerous anti-Manchu revolutionary, Sun then began to travel among the scattered communities of Overseas Chinese from Southeast Asia to Europe and the United States. It was these communities which became Sun's primary constituency, rather than the Chinese students and intellectuals who have most intrigued Western scholars of the revolution. These groups of Overseas Chinese were not particularly concerned with political theory, but in the strength of Suns' anti-Manchuism and in the immediate question of how it was that he proposed to drive out the Ch'ing.

These people, in general the poorer and more down-trodden segments of their communities, were to be the major source of Sun's support until the fall of the dynasty in 1911. When not actively engaged in facilitating armed risings, Sun was generally touring these foreign enclaves raising funds or building organizational support. In this process he found the Three People's Principles to be of minimal utility and he had no reason to elaborate upon, or to define them further.

This lack of a highly developed body of political thought in the period before the fall of the Manchu did not really cause Sun concern, for he felt that the revolution was a two-stage process. In the first stage, which he labelled the period of "destruction," the Ch'ing dynasty was to be overthrown. In the second period, "construction," China would be given, by Sun, more modern political forms and values.[15] Sun felt the Three People's Principles to be relevant only to this second period. That Sun was not at that time advocating a comprehensive program, which united both the process of revolution, and its ultimate goals should not surprise us. It must have seemed to Sun, as to so many others, such an overwhelming task to overthrow the old system, that speculation as to ultimate goals would be no more than potentially divisive conjecture.

The 1911 revolution then forms a sort of watershed in Sun Yat-sen's thought. His writings before that time consist primarily of communications with other radical individuals and groups, vague political tracts and fiery speeches, all intended to serve the immediate purpose of rallying support with which to overthrow the Ch'ing. Sun clearly had expected that his activities would not only overthrow the dynasty, but would also assure his ability to guide China's destiny after the revolution. This proved not to be the case, but rather China descended into the long period of warlordism which was not to end until after his death. As Sun said later of this crucial transition after the fall of the Dynasty:

> At first it seemed as if I, the leader, would be able very easily to give effect to the programme of the revolutionary party...as well as to solve the problems created by the Revolution...But, unfortunately, the Revolution was scarcely completed when the members of our party unexpectedly turned out to be of a different opinion from myself, considering my ideals too elevated and unattainable for the reconstruction of modern China.[16]

The chaos following the revolution forced Sun to consider not only the again immediate problem of gaining control of the government, but also why it was that China had not moved smoothly into a period of peaceful and modern development. It is in this period, generally after 1918, that Sun was to write the major works in which we can see his political thought better developed and focussed upon broader problems.

The world view of Sun in these latter days is almost unremittingly harsh and apocalyptic. He felt, as he always had, that China was in critical danger. As he put it,

> Now that we realize the seriousness of political domination and the even greater seriousness of economic domination, we cannot boast that China's four hundred millions will not be easily exterminated. Never before in all her millenniums of history has China felt the weight of...such forces at one and the same time.[17]

This sense of crisis, even of an impending doom, was in response to two interrelated factors: a Darwinian racial competition, and Western imperialism. The argument that man's history was marked and in part determined by racial competition which was an aspect of Darwinian natural selection was absolute orthodoxy in the West. The theory shaped the ideas of such influential scholars of international affairs as Admiral Mahan, and through them, politicians like Theodore Roosevelt. It was a major factor in international relations for some time and was to complicate interaction between Whites and Asians. The analysis had entered China in the nineteenth century when the great scholar Yen Fu translated some of the basic works of Social Darwinism into Chinese.[18]

Although Sun accepted the basics of Racial Darwinism, his thoughts on race are often confusing. It is never clear for example whether he considers Manchus and Han Chinese one race or distinct branches of an Asian race. He did see a clear distinction between Anglo-Saxon and Asian races, however, and believed that in the great competition between them, the Chinese were in danger of extinction.[19]

This fear of losing a competition between races, the penalty for which was extinction, was a constant concern of Sun Yat-sen. It provided the structure in which he viewed the more immediate dangers created by Western imperialism. It is perhaps difficult for us today to take seriously his concern, or his strident language; but he was responding to the major reality facing China from the 1840's to the time in which he lived. Western pressure had been unremitting and had caused China the most serious political, social and economic damage. Sun's life-long attempt to unite the Chinese people under a republican form of government had often been frustrated by the remarkable degree to which foreigners exercised politica and economic power in China.

Although Americans have most usually seen Sun Yat-sen as a pro-Western and rather amiable figure (by way of contrast to the inimical and foreboding China of Mao Tse-tung), he was in his day more often regarded as an anti-Western Chinese nationalist. To the Englishmen and Americans of the period before the late 1920's, "Nationalist" was often used interchangeably with "Bolshevik," by which the foreigners meant a dangerous revolutionary.

Sun saw that Western nations alternately used political and economic pressures against China, which had the effect of retarding her development and thus her control over her own future. In his words,

> After the Manchu government had carried on wars with foreign nations and had been defeated, China was forced to sign many unequal treaties. Foreign nations are still using these treaties to bind China, and as a result, China fails at whatever she attempts. If China stood on an equal basis with other nations, she could compete freely with them in the economic field and be able to hold her own without failure. But as soon as foreign nations use political power as a shield for their economic designs, then China is at a loss how to resist or to compete successfully with them.[20]

It is not completely clear from Sun's writings why this fundamental conflict has come about. It was such a constant feature of the Chinese world from the mid-nineteenth century that few Chinese tried to analyze it. A systematic theoretical development was to be left to Lenin in his work, "*Imperialism, The Highest Stage of Capitalism*," first published in 1916.[21] This work provided many Chinese (and Vietnamese) anti-colonialists, with the structural framework in which to view Western actions. The generally anti-Western behavior of the new Soviet government and its announced readiness to renounce unequal treaties imposed upon China by the Czarist government ensured Soviet political theory a ready audience in China as well as in other colonial and semi-colonial nations. Sun referred to China as a "hypo-colony", by which he meant a status worse than "semi-colony," domination not by one nation but by many.[22]

If Sun saw China's problems as having their origins in the West, he also saw the solution as emanating from the same quarter. To

Sun, as to most Chinese after about 1895, China could best meet the Western challenge by modernizing herself. He felt the sine qua non of Chinese modernization to be the development of a sense of national identity. As Sun lamented, too many Chinese still identified with traditional values such as regionalism and familism rather than with their nation, China. This was so because traditionally China had viewed herself not as a nation-state, but as a culture, as civilization itself. To move from Confucian culturalism to Chinese nationalism was not easy in a large land divided by geography, language and local cultures, a land where the peasant was suspicious of everyone outside his own family. Sun himself often confused "nation" with "race," and was seemingly unsure as to just what groups truly made up the Chinese nation.[23]

Sun's answer to China's lack of national cohesion was to build upon pre-existing loyalties, particularly upon loyalty to the clan, the extended family grouping, especially powerful in south China. What Sun termed "clanism" has rarely been viewed as a potential advantage to political centralization in China, but usually as a major obstacle. A sense of national identity in the modern sense was very slow to emerge in China, and was most basically a result of the Japanese invasion of the late 1930's. One of the many anomalies of the nationalist revolution begun in part by Sun Yat-sen has been that his political heirs, the Kuomintang or Chinese Nationalist Party led by Chiang K'ai-shek did not succeed in harnessing that nascent Chinese nationalism, but rather fell before the Chinese Communist Party which did use it effectively.

Sun Yat-sen felt that Chinese nationalism could in part emerge from the creation of more modern political forms which would provide the Chinese with a strong and progressive central government meriting their loyalty and confidence. For these new institutions, Sun looked once more to the West.

Sun was not a slavish imitator of things Western; he frequently deplored the tendency of enthusiastic modernizers to uncritically copy foreign models. He felt that while Western, particularly American, political institutions were necessary to progress in China, they had to be modified. He was especially concerned that many of these institutions were ultimately too democratic for the good of the West as well as of China. Many Chinese intellectuals, struck by the chaos of warlordism, and the generalized social anarchy which had followed the dissolution of the old imperial system, agreed with him. To them, China needed both democracy and a strong central government.

Sun showed a very Confucian regard for the differing levels of ability found among the Chinese social classes. A recurrent theme in his writings is that most people are simply not capable of self-government. "If we divide people according to their individualities", Sun wrote, "we shall find three groups: the first, those who create and invent (they are called pioneers and leaders), the second, those who transmit or disseminate new ideas and inventions (these are called disciples), and the third are those who carry out what they receive from the people of the first two groups, without doubt and without hesitating (these are called unconscious performers and people of action)."[24]

Sun felt that the West had not devised institutions to give the masses of the people both freedom and proper leadership and that Western progress had begun to slow, hampered by an excess of liberty.[25] To provide the proper balance of freedom and direction, Sun borrowed from the Chinese past and the Western present, arriving at the "Five Power Constitution." Sun described this system as two-tiered, consisting of the people at the first level, protected by such progressive institutions as suffrage, recall, initiative and referendum. The second level was the governmental administration consisting of five departments: the legislature, the judiciary and the executive, all essentially similar to contemporary American examples, and two more drawn from the Chinese tradition: censorship and civil service examinations.

Civil service was to choose government employees by examination, and censorship was to act as an internal check on corruption and malfeasance. In Sun's judgment, such a system, instituted after a short period of military control and tutelage, would guarantee the people ultimate control over their government, which, however, would have the necessary centralization of power to function in troubled China.

Another necessity for China's future progress as Sun viewed it was the rapid adoption of scientific methods. The two important metaphors to the Chinese of the May Fourth period were "Mr. Democracy" and "Mr. Science," and Sun was no exception. Many Chinese of his generation yet harbored some doubts about the ultimate benefits of science, but Sun was not among them. He felt that scientific progress was not only the key to resisting the West but also the solution to China's eternal poverty. To Sun, science meant primarily economic progress which would permit China to protect herself from Western products and to develop further her own industry and markets.[26]

The third of the Three People's Principles is "Livelihood," a problem to which Sun devoted much thought. By this term he meant essentially the achievement of a minimum standard of living for the peasantry. He believed that this could be attained through the development of industry, transportation and communication. His book, *The International Development of China*, was devoted entirely to a program of development. Obviously assembled with considerable technical advice, the book is a detailed plan for the nurturance of communications, river conservancy, harbors, urbanization, electrification, heavy industry, mining, agriculture, irrigation and reforestation.[27]

Sun's economic conceptions, like his political ones, were eclectic. Again he assembled bits and pieces of modern Western and traditional Chinese ideas and institutions. By his death, he had accepted the basic elements of the Marxist analysis although he disagreed with it at several crucial points. He believed in a historical process which we can term materialist, and he agreed with Marx and Lenin that the economic mode of production was the primary factor in any particular situation. He also seems to have accepted the Leninist argument that the Western powers were seeking markets for surplus production and capital.

Again like Marx and Lenin, he advocated a fundamentally socialist society. As he was always careful to assert the primacy of his contribution, he usually argued that his views were unique and without progenitors. For example, he states, "Socialism is similar to the Principle of the People's Livelihood which I have been advocating."[28] Although Sun's clear debt to Marxist theory has sometimes discomfited his political heirs, the most fervent of anti-communists, the critical issue has always been his ties to the Soviet Union.

Sun was aware that no successful nationalist movement in China could stand against the foreign-backed warlords, or a united foreign opposition, and he had searched for allies in every possible quarter. Rebuffed over the years by French imperialists, Japanese expansionists, American presidents and businessmen, he found himself at the last working closely with the Soviet Union. Sun was concerned about the dangers of Soviet assistance, but he was in need of money, weapons and advisors, all of which the Soviets provided. The Soviet Union too desired allies, isolated as it was by European and American hostility. It saw in Sun Yat-sen not only the potential leader of the world's most populous nation, but also a man whose nationalism would damage Great Britain's empire in the East.

Unlike the Western powers Sun was not terribly concerned by the revolutionary nature of Soviet ideology because he felt that history had already pronounced its judgment on critical aspects of the Marxist-Leninist position. Like many European socialists, Sun felt that class war was not inherent in socialism and that the experience of Europe and America demonstrated that in fact capitalists would share with their workers and yield where necessary to non-violent reform. In support of his argument, Sun cited a contemporary American scholar, Maurice Williams, whose work *Social Interpretation of History* persuaded him that Marx' prediction of inevitable class warfare could be avoided.[29] In making his analysis of Marxism, Sun was sometimes incisive and persuasive; at other times his arguments grew muddled as he asserted the primacy of his own ill-defined Principle of Livelihood.

Ultimately the question as to the exact nature of Sun's commitment to Soviet assistance and socialist ideals is moot. He sometimes asserts that "socialism is similar to the Principle of the People's Livelihood...," and then again, "...we have not championed socialism but the *Min Sheng* (People's Livelihood) Principle."[30] At another point he states, "When the people share everything in the state, then will we truly reach the goal of the *Min Sheng* Principle, which is Confucius' hope of a 'great commonwealth.'"[31] Just when the reader decides that Sun is fundamentally critical of the Soviet position, he then adds,

> The communism of her initial stage, has in the course of six years, been modified to such an extent that it accords with our Principle of the People's Livelihood. It may be said that the Russian Revolution was in actual fact a *San Min Chu I* (Three Principles of the People) revolution...[32]

Some elements of Sun's economic views are quite clear. He advocated state ownership of the basic factors of production, a socialized method of distribution—principally cooperatives—and redistribution of land. Sun was greatly influenced by the progressive American thinker Henry George. He saw George's Single Tax, a tax upon "unearned increments," increases in the value of real property, as the solution to economic reform. Armed with the funds generated by the Single Tax the Chinese government could then buy up agricultural land and redistribute it to the tenant-peasant, creating a nation of small free-holders.[33]

Sun, in all his thinking, shows a tremendous tension between an enthusiastic commitment to Western values, and a resentment at Western Intrusions into China. As might be expected, his attitude toward his own country is also ambivalent. He was captivated by the inchoate Chinese utopianism of the "Great Unity." The slogan most commonly associated with Sun is *T'ien-hsia wei-kung*—"All under heaven belongs to the People." The slogan hearkens back to the Golden Age of the mythical founding ancestors, the Emperors Yao and Shun, when Sun states "There was perfect peace, and the people enjoyed equality and liberty to the greatest extent."[34] For many Chinese, life from that time had been the story of the fall from grace into the suffering and disorder of early twentieth century China. Many Confucians, and Sun Yat-sen, felt that to achieve "good government" was eventually to usher the world into another era of "perfect peace."

In developing his case for the adoption of Western-style institutions, Sun constantly mentioned Chinese equivalents and precedents for them. In the final analysis, however, Sun Yat-sen saw China as backward, and in a certain sense, degenerate—the remains of a once-great culture whose light had pervaded Asia. This backwardness was reflected primarily in the disorder of Chinese politics, but also in the personal culture of her people. The gap between the Victorian manners of Sun's day and the spontaneity of the Chinese who gaped at foreigners and unashamedly performed virtually every natural function in public upset Sun, the cosmopolite. As he said, "Every word and act of a Chinese shows absence of refinement; one contact with Chinese people is enough to reveal this."[35]

Sun's personal morality was sometimes a matter of some dispute. There were those among his political enemies, and sometimes his allies, who felt that he was too lax in handling and accounting for the funds which he raised for the revolution.[36] There is no real evidence, however, that he was ever less than upright, if occasionally cavalier of others' opinions and sensitivities.

Although modern in his economics and politics, Sun was unabashedly conservative in his moral standards. He held that it was the power of Chinese morality, the superior virtue (*de*) of the Confucian system which had been successful for its cultural brilliance and its long survival. Sun lists among the important virtues, Loyalty, Filiality, Kindness, Love, Faithfulness and Justice, as well as the Love of Harmony and Peace.[37] In each case, Sun pointed out that the focus of those virtues could and should be transferred to the state from their previous foci in traditional society.

Sun also felt that ancient learning should be revived as well as ancient virtues. He saw the combination of learning and virtue as being the inner essence of the sage, necessary for the great man to contribute to the political system and national progress. As he said, "This calls upon a man to develop from within outward, to begin with his inner nature and not cease until the world is at peace."[38] This is the classical Confucian view, the image of the sage-king who calms the realm and subdues the outer barbarian through his radiant virtue.

Sun's blending of Western political forms and Chinese morality creates a number of seeming contradictions. The moral structure of Confucian China was eminently suitable for a society controlled not by law or government but by the customs and mores of an agrarian folk society. The Confucian virtues are most relevant to one-to-one relationships, such as that between husband and wife or father and son. The difficulty with the moral structure had always been that while it nourished and protected those within the circle of one-to-one relationships, it was often at the expense of those without. Family relationship thus vitiated the ability of the state to govern. Sun did perceive that the essence of modernization was to persuade citizens to work and sacrifice for the common good, but he did not see that traditional morality much restricted the desire and the ability of Chinese to do just that.

Although at this level Sun can be said to have blended Western economic and political values with traditional Chinese morality, there were rather severe limits to this eclecticism. While Sun was attracted to Western thought and thinkers he always subordinated them to his own program for China. He used them not to define necessary reforms stemming from Western attitudes as such, but to buttress his own arguments. The few Western scholars or political philosophers whom he mentions directly in his many works are the classical authorities and not the modern reformers who interested many other Chinese intellectuals, although there are some few exceptions such as Henry George. For example, the *Three Principles of the People* contains a long treatise comparing Hamiltonian and Jeffersonian attitudes toward democracy (Sun opts for Hamilton), but no mention of John Dewey who was the primary Western influence upon many Chinese intellectuals of Sun's day.

It is probable that Sun found the tendencies evidenced in the Western philosophy of the period after the First World War disturbing. Some Western liberals had begun to envision a sort of philosophic synthesis, which would include Western scientism but would buffer it with Eastern spirituality, to prevent excesses of the sort which it was widely believed had led up to the Great War. These men, including Bertrand Russell who travelled and lectured in China, and the influential German philosophers Rudolf Eucken and Hans Dreish, as well as major educators like Maynard Metcalf of Oberlin and Irving Babbit of Harvard; and publicists like the editor of *The Nation*, Oswald Garrison Villard, espoused a sort of world synthesis of Eastern and Western cultures.[39]

Such ideas were both appealing and appalling to the Chinese intellectuals of the period. Many of the currents of Western philosophy associated with the cultural synthesis moved closer to the traditional Chinese world-view. Thinkers such as Eucken, Dreish, Boutroux and Bergson shared a distrust of the scientific method as a means of acquiring knowledge, and an emphasis upon thought, intuition, things of the "spirit." Eucken and Dreish styled themselves "Vitalists" and Boutroux and Bergson were members of the French Spiritualist school.[40] While many Chinese intellectuals approved of Western concepts which seemed to add value to their own philosophical tradition, others recognized that such ideas ran counter to the spirit of the May Fourth movement which they saw as essential to reform.

On the surface, such ideas might seem attractive to Sun Yat-sen and useful to his synthesis of Western institutions and traditional Confucian morality. Sun is seemingly in fact unconcerned with the whole issue and mentions it hardly at all. There would appear to be two reasons why Sun ignored such an opportunity to bolster his position with Western authorities. First, he had little interest in abstract thought, and second, he may not have read the necessary materials.

More importantly, Sun had basically abrogated the field of abstract argument on political affairs and philosophy, such as the recurring debates between Chinese conservatives and reformers, to men with more formal credentials than he possessed—men like Liang Ch'i-ch'ao, Hu Shih, V.K. Ting, Chang Chün-mai and Ts'ai Yuan-p'ei. Sun was not seen as a major philosopher by the men of his time but primarily as an activist. Those who did follow the struggles between the schools of the Left and the Right viewed Sun as an uncouth lower-class rebel, closer to a secret society bandit than to political philosophers like Wang Yang-ming or K'ang Yu-wei.

Sun was himself dubious that the cosmopolitan synthesis proposed by the proponents of a cultural blending would be good for China. He saw it in part as another clever strategy designed to further obstruct Chinese nationalism and thus to continue to expose China to Western domination.[41] In this Sun was as always more realistic than the Chinese pure philosophers of his day. The East-West synthesis was in fact ultimately a minor strain in Western thought, and quite secondary to the great issues of international competition, and the search for markets. The cultural synthesis was an attractive idea, one which continues to circulate to this day—witness the many American young people who espouse Eastern religions or some mixture of Eastern and Western religions as an antidote to the mindless materialism of America in the seventies.

In the last analysis, Sun Yat-sen defies easy categorization. In reading his works one frequently encounters crude eclecticisms and myriad contradictions, learned discourses on Western history and science, followed by references to the mythical golden age of China. The key to Sun Yat-sen may be that he was essentially a transitional figure who stood between the Chinese past and its future, between East and West. He borrowed freely and was inspired by the entire range of all the world's ideas in an effort to protect his China. Sun was fundamentally not a thinker at all, but an inspirational political actor, who constantly adapted over a long and active life, to discontinuous shifts within the contexts in which he lived. Despite setbacks and shifts in circumstances which reduced many others to inaction, Sun never stopped struggling. As he himself said,

> Now, the key to success is action, and the essential in action is perseverance.[42]

NOTES

1. William Theodore DeBary, "Individualism and Humanitarianism in Late Ming Thought," in *Self and Society in Ming Thought*, ed. William Theodore DeBary (New York: Columbia University Press, 1970).

2. Frederick Wakeman, *History and Will* (Berkeley: University of California Press, 1973), pp. 101-137.

3. For biographical details, see Harold Z. Schiffrin, *Sun Yat-sen and the Origins of the Chinese Revolution* (Berkeley: University of California Press, 1968); see also C. Martin Wilbur, *Sun Yat Sen: Frustrated Patriot* (New York: Columbia University Press, 1976).

4. Jeffrey G. Barlow, "*Sun Yat-sen and the French in Viet-nam*" (Center for Chinese Studies, University of California, Berkeley), forthcoming.

5. Jerome B. Grieder, *Hu Shih and the Chinese Renaissance* (Cambridge: Harvard University Press, 1970).

6. Sun Yat-sen, *The International Development of China* (New York and London: G.P. Putnam's Sons, 1929).

7. D.W.Y. Kwok, *Scientism in Chinese Thought*, 1900-1950 (New Haven: Yale University Press, 1965); see also Leon Wieger, *Chine Moderne*, seven volumes, published from 1922-1937 in Hsien-hsien, China.

8. *Kuo-fu ch'üan-chi* (The Complete Collected Works of Sun Yat-sen) (Taipei: 1965), 3rd ts'e.

9. Sun Yat-sen, *San Min Chu I* (The Three People's Principles) (Taipei: China Publishing Co. reprint of 1927 edition [n.d.), p. 1.

10. Lo Chia-lun, ed., *Kuo-fu nien-pu'*, 2 vols. (Chronological Biography of Sun Yat-sen) (Taipei: 1969), I, p. 90.

11. Feng Tzu-yu, *Ke-ming i-shih* (Unofficial History of the Revolution), 5 vols. (Taiwan: 1969), Vol. II, p. 144.

12. Harold Z. Schiffrin, "The Enigma of Sun Yat-sen," in *China in Revolution*, ed. Mary Wright (New Haven: Yale University Press, 1968), p. 463.

13. *Min-pao* (The People's Journal), Tokyo, 1905-1910. Reprint (Taipei: 1969), 1st ts'e, 3rd ch'i.
14. Martin Bernal, "The Triumph of Anarchism over Marxism, 1906-1907," in *China in Revolution*, ed. Mary Wright (New Haven: Yale University Press, 1968), pp. 103-106.
15. Sun Yat-sen, *Memoirs of a Chinese Revolutionary* (New York: AMS Press, Inc., 1970). Reprinted from the 1927 London edition, p. 7.
16. *Ibid.*, p. 5.
17. Sun Yat-sen, *San Min Chu I*, p. 13.
18. Benjamin I. Schwartz, *In Search of Wealth and Power. Yen Fu and the West* (Cambridge: Harvard University Press, 1961), p. 45.
19. Sun Yat-sen, *San Min Chu I*, p. 6.
20. *Ibid.*, p. 208.
21. V. I. Lenin, *Imperialism, the Highest Stage of Capitalism* (Peking: Foreign Language Press, 1969). From Selected Works, Vol. I, Part II, Moscow: 1952.
22. Sun Yat-sen, *San Min Chu I*, p. 10.
23. *Ibid.*, Lecture 1.
24. Sun Yat-sen, *Memoirs of a Chinese Revolutionary*, p. 112.
25. Sun Yat-sen, *San Min Chu I*, p. 110.
26. *Ibid.*, p. 208.
27. Sun Yat-sen, *The International Development of China* (New York and London: G.P. Putnam's Sons, 1929).
28. Sun Yat-sen, *San Min Chu I*, p. 103.
29. *Ibid.*, pp. 155-169.
30. *Ibid.*, p. 155.
31. *Ibid.*, p. 184.
32. Sun Yat-sen, *Fundamentals of National Reconstruction* (Taipei- Sino-American Publishing Co., 1953), p. 162.
33. Sun Yat-sen, *San Min Chu I*, pp. 175-178.
34. Sun Yat-sen, *Fundamentals of National Reconstruction*, p. 32.
35. Sun Yat-sen, *San Min Chu I*, p. 43.
36. *Kuo-fu ch'uan-chi*, Vol. I, p. 421.
37. Sun Yat-sen, *San Min Chu I*, pp. 37-40.
38. *Ibid.*, p. 42.
39. Leon Wieger, *Chine Moderne*, Vol. VIII, p. 179; see also H.C. Meng, "The New Literary Movement in China," in *The Weekly Review of the Far East*, XX, No. 7 (April 15, 1922), p. 250; see also Chang Hsin-hai, "Chinese Political Thought and the West," *The Nation*, CXIV, No. 1965 (May 3, 1922), p. 527.
40. John Passmore, *A Hundred Years of Philosophy* (London: Gerald Duckworth and Co., Ltd., 1957), p. 105.
41. Sun Yat-sen, *San Min Chu I*, p. 17.
42. Sun Yat-sen, *Fundamentals of National Reconstruction*, p. 203.

15
HU SHIH

SUNG-PENG HSU

A. HU SHIH'S LIFE

Hu Shih (1891-1962) was born in Shanghai, where his father was a minor official of the Ch'ing Dynasty. His ancestral home was Chi-hsi in Anhwei Province. He was the only child of his father's third wife, who married him at the age of seventeen. As his father died when he was only four years old, Hu Shih was raised under the care of his young mother. The mother was an illiterate peasant woman and a devotee of the Buddhist Bodhisattva, Kuan-yin (Avalokiteśvara), commonly worshipped as a goddess in China since about the tenth century. Hu Shih used to accompany her to pay homage to Kuan-yin. In spite of her personal faith in popular Buddhism, the mother was determined to follow her husband's will, that Hu Shih be given a good education so that he would become a great Confucian scholar. Every morning she would tell the son all she knew about his father and remind him to follow in his father's footsteps.[1]

Hu Shih's early childhood was much influenced by the Buddhist ideas of heavens, hells, rebirth and Pure Land. But his education was strictly Confucian. Before he was three, he had learned over eight hundred characters from his father. A little after three, he was already in school in Chi-hsi. His mother paid the teacher more than the usual tuition, in order that the teacher would not teach him by rote (memory) alone, and would explain the meaning of the classical texts to him. Before the age of eight, Hu Shih could read almost everything with very little assistance. He read many books other than the Four Books and the Five Classics and became absorbed in vernacular novels. This interest in colloquial literature led him eventually to advocating what was later known as the Literary Revolution in China.

At the age of thirteen Hu Shih was sent to Shanghai for further education where he was exposed to a new world. He studied in three schools that offered courses in Western culture and came under the influence of the reformist and revolutionary ideas advocated by Liang Ch'i-ch'ao (1873-1929) and Sun Yat-sen (1866-1925). The Darwinian theory of evolution was a favorite subject among students. Hu Shih's personal name, Shih or Shih-chih, was adopted from the idea of "fitness" in the phrase "survival of the fittest."

From 1908 to 1910 Hu gave up his studies and taught English and Chinese in order to support himself and his mother. He became very much depressed with his personal life, and pessimistic about the future of China. In his despair he composed a poem that contained this line: "How proudly does the wintry frost scorn the powerless rays of the sun!" One evening, he became dead drunk and fought with a policeman in the street. He was jailed for the night. The next morning he went home and saw in the mirror the bruises on his face. The following line from Li Po's "Drinking Song" came to his mind: "Some use might yet be made of this material born in me."[2] He decided to take the examination in Peking for the scholarship, founded on the returned portion of the Boxer Indemnity, to study in the United States.[3] After a month of hard work, he succeeded in the examination and became one of the seventy chosen in 1910.

Hu Shih began his study in the College of Agriculture at Cornell University in September 1910. He had planned to learn something useful for the salvation of China. But his greater interest and ability in literary and philosophical subjects, prompted him to change his area of study. He completed the B.A. degree in philosophy in February 1914, and went on to the graduate program. Since he became dissatisfied with the idealistic emphasis in the Sage School at Cornell, he transferred to Columbia University the next year to study with John Dewey. Two years later, in 1917, he completed his doctoral program with the dissertation, "The Development of the Logical Method in Ancient China."

Before his return to China in the summer of 1917, Hu Shih was already involved in the problem of Chinese language reform. His article "Tentative Proposals for the Improvement of Literature" was published in January 1917 in the *New Youth* founded by Ch'en Tu-hsiu (1879-1942) in 1915. This article has generally been regarded as the formal call of the Literary Revolution.

When he began his teaching at the National Peking University, Hu Shih was already hailed as an intellectual leader in China. The Literary Revolution was unexpectedly successful. The classical language was pronounced dead. In a few years the colloquial language was widely used in newspapers, magazines, and literature. The Peking government in 1911 ordered that the colloquial be taught in schools. In fact, the Literary Revolution was a part of a general movement usually called New Culture Movement, which covered the period from about 1915 to 1923. The *New Youth* was the leading periodical of the Movement. Through the vernacular language the intellectuals consciously introduced new ideas to the masses. Gradually, the "literary revolution" became "revolutionary literature."

The New Culture Movement was given an additional impetus by the May Fourth Movement in 1919, which was originally a nationwide protest against the Paris Peace Conference held after the First World War. The Conference had decided to grant Japan's claim on Shantung. The May Fourth Movement forced the Chinese government not to sign the peace treaty. It also generated greater effects on the various social, cultural, and political forces in China. Quite a few important intellectuals became disillusioned with the democratic countries that attended the Paris Peace Conference. Many of them turned to Communism for the salvation of China. Ch'en Tu-hsiu was converted to Communism and with others organized the Chinese Communist Party in 1920.[4]

Hu Shih's reputation was established when he taught at Peking University from 1917 to 1926. He was generally regarded as one of the foremost spokesmen of the Literary Revolution, the New Culture Movement, and the May Fourth Movement. After that productive period, he served in many different positions, including the deanship and presidency of Peking University. During the Second World War, he was appointed ambassador to the United States (from 1938 to 1942). He lectured and taught in several major universities in America. After the Communist victory in 1949, Hu Shih lived in the United States. In 1957 he accepted the invitation from the Nationalists in Taiwan to become the director of the Academia Sinica. Before his death in 1962, he had received thirty-five honorary degrees from various universities in the world.

B. Hu Shih's Conception of Philosophy

Hu Shih lived in a turbulent period of Chinese history. In such a situation, one could have responded with a philosophy of resignation. But that was not the kind of philosophy Hu Shih advocated. We can find two basic points in his conception of philosophy. First, he insists that in doing philosophy we must concentrate on the actual problems that we are confronted with in our life. The task of philosophy is to solve those problems. Second, he maintains that all answers to the problems are hypothetical and instrumental in nature. They should not be taken as absolute. They are true or good only if they can solve our problems. If they cannot solve our problems, we should reject them, or revise and improve them. These two points are expressed in many different contexts in his writings.

In his *Outline of the History of Chinese Philosophy* published in 1919 Hu Shih defines philosophy as "the kind of learning that investigates the basic and crucial problems of human life and seeks a fundamental solution to them from a fundamental point of view."[5] He lists the following six points as the basic problems of philosophy:

1. What is the origin of the universe and the myriad things?
2. What is the extent, function, and method of knowledge and thought?
3. What ought man to do in this world?
4. How can we educate people to gain knowledge, to think, and to do what is good and to avoid what is bad?
5. How should man organize and maintain a society or state?
6. What is the ultimate destiny of human life?

Hu Shih did not write any book to answer these questions in any systematic manner. But his views can be found in his various writings about his own life and about his attempts to solve China's problems. He was eager to defend his views against criticism, but he was careful to admit that his views were not absolute.

Hu Shih holds that his personal views about the basic problems of philosophy can be separated from the method of thinking that he advocates. This method of thinking is summarized in eight Chinese characters: Ta-tan chia-she, hsiao-hsin ch'iu-cheng (boldness in proposing hypothesis and carefulness in seeking verification). This statement has become a familiar slogan and a mark of Hu Shih's teachings. Hu believes that, if the Chinese people would accept this method of thinking to solve their problems, a new culture could be created in China and China could be saved. It is not important whether Hu Shih's personal philosophy is accepted.

Hu Shih acknowledges that Thomas Huxley and John Dewey were the two most important persons who had taught him how to think honestly and think well. Huxley taught him the spirit of doubting everything that has insufficient evidence. Dewey taught him to focus attention on the actual problems at hand, to regard all theories or ideals as hypotheses yet to be verified and to be concerned with the effects of thought. According to Hu Shih, Dewey's method of thinking is not only true of discoveries in the experimental sciences but also of the best researches in the historical sciences such as textual criticism, philological reconstruction and higher criticism. He gives Dewey's instrumental logic credit for having turned him into a historical worker. Hu learned to think genetically and he attributed to the genetic habit of thinking the key to success in all his work in the history of thought and literature.[6]

An important aspect of the New Culture Movement was to introduce new ideas from the West. As a result, many "isms" were preached by the enthusiasts of Western culture. Hu Shih saw great dangers in talking about isms to the extent of neglecting actual problems. In a series of articles written in 1919 entitled "Problems and Isms" Hu Shih called on the Chinese intellectuals to exert more energy and spend more time on studying the actual problems in China and less on isms. He said,

"We do not study the livelihood of rickshaw drivers, but we make an abstract talk about Socialism. We do not study how to liberate women or improve family system, but we make an abstract talk about the isms of sharing wives and free love. We do not study how to liberate the Anfu Club of the warlords or how ot solve the civil war between the south and the north, but we make an abstract talk about anarchism. Yet we boast that we are talking about fundamental 'solution.' To tell the truth, it is just a dream talk that deceives oneself as well as others. It is a solid evidence of the bankruptcy of Chinese thought. It is a death sentence to the cause of improving Chinese society."[7]

Hu Shih asserted that the reason that so many people were fond of talking about isms was their laziness. It is easy to talk about isms because a parrot or a record player can also do it.

According to Hu Shih, all isms were originally formulated in response to actual problems in concrete historical situations. Those who were concerned about the evil conditions of the times investigated the causes of the problems and offered a method of solution. When the method was propagated to a large number of people, the proposal was summarized in a few words for the sake of simplicity and convenience. In this way, a proposal became an ism, and a concrete plan became an abstract term. Here lies the danger and weakness of isms.

Hu Shih challenged the Chinese intellectuals to produce original thought in response to the peculiar problems in China. According to him, the first step of thought is to investigate all the aspects of the problems, to find out the causes of the evil conditions. The next is to propose all possible prescriptions on the basis of one's experience and knowledge. Then one should use one's imagination, together with one's experience and knowledge, to infer the possible consequences of each prescription and to determine whether it could solve the actual problems. Finally, one chooses a particular method of solution to be one's proposal.

Hu Shih did not really oppose the study of isms. Isms are worthy of study as long as they are regarded as theories, hypotheses, or instrumentalities. The knowledge of many isms would enable us to find a good solution to our problems. One should however avoid "hanging an ism on one's lips" and believing it dogmatically. Hu Shih suggests that when we study a theory, we must take three things into consideration. First, we must know the historical circumstances in which the theory was formulated. Second, we must consider the biographical and cultural background of the person who formulated the theory. Finally, we must investigate the effects the theory has produced. These three points constitute what he calls the "historical attitude" or "genetic method."[8] This attitude or method should be applied to the study of the theories imported from the West as well as to the study of the philosophies found in the Chinese tradition.[9]

In Hu Shih's judgment, the greatest problems or evils in China that await solutions are poverty, disease, ignorance, corruption and disorder.[10] He believed that nothing less than a total transformation of Chinese culture could eliminate these evils. This is why Hu Shih was such a fervent advocate of a new culture. To him, the Literary Revolution was not simply to replace the classical language with the colloquial language. It was also to replace the mode of thinking embodied in the old culture, with a new mode of thinking that was to be developed in the vernacular literature. In his *"Tentative Proposals for the Improvement of Literature"* written in 1917, Hu Shih listed the following eight points for emphasis:

1. Write with substance; do not write when there is nothing substantial to say.
2. Do not imitate the ancients.
3. Write with a grammatical structure.
4. Do not use gloomy language when there is nothing to complain.
5. Eliminate rotten expressions and conventional phrases.
6. Do not use ancient allusions or quotations.
7. Do not use the ancient rules of couplets and parallelisms in poetry.
8. Do not shun vernacular words or phrases.[11]

It is clear that these rules were intended to break loose the traditional mode of thinking. A year later, Hu Shih mentioned the following four points in order to emphasize the constructive spirit of the revolution:

1. Speak only if there is something to say.
2. Say what there is to say and say the way it is to be said.
3. Speak your own words; do not repeat what others say.
4. Use the living language of our own times.[12]

Hu Shih obviously hoped that the development of a vernacular language and a new literature would help the transformation of Chinese culture, which in turn would help to eliminate poverty, disease, ignorance, corruption, and disorder.[13] In a sense, the New

Culture Movement that Hu Shih promoted tried to accomplish the combined results of the Renaissance, Reformation, Enlightenment, Industrial Revolution, etc. in the West.

Unlike some other people, Hu Shih did not regard capitalism and imperialism as the major causes of the evils in China. In his view, capitalism had not yet been developed enough in China to become a major cause of China's problems. The Western and Japanese invasions of China were in his judgment mainly due to the weakness of China herself.[14] Hu Shih may have underestimated the close connection between domestic affairs and international situations. But he may have wanted to emphasize the importance of putting one's own house into order rather than blame others for the mess. In any case, he has often been criticized as an agent of Japanese or Western imperialism.

C. SCIENCE AND PHILOSOPHY OF LIFE

After the Opium War with England in 1840, China was forced to open her doors to the Western powers. The Chinese were first impressed by the gunpowder and warships of Western civilization. Then they realized that behind the military equipment were science and democracy. The superiority of Western culture was gradually conceded. The traditional conception that China was the center of the world became a myth. China had to learn from the West not only technology but also science and a way of life. By the time of the New Culture Movement there was already a widespread acceptance of science and democracy among Chinese intellectuals. The famous slogans in the movement were "Mr. Science" and "Mr. Democracy." In the names of Mr. Science and Mr. Democracy, the enthusiasts hoped to drive away the "evil spirit" of the old culture by chanting "Down with the curiosity shop of Confucius!" Hu Shih was one of the enthusiasts, but in general his radical position was somewhat balanced by a tolerant, moderate, conciliatory, and scholarly attitude—a seemingly paradoxical combination in his personality.[15]

The emphasis on science and democracy was challenged however by the defenders of Chinese tradition, especially after the First World War. Liang Ch'i-ch'ao, who had been a strong supporter of science, led a group of Chinese intellectuals to visit postwar Europe. After his return, he published *Impressions of My*

European Journey in 1919, in which he presented the views expressed by many European thinkers, that Western civilization was bankrupt and that it was time for the West to look towards the East for salvation.[16] This book was used by the traditionalists to support their cause. In 1921, Liang Sou-ming, professor of Indian and Chinese philosophies at Peking University, published *Eastern and Western Civilizations and Their Philosophies* in which he argued that the world civilization of the future should be a rejuvenated Chinese culture. According to him, Western civilization since the Renaissance represents a way of life in which the will seeks satisfaction by the conquest of nature and struggle for existence. On the other hand, the Indian civilization represents a way of life in which the will seeks to suppress human desires and ignore actual problems in the present world. The Chinese civilization is most reasonable because it represents a way of life in which the will seeks equilibrium and self-contentment.[17] This book added another weapon on the side of the traditionalists.

The conflict between the promoters of a new culture (often called "modernists" or "westernizers") and the traditionalists took the form of a debate on science and philosophy of life in 1923 after Carsun Chang (Chang Chun-mai, 1886-   ) delivered a lecture entitled "The Philosophy of Life" to the students at Tsing Hua University. According to him, there is a qualitative difference between the impersonal and materialistic nature of science (Not-I) and the personal and spiritual nature of philosophy of life (I). The former is said to be objective, logical, analytical, causal, and uniform in character; the latter is said to be subjective, intuitive, synthetic, based on freedom of the will and rising from the uniqueness of human personality. Because of this difference, Chang argued, science cannot and should not determine the question of values that constitute a philosophy of life.

Chang's view was quickly attacked by Ting Wen-chiang (V.K. Ting, 1887-1936), a famous geologist, who found in Chang's view a "metaphysical ghost" who had long been unemployed in the West and suddenly appeared in China. In less than a year, virtually all the major intellectuals in China joined in the battle. At the end of 1923, the major articles in this debate were collected and published as *Science and Philosophy of Life*, which amounts to 250,000 words. Hu Shih and Ch'en Tu-hsiu were asked to write introductions to it. During the debate Hu Shih was not actively involved because of his illness, but he was certainly in the pro-science camp.[18]

An important issue in the debate is the nature of science. It is possible for a traditionalist to define science so narrowly that the question of values is entirely beyond its boundary. The modernists tended to hold a broader conception of science, including natural as well as social and human sciences. Another important issue concerns the place of human will in the natural world. The traditionalists generally emphasized freedom of the will to such an extent that there was an absolute dichotomy between body and spirit in man. The modernists tended to minimize the importance of human will or understand it within the context of the natural world.

Hu Shih's position will be analyzed in detail later. In general, his view is similar to John Dewey's. Like Dewey, Hu rejected the dualism of body and spirit. If there is no such dualism, there would be no reason why science, understood broadly as in Pragmatism, could not deal with the spiritual aspect of man. In *Reconstruction in Philosophy* published in 1919, Dewey in fact advocated an American "new culture movement" mainly because, in his view, the traditional dichotomy between body and soul could no longer be the foundation of philosophy. Dewey admitted that the methods used in natural sciences were inadequate for the study of social and human problems, but he was confident that it would be possible to develop, form, and produce "the intellectual instrumentalities which will progressively direct inquiry into the deeply and inclusively human—that is to say, moral—facts of the present scene and situation."[19]

Hu Shih believed in the freedom of human will, but he held that the will should be understood within the general framework of a naturalistic universe. The naturalistic tendency in Hu's thought began very early in his life. The first seed was sown by the rationalistic and naturalistic elements in Confucianism. In his childhood, Hu Shih was very much terrified by the vivid descriptions of various hells, and ugly and fierce gods in popular Buddhism. At the age of eleven, while rereading aloud *The Elementary Lessons* of Chu Hsi, he came upon a passage where Chu Hsi quoted Ssu-ma Kuang in an attack on the popular belief in heaven and hell. The quotation reads: "When the body has decayed, the spirit fades away. Even if there be such cruel tortures in Hell as Chiseling, Burning, Pounding, and Grinding, whereon are these to be inflicted?" Hu Shih began to doubt the idea of judgment after death.[20] Shortly afterward, when he was reading Ssu-ma Kuang's *The General Mirror for Government*, he came upon a passage which he credited to making him an atheist. The passage tells a philosopher of the fifth century A.D. named Fan Chen who championed the theory of the destructibility of the spirit or soul against the whole Imperial Court, which was then patronizing Mahāyāna Buddhism. Fan Chen's view was summed up by Ssu-ma Kuang in these words: "The body is the material basis of the spirit, and the spirit is only the functioning of the body. The spirit is to the body what sharpness is to a sharp knife. We have never known the existence of sharpness after the destruction of the knife. How can we admit the survival of the spirit when the body is gone?" Fan Chen also attacked the Buddhist doctrine of *karma*, and Hu Shih found his argument convincing.[21]

Hu Shih's naturalistic orientation was of course later reinforced by the Darwinian theory of biological evolution and Dewey's philosophy.

D. HU SHIH'S BASIC PHILOSOPHICAL POSITION

Hu Shih's basic philosophical position is most fully expressed in his introductory article for *Science and Philosophy of Life*. In examining the views expressed in the great debate, he felt that there was a common defect among the defenders of science in that they concentrated too much on the general and abstract question whether it is possible for science to deal with human values. He suggested that they should go a step further to state what was actually a scientific philosophy of life, so that the debate would be on more concrete issues. He detected that the defenders of science were reluctant to state their views of life on the basis of science because they were not sure what a scientific philosophy of life was, and also because they were afraid to get into the territory of metaphysics that they were attacking. He agreed with Ch'en-Tu-hsiu when Ch'en said that, if the scientists failed to provide a scientific view of life, then the metaphysicans would have the monopoly of answering all the problems of human life.[22]

According to Hu Shih, those who believe in science should be willing to develop a grand hypothesis about the universe and man's place in it, which is a philosophy of life. As long as the hypothesis is based on the facts already known, and can be revised and improved on the basis of new evidence, there is no reason why the scientists should not enter the realm of the so-called "unknown," the realm that has been unwittingly conceded to the metaphysicians. Hu Shih highly recommended Wu Chih-hui (1865-1953), a philosophical materialist, because he was the only person boldly stating his "materialistic and mechanistic philosophy of life" to combat the "metaphysical ghosts." In this way, the real or crucial issue is no longer whether science can solve human problems. The issues become whether there is God, whether there are spirits and ghosts, whether there are souls.

Hu Shih took up his own challenge, and formulated his philosophy of life on the foundation of available scientific knowledge. He proposed it as a grand hypothesis and called it "the naturalistic conception of life and the universe." Since the hypothesis is stated in ten points and is very anti-religion in tone, hostile Christian missionaries called it "Hu Shih's New Decalogue." The ten points are:

"1. On the basis of our knowledge of astronomy and physics, we should recognize that the world of space is infinitely large.
2. On the basis of our geological and paleontological knowledge, we should recognize that the universe extends over infinite time.
3. On the basis of all our verifiable scientific knowledge, we should recognize that the universe and everything in it follow natural laws of movement and change—'natural' in the Chinese sense of 'being so of themselves'—and that there is no need for the concept of a supernatural Ruler or Creator.
4. On the basis of the biological sciences, we should recognize the terrific wastefulness and brutality in the struggle for existence in the biological world, and consequently the untenability of the hypothesis of a benevolent Ruler.
5. On the basis of the biological, physiological, and psychological sciences, we should recognize that man is only one

species in the animal kingdom and differs from the other species only in degree, but not in kind.
6. On the basis of the knowledge derived from anthropology, sociology, and the biological sciences, we should understand the history and causes of the evolution of living organisms and of human society.
7. On the basis of the biological and psychological sciences, we should recognize that all psychological phenomena are explainable through the law of causality.
8. On the basis of biological and historical knowledge, we should recognize that morality and religion are subject to change, and that the causes of such change can be scientifically studied.
9. On the basis of our newer knowledge of physics and chemistry, we should recognize that matter is full of motion and not static.
10. On the basis of biological, sociological, and historical knowledge, we should recognize that the individual self is subject to death and decay, but the sum total of individual achievement, for better or for worse, lives on in the immortality or the Larger Self; that to live for the sake of the species and posterity is religion of the highest kind; and that those religions which seek a future life either in Heaven or in the Pure Land, are selfish religions."[23]

In spite of his atheistic and naturalistic stand, Hu Shih was very much interested in the function of religion in human society and was also concerned with the problem of ultimate human destiny. Living in depressing times in China, Hu Shih was at first quite pessimistic about the meaning of life. After he went to study at Cornell, he found it difficult to cheer and shout with the crowd while watching football games. In the summer of 1911, after the semester was over, he was invited to attend a conference of the Chinese Christian Students' Association held at Pocono Pines, Pennsylvania. Moved by a testimony about a new life in Jesus Christ, Hu stood up and declared his desire to become a Christian. But later he drifted away from Christianity and came to think that in that episode he was a victim of a trap set up by the preacher on the basis of human emotion.[24] Gradually, he became caught up with the optimistic spirit of America. In 1915 he wrote the essay "*In Defense of Browning's Optimism,*" and was awarded the Hiram Corson Prize for the best essay on Robert Browning. From then on, he was able to face the "terrific wastefulness and brutality in the struggle for existence in the biological world" with an optimistic view.

For many years, Hu Shih had contented himself with an ancient Chinese doctrine of "three immortalities" found in the Tso Commentary of the *Spring and Autumn Annals*: the immortality of virtue, of service, and of wise speech. In 1918, when his mother died, Hu Shih felt that this doctrine was in need of revision because it neglected the common people who did not have great virtue, service, or wise speech for the posterity to remember, and because it failed to "furnish any negative check on human conduct." He came to believe that everything we do, whether great or small, good or bad, would have direct or indirect effects on other people. What we are today is the result of what our forefathers consciously or unconsciously did. For this reason Hu Shih often blamed the Chinese forefathers for the great evils that the Chinese people suffer today. He also urged the Chinese to "create new (good) causes" so that our posterity would enjoy a better life.[25] He said,

> "As I reviewed the life of my dead mother, whose activities had never gone beyond the trivial details of the home but whose influence could be clearly seen on the faces of those men and women who came to mourn her death, and as I recalled the personal influence of my father on her whole life and its lasting effect on myself, I came to the conviction that everything is immortal. Everything that we are, everything that we do, and everything that we say is immortal in the sense that it has an effect everywhere in this world, and that effect in true will have its results somewhere else, and the thing goes on in infinite time and space."[26]

For Hu Shih, the Larger Self is basically the human society, but it could also be extended to mean the natural universe as a whole. To live for the good of the Larger Self is in his view religion of the highest kind.

E. HU SHIH'S THOUGHT AND COMMUNISM

The two most important figures in the New Culture Movement were Ch'en Tu-hsiu and Hu Shih. Hu Shih's rise was to a large extent aided by Ch'en, then a dean of Peking University and the editor of the *New Youth*. After 1919, Ch'en turned from Mr. Democracy to Communism largely because of his disappointment at the Versailles decision in which the democratic nations betrayed China by granting Japan's demand for the Shantung Peninsula.

During the great debate in 1923, both Hu and Ch'en were on the side of science and both were invited to write an introduction to *Sceince and Philosophy of Life*. But one finds significant differences between them, especially on the questions of human will and the place of culture in the universe.

According to Hu Shih, freedom of the will is very limited, but it is very important for creating a new culture and for transforming Chinese society. Hu's optimism lies mainly in his confidence that man can "create new causes" for the good of the future. Man can use his intelligence to create new ideas and through the ideas to master the natural forces for human happiness. He said,

> "In this naturalistic universe, in this universe of infinite space and time, man, the two-handed animal whose average height is about five feet and a half and whose age rarely exceeds a hundred years, is indeed a mere infinitesimal microbe. In this naturalistic universe, where every motion in the heavens has its regular course and every change follows laws of nature, where causality governs man's life and the struggle for existence spurs his activities—in such a universe man has very little freedom indeed.
>
> "Yet this tiny animal of two hands has his proper place and worth in that world of infinite magnitude. Making good use of his hands and a large brain, he has actually succeeded in making a number of tools, thinking out ways and means, and creating his own civilization. He has not only domesticated the wild animals, but he has also studied and discovered a considerable number of the secrets and laws of nature by means of which he has become a master of the natural forces and is now ordering electricity to drive his carriage and ether to deliver his message.

"The increase of his knowledge has extended his power, but it has also widened his vision and elevated his imagination. There were times when he worshipped stones and animals and was afraid of the gods and ghosts. But he is now moving away from these childish habits, and is slowly coming to a realization that the infinity of space only enhances his aesthetic appreciation of the universe, the infinite length of geological and archaeological time only makes him better understand the terrific hardship his forefathers had to encounter in building up this human inheritance, and the regularity of the movements and changes in the heavens and on earth only furnishes him the key to his dominion over nature.

"Even the absolute universality of the law of causality does not necessarily limit his freedom, because the law of causality not only enables him to explain the past and predict the future, but also encourages him to use his intelligence to create new causes and attain new results. Even the apparent cruelty in the struggle for existence does not necessarily make him a hardened brute; on the contrary, it may intensify his sympathy for his fellow men, make him believe more firmly in the necessity of cooperation, and convince him of the importance of conscious human endeavour as the only means of reducing the brutality and wastefulness of the natural struggles. In short, this naturalistic conception of the universe and life is not necessarily devoid of beauty, of poetry, of moral responsibility, and of the fullest opportunity for the exercise of the creative intelligence of man."[27]

It is significant to note that Hu Shih has not tried to derive human values logically from facts about the natural universe. He is only pointing to the possibility of creating values in such a universe. It is possible for a person, such as a Buddhist, to agree with Hu Shih on everything he has said about the natural universe, and yet to believe that it would be futile to find happiness in this world. This is the major difference between Hu Shih's philosophy and a philosophy such as Buddhism.

Hu Shih's view that man can use his will and freedom to create a desirable civilization was attacked by Ch'en Tu-hsiu from the Marxist point of view. In his introductory essay for *Science and Philosophy of Life*, Ch'en used the theory of Dialectical Materialism to reject Chang Chung-mai's view that philosophy of life is subjective, intuitive, synthetic, based on the freedom of the will and arisen from the uniqueness of human personality. According to Ch'en, all the different philosophies of life mentioned by Chang were determined by "objective material causes," namely the economic conditions of the times. He rejected the idea that there was such a thing as conscience, intuition, or the freedom of the will that could determine a philosophy of life, explain history, or change a society. At the end of his article, he accused Ting Wen-chiang and indirectly Hu Shih of an "idealistic" tendency because they failed to explain the formation of a philosophy of life exclusively in terms of "objective material conditions."[28]

Ch'en's accusation gave rise to a round of debate between Ch'en and Hu. In his reply, Hu Shih says that the issue depends very much on what is meant by "objective material causes." He states that it is no problem for him to regard the mind as a manifestation of matter. He goes on to say that just because of this, when one talks about "objective material causes," one must include all the activities of the mind, such as knowledge, thought, speech, education, etc. He objects to Ch'en's method of reducing "matter" to "economic forces." According to Hu, the Marxist interpretation of history in terms of economics can at most explain a majority of historical phenomena but not the whole. Finally, he asks Ch'en if Ch'en had not really believed that knowledge, thought, speech, and education could change a society, explain history, and determine a philosophy of life, then he should have sat down in an armchair and just observed the changing process of economic conditions. He should not have worked so hard for propagating new ideas and for creating a new culture.[29]

In his reply, Ch'en Tu-hsiu reiterates his view that economics is the cause of all changes in knowledge, thought, speech and education of a given historical period, and denies that it is only one of many causes along with knowledge, thought, etc. He calls the former view "monism" and the latter "pluralism." Ch'en, however, admits that human effort and the exercise of intelligence are necessary for the progress of society, and adds that their effects are limited to the extent made possible by the material conditions of the society.[30]

The basic issue in the debate between Ch'en and Hu is on the nature of human will in the natural world. This is a perennial philosophical problem. Neither Hu Shih nor Ch'en Tu-hsiu has gone into a detailed analysis of the problem. Whatever the theoretical difficulties in their respective philosophical systems, it is clear that both Hu and Ch'en theoretically recognize much less freedom of the will than the traditionalists do. Between Hu and Ch'en, Hu acknowledges a greater role of the free will than Ch'en does. But in practice, Hu Shih was the strongest advocate of the freedom of the will in the form of individualism. Following the tradition of liberalism in the West, Hu Shih holds that a good society must consist of individuals who are free to express their views and to create new ideas for the improvement of human life. The traditionalists tended to emphasize the need for individuals to confrom to ancient teachings. The Communists believe in Marxism, Leninism, Stalinism and later Maoism as the absolute truth. It is indeed very paradoxical that, while theoretically discounting the importance of ideas in changing a society, the Communists, in practice, resort to the most careful control of thought and use of propaganda to create and maintain a society. This dogmatic and authoritarian orientation in Communism is one reason Hu Shih was so much opposed to it.

In proposing his philosophy of life, Hu Shih did not mean to assert an absolute truth based on science. Apart from the fact that it was proposed as a hypothesis, he stated that the ten points that he had formulated were only intended to be the "minimum" common ground for building a view of life. The implication is that each individual is to a certain degree free to "create new causes" for making life happy. Hu Shih's universe is therefore a universe open to novelty. The biological world is wasteful and brutal, but man can overcome the evils. In spite of the tension between the biological world and the ideal society, Hu Shih resisted a bifurcation between body and mind in his philosophy.

In 1930 Hu Shih wrote an article introducing his own thought. He said that Ch'en Tu-hsiu had at one time made the suggestion that, since Pragmatism and Dialectical Materialism were the two most important methods of thought in the modern world, the two methods should make an alliance to fight against traditional thought. Hu rejected the idea, saying that the Dialectical Method had originated in Hegel's philosophy and was a metaphysical method established before the development of Darwin's theory of evolution. Pragmatism or Experimentalism was, on the other hand, a scientific method developed after the evolutionary theory was established. He said,

> "Darwin's theory of biological evolution taught us a great lesson, namely that biological evolution, whether through natural development or human selection, is a gradual process of small changes one at a time. It is a very complex phenomenon. There is no simple goal that can be attained by a giant leap, nor is there any permanent state that can be reached after such a leap. The philosophy of Dialectical Method was originally a theory of evolution established before the development of biology. According to its own theory, the process of changes between thesis and antithesis should continue without an end. But the Communists of the narrow kind seem to have forgotten this principle. They dogmatically and illusorily set up an ideal world of shared production and shared ownership. They believe that it can be easily attained by the means of class struggle, and that, when it has been attained, it can be kept from further changes under the dictatorship of a class. To reduce the complex to the simple and to deny the continuous process of changes is one hundred per cent a dogmatic thought before the rise of Darwinism. It is much more dogmatic than Hegel's philosophy."[31]

One may properly raise the question whether Hu Shih had adequately understood Communism or whether his interpretation of Darwinism was sound. In any case, it is clear that his criticism of Communism and his interpretation of Darwinism do reflect his own philosophical orientation. Like Dewey, Hu believed that society should be changed and reformed through a piecemeal process. Hu Shih said,

> "A culture is not formed altogether at once. It is formed little by little. Evolution is not completed altogether overnight. It takes place little by little. People today love to talk about 'liberation' and 'reform'. One must realize that liberation is not liberation altogether and that reform is not reform altogether. Liberation is the liberation of this or that institution, this or that thought, this or that person. It must be a gradual liberation,

little by little. Reform is the reform of this or that institution, this or that thought, this or that person. It must be a gradual reform, little by little."[32]

Ch'en Tu-hsiu did not have such great patience for gradual changes. Nor did the Communists.

In 1949 the Communists succeeded in bringing about the most drastic revolution in Chinese history. Hu Shih fled to the United States. The Communists did not forget him, nor was his thought forgotten in China. In 1951, the Communists launched a nationwide campaign to purge Hu Shih's thought from China. It began with an attack on a work written by one of Hu's former students at Peking University, a work about the famous novel *The Dream of the Red Chamber*. Hu Shih's philosophy was allegedly found in it. As the campaign went on, his thought was found in almost every area of cultural and scholarly activities, in philosophy, history, literature, arts, language and politics. One of the many people persecuted was a person called Hu Feng, someone not personally know to Hu Shih. His name literally means "the wind of Hu." He was criticized for having advocated freedom of expression in the arts and literature. According to Hu's own calculation, the government-sponsored campaign against his thought from 1951 to 1955 produced articles and volumes in China amounting to at least seven to eight million words. Hu Shih's thought was denounced as reactionary, bourgeois, capitalistic, imperialistic, and anti-Chinese.[33]

F. HU SHIH'S EVALUATION OF CHINESE CULTURE

There is a certain dilemma in Hu Shih's attitude toward traditional Chinese culture. On the one hand, in order to promote a new culture, he attacked it as strongly as possible so that his countrymen would realize its bankruptcy and the need to learn from the West. On the other hand, being a historian of thought, he knew that there could be some continuity between the old and the new by emphasizing certain aspects of the old culture. This could also be a good strategy of gaining some sympathy from the tradition-minded people.

In *The Development of the Logical Method in Ancient China* written in 1917, Hu Shih raised the question: "How can we best assimilate modern civilization in such a manner as to make it congenial and congruous and continuous with the civilization of our own making?"[34] He expressed the fear that an abrupt acceptance of the new would cause the disappearance of the good in the old. He learned later that to emphasize continuity tended to strengthen the traditionalist position that it was only necessary to revive the old as the "foundation" and to adopt the good from the West as the "branches."

Thus Hu Shih became more and more impatient with the problem of preserving the good elements in the old. He argued in 1935 that the thing we should worry about was not how to preserve the good thing in the old but how to deal with the inertia of the old culture because it was the very nature of the old culture to preserve itself.[35] Hu Shih was willing to throw away the gems together with the trash in order to create a new civilization, for the gems would in any case be picked up again later. Hu Shih has often been regarded as one of those who advocated "wholesale westernization" of China. In an article written in 1935, he suggested that the phrase "wholehearted modernization" would be a better description of his position.[36]

It would be reasonable to say that of all the philosophies in China, Confucianism is closest to Hu Shih's thought. But there was a great controversy as to what Confucianism actually means. Does it refer to the teachings of Confucius himself, or Mencius, or Hsun Tzu, or Tung Chung-shu, or Chu Hsi or Wang Yang-ming? Does it also mean the state cult, the civil service examination, the eight-legged style of writing, etc.? Should Confucianism be blamed for concubinage, footbinding of women, prostitution or the eunuch system? Since Confucianism stands for the main tradition of China for more than two thousand years, it is always easy to find something in it to criticize or praise. In the battle cry against the old tradition, Hu Shih was able to shout with his fellow modernists, "Down with Confucius and Sons!" But in his sober and scholarly works Hu was willing to admit that his own thought was very influenced by Confucian philosophy and that Confucianism had been a very important civilizing force in China.

In an article on Chinese thought written in 1946 for Western readers, he approvingly stressed the basically rationalistic, naturalistic, and humanistic orientation of Confucian thought.[37] The failures to produce natural sciences and to develop a democratic system of society were usually mentioned as its shortcomings. He also pointed out that the rationalistic Neo-Confucianism tended to be dogmatic, authoritarian and metaphysical. For this reason, he was more sympathetic to the empirical-oriented, anti-rationalistic and anti-metaphysical thinkers of the Ch'ing Dynasty such as Tai Chen (1724-1777).[38] Hu Shih recognized that some democratic ideas did exist in Confucianism as in Mencius' thought and that some scientific spirit could be found in Chu Hsi's philosophy and the Ch'ing Confucian thought.[39]

Partly to show varieties in the Chinese heritage and partly to put down the dominant position of Confucianism, Hu Shih gave equal or even more favourable treatment of non-Confucian schools in his study of classical Chinese philosophy. He applied the "genetic method" to the major schools of thought. In so doing, he opened up new problems, new perspectives, and new interpretations, and stimulated many controversies and further research by other scholars. Hu Shih emphasized Lao Tzu's and Chuang Tzu's roles as a critic of contemporary society and went so far as to characterize them, especially Lao Tzu, as a "revolutionary," apparently in the sense of advocating individual freedom against social conformity and the ruler's power. The mystical aspect of their teaching was either discounted or minimized. Their naturalistic thought was highly stressed. He found in Chuang Tzu's thought a theory of biological evolution comparable to Darwin's theory. But he later admitted that he had gone too far in making the comparison.[40]

Hu Shih was mainly responsible for bringing scholars' attention to the logical theories developed in Later Mohism. The Mohist principles of universal love and utilitarianism were also appreciated.[41] As to the "Legalist School," Hu was sympathetic to its position that all men should be equal before the law. The Legalists also advocated that a new culture should be created according to the needs of the new historical circumstances.[42]

Needless to say, Hu Shih did not believe that any of the ancient philosophies was adequate for solving the problems of twentieth-century China. He could not endorse the dictatorial view of government advocated in the Legalist School, the personalistic conception of Heaven in Mohism or the negative and passive attitude toward human civilization in Taoism.

Although his own philosophy is strongly anti-Buddhist, Hu did considerable research on Chinese Buddhism. He regarded the introduction of Buddhism into China as an unfortunate event and blamed Buddhism for the "religious fanaticism" in the Medieval Period, such as cutting off one's own arm or setting oneself on fire for the faith. The "Indianization" of China was compared by him to the Christianization of Europe in the Middle Ages. In both cases, it was regarded as a dark age. "Modernization" was seen by him largely as a liberation from medieval thought. Hu Shih gave credit to Neo-Confucianism for restoring some rationality and humanity to China.[43]

Hu Shih's historical research covered philosophy, religion, literature, arts and politics. He made contributions and aroused criticism in every field. He had the gift and the patience needed for combing a vast amount of historical materials. No wonder that, when the Communists decided to purge his influence from China, they found his ghost everywhere.

G. CIVILIZATIONS EAST AND WEST

It has often been said that Eastern civilization is "spiritual" and that Western civilization is "materialistic." Such a view was expressed by many European thinkers after the First World War and was reflected in Liang Ch'i-ch'ao's *Impressions of My European Journey*, and in Liang Sou-ming's *Eastern and Western Civilizations*. Hu Shih felt that such a view was a dangerous "myth" that would prevent China from modernization. So in 1926 he wrote an article in Chinese entitled "Our Attitude toward the Modern Civilization of the West." A revised English version was published in 1928 as "The Civilizations of the East and the West." These articles provoked bitter reactions both in the East and the West.

Consistent with his rejection of the dualism of body and mind, Hu Shih holds that a civilization is really a joint product of the material and the spiritual. It is "simply the sum-product of (a race's) achievement in adjusting itself to its environment."[44] Our intelligence, which is spiritual, is essentially for the invention of the "necessary and effective tools" to adjust or control the environment. Advancement in civilization depends upon "the improvement of tools." No civilization is purely spiritual, for the spiritual must be expressed in the material.

The term "tools" may mean "theories", as in the Pragmatist theory of knowledge. But Hu Shih uses it here to mean material tools, such as stone, fire, agriculture, writing, printing, telescope, etc. For him, such names as the Stone Age, the Bronze Age, the Iron Age and the Steam and Electricity Age tell the tale of the development of civilization. Thus the difference between the Eastern and Western civilizations is not that between the spiritual and the material but that between the tools used. Since the West has moved far ahead in the invention of new tools to conquer nature in the last two hundred years, a major difference between the East and the West is that between the use of human labor and the use of machinery as the source of power.

To use vivid language, Hu Shih calls the Oriental civilization a rickshaw civilization and the Occidental civilization a motot-car civilization. He says that when we call a motor-car material, we are only refering to the physical aspect of the car. He adds that a motor-car really presupposes a quality of human intelligence that is not inferior to the mind that composes a poem. There is therefore no point for the person riding a rickshaw to boast about his "spiritual" life and laugh at the person who has invented and is driving a motor vehicle.[45]

Hu Shih not only argues that the spirituality presupposed in the making of a car is superior to the spirituality presupposed in the making of a rickshaw, he also argues that in science, morality, literature, arts and music, the West is more spiritual than the East. Nothing is more spiritual than to know the truth that science has discovered, and nothing is more spiritual than the dignity of human life that a democratic society has provided.

Hu Shih goes on to attack the so-called "spirituality" in Oriental religions such as Buddhism. He asks: "What spirituality is there, let us say, in the old beggar-woman who dies while still mumbling, 'Nama Amita Buddha!', and in the clear conviction that she will surely enter that blissful paradise presided over by the Amita Buddha? Do we earnestly think it moral or spiritual to inculcate in that beggar-woman a false belief which shall so hypnotize her as to make her willingly live and die in such dire conditions where she ought not to have been had she been born in a different civilization?"[46] According to Hu Shih, such a religion is "hypnotic" in character. It is defeatism, conceding that man cannot control his own life and cannot build a good society on earth. Hu includes Christianity among the hypnotic religions, and he quotes a revolutionary song to make his point:

> I fight alone, and win or sink,
> I need no one to make me free;
> I want no Jesus Christ to think
> That he could ever die for me.[47]

According to Hu Shih, the West has largely freed itself from the Christianity that dominated the West in the Medieval ages, but the East is still very much under the power of Medieval hypnotic religions.

Hu Shih suggests that the term "material civilization" ought to have a purely neutral meaning because all tools of civilization are material embodiments of ideas. But the phrase "materialistic civilization" is a more appropriate name for Eastern than Western civilizations, because the former are under the control of matter and incapable of mastering it. To try to transcend matter by means of gods and a future life is only an illusory solution. The truly spiritual civilization is to make full use of human intelligence for the conquest of nature and for the improvement of the conditions of man.

CONCLUSION

A figure like Hu Shih is bound to be evaluated by many people from their partisan point of view. He has been regarded as the champion of the liberal cause in the twentieth-century China. The Communists have attacked him as a reactionary and a running dog of Western imperialism. The traditionalists and the Nationalists tend to blame him for the mess and eventually the loss of China to the Communists. One may also find that at the bottom of his heart Hu Shih was a Confucian gentleman. Whatever one's evaluation of his life and thought, there is no doubt that he will be long remembered for the role he played in the New Culture Movement.

Hu Shih believes that the task of philosophy is to solve problems. In his attempt to solve China's problems, he has answered most of the fundamental questions of philosophy. He tried to convince other people to accept his views, but he was more concerned that other people would think for themselves according to the method of thinking that he advocated. In the 1930 article, in which he introduced his own thought to the young people of China, Hu Shih concluded by saying,

"A Ch'an monk once said, 'Bodhidharma came to China just for the purpose of finding a person who would not be deluded.' In my works that amount to hundreds of thousands of words, I am also only teaching people a method by which they would not be deluded. It is certainly not good to be led by Confucius and Chu Hsi by the nose. To be led by Marx, Lenin, and Stalin by the nose is not a great man either. I myself never intend to lead anybody by the nose. I am only hoping that through my humble effort the young people will be taught an ability to defend themselves so that they would strive to become a person who cannot be deluded."[48]

NOTES

1. For Hu Shih's life, see his own article "Hu Shih" in Albert Einstein, etc., *Living Philosophies* (Forum Publishing Co., 1930; Simon & Schuster, Inc., 1931), 235-263. For further information, see Jerome B. Grieder, *Hu Shih and the Chinese Renaissance* (Harvard University Press, 1970) and Fan Kuang-huan, *A Study of Hu Shih's Thought* (New York University, Ph.D. dissertation, 1963).
2. *Living Philosophies*, 250.
3. The Boxer Rebellion against the foreigners took place in 1900. As a result, China paid a large amount of indemnity to many nations. The United States returned her portion to establish scholarships.
4. On the May Fourth Movement, see Tse-tsung Chow, *The May Fourth Movement* (Harvard University Press, 1960). Also Hu Shih, *The Chinese Renaissance* (University of Chicago Press, 1934; Paragon Book Co., 1963).
5. Hu Shih, *Chung-kuo che-hsüeh-shih ta-kang* (Outline of the History of Chinese Philosophy). Since only the first part has been published, it is also called *Chung-kuo ku-tai che-hsüeh shih* (History of Ancient Chinese Philosophy). The edition used here was published in 1958 by the Commercial Press in Taiwan; p. 1.
6. *Living Philosophies*, 254-256.
7. "Wen-t'i yü chu-i" (Problems and Isms), in *Hu Shih wen-ts'un* (Collection of Hu Shih's Works, hereafter *HSWT*; the edition used here was published in 1953 by Yuan-tung Book Co. in Taiwan), I, 345.

8. *Ibid.*, I, 374-378.
9. Basically the same method is discussed in his *Outline of the History of Chinese Philosophy*, 3-5.
10. See "Wo-men tsou na-t'iao lu?" (Which Road Should We Take?, written in 1930), *HSWT*, IV, 431-432.
11. "Wen-hsüeh kai-liang ch'u-i" (Tentative Proposals for the Improvement of Literature), *HSWT*, I, 5.
12. "Chien-she-ti wen-hsüeh ko-ming lun" (On Constructive Literary Revolution), *HSWT*, I, 56.
13. Hu Shih was an admirer of Henrik Ibsen, and advocated Ibsenism, which stands for realism and naturalism in literature and individualism in social philosophy. See "I-pu-sheng-chu-i" (Ibsenism, written in 1918), *HSWT*, I, 629-647.
14. "Which Road Should We Take?", *HSWT*, IV, 432.
15. For the various responses to science in China, see D.W.Y. Kwok, *Scientism in Chinese Thought: 1900-1950* (Yale University Press, 1965).
16. *Ou-yu hsin-ying lu* (Impressions of My European Journey). A condensed version is in his *Yin,ping-shih ho-chi* (Collected Works from the Ice-drinker's Studio). For Hu Shih's response, see *HSWT*, II, 121-124.
17. *Tung hsi wen-hua chi ch'i che-hsüeh* (Eastern and Western Civilizations and Their Philosophies; Shanghai: Commercial Press, 1922). For Hu Shih's response, see *HSWT*, II, 158-177.
18. *K'o-hsüeh yü jen-sheng-kuan* (Science and Philosophy of Life, 2 vols.; Shanghai: Ya-tung, 1923). Hu Shih's preface or introductory essay is also found in *HSWT*, II, 120-139.
19. John Dewey, *Reconstruction in Philosophy* (enlarged edition, Beacon Press, 1948), xxvii (from his 1948 Introduction).
20. *Living Philosophies*, 243.
21. *Ibid.*, 243-244.
22. *HSWT*, II, 127-129.
23. *HSWT*, II, 136-137. The translation here was by Hu Shih himself in *Living Philosophies*, 260-261.
24. *Hu Shih liu-hsüeh jih-chi* (Hu Shih's Diary While Studying Abroad; Shanghai: Ya-tung, 1939; Commercial Press, 1947), I, 50. Also Tuan Hung-chün, ed., *Hu Shih yü-ts'ui* (Hu Shih's Selected Works; Taipei: Ta-hsi-yang, 1970), 113-115.
25. *HSWT*, IV, 452, 463.
26. *Living Philosophies*, 257. Cf., "Pu-hsiu: wo-ti tsung-chiao" (Immortality: My Religion, published in 1919), *HSWT*, I, 693-702.
27. *Living Philosophies*, 262-263. Cf., *HSWT*, II, 137-138.
28. Ch'en Tu-hsiu's preface is found in *HSWT*, II, 139-147.
29. *HSWT*, II, 147-149.
30. *HSWT*, II, 149-154.
31. "Chieh-shao we tzu-chi ti ssu-hsiang" (Introducing My Own Thought), *HSWT*, IV, 608-609.
32. *Ibid.*, IV, 609.
33. Tuan Hung-chün, *op. cit.*, 289-291. Also Chan Lien, "Chinese Com-

munism Versus Pragmatism: The Criticism of Hu Shih's Philosophy, 1950-1958," *Journal of Asian Studies*, 27:3 (May, 1968), 551-570.

34. Hu Shih, *The Development of the Logical Method in Ancient China* (Shanghai: Oriental Book Co., 1922; reprint, Paragon Book Co., 1963), 7.

35. *HSWT*, IV, 535-540.

36. *HSWT*, IV, 541-544.

37. Hu Shih "Chinese Thought," in Harley F. MacNair, *China* (University of California Press, 1946,) 221-230.

38. See "Chi-ko fan li-hsüeh ti ssu-hsiang-chia" (Several Anti-rationalistic Thinkers), *HSWT*, I, 53-108.

39. See Hu Shih, "Chinese Thought," *op. cit.* Also see the following articles by Hu Shih: "The Scientific Spirit and Method in Chinese Philosophy," in Charles A. Moore, ed., *Philosophy and Culture—East and West* (University of Hawaii Press, 1962), 199-222; "The Right to Doubt in Ancient Chinese Thought," *Philosophy East and West*, 12:4 (Jan., 1963), 295-300.

40. See his 1958 preface to the *Outlines of the History of Chinese Philosophy*, 2-3. Also *Outline*, I, 43-63; II, 109-133.

41. See his *Development of the Logical Method*, 53-130; *Outline*, II, 1-30; 39-108.

42. See *Outline*, III, 78-100.

43. "Chinese Thought," *op. cit.*, 228.

44. Hu Shih, "The Civilizations of the East and the West," in Charles A. Beard, ed., *Whither Mankind* (Longmans, Green, and Co., 1928), 27. Cf., "Wo-men tui-yü hsi-yang chih-tai wen-ming ti-t'ai-tu" (Our Attitude toward the Modern Civilization of the West), *HSWT*, III, 1-15.

45. Hu Shih, "The Civilizations of the East and the West," *op. cit.*, 27-29.

46. *Ibid.*, 30.

47. *Ibid.*, 31.

48. *HSWT*, IV, 623-624.

16
MAO TSE-TUNG
AND THE CHINESE TRADITION

D. BISHOP

Before taking up the question of Maoism and traditional Chinese thought I would like to outline a philosophical context within which the question may be discussed. Two primary areas of philosophy are metaphysics and epistemology. "What is the nature of reality?" is the central question of metaphysics, and "How do we know reality?" of epistemology. Regarding the former, three major answers have been given—monism, dualism and pluralism. Monism is the view that reality is basically one. It is inter-related and inter-dependent. The principle of identity is primary. Thus similarities, the things men have in common for example, are much more numerous and significant or important than differences.

The monist emphasizes the organic unity of reality. Everything is an extension of everything else. "There is no self that I am not and no self that is not I", as the Buddhist says. The monist might say that reality can be validly conceived of in terms of one category—consciousness, being or existence and that differences are of degree or kind. One implication of monism in regard to human reality is that all men are alike in that they have the same essential needs and ends; differences are in the means persons use to reach those ends.

According to the pluralist only particulars exist. Reality consists of innumerable, isolated entities. It is not inter-related or inter-dependent. It has no organic unity. Relations are accidental or "conjunctive", to use William James' term. The pluralist holds to an individualistic view of man. Persons are conceived of as separate, independent, self-contained units. As might be expected, the pluralist picks out and magnifies differences. Pluralism in the Modern Period, the twentieth century especially, has taken the form of Positivism and has become quite widespread.

Dualism is the view that reality consists of pairs or sets such as up/down, good/bad, friend/enemy, nautral/supernatural. It is important to note that there are two types of dualists, exclusionist and inclusionist. The exclusionist thinks in terms of absolutes and opposites. He describes reality in the language of either/or,—right or wrong, villain or hero, body or soul. Reality, then, is permeated by mutual exclusion and contradictions predominate. It is easy for the exclusionist to pass from the notion of opposites to opposition. And because the two parts of the set are opposites and mutually exclusive, conflict between them is believed inevitable.

The inclusionist type dualist, however, while he admits the reality of sets—this/that, you/I—insists that their relationship is supplementary or complementary and not mutually exclusive. The inclusionist does not view reality in terms of absolutism, irreconcilability and conflict. It is not a matter of this or that but rather both/and. His connective is not "or" but "and".

Regarding epistemology we find to the questions of how and what we can know three major answers—empiricism, rationalism and trans-rationalism. Briefly, the empiricist holds that we know through the senses and what we know is the objects the senses perceive. The only knowledge we can have is of the material world as known via the senses. This kind of knowledge may be referred to as perceptual knowledge. More broadly, the empiricist holds that the source of knowledge, truth or our ideas is observation and experience.

The rationalist asserts that true knowledge consists of concepts not derived from empirical reality but which exist a priori, and which are used to analyze and understand empirical and other types of reality. He claims that there are universal, necessary truths existing independent of or not known through experience (a thing cannot both be and not be at the same time) but which are relevant to experience. The rationalist emphasizes the priority of immaterial reality as known via the mind. He believes reason can give us sure knowledge, acting on the information supplied by the senses or experience and using a priori truths or principles. His method is the deductive one, the going from the general to the particular.

There are other epistemological approaches. Religions such as Islam and Christianity stress revelation and revealed knowledge.

There are some truths which God has revealed to his chosen, infallible recipients who in turn convey them to the non-elect. Intuition is considered by some as the best source of truth. The intuitionist emphasizes direct knowledge or understanding. Truth can be known immediately or straight-forwardly. A person can know intuitively what is right and wrong for example, without having to appeal to experience. He does not need to rationalize or reflect about it but can have direct insight into the good.

II MAO'S EPISTEMOLOGICAL VIEWS

What is Mao's metaphysical and epistemological position? Let us consider epistemology first. His attitude toward revelation and intuition can be readily discerned from the following. In one essay he writes, "Where do correct ideas come from? Do they drop from the skies? No. Are they innate in the mind? No. They come from social practice and from it alone."[1] In another he writes, "The truth of any knowledge or theory is not determined by subjective feelings, but by objective results in social practice. Only social practice can be the criterion of truth." By such statements Mao, like contemporary social scientists generally, quickly dispenses with revelation and revealed knowledge, and intuition and intuitive knowledge.

What about empiricism and rationalism? Again let us quote from Mao himself. In the essays On Practice, On Contradiction and Where Do Correct Ideas Come From, he writes—"Knowledge begins with experience"; "All genuine knowledge originates in direct experiences"; "There can be no knowledge apart from practice"; "All knowledge originates in perception of the objective external world through man's physical sense organs"; "...the first step in the process of cognition is contact with the objects of the external world; this belongs to the stage of perception. The second step is to synthesize the data of perception by arranging and reconstructing them; this belongs to the stages of conception, judgement and inference"; "As regards the sequence in the movement of man's knowledge, there is always a gradual growth from the knowledge of individual and particular things to the knowledge of things in general. Only after man knows the particular essence of many different things can he proceed to generalization and know the common essence of things"; "Logical knowledge differs from perceptual knowledge in that perceptual knowledge pertains to the separate aspects, the phenomena and the external relations of things, whereas logical knowledge takes a big stride forward to reach the totality, the essence and the internal relations of things ..."; "Knowledge begins with practice and theoretical knowledge is acquired through practice and then must return to practice"; "Perception only solves the problem of phenomena; theory alone can solve the problem of essence. The solving of both these problems is not separable in the slightest degree from practice"; "Discover the truth through practice, and again through practice verify and develop the truth. Start from perceptual knowledge and actively guide revolutionary practice to change both the subjective and objective world."

The above statements show that Mao did not choose either empiricism or rationalism but rather a combination of the two. Cognition involves two steps—perception and conception, induction and deduction, going from the particular to the general, gathering facts and developing theories from them. Both steps are necessary. Knowledge is of two types, perceptual and logical. The second is impossible without the first, since it is derived from the first. The first is incomplete without the second, as the second is an extension of the first. In addition, of course, verification comes from returning to practice or the "test of practice".

His combining of empiricism and rationalism led Mao to criticize two groups in the Chinese Communist party, the dogmatists and empiricists. The empiricists think "...that knowledge can stop at the lower, perceptual knowledge." Such "...practical men respect experience but despise theory, and therefore cannot have a comprehensive view of an entire objective process, lack clear direction and long-range perspective, and are complacent over occasional successes and glimpses of the truth." They "...mistake fragmentary experience for universal truth." They see only externals and not the essence of things.

On the other hand the "dogmatists (rationalists and idealists)... are lazy bones. They refuse to undertake any painstaking study of concrete things, they regard general truths as emerging out of the void; they turn them into purely abstract unfathomable formulas, and thereby completely deny and reverse the normal sequence by which man comes to know the truth." They do not "...understand the interconnection of the two processes in cognition—from the particular to the general and then from the general to the particular." They "...never use their brains to analyze anything concretely, and in their writings and speeches they always use stereotypes devoid of content..." Of such people in the Red Army Mao wrote that they "...are content to leave things as they are...do not seek to understand anything thoroughly...eat their fill and sit dozing in their offices all day long without ever moving a step and going out among the masses to investigate...To awaken these comrades we must raise our voices and cry out to them...Go among the masses and investigate the facts."

What Mao was referring to might be stated differently by saying that he constantly urged his followers to see things as a whole. One should recognize the complexity of reality and should not be satisfied with understanding but one or several parts of a problem. A problem or event, for example, should be looked at from all sides not just one. A person should see the forest and not just the trees, to use Mao's analogy. Mao criticized the "subjectivists" for seeing only one side of a problem or contradiction. Thus their views are superficial, incomplete and biased. Because they "...often look at problems one-sidedly" they "...often run into snags". A subjectivist understands only one side of the contradiction. He does not understand the other or the inter-relations between the two.

Another aspect of Mao's epistemology is his insistence on the union of knowledge and practice. A rather striking example of this is his speech of 1930 titled "Oppose Book Worship" in which he said "Whatever is written in a book is right—such is still the mentality of culturally backward Chinese peasants." Even "...within the Communist Party there are also people" of such mind. "Of course we should study Marxist books", Mao said, "...but this study must be integrated with our country's actual conditions. We need books, but we must overcome book worship...How can we overcome book worship? The only way is to investigate the actual situation."

Regarding knowledge and practice Mao cautioned his followers against the influence of the Deborin school among the Russian communists which had infiltrated the Chinese communist party. Deborin's basic error was separating theory from practice. It was reflected among the "right opportunists" in that their "thinking was divorced from social practice." This was a major fault of the philosophical Idealists too. Neither they nor the opportunists realize that knowledge arises from experience and must return to it for verification. The knowing process is not just one of beginning with perception and going to conception or from the particular to the general. There is a third step, the return to practice, the particular, to experience.

In summary Mao's epistemological position may well be characterized by the term pragmatism. The source of knowledge is external reality. Knowledge arises from a context. That context is one's environment and for Mao one's socio-economic environment primarily. The pragmatist conceives of the role of knowledge as an active one. The function of reason is to solve practical human problems. "The one and only purpose of the proletariat in knowing the world is to change it", Mao asserted. The goal of knowledge is not "knowledge for its own sake" but solving existential problems and improving the world. The test of a truth (theory or assertion is whether it works in practice to bring about accepted social goals; to quote Mao, "The truth of any knowledge or theory is determined not by subjective feelings but by objective results in social practice."

III MAO'S METAPHYSICAL VIEWS

Mao's metaphysical position or his views regarding the nature of reality are seen in the following statements:

"Contradiction is universal and absolute; it is present in the process of development of all things and permeates every process from beginning to end."

"The law of contradiction in things, that is, the law of the unity of opposites, is the fundamental law of nature and of society and therefore also the fundamental law of thought."

"The question is one of different kinds of contradiction, not the presence or the absence of contradiction."

"Since the particular is united with the universal and since the universality as well as the particularity of contradiction is inherent in everything, universality residing in particularity, we should, when studying an object, try to discover both the particular and the universal and their interconnection..."

"The movement of change in the world of objective reality is never ending and so is man's cognition of truth through practice."

"All processes have a beginning and an end, all processes transform themselves into each other and the nature of the thing changes accordingly."

"Processes change, old processes and old contradictions disappear, new processes and new contradictions emerge."

"The supersession of the old by the new is a general, eternal and inviolable law of the universe."

"What is universal in one context becomes particular in another. Conversely, what is particular in one context becomes universal in another."

"In any given phenomenon or thing, the unity of opposites is conditional, temporary and transitional, and hence relative..."

"In given conditions, opposites possess identity, and consequently can coexist in a single entity and can transform themselves into each other."

"All objective things are actually interconnected and are governed by inner laws..."

"The fundamental cause of the development of a thing is not external but internal..."

The statements above indicate several aspects of Mao's metaphysics. One is that reality is constantly changing. It is dynamic, moving, always in flux. Coming into being and going out of existence is a never ending process in nature.

Mao stressed four important aspects of change. One is change as an emergence of the new from the old. Another is change as development or progression from lower to higher levels. The third is change as teleological, purposive or directed toward ends or goals. The fourth is change due to forces immanent in reality and not a result of the impingement of some external force or being.

This "process" view led Mao to criticize several groups, the rightists or reactionaries, the leftists, the metaphysicans and the empiricists or mechanists. The first were behind in their thinking. It had not kept up with changes. Of them Mao said, "We oppose the die-hards in the revolutionary ranks whose ideas, failing to advance with the changing objective circumstances, manifest themselves historically as 'right' opportunism."[2] The leftists on the other hand were too far ahead. They set up proposals which could "...only be realized in the future." As a result they became unrealistic and "adventurist in their action" and alienated themselves from "...the current practice of the majority of the people and the realities of the day."

Mao criticized the metaphysicians for insisting that reality is static and immutable. They hold "that all the different kinds of things in the universe and all their characteristics have been the same ever since they first came into being." They insist that "a thing can only keep on repeating itself as the same kind of thing..." Thus since "...capitalist exploitation, capitalist competition, the individualist ideology of capitalist society and so on, can all be found in ancient slave society......" and exists up to the present, it will inevitably continue in the future. Mao rebuked the empiricists along with the metaphysicians for their allowing of only mechanical change and external causation. According to the empiricists there is only quantitative change, a change in time and space of an entity and not qualitative or internal change. According to the metaphysicians change is due to some external cause, God or the Absolute or mechanical force or pressure and not to forces inherent in reality itself.

A second aspect of Mao's metaphysics is his view of reality as an organism. Reality is like an organism in that it consists of many interconnected, inter-related, inter-dependent parts or entities. Mao rejected a Positivist or atomist view which asserts that only particulars exist. Universals have as real an existence as particulars. In terms of inter-relatedness, unities or relationships are as real as the things which are held together. Inter-relatedness, then, is an essential not just an accidental characteristic of reality, or the inter-relatedness of reality is not just a matter of expediency or utility but goes much deeper. Conceiving of reality as an organism led Mao to insist that the principle of identity is a basic one. From such a standpoint differences are variations and are relative, not absolute. And by relating teleology to organicism Mao was led to affirm the reality of some final cause or end. Final causes or a final cause, not just efficient causes exist. The final cause might, for example, be the realization of Harmony, whether in nature or among men.

Mao's organicist metaphysics led him to criticize the metaphysicians for taking a compartmentalized or separatist view of reality. To them "all things in the universe" are "eternally isolated from one another." On the same basis he criticized the empiricists for seeing "only individual parts but not the whole", or only one and not "both aspects of a contradiction." They do not undertake the task of "reflecting on things as they really are", but "only look at things one-sidedly or superficially and know neither their interconnections nor their inner laws."

A third aspect of Mao's metaphysics is his emphasis on transformation and subsumption. As noted above, change is constant in the universe. Change, to Mao, is a matter of becoming. Everything has within it that which, given the right environment, enables it to become something different or what it is not at the present moment. The fertilized egg may become a chicken, the acorn an oak tree. Potentiality, then, is a very important concept for Mao and it underlies the notion of transformation. It stimulates or is the condition for change; without potentiality there would be only quantitative and not qualitative change as well.

The idea of transformation is especially significant as far as Mao's concept of contradictions is concerned for it means that contradictions can be resolved by one aspect of the contradiction being transformed or changed into its opposite. Thus the eradication or elimination of the one by the other is not necessary. The resolution of a contradiction can be achieved through transformation instead.

A very important, if not the most important aspect of Mao's metaphysics is the kind of dualism he affirms. That he is a dualist rather than monist or pluralist is evidenced by his constant use of the concept or term "contradictions". Moreover, his many statements stressing the unity of opposites indicates that he is the second, inclusionist type dualist described previously.

Mao believes the "both/and" type of dualism to be the true one for at least two reasons. First because the principle of identity, not dissimilarity, is primary in reality; and second, because one aspect of a contradiction is simply the condition or prerequisite for or ground of the other. One could not be without the other. The existence of one is dependent on the existence of the other. Thus there is a unity or identity of opposites. To illustrate the point Mao uses such examples as, "Without life, there would be no death, without death, there would be no life. Without above, there would be no below; without below, there would be no above. Without misfortune, there would be no good fortune; without good fortune, there would be no misfortune." Opposites exist in a relationship of both potentiality and actuality and are always set within a context of time and change. Both aspects of the contradiction have a real existence at time A; at the same time they have the potential of becoming the other at a later point in time when certain changes have taken place.

Thus a contradiction to Mao does not consist of a set of entities diametrically and eternally the opposite of or opposed to each other as supposed by Western thinkers. Instead a contradiction is a set, one aspect of which can be transformed, united with or changed into the other. Thus contradictions for Mao are in reality contraries, a term which might well have been used instead of contradiction. The exclusionist type dualist sees reality in terms of contradictions, the inclusionist type in terms of contraries. As contraries they are relative not absolute, relative in the sense that they are related and relative in the second sense of being impermanent and therefore transformable into their opposite. Thus their original opposition is not a permanent, absolute one. To use Mao's words, "All contradictory things are interconnected; not only do they coexist in a single entity in given conditions, but in other given conditions, they also transform themselves into each other."

While Mao generally uses the term "contradiction", he does occasionally use such words as differences, antagonism, struggle and tensions. He distinguishes two types, principal and non-principal contradictions, those which involve open antagonism and those which do not. Principal contradictions are much harder to resolve and may require conflict or revolution. The second type do not. And it is the tensions within a contradiction which, when it reaches a certain point, gives rise to change.

Mao's view of contradictions as contraries led him to criticize both the "Rightists" and "Leftists". The Rightists blur contradictions and thus "...make no distinction between ourselves and the enemy and take the enemy for our own people. They regard as friends the very persons whom the broad masses regard as enemies." On the other hand the Leftists "...magnify contradictions between ourselves and the enemy, and regard as counter-revolutionaries persons who are not really counter-revolutionaries. Both these views are wrong."

IV THE CHINESE EPISTEMOLOGICAL TRADITION

We are now at the point where we can ask how Mao's epistemological and metaphysical views compare with those of Confucius and the Chinese tradition. To begin with we might note that the "both/and" emphasis in metaphysics has its correlate in epistemology in the traditional combination of knowledge and practice or rationalism and empiricism. Knowledge cannot be separated from practice either in origins or verification and the senses and mind must supplement one another as the means of knowing.

That knowledge begins with the senses, i.e., observation and experience, has been constantly emphasized in the Chinese tradition. Professor Creel points out that "Confucius stayed closer to the concrete", and that he "emphasized the role of experience and observation as means by which the individual could attain to a knowledge of the true and the good."[3] Interestingly Mao exhorted his cadres to "...get moving on your two legs, go the rounds of every section placed under your charge and 'inquire into everything' as Confucius did, and then you will be able to solve problems."

The Great Learning, which the Neo-Confucianists attributed to Tseng Tsu, a disciple of Confucius, insists that the "...extension of knowledge lay in the investigation of things. Things being investigated, knowledge became complete."[4] This early pragmaticism was the foundation on which the Neo-Confucianists added their rationalism. Shao Yung stated that "Forms and numbers in the universe can be calculated but their wonderful operations cannot be fathomed. The universe can be fully investigated through principles but not through corporeal forms. How can it be fully investigated through external observation?" Shao Yung's view is that empirical knowledge by itself or that knowledge of things only is not enough. A knowledge of principles, theories or laws must be added to it.

Chu Hsi, in commenting on *The Great Learning*, noted that "*The Great Learning* speaks of the investigation of things but not of the investigation of Li. The reason is that to investigate Li is like clutching at emptiness in which threre is nothing to catch hold. When it simply speaks of 'the investigation of things', it means that we should seek for 'what is above shapes' through 'what is within shapes'."[5] Li refers to the abstract "above shapes" and things to the concrete "within shapes!" The abstract is investigated through the concrete, or knowledge begins with concrete, particular things.

Chu Hsi was a Neo-Confucianist who, like Mao, recognized that a third step must be taken to attain true knowledge. He wrote: "When one knows something but has not yet acted on it, his knowledge is still shallow. After he has experienced it, his knowledge will be increasingly clear, and its character will be different from what it was before." also, "Knowledge and action always require each other. It is like a person who cannot walk without legs although he has eyes, and who cannot see without eyes although he has legs."[6] Chu Hsi's point is that theory must return to practice and be verified by it. His statements have the same ring as Mao's "Discover the truth through practice, and again through practice verify and develop the truth."

The emphasis on the material and the concrete or particular was continued in the post Neo-Confucian period by men such as Wang Fu-chich (1619-1692), Yen Yuan (1635-1704) and Tai Chen (1723-1777). Wang is known through his statement, "The world consists of only concrete things." Thus our knowledge begins with them. Yen's criticism of book learning and scholars who only read books and claim to be knowledgeable sound very much like those of Mao's in his speech called Oppose Book Worship. A person may read many books about learning to play a musical instrument but he will never learn to play one until he takes the instrument in his hands, Yen stated. Similarly one must put into practice what one learns in the *Classics* if that learning is to be meaningful.

Tai Chen was an outstanding leader of the movement called: Investigations Based On Evidence. It emphasized objective analysis and the method of induction (going from the particular to the general). To Tai Li (principle) was not an abstraction or some transcendental entity but simply the order or orderliness we find in everyday, ordinary things. Moreover Tai, like Mao, believed strongly that knowledge has a social end or purpose. Professor Creel notes that "As Fang Chao-ying has pointed out, Tai Chen had the conviction that these studies were not ends in themselves but must be used to develop a new philosophy whose aim should be the betterment of society."[7]

Pragmatists in early twentieth century China include both Hu Shih and Sun Yat-Sen. The former was greatly influenced by John Dewey's instrumentalism, seeing in it parallels to his own tradition. Sun, speaking of the relationship between knowing and acting, asserted that "It is easy to act but difficult to know."[8] and "We cannot decide whether an idea is good or not without seeing it in practice. If the idea is of practical value to us, it is good; if it is impractical, it is bad."[9]

"Pragmatic monism" might be one characterization of the major thrust of the Chinese epistemological tradition; pragmatic in the sense that knowledge starts with the world of immediate, everyday experience, monistic in that there is no sharp epistemological bifurcation. Fung Yu-lan refers to the latter when he writes that epistemology never developed extensively in Chinese philosophy because "...epistemological problems arise only when a demarcation between the subject and object is emphasized."[10] In the aesthetic continuum which characterizes Chinese epistemology "...there is no such demarcation. In it the knower and the known is one whole."[11] Chang Tung-Sun, who lived from 1886-1962 wrote that "Scholars have generally divided knowledge into two general types. One is called direct acquaintance and the other indirect comprehension." He insisted, however, that "direct acquaintance and discrimination cannot be separated."[12]

Francis Hsu's statement in his book *Americans and Chinese* is in a similar vein: "The Chinese are not motivated by abstract principles. They do not see the world or mankind as irreparably divided between the good and evil, the just and the unjust."[13] And in his essay "Chinese Theory and Practice" Professor Chan writes: "It is often said that there is a closer relationship between philosophical theories and practice in China than in other lands. Whether this is true or not, it is certainly a fact that the relationship between philosophical doctrines and actual practice in China has been very close indeed".[14] The reason he gives for it is the Chinese concept of truth, "First of all, truth is not understood as something revealed from above or as an abstract principle, however logically consistent, but as a discoverable and demonstrable principle in human affairs."[15]

Professor Creel points out that the Chinese view is quite different from the one found in the Occident where "...we have tended to think of truth as being immutable, and to think that a god or a very wise man must partake of the unbending character of absolute truth."[16] He notes that the Chinese character for right denotes the right not in some metaphysical, absolute sense but as being what is fitting or suitable. The right is what is appropriate in a particular situation. It may differ in another situation. Hu Shih serves as a twentieth century example of this view as is seen in his statement, "Only when we realize there is no eternal, unchanging truth or absolute truth can we arouse in ourselves a sense of intellectual responsibility. The knowledge that mankind needs is not the way or principle which has an absolute existence but the particular truths for here and now and for particular individuals."[17] Such a view was applied to political institutions by Wang Fu-chih living three centuries earlier when he wrote in his essay On the Inapplicability of Ancient Institutions To Modern Times, "The ancient institutions were designed to govern the ancient world, and cannot be applied to the present day. One uses what is right for today to govern the world of today, but this does not mean it will be right for a later day."[18]

This is what might be called a "social" criterion of the truth. Truth to the Chinese, Nakamura observes, is not associated with "cold, logical considerations" but with the social and political context in which man lives. Mao follows this tradition in that he is not primarily concerned with abstract right or truth. He associated the truth with "the interests of the people", and conceived of it in terms of the social, political and economic realities of the twentieth century.

The epistemological tradition of China is admittedly a diverse one. It includes intuitionism and rationalism; empiricism, however, has found greatest favour. This seems to be true especially during times of crisis when the people and nation are confronted by pressing practical problems demanding close investigation and scrutiny for their solution. It is not to be wondered that the School of Investigation Based on Evidence has dominated Chinese philosophy for the last three centuries. Mao falls squarely within that tradition.

V. CHINESE METAPHYSICAL VIEWS

In metaphysics one of the most obvious resemblances is between Mao's inclusionist type dualism and the Yin-Yang view of reality. The Yin-Yang school arose very early in Chinese history. Fung Yu-lan suggests that it originated with the occultists of the Chow dynasty and that it represented an early scientific, naturalistic tendency. Wing Tsit Chan states that "The Yin-Yang doctrine is very simple but its influence has been extensive. No aspect of Chinese culture...has escaped its imprint."[19] Fung Yu-lan describes Yin-Yang as follows: "The word Yang meant sunshine, or what pertains to sunshine and light; that of Yin meant the absence of sunshine, i.e., shadow or darkness. In later development, the Yang and the Yin came to be regarded as two cosmic principles or forces, respectively representing masculinity, activity, heat, brightness, dryness, hardness, etc., for the Yang, and femininity, passivity, cold, darkness, wetness, softness, etc., for the Yin. Through the interaction of these two primary principles, all phenomena of the universe are produced. This concept has remained dominant in Chinese cosmological speculation down to recent times."[20]

Wing-Tsit Chan characterizes the Yin-Yang theory more briefly: "...the doctrine teaches that all things and events are products of two elements, forces or principles: Yin, which is negative, passive, weak, and destructive and Yang, which is positive, active, strong, and constructive."[21] And an early statement of the view is found in the *Appended Remarks to The Book of Changes*:

"Heaven is high, the earth is low, and thus ch'ien (Heaven) and K'un (Earth) are fixed. As high and low are thus made clear, the honorable and the humble have their places accordingly. As activity and tranquility have their constancy, the strong and the weak are thus differentiated. Ways come together according to their kinds, and things are divided according to their classes. Hence good fortune and evil fortune emerge. In the heavens, forms (heavenly bodies) appear and on earth shapes (creatures) occur. In them change and transformation can be seen. Therefore the strong and the weak interact and the Eight Trigrams activate each other. Things are stimulated by thunder and lightning and enriched by the influence of wind and rain. Sun and moon revolve on their course and cold and hot seasons take their turn. The way of ch'ien constitutes the male, while the way of k'un constitutes the female. Ch'ien knows the great beginning, and k'un acts to bring things to completion. Ch'ien knows through the easy, and k'un accomplishes through the simple."[22]

What we see in such statements is, again, the viewing of reality in terms of twos—heaven, earth; high, low; active, passive and the relating of them in terms of "and" not "or"—"Sun and moon", "cold and hot". The two parts of the equation in each instance supplement rather than oppose each other, thus making a harmonious whole. Tung Chung-shu (179-104 B.C.) a philosopher of the Han dynasty used the term "correlates" and extended the theory into the social and political realms:

"In all things there must be correlates. Thus if there is the upper, there must be the lower. If there is the left, there must be the right. If there is cold, there must be heat. If there is day, there must be night. These are all correlates. The Yin is the correlate of the Yang, the wife of the husband, the subject of the sovereign. There is nothing that does not have a correlate, and in each correlation there is the Yin and Yang. Thus the relationships between sovereign and subject, father and son, and husband and wife, are all derived from the principles of the Yin and Yang."[23]

Tung Chung-shu's term "correlates" has the same meaning as the words supplementary or complementary as we use them today; and Mao's statement is significant in this respect—"We Chinese often say, things that oppose each other also complement each other."

A second example of inclusionist dualism in Chinese philosophy is the viewing of reality in terms of li and chi. This is found, for example, in the *Appended Remarks to The Book of Changes* in which we read that "Essence and material force are combined to become things."[24] King-sun Lung, one of the leaders of the School of Names, used the terms Chih and wu to distinguish between things and universals. The Han philosophers also emphasized chi as the basic substance of all creation and its union with li or principle.

The Neo-Confucianists, however, were the ones who may have

stressed the unity of chi and li most. In his discussion of them Chu Hsi stated that "principle has never been separated from material force...Principle is not a separate entity. It exists right in material force...Principle attaches to material force and thus operates. Throughout the universe there are both principle and material force. Principle refers to the Way, which exists before physical form and is the root from which all things are produced. Material force refers to material objects, which exists after physical form; it is the instrument by which things are produced...What are called principle and material force are certainly two different entities. But considered from the standpoint of things, the two entities are merged one with another and cannot be separated with each in a different place."[25] Such statements remind one of Mao's—"All objective things are interconnected and are governed by inner laws."

The question involved here is that of particulars and universals. Does reality consist solely of individual, concrete, material things or objects or do we find in reality also universal principles, laws, or abstractions either inherent in things or of which things are manifestations. Chinese philosophers generally have agreed that reality does not consist in one or the other alone but that they exist in combination. Just as, in Ch'eng I's words, "There is no Way independent of Yin and Yang", so there are in reality both the particular and the universal.

The Yin-Yang view was instrumental in stimulating two other metaphysical concepts, organicism and change. In Wing-tsit Chan's words, the Yin-Yang theory "...helped to develop the view that things are related and the reality is a process of constant transformation."[26] As noted earlier, organicism is the view that reality is both pluralistic and monistic. It consists of many inter-related and inter-dependent parts which form a whole.

The view that reality is pluralistic may be traced back to the Five Agents school. When this was combined with the Yin-Yang view in the first century B.C. by men such as Tsou-Yen, new dimensions were added to the Chinese metaphysical outlook. On the one hand the Yin and Yang were traced back to a single source such as the Great Ultimate, and on the other they were extended forward in the belief that from the Five Agents sprang all things. Numerous statements of this can be found. In the *Great Appendix to The Book of Changes* we read "Therefore in the Changes there is the Supreme Ultimate. This generates the two primary forms, the Yin and the Yang. The two primary forms generate the four modes, major and minor Yin and Yang. The four modes generate the eight trigrams...."[27] In a similar vein the Neo-Confucianist Chou Tun I wrote "By the transformation of Yang and its union with Yin, the Five Agents of Water, Fire, Wood, Metal and Earth arise. When these five material forces are distributed in harmonious order, the four seasons run their course. The Five Agents constitute one system of Yin and Yang, and Yin and Yang constitute one Great Ultimate."[28] The "Great Unity" philosophy of K'ang Yu-Wei three hundred years later continues this organicism; and it is interesting to note that in supporting his views he refers back to Confucius—"Confucius said, Earth contains spiritual energy, which produces the wind and thunder. As a result of movements of wind and thunder, a countless variety of things in their changing configurations ensue, and the myriad things show the appearance of life".[29]

The dominant Chinese view is, then, that reality is made up of a plurality of natural, human, metaphysical and spiritual entities made one in the Great Ultimate. *The Commentaries on The Book of Changes* states: "Great is ch'ien, the originator. All things obtain their beginning from it. It unites and commands all things under heaven. The clouds move and the rain is distributed, and the various things are evolved in their respective forms. Ch'ien at all times rides the six dragons and controls all things under heaven."[30] Of the later Yin-Yang Wing-Tsit Chan writes: "In the Yin Yang school, the universe is conceived of as a well-coordinated system in which everything is related to everything else."[31] In their account of creation the Han Philosophers wrote: "When heaven and earth were joined in emptiness and all was unwrought simplicity, then without having been created, things came into being. This was the Great Oneness. All things issued from this oneness but all become different, being divided into various species of fish, birds and beasts..."[32] Yu Lan noted of the Han philosophers: "According to their way of thinking, the universe is an organic structure, and the controlling power in this structure is Heaven". and "Man and Heaven complement each other."[33]

The universe, then, is one but its manifestations are many. Unity exists alongside of plurality, plurality alongside of unity. One supplements, not denies the other. Unity makes it possible to join the particular and the universal, man and nature, the two sides of a contradiction, universals into a single Universal. As Chu Hsi put it, "Considering the fact that all things come from one source, we see that their principle is the same but their material force is different. There is only one Great Ultimate, yet each of the myriad things has been endowed with it and each in itself possesses the Great Ultimate in its entirety."[34]

Chinese philosophers introduced the concept of harmony as the basis for their insistence that unity does not deny or exclude particularity, diversity, individuality or differences. There can be unity in diversity. That harmony is not sameness is pointed up in a very homely illustration in the *Tao Chuan:* "Harmony is different from sameness...Harmony is like soup. There being water and heat, sour flavoring and pickles, salt and peaches, with a bright fire of wood, the cook harmonizing all the ingredients in the cooking of the fish and the flesh. If water be used to help out water, who could eat it? If the harp and the lute were the same, who would delight in them?" Moreover harmony is associated with balance, equilibrium or the "mean". As Fung Yu-lan points out, "A harmony includes differences, with all the differences harmonized to produce a state of harmony. Nonetheless, if differences are to produce a state of harmony, then it is necessary that all differences should have each of its own due proportion and be 'exactly good' to that extent, neither exceeding nor coming short. What is described as 'achieving the mean', and also as 'in due proportion' amounts to all the differences being neither too much nor too little, if a state of harmony is to be achieved."

In Chinese thought vitalism or dynamism has usually been associated with organicism. Reality is alive, moving, constantly changing. Wang Fu-Chih's view that different political institutions are required at different times was based on his premise that "Times change; conditions are different."[35] The basic theme of the *Commentaries and Appended Remarks to The Book of Changes* is the constancy and universality of change, a view Buddhism reinforced with its doctrine of Anicca. Change in *The Book of Changes* is conceived of as transformation not eradication. An entity is not eradicated in the sense of being completely destroyed but as being changed into something else. Wing-tsit Chan writes that "In the

Yin Yang school, the universe is conceived of as a well-coordinated system in which everything is related to everything else. In *The Book of Changes* this order is conceived of as a process of transformation. In *Tung Chung-shu*, however, both ideas take a step forward: the universe is treated as an organic whole."[36] Transformation, of course, presupposes potentiality and therefore continuity.

Many Chinese philosophers conceived of changes as union or combination. As indicated in the *Commentaries on The Book of Changes*, "Essence and material force are combined to become things." Moreover change was associated with progression or advance. The progression may be cyclical or linear. The Yin-Yang philosophers conceived of the five agents acting in terms of a cycle of mutual production and mutual overcoming. Tung Chung-Shu (c. 179-c. 104 B.C.), however, interpreted their action as linear and was led to believe that civilization is constantly advancing to ever higher levels. In both cases it was a matter of mutual production and overcoming—one being replaced by another.

The process of change also was conceived of as being dialectical, although it led to a state of monism, "a dynamic monism through the dialectic", to use Wing-tsit Chan's words. The meaning of dialectic is indicated in De Bary's book—"Each force as it reaches its extreme produces its opposite and the two continue to succeed each other in a never ending cycle" and "The doctrine that extremes produce opposite reactions, that each object or situation invariably gives birth to its antithesis, cautioned the scholar to choose a central course, a golden mean between the extremes, which would be timely and in accordance with the situation at the moment."[37]

A good example of the dialectical movement in reality is seen in Chou Tun-Yi's *Explanation of the Diagram of the Great Ultimate:* "The Non-ultimate! And also the Great Ultimate. The Great Ultimate through movement generates the Yang. When its activity reaches its limit, it becomes tranquil. Through tranquility the Great Ultimate generates the Yin. When tranquility reaches its limit, activity begins again. This movement and tranquility alternate and become the root of each other, giving rise to the distinction of Yin and Yang, and these two modes are thus established." Reality then is going through a constant process of rest and motion, equilibrium and non-equilibrium, tranquility and turbulence. One stage is reached and continues for a while and gives rise to its opposite. One is inherent in the other and because of an inner dynamism and tension brings about the other.

VI Mao and the Chinese Tradition

One of the most strking similarities between Mao's and traditional Chinese thought is his emphasis on dialectical change. This is really what he is referring to in his discussion of contradictions. For a contradiction is a set of opposites, one aspect of which, because of its underlying affinity or identity, changes under certain conditions into the other or gives rise to a new entity or situation. This process is one of transformation and progression or "supersession", to use Mao's term.

Mao related the concepts of dialectical change, transformation and supersession especially to the social and political scene in twentieth century China. They led him to declare that "...old China will inevitably change into New China"; The "semi-feudal society will change into a new democratic society"; "The old feudal landlord class will be overthrown, and from being the ruler it will change into being the ruled"; "...the landlord class owning the land is transformed into a class that has lost its land, while the peasants who once lost their land are transformed into small holders who have acquired land..."; "under socialism, private peasant ownership is transformed into the public ownership of socialist agriculture"; "The proletariat...initially subordinate to the bourgeoise...becomes an independent class...seizes political power and becomes the ruling class"; "...the power of the Chinese people...will inevitably change China from a semi-colony into an independent country...imperialism will be overthrown..." Through such changes there will be a gradual moral and social development of Chinese culture.

Mao's views are in many ways an expression of organicism as well. This is apparent when its ethical implications or corollaries are clarified, namely that the good is to be conceived of in terms of the good of all, and that a person should be concerned not just about his own but everyone's well-being. This is reflected in Confucius' emphasis on righteousness not profit and in his statement, "The man of perfect virtue wishing to establish himself, seeks also to establish others."[38] Its likeness to Tai Chen's (1724-1777) statement "The benevolent man, wishing to live his own life fully, helps other men to live their lives to the full"[39] is obvious. The ethical implications of organicism are seen in Motzu's writings on Universal Love, in Mencius' claim that the sense of commiseration and the other three "beginnings" are found in all men and in K'ang Yu-wei's essay *The Mind that cannot Bear to See the Suffering of Others*. Each emphasizes that man is truly virtuous only when he is not motivated by self-gain but when he acts in terms of the good of the whole or on the level of the universal. A person may love himself but if his love and concerns do not extend to his family, community, nation and all mankind, he is not a man of Jen.

Mao's continuation of this emphasis is reflected in his cautioning that "a dangerous tendency had shown itself of late among many of our personnel—an unwillingness to share the joys and hardships of the masses, a concern for personal fame and gain." It is seen in his definition of a revolutionary as one who "...must not have a single grain of selfishness or exaggerate his own role and must work honestly for the masses", and of a collectivist as one who "...must do his utmost to acquire the knowledge which is useful to the people and to devote his ability to the revolution." Mao defines a "truly modest man" as one who "enthusiastically, unconditionally, loyally, and actively works for the cause of the party, the people and the collective. He works not to show off or for awards and fame, not for any selfish desire, but wholeheartedly for the happiness and interests of the people." Moreover, "He considers nothing more than how to serve the people better." The emphasis on serving is seen also in Mao's exhortation to the cadres: "We must never detach ourselves from the masses, so that we may know them, understand them, be with them, and serve them well." To be a true Communist, Mao said, one must be "...more concerned about others than himself", and "...to die for the people's sake is to die a worthy death." The statements above are but a few of many which might be quoted to demonstrate Mao's continuing of traditional Chinese ethical organicism with its priority on the good of the whole or the masses. The concept assumes an identity of interests and needs among men, and the good of the individual and the group are not, therefore, necessarily in conflict.

In regard to the socio-political correlates of organicism several items may be noted. From the standpoint of organicism, society is made up of a number of supplementary or mutually supporting groups. Each in its own way contributes to the good of the whole. The result is a basic unity or solidarity stemming from a common goal reached in various ways. K'ang Yuwei's philosophy serves as an example of this view. He was concerned about the turmoil and conflict of his time and how it might be resolved. His view is seen in the following statement:

"Having been born in an age of disorder, and seeing with my own eyes the path of suffering in the world, I wish to find a way to save it. I have thought deeply and believe the only way is to practise the way of Great Unity and Great Peace. Looking over all ways and means in the world, I believe that aside from the way of Great Unity there is no other method to save living men from their sufferings or to seek their great happiness. The way of Great Unity is perfect equality, perfect impartiality, perfect humanity, and good government in the highest degree. Although there are good ways, none can be superior."[40]

What K'ang is pointing to is what has been called here an organic society.

The earlier quotations from Mao presuppose that concept also. One other example may be used, Mao's formula "unity, criticism, unity." Mao declared that it epitomized the "democratic method of resolving contradictions through criticism or struggle and arriving at a new unity on a new basis." As to its use he wrote: "Since the liberation of the whole country, we have employed this same method of 'unity, criticism, unity' in our relations with the democratic parties and with the industrial and commercial circles. Our task now is to continue to extend and make still better use of this method throughout the ranks of the people; we want all our factories, cooperatives, business establishments, schools, government offices and public organizations, in a word, all our six hundred million people, to use it in resolving contradictions among themselves."

Mao's statements on criticism and his exhortation to cadres to not fear it, as one learns through mistakes, is reminiscent of Confucius' emphasis on self-examination, "Everyday I examine myself on these three points: in acting on behalf of others, have I always been loyal to their interests? In intercourse with my friends, have I always been true to my word? Have I failed to repeat the precepts that have been handed down to me?" The Doctrine of Rectification in the *Great Learning* emphasizes the same theme—"The ancients who wished to illustrate illustrious virtue throughout the kingdom, first ordered well their own states. Wishing to order well their states...they first cultivated their persons. Wishing to cultivate their persons, they first rectified their hearts... That at least one emperor seems to have heeded the injunction is reflected in the account in the second chapter of the *Great Learning* of king T'ang on whose bathtub was engraved "If you can one day renovate yourself, do so from day to day. Yes, let there be daily renovation."

The concept of an organic society led Mao to sharply criticize what he called "the individualist ideology of capitalist society" which moves the individual to put his good before that of others or the whole. Such individualism is a species of self-pride. Mao declared that "Conceit is based on the bourgeois, idealist world view." It "...is derived from individualism and nurses the growth of individualism." The truly modest man, however, is concerned "for the happiness and interests of the people."

The political correlation of organicism is the view that the function of government or the state is to ensure the good, not of just a few or a minority but of all the people. The government is the means the people use to collectively ensure their well-being. Its task, to use K'ang's phrase, is to "cherish the people". Mao's statements above indicate this view also. Others might be quoted. Mao wrote that "to maintain public order and safeguard the interests of the people, it is necessary to exercise dictatorship over embezzlers, swindlers, arsonists, murderers, criminal gangs and other scoundrels who seriously disrupt public order." In distinguishing right from wrong words and deeds, the criterion to be used is "the point of view of the broad massess of people." Members of the party should be good at "...discussing and handling affairs with the masses; they must not at any time detach themselves from the masses. The relationship between the party and the masses is comparable to that between fish and water." Mao declared the aim of his government is "...to protect all our people so that they can devote themselves to peaceful labour and build China into a socialist country with a modern industry, agriculture, science, and culture." Finally, Mao pointed out that "...the organs of the state must practise democratic centralism, that they must rely on the masses and that their personnel must serve the people."

Mao extended the organicist model to the world level also. Like K'ang Yu-wei he conceives of the world as a "Great Unity". Mao does not go as far as K'ang Yu-wei, however, who advocated "no divisions into national states" but a single "world government" instead. Instead he stressed the idea of peaceful coexistence, even with nations with a different form of government—"As for the imperialist countries, we should unite with their peoples and strive to coexist peacefully with those countries, do business with them and prevent any possible war, but under no circumstances should we harbour any unrealistic notions about them." At the same time the effort should be continued to "help the broad masses of exploited throughout the world" and promote "international socialist unity and the unity of the peace-loving people of the world."

The last statement presupposes what might be called an "organic" view of man. It holds that the individual is a composite or a harmonious whole, and so is mankind. There is a basic unity among men which should transcend all barriers of race, creed and nation. In essence men are alike although they may differ externally. In his essence the individual is a member of the category of the universal. By accident he is a member of the category of the particular.

The individual is a composite in that he is made up of body and mind, emotions, feelings, desires, senses, reason, intuition, etc. Each has its appropriate part or role. They are not at odds with each other. The individual in Chinese thought is not a duality of contending parts as asserted by some Western schools of thought. As a composite the individual is a microcosm of the universe. "Heaven is my father and earth is my mother, and even such a small creature as I finds an intimate place in their midst. Therefore that which extends throughout the universe I regard as my body and that which directs the universe I consider as my nature", Chang Tsai wrote.[41] Ch'eng Yi asserted that "The mind of one man is one with the mind of Heaven and Earth", and the Taoist

Huai-Nan Tzu declared "Heaven, earth, infinite space, and infinite time are the body of one person, and the space within the six cardinal points is the form of one man."[42]

Just as the individual is a microcosm of the universe so is he also a part of humanity or mankind. Chang Tsai wrote in *The Western Inscription* that "All people are my brothers and sisters, and all things my companions." In describing the man of *jen*, Ch'eng Hao said "The man of jen forms one body with all things without any differentiation." K'ang Yu-wei pointed out that "The word jen consists of one part meaning man and another part meaning many. It means that the way of men is to live together." And Wang Yang-Ming declared that "The great man regards Heaven and Earth and the myriad things as one body. He regards the world as one family and the country as one person." The relationship of the individual and mankind is seen further in the Chinese concept of duties. The individual has four duties—duties toward himself, his family, his nation and the world.

A traditional theme has been that the unity of mankind is promoted through universal love. Wing-tsit Chan writes that "In the traditional Confucian theory of love, one proceeds from affection for one's parents to being humane to all people, and finally kindness to all creatures."[43] Motzu was an outstanding early proponent of universal love—loving all men equally, others' parents as much as one's own. This is reflected later in Han Yu's statement, "Universal love is called humanity. To practice this in the proper manner is called righteousness. To proceed according to this is called the Way."[44] Several centuries later K'ang Yu-wei pictured universal love as a catalyst for a unified and peaceful world—"In the world of Great Unity, the whole world becomes a great unity... There will be no war...There is no competition at all...All people are equal and do not consider position or rank an honor...In the Age of Great Peace, all creatures form a unity and therefore people feel love for all creatures as well."[45]

There is much of this outlook reflected in Mao's writings. "Our Congress", Mao said, "should teach every comrade to love the people and listen attentively to the voice of the masses..." Mao looks forward to a time when all contradictions will disappear and he envisions a social utopia made up of a classless world society of the proletariat. All will "join in common effort with the other members." Revolutions and revolutionary wars "inevitable in class society" will be absent. The "state of universal fraternity" will be realized. Selfishness and competition will cease. Virtue will abound.

An organicist view holds that, as a product of the cosmos, man is good and that he has a proper place in the universe as a whole. In the *Commentaries on The Book of Changes*, as Wing-tsit Chan points out, the universe is considered as one "of constant change and whatever issues from it is good." In an organic scheme man is significant but not dominant; in Chou Tun-yi's words, "It is man alone who receives the material forces in their highest excellence..." or, as Shao Yung put it, "Man occupies the most honored position in the scheme of things because he combines in him the principles of all species." Classical Chinese art illustrates very well that man is a part of nature and not apart from it as its master.

Chinese philosophy holds that man is a part of reality yet he is not determined by it. He can remould reality to better meet his ends. Mao sets this emphasis on man's free will in a sociological rather than metaphysical context. He asserts that through self-will, discipline and effort, men can change the social, economic and political environment in which he lives for the better.

Mao's own view of man is a continuation of the traditional optimistic one. "Of all things in the world, people are the most precious", he wrote. He had much faith in the masses. He exhorted cadres to take them into their confidence— "...we must carry on lively and effective political education among the masses and should always tell them the truth about the difficulties that crop up and discuss with them how to surmount those difficulties." Even most "reactionaries", he believed, could be rationally appealed to and led to "re-educate themselves into new persons..."

VII SUMMARY

So far a number of parallels between Mao and Confucianism have been discussed. In metaphysics similarities have been drawn between a non-exclusionist type dualism and the Yin Yang and chi and li views of reality. Mao and Confucianism both accept a non-exclusionist epistemology consisting of empiricism and rationalism. Both view reality [as organic and constantly in flux and they agree in the ethical, social, political and humanistic implications of organicism and change.

Other similarities may be touched on briefly. One is the emphasis on moral government or the view that the ruler or leaders must be virtuous. They must not rule for personal gain or fame but must have the well-being of the people at heart. Any government, no matter what its type, which does not, will eventually fail. Regarding type of government it might be pointed out that the difference may not be as great as some suppose. It has always been authoritarian. Benjamin Schwartz points out that long before Mao "...the Chinese accepted the idea of absolute obedience to absolute rulers."[46] The present government is still paternalistic and authoritarian, although it is not a monarchy.

Another parallel is the acceptance of the "Great Man" theory of society. This holds that a society progresses through the leadership and example of an outstanding man or group of men. They embody the idealized virtues, set up goals and ends and lead the masses in their realization. Along with this is the belief that a society progresses only as the masses and not just a few do. The good of all and not just a minority is the basic criterion.

Parallels of a general type might be noted such as a continuation of the tendency to look outward rather than inward, to be less interested in ultimate than immediate type explanations, to offer rational, scientific rather than speculative, theoretical explanations, to not view reality in terms of absolutes but relatives. The quest for a better society goes on. The concern for the quality of human relations remains fundamental. The doctrine of the mean, moderation or refraining from extremes carries over. China still remains a group rather than individualistically oriented society. Society continues to be "sharing" or cooperative rather than competitive oriented. Finally the tendency to "Sinocize" the alien or the intruder continues. Schwartz notes that "Mao taught his Communist disciples that their task was to 'make Marxism Chinese'." Marxism, then, is not accepted in its Russian form but is remoulded to fit Chinese conditions. Perhaps, to sum up, the best terms to use would be that there is continuation and extension of traditional Chinese humanism and pragmaticism.

Mao's final place in the history of China and her thought has not yet been determined because of the disruptive events following his death. More time and distance between them is needed. No one will deny that his influence has been great, however. A genuinely objective evaluation of his influence still needs to be done. Here the main emphasis has been on a description of his views and how they do or do not fit into the Chinese tradition.

NOTES

1. Statements by Mao quoted in this chapter have been taken mainly from Mao Tse-tung, *Four Essays on Philosophy*, (Peking: Foreign Language Press, 1968). There are a number of reproductions of Mao's works available now. A very handy one containing his four philosophical essays is Anne Fremantle, *Mao Tse-tung; An Anthology of His Writings*, New York, The New American Library of World Literature, Inc. 1963.
2. Wm. Theodore de Bary, *Sources of Chinese Tradition*, (New York, Columbia University Press, 1960), Vol. II, p. 247.
3. H.G. Creel, *Chinese Thought from Confucius to Mao Tse-tung*, (New York, New American Library of World Literature, Inc., 1960), pp. 39.186.
4. James Legge, *The Four Books*, (Hong Kong, Chinese Book Co.), pp. 312-313.
5. Fung Yu-Lan, *A Short History of Chinese Philosophy*, (N.Y. Macmillan Comp., 1962), pp. 305-306.
6. Wing-Tsit Chan, *A Sourcebook in Chinese Philosophy*, Princeton University Press, 1963), p. 609.
7. H.G. Creel, *op. cit.*, pp. 187-90.
8. Wade Bashin, editor, *Classics in Chinese Philosophy*, (New York, Philosophical Library, 1972), p. 645.
9. *Ibid.*, p. 647.
10. Fung Yu-Lan, *op. cit.*, p. 25.
11. *Op. cit.*
12. Chan, *op. cit.*, p. 747.
13. Francis L.K. Hsu, *Americans and Chinese*, (New York, Henry Schuman, 1953) p. 435.
14. Charles Moore, ed., *Philosophy and Culture, East and West*, (Honolulu, University of Hawaii Press, 1968), p. 81.
15. *Op. cit.*
16. H.G. Creel, *Confucius and the Chinese Way*, (New York, Harper and Brothers, 1949), p. 137.
17. Bashin, *op. cit.*, p. 660.
18. *Ibid.*, p. 620.
19. Chan, *op. cit.*, p. 244.
20. Fung Yu-Lan, *op. cit.*
21. Chan, *op. cit.*, p. 244.
22. *Ibid.*, p. 248.
23. Fung Yu-Lan, *op. cit.*, p. 196.
24. Chan, *op. cit.*, p. 265.

25. *Ibid.*, p. 637.
26. *Ibid.*, p. 246.
27. De Bary, *op. cit.*, p. 196.
28. Chan, *op. cit.*, p. 463.
29. *Ibid.*, p. 730.
30. *Ibid.*, p. 264.
31. *Ibid.*, p. 272.
32. De Bary, *op. cit.*, p. 193.
33. Fung Yu-Lan, *The Spirit of Chinese Philosophy*, (Boston, Beacon Press, 1962), p. 121.
34. Chan, *op. cit.*, p. 637.
35. Baskin, *op. cit.*, p. 620.
36. Chan, *op. cit.*, p. 271.
37. De Bary, *op. cit.*, p. 192.
38. Legge, *op. cit.*, p. 77.
39. Creel, *op. cit.*, p. 185.
40. Lawrence Thompson, translator, *One World Philosopher of K'ang Yu-Wi*, (London, Allen and Unwin, 1958), p. 72.
41. Baskin, *op. cit.*, p. 463.
42. De Bary., *op. cit.*, p. 472.
43. *Ibid.*, p. 725.
44. *Ibid.*, p. 454.
45. *Ibid.*, p. 734.
46. Benjamin Schwartz, *China: An Introduction*, (New York, Atheneum, 1965), p. 29.

17
CONTEMPORARY PHILOSOPHERS OUTSIDE THE MAINLAND

JOSEPH WU

Chinese philosophy outside the mainland is a panoramic scene of multiplicity. In giving an account of this scene it is in need of a geographical limit. Thus the geographical scope of this account will be limited to three places—Hong Kong, Taiwan and the United States. The development of Chinese philosophy in other countries such as Japan, France and Germany will not be included. The two islands outside the Chinese mainland are important bases for the continuous development of Chinese culture. We find on those two islands many thinkers and scholars who left the mainland when the communists gained full control in 1949. Thus an account of Chinese philosophy being carried on there is only natural. But what is the justification for including the United States which is neither a Chinese speaking nation nor a colony of Chinese culture?

A major reason is that the United States is a great melting pot of ideas and values of our times. In it, one can find varieties of cultural specialities from every corner of the world. Regarding Chinese philosophy, the United States is probably the only non-Chinese speaking country which has so many college teachers in that field.[1] This is probably due to the political reason that many Chinese philosophy students, after getting their doctoral degree, remain a permanent member of the American academic world. As a result, the effort devoted to the promotion of Chinese philosophy has become strikingly phenomenal. Within a short period of the last three years, *The Journal of Chinese Philosophy* was established and the *International Society for Chinese Philosophy* was founded.[2]

In spite of the multiplicity and diversity in the panorama of contemporary Chinese philosophy, this chapter will be divided into the following four sections: Chinese Buddhism, Chinese Scholasticism, Neo-Sunism, and Contemporary Confucianism. Some individual thinkers who are hard to classify in the above categories will be discussed briefly as well.

II Chinese Buddhism

During the early period of the founding of the Republic of China, Buddhism in China had an exuberant revival in which Auyang Ching-wu and Master T'ai-hsu were the central figures. Since 1949, it has continued its gradual development in Taiwan and Hong Kong. The main representative in Taiwan is Master Yin Hsun, a very learned scholarly monk who was a graduate from Wu Ching Buddhist Academy and who earned his doctoral degree from a Japanese university. Nearly eighty years old, he is still active in lecturing and writing, with a chair in philosophy at the College of Chinese Culture. Master Yin Hsun has written volumes on Buddhism and his most recent work *The History of Ch'an Buddhism in China* exhibits much more substantial scholarship than other works of the same kind.[3] Following Master T'ai-hsu, Yin Hsun advocates Buddhism as a means to the creation of a new world culture. From his viewpoint, Brahmanism was a local product of the Hindu people and Judaism a local product of the Jewish people. Although Hinduism and Christianity attempted to break local limits, they still exhibit much intolerance and exclusiveness. Buddhism is the only religion in the world which is all-tolerant and all-inclusive. A convert does not need to abandon his previous religious beliefs, since Buddhism recognizes the genuine values of all other religions. Therefore, the promotion of Buddhism can lead to the creation of a new world culture which features genuine love, freedom, and equality.[4]

A very unique Buddhist personality is a female scholar, an artist-nun, whose religious name is Shig Hiu Wan (Cantonese pronunciation—Mandarian should be "Shih Shao-yun"). Instead of being trained in a monastery in her youth, she was a graduate of two art institutes of South China, including one in Hong Kong. After her college years in Canton, she went to India to study art. Having been a visiting professor of art in India, she is now the director of the Institute for the Study of Buddhist Culture of the China Academy and a professor of the College of Chinese Culture. Her academic field in Buddhist studies is the T'ien school, but her genuine and unique contribution lies in her blending of Buddhist culture with the artistic spirit of the Chinese tradition. In recent years, she advocates the philosophy of "field and garden" (*t'ien-yuan hsu hsiang*) which originated in naturalist poets like T'ao Yuan-ming. This type of philosophy could not have been produced by a Buddhist without in-depth cultivation in Chinese culture. Shig Hiu Wan herself is an excellent painter and a writer, as well as a nun of a very high religious level. Nevertheless, her disciples or laymen await the future when her position is more appreciated and recognized by the intellectual world which has been male-dominated.

Another scholar who synthesizes Buddhism and Chinese culture together is Professor Hu-t'ien Pa who has been a professor of National Taiwan Normal University, National Taiwan University, and Tunghai University. While Shig Hiu Wan has blended Chinese painting and T'ien T'ai Buddhism, Pa in himself has synthesized Ch'an Buddhism and Chinese poetry. Although he never published extensively, his short papers were written with a high degree of clarity and penetration, so his readers and students recognize him as a top authority in Ch'an Buddhism. His writings were anthologized by himself into a volume called *I Hai Wei Lan* (*Mild Waves in the Ocean of Literature*) with a subtitle "*Ch'an and Poetry*."[5] It might well be that the greatest contribution to Ch'an by Professor Pa is his interpretation of *kung-ans* (konas). Unlike Japanese scholars (e.g. D.T. Suzuki) who mystified and obscured the specific meanings in a *kung-an* with general remarks about the irrational nature of Ch'an, Professor Pa is able to render each *kung-an* in a clear and intelligible manner with his solid scholarship in Buddhism and his keen awareness of the poetic ways of using language. After his retirement from university teaching in Taiwan, he became an immigrant of the United States residing in Las Vegas, which to him is the same as an old temple amid the mountains.

In Hong Kong, the most influential and reputed scholar in Buddhism is Professor Lo-Shih-hsien, a student of the late Master T'ai-hsu and a follower of Au-yang Ching-wu. In addition to his writings promoting Wei-shih Buddhism (Yogācāra School), Lo tirelessly gave lectures on the glorious classic *Chen Wei Shih Lun* every Monday for a continuous period of over ten years. His student, the late Professor Wai Tat, after attending his lectures, rendered the entirety of this important classic into English. Lo and his students seventeen years ago founded the Society for Fa Hsiang Buddhism which is probably the only academic society for Buddhism in the British Colony of Hong Kong. Now in his sixties, Lo is still actively engaging himself in a very ambitious publishing project, an extended commentary on the *Shu Chi* of Kwei Chi. This is a ten-volume project, the first volume of which has been completed.[6] Lo's most brilliant and learned student (also a student of T'ang Chun-i who will be reported under contemporary Confucianism), Tou-hui Fok, a lecturer at New Asia College of the Chinese University of Hong Kong, has been very active in the academic field of Buddhist philosophy and has published many articles which have contributed much to Buddhist studies.

Regarding Buddhism in the United States, it seems to have been dominated by the Japanese, yet we find a very important exception. This is Master Hsuan Hua, the head monk of the Gold Mountain Monastery of San Francisco. Hsuan Hua, who was known as Tu-lun in Northern China, went to Hong Kong after the Maoists captured mainland China. Being at odds with the Hong Kong environment, he came to the United States to acquaint American people with Buddhist philosophy. As a result of his pedagogic effort, a number of young American scholars became his disciples, among whom Ronald Epstein, who holds a Ph.D. from University of California, Berkeley, is probably the most prominent. In addition Hsuan Hua started an ambitious project of founding the first Buddhist University in the Western world. This is Dharma Realm University located two miles east of Ukiah, California. Recruited on its faculty were such prominent scholars as Professor Yi Wu, formerly a teacher of Chinese philosophy at the Chinese Culture University who became chairman of the Department of Chinese Philosophy and Religion.

III CHINESE SCHOLASTICISM

Another movement of religious philosophy in contemporary Chinese philosophy is "Chinese Scholasticism." This term is used for two reasons. First, the major representatives in this movement have a great respect for, and a good understanding of Chinese cultural traditions. Secondly, the effort is not a mere promotion of Catholicism or Scholasticism in China. Rather, it is an effort to fuse the basic spirit of Scholasticism with the traditional values of Chinese culture, particularly those of the Confucian tradition. This philosophic movement has its institutional basis at the Catholic Fu Jen University and has a journal of its own—UNIVERSITAS: Monthly Review of Philosophy and Culture.

The chief exponent of this philosophic trend is Dr. S. Lokuang, the publisher of UNIVERSITAS and the archbishop of Taipei. Bishop Lokuang is a very learned scholar in both Eastern and Western philosophy and has published many philosophic treatises. His most recent work *The Future of Chinese Philosophy* (*Chung Kuo Che Hsueh te Chien Wang*, published by Hsueh Sheng Shu Chu of Taipei) suggests an attempt to synthesize the East and the West through blending together Confucianism and Christianity.

Other active exponents include John C. Wu, director of the doctoral program in philosophy at Chinese Culture University, Albert Chao and Thaddeus Hang of National Cheng-chi University and Cheng-tung Chang and Chih-tsun Ch'ien of Catholic Fu Jen University. There are still many others in this group. Wu was a professor of international law at Seton Hall University until his retirement. In addition to his publications in his major field, he has devoted the rest of his academic energy to philosophy, introducing Taoism and Ch'an to the West and Christian philosophy to China. Albert Chao has written extensively on many topics in philosophy. His philosophic position is quite humanistic in spite of his position as a Catholic priest. He regards religion as an important part of humanity, and the concept of humanism should be broadened to include religion which is an expression of the humanistic spirit.

In regard to a philosophic guideline for a synthesis of scholasticism and traditional Chinese philosophy, several suggestions have been made. The most systematic and all-encompassing is found in a recent article "Chinese Thought and the Christian Religion" (*Chung Kuo Hsi Hsiang yu Chi Tu Tsung Chiao*).[7] Its author is Peiyung Fu, the former editor of UNIVERSITAS, currently instructor in philosophy at National Taiwan University. In this article, Fu suggested ten points for consideration:[8]

(1) Problem of Human Nature: Confucianism maintains that human nature is originally good, while Christian philosophy believes in original sin. There appears a serious incompatibility between the two. Fu suggests that since the theory of

original sin has been reinterpreted through the centuries and the Christian theory of human nature can be modified to emphasize the idea of man as created after the image of God. This will be more acceptable by the Confucians yet this idea is originally a part of Christian doctrine.

(2) Self-Reliance and Reliance on God: Recognizing the innate goodness of human nature, Confucianism emphasizes self-reliance in self-realization while Christianity emphasizes reliance on God. But a careful reading of Jesus' sayings in the *New Testament* will reveal that self-reliance is equally important in Christianity. The common saying "God helps those who help themselves" demonstrates this point.

(3) Immanence and Transcendence: Transcendence features Christianity, while traditional Chinese thought as influenced by Confucian humanism and Mahāyāna Buddhism emphasizes immanence. Nevertheless, the difficult situation of contemporary philosophy tends to compel Chinese thinkers to seek the path of transcendence. This means that the two are hopefully getting closer.

(4) T'ien-Jen as One and God-Man as One: One of the main themes of traditional Chinese thought is that *T'ien* (Heaven, Sky, Nature, or Supernature, no exact English equivalent) and Man are not separate from each other. The ultimate moral purpose of man is to attain all the virtues of T'ien. Being with God through Jesus Christ is a fundamental belief for all Christians. Therefore, this is a good meeting ground for Christianity and Confucianism.

(5) Harmony in One and Being one with God: Both represent a form of mystical experience. Although Confucian philosophers de-emphasize experience of this kind, yet it is quite fundamental in Taoism. Being one with God as mystical union is very fundamental to the Christian mystics.

(6) The Problem of Creation: In traditional Chinese cosmology, man is the co-creator (together with T'ien and Ti) of the universe. In Christianity man is a creature of God rather than a creator. These two philosophies appear in conflict with each other. But Fu maintains that it was only the same process viewed from different angles.

(7) Confucius and Jesus Christ: Confucius is the greatest sage of

the Chinese tradition, but he never claimed himself as a divine being. We can say, suggests Fu, the birth of Confucius in China was indeed God's gift to the Chinese people. This means God sent Confucius to educate the Chinese people.

(8) Confucian Jen and Christian Love: While Jen represents the never-ceasing process of life, love is the ever-existing process of reality. The two in fact bear striking similarities. This is again a very good meeting ground for Christianity and Confucianism.

(9) Religion as based on Morality and Morality as based on Religion: The former is the way of Christianity, and the latter, Confucianism. They appear very different from each other, yet a good balance and compromise between the two will create a more ideal morality as well as a more healthy religion.

(10) The Unity of Knowledge and Action and the Unity of Belief and Deed: Both Confucianism and Christianity emphasize philosophy lived rather than philosophy theorized. This is also a feature of the religious aspect of Confucianism.

These ten points are, according to Fu, suggested for speculation or theorization. Any fruit generated from this suggestion awaits the efforts of both Catholic thinkers and scholars in the Confucian tradition. But, in order that Christianity can become a part of Chinese culture, a meeting between Christianity and Confucianism is not enough. Therefore, a meeting between Christianity and Buddhism is necessary before Christianity can become a part of the Chinese tradition. Unfortunately as Fu pointed out correctly, most of the exponents (possibly all) of Chinese Scholasticism do not know Buddhist philosophy well. What is more, since most of the Chinese Catholic thinkers received their doctoral degree from Europe, they seem well satisfied with what they imbibed from European philosophy. Consequently they developed an attitude of ignoring the philosophic panorama of the United States, for they mistakenly think that the only philosophy in the United States is analytic philosophy accompanied by some declining types of pragmatism.

IV Neo-Sunism

The term "Sunism" may be used in reference to the thought of

Dr. Sun Yat-sen, the founder of the Republic of China. Unlike Mao Tse-tung who drew on Marxism-Leninism, Sun was a thinker with originality, as his *San Min Chu I* (The Three People's Principles) is a comprehensive synthesis of diverse cultural values, Western and Chinese. It had become the official ideology of the Republic of China before the Maoists took over the mainland.

Dr. Sun's doctrines were originally delivered in very plain language. They were intended as ideological instruments for the Nationalist revolution. Nevertheless, after the Nationalist government moved to Taiwan, his thought has become a subject matter of academic studies. *San Min Chu I* is now a required course for every college student getting a bachelor's degree. In recent years, universities established graduate programs leading toward master and doctoral degrees in this field.

There are many representative scholars in this school of thought. They are largely high-ranked officials in the government, members of the Nationalist party, or professors teaching *San Min Chu I* or related subjects in a college or university. Among them, Professor Jen Cho-hsuan is the most prominent and productive one. His systematic interpretation of Sun's thought was first published in 1942, and was revised and published under the title of *Sun Che Hsueh Yuan Li* (*The Philosophical Theory of Sun Yatsen*).[9] In 1976, Jen wrote an article "The Philosophy of *San Min Chu I*"[10] summarizing the main points of his major work. In what follows a summary will be given of his own summary which provides an interpretation of Sun's thought in accordance with the following six points:

(1) *Hsin Wu Ho I Lun* or "Mind and Matter in One": Sun rejects materialism and idealism as extreme positions, resulting from selective emphasis on one at the cost of the other. If we examine the fundamental existence of a person, we shall realize that Mind and Matter require each other, supplement each other, and complete each other. But Sun tends to place more weight on the role of the mind or spiritual power by calling our attention to some historical battles where the more spirited side (but less armed side) gained an eventual victory.

(2) *Yu Chou Chin Hua Lun* or "Evolutionary View of the Universe": Sun maintains the universe is an evolutionary process

which can be conceived in three stages. The first stage is the evolution of pure matter or inorganic existence. Inorganic activities consist in the interaction of atoms with one another. The second stage is the evolution of organic matter or biological existence. The emergence of life is the feature of this stage. The third stage is the evolution of man. This is marked by the emergence of spirituality. Sun's theory might have been influenced by Charles Darwin, Samuel Alexander, and Lloyd Morgan with the emphasis on spirituality as the essence of man.

(3) *Jen Lei Sheng Tsun Lun* or "Theory of Human Survival": Rejecting the Marxist theory of historical materialism, Sun maintains that the problem of human survival occupies the center of history. Human survival, Sun holds, plays a very important role in economics, politics and social progress. Nevertheless, human activities, energized by the urge to survive, are not merely physical. Instead, both the physical and the mental (or the spiritual) are involved in the survival process.

(4) *Jen Lei Hsing Wei Lun* or "Theory of Human Action": In order to motivate his followers to participate in revolutionary activities, Sun elaborated his theory of action which has been known as *Chih Nan Hsing I Shuo*—the theory that action is easy but knowledge is difficult. He has worked out ten arguments to support this thesis, reminding us of the fact that many people developed the habit of doing something without knowing of it. Due to some logical difficulties, the late president Chiang Kai-shek has modified this into a more pragmatic and vitalistic theory called Li Hsing Che Hsueh or "Philosophy of Effortful Action."

(5) *Jen Lei Hu Tsu Lun* or "Theory of Cooperation": Sun conceives human survival as a social problem rather than an individual problem. It is an ironic fact that human beings need to rely on one another in order to survive. This logically leads to the thesis that we need to cooperate in order to survive. This concept automatically rejects any theory which advocates hatred, struggle, or violence. Once Sun rejects Karl Marx's saying that "class struggle" is only a symptom of a sick society but not the normal discourse of social progress, it follows that Marx can only be a pathologist rather than a physiologist of human society.

(6) *Shih Chien Jen Shih Lun* or "Pragmatic Theory of Knowledge": Sun speculates that primitive people lived the life of doing without knowing. Later, with further development and progress, people gained knowledge from doing. This means knowledge is gained though inductive generalization. After the rise and development of science, we can have knowledge before we proceed to do anything. Modern man, Sun suggests, should fully utilize his knowledge to guide his action.

Being a follower of Sun in both theory and action, Chiang Kai-shek has developed Sun's philosophy much further. For brevity's sake, only two points of importance need mention: First, regarding a theory of reality, Chiang has substantiated Sun's evolutionary view of the universe with the reputed Chinese classic *I Ching* or *The Book of Changes*. In his theory of knowing, Chiang goes back to the celebrated Chinese philosopher Wang Yang-ming for a stronger theory of knowledge and action. In addition, Chiang has contributed a great deal in his promotion of Confucianism, particularly the Confucian theory as contained in the two classical essays *Ta Hsueh* (Great Learning) and *Chung Yung* (Doctrine of the Mean).[11] After his death, there have appeared in Taiwan a number of scholarly articles devoted to the exposition and interpretation of his thought.

V Contemporary Confucianism

The term "contemporary Confucianism" is used deliberately in order to make a distinction between Confucianism today and the kind of Confucianism developed by Sung and Ming philosophers. Since the term "Neo-Confucianism" has been conventionally used for Sun-Ming Confucian philosophy (Sun-Ming Li Hsueh), its unqualified use for the Confucianism of the twentieth century would result in linguistic confusion. Thus "contemporary Confucianism" will be used for the Confucian philosophy of our age.

Contemporary Confucianism is probably the most influential and widely spread trend of thought outside mainland China. In addition to its large number of exponents and adherents, it has maintained its prominent and prestigious status through the educational system of Taiwan, and with certain limits, the curriculum of the schools in Hong Kong. *The Four Books*, *The Confucian*

Analects, Mencius, The Great Learning, and *The Doctrine of the Mean* constitute a three-year course (in fact three different one-year courses) required of all the students in National Taiwan Normal University which has been the major cradle of high school teachers. National Taiwan University, which is characterized by a more liberal spirit perhaps inherited from the May Fourth Movement, still requires Mencius as a text for freshman Chinese. Confucian doctrines are also taught on the high school level both in Taiwan and in Hong Kong. A Hong Kong high school even required the *Hsiao Ching* (*The Book of Filial Piety*) be taught as a part of the course of Chinese Literature.[12] From all these we can observe, in spite of the Maoists' demotion of Confucius, Chinese people still respect and honor their sage.

There are too many accomplished scholars in this trend of thought for this brief account. So, in this short section, I will present only five very prominent individuals: Professor Chen Ta-chi and Hsieh Yu-wei of Taiwan, Professors Mou tsung-san and T'ang Chun-i of Hong Kong, and Professor Wing-tsit Chan of the United States.

Professor Chen Ta-chi, being well-trained in logic in both Western and Hindu traditions, is probably the most clear and fluent writer among contemporary Chinese thinkers. He is very well educated in classical Chinese thinkers. Being very well educated in classical Chinese culture, he is able to clarify the subtle problems in classical writings. He has published numerous articles elucidating major concepts and problems in classical Confucian philosophy.[13] Unlike some other Confucian scholars who attempt to fit Confucius into some ready made schemes, Chen tries his best to disclose the original ideas of Confucius without westernizing or modernizing the sage. It is not surprising that when the Society for Confucius and Mencius was founded, he was elected its first president.

The late Professor Hsieh Yu-wei, being once a student of Alfred North Whitehead at Harvard, contributed to the Chinese academic world through his tireless introduction of Western thinkers to Chinese readers. Nevertheless, his philosophic position was a Confucian one. He gained his reputation as a Confucianist by his persistent promotion of the philosophy of filial piety. According to Hsieh himself, he came by the idea of promoting "filial piety" in 1934 when he wrote on the philosophy of loyalty advocated by Josiah Royce. He published his first article on "Filial Piety and Chinese Culture" in *Hsi Hsiang Yu Shih Tai* (*Thought and Time*) in 1943. His second article was written in English and was presented to the third East-West Conference at the University of Hawaii in 1959.[14] This article aroused much controversy in the conference and since then Hsieh has become a confirmed advocate of filial piety. Later in Hong Kong, Hsieh published a third article (in Chinese) explaining the compatibility between filial piety and democracy. After his retirement from the Chinese University of Hong Kong in 1969, he continued his teaching at the Chinese Culture University in Taiwan until his death. In Taiwan, he continued his philosophizing in the hope that he would write a book on this concept some day. Unfortunately he was unable to fulfill this wish, for he died in 1976 at the age of seventy-three. His last article on filial piety, "The Nature of Filial Piety and the Need of It" (*Hsiao Chih Hsing Chih chi ch'i Ssu Yao*) published shortly before his death.[15]

Professor Mou Tsung-san is a very talented original thinker. He is very well-trained in logic like Professor Chen Ta-ch'i. But unlike Chen who tries to disclose the original meanings of ancient philosophical classics, Mou is more inclined to conceptualize previous philosophers in order to reconstruct their philosophy according to his wish. In his college days, he studied mathematical logic with untiring effort. But he found the logic of the Whitehead-Russell tradition unrewarding because it fails to account for the knowing subject. Then he turned to the study of Kant and has since been intoxicated with the philosophy of subjectivity. Being a student of Hsiung Shih-li who reconstruced Confucianism with the concepts and methods of Yogācāra (Wei-shih) Buddhism, Mou attempted to reconstruct Confucianism with Kant's method and some Kantian modes of thinking. His main contribution is the affirmation of the validity of moral knowledge attainable by intuition. His representative works are the three-volume work *Hsin-Ti yu Hsing-Ti* and *Chih te Chih Chueh yu Chung Kuo Che Hsueh*.[16]

Professor T'ang Chün-i, who died February 2, 1978, is probably the greatest Confucian philosopher China has produced since Chu Hsi and Wang Yang-ming. Different from Mou who took a short-cut through Kant, T'ang developed his version of Confucian philosophy through a very careful and judicial assessment of each philosophic position of both Eastern and Western philosophy. His mode of philosophizing has been influenced by Hegel, but his ideas are so existentially and culturally grounded that in his philosophy we find an unprecedented comprehensive synthesis of the East and the West. In addition to a systematic re-interpretation of the entire Chinese philosophic tradition in his six-volume work *Chun Kuo Che Hsueh Yuan Lun*,[17] he has developed a comprehensive theory of culture through which the reconstruction of Chinese culture is possible. His masterpiece, two-volume work entitled *The Existence of Life and the World of Spirituality* (*Sheng Ming Tsun Tsai yu Hsin Ning Ching Chieh*) was published several months before his death.[18] This is a rare product of top originality with persistent effort in moral cultivation, philosophic discipline and ultimate concern for the destiny of man. It is a piece of work which should be placed among Plato's *Republic*, Kant's *Critique of Pure Reason*, Heidegger's *Being and Time* and Whitehead's *Process and Reality*. Some selections from T'ang writings were translated into English and were published in 1973 and 1974 in Chinese Studies of Philosophy.[19] In spite of his difficult writing style, his influence has been far-reaching because his written works cover the entire range of human culture and experience, ranging from philosophy, history, art, literature, education, morality, law, politics, international relations and even architecture and landscaping. It is a great pity that none of his works has been translated in its entirety for readers of the English speaking world.

Professor Wing-tsit Chan of Chatham College, Pennsylvania, is a very important figure in contemporary Chinese philosophy. He has added a new but significant dimension to the development of Chinese philosophy outside mainland China. His selection, compilation and translation of Chinese classical writings from Confucius to the twentieth century has laid down the foundation for the development of Chinese philosophy in the English-speaking world, particularly the United States. With a solid background in the English language and a study of history of ideas, Chan's translation (most of the time with annotations and comments) demonstrates admirable scholarship and a high degree of accuracy. Without his *Source Book in Chinese Philosophy*,[20] the teaching of Chinese philosophy in the English-speaking world would be limited to early Confucianism in scope and Arthur Waley or James Legge in texts. Besides his contribution in the *Source Book*, Chan's articles elucidating problematic facets of historical figures and important concepts in Chinese philosophy have demonstrated an unprecedented reservoir of cultural information and scholarship in the history of Chinese thought.[21] In addition, he has written extensively in providing truthful descriptive accounts of Chinese philosophers and philosophical movements and has compiled extensive bibliographies which facilitate greatly the research in Chinese philosophy in the English publishing world.[22] In spite of his historical knowledge of Buddhism and Taoism, his position is one of Confucianism. In one of his recent poems, he even confessed that the people who often appeared in his dreams were Chou tun-i, the Ch'eng brothers, Chu Hsi, Lu Chiu-yuan, and Wang Yang-ming.

It is an obvious fact that Confucianism still plays a very significant role in contemporary Chinese philosophy. Even the adherents of Chinese Buddhism, Sunism, and Chinese Scholasticism are Confucian to a certain extent. The influence of Confucianism in the West today cannot be directly measured. But in terms of this author's experiences, American philosophers and scholars are quite capable of understanding Confucian philosophy even without knowing the Chinese language. When the author was a teaching assistant to an American professor teaching Chinese philosophy, he was surprised that the American professor represented and spoke for Confucius in so truthful, vivid, and moving a manner that one might suspect Confucius was incarnated in the English speaking world. What is more surprising is that this professor did not have any knowledge of the Chinese language.[23] This indicates that Confucian philosophy has a universal appeal.

VI Conclusion

It is inevitable that, in this limited discussion, some accomplished scholars who deserve at least mentioning have been omitted. Also, a few unclassifiable scholars have not been taken up; nor has anything been said about comparative philosophy. We turn to both of these items now.

The first unclassifiable thinker is the late Professor Thomé H. Fang of National Taiwan University. He had a Confucian family tradition, a personally preferred Taoist way of life, a Buddhist religion, and a Western philosophic discipline. In spite of the fact that his published works are incomparable in quantity to most of those individuals mentioned in this paper, he has exercised tremendous influence through his classroom teaching. For over thirty years, he taught at National Taiwan University which was the only university having a philosophy department until recently. Therefore many of the younger scholars teaching Chinese philosophy today were once his students and are still his admirers or followers. Although he did not publish many volumes, his published works like *Che Hsueh San Wei* (*Three Sources of Philosophic Wisdom*),[24] *Creativity in Man and Nature* and *The Chinese View of Life*[25] demonstrated his originality and comprehensive knowledge of philosophic traditions, both East and West. Besides, in the East-West Conferences he impressed his fellow participants greatly with his eloquence, humour, and philosophic sharpness, together with his enthusiastic defence of Chinese philosophy. Immediately after his death in July 1977, his students, headed by Professor Chen-hua Huang, the renowned Kantian-Confucian scholar and chairman of the Department of Philosophy at National Taiwan University, started gathering all his tape-recorded lectures, fragmentary notes, published or unpublished, in order to compile *The Complete Work of Thomé H. Fang*. So, Fang's position in contemporary Chinese philosophy may still be too early to assess.

The second unclassifiable individual thinker is Professor Constant C.C. Chang of National Taiwan Normal University. Chang started earning an academic reputation as a scholar in the philosophy of Lao Tzu, although his personality is far from being Taoistic. Later, co-authoring with his student Yi Wu (mentioned under Chinese Buddhism), he published a very well-written book called *A Story of Chinese Philosophy* which has become one of the best-sellers in the intellectual world of Taiwan.[26] In recent years, he has developed his ideas of *Ta T"Tung* (Great Commonness Society). In 1972, he was invited to give a series of television talks on his own theory, and since then he has become a popular social philosopher among the younger generation. Chang at the same time founded The Academic Society for *Ta T'ung* in the February of 1974. Participants included Confucianists, Buddhists, Neo-Sunists, and Catholics. The archbishop Yu-pin was elected the chairman of the executive committee, and Chang himself, the secretary. In one of his published articles, Chang has outlined his fundamental principles and a program for further research and action.[27] With his continuous effort and with support and cooperation from other Chinese thinkers, particularly thinkers of the younger generation, Chang's philosophical movement can become a strong intellectual force in our age.

The third and last unclassifiable thinker to be mentioned is Professor Hsu Fu-kuan of the New Asia Research Institute of Advanced Chinese Studies in Hong Kong founded by Professor T'ang Chün-i. He is generally known as a scholar in the Confucian tradition. But he is much more than a Confucian scholar. Unlike most of the Confucian scholars who concentrate on ethics and metaphysics of morals, Hsu contributed tremendously to art theory and Chinese esthetics. Professor Hsu's *The Spirit of Chinese Art* (*Chung Kuo I Shu Ching Shen*) and his interpreation of the principle of *Chi Yun Sheng Tung* is interesting, refreshing, penetrating, with a high degree of originality. Besides, Hsu is an excellent writer for editorial comments on current events, public affairs and international situations. He has attracted many admirers partly because of his originality and partly because of his sharpness in rhetoric. Although Hsu is not readily classifiable, yet he is a valuable asset of the Chinese intellectual world today.

The second point which has to be mentioned in this concluding section is the continuous effort in comparative philosophy. Comparative studies of philosophy and culture started very early in the Chinese academic world due to the need for a re-evaluation of traditional values and the importation of new values from the West. Several distinguished works were published before the Maoists took over the mainland. Thereafter, being inspired by the East-West Conferences taking place at the University of Hawaii, Chinese scholars have continued their effort in comparative studies. The Society for Asian and Comparative Society in the United States was founded in the academic year of 1968-69, quite a few younger Chinese scholars becoming members and actively participating in the annual workshops. At the same time, there have appeared study type papers by Chinese scholars in journals like *Philosophy East and West*, *International Philosophical Quarterly* and the recently founded *Journal of Chinese Philosophy*. *Inquiry*, a celebrated international journal with its headquarters in Europe, also devoted a special issue to comparative studies in the year 1971.[28]

Scholars and students in Taiwan have also been fascinated by the comparative approach. The journal UNIVERSITAS purposely selected articles in this area and suggestions have been made to institute a course in comparative philosophy in Taiwan universities.[29] From the viewpoint of this author, comparative philosophy is more a method of approach than a branch of philosophy. This method can apply to any branch of philosophic inquiry and is not restricted to a comparison between the East and the West. With proper use of it as a method, together with a judicial and tolerant attitude, it may bear substantive fruit in research. But if it is employed improperly, comparative philosophy can become a mere battlefield for the cultural chauvinists, or a gymnasium for the intellectual gymnasts with "academic vanity" as the hidden motive. So the assessment of the results of this approach still waits for the future.

In concluding this chapter the author would like to express his hope that it has succeeded in giving the reader an initial acquaintance with the labors of Chinese philosophers outside the mainland. Much more work needs to be done to bring their contributions to the attention of the public; hopefully this has been a start.

Notes

1. According to the *Directory of American Philosophers*, (1976-77), there have been over 200 philosophy scholars claiming a speciality in Oriental philosophy and over 20 of them specifically in Chinese Philosophy. In 1976-77 this author had an opportunity to have direct contacts with the philosophy circles of both Hong Kong and Taiwan. He spent the entire academic year in doing research work and lecturing there where he was a student in his youth under some prominent philosophers. As a visitor from the United States he was welcomed by the Catholics as well as the Buddhists, the liberals as well as the conservatives, the Confucianists and the followers of Dr. Sun Yat-sen. So, this article is in a way a report of his direct experience of his Sabbatical leave. Nevertheless, these observations have been prepared on the basis of a continuous attention to the development of Chinese philosophy in these

two places and tireless study of the important philosophical works written by prominent contemporary Chinese thinkers.

2. *The Journal of Chinese Philosophy* was founded by Chung-ying Cheng of the University of Hawaii. In spite of its immature status and modest academic prestige, it is the only journal devoted to Chinese philosophy in the English publishing world. The International Society for Chinese Philosophy had its first annual meeting at Fairfield University from May 30 to June 4, 1978, with the theme "Being and Nothingness in Chinese and Western Thought."

3. Yin Hsun, *Chung Kuo Ch'an Chung Shih* or *History of Chinese Ch'an Buddhism* (Taipei, 1971 first printing, 1975 second printing).

4. Yin Hsun, "Promotion of Buddhism as means to Create New World Culture," *Che Hsueh Lun Chi* or *Collected Essays in Philosophy*, edited by Yi Wu, Hua Kang Publishing Company, 1976. This collection of essays consists of fifty essays written by contemporary Chinese thinkers representing all trends in contemporary Chinese philosophy except Maoism. Most of the essays were invited to write and a few of them were selected from published works.

5. Hu-t'ien Pa, *I Hai Wei Lan* or *Mild Waves in the Ocean of Literature* (Taipei, Kwang Wen Book Company, 1971).

6. Shih-hsien Lo, *Cheng Wei Shih Lun Shu Chi Shuan Chu*, Vol. I (Hong Kong: Fa Hsiang Academic Society, 1977).

7. Pei-yung Fu, "Chinese Thought and the Christian Religion," *UNIVERSITAS* Vol. IV, No. 7 (July, 1977); reprinted in *Fu Jen Ta Hsueh Shen Hsueh Lun Chi* or *Theological Essays of Catholic Fu Jen University*. Quotations will be from the latter.

8. *Fu Jen Ta Hsueh Shen Hsueh Lun Chi*, pp. 214-216.

9. Cho-hsuan Jen, *Sun Chung San Che Hsueh Yuan Li* or *The Philosophical Theory of Sun Yat-sen* (Taipei, Po Mi Erh Book Co., 1960).

10. Cho-hsuan Jen, "The Philosophy of San Min Chu I," *Che Hsueh Lun Chi*, pp. 19-33.

11. Chang Tsai-yu wrote an article on Chiang's contribution to *Ta Hsueh* and *Chung Yung* and is included in *Che Hsueh Lun Chi* pp. 93-108.

12. This is Tak Ming Secondary School (called Tak Ming College).

13. Chen Ta-ch'i *Kung Tzu Hsueh Shuo* or *The Theory of Confucius* (Taipei, Cheng Chung Publishing Company, 1964).

14. Hsieh Yu-wei, "Filial Piety and Chinese Society,' in *Chinese Mind*, edited by Charles A. Moore, (Honolulu: East-West Center Press, 1967), pp. 167-187. This article has its Chinese version published in *Hsin Ya Hsueh Pao*, Vol. IV, No. 1 (August, 1958).

15. Hsieh Yu-wei, "The Nature of Filial Piety and the Need of it," in *Che Hsueh Lun Chi*, pp. 425-439.

16. Mou Tsung-san, *Hsin Ti yu Hsing Ti* or *Mind and Nature*, 3 volumes, (Taipei: Cheng Chung Book Company, 1968-69). Also, *Chih te Chih Chueh vu Chung Kuo Che Hsueh* (Taipei, The Commercial Press, 1971).

17. T'ang Chün-i, *Chüng Kuo Che Hsueh Yuan Lun* or *The Origin and Development of the Basic Concepts in Chinese Philosophy*, 6 volumes, 1966-

1973, initially published by New Asia Research Institute of Hong Kong. Since 1976, copyright goes to Hsueh Sheng Shu Chu of Taipei.

18. T'ang Chün-i, *Sheng Ming Tsun Tsai yu Hsin Ning Ching* or *The Existence of Life and the World of Spirituality* (Taipei: Hsueh Sheng Shu Chu, 1977).

19. *Chinese Studies of Philosophy: A Journal of Translation*, Vol. V, No. 1 (Fall, 1973) and No. 4 (Summer, 1974), were entirely devoted to the publication of the translation of selections from Professor T'ang's writings.

20. Wing-tsit Chan, *Source Book in Chinese Philosophy* (Princeton: Princeton University Press, 1963).

21. Professor Chan's scholarship as exhibited in his English articles is well-known to scholars in the English publishing world. Professor Chan's articles written in Chinese even exhibit more solid scholarship. In his recent Chinese aritlce "Confucianism in the Early Period" in *The Bulletin of the Institute of History of Philology*, Vol. XLVII, Part 4, pp. 707-782, published in 1976 by Academic Sinica demonstrated unprecedented scholarship in history of Chinese philosophy. This article is a result of using 148 published items, with 683 footnotes of documentation.

22. Professor Chan has contributed many articles to Encyclopedias, chapters to books providing truthful accounts of Chinese philosophic activities and movements. Besides, his compilation of bibliographies in Chinese philosophy is admirable. The following two items are particularly important: *An Outline and Annotated Bibliography of Chinese Philosophy*, rev. ed., 1969, by the Far Eastern Publication of Yale University, and *Chinese Philosophy 1947-1963* (Honolulu: East-West Center Press, 1967).

23. This American philosopher is Professor William H. Forthman, now the chairman of the Department of Philosophy of California State University at Northridge.

24. Fang Tung-mei (Thome II. Fang), *Che Hsueh San Hui* or *Three Sources of Philosophic Wisdom* (Taipei: Hsin Chung Kuo Ch'u Pan She, 1968).

25. Thomé H. Fang, *The Chinese View of Life* (Hong Kong: The Union Press, 1957). Fang's monumental work *Chinese Philosophy: Its Spirit and Development* was published posthumously in 1981, Linking Publishing Co., Taipei.

26. Chang Ch'i-chun (Constant C.C. Chang) and Wu Yi, *Chung Kuo Che Hsueh Shih Hua* or *The Story of Chinese Philosophy* (Taipei: Hsin T'ien Ti Ch'u Pan She, 1964 first printing, 1973 fifth printing).

27. Chang Ch'i-chun, Toward a Ta Tung World," in *Che Hsueh Lun Chi*, pp. 307-325.

28. *Inquiry*, Vol. 14 (1971), Nos. 1-2.

29. In regard to the study of comparative philosophy in Taiwan, this author was offered a visiting professorship to start the teaching of a course in *Pi Chiao Che Hsueh* (Comparative Philosophy) for the graduate program of National Taiwan University. In addition, he has written a book on the subject titled *Pi Chiao Che Hsueh yu Wen Hua* or *Comparative Philosophy and Culture* (Taipei: Tung Ta Publishing Co., 1978).

18

THE CHINESE CONTRIBUTION TO WORLD THOUGHT

D. BISHOP

I

We have seen that a major strand of Chinese philosophy in the Modern Period from 1600 onwards emphasized a practicalism in its asserting, for example, the unity of knowledge and action.[1] The pressing problems facing China in the 19th and 20th centuries made it difficult, if not impossible, for thinkers to pursue knowledge for its own sake or to be concerned with only a personal ethics and not an ethics of society. We can take Wang Fu-chih as the initiator of this trend toward practicalism, and it would seem quite valid to claim Mao Tse-tung as being within this tradition, perhaps even its culmination, with his emphasis on the unity of knowing and doing, theory and practice, discovering and verifying truth through practice and his insistence on philosophy's being of practical use to the masses.

Moreover both Mao and Wang, becuase they lived in tumultuous times, were concerned over order, progress, peace and prosperity in society. They believed the place to start in order to reach those ends is with things as they are. This kind of realistic emphasis took the form of a movement which Wang Fu-chih deserves credit for stimulating and which had Ku Yen-wu (1613-1682) and Yen Jo-ch'u (1636-1704) as early leaders, and Tai Chen (1723-1777) as its most prominent one. The movement was known on the one hand as the Han Learning because its leaders rejected many of the views and interpretations of the Sung Neo-Confucianists and attempted to get back to the truths of the original Classics as reconstituted by the scholars of the Han dynasty.[2] And it was given the second title because its adherents insisted on basing truth on the factual and not the theoretical, on the concrete and objective and not the subjective or conjectural.

Both titles imply the answers given by the movement's leaders to the questions noted at the end of the Introduction to the Modern Period. The first title shows that these thinkers did believe in social continuity, that the past has something to offer the present and future. One must have a right understanding of the past, however; it being in this case that the ancient philosophers, as the Han scholars interpreted them, were of a practical orientation in their concern for the rectification of names, investigation of things and seeing and dealing with reality as it is and not just as we dream or wish it to be.

If this movement may be fairly described as being centered around a philosophy of the particular and the concrete, K'ang Y-wei may also be taken as an example of both an impulse in the opposite direction in the Modern Period and how persons are influenced by changes in the times. For K'ang lived in an era when the Chinese, because of the intrusion of the west, were, by necessity if for no other reason, learning more about the West. One result, which K'ang epitomizes, was the rise of thinkers who took the whole world as their subject, whose thought took a universalistic, synthetic dimension which lifted it above narrowness and provincialism in both content and attitude. Kang's concern was all mankind, not the Chinese only; how the whole world, not just China, might be a better place in which to live. This universalistic concern injected into Chinese veins was one positive result of the interaction between China and the West.[3]

A discussion of Chinese philosophy or thought in the Ch'ing of the 19th and 20th centuries cannot omit the introduction and effects of Western philosophers or schools of thought. For Chinese students not only studied in the West but Western thinkers such as Dewey and Russell lectured in China as well.[4] Furthermore, the writings of many Westerners were brought to China and were translated into Chinese. Yen Fu (1853-1921) translated Huxley's *Evolution and Ethics* in 1898 and soon afterward essays by Spencer, Mill and Montesquieu.[5] The major British and Continental philosophers quickly became known to Chinese intellectuals. Among the "isms" imported and expounded were Social Darwinism, Evolutionism, Ethical Relativism, Classical Liberalism, Continental Idealism (Kant), Platonism, Pragmatism, Naturalism, Instrumentalism, Positivism, Marxism, Leninism, Vitalism,

The Chinese Contribution

Pacifism, Scepticism, Utilitarianism, Existentialism, Scientism, Process Philosophy, Organicism, Utopianism, Capitalism, Socialism, Communism and Christianity. Some of these were quite new; others were not. Some were a variant form of traditional Chinese themes.[6] Each tended to have a band of followers.

We have seen in the chapters on the Modern Period the impact of many of these "isms." The Chinese reaction may be reduced for practical purposes to three types—complete acceptance or nearly so, a syncretism and the other extreme of rejection.[7] The first was headed by young Chinese who went to the West to study or attended universities in China modeled on Western lines. The result was the same in either case, Westernization or an almost complete acceptance of Western ways, an attempt to remake China after them, and a complete or nearly so repudiation of anything traditionally Chinese. Two examples of movements illustrating this alternative are the New Culture Movement and the Literary Reform Movement.[8] The latter was headed by Hu Shih and has been sufficiently discussed already. The New Culture Movement, mentioned previously also, flourished in the second decade of the 20th century, was headed by Ch'en Tu-hsui (1879-1942), editor of the monthly, *The New Youth*, was influenced by Western scientism, materialism and positivism, and attacked and attempted to discredit all aspects of traditional Confucianism, its ethics, filial piety, political authoritarianism, paternalism and ritualism. Both Hu Shih and Ch'en were strongly influenced also by British Liberalism with its exultation of individualism, individual right and belief in inevitable progress with science and technology as the means and democracy as its political concomitant.

Syncretism as another alternative was an attempt to bring together what its adherents believed was the best and most relevant in the West with the same in the Chinese tradition. K'ang Y-wei has already been noted as an example of this. Sun Yat-sen may be cited also, for, while he accepted Western democracy, he would not let it stand alone and so he combined political tutelage with it. Moreover, he based his political views on Confucian ethics. Mao Tse-tung, of course, may be pointed to as a third, for he accepted Western Marxism and communism but modified them to fit the Chinese setting. In fact, as has been rightly observed, most of the syncretists proposed a mixture containing a greater Chinese than Western portion.

The rejection of the West, the third alternative, took the form of the "Traditionalist Movement." It was spurred on by attacks on Confucianism coming from the first group. The traditionalists rejected the second alternative because they saw little of value in the West except perhaps elements of its science and technology which might be adopted only as a means to Confucian ends. And they believed, in the third place, that traditional Confucianism was the key to national revival and greatness, if only that Confucianism would be made clear and convincing to the masses.

Traditionalists thus believed in cultural continuity and the projecting of the best of the past as a model for the future. They repudiated ethical individualism and believed traditional Confucian ethics to be superior to contemporary Western liberal ones. They saw no use for changing institutions, for in their moral scheme they asserted starting with the individual and self-rectification as the way to guarantee good institutions. Refurbishing traditional institutions with men of leadership ability and moral stature would be the way to meet the challenges of the times. Their view was that, just as society must be grounded in virtue and not secularism if it is to endure, so the right way politically is government based on morality and not power as in the West where "power politics" reigned supreme.

In philosophy two philosophers whose attention was given primarily to their own tradition and who, therefore, can be placed in the category of traditionalists are Hsiung Shih Li and Fung Yu-lan, although caution must be taken in regard to making a final statement about them. Fung followed the rationalistic wing of Neo-Confucianism and Hsiung the idealistic. Prior to them we have as espousers of traditionalism T'an Ssu-t'ung, Liang Sou-ming, Ou-yang Ching-yu and the Abbot T'ai-hsu.

Chiang Kai-Shek and his New Life Movement is also an example of the traditionalist attitude that Western individualism and materialism were a threat to Chinese civilization, that they should be rejected therefore and that a return to orthodox Confucianism was in order.[9] He saw no need for changing social and political institutions but would have a people transformed inwardly and supporting worthy rulers such as he conceived himself to be. And

Liang Ch'i-ch'ao, who had at first ardently championed westernization, turned to the opposite after his trip to the post-World-war-I West which he believed had become a victim of its own fanatic nationalism, materialism and individualism.

While there were disagreements among traditionalists, they were minor. They all agreed that there was an urgent need to develop a sense of nationalism, self-identity or national unity. They were unanimous in their rejecting of ethical relativity and asserted, as was mentioned before, that society must be grounded in morality not utility. They were concerned that the traditional extended family system was being endangered and that the sentiment of filial piety was being weakened. They were apprehensive of the Western individualistic as compared to their own group-oriented society. They believed greater emphasis should be given to the five "great relationships" and that duties had precedence over rights. Few among them felt any overwhelming attraction for the alien faith of orthodox Christianity, three reasons being among others its dim view of man which contrasted with the more optimistic Chinese one, its denial of filial piety as seen in such statements of Jesus as "I came to set a man at variance with father and the daughter against her mother", and "He that loveth father and mother more than me is not worth of me", and its doctrine of the vicarious atonement of Christ which was seen as an abrogation of individual moral responsiblity. The traditionalists reiterated instead their own pluralistic tradition of the "Three Ways," Taoism, Buddhism and Confucianism.[10]

The closing of China to the West for nearly three decades after 1949 represents on the one hand a revolt against Western ideas and influences and on the other hand a combination of syncretism and traditionalism. For it was a period in which China turned in upon itself, sought to consolidate herself, restore national stability, unity and identity, and attempted to digest those foreign influences she had already accepted. She shut off the flow of external "isms" and influences, attempted to restore self-confidence by pulling herself up through her own efforts and engaged in a sorting out of her past to discover that which was relevant and valuable for the present. Thus we have Mao affirming the traditional and recurring doctrine of Chinese philosophy on the unity of knowledge and practice and at the same time his accepting Western type industrialization, to be instigated gradually and not abruptly however.

II

A study of Chinese thought and philosophy and its relationship to Chinese culture and history inevitably raises questions of a comparative type or leads a non-Chinese reader especially to make comparisons between his own culture and the philosophy or culture studied.[11] The contemporary world is one in which technology has made cultural interaction relatively easy also. As to the nature of the world of the future, one wonders if it will be a monotonously monolithic one of the Western urban-industrialized type, or a pluralistic one in which various cultures retain their own basic identity although at the same time accepting that which may be best from other cultures, and contributing what is good from their own to the rest. The result would be a cultural pluralism along with a syncretism. Assuming this latter as the better alternative, what the Chinese tradition can offer for a hopefully better world is the theme to be dealt with now.

In comparing Chinese and non-Chinese views, we might start with the traditional view of man and emphasize what has been mentioned only briefly before that it differs from such views as the orthodox Christian view of man as sinner, the Darwinian view of man as animal, and the dialectical view of man as master of all he surveys, all of which have been extremely influential in the West. The Chinese tradition on the other hand asserts an optimistic anthropology, rejects the man-animal distinction, and places man in, not apart from, nature.[12]

Mencius typifies the Chinese view. "Man's nature is naturally good just as water naturally flows downward," he said. He added, furthermore, that "All men have a mind which cannot bear to see the sufferings of others" and pointed to the feeling of distress everyone experiences on seeing a child about to fall into a well. Mencius' doctrine of the four beginnings asserts man's natural virtue in four respects: "...we see that no man is without a sense of compassion, or a sense of shame, or a sense of courtesy, or a sense of right and wrong. Every man has within himself these four beginnings, just as he has four limbs." Mencius' view of man's innate virtuosity became the classical Chinese one, and it poses an obvious challenge today to those cultures or traditions which assert the opposite.

Many Chinese Buddhists as well as the Neo-Confucianists asserted an anti-Darwinian, anti-dialectical, optimistic view of man. Typical of the former are the affirmations that "Non-attachment is man's original nature...our nature is originally pure...self-nature is always pure, just as the sun and moon are always shining." Among the Neo-Confucianists Shao Yung wrote, "The nature of all things is complete in the human species...Man occupies the most honoured position in the scheme of things because he combines in him the principles of all species...Man is central in the universe, and the mind is central in man...The spirit of man is the same as the spirit of Heaven and earth." Chou Tun-yi declared, "It is man alone who receives [the material forces] in their highest excellence, and therefore he is most intelligent." Ch'eng Hao stated that "Man is not the only perfectly intelligent creature in the universe. The human mind (in essence) is the same as that of plants and trees." As noted before, Chang Tsai asserted, "Heaven is my father and earth is my mother, and even such a small creature as I find an intimate place in their midst." And Wang Yang-ming believed that "The nature endowed in us by Heaven is pure and perfect."

The statements above present no picture of man as an animal. Rather they attribute to man a high or exalted but not unique or superior position in the universe. He forms a trinity with Heaven and earth. He is one with all things because he is made of the same substance as other things. The Western man-animal distinction is absent, as is a sharp animate-inanimate dichotomy. Man is a part of and not apart from the rest of the universe. He is not isolated from and set in a dialectical relationship of conflict with the rest of reality. This is significant in regard to man's attitude toward nature. He does not view himself as its master and conqueror. Instead he seeks to establish a harmonious, working relationship with it. The theme of the harmony of man and nature found sypathetic support in Taoism. Its artistic expression is the great landscape paintings of Ma Yuan, Chao Po-chu, Hsia Kuei, and others in which man is present in but does not dominate the scene. Placed in such a position, man's egoism is not stimulated. At the same time he has a place in the universe. It is his home. He belongs to it, although it does not belong to him. It is not alien to him and he is not alienated from it.

The Chinese view of man may be described further as a teleological one in that it declares man's goal is to become fully man. Man's task is to realize his inherent humanness or humaneness; in Buddhist terminology he is to achieve Buddhahood. The roots or beginnings of wisdom, virtue, and sageliness are in each of us. How much they grow varies with individuals. Confucius noted this in his observation that "Men are by nature very similar, but by practice they come to be very different."

The means by which man becomes fully man is self-rectification. Confucius emphasized daily examination in three respects, as has been noted already. It is the first lesson taught in the *Great Learning*. Buddhism reinforced the theme in such statements of Buddha's as "As rain breaks through an ill-thatched house, passion will break through an unreflecting mind.[13] As rain does not break through a well-thatched house, passion will not break through a well-reflecting mind...Let a wise man blow off the impurities of his self, as a smith blows off the impurities of silver, one by one, little by little, and from time to time." Wang Yang-ming continued the theme of mental discipline in his assertion that "The main thing is for the mind to make an effort to get rid of selfish human desires and preserve the Principle of Nature," and his query "...how can anyone who does not watch over himself carefully when alone...attain to such a state of perfection ?"

The teleological view which upholds an initial goodness in man is at variance with the Western Calvinist view of man as inherent sinner and utterly depraved, completely dependent on God for self-realization and salvation from evil. The former's value is that it places moral responsibility upon the individual and does not allow him the many excuse philosophies we find today: the placing of blame on environment, fate, circumstances, God's will, childhood conditioning, government, or animal nature rather than ourselves. It insists that we start with ourselves and not others and that we take our share of the blame rather than locating it all elsewhere.

In this respect Confucius' "Superior Man" is a relevant and instructive figure. The superior or "Great" man "...demands it of himself; Petty man, of others," Confucius said. Moreover, the superior man is impartial, the petty man partial. The superior man "...cherishes excellence; Petty man his own comfort." The Great Man "...is dignified but not proud. Petty man is proud but not dignified." The superior man "...is accommodating, but he is not one of the crowd. Petty man is one of the crowd, but he is also a source of discord." The Great Man "is conscious only of justice; petty man only of self-interest."

It is significant that Confucius uses virtue as a test of greatness. The "Superior Man" is a paradigm of morality. In Chinese thought magnanimity is associated with virtue, not utility.[14] Such characteristics as aggressiveness, forcefulness, assertiveness and others are not extolled as marks of eminence, as is often the case today. Thus the Chinese tradition presents us with a much needed reminder that greatness is qualitative, not quantitative in nature.

It may be noted further that Confucius' distinctions between the superior and inferior man are as valid today as in Confucius' time. Confucius presented the Chinese tradition with a model of what man might be. Experience would seem to confirm the assertion that the model might well be a universally adoptable one.

The emphasis on self-rectification is one clue to the Chinese solution to the problem of evil. If man is good and nature is benign, how does one account for suffering and wrong in the world? Mencius argued it was due to man's failure to develop his original nature. "It is only neglect and abuse of this innate goodness which leads men into evil ways...Let every man but attend to expanding and developing these four beginnings that are in our very being, and they will issue forth like a conflagration being kindled and a spring being opened up. If they can be fully developed, these virtues are capable of safeguarding all within the four seas; if allowed to remain undevoloped, they will not suffice even for serving one's parents."

Confucius had earlier formulated the Mencian view. He also sympathized with the tradition that emphasized evil as a result of deviating from the mean or path of moderation. Confucius described the superior man as one who "embodies the course of the mean" while "the mean man acts contrary to the course of the mean." In the classic *Doctrine of The Mean* the sage king Shun is praised as one who "...determined the mean and employed it in his government of the people." Chinese Buddhists also extolled the "Middle Way" as the way of avoiding evil. Neo-Confucianists such as Ch'eng Hao continued the theme as we see in his statements, "Good and evil in the world are both the Principle of Nature. What is called evil is not original evil. It becomes evil only because of deviation from the Mean."

Others offered a psychological explanation of evil. Wang Yang-ming declared that when man's mind "...is aroused by desire and obscured by selfishness, compelled by greed for gain and fear of harm, and stirred by anger, he will destroy things, kill members of his own species, and will do everything." Earlier Shao Yung had written "Our nature views things as they are, but our passion causes us to see things subjectively and egotistically. Our nature is impartial and enlightened, but our passions are partial and deceived." He brought in the Yang-Yin, too, for "If yang predominates, he will be off balance toward weakness." When a man reaches a balance between the two forces he will not be ruled by passions and partiality but will be impartial and reasonable. Yen Yuan offered a similar view when he wrote that "...physical nature is a concentration of the two material forces (yin and yang or passive and active cosmic forces) and the four virtues. How can we say that it is evil? Evil is due to attraction, obscuration, and bad influence." A century later Tai Chen wrote "The greatest troubles of people in the world, whether past or present, are the two items of selfishness and obscuration. Selfishness is the product of error in desire, and obscuration is the product of error in knowledge."

A Buddhist contribution to Chinese thought was its teaching that suffering has both a discernible cause and cure. It is due to craving, and the way to alleviate suffering is to curb our desires and stop craving for things which are unnecessary. Taoism, too, emphasized the minimizing of one's wants and demands. In Lao Tzu's words, "Let people hold on to these: Manifest plainnes , embrace simplicity, reduce selfishness, have few desires."

One might summarize the Chinese tradition in this matter by saying it views evil humanistically. The Chinese do not solicit an all-powerful God to vindicate evil. Nor do they posit a Satan as its source. Instead, wrong is created by man and is, therefore, resolvable by him. It is a result of ignorance, whose cure is education as

Confucius would say, or enlightenment if you prefer the Buddhist alternative. It is due to disharmony, to imbalance. Evil is man's responsibility. Since he caused it, he must assuage it.

The Chinese view of evil, then is in contrast to the dominant Western theistic view which incorporates the God-Satan dichotomy and presupposes good and evil as absolutes and antithetical. To the Chinese the absolutizing of good and evil is undesirable. For if to be good is to always be battling evil, then one is consigned to a life of constant warfare with evils which may often be more imagined than real. Moreover, the emphasis highlighted by Chinese Buddhism on evil being a result of craving is especially relevant to today's world in which man makes exorbitant demands on his universe and esteems self-assertion and the exercise of the will as a means of satisfying his demands.

III

In discussing the Chinese religious tradition one might note that it is characterized by pluralism and diffusion. Pluralism is reflected in the classical view that there is not just one religion or way but three, the three "Ways" of Confucianism, Taoism, and Buddhism. Diffusion found expression in the numerous temples scattered throughout the countryside, independent of each other, and in which it was not uncommon to find statues of numerous deities. The absence of a single, highly centralized or institutional religion meant there was no religious autocracy exercising great, direct influence on the State. Even Buddhism at its peak was unable to.

The external form of a Trinitarian diffusion which religion took in China may well have been a result of several tenets around which the religious tradition centered. One was the refusal to accept the Western disjunction between the One true God and the many false gods. Another was the disinclination to see religious truth as revealed truth. A third was the hesitancy to separate the sacred and the profane.[15] A fourtth was the failure to anthropomorphize and exult God, to conceive of the one God as a being on high with the same attributes as man. A fifth was the prevalence of a functional rather than idealistic relationship with the Divine.

Without the first distinction there could be no soldiers of the One True God engaging in battle the pagan followers of the many false gods. However, if there are many gods rather than one, as the Christian believes, a person's faith need not be limited to just one; and there would be no compulsion toward quarreling with others whose experiences with a different god were equally meaningful.[16]

Without the second tendency to see religion as revelation there could be no especially chosen people to whom God has revealed himself, whose duty and destiny was to proselytize and insure, in whatever ways circumstances demanded, that all people recognize and accept that revelation. Instead truth could be accepted as subjective and personal and each could traverse the path of truth clearest to him. Further, absence of revelation in the Chinese religious tradition meant that there was no single, sacred scripture which embodies that revelation serving as a standard against which all other purported scriptures were measured and found wanting. There was no requirement of assent to such a scripture in order to be a true believer and the persecuting as heretics of those who dissented. In a religious tradition in which such features are absent, the attitude of superiority is not elicited, for there is little present to stimulate such.

The failure to sharply distinguish between the secular and divine, this life and the next, or this world and some other made possible a belief in hovering spirits, in ancestor reverence, fatalism and ritualism which have been discussed earlier.[17]

The absence of belief in a single personal Deity on high had several implications. It meant that such a Being could not be used by man as a model for his actions. It meant that men could not confuse their wills with God's and rationalize their actions as the carrying out of God's will rather than their own. If there was no God characterized by jealousy, man could not be jealous of and vindictive toward others whose faiths were different.

The functional rather than idealistic orientation of Chinese religion meant that the Gods are not wholly transcendent.[18] Instead, being little more than men, they can be bargained with for favors and dispensed with when not needed for such. On a conceptual level, it meant that religion is not a matter of truth or falsehood, or that the categories of true and false are relevant to religion. Instead, meaningfulness is the central criterion. If one's relationship to a god is meaningful and fruitful, continue with it. If not, strike up a relationship with a different deity. The absence of the categories of truth and falsehood as related to religion made for a religious tradition in China in which neither dogma nor dogmatism were prevalent. An elaborate dogma or theology can develop only where such dualities as revealed or not revealed, right or wrong, transcendent or immanent are the roots of religion. Where a religious tradition is functionally oriented, they do not. Similarly the heretic-true believer distinction and wars of religion can be present in the former but not the latter.

The associating of religion with antithetical forces eternally at war with one another, the notion of one God, holy and transcendent, to whom one gives single, absolute loyalty and devotion and on whom one is completely dependent, these and other beliefs like those sketched above were unfamiliar to the Chinese. They made the majority of Chinese reluctant to accept Western Christianity as it came to China in the 19th century and finally in the 20th century to exclude it. Such particularistic, absolute, exclusivist religion was too much for the Chinese people to bear.

The technological revolution of the 20th century has led to a growing awareness among people of the differing religious traditions throughout the world. It has brought into focus several questions. What are valid criteria for evaluating religion? What are some possible types of attitudes and relationships between the adherents of different faiths? Are we to have a pluralistic or monolithic religious world? A central contribution of Chinese religion is that it forces the adherents of other, differing religious tradition to re-examine or re-evaluate their beliefs, and it serves notice that imperialism in religion as in other aspects of life is unacceptable and fruitless.

IV

Running through Chinese thought are several recurring themes regarding the nature of reality. The tracing of all existences to a single one; attributing preeminence to the two forces Yin and Yang; seeing nature as an organism, an inter-related, interdependent totality of many parts in which non-dialectical or reciprocal forces are at work; viewing reality in terms of balance, harmony, complementaries, unity in diversity; change as emergence and nature as good or benign are some.[19]

The extensive literature of China offers many examples of these views. The *Book of Changes* declares, "Through the movement and repose of their interaction come all things between Heaven and Earth." We read in the *Doctrine of The Mean*: "All things are nourished together without their injuring one another. The courses of the seasons, and of the sun and moon, are pursued without any collision among them." Moreover, "...a happy order will prevail throughout heaven and earth, and all things will be nourished and flourish" when "...the states of equilibrium and harmony exist in perfection..."

For Lao Tzu primal reality is the *Tao*, the central unity—"There was someting undifferentiated and yet complete, which existed before heaven and earth. Soundless and formless, it depends on nothing and does not change." He declared, further, that "Being and non-being produce each other; difficult and easy complete each other...sound and voice harmonize each other; front and behind accompany each other." Of the named and nameless, being and non-being, he said "The two are the same, but after they are produced, they have different names."

Chinese Buddhists such as Hua-yen continued these themes in their own way. In discussing the *Rounded Doctrine of the One Vehicle* he said, "The all is the one...and the one is the all, for the relation between cause and effect is clear." Reality is inter-related in terms of cause and effect or the principle of Dependent Origination. Given this, that follows. His reference to the "gate of different formation of separate dharmas in ten ages" is an example —"Altogether there are three times three units, thus forming nine ages, and these, grouped together, become the total gate to truth. Although there are nine ages, each separate from the other, yet, since they are formed because of one another, they are harmoniously merged and mutually penetrated without obstacle and together constitute one instant of time."

In Medieval China such views were propagated by the Neo-Confucianists. Chou Tun yi's declaration, "Great is the ch'ien, the originator! All things obtain their beginning from it," has been noted earlier. Ch'eng I asserted that "Principle is one but its manifestations are many" and "Although things involve many events and events go through infinite variations, when they are united by the one, there cannot be any contradiction." According to Chu Hsi "...there is only one Great Ultimate, yet each of the myriad things has been endowed with it..." and "Principle has never been separated from material force...Fundamentally principle and material force cannot be spoken of as prior or posterior."

These views were taken up by later thinkers too. Yen Yuan wrote that "The nature of the ten thousand things is an endowment of principle, and their physical nature is a consolidation of material force. What is balanced is this principle and material force...what is mixed is none other than this principle and this material force..." T'an Ssu-t'ung stated that "Throughout the realms of elements of existence...there is something supremely refined and subtle, which makes everything adhere, penetrates everything, and connects everything so that all is permeated by it. ...The realms of elements of existence, empty space, and sentient beings all issue from it." Of the Primal Ch'i K'ang Yu-wei wrote, "Although individual forms may differ in size, still, they are all but parts of the all-embracing ch'i of the ultimate beginning of the universe."

The significance and relevance of these Chinese metaphysical views becomes apparent when we contrast them with the dialectical dualism which has dominated and to a large extent still dominates Western metaphysical thought.[20] Dialectical dualism is based on the law of the excluded middle and the method of compartmentalization. It holds that reality can be divided legitimately into parts or categories, each with distinctive features, a major division being between the animate and inanimate. The either/or distinction is asserted to be universal—this or that, true or false, good or bad, right or wrong, hero or villain, saved or redeemed; there is no middle ground.

Such thinking facilitates the extending of the notion of differences into opposites, opposition, hostility, inevitable conflict and war. In the end it leads to seeing reality as characterized by particularism, exclusiveness, absolutes, polarities, disharmony and antagonism. The significance of such metaphysical views is underlined when they are carried over into the realm of human reality, as was done by the Social Darwinist of the West in the nineteenth century. It led them to set life and human relations into a context of brute force, rule by the strongest, survival of the fittest, competition and self-interest, nature being used as a rationalization for such. Since competition for survival is the law of the jungle, an economic system based on that principle is quite acceptable. Power politics is a correlate of rule by the strongest in nature. Classism or social classes are inevitable since there are distinctions between species in nature as well. Exploitative relationships in society need cause no alarm, since the domination of the more by the less fit is nature's way.

On the other hand, much has been said already about the Chinese way of viewing reality in terms of the principle of inclusion, complementaries, and a plurality which are manifestations of a One. Exclusivism and dialecticalism (the presence of opposite, inevitably conflicting forces) were rejected in metaphysics as in religion. Social Darwinism would be an impossible implication of such a view, and the question Chinese metaphysics presents us with is not only whether its view is valid but also whether it may not be a more profitable or fruitful view. Is reality most truly and best characterized by logical, rational, spatial categories or by what might be called ontological-existential ones? Are human institutions based on a Darwinian view of nature desirable or the best man can devise?

Questions regarding the nature of reality cannot be separated from the question of man's relationship to reality or nature, especially today. The Chinese tradition is relevant to the second question, too. It has been noted already that, as classical Chinese landscape painting suggests, man is viewed as not a master of, but co-worker with, nature. Man's relationship to nature is not a dualistic, dialectical one. He is not separate from it and is not its supreme Lord. It does not exist to be manipulated and exploited by him. It is not there for him alone.[21]

One aspect of Chinese Buddhism is its view that man shares reality with other sentient beings; it is not solely man's. It is not his exclusive possession; in fact, it does not exist to be possessed but rather to be involved with, to become one with and share in its effluence. When nature is seen in this light, man's reaction to it is one of gratitude, obligation, praise, and sharing, an aesthetic as much as utilitarian response.

On the other hand, its dualistic metaphysics has led Western man to see himself as distinct and set apart from nature as its sovereign master. His relationship to nature is an acquisitive, exploitative, primarily utilitarian one. In an era in which we are beginning to question and become concerned over the resources nature has to offer us, the Chinese tradition poses the question of what is the most desirable attitude to have toward nature, an exploitative or appreciative one.

V

Associated with the question of man's relationship to nature is the problem of the function of the mind in relation to reality. One way of looking at the matter is to assert that the role of the mind is to analyze in order to control and exploit. The mind is to be used for the production of sense data with which we can manipulate and utilize the external world.

From a second perspective, however, the proper task of the mind is to understand in order to appreciate and become one with. The more we understand the universe, the more we are struck by its wonder, grandeur, intricacy, and magnificence, and the less we wish to selfishly manipulate it.

The Chinese tradition favors the second alternative more. Shao Yung's assertion illustrates this—"The learning of a gentleman aims precisely at enriching his personality. The rest, such as governing people and handling things, is all secondary." According to his statement the purpose of knowing is first a moral-spiritual one and secondly a practical one. The developing of character and the ordering of human relations is the first task of the intellect. All else follows from it.

The relevance and import of this view to today's world is obvious. It is one in which materialism holds increasing sway, resulting in a growing, monolithic world culture empirically oriented, based on science and technology, in which the principal function of the mind is believed to be an expedient and utilitarian one. The vast reservoir of human intelligence is used much more for the production of external paraphernalia than for the sensitizing of life and the perfecting of human relationships.[22] The Chinese view raises a question regarding the desirability of such a development and end, not denying the pragmatic function of the mind but insisting on the non-utilitarian as well. For the mind which is motivated solely by gain becomes a decadent mind, since it is rooted in selfishness; and selfishness, as Mo Tzu and other Chinese have pointed out is self-defeating in the end.

A second aspect of the Chinese epistemological tradition is its emphasis upon viewing totalistically.[23] If reality is whole, then knowledge to be genuine must be knowledge of the whole. Confucius and Chuang Tzu may be cited in this respect. Confucius said, "Great man reaches complete understanding of the main issues; petty man reaches complete understanding of the minute details" and "Those born with an understanding of the universe belong to the highest type of humanity. Those who understand it as the result of study come second. Those who study it with great difficulty come third." In each utterance, understanding is associated with breadth of vision and has a moral connotation as well.

Chuang Tzu put the matter thus—"Great knowledge embraces the whole: small knowledge, a part only. Great speech is universal: small speech is particular." "Only the truly intelligent understand this principle of the identity of all things..." and "To wear out one's intellect is an obstinate adherence to the individuality of things, not recognizing the fact that all things are one..." These statements indicate that Chuang Tzu saw reality as an organic whole and that, consequently, true knowledge embraces the whole.

Chinese Buddhists such as Hui-ssu continued this tendency toward epistemological and metaphysical non-dualism. He wrote, "As to the function of concentration and insight: It means that because of the accomplishment of concentration, the Pure Mind is realized in substance, the nature which is without duality is harmonized through principle (li, rational nature of things), these and all sentient beings are harmoniously identified to form a body of one single character. Thereupon the Three Treasures are merged together without being three, and because of this the Two Levels of Truth are fused without being two. How calm, still, and pure! How deep, stable, and quiet! How pure and clear the inner silence! It functions without the character of functioning, and acts without the character of acting. It is so because all dharmas are from the very beginning the same and not differentiated and because the nature of the mind is naturally so. This is the substance of the most profound Dharma-nature."

For the Chinese, totalistic-type thinking involves not making an absolute distinction between subject and object, perceiver and perceived in the sense that Chuang Tzu meant when he said, "So it is that to place oneself in subjective relation with externals, without consciousness of their objectivity—this is the Tao." Totalistic thinking incorporates synthesis as well as analysis, not stopping with parts but bringing them together into an integral whole. For reality consists of both the inner and outer, material and immaterial, subjective and objective, an entity and its context, the particular and the universal.

From a Chinese view the positivism and empiricism which dominates much of modern thinking is far too one-sided. It assumes and concentrates on one type of reality only. The method of analysis is too limiting a one, for it separates and divides reality and focuses on details severed from the whole. The method of categorization is questionable for it assumes the complete comprehensibility of reality and may involve man's creating and forcing distinctions upon reality which may not be present in it. And the importance attributed to words is excessive and egoistic, for it leads man to believe that he can name everything that is and that whatever cannot be named does not exist, an attitude that takes no account of Lao Tzu's assertion, "The Tao that can be told is not the eternal Tao; the name that can be named is not the eternal name."

There is another aspect of the Chinese epistemological tradition which is significant and relevant. In one of his books Professor Creel writes, "In the Occident we have tended to think of truth as being immutable, and to think that a god or a very wise man must partake of the unbending character of absolute truth." This is what might be called epistemological absolution. It leads the Westerner to think in terms of fixed standards of truth, that truth is something one gets at a certain point in time by doing this or that, that truth and falsehood are opposites and that falsehood is on one side and truth on another—usually his—and that compromise is bad and to be disavowed. There is another way of looking at the truth, however, one which is more in keeping with the Chinese view. The true and the right are not to be conceived of in terms of the categories of eternal and immutable, but rather fitting and suitable. Moreover, what is fitting and suitable at one time may not be at another, and similarly with persons. It is not a matter of truth being non-existent. The notion of truth is eternal and universal; its content varies in time and place. And since truth is always related to context, the functional concept of truth is the preferable one.

It follows from this that truth seeking is what is important. Truth is a goal we aim at and never quite reach. The failure to do so does not keep us from trying, however. And perhaps it is better that truth is ultimately elusive, for this discourages epistemological arrogance and dictatorship. The point here is that, while the Chinese view advocates seeing as a whole, it rejects epistemological, as well as metaphysical and theological, absolutism and exclusivism. It does not demand ultimate explanations but is content with functional ones enabling man to live the best that time and circumstances allow.

Chinese thinkers also remind us that epistemology and ethics are correlated in that truth cannot be attained without inner purification. Confucius' statement may be taken as an example of this—"The true gentleman, in the world, is neither predisposed for anything nor against anything; he will side with whatever is right." The mind must be freed of biases or preconceptions in order to be able to discern what is right or wrong in a given situation. Ridding oneself of undesirable mental states was expressed differently by Wang Yang-ming—"If now we concentrate our thoughts upon extending intuitive knowledge, so as to sweep away all the barriers caused by selfish desires, the original state will then again be restored, and we will again become part of the profundity of Heaven." Here the emphasis is upon ridding oneself of certain desires in order to know truth.

Chinese Buddhists strongly emphasized mental purity or the need to free the mind from craving and worldly attachment. Fa-Tsang declared to the empress, "By avoiding both attachment and renunciation, one, along this very road, flows into the sea of perfect knowledge." Hui-neng wrote, "If one is externally attached to phenomena, the inner mind will at once be disturbed, but if one is externally free from phenomena, the inner nature will not be perturbed." And a statement from the *Platform Scripture* which has both ethical and epistemological connotations and contemporary significance is: "Self-enlightenment and practice do not consist in argument. If one is concerned about which comes first, he is a deluded person. If he is not freed from the consideration of victory or defeat, he will produce the dharmas as real entities and cannot be free from the Four Characters (of coming into existence' remaining in the same state, change, and going out of existence)."

Neo-Confucianists found themselves in agreement with Buddhists on the need for mental purification. Shao Yung wrote, "When the mind retains its unity and is not disturbed, it can act on, and react to, all things harmoniously" and "The human mind should be as calm as still water. Being calm, it will be tranquil, it will be enlightened." Calmness is a result of not being disturbed by passions such as selfish desires or ambitions which lead us to bend reality to our ends.

The point that the Chinese thinkers are making is that epistemology and ethics are related, that turth can be attained only when the truth-seeker is freed from bias. Mental purity is a prerequisite to true knowledge, a maxim as relevant today as before.

VI

A further correlation between epistemology and ethics is reflected in K'ang Yu-wei's statement, "Those whose perceptiveness and awareness is small, their loving mind is also small; those whose perceptiveness and awareness is great, their jen-mind is also great. Boundless love goes with boundless perceptiveness." In terms of K'ang's assertion, knowing is defined as sensing or being aware of and sensitive to. Chinese Buddhists stressed this also, for to perceive is to be aware of the misfortunes of mankind and to identify with and respond in love to suffering mankind. The greater one's awareness, then, the greater one's love. This suggests in turn that a non-dualistic epistemology in which subject and object are not viewed as separate in consciousness is more likely to lead to an ethics of love.

In discussing the nature and relevance of Chinese ethical thought several further points may be made. One is that we see several attributes extolled by Confucianist, Buddhist, and Taoist alike such as sincerity, human-heartedness, compassion, loyalty, gentleness, mutuality, generosity, dutifulness, harmony and moderation. These characteristics were accepted universally as desirable. The Sage and "Superior Man" embody them; all should strive for them.

This does not mean that Chinese ethical thought is absolutistic and dogmatic, however. Professor Creel points out that the Chinese disavow the Western view that "truth and virtue are somehow fixed and absolute things with which the wise and good man has established communion." Instead virtue, like truth, is conceived of functionally. There is a right and wrong, in the sense of appropriateness for each situation. It may not be the same, however, in every situation; for no two situations or persons are exactly alike. Confucius was very aware of this. It was one reason for his advocating the mean or the middle course, although admitting at the same time that what may be the mean for one person may not be for another.

If there are no ethical absolutes or universals, does this mean the good is completely relative? No, the Chinese ethical tradition does not admit this. It holds instead to what might be called a relative-absolutism. There are values such as sincerity which are good in all times and places; what action is required by sincerity in one situation may not be exactly the same in another.

Such a modesty in ethics makes for more flexibility in human relationships. It permits greater consideration for individual differences. While setting limits, it allows for room within them. It necessitates greater moral responsibility on the part of the individual, however; and moral decisions become harder to make. However, if man does possess reason and a moral faculty, a relative-absolutism ethics gives man both an opportunity and obligation to exercise them.

The relevance of this type of ethical system would seem obvious. One can see in the West in the last two centuries almost a full swing of the pendulum from an absolutist to relativist ethics. The belief in universal moral laws binding on all yielded to an ethical anarchy under which each one sets himself up as the sole arbiter of right and wrong. The Chinese ethical tradition reflects a path which strikes a balance between the two extremes.

One is reminded by this of the distinction between rights and duties. The liberal Western tradition of the past two centuries has emphasized the rights much more than the duties of the individual. The growth of ethical relativism is an indication of this. By contrast, the emphasis in the Chinese tradition is upon duties. The individual is set within and not apart from the group and his relation to the group is a duties-oriented relation, e.g. the children's obligation to parents, the subjects' to the sovereign, and vice-versa. What Chinese ethics reminds us of is that the ethics of individual rights may have been carried too far and needs to be counter-balanced by an ethics of obligation. Individuals may have rights, but they have duties also. In fact, for each right is there not a concomitant duty? The Chinese tradition answers in the affirmative.

A tacit implication of ethical relativism is the premise of the individual over the common good. There are both possible and actual examples of societies in which greater emphasis is on the good of the individual and others in which the good of the individual is subsumed in the common good. Modern Western liberalism has tended toward the former, granting a lower priority to the common good and exulting the individual's.

The Chinese tradition, on the other hand, has upheld as a correlate to an ethics of duties an ethics of the whole. Duties to self are at the lower end of the scale of duties. Again, a contribution the Chinese tradition can make today is to question the appropriateness of the Western liberal view. In the process of doing so it can point out that the dichotomy often affirmed by the liberal between the good of the individual and the group may be a false one. It is based on an invalid separation of the two. In actuality, individuals seldom live in isolation. A person's actions always affect others to one degree or another; therefore, he cannot realistically assert absolute sovereignty for himself, and his good or well-being is always interrelated with others.

One concern of ethics is motivation. Assuming general agreement as to the good, a subsequent question is why do the good. The profit-righteousness (li-yi) distinction found in Chinese ethics indicates two possible motives, the expedient and the idealistic. One does the right in order to get something from doing so or simply for its own sake. That man is constantly facing a choice between the two is illustrated amply in Chinese literature. Confucius noted "He who engages solely in self-interest actions will make himself many enemies" and "He who concentrates upon the task and forgets about reward may be called Man-at-his-best." Chuang Tzu represented the Taoist tradition in his statement, "He who calculates opportunity is not a worthy person." Lao Tzu himself advised, "Abandon skill and discard profit," and in distinguishing between the two types asserted, "The man of inferior virtue takes action and has an ulterior motive to do so. The man of superior humanity takes action, but has no ulterior motive to do so".

Mencius was especially outspoken in his disdain of the profit motive. When on a visit to him, King Hwuy asked for words of counsel "to profit my kingdom", Mencius replied, "Why must your Majesty use that word profit? What I am likewise provided with are counsels to benevolence and righteousness, and these are my only topics." Later in the *Book of Mencius* we read his assertion, "The regular path of virtue is to be pursued without any bend, and from no view to emolument." A later statement of the same theme is Wang Yang-ming's, "The reason the great man is able to be one with Heaven, Earth, and all things, is not that he is thus for some purpose, but because the human-heartedness of his mind is naturally so."

There is agreement in the statements above that an act and its consequences cannot be separated from motives and that the idealistic is the more desirable motive. Of course the Confucianist recognized that good will usually come to one from doing good. But this is because of the law of cause and effect or the principle of reciprocity. The Buddhist calls this the principle of the Dependent Origination, as exemplified in Buddha's words, "Since it is impossible to escape the results of our deeds, let us practice good work."

Expediency and egoism seem to dominate our ethics today. We tend to approach situations from the "what can be gotten out of it for me," attitude. The results are not always the best. For, if a person is motivated by profits only, he is much less apt to do the good, as Kant pointed out, at those times, which are many, when he will get nothing from doing so. He will more likely place his above the general good. He is more apt to be turned inward and devoid of compassion and concern for his fellowmen. Confucianism offers an ethics of idealism which, even from a pragmatic standpoint, may be more desirable.

Another concern of ethics is the criteria of the good. Utilitarianism is one. The Chinese attitude toward the utilitarian criterion is that it is, by itself, an incomplete one. One of its dangers is that it may be used for evaluating human as well as material reality. This seems to predominate in the West today, and in other areas where a technological culture is developing. We are so habitualized to evaluating things in terms of their usefulness that we carry it over into evaluating persons as well. The utilitarian test may be valid

...ersons are not things or objects to
... seful they are to someone else.
... idual and insist on a social as well
... od, as has been noted already.[24] The
... n is seen in Chuang Tzu's question,
... with me. If you beat me, instead of my
... cessarily right and am I necessarily wrong?
... not you me, am I necessarily right, and are
... rong?" What his words point to is that a victory
... er is not necessarily a triumph of truth or goodness.
Truth is not enthroned by force. A superiority of power does not determine the right, personally or nationally, an admonition which the so-called "great" nations of the world today might well be reminded of.

Many authors point out the absence of wars of external aggression and a war hero mythology in Chinese history. The soldier has been traditionally looked down upon. Wars and warfare have been condemned by Confucianist, Mohist, Buddhist, and Taoist alike. Lao Tzu wrote, "He who assists the ruler with Tao does not dominate the world with force...Fine weapons are instruments of evil...when he uses them unavoidably, he regards calm restraint as the best principle. Even when he is victorious, he does not regard it as praiseworthy, for to praise victory is to delight in the slaughter of men." Thus even a so-called "righteous" war is lamented, and war as a means of solving problems is seen as an inferior one.

The test or criterion of means is a further one with which the Chinese tradition has been concerned. The general tendency has been to insist on the correlation and consistency of means and ends. If evil means are used, it will lead to bad ends. Only good means should be used to achieve good ends. Evil means should not be used to achieve a good end. Confucius was concerned about means—"Look at the means which a man employs; consider his motives; observe his pleasures. A man simply cannot conceal himself!"—and pointed out that "Wealth and honors are what men desire; but if they come undeserved, don't keep them. Poverty and low estate are what men dislike; but if they come misdeserved, don't flee them."

The question of criteria or tests for determining the good or

right is as significant today as ~~~
contribution to make in its insiste~~
sal to limit the criteria to the emp~~
nating today. It insists on a qualitat~~
terion of the good.

A further relevant feature of traditio~~
conceiving of ethics in terms of attitude~~
virtuous is to have a certain set of attitudes~~
he or she approaches a situation requiring a ch~~
attitudes such as sincerity and human-heartedness,~~
ed on by Confucianist, Taoist, and Buddhist alike, have been noted already. If those attitudes have become ingrained in one or so much a part of one that one acts unconsciously in terms of them, he will not need rules or injunctions to determine what to do in a given situation. The better way will be immediately apparent to him.

This trans-legalism or attitudinal ethics, which is a major feature of the Chinese moral tradition, is appropriate and valuable today. Because it is not based on an exclusivist dualism, it avoids the pitfalls of absolutism which have been indicated previously. Non-absolutism in ethics, as in religion, metaphysics, and epistemology, is a contribution of the Chinese tradition.

VII

As to social thought, one aspect of the Chinese tradition which merits consideration today is its insistence that a society must be grounded ultimately in virtue not utility, if it is to endure.[25] The statement in *The Great Learning* that "In a state pecuniary gain is not to be considered prosperity, but its prosperity will be found in righteousness" is an indication of this. The same text, as noted earlier, points out that "Virtue is the root, wealth is the result," implying that stability is less likely in a society in which ends are subordinated to means and wrong means are justified in terms of a good end. Confucius' statement about wealth and honor is a refutation of such as is the Buddha's injunction, "Exult not thyself by trampling others down."[26] A society grounded in utility and expediency is more apt to accept questionable means to good ends than would one grounded in virtue.

The criterion of virtue is significant today also in relation to the question of the nature and means of progress. What is social progress to be measured in terms of? From the Chinese tradition come several answers. First, true progress occurs only when, not a minority, or even a majority, but all progress. There is not genuine progress unless everyone benefits. Otherwise, there will be some who are envious of others. Conflict results, leading to regress, not progress.

Secondly, progress, to use earlier terms, is qualitative as much as quantitative. Fung Yu-lan points out that Chinese philosophy "...has always emphasized what man is rather than what man has, and has extensively discussed the problem of how to live." Lin Yutang writes, too, that "Chinese humanism, or Confucianism, concentrates on certain human values" and "Chinese Humanism in its essence is a study of human relations..." What both are pointing to is the Chinese view that a society progresses only when relationships between people become characterized less and less by jealously, greed, animosity, and violence. Societies highly advanced technologically and scientifically who desire and use weapons of wholesale destruction cannot be called progressive.

Thirdly, progress is not a result to the clash of diametrically opposed forces, one rising victoriously over the defeat and elimination of the other. Progress is not based on the Darwinian law of the jungle and does not come through the fury and din of conflict and war. Rather it is a result of divergent views being synthesized through the process of mediation and compromise into a more inclusive whole.

There are many today who associate progress with encounter, complexity, size and amount. The bigger and the more, the better. Modernization is connected with the proliferation of things and their means of production. There is also a lamentable lack of concern about the beneficiaries of progress, the more general attitude being "each one for himself and get as much as you can for yourself before others do." From a Chinese perspective this is not progress, for if such means are required and such production reduces the quality of human relationships and the environment in which man lives, how can it be called progress?

The conceiving of society as an organism is an important contribution of Chinese thought. It serves to counterbalance what many feel is the excessively individualistic orientation of modern,

Western liberal thought and many so-called modern societies. They extoll unfettered individualism, an ideal which may be as unrealistic as undesirable.

We can delineate two types of societies, one which tends toward setting the individual up as sovereign, the other which assigns that status to the group. In the first the tendency is to maximize the independence and separateness of individuals. In the second, which the Chinese tradition typifies, emphasis is upon the interdependence and inter-relatedness of individuals. Each person is viewed as part of a group or groups, with duties toward them. Classical Chinese thought delineated five "great" relationships and their corresponding virtues. The relationships were conceived in terms of duties not rights.

The Chinese tradition raises the question of whether a rights-oriented individualism, especially when it becomes extreme, is conducive to social stability and continuity. Can a society endure if aggressiveness, the self-contained individual, self-interest and self-assertion are extolled as virtuous? The alternative may not be to go to the other extreme. Is not a balance between the two a better alternative? This has been the goal sought in traditional Chinese social thought.

What this raises is a question regarding modern Western liberalism's concepts of individual equality, freedom and rights and their alleged superiority. They are central values around which Western societies have tried to organize themselves in the last three centuries. But there are other ideals a society may be established on, as Professor Hsu implies in his statement, "The other factor is the concept of equality as an active ideal, which has been as important in America as it has been insignificant in China." He adds, regarding Protestant ethics and the growth of capitalism, that they "are twin consequences of an individualistic orientation fundamental to Western life, another outgrowth of which is American self-reliance" and "The personal security of the individual American lies in the conquest of the physical environment because of his premise of self-reliance; just as his Chinese counterpart must find security within the kinship and primary circle because of his premise of mutual dependence."[27]

Among other things, what Professor Hsu is indicating in the above is that there does exist in the world, in fact as well as theory, more than one kind of society or cultural pattern. The very existence of such a variety is a challenge to any absolutistic claim of supremacy made by any one of them. Two obvious contrasts are societies individualistically oriented on the one hand and group on the other, rights on the one hand and duties on the other. Each has its strengths and weaknesses; neither can claim finality for its own. Moreover, such concepts themselves as equality, freedom and rights may have different connotations and degrees of significance in different societies and even at different times in the same society, and not every society may consider those attributes to be the most desirable values to be centered around.

The fact that Chinese culture, as a group- and duties-oriented one, has a continuous existence of more than twenty centuries, makes questionable any ethnocentric claim such as is still heard in the West of the indubitable superiority of its type of culture. The Chinese contribution may be two-fold, forcing the West to acknowledge and accept cultural diversity on the one hand and helping mankind to grow toward a world society which would utilize and combine the better aspects of existing societies on the other.

As might be expected, one finds parallel themes in Chinese economic thought which pose a challenge to generally accepted Western economic truisms. A central one is the notion of private ownership on which competitive capitalism is based. Professor Creel points out that "From time immemorial both the Chinese people and their government have looked with distrust upon the concentration of economic wealth and power in private hands." Moreover, "Confucians, as far back as Confucius and Mencius and continuing over the centuries, have denounced the economic exploitation of the masses" which occurs when competitive practices have been replaced by monopolistic ones in a supposedly free society, and wealth becomes concentrated in a minority. Professor Creel adds that "In the twentieth century China's political leaders even those who looked most to the West—have in general considered private ownership of large enterprises an evil, and have been determined that their control should rest with the state. On this point the pronouncements of Sun Yat-sen, Chiang Kai-shek, and Mao Tse-tung show remarkable similarities."[28]

Apart from views in direct contrast to Western capitalist ones, is there what might be called a basic, traditional Chinese economic philosophy and, if so, of what does it consist? An affirmative answer may begin with the statement in the *Great Learning*, "the accumulation of wealth is the way to scatter the people; and the letting it be scattered among them is the way to collect the people." This statement implies the principle of equity and the immorality and danger of an inequitable distribution of wealth. It is unethical for some to have much more than they need while others have much less. It is inadvisable as well; for divisions will occur in a society and dissension will set in when the many exploit the few.

A second aspect of that traditional economic philosophy is reflected in the Taoist ideal "To produce things and to rear them. To produce, but not to take possession of them. To act, but not to rely on one's own ability. To lead them, but not to master them ...This is called profound and secret virtue." Implicit or explicit in those passages is the emphasis on the virtue of contentment,[29] the desirability of not demanding too much, not becoming so attached to things that they overpower and blind us, not letting one's happiness being determined almost exclusively by things, not always being motivated by gain. By viewing reality as impermanent and constantly changing, Buddhism supports this non-absolutistic attitude toward possessions. It, too, emphasized the attitude of non- or trans-attachment.

A third aspect of traditional economic philosophy is its grounding in a metaphysical view which conceives of reality as a given and man's response as gratitude and stewardship. Reality is good; it is characterized by sufficiency. There is enough, either in actuality or potentiality, for everyone. For this effluence of nature man is to be thankful and to recognize the obligation a benevolent nature places on him to nurture and share it equitably.

These and other traditional themes were reinforced by the actual situation. Group-centeredness in society as a whole was reflected in a group-centered economic system. In the extended family, the land was neither tilled or owned by a single person. Rather, work and its fruits were shared in common. Cooperative rather than competitive type relationships and attitudes predominated. The individual found economic as well as psychological security in shared or mutual relationships and activities.[30]

The Chinese economic tradition poses the same reminder and

The Chinese Contribution

raises the same question as elicited by the Chinese social tradition. It forces us to admit the fact of economic systems, differing in regard to both method and motive, whose good is the same, the meeting of human needs. There is a plurality of means but a singular end. Is there a better or best means? The absolutist would say yes, obviously his own. The Chinese tradition would gently remind him that such arrogance and exclusivenesss is outdated and unprofitable in economics also. Why not an economically pluralistic world in which each culture adheres to but at the same time modifies and refines its economic traditions to better suit the changing conditions in a constantly evolving world?

Features of the early Chinese political tradition have been discussed already. They included themes such as the ruler must be moral; ability and virtue are both necessary in governing the relationship of Heaven and the state; the need for self-rectification by ruler and subject alike; the power of example, especially the ruler's; the reciprocal relationship between ruler and subject; rule by li rather than fa; the importance of the people; benevolence and a paternalistic authoritarian form of government.

These themes were continued by Confucius and Mencius. Confucius said, for example, "If a ruler himself is upright, all will go well..." and "A government is good when those near are happy and those far off are attracted." Mencius asserted that "If the sovereign be benevolent, all will be benevolent. If the sovereign be righteous, all will be righteous." However, "If the emperor be not benevolent, he cannot preserve the empire from passing from him." Moreover, "If a ruler gave honor to men of talents and virtue and employed the able...then all the scholars of the empire will be pleased and wish to stand in his court." We see other themes continued in his statements, "The people are the most important element in a nation; the spirits of the land and grain are the next; the sovereign is the lightest" and, in relation to the prince and his ministers, "when he regards them as the ground or as the grass, they regard him as a robber and an enemy."

From Mencius onward these themes became deeply rooted in the Chinese tradition. They were extolled by the Neo-Confucianists and by a host of thinkers up and into the twentieth century. Huang Tsung-hsi, living in the seventeenth century wrote, "Whether there is peace or disorder in the world does not depend on the rise and fall of dynasties, but on the happiness or distress of the people...If a minister ignores the plight of the people, then even if he succeeds in assisting his prince's rise to power or follows him to final ruin, it still can never be said that he has followed the true Way of the minister." His contemporary Ku Yen-Wu lamented that "what the world needs most urgently are local officials who will personally look after the people." In the nineteenth century Yeh Te-Hui asserted, "If one keeps to kingly rule (relying on virtue) there will be order; if one follows the way of the overlord (relying on power) there will be disorder." And Sun Yat-sen's basic political philosophy reflected much of the old tradition, as does Mao Tse-Tung's.

The contribution traditional Chinese political thought can make today is at least three-fold. Its role as a critic is one. Yeh Te-hui, for example, said, "The Western system of election has many defects. Under that system it is difficult to prevent favoritism and to uphold integrity": and Chang Chih-Tung declared, "The theory of people's rights will bring us not a particle of good but a hundred evils." However disturbing or stinging such criticisms may be to those toward whom they are directed, they, if valid, may bring about good results in the end, just as Western criticisms of non-Western traditions may.

A second contribution is its presenting to the world stream of thought political concepts or truisms which are universally valid. Among these would be that government must be grounded in virtue; that its leaders must be moral; that expediency is insufficient and self-defeating; that the final justification for a government's existence, no matter what the type, is the people; that duties are as important as rights; that a nation's greatness is determined as much by qualitative as by quantitative criteria. Such truths cannot be disregarded by any government or people.

Its third contribution is to remind us of the fact of political pluralism and to forewarn us of the danger and tendency toward political ethnocentrism. Following his criticism of the Western electoral system, Yeh Te-hui added, "At any rate each nation has its own governmental system, and one should not compel uniformity among them." His point is obvious. There are different, viable political systems which have been worked out by the people of the world; and, in an era in which interaction between nations is increasing, there is a tendency for adherents of the different traditions to think of their own as best. The ideal, however, is a pluralistic world, politically as well as economically. In it each nation starts from its own political roots, trimming and pruning the growth which has already emanated from them, forming it into a more fruitful tree. Trans-cultural criticism may be helpful in such a process.

VIII

There is a basic distinction made which one finds made in many cultures. It may be referred to variously as the tension between the particular and the universal; the tendency toward separation and the tendency toward unity; the small mind-great mind; the parts and the whole; partiality and impartiality; the I-you or we-them disjunction; the one and the many; expansion and contraction.

The Chinese tradition is no exception to this penchant toward bifurcation. We see it in Confucius' graded or partial and Mo Tzu's universal love. It is reflected in definitions in the *Doctrine of The Mean* which universalists would reject—"Benevolence is the characteristic element of humanity and the great exercise of it is in loving relatives...The decreasing measures of the love due to relatives, and the steps in the honor due to the worthy, are produced by the principle of propriety."

What are the differences between the particularist and the universalist and on what grounds do the universalists argue their case? The disagreement between Confucius and Mo Tzu offers a clear example. Briefly, according to Confucius, it is only natural and proper to be more concerned for and love one's own kin, relatives, family, and parents more than others. Mo Tzu, however, asserted that our love ought to go out to everyone and to everyone equally. Mencius, of course, disagreed even more sharply with Mo Tzu, arguing it would be plainly immoral to treat others' parents as lovingly as one's own.

The grounds or justifications for universal love offered by Mo Tzu and others are several. A favorite of Mo Tzu's was the argument from Heaven. "Heaven," he said, "loves the whole world universally" and "The will of Heaven abominates the large state which attacks small states." This being Heaven's nature, will, or way, man as Heaven's creation should follow it. A parallel position which might be called the metaphysical argument or argument from nature is seen in Chang Tsai's Western Inscription which may well be repeated—"Heaven is my father and Earth is my mother, and even such a small creature as I finds an ultimate place in their midst. Therefore, that which fills the universe I regard as my body and that which directs the universe I consider as my nature. All people are my brothers and sisters, and all things are my companions." Here the oneness, impartiality, non-separateness of nature provides a model for man's actions.

An ethical argument centered around the concept of jen is offered also. Chuang Tzu wrote, "He who shows (special) affection (to anyone) is not a man of humanity." Similarly, Ch'eng Ming-tao said, "The man of humanity regards Heaven, Earth, and all things as one body", and Wang Yang-ming asserted, "To manifest the illustrious virtue is to establish one's state of unity with Heaven, Earth, and all things." In these, virtue is purported to have the character of the universal not the particular.

Mo Tzu also rejected graded love on the grounds of egoism. Found in Mo Tzu's words is an interesting discussion between himself and Wu Matse in which the latter baldly admits that "I love my parents better than other members of my family, and myself better than my parents." And if it came to a choice between who was to be beaten or killed, Wu Matse stated he would rather it be his parents than himself. Mo Tzu abhorred such a view as the heights of egotism and impracticality. For, if everyone took such a view, everyone would be quite willing to have everyone else sacrificed and no one would be safe.

What might be called the "argument from context" is a further one and is reflected in K'ang Yu-wei's statements, "And being that I was born into a family, and by virtue of receiving the nurture of others was able to have this life, I then have the responsibilities of a family member...Being that I was born on earth, then mankind in the ten thousand countries of earth are all my brothers. Being that I have knowledge of them, then I have love for them." One point of his statements is that no one lives in isolation. We live in a variety of contexts—family, city, nation, world and in a variety of relationships—parent, sibling, civil. The principle of consistency or identity requires that what is true, good or appropriate in one is likewise in other contexts.

A further justification for universalism and universal love is the argument from tradition. Over and over in the ancient texts the three sage kings are held up as models of such. Mo Tzu was aware of this and was not hesitant in reminding his listeners, "Who are those that love the people and benefit the people, obey the will of Heaven and obtain reward from Heaven? They are the ancient sage-kings of the three dynasties, Yao-Shun, Yu T'ang, Wen and Wu. What did Yao, Shun, Yu, T'ang, Wen and Wu do? They engaged themselves in universality and not partiality in love...Therefore universal love is the way of the sage-kings." The standard set up by the early kings was held up constantly to rulers through the centuries to remind them to the "kingly" way they should follow.

Mo Tzu appealed also to the nature of man as another rationale for universal love. "Every creature living between Heaven and earth and within the four seas partakes of the nature of Heaven and earth and the harmony of the Yin and Yang. Even the sages cannot alter this", he asserted. Chinese Buddhist reiterated this view as reflected in a statement from the Platform Scripture regarding the three bodies—"It has always been the case that the three bodies lie in one's own nature. Everyone had them, yet because they are deluded they do not see, and they seek the three bodies of the Tathāgata externally, without realizing that the three bodies are inherent in one's own physical body." Wang Yang-ming's is an especially pointed statement to this effect which has been referred to previously—"The great man regards Heaven and earth and the myriad things as one body. He regards the world as one family and the country as one person. As to those who make a cleavage between objects and distinguish between self and others, they are small men. That the great man can regard Heaven, earth, and the myriad things as one body is not because he deliberately wants to do so, but because it is natural with the human nature of his mind that he should form a unity with Heaven, earth, and the myriad things." The sage, of course, was one who had fully realized his universal nature for, as we read in the Li Ki, "A sage can look on all under the sky as one family."

The view generally accepted by the Chinese of the essential goodness of man has been discussed already. If it is true, it means that the potentiality of universality exists in all men. It means that man's universal nature transcends and has priority over his particular nature, inasmuch as the particular is grounded in and is a manifestation of the universal. It also means, and this is very relevant and significant, that universal love is natural to man while graded or partial love is unnatural and is taught, conditioned, or learned.

The pragmatic was the argument for universality which perhaps was appealed to most. Mo Tzu did not hesitate to use it. He declared that "When feudal lords love one another, there will be no more war...when individuals love one another, there will be no more mutual injury...when all the people in the world love one another, the strong will not overpower the weak, the many will not oppress the few..." Lao Tzu associated universality and impartiality with the Tao and pointed to the many benefits of practising it. And as but one further example, Wang Fu-chih may be quoted—"Thus in sound, flavor, and fragrance, we can broadly see the open desires of all creatures, and at the same time they also constitute the impartial principle for all of them. Let us be broad and greatly impartial, respond to things as they come, look at them, and listen to them and follow this way in words and action..."

The justification for universality and universal love discussed above are both idealistic and pragmatic in character. One might close on the latter note by pointing to the urgent need among individuals for a universalistic-type mind, consciousness, awareness or outlook today. Our world is still too much engulfed in nationalism, ethnocentrism and chauvinism. It is not time to take seriously and to implement the vision projected in Mo Tzu's declaration that "Heaven loves all people universally", Chang's assertion that "All people are my brothers and sisters", Wang's description of the man of Jen as one who "regards all things as one body", and Kang's affirmation that, having been born in a "uni"-verse not "multi"-verse, "mankind in the ten thousand countries...are all my brothers." This universalism can surely be a special contribution of Chinese thought to a world which is still bound by the confines of dualism and particularism.

At the beginning of this volume in the discussion on the Pre-Confucian Chinese tradition it was suggested that there was an "early wisdom", an "ancient tradition" which the authors point to as having existed not only in China but in such locales as India and elsewhere where early man formed communities. People in them lived close to nature and the earth which led them to adopt a *weltanschauung* in which harmony, orderliness, unity, oneness, inter-relatedness, wholeness, empathy, beneficence and mutuality were characteristics attributed to reality and human existence. It was suggested subsequently that in China Taoism and Mohism or Mo Tzu's views most nearly approximated that wisdom or tradition and were the chief vehicle of its transmission through the many centuries of Chinese cultural existence. Finally, it has been implied, if not openly affirmed, that in the so-called "modern" period with the advent, proliferation and domination of science, technology, industrialization and urbanization in the world the ancient wisdom has been nearly obliterated. If that wisdom is valuable and relevant, we are faced with the question of how it can be revitalized and implemented and who is to do this, so that it may be a decisive factor in the world of tomorrow.[31]

The question now is: Which are the areas that still remain in the world today in which the modernization of the type indicated above has not completely eroded, engulfed or ravaged, depending on how strong a term one wishes to use, traditional cultures? One answer is: Mainland China, in part because it closed itself off for three decades, is one of them and it is perhaps from there and other less modernized, urbanized, less technological, less impersonal, less polluted regions of the earth that the ancient wisdom may still be carried on.

Notes

1. In his *Source Book* (p. 703) Chan points out "the growing trend toward practical learning" beginning at this time, saying "In reaction to the speculative Neo-Confucianism of Sung and Ming times and to some extent under the influence of Western knowledge introdueced by Jesuits, Confucianists in the seventeenth century turned to practical learning and objective truth."

2. Clarence Burton Day characterizes the change in the philosophical outlook as "Empirical Realism". See pp. 229-250, *Philosophers of China*, Secaucus, Citadel Press, 1978. His discussion of Han Learning is on pp. 229-230.

3. T'an Ssu-T'ung's Jen-hsueh (Philosophy of Humanity) is an example of this universalism in China. See De Bary, *Sources of the Chinese Tradition*, Vol. II, 1964, pp. 88 ff.

4. Dewey's lectures in China have been published in book form—*Lectures in China*, 1919-1920, University Press of Hawaii, 1973. Translated by Robert Clopton and Tsuin-chen Ou.

5. Chan, *op. cit.*, p. 743.

6. Day, *op. cit.*, pp. 274-276.

7. Day characterizes the activities in the first three decades of the twentieth century as consisting of two main trends "...a horizontal comparison and harmonizing of Eastern and Western philosophies and a vertical harmonizing of the ancient, classical philosophy with modern thought...", *op. cit.*, p. 263.

8. For a discussion of the New Culture Movement and the Literary Reform Movement see De Bary, chapter XXIV and Day, chapter 13. See also Creel H. G., *Chinese Thought from Confucius to Mao Tse-Tung*, New York, Mentor Book, 1960, pp. 190-199 for a good, concise discussion of the 20th century reaction of China to the Western intrusion.

9. For a discussion of Chiang Kai-shek's ideas see De Bary, 134-142 and Day 270-273.

10. For a good discussion of Christianity and the Chinese revolution see Fitzgerald, C.P., *The Birth of Communist China*, Baltimore, Penguin Books, 1964, chapter 5.

11. The importance of a knowledge of Chinese philosophy if a philosopher would be "worthy of the title philosopher" is emphasized by Charles A. Moore in his Introduction to the volume, *The Chinese Mind*, Honolulu, East-West Center Press, 1967, p. 1.

12. For a concise discussion of the concept of man in Chinese religious thought see the chapter titled "The Individual in Chinese Religious Thought" by Wing-Tsit Chan in *The Chinese Mind*.

13. Found in the Dhammapada section in Carus Paul, *The Gospel of Buddha*, Chicago, Open Court Company, 1915, p. 132.

14. Creel, *Chinese Thought*, p. 208.

15. Joseph Wu in *Clarification and Enlightenment*, Tunghai, Tunghai University Press, 1979, writes that for the Chinese "...the supernatural world and the natural world do not seem very sharply distinct from each other", p. 76.

16. See Hsu, Francis L.K., *Americans and Chinese, Two Ways of Life*, New York, Henry Schuman, 1953, chapters IX and X on religion.

17. Wu, *op. cit.*, p. 76.

18. C.K. Yang in *Religion in Chinese Society*, Berkeley, University of California Press, 1961, emphasizes the functional aspect of Chinese religion.

19. In his essay "Syntheses in Chinese Metaphysics" Wing-Tsit Chan writes "...one of the outstanding facts in the history of Chinese philosophy has been its tendency and ability to synthesize." *The Chinese Mind*, p. 132.

20. The effect of dialectical dualism on Western religious thought is pointed out by Hsu, *op. cit.*, pp. 250 ff.

21. Thome H. Fang represented this view at the 4th East-West Philosophers' Conference in 1964 at the University of Hawaii in his paper "The World and the Individual in Chinese Metaphysics" which closed with the statement, "As to the nature and status of man, the Chinese, either as a unique person or as a social being, takes no pride in being a type of individual in estrangement from the world he lives in or from the other fellows he associates with. He is intent on embracing within the full range of his vital experience all aspects of plentitude in the nature of the whole cosmos and all aspects of richness in the worth of noble personality." *The Status of The Individual in East and West*, Charles A. Moore, editor, Honolulu, University of Hawaii Press, 1968, p. 43.

22. Creel writes of the West that "We have been so busy building machines and creating wealth that we have paid little attention to relations between men...The emphasis of Chinese civilization has been almost the opposite. There has been little attempt to conquer nature; instead, the Chinese have sought to live in harmony with it." *Chinese Thought*, p. 26.

23. An interesting account of Chinese epistemology is by T'ang Chunititled "The Individual and the World in Chinese Methodology" found in the book *The Chinese Mind*.

24. The mutual relationship between the good of the individual and the good of society is the central theme of Hsieh Yu-Wei's essay "The Status of the Individual in Chinese Ethics" in the book *The Status of the Individual in East and West*.

25. 20th century traditionalists such as Yeh Te-Hui and Chang Chih-Tung in arguing with their fellow Chinese who would replace everything Chinese with Western asserted that Western society is too utilitarian-oriented to be copied by the Chinese.

26. Carus, *op. cit.*, p. 62.
27. Hsu, *op. cit.*, p. 311.
28. Creel, *Chinese Thought*, p. 198.
29. Creel writes that "Most Chinese philosophers have preached the virtue of contentment and most Chinese have practiced it to a remarkable degree." *Chinese Thought*, pp. 209.
30. For a good discussion of Chinese economic philosophy see Hsu, *op. cit.*, chapter 4.
31. For a good discussion of this see, *The Marriage of East and West*, by Bede Griffiths (Templegate Publishers, Springfield, Illinois, 1982).

INDEX

abhi-dharma, 187
Amitābha, 211
Amoghavajra, 215
Analects, 15, 16, 17, 110
ancestor reverence, 172
ancient wisdom, 6, 11, 13n
An Yang, 4
archaeology, 4
Aristotle, 263, 281, 290
Asaṅga, 189
Au-yang Ching-wu, 406

Bergson, 57
Berkeley, 285
bodhidharma, 217
Book of Changes, 28, 30n, 156, 241, 246, 259, 410-11
Boxer Rebellion, 389n
Buddha, 184, 288
Buddhism in China, 184ff; impact on China, 226ff; in India, 185ff; Neo-Confucianist criticisms of, 244ff; and Wang Yang-ming, 297; contemporary Buddhism, 423ff, 451, 455, 458
Bull Mountain, 69
burning of the books, 3
Burtt, E, 40, 57n

Chan Buddhism, 217ff
Chang Chun-mai, (Carson Chang), 347, 372
Chang Constant C.C., 436
Chang Ling, (Chang Tao-ling), 56n
Chang Tsai, 245, 246, 255ff, 285, 289, 416, 443
Chan Jo-shui, 298
Chao Albert, 426
Ch'eng Hao, 246, 258ff, 298
Chen-hua Heng, 436
Ch'eng Ming-tao, 294
Cheng-tung Chang, 46
Chen Tai-chi, 432
Ch'en Tu-hsui, 346, 374, 378, 379ff, 440
Chen-yen Buddhism, 213ff
Ch'eng Yi, 247, 262ff, 266
ch'i, 256, 262ff, 292, 294, 312, 336, 338
Chiang Kai-shek, 430, 441
ch'ien, 285
chih, 156, 238
Ch'ien Te-hung,

Chinese arts, 4, 226, 305ff
Chinese religion, 4, 169ff, 183n, 446ff
ching, 50, 52, 54
Chi-tsang, 201
Chou dynasty, 4, 5, 11
Chou Tun-yi, 245, 252-5, 295
Christianity, 54, 338n; and Confucianism, 426-27
Chu Hsi, 30n, 227, 245, 248ff, 264ff, 277, 290, 305-8, 373ff, 402, 454
Chu Tzu, 293-4
Chuang Tzu, 34, 41, 43, 47, 54, 56n, 57n, 58n, 166, 178, 193, 277, 284, 458, 465, 474
chung 20, 21
classes, 176ff
Confucius, 6, 12, 14; and jen 17ff; and religion, 23ff; and Heaven, 26ff, 67, 72, 445, 455, 461, 466
Creel, H.G., 92, 93, 103, 106n, 107n, 454, 456, 478n

Darwinianism, 352, 382, 439n
Dewey, John, 368, 373, 439n
Dhammapada, 191, 229n
dharma, 190, 228n
disinterest, 52, 54
divination, 172, 174
doctrine of the mean, 283, 449, 473
Dream of The Red Chamber, 44, 57n, 383

eightfold path, 192
existentialism, 41

fa, 90, 207
Fa-chia, 81ff
Fa-hsiang, 239
Fang, Thome, 435, 479n
Fa-tsang, 208, 455
five classics, 3, 6, 274n
five constant virtues, 274n
five elements, 241, 408
five great relationships, 441
four books, 3, 30n
four noble truths, 185, 190
Fung Yu-lan, 223, 230n, 231n, 290, 420n

God, in Western religions, 39; in early Chinese religion, 171ff; 292, 441, 462

great ultimate, 244, 252, 268, 273n, 294, 410, 450
great wall, 154

Han dynasty, 153-4, 184, 193
Han Fei, 39, 82, 96ff, 108n
Han Fei Tzu, 93, 97ff, 159, 301n
Han historians, 3, 153
Han Yu, 237
Hang, Thaddeus, 426
harmony, 8, 9
heaven, and Mo-Tzu, 61ff; and Mencius, 125ff; and Hsun Tzu, 159
Hegel, 277, 293, 300n, 381, 434
Heidegger, 283, 300n
Hobbes, 77n
Ho Yen, 194
Hsiang Hsiu, 194
hsiao, 40
Hsiao Ching, 432
Hsieh Yu-wei, 432
Hsiung Shih- Li, 433, 444
hsu, 50, 51, 54
Hsu, Francis, L.K., 478
Hsuan Hua, 425
Hsuan-tsang, 202
hsu hsin, 50
Hsun Tzu, 101, 108n, 131, 159ff, 287
hsu tzu, 50
Huang Tsung-hsi, 471
Hua-yen Buddhism, 267
Hui-kwo, 216
Hui-wen, 206
Hui-ssu, 208, 458
hundred schools of thought, 6, 11
Hung-jen, 219
Husserl, 283
Hu Shih, 217-8, 233n, 362n, 364ff; and religion, 377
Hu-t'ien, 424
Hu Yuan, 306-7

Ibsen, 390n

James, William, 55, 58n
jen, 17ff, 29n, 40, 156, 240, 258-9, 287, 318

K'ang Yu-wei, 323ff; and man's nature, 325; social philosophy, 329; political philosophy, 331; economic philosophy, 333; metaphysics, 335, 412, 439n, 470
Kant, 58n, 298, 301n, 433, 442
Ko-wu, 278
Kuan-tzu, 41
Kuang Wu-tl, 153
Kumārajīva, 199
Kuo Hsiang, 195
Kuomintang, 344

Ku Yen-wu, 441, 472

landscape painting, 447
Lao Tzu, 12; and the Tao, 34ff; and freedom, 40ff, 178ff, 287
Legalists, 81ff, 193, 296
li, 40, 156, 238, 262, 266-7, 287, 290, 307, 407, 458
liang chih, 284ff
Liang Chi-chao, 65, 76n, 77n, 320n, 321n, 351, 386
Li Ssu, 159
Literary Reform Movement, 443
logicians (Mohists), 162, 385
Lokuang S., 426
Lo Shih-hsin, 424
lung shan culture, 4
Lu Hsing-shan, 249-250, 290

Mahāyāna, 205, 223, 240
mandate of heaven, 157
Mao Tse Tung, 392ff; epistemology, 394ff; metaphysical views, 397ff; social philosophy, 415ff; and man, 416ff; and Confucianism 425ff, 428, 439n, 442, 467
Marx, 104, 356, 379, 389
May Fourth Movement, 366
Mencius, 110; discourses of, 113ff; method of categorization, 118ff; and rectification of names, 121ff; and fate, 122ff; and nature 123ff; and heaven, 131ff; and government, 133ff; and well field system, 142; and attack on Mo Tzu, 144, 239, 286, 289, 443
middle kingdom, 154
middle path, 190, 192, 462
Mill, 339n
moderation, in Buddhism, 191ff
Mou tsung-san, 432
Mo Tzu, 12, and ethics, 61ff; and metaphysics, 62ff; and war, 67ff; concept of man, 67; and social philosophy, 69ff; decline of mohism, 72ff, 101, 180ff, 287, 298, 468, 471
mysticism, 55

Nāgārjuna 199, 201
nature's way, 10
Neo-Confucianism, 235ff, 431
Neo-Taoism, 166ff, 192ff, 229n
New Culture Movement, 366, 378, 443, 478n
New Script School, 154, 159
nirvāṇa, 190, 208, 211, 230n

Ockham, 48
Old Script School, 154

Index

opium wars, 342, 371
oracle bones, 4
order in nature, 7
Ortega Y Gasset, 52

Pei-yung Fu, 426
Po Chu-i, 226
positivism, 313, 454
pure land Buddhism, 210ff

Ricci, Mathew, 307
Royce, Josiah, 433
Russell, 433, 443

sacrifices, 170
sage kings, 5, 18, 29n, 79n, 114, 445, 475
sangha, 190
San-Lun school, 201
school of mind, 271ff
science, 372, 374
Seng-chao, 199ff
Shang dynasty, 5
Shang Yang, 82ff
Shan-tao, 212
Shao Yung, 246, 450, 457, 461
Shen-hui, 218
Shen Pu-lia, 90
Shig Hui Wan, 423
Shih Huang Ti, 159
shu, 20, 21
Spinoza, 39, 42
spirits, 170
spring and autumn era, 6
Ssu-ma Ch'ien, 29n, 56n, 82, 96, 103, 106n, 154
Ssu-ma Kuang, 306
Sung dynasty, 30n, 305ff
śūnyatā, 240
Sun Yat-sen, 340ff, 429-31, 407, 472
superior man, 17ff, 29n, 72, 445, 448ff
Suzuki, 217

Tai-Chen, 403, 441
T'ang dynasty, 306
T'ang Chun-i, 433
tao, 32, 35ff, 55, 163, 178, 181, 184, 193, 195, 223, 240, 283, 286, 288, 290
Taoism, 32ff; and language, 33; and tao, 34ff; and wu-wei, 47ff; and religion, 167ff, 236, 319n, 449, 460, 465

tao-sheng, 200
te, 41
ten gates, 232n
T'ien-t'ai Buddhism, 204ff, 424
three ancient dynasties, 5, 13n, 141
three people's principles, 347ff
three ways, 3
traditionalist movement, 444
Tsung Tzu, 29n
Tsou Yen, 156
Tung Chung-shu, 155, 157ff, 192, 229n, 240, 241
T'ung Ming Hui, 344

utilitarianism, and Mo Tzu, 59ff

Vajrabodhi, 214
Vasubandhu, 189
vitalism, 7, 10

Waley, Arthur, 12n
Wang Chi, 298
Wang Ch'ung, 159
Wang Fu-chih, 301n, 308, 311ff, 322n; and metaphysics, 312; and social philosophy, 317, 403, 441
Wang Pi, 57n, 194
Wang Yang-ming, 250ff, 276ff, 455, 474-5
warring states period, 6, 78n, 110, 133, 153
well field system, 106n, 142, 155,
Western inscription, 256
Whitehead, 39
Wing-tsit Chan, 434, 478n
Wu Chih-hui, 375
Wu John C., 426
Wu Matse, 64
Wu Ti, 156
wu-wei, 47ff, 92, 163, 164, 200, 319n

Yang Hsuing, 154
Yang Shao, 4, 5
Yen Fu, 41
Yen Hui, 46
Yen Jo-ch'u, 309
Yen Yuan, 29n, 309, 321, 403
yi, 40, 156, 238, 461
Yin Hsun, 423
yin-yang, 156, 157, 241, 242, 253, 406, 408, 409
Yogācāra, 202, 433

ERRATA

Page	Line	Incorrect	Correct
69	12 from top	o	of
97	2 from bottom	sances	stances
105	16 ,, ,,	enoble	ennoble
	12 ,, ,,	on	in
108	Note 39, line 2	sustenable	sustainable
	,, ,, 4	reflected	reflecting
	Note 42, line 5	gentiality	geniality
122	18 from top	trom	from
131	12 ,, ,,	informing	in forming
193	24 ,, ,,	*Tao-Ten-Ching*	*Tao-Te-Ching*
271	10 ,, ,,	bccause	because
307	15 ,, ,,	measure	measures
311	6 ,, ,,	over-changing	everchanging
316	23 ,, ,,	insrumentalism	instrumentalism
326	13 ,, bottom	theological	teleological
329	9 ,, top	own contributes	own way contributes
330	5 ,, ,,	illustion	illusion
	6-7 ,, ,,	insight of…	insight-ful
331	3 ,, ,,	heys	keys
343	top line	mos	most
352	last line	pol itica	political
387	16 from top	motot-car	motor-car
450	7 ,, bottom	plainnes	plainness
451	7 ,, ,,	fourtth	fourth
467	20 ,, top	result to	result of
471	3 ,, ,,	good	goal